InStyle
WEDDINGS

InStyle
WEDDINGS

FROM THE EDITORS OF IN STYLE

WRITTEN BY
HILARY STERNE

Produced by Melcher Media for
In Style Books and Time Inc. Home Entertainment

CONTEMPORARY CUTS

PRINCESS

Designed in 1961 in London by jeweler Arpad Nagy, the princess is a square cut with a multitude of brilliant-cut facets, resulting in a glittering light show. Such flirty flash has made the princess a consistently sought after shape for engagement rings since it first debuted, especially since the brilliance can make the stone seem bigger than it actually is. Princess stones are particularly scintillating when used in eternity bands, because the edges of each square diamond line up to create a solid wall of gems.

SIGNATURE

Jewelers looking to make a bold design statement have begun offering exclusive, often patented cuts of diamond solitaires set in distinctive bands. These shapes—glittering reinterpretations of classic cuts—are typically named after the company that created them, such as David Yurman's modified cushion (far left, bottom), Movado's variation on the round brilliant (far left, top) and Asprey's own dazzling, 61-facet take on the cushion cut (second from far left, top). The Rand Round Brilliant Zero Tolerance diamond takes its designation from the proprietary cutting technique used to create it, which ensures that each facet is precisely the same size as all the other facets of the same shape, resulting in a particularly sparkling diamond (far right, top and middle). Other signature cuts have a more romantic connotation: Lucida, for example, the name of the wide-cornered square cut by Tiffany & Co., is also the term for the brightest star in a constellation (far right, bottom).

RING STYLES

CLASSIC SOLITAIRE

While this iconic style may now seem timeless, the custom of a single diamond gracing a metal band really only dates back to the 19th century. Not only were diamonds large enough to be set as solitaires suddenly more plentiful and affordable thanks to the discovery of huge African diamond mines in the 1870s, but it was in this era that advances were made in cutting and polishing techniques. The result: highly brilliant diamonds more able to stand alone. While round brilliants are most commonly used for solitaires, any shape of diamond can work in this simple presentation.

SIDE STONES

This design, which made its mark in the ladylike late '40s, uses two smaller stones to flank the main one, thus flooding it with light and making it sparkle even more. The most traditional version features a round diamond sandwiched by two tapered stones known as baguettes because they resemble the classic loaf of French bread. Nevertheless, emerald-cut center stones and other shapes are also popular. Marc Anthony gave Jennifer Lopez a ring with side stones.

VINTAGE

Whether a delicate, lacy Edwardian design or a glamorous art deco look, vintage rings have recently caught on with brides looking for something different that nevertheless has a whiff of romance about it. Keep in mind that stones cut in the 19th century and earlier— including those with Asscher, rose and cushion shapes—give off a softer glow than the more fiery contemporary versions of these styles. That's because the technology didn't exist then to facet stones the way jewelers can today.

WIDE BAND SOLITAIRE

Sleek and modern, this style, which embeds a single diamond in a thick metal band, is ideal for brides who prefer not to stack an engagement ring with a wedding band since it's strong enough to stand alone. It's also flattering on women with large hands and fingers who might not feel comfortable wearing a daintier style. And it allows plenty of room for engraving.

MICRO-PAVÉ

Invented in Paris about 20 years ago, micro-pavé is a stone-setting technique that involves placing many tiny stones closely together on a ring so that it looks covered with diamonds. The gems can appear everywhere: the band (as shown here), which is usually very thin, the prongs, encircling the main stone—even underneath the gem. Note that the resulting ring can be quite fragile, though this fact didn't deter Ashley Judd, who wears a micro-pavé engagement ring.

MORE RING STYLES

THREE-STONE

Symbolizing a couple's past, present and future, this style, unlike those that display a center stone with flanking side stones, features stones of roughly the same size and shape (most often round). Three-stone rings have existed for hundreds of years, but the look works for women as stylish and up-to-the-minute as Madonna, who wears an Edwardian-era three-stone ring chosen for her by husband Guy Ritchie.

CREATIVE

A ring that features an unusual design motif, such as a star- or vine-shaped setting, intricate engraving, crossover bands, or what's known as a split shank—a band that divides into two with stone nestled in between—offers an unusual way to announce you're spoken for. Not only will you wear something that's yours and yours alone, these styles, which often don't feature a center stone, can offer relative value, especially since many are striking enough to be worn without a band.

COLORED DIAMONDS

Pink and yellow diamonds, also known as fancy colored diamonds, are extremely rare (with pink ones even less common than yellow, also known as canaries). Though yellow diamonds have been used in jewelry for 100 years, only recently have they become the It stone for engagement rings: Heidi Klum wears an eyecatching canary diamond. Even rarer are blue and green diamonds. A .9-carat green diamond sold in 2000 for $600,000. (The legendary 45.52-carat Hope diamond is the most well-known blue diamond.)

COLORED DIAMONDS, CLOCKWISE FROM TOP: Round diamonds with round pink diamonds in white-gold-and-rose-gold band. Platinum eternity band with brilliant-cut pink diamonds. Oval pink diamond with trapezoid-cut white side stones in pink-gold-and-platinum band. Radiant-cut yellow diamonds in platinum band. Radiant-cut yellow diamond in gold band. Cushion-cut pink diamond in white-gold band.

SMALL PRICE, BIG IMPACT

BUY JUST UNDER A CARAT

Clarity and color being equal, a stone just under a carat will cost significantly less than one that weighs in at that seemingly magical number. The same goes for stones that weigh fractionally less than two carats, three and so on. And since only a jeweler will be able to tell the difference between a diamond that weighs a full carat and one that weighs slightly less, no one will be the wiser.

DARE TO COMPARE

Most experts agree that the untrained eye can't distinguish between the first several color grades (that is, those designated D through I, which is somewhat yellower than a colorless D). The same goes for clarity. Stones at the very top of the range (an internally flawless "FL" or "IF" stone, or one with a very, very slight inclusion—VVS1 or VVS2) will cost you significantly more than those with SI grades, which stands for "slight inclusion," even though the visible difference is negligible. As an example, a D, internally flawless, round brilliant-cut 1-carat diamond will cost approximately 30 percent more than an E diamond of the same weight, clarity and cut and 50 percent more than a comparable F diamond.

BELOW, FROM LEFT: .33-carat diamond set in 18kt white gold with matching wedding band. Diamonds set in 18kt white gold (1.13 total carat weight). 18kt white-gold bands with pavé-diamond balls.

KNOW YOUR SETTINGS...

Channel settings, those with stones set side-by-side and held between two slim bands of metal, are the most expensive type. Bezel or collet settings, with a band that encircles the gem, are less costly, as are classic prong settings. Pavé settings, in which the metal is "paved" with dozens of tiny stones, resulting in lots of glitter, offer the best value for the price.

...AND YOUR CUTS

Though the most popular and traditional of shapes—as well as one of the most brilliant—a round-cut stone the same size as one with a different cut can often seem smaller on the hand. Seek out unusual cuts instead: Carat for carat, a rose cut, for instance, is typically less expensive than other shapes.

CONSIDER AN ETERNITY BAND

A good 1-carat solitaire ring can cost five figures and up, whereas a ring with smaller stones that together add up to a total weight of 1 carat can cost a half to a tenth of that. Factor in that you can wear an eternity ring as both an engagement and wedding band, and you've got yourself a relative bargain.

TEST YOUR METALS

Depending on the karat, the designation for its pureness, a gold ring will generally cost about half of what a comparable platinum one does. (The downside is that gold is softer, causing it to nick more easily and lending itself less easily to ornate designs.) Some maintain that a less-white diamond looks better in a yellow-gold setting, which, by contrast, makes it look whiter, while others think white metals set off a diamond best no matter the color.

THINK BEYOND A DIAMOND

While diamonds are the classic choice for engagement rings, any sort of gemstone can be showcased on the left ring finger. The most popular, however, are other precious stones: sapphires followed by rubies. (Sapphires are actually the least expensive of all the precious gems, and their navy hue means they coordinate easily with most wardrobes.)

CLOCKWISE FROM ABOVE: .3 total carats of diamonds in 18kt yellow-gold band. 18kt yellow-gold eternity band with diamonds and 18kt yellow-gold flower band with diamonds. Round sapphire in platinum-and-diamond ring with matching platinum-and-diamond wedding band.

WEDDING BANDS

PLAIN BAND

The basic band, in either yellow gold, white gold or platinum, is favored by both minimalists, who love it for its simplicity, and jewelry-loving brides, who want a ring that goes with everything. A plain band can have a rounded shape, appear flat or have a bevel—what's known as knife-edged. It can also feature millegraining—tiny beadwork along the top and bottom edges that give an antique look.

ENGRAVED BAND

Bands with carving or engraving on the outside can incorporate design motifs—dainty floral ones or sinuous Celtic ones, for instance—or words, initials or phrases, the letters working as decorative elements as well as bearers of meaning. Consider displaying your initials, your wedding date in Roman numerals, or a few words from a poem that's meaningful to you as a couple. You'll have a ring that's one of a kind.

ETERNITY

In the 1950s, Marilyn Monroe and Audrey Hepburn popularized this style, which features diamonds (often channel-set ones) all the way around the band—meant to symbolize endless love. Eternity bands can showcase round, emerald or princess cuts, or even tiny pavé stones. Because they rely on a collection of relatively small diamonds to dazzle, eternity bands can be an affordable alternative to a solitaire.

OPENWORK BAND

Wide bands with airy filigree and organic motifs that recall antique styles have caught on recently—perhaps because they manage to be both delicate and substantial at once. While often covered with diamonds, creating an enchanting pattern of sparkle and space, the gems used are generally small, which means they can give glitter without a big price tag. (Keep in mind, however, that rings featuring exceptional workmanship are never inexpensive.)

A SENTIMENTAL MOOD

MARISKA HARGITAY AND PETER HERMANN

On the sun-dappled grounds of the private estate where actors Mariska Hargitay and Peter Hermann held their wedding reception sits a swan pond filled with those long-necked creatures known to mate for life. It wasn't the day's only sweetly sentimental detail. Hargitay donned a strapless Carolina Herrera gown in a pretty blush hue, a favorite shade of her late mother, actress Jayne Mansfield. She pinned to it a locket holding photos of both her mother and her grandmother, a gift from her friend Joely Fisher. Encircling her finger was her engagement ring, a weathered platinum band by Karen Karch for N.Y.C. jeweler Push that was set with nine evenly spaced round diamonds meant to symbolize that though she and Hermann will encounter rough patches, there will always be happy moments ahead.

The first sparkling stop along the way: Santa Barbara's Unitarian Historical Chapel for the ceremony, at which Hargitay's father, Mickey, read an e.e. cummings poem and that ended with a 12-member gospel choir singing a rousing rendition of "Ain't No Mountain High Enough." Hilary Swank, Chad Lowe and Jodie Foster were among the guests who then traveled to the nearby reception site, where dining tables were dotted with Depression-glass vases of dahlias, roses and lily of the valley, and the menu included seared Alaskan halibut with a tomato-basil relish.

"Weddings have a tendency to be uptight and stodgy, and I'm not like that," says Hargitay. "The one thing I wanted our wedding to be was fun." And that it was. At a Mexican-themed buffet dinner the night before the ceremony, the groom was literally head over heels, jumping on a trampoline rented for the event by wedding planner Yifat Oren. At the reception, revelers danced the night away to R&B favorites. Even the pièce de résistance, a six-tiered chocolate-and-vanilla wedding cake, was designed with a decided Dr. Seussian tilt. The crowning touch: a Swarovski crystal–studded topper in the shape of the couple's initials.

ABOVE: Hermann gave Hargitay a platinum wedding band by jeweler Loree Rodkin to wear with her diamond-studded engagement ring. BELOW, LEFT TO RIGHT: Very Different Cakes created the lavish, crystal-adorned dessert; young revelers on the mahogany dance floor; at the reception, the bridal couple and their guests enjoyed R&B favorites following the first dance to "Over the Rainbow." OPPOSITE: The bride and groom exchange their first kiss as newlyweds.

THE
INVITATION

Like the trumpet fanfare that announces the queen's approaching carriage or the searchlight beams scudding across the night sky above an Old Hollywood movie pre-mière, a wedding invitation heralds something special. Its arrival, in a thick envelope covered with loops of graceful script or sculptural blocks of print, is a signal to your friends and family that the day you've talked about for months is almost here. And the way you decide to make that announcement—through your choice of paper, format, type style, printing method and embellishment—will make a first and lasting impression of your wedding, hinting at the tone of the event just weeks away and serving as a keepsake for years to come.

Until recently, tradition deemed only a few choices appropriate for the formality of this occasion: white or ecru paper in one or two standard sizes engraved with either black or charcoal script. If your wedding is an ultra-formal affair, you may want to stick with one of these classic and always elegant combinations. But because the rules have now relaxed, an invitation offers the engaged couple an opportunity to get creative—to play with design elements in a way that reveals something about their per-sonalities and about the kind of wedding they're planning.

Maybe you're looking for something luxe to make a grand opening statement: a stiff, cream-colored card with a beveled edge lined in gold and a curlicue monogram at

The wedding program, which often takes its cues in style and palette from the invitation, is not strictly necessary, but can be a pretty way to greet guests at the ceremony.

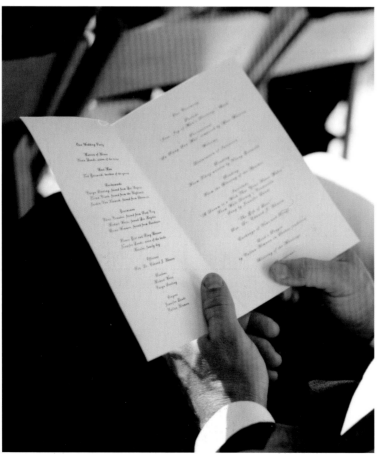

The different decorative elements of the printed and hand-lettered material used at a wedding imbue the event with a subtle note of distinction, including (clockwise from top left) a delicate, garland-shaped motif on an invitation, an ornate capital letter on a name card, and the flowing script on a program. Simple escort cards (opposite) can be dressed up with something as ordinary but pleasing as a green apple used to support it.

the top has the same effect as a gold-fringed velvet curtain opening on the first act at La Scala. If that's not your style, how about the Zenlike appeal of translucent rice paper embellished with the pale pink outline of cherry blossoms? Or are you an ultraminimalist? You might prefer a square card with no embellishments whatsoever, relying instead on a crisp combination of sky-blue ink and navy paper for drama.

Given the staggering number of possibilities, it's sometimes tough to know where to start. Think first of the wedding itself—the style, the setting, the season in which it will be held, the formality. Black-tie or beach attire? Indoors or out? Does your guest list number 200 or is your wedding a more intimate affair? Kyle MacLachlan's invitation was printed in sea-green ink, a nod to the wedding's location of Coral Gables, Fla., while the one chosen by Brooke Shields, whose low-key marriage to TV writer Chris Henchy also took place in a seaside setting, featured a drawing of a palm tree on the front. Look at samples at local stationery stores and online. Make a note of the colors, types of paper and fonts that appeal to you. Then begin to experiment with different elements.

A square fuchsia invitation that uses modestly priced offset printing in bright white ink with a crisp, dotted border and lowercase sans-serif type looks cheerful and casual, suggesting a sunny summer day. A letterpress invitation that relies on a classic typeface but an unusual mix of light blue paper and brown type, on the other hand, conveys a feeling that's sophisticated but not overly formal, perfect for an afternoon city wedding. You may notice

Escort cards are par for the course, but the way NASCAR driver Jimmie Johnson and bride Chandra Janway decorated theirs—tied with ribbons to dried starfish and displayed in a sandbox for their beach wedding (left, top)—shows true creativity. Just as unexpected is this cocktail menu (left, bottom) adorned with a delicate floral motif and martini glasses. Other fun ways to personalize your wedding (opposite, clockwise from top left): cocktail napkins printed with the names of the bride and groom, menu cards bedecked with fresh herb bouquets, antique figurine place-card holders, and place cards printed on ribbons that encircle fresh limes.

as you sort through sheaves of samples that sometimes a tiny tweak is enough to change the mood. Brown type on blue paper speaks of refinement, while blue on brown looks decidedly hip. Shifting the text from centered to aligned on the left can also swing the mood from traditional to modern. Mixing typefaces, breaking text into blocks, or adding a vellum overlay are other ways to get a contemporary look, while ribbons, pressed flower appliqués and deckled (or ragged) edges set a more romantic, old-fashioned tone. Keep in mind that the type of paper you choose will affect what printing methods are available to you, so if you don't know which design element to start with, this one might be your best bet.

If your wedding is small and informal, you might consider hand-writing the invitations yourself or hiring a calligrapher to do them. (Long after the advent of the printing press, the aristocracy continued to have their invitations hand-lettered as a sign of status. In fact, traditional script fonts used for engraving, such as Copperplate, were designed to emulate handwriting.) You could also design and print invitations yourself using software made for such a task, or have an artistic friend design a template that you could take to a local printer. If you're feeling ambitious, you might even get out scissors and paste to create something handmade. Actress Leslie Bibb and her husband, Rob Born, made the invitations to their wedding in Mexico by sandwiching a reproduction of a Diego Rivera painting between vellum.

Remember too that there's more to your wedding stationery trousseau than the invitation. Depending on the size, type and formality of the wedding, as well as your personal preference, you may want reply cards (technically not proper, but practically a necessity in this day and age), programs, place cards, table cards, menu cards and save-the-date cards. One elegant and popular way of tying all these elements together is with a motif or ornament, such as a monogram or something meaningful to you: a seashell to evoke the place you first met or a sunflower to echo the reception table centerpieces. Music mogul Antonio "L.A." Reid, who married in Capri, used an outline of the cliffs that dot that Mediterranean island, while Laurence Fishburne and his wife, Gina Torres, picked an infinity symbol (a sideways figure eight), intended to suggest the eternal nature of marriage. A selection of basic ornaments is available at most stationers, or you can often supply a piece of camera-ready artwork yourself. Be sure to order thank-you cards too, which can also be custom-made to coordinate with your invitation and other printed material. Pick a pretty design for these and you may want to start sending them out before you've even returned from your honeymoon. Who knew a petal-thin piece of paper could be so inspiring?

Consider adding cheerful messages to your menu cards, such as this one (above), which reads "eat, drink and be married." Or try an unusual way of arranging the type on them instead. This example (opposite) features bold blocks of type in which the words run together, rather than the traditional single lines for each course.

WEDDING STATIONERY TROUSSEAU

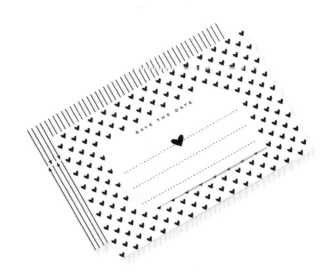

WHAT TO ORDER

The elements of a wedding stationery trousseau can include save-the-date cards, the invitation, response cards, programs, seating cards, place cards, menu cards and thank-you notes. Ordering everything from one stationer imparts a unified theme to all of your stationery (opposite).

WHEN TO SEND

If you're planning a destination wedding or will be inviting lots of out-of-towners, save-the-date cards (shown at right) can be a thoughtful gesture, giving guests plenty of time to book flights and hotels. The cards should be sent no later than three months in advance of the wedding day, and up to six months beforehand if you have picked a popular destination or a holiday weekend for your wedding. Firm up your guest list and order the cards at least six weeks before that to allow for any printers' errors. Wedding invitations should be ordered at least three months prior, again to allow for any mistakes to be corrected and for envelopes to be addressed by a calligrapher if you plan to use one. (Figure on allotting two weeks for this service, to be safe.) They should be mailed out six to eight weeks before the wedding, and invitations to the rehearsal dinner two to three weeks after that. Many brides wonder if it's acceptable to send invitations to "A-list" friends and relatives first, wait to see who declines, then send a batch to those on the B list. The answer is yes, as long as you're discreet and as long as you send the second round out promptly. Mail the first invitations out at least eight weeks ahead of time. Then mail those to any additional names you'd like to add to your list as soon as any regrets come in, and no later than five weeks before the wedding to ensure that no guest feels like an afterthought.

THIS PAGE, FROM TOP: Letterpress save-the-date card. Hand-lettered save-the-date card. Letterpress invitation and directions to ceremony in Thai-paper pocket with bow and tag.

OPPOSITE, CLOCKWISE FROM TOP RIGHT: A wedding stationery trousseau, with two-color offset printing, includes invitation, reception and reply cards, thank-you note, menu card, place card and seating card with envelope, favor tag, program, save-the-date card and map.

Save the date

Laura Litzky & Dave Hoberecht
PLAN TO BE WED
SATURDAY, AUGUST 17, 2002
ORCAS ISLAND, WASHINGTON

Dear Family & Friends,

We're getting married and would like you
to join in our celebration.

As summer is popular time to visit
the San Juan Islands and lodging options
are extremely limited, we encourage you
to make reservations soon!

Included is some helpful information
about travel and accommodations.
Plan to spend a few days on
the island if you can, as it is a wonderful
place to explore and experience.
We hope you will join us.

Laura & Dave

invitation to follow early summer

7336 14th Avenue NE, Seattle, Washington 98155

LEWIS AND SUZANNE LITZKY

SHARON SAVAGE

HAPPILY INVITE YOU TO CELEBRATE

THE MARRIAGE OF

Laura Litzky & David Hoberecht

SON OF PHILIP AND BARBARA HOBERECHT

SATURDAY, THE SEVENTEENTH OF AUGUST

TWO THOUSAND AND TWO

AT FIVE O'CLOCK

ATOP MOUNT CONSTITUTION

ORCAS ISLAND, WASHINGTON

BAR-B-QUE AND DANCING TO FOLLOW

ODDFELLOW'S HALL

EASTSOUND, ORCAS ISLAND

Directions

FROM SEATTLE:
Take Interstate 5 north approximately 80 miles
to exit 230 (Burlington/Anacortes). Go
west on highway 20 into Anacortes and
follow signs to the ferry terminal. Take
ferry to Orcas Island.

Allow 2-3 hours for boarding.
If by vehicle, 20 minutes
if foot passengers.

From the island follow the
roads and signs into
Eastsound.

Ceremony will be
atop Mt. Constitution.
Reception site is located in
Eastsound on Haven Road, one
block off of Main Street.

AIRPORT

ODDFELLOW'S HALL
Reception on Haven Road

KAYAK RENTALS
on Ship Bay

MT. CONSTITUTION
Ceremony held at the top
~ 2407 feet ~

Summit Lake

Mountain Lake

Deer
Harbor

West Beach

Westsound

Cascade
Lake

Olga

Doe Bay

MORAN STATE PARK
DAY USE AREA
on Cascade Lake

Orcas Village

ORCAS
FERRY DOCK
arrival/departure point

Obstruction
Pass

ORCAS ISLAND

Kindly reply by July 20th

Reception and Dinner

IMMEDIATELY FOLLOWING THE CEREMONY

ODDFELLOW'S HALL

EASTSOUND, ORCAS ISLAND

Laura & David

Laura and Dave Hoberecht
August 17, 2002

Hoberecht
ORCAS ISLAND
AUGUST 17, 2002

PACIFIC NORTHWEST OYSTERS
served on the half shell with chipotle aioli

DUNGENESS CRAB COCKTAILS
*with avocado basil sauce, watercress,
and lemon vinaigrette*

SEA BASS AND PACIFIC SALMON BROCHETTES
with summer vegetables and potato risotto

MINIATURE FRUIT AND BLACKBERRY TARTS
AND CHOCOLATE SWEETS
espresso, coffee and tea

WEDDING CAKE

Table

Mrs. Lea Dirken

Laura & Dave Hoberecht
August 17, 2002

ALL ABOUT PAPER

STOCK

Paper can be made of many different materials and comes in all sorts of textures, finishes and weights—each of which, along with how it's manufactured, affects the price. "Stock" refers to how many pounds a ream (500 sheets) of a particular paper weighs. In general, the heavier the stock, the more expensive the paper. Lighter stocks (for example, 24 to 32 lb.) generally work best for folded or layered invitations and offset printing, while heavier paper (60 lb. and higher) lends itself to single-panel styles, perfect for engraving or letterpress. (See more about printing methods on pages 48 and 49.) You can print an invitation on anything from vellum (a translucent cellulose paper) to rice paper (a soft paper ideal for letterpress). Still, most brides choose opaque cotton paper, also known as rag, which is more refined than that made from wood pulp. Acid-free paper that is 100 percent cotton lasts longest, so it's best for keepsakes.

SHAPES

Traditional invitations, with printing appearing on the first page of a folded sheet or on a single sheet of heavy paper, are either 4½" x 6¼" or 5½" x 7½" rectangles, known as classic and embassy sizes, respectively. But you're certainly not limited to these two choices. The square has increased in popularity, as has the tea-length style, a long rectangle that measures about 4" x 9¼". Keep in mind that large or unusually shaped invitations often require costly custom-made envelopes or additional postage. If you need to convey lots of information—such as listing two sets of parents as hosts, for instance, or adding information regarding a foreign ceremony site—consider a folded card. In addition to the simple bifold, formats include the accordion-pleated style, the tri- or C-fold (which opens like a gate to reveal three panels), and the French fold—a double-folded, four-panel card. (Information such as maps and driving directions is usually best confined to a separate sheet of paper, which is fine to print using a laser printer and can be included with the invitation or sent separately after your responses come in.)

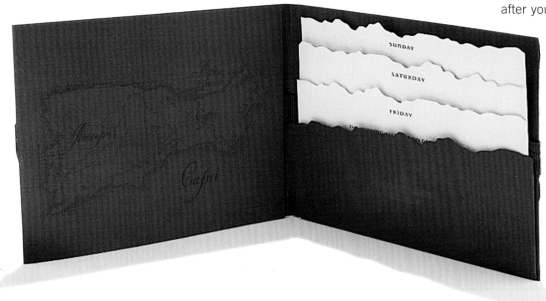

ABOVE: Music executive L.A. Reid's custom-folder invitation re-created Capri's cliffs in coral hues, giving guests a preview of their destination.

OPPOSITE, CLOCKWISE FROM TOP: Trifold invitation. Accordion-fold invitation. Petal-fold invitation. Bifold invitation. Trifold invitation with pocket. Bamboo scroll on rice paper.

PRINTING METHODS

While many elements of a wedding invitation can vary, including the size, shape, color, weight and material from which it's made, when it comes to putting ink to paper, these are your four basic options.

ENGRAVING
The most formal and typically most expensive option, engraving is made by etching type into metal plates, which are then impressed on paper. (The "bruising," or indentation, on the back of the paper and the raised type that results are the telltale signs that an invitation has been engraved.) This process produces crisp, matte type, which makes it ideal for use with white ink on dark paper, metallic inks and, of course, the classic pairing of black ink on ivory paper. Engraving requires paper with substantial weight, such as card stock. This method is traditionally used with time-honored scripts, but contemporary fonts are increasingly popular.

Espresso brown invitation engraved with light blue and ecru inks on 100 percent cotton stock with matching lined envelope.

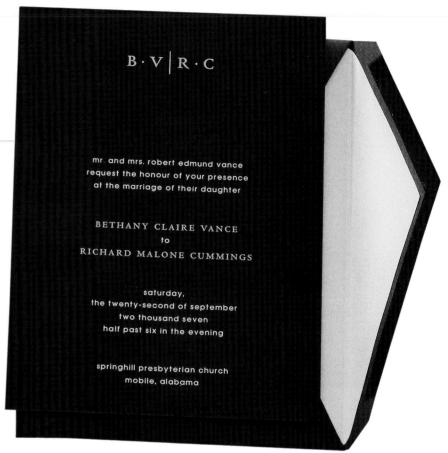

LETTERPRESS
Like engraving, letterpress is an age-old technique that is labor-intensive and costly—and can sometimes be as expensive as engraving. But while engraved printing appears raised, letterpress type is created by manual impression, producing indented type. A letterpress invitation can be either formally worded or casual, but it has a certain handmade look about it: The type often appears slightly weathered and the ink somewhat diffuse. A heavier, softer paper is ideal with this type of printing.

Smooth, bright white invitation printed with letterpress type on heavy card stock with multi-colored stripe detail and coordinating pink envelope.

OFFSET LITHOGRAPHY

Also known as flat printing or litho, offset lithography is what you'll find on such everyday items as standard store-bought greeting cards and magazines. It is the least expensive, most adaptable and widely available option—100 invitations can be had for around $100. Though not as elegant in appearance as engraving, offset printing can look quite modern, depending on the design of your invitation, and is ideal for those you design yourself. Use smooth, strong paper to achieve the best result.

Square, hot-pink invitation with offset lithography type on heavy card stock.

TOGETHER WITH THEIR PARENTS

jennifer lynn di leva
&
rory jason radcliff

REQUEST THE HONOR OF YOUR PRESENCE AT THEIR WEDDING

*

Saturday morning, the sixth of March
Two thousand and four
at ten o'clock

*

THE NEIGHBORHOOD CHURCH
PALOS VERDES ESTATES, CALIFORNIA

Lunch & merriment to follow
Hyatt Regency Long Beach

MR. AND MRS. DONALD FINDLAY

REQUEST THE HONOUR OF YOUR PRESENCE

AT THE NUPTIAL MASS UNITING THEIR DAUGHTER

Cari Natalie

AND

Mr. Daniel Harper Boylan

IN THE SACRAMENT OF HOLY MATRIMONY

SATURDAY, THE TWENTY-SIXTH OF AUGUST

TWO THOUSAND AND SIX

AT ELEVEN O'CLOCK IN THE MORNING

SAINT PATRICK'S CATHEDRAL

CHARLOTTE, NORTH CAROLINA

THERMOGRAPHY

If you love the look of engraving but your budget won't allow it, thermography is a cost-effective alternative that uses a heat-based process and resin powder to create raised lettering. Thermographic type doesn't have the crispness of engraving and is shiny rather than matte, but it can cost nearly 50 percent less. Midweight, smooth paper is preferable to use with thermography, because it allows the resin to adhere properly.

Prussian-blue card with thin white border and brown thermography type on heavy acid-free paper with blue envelopes lined in matching brown.

WORDING

The invitation is most often issued by those paying for the wedding. Traditionally, that means the parents of the bride, and thus their names usually appear on the first line:

Mr. and Mrs. James Colin Reynolds
request the honor of your presence
at the marriage of their daughter
Corinne Chase
to
Mr. Stephen Frederick Bradshaw III

Lines indicating the date and time of the ceremony and the name and address of the place where it will be held follow. (A separate reception card is traditionally included as an insert if the ceremony and reception take place at different locations.) Note that while the groom's name is preceded by an honorific, the bride's name is not.

But the invitation can also be sent out by both sets of parents, in which case the bride's parents' names appear on the first line (assuming they are picking up or splitting the tab) and the groom's parents' on the third, separated by the word "and" on the second line. Or, as is increasingly the case with older brides and grooms who are hosting the wedding themselves, the couple issues the invitation. In this case the bride's name and honorific ("Ms. Corinne Chase Reynolds") appears on the first line, and the groom's ("Mr. Stephen Frederick Bradshaw III") on the third, again, separated by the word "and." Or it might read: "You are cordially invited to celebrate the wedding of" followed by the same sequence of names.

While these wordings are the most traditional, there's certainly plenty of leeway these days for families looking for something different. A more informal invitation issued by the bride's parents might start with the lines:

Our joy will be more complete
if you will share in the marriage of our daughter

These would then be followed by the bride's and groom's names. Or if the bride and groom are the hosts, they might drop the honorifics and begin, "Corinne Chase Reynolds and Stephen Frederick Bradshaw III invite you to celebrate their wedding," then proceed with lines indicating the time and place of the ceremony.

Of course every couple's family situations differ, and when divorced, widowed or remarried parents host the wedding, you will need to alter the standard wording to reflect such circumstances. For more information consult a good wedding etiquette guide, such as *Emily Post's Wedding Etiquette: Cherished Traditions and Contemporary Ideas for a Joyous Celebration,* by Peggy Post.

BELOW: Three-color letterpress invitation with poppy motif, issued by couple with their families.

OPPOSITE, TOP ROW: Gold-engraved invitation with gold beveled edge, issued by the bride's parents. Letterpress invitation and envelope in blossom and chocolate inks, issued by couple.

OPPOSITE, BOTTOM ROW: Two-color letterpress invitation, issued by couple. Letterpress invitation on cotton finished paper with plum type and fall leaves motif, issued by couple with their families.

Lily Mei & Christopher Quimby

TOGETHER WITH THEIR FAMILIES
LILY AND CHRISTOPHER
INVITE YOU TO CELEBRATE THEIR MARRIAGE
SATURDAY, AUGUST 27TH, 2005
7 O'CLOCK PM
CLASSICAL CHINESE GARDEN
PORTLAND, OREGON

DINNER AND DANCING TO FOLLOW

Mr. and Mrs. John Kenneth Upham
request the honour of your presence
at the marriage of their daughter
Elizabeth Ann
to
Mr. Paul Niles Howell
Saturday, the twenty-second of June
Two thousand and two
at five o'clock
Fall River Club
Denver, Colorado

HEATHER AND ETHAN
delacroix   matheson

request the pleasure of your company
at the celebration of their marriage
saturday, march 20, 2004 at five o'clock
in the japanese tea gardens
in golden gate park
san francisco, california

DINNER & DANCING TO FOLLOW

LAYLA & JAMES

You are invited to share in the joy as
Layla Nolan and James Ball join their lives in marriage
Saturday, the twenty ninth of June, Two thousand and three
at half past the hour of six o'clock in the evening

06.29.03

Lido Beach Golf Club • Lido Beach, New York
Reception and Celebration to follow

Suzanne Marie McAllister

and

Michael John DiMaio

together with their families

request the honor of your presence

at their marriage

Saturday, the twelfth of October

Two thousand and two

at two o'clock

Beaulieu Gardens

Rutherford, California

HOLLYWOOD AND VINES

AMY ACKER AND JAMES CARPINELLO

You might say that on Amy Acker's wedding day the bride herself was something blue. Bundled up in blankets in a cold, dark guest cottage on a Napa Valley vineyard, just hours before her nuptials to actor James Carpinello, the actress and her bridal party waited for a raging storm to end and the power—and heat—to return. "It was 35 degrees, and no one had the courage to get dressed!" says Acker. Then, five minutes before the ceremony was set to start, the clouds parted and the power flickered on.

Sunlight at last streamed through the rose- and moss-adorned tent set up on the Giverny-like grounds as Acker, carrying red roses and chocolate cosmos, walked down an aisle covered with red douppioni silk. During the marriage rites, an all-family bridal party surrounded the couple, and Carpinello's childhood friend, Broadway singer Tim Fitz-Gerald, offered a rendition of Andrea Bocelli and Celine Dion's "The Prayer."

Guests later enjoyed a three-course dinner served in a wine cave, once used to store barrels but now outfitted with a 56-foot-long mosaic table laden with crystals and candles. At each place setting: a menu card printed by Exclamation Invitations of Petaluma, Calif., with a Gothic-style monogram of the letters "AC"—for the bride's and the groom's last names. The motif, which had appeared on the invitations, was repeated on cookie favors and projected in light onto the wall of the cave. "It made the event more personal," explains wedding planner Sasha Souza.

The party kicked into full swing when guests break-danced and limboed across the room and Carpinello announced the opening of a food station called the A&J Diner, serving mini grilled ham-and-cheese sandwiches and french fries. "I've been to weddings where all people do is look at the clock because they can't wait until the bride and groom cut the cake," said actress Alyson Hannigan, a guest. "But this is the kind where no one wants to leave."

> **ABOVE:** Along the single red mosaic dining table sat menu cards with a monogrammed motif, which also appeared on the couple's place cards. **BELOW, LEFT TO RIGHT:** Both the bride's bouquet and the cake featured red roses; the couple shares a kiss. **OPPOSITE:** The bride and groom lead guests to the reception through the vineyard's garden.

THE
DRESS

Duchesse satin, slipper satin, taffeta, organza, chiffon, douppioni, broderie Anglais, peau de soie. Just the names of wedding dress fabrics sound shimmering and magical, like something out of Hans Christian Andersen by way of Christian Lacroix. You may have the diamond on your finger and a deposit with the caterer, but until you step out of a dressing room to the tears and cheers of your mother or your best friend, you may not feel like you're really a bride-to-be. And yet, if the fantasy of a wedding gown is the stuff of little girls' daydreams, the reality of choosing the right one usually requires some steely determination and a very grown-up mindset indeed.

Typically made of about five to seven yards of fabric, a dress, perhaps more than any other wedding element, conveys how you want to be perceived on one of the most important—and highly scrutinized—days of your life. In the past, when there were rules and rituals about such things, a wedding gown was white and modest and fairly predictable. Queen Victoria, the monarch who first shed fusty, fur-trimmed robes as royal wedding garb, popularized the long white dress with full train, and the style remained pretty much the same for more than a hundred years.

Now a bride can march down the aisle in anything from a breezy shift to something so cumbersome it requires special furniture to allow the bride to sit in it, as Melania Trump's 60-pound, crystal-encrusted, duchesse satin dress

Floral embroidery and tiny, covered buttons create a delicate, snowy white pattern that plays off the flowers in the bridal bouquet.

The simplest of details—a thin ribbon or sash around the waist (above) or a lacy hem grazing a pair of strappy sandals (right)—can make a gown extraordinary. News correspondent Elizabeth Vargas's strapless Vera Wang gown (opposite) relied on a streamlined silhouette, a waist-hugging cummerbund and layers of airy chiffon for its understated beauty.

famously did. Perhaps your big-day ideal is a Russian princess–style satin ballgown topped by a shawl-collared coat with a grand flourish of a train, à la Kate Hudson. Or would you, like model Kirsty Hume, prefer to see yourself as a modern-day Guinevere? Maybe you're the type who fancies herself a 1940s screen goddess in body-skimming, bias-cut satin as Jenny McCarthy did on her wedding day, or are you a thoroughly modern Millie who would no sooner wear a bustle than a beehive hair-do?

Keep in mind that even a bride who thinks she knows herself well might be surprised by what she ends up choosing. "I had an idea of what I wanted, and it was nothing like what I ended up with," recalls actress Jennie Garth of her search for the right dress for her wedding to Peter Facinelli. "I wanted something simple, low-key," she explains. But when she saw the lavish, exquisitely embel-

A veil is often thought of as a traditional accessory, intended to be worn with a classic dress such as this boatneck, A-line style (above). But a sweeping version (opposite) can lend an exotic touch to a more modern slip dress.

The drama of embellishment: Ruffles dress up a train that recalls a flamenco dancer's (above, left), while shells in a floral pattern bedeck a pair of dainty sandals (above, right). Actress Kimberly Williams wore a nearly unadorned gown by Monique Lhuillier when she wed singer Brad Paisley, then changed for the reception into a Mark Zunino dress appliquéd with denim flowers and matching denim coat, lined in paisley to match her husband's tie (opposite).

lished styles by designer Reem Acra, who dressed actresses Melissa Joan Hart and Christina Applegate for their wedding days, she changed her mind. Ultimately she chose a custom-made ivory satin ballgown with a sweeping train. The fitted bodice twinkled with a scattering of Swarovski crystals and arabesques of silver embroidery inspired by ancient Turkish upholstery patterns. Wispy cap sleeves added a dollop of delicacy to the gown's ornate richness.

Garth is not the only bride to surprise her fans and admirers and perhaps herself. Who would have guessed, for instance, that siren Marilyn Monroe would wed Joe DiMaggio in a demure fur-collared brown suit, or that belly-baring neo-punk pop star Gwen Stefani would channel her inner princess in a pink and white full-skirted silk faille number? Of course, some women are either so sure of—or so casual about—their big-day look, endless shopping isn't an issue. Says Tori Spelling, "I knew from the beginning that I wanted to create a 1920s feel with

my dress." So she shared her ideas with Mark Badgley and James Mischka of the design team Badgley-Mischka, who then turned out her dream in diaphanous, hand-beaded silk with a bejeweled Empire waist, a v-neck with embroidered illusion inset, and feathery cap sleeves. Meanwhile Talisa Soto bought her silk chiffon dress—which she wore with flip-flops at her simple, outdoor wedding to Benjamin Bratt—off the rack, without any hand-wringing whatsoever.

Nevertheless, if you're like most brides, you'll try on about 12 gowns before you find the one of your dreams, and you may, of course, wriggle your way through many more swaths of satin and acres of Alençon lace than that before you have your "aha!" moment, standing ballerina-like on that pedestal before the three-way mirror. Besides bridal salons, you'll want to check out department stores, sample sales, and—if the thought of a one-of-kind dress appeals—dressmakers' ateliers, vintage shops and even perhaps your mother's closet. (Actress Sharon Lawrence wed in an altered version of the candlelight satin style her mother had worn more than 40 years earlier.) Your taste will determine what styles you gravitate towards, of course, but so should your budget, your figure and the setting of the wedding.

As with most items on your wedding-day checklist, your choice will depend to a large extent on your budget. The average cost of a wedding dress now hovers at just under $900, though many brides are willing to splurge on this singularly important purchase, spending upwards of five figures on a creation made especially for them, with custom touches like a train hand-sewn with crystals to form a monogram. Others, of course, happily find beautiful, albeit simple, styles for a few hundred dollars. Whatever your price range, give yourself enough time so that you can

For her marriage on the Italian Riviera to writer Rick Marin, writer and entrepreneur Ilene Rosenzweig donned a gown of Italian lace designed and hand-painted by her business partner, fashion designer Cynthia Rowley. Beneath its hem is a pair of Manolo Blahnik heels dyed pale green, one of her favorite colors.

zero in on The One at least six months before your wedding day, which will allow plenty of time for alterations (plan on three fittings for anything that's not cash and carry), and decide what you're willing to spend early on, so as not to waste time and effort pursuing things you can't afford.

Most important, know what it is your money can buy you. For $1,000, you can have a lovely gown with a few well-placed details—a dusting of sequins on the bodice or floral appliqués along the hem—but high-quality head-to-toe lace is pretty much out of the question, as is heavy beadwork or dense embroidery. Luckily, more and more design firms are offering beautiful gowns for mere hundreds rather than thousands, and they're often made of real silk. Remember that shiny fabrics, such as satin, tend to look cheaper when they aren't of high quality, while the differences between expensive and more modest matte fabrics, such as chiffon, are harder to discern.

As for finding a style that's flattering, take someone whom you trust shopping with you and try on as many different kinds of styles as you have the patience for—even the ones you need to be talked into. Corseted bodices will help hold in a round tummy, draped necklines can disguise a small bustline, and Empire styles work to downplay a short waist. But these are only guidelines, and every bride-to-be should remain open to possibilities above all else. What looks so-so on the hanger can be enchanting on the body. If you're unsure what works best, remember two pieces of advice from one of the world's foremost authorities on the subject, designer Vera Wang, whose bridal clients have included Kate Beckinsale and Angie Harmon. "An A-line dress is the all-time biggest problem solver, whether full and constructed or soft and deconstructed," she says. And if you want to show some skin, she points out that the area around the clavicle is attractive on almost every woman—one reason strapless styles are perennially popular with brides from Joan Lunden to Renée Zellweger.

Additionally, you shouldn't forget where it is you'll be exchanging vows. A cream puff of a ballgown, with

A classic sheer tulle veil complemented the Badgley Mischka goddess gown dusted with crystal rosettes worn by actress Idina Menzel for her marriage to actor Taye Diggs (below) in Montego Bay, Jamaica, and also sets off modern "shredded ruffles" on the custom-designed wedding dress of a New York City bride posing before the Brooklyn Bridge (opposite).

millefeuilles of crinoline, looks as silly on the beach as a knee-length slipdress and beaded flip-flops do in a cathedral. And although Monique Lhuillier, couturier to Sarah Jessica Parker and Angelina Jolie, applauds the decline of what she calls "dowdy" bridal fashion—"sleeves that are too big, bodices junked up with too many beads"—think carefully about wearing a super-sexy ensemble on your wedding day. "A wedding gown should have a certain propriety built in," says Wang. In other words, you should probably err on the side of dignified rather than daring. What's the final rule? Relax your notion of the rules. "The goal is to discover the right combination of neckline, waistline and skirt style that come together to create the perfect gown for your day," says designer Helen Morley. "You can't always predict the outcome by arming yourself with a set of preconceived notions." Arm yourself instead with an open mind, an honest friend and the willingness to be utterly transformed before your very eyes. As with the man you'll meet at the end of the aisle, there's a perfect match for you out there somewhere. All you have to do is find it.

Fresh flowers tucked into the hair set off an unstudied wedding look (above), yet they add an appropriate flourish to a more formal gown, too, such as Mariska Hargitay's silk version with inverted back pleat (opposite). "It was such a great dress," actor Peter Hermann says of her choice.

SILHOUETTES

These six examples, form-fitting to full-skirted, represent the basic styles when it comes to wedding gowns. Find the one that flatters you best.

BALLGOWN
The most classic of wedding dress shapes, the ballgown features a close-fitting bodice, with either a natural, dropped or Basque (v-shaped) waist, and a very full skirt. The skirt helps to hide curvy hips, and the volume can make a thick middle look less so by comparison. Nevertheless, heavy brides—as well as very tall ones—should consider something less imposing, while petite figures can be overwhelmed by this style.

Sleeveless ballgown with slightly dropped waist and skirt with tulle overlay.

MERMAID
Evocative of '30s screen goddesses, this sexy style hugs the body to about mid-thigh, then flares out slightly (looking at the hem a bit like a mermaid's tail). A mermaid silhouette is most appealing on slim or hourglass figures.

Satin fishtail gown with chiffon wraparound ties (left).

SHEATH
The clean-lined sheath made its mark on fashion in the 1950s. It features a straight skirt and no waist seam and employs darts and seaming to achieve a proper fit. Those with balanced proportions can wear this one well, especially petite brides, for whom this style helps give the illusion of height.

Ivory mikado silk shantung gown with boatneck (far left).

The accent in a bouquet can come by way of a single contrasting bloom—white stephanotis blossoms amidst purple hydrangea (above, left) or the curved pink petals of cattleya orchids against a background of green viburnum (above, right)—or even something so small as pom-poms dangling from the cuff that wraps the stems (opposite).

fruit can evoke a Dutch still-life, and a centerpiece accented with sprigs of mint and rosemary makes for a lovely summertime display. If your ceremony is taking place in a house of worship, you may want substantial arrangements to flank the altar or chuppah and garlands to hang from pews or chair backs. Or, depending on the interior design, you may decide to keep things simple: When the late Carolyn Bessette and John Kennedy married in a rustic clapboard chapel on Georgia's Cumberland Island, a few spare arrangements of wildflowers and trailing vines served as the only decoration. At an outdoor wedding, consider building a flower-twined arbor to mark the place where you'll exchange your vows, and if you plan a wedding reception on the beach, remember that tall arrangements aren't windproof: Single gardenias floating in glass bowls make a more practical choice.

Whatever your ceremony and reception venues, take a survey of the site or sites with your florist, noting the style of the décor or the mood of the natural surroundings. If you've booked a ballroom as your reception site, are there entryways or wall niches that cry out for formal arrangements? Or if the local park is where you'll wed, would bunches of plush-petaled ranunculus help dress up plain black fence railings? Assuming you have a table for escort cards, how do you plan to adorn it? Note that if you choose a place that's essentially a blank canvas, such as an empty, white-walled photo studio, you've got more range when it comes to types of flowers, but you'll probably need more of them to keep the space from feeling empty. There's nothing worse than meager arrangements that seem lost in their surroundings. Flowers convey the message of celebration, after all.

In fact, in prim Victorian society, flowers were assigned symbolic meanings, and lovers who were otherwise unable to express their feelings felt free to do so using doily-wrapped bouquets—or "tussy mussies"— as their medium. Few know that daisies say "I share your sentiment," that carnations symbolize pure love, or that irises represent a promise. But at a wedding, everyone understands and appreciates the silent declarations made by the flowers on display, whether daisies or dahlias, lilies or lisianthus: Exuberance, bliss, celebration, love—the language of flowers needs no translation.

Rose petals are a romantic way to incorporate flowers into the ceremony. This bride uses just a delicate smattering, but to completely blanket the aisle, figure on spending between $2,000 and $3,000, says celebrity wedding planner Preston Bailey.

CLASSIC BLOOMS

ROSE The classic wedding flower, the rose comes in hundreds of varieties and shades to match nearly every color scheme. Hybrid tea roses, grown commercially, are readily available, will last throughout the day and, with their tightly furled heads, tend to be uniform in shape and size. The downside: They have only a subtle aroma or none at all. Lush, full-headed garden roses are more fragile, more expensive, less uniform and have a delicious scent. They're particularly nice for more informal weddings. Availability: hybrid roses, year-round; garden rose, May through early July.

Classic red roses (below). Cheryl Hines with her ring bearers, cousins Griffith and Graham Hines (right). She carried a bouquet of red roses bound by a blue ribbon created by her florist and makeup artist, Tom Kolarek.

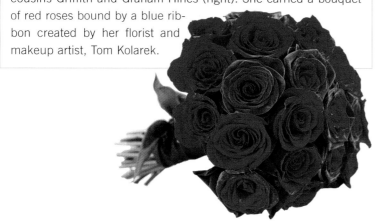

LILY The heavy perfume of lilies—particularly Casablanca and Stargazer varieties—makes them either an instant turn-off or a favorite, and with three to seven heads on one stem, they offer good value as a wedding bloom. Oriental lilies, available in white, pinks and red, are priciest, while Asiatic varieties—the sort sold at grocery stores—make for a relative bargain. As accents, white lilies provide a glamorous touch to classic bouquets; used alone in bright hues, they can look quite modern. Be careful of their stamens: The pollen spills easily and tends to stain. Availability: year-round, but best in spring and summer.

Asiatic, nerine and gloriosa lilies mixed with calla lilies.

LILY OF THE VALLEY
With their dainty, bell-shaped florets and their heavenly fragrance, lily of the valley look pretty alone (as a ribbon-wrapped posy) or mixed with other relaxed-looking blooms, such as sweet pea or garden roses. Though typically pure white, there exists a rarer pink version. The high price and short growing season of lily of the valley means it isn't the best option for every bride. Availability: late April through late May.

Lily of the valley with hyacinth.

TULIP
Tulips, with their clean, cup-shaped heads and sleek stems, are versatile wedding flowers, working well in both formal and more casual settings. Dutch tulips are by far the most common type; they are known for their small, compact heads, short stems and variety of shades. Elegant—and more expensive—French tulips have longer, tapered heads and stems that can measure twelve inches or more. They're most often white or pastel-hued. Parrot tulips feature ruffled, brightly striped petals, and while they're showy, their heavy heads mean they tend to sag. Availability: year-round, but best in fall, winter and spring.

Parrot tulips in citrus tones (above). Cream-colored tulips dotted with grape hyacinths and surrounded by variegated ivy (right).

MORE CLASSIC BLOOMS

ORCHID Perhaps the most exotic, seductive-looking wedding-day blooms, orchids come in shades from white to vibrant pink to chartreuse. While they are cultivated in thousands of species, only a few are typically used for weddings. Fragrant, star-shaped cymbidium orchids and wide, flat-petaled phalaenopsis orchids are the most expensive. Though both are quite hardy, they can perish in cold weather. Long-stemmed dendrobiums—perfect for a cascade bouquet—and cattleya orchids, with their thin, curved petals, are a relative bargain. Tiny oncidium orchids, known as spray orchids, are most often used as accents. Availability: year-round.

A cascade of cattleya orchids and cyclamen leaves (right). Cymbidium orchids, camellia, kalanchoe and miniature ranunculus (far right).

CALLA LILY These long-stemmed, trumpet-shaped flowers, popular in imagery from the Art Nouveau period, make a bold statement when carried in the crook of the arm as a pageant bouquet set off by a sleek, fitted gown. Mini calla lilies, which have shorter stems and smaller heads, make striking nosegays, though their long, narrow shape means it takes at least 30 stems to make a bouquet. To save money, use them as accents: Their pointed tips can add nice texture to a round bouquet. Ivory is the most popular color, but calla lilies come in shades ranging from yellow to mauve to dark purple. Availability: year-round, though best in winter to late spring.

Burgundy calla lilies accented with orange freesia (left). Richly hued, short-stemmed miniature calla lilies (right).

HYDRANGEA

Round, bushy heads of scent-free blossoms characterize this garden favorite, which is most often found in shades of blue, pink, purple or white (though green ones can also look chic in a like-hued or white bouquet). Moderately priced with a casual, romantic feel, hydrangea works nicely with lilacs, delphinium and other garden blooms, but can also help to fill out bouquets composed of more formal-looking flowers. Availability: July through November.

Gloriosa lilies, hydrangea and nerine lilies (below). Green hydrangea gathered with butter-yellow hyacinths and green viburnum (right, top); purple hydrangea, anemones and viburnum berries (right, bottom).

GARDENIA

Creamy-petaled, ivory-hued gardenias have a rich perfume and a high price tag. To keep costs down, use them sparingly: Two or three floating in a low bowl makes a clean, modern centerpiece, while a smaller posy, off-set by the flower's waxy green leaves, can be quite pretty as a bouquet. Because they tend to wilt and bruise easily, think twice before carrying gardenias in hot, humid weather, and wet your fingers before handling them: even oil from your skin can harm the petals. Gardenias show especially well at a softly lit nighttime wedding. Availability: year-round.

An arrangement of gardenias, silver dusty miller and green amaranthus.

PALE BOUQUETS

Gatherings of such ultrafeminine flowers as roses, lilies and tulips in white or pale pastels may be the classic choice for a bridal bouquet, but depending on the flowers and the way they're arranged, monochromatic mixes of light-hued blooms can also look quite modern.

ABOVE: Vendella roses and green hydrangea tied with white French satin ribbon.

OPPOSITE, TOP ROW, FROM LEFT: White calla lilies. Cymbidium orchids, roses and hydrangea. Femma roses.

MIDDLE ROW, FROM LEFT: Chartreuse cymbidium orchids accent arabicum and limona roses. Cream spray roses tied with blue taffeta ribbon. Lily of the valley and lisianthus with a collar of white feathers.

BOTTOM ROW, FROM LEFT: Lily of the valley and bouvardia. Peonies, calla lilies and garden roses. Lavender sweet pea.

BRIGHT BOUQUETS

Deep red roses, tropical-hued orchids or vivid bunches of calla lilies make a splash when carried by the bride. "A vibrant bouquet contrasts nicely with a white gown and is a modern twist on tradition," says celebrity wedding planner Jo Gartin, who owns Love, Luck and Angels in Los Angeles and whose past clients include comedian Molly Shannon and actors Fred Savage and Elizabeth Banks. If you want to use color in your bouquet, remember that using one basic hue or those from the same color family tends to look more sophisticated than a mix of many contrasting shades.

RIGHT: A beachy bouquet of peach plumeria, pale green anemones, green pompon mums, gold-tinged lady's mantle and seeded mini-Brazilla accented with polished South African turban shells.

OPPOSITE, TOP ROW, FROM LEFT: Cappuccino ranunculus, myrtle, calla lilies and orinthogalum entwined with spring grasses (top); yellow ranunculus, hyacinth, Limbo roses, and mimosa wrapped in a leaf cuff (bottom). Black Beauty and Black Magic roses with chartreuse lady's mantle. Gerber daisies, Oriental lilies, rosemary and Lipstick roses.

MIDDLE ROW, FROM LEFT: Faux amethysts nestled in a bouquet of pink heliborus and mauve Allure and Curiosa roses. Grape-hyacinth nosegay bound with a lavender satin cuff (left); anemones, sweet pea, hydrangea, lisianthus and veronica (right). Black calla lilies with ranunculus, tulips, seeded eucalyptus, miniature artichokes, scented geraniums and fern fronds.

BOTTOM ROW, FROM LEFT: Purple-haze calla lilies. Roses, bittersweet, cymbidium orchids, and acorns draped in green glass seed beads. Orange, coral and golden Iceland poppies bound with glass seed beads (left); ranunculus and miniature mandarin oranges (right).

DÉCOR

No matter what flowers you use for center-pieces and other decorative arrangements, keep a few simple rules in mind. In general, the ceiling height in the room will determine how tall your centerpieces should be, but remember that your guests need to be able to look over or under any arrangement. Either less than 14 inches in height or more than 20 inches usually allows guests to see one another across the table. Consider varying the heights and shapes of your centerpieces. It gives a space visual rhythm and creates less of a hotel convention room look. Don't feel compelled to use traditional vases. Vessels can range from containers on stone pedestals to lacquered boxes to low bowls to antique silver urns depending on the style of the arrangements and the room's décor. For grander arrangements, such as those used to flank an altar, large-headed, long-stemmed flowers work best (and white or bright colors are good choices in houses of worship, which are often dimly lit), while garlands often include smaller blooms, like stephanotis, along with smilax, ivy and other greenery.

ABOVE, TOP ROW, FROM LEFT: White roses in a bronze urn. A cupid crowned with a floral wreath of yellow roses, kumquat and mixed leaves.

LEFT: Peach roses and red dahlias line a long banquet table.

BOTTOM ROW, FROM LEFT: Flowered candelabras, designed by London florist Rob Van Helden, lined the aisle of Ireland's Ballintubber Abbey, as Pierce Brosnan and Keely Shaye Smith exchanged vows. A heart-shaped wreath of roses.

OPPOSITE, TOP: Actress Mel Harris presented a 1958 Dodge Power Wagon to her new husband, Michael Toomey. Her friend and florist, actress Gail Grady, decorated it with wildflowers and guests filled it with wedding presents.

OPPOSITE, BOTTOM ROW, FROM LEFT: Rose petals brighten an escort card table. A gardenia accents a simple place setting. Garlands of greenery and gardenias work to beautifully set off a seating area.

BUDGET TIPS

BUY IN SEASON

Choosing flowers that grow naturally at the time of your wedding can save you up to 40 percent. To ensure you get the best deal, avoid pre-ordering specific blooms. Instead, ask your florist to purchase the best of what's available in your color palette a day or two before your wedding.

FAKE IT

Many inexpensive blooms can easily substitute for pricier picks. Ranunculus look similar to roses, for example; stephanotis can double for more costly lily of the valley for less than half the price; and you won't spend as much on dendrobium orchids as cymbidiums, though you'll still have a gorgeous bouquet.

THINK BIG

Masses of smaller blooms, such as freesia, stephanotis, lily of the valley or miniature calla lilies, can inflate your budget. For an outdoor wedding, place a few large flowers, such as open roses, peonies, lilies or hydrangea (a particularly large and cost-effective bloom) in vintage rusted urns or hand-painted terracotta pots and you'll need only a few stems to make a pretty presentation. For something more modern, try potted amaryllis or orchids.

LOOK AGAIN

Some modest blooms, like carnations and baby's breath, suffer from a reputation as being either cheap or cliché. But a bouquet made exclusively of either of these well-priced flowers makes a striking, modern arrangement that's anything but tired. Other once-maligned blooms worth a second look: velvety, rippled coxcomb, gladioli and chrysanthemums.

GET CREATIVE

Heap groupings of pears, apples or plums glazed in sugar in footed glass bowls for a pretty alternative to flowers, or nestle lemons or limes in among flowers in a centerpiece to stretch your budget. Use ivy and other greens to give a lush look with fewer blooms, which can be lovelier than a tight arrangement. Berries on stems are another attractive accent, or beautiful on their own. Rent potted plants or place two or three huge elephant leaves in simple glass vases to dress up a room rather than relying on tall floral arrangements. For a moderately priced centerpiece, display pillar candles in varying heights on silver trays.

BELOW, FROM LEFT: Miniature peach Italian ranunculus with celadon centers. Viburnum berries. Zinnias bound with raffia (left); celosia tied with a plaid ribbon (right).

USE YOUR SETTING

If you like the idea of marrying in a park, a garden or a vineyard, plan your wedding for a time when trees and flowers will be in bloom or, in the case of a vineyard, when the grapes are ready to be harvested. (Or hold your ceremony in a backyard garden, where friends can pick blooming plants and flowers to use as boutonnieres or small arrangements.) At night, play up the beauty of towering trees by stringing a few sets of Christmas lights or lanterns in them.

AVOID THE HOLIDAYS

Remember that prices for flowers always soar around Valentine's Day and Mother's Day, so plan accordingly.

CLOCKWISE FROM TOP RIGHT: Cherry roses and limes in a silver vase. Yellow ranunculus wrapped in horse tail, parrot tulips, gloriosa lilies and orange protea reflect the colorful Chinese lanterns that are as successful at scene-setting as an abundant floral décor. Ivy, peonies and amaryllis in an irridescent glazed china vase.

A NOVEL IDEA

TORI SPELLING
AND CHARLIE SHANIAN

What bride but Tori Spelling could host a pre-ceremony cocktail party in an all-white lounge that usually serves as the family's 10-car garage? Even without a Corniche or a Corvette, Spelling was riding high on the day she wed actor-writer Charlie Shanian in a setting meant to mimic the glamour of Gatsby's slice of West Egg, right down to the period-perfect shallow champagne *coupes*. Says Spelling, "They spill a little, but, darn, they look good!"

The radiant bride almost took a spill herself when her father, legendary TV producer Aaron Spelling, stepped on the train of her crystal-beaded Chantilly lace Badgley Mischka dress as he kissed her at the head of the aisle. "My dad was so cute—he was nervous," explains the actress, who carried a frothy clutch of lily of the valley to join her groom, whom she first met when she co-starred in a play he co-wrote called, auspiciously, *Maybe Baby, It's You*. The Jewish and Christian ceremony included self-written vows, a reading of a Native American blessing by Tori's younger brother, Randy, and the breaking of the glass under a chuppah dripping with armloads of fragrant white flowers.

Former *Beverly Hills 90210* co-stars Jennie Garth, Tiffani Thiessen and Jason Priestley, along with more than 300 other guests, were then ushered to a gauzy tent where wedding planner Mindy Weiss had bedecked tables with luscious centerpieces of white roses, hydrangea and lily of the valley. While cabaret crooner Michael Feinstein sang Irving Berlin's "What'll I Do?" (which was on the *The Great*

Gatsby soundtrack), waiters served courses of *loup de mer en croûte* with caviar sauce and sweet-corn-and-mascarpone agnolotti with truffle oil, followed by lemon tarts and a slice from the five-tier, white-frosted cake.

"My parents never really had a grand event here," Spelling says of the 56,500-square-foot home renowned for its bowling alley, ice rink and two gift-wrapping rooms. And how did the Spelling production rate? Says this Charlie's angel, "It was pure perfection."

> **ABOVE:** Spelling and Shanian at one of the dining tables, which were set with a candle in a silver holder and a matchbook for each guest reading "Tori and Charlie: A Perfect Match." **BELOW, LEFT TO RIGHT:** White sugar flowers on the five-tiered cake echoed the lily of the valley in Spelling's bouquet and the centerpieces. Their self-written vows included Spelling referring to Shanian as "my protector." **OPPOSITE:** The couple walked back up the aisle to "I Got You Babe."

THE CAKE

Catherine Zeta-Jones is Hollywood the way it used to be: big diamonds, thrilling dresses, no apologies. "No little barrettes in the hair for me. People want to see a movie star," Zeta-Jones has said of her glamorous look. "I came out of the womb wearing makeup." So when she asked for a wedding cake that was "spectacular," Sylvia Weinstock, the reigning queen of matrimonial confections, made sure it was larger than life—or at least larger than the doors of the Grand Ballroom in New York's Plaza hotel, site of the lavish reception for her wedding to Michael Douglas.

Rising nine feet and 12 tiers high, the creation was a heady mix of dense chocolate cake layered with creamy chocolate ganache, yellow butter cake enlivened with the tart taste of both blood orange and Key lime, and bitter-sweet espresso tiers made even richer with a silky hazelnut filling, all blanketed in a stunning profusion of filigreelike white sugar flowers—tulips, lilies, lily of the valley and baby's breath. It was spectacular. In other words, it was the perfect reflection of the bride who commissioned it.

Certainly a wedding doesn't require so grand a gesture. Rosettes made of sculpted frosting glistening with sugar crystal dewdrops, raspberry jam filling, layers of angel food as light as Chantilly lace—it's all, so to speak, icing on the cake of the day meant to consecrate the bond between you and your groom. Yet this somewhat frivolous accoutrement, with its towering tiers and spun sugar sculptures, can represent one of your wedding's most personal touches. What's more, a wedding cake rarely fails to inspire pure delight, particularly when the moment to cut it arrives.

Actress Natasha Gregson Wagner's cake, made by Very Different Cakes, evoked the enchantment of Belle Époque Paris with dangling beads, feathers and a pair of lovebirds on top.

however, you should know what kind of photography you like before you begin your search. Some artists produce crisp, finely detailed color images, while others' work is soft, slightly blurry and done in black and white. Perhaps gritty photojournalistic shots are the way you want to remember the day, though you may prefer photos that take their cue from fashion pictorials in glossy magazines.

The reason you have such luxury when it comes to choosing a style is that wedding photography has evolved since the formal, posed portraits of your parents' and grandparents' generation. In those days, the shots followed a script from which photographers rarely deviated: the first kiss, the walk back up the aisle, the cutting of the cake—and not much more. Now, wedding photographers, whose ranks have doubled in the past 20 years, often shoot the sort of tiny details your parents might not have thought grand enough to record, but which together with more traditional shots can paint a rich picture of the day. The swirls of calligraphy on an escort card lying casually on a table, the gleaming toe of a satin pump peeking out from under the hem of a gown—while they may seem peripheral, such images can instantly telegraph a mood.

Candid shots have also become a more important part of the mix; often they convey more immediacy and a better sense of emotions than posed ones can. Nevertheless, you will probably want to have formal portraits taken too, to give to family members whose taste may be more traditional and also to ensure that you have photos in which certain family members are grouped together. When it comes to the question of black-and-white or color, many couples choose to have their photographer work in both mediums, as each has its distinct appeal. (A shot of the ceremony at sunset will dazzle in color, while a candid portrait of a guest may seem more refined in black and white.)

And while more and more photographers use digital cameras these days, making it easier for them to print and share images (as well as see images as they're shooting

A posed portrait that includes your wedding party can be as casual (above) or as formal (below) as you wish.

them and correct lighting and contrast accordingly), many still use film or a combination of the two. Advances in technology mean digital prints and ones made from film are virtually indistinguishable, especially to a nonprofessional eye, so usually it comes down to a matter of your photographer's preference. If you do choose a photographer who will work with a digital camera, inquire as to how long he has been doing so, and ask to see images he's shot on film and digitally so you can compare the two.

In your search for a photographer, bring along images that have caught your eye, and take a good look at albums of a candidate's past clients so that you can understand her style as well as the sorts of subjects she tends to shoot. Look at candid and posed shots, indoor and outdoor ones, close-ups and panoramas—as many different kinds of photographs as you can, since your album will probably consist of a combination. Ask to see traditional shots to get an idea of how creative a photographer is when faced with what can seem hoary subject matter. Is the one of the cake simply a dead-on view of four tiers resting square within the frame? Or does the cake sit in the foreground at the edge of the frame while behind it a whirling party takes place, giving a sense of its stolid grandness within the context of a kinetic celebration?

Discuss with candidates the sorts of details you think might be worth recording, and once you've hired someone, be sure to give him a "cheat sheet" with thumbnail photos of the people you want shot during the day. Brides sometimes assume that a photographer either knows instinctively whom to photograph or that everyone will be caught on film at least once during the day, which often isn't the case. Discuss, too, any specific shots you may want taken. Most pros know to take the standard ones of the bouquet toss and the cake-cutting, for example, but if you want a shot of your hand-lettered menus or of your

Candid portraits often show unguarded emotions (above), but just because a group poses for the camera, as the bridesmaids at the wedding of actor Brad Rowe and stylist Lisa Fiori did (below), doesn't mean the shot that results will lack a sense of fun.

Hiring a photographer with a photojournalistic approach will result in photos that have a certain spontaneity about them: from a romantic moment alone between the bride and groom (above) to (opposite, clockwise from top left) bridesmaids thrilled at the first sight of their friend in her wedding dress, a happy moment on the dance floor, a bashfully excited girl who gets to shine as flower girl, and a father's pride.

parents dancing to what was played for the first dance at their wedding, you should make this clear to your photographer ahead of time.

As for videography, you may view this method of documenting the day as an extravagance or you may appreciate the immediacy it offers that still images can't always achieve, particularly since so many developments have been made in the field of videography over the past several years. If you decide to hire a videographer, look for someone who uses digital video editing equipment, which allows for smoother transitions between scenes and the option of using more sophisticated special effects, and discuss such things as music and still images you might want to incorporate into the final cut.

One retro trend that's caught the fancy of actresses such as Mariska Hargitay and Marley Shelton is the use of film rather than video, particularly Super 8 film, which produces the grainy look of a home movie. Though the technology is old-fashioned, the prices aren't: The few companies that offer this service generally charge several thousand dollars for a half-hour of film (the average price for a video is about $1,200 or so, depending on the length, any special effects, and where you live). To avoid putting a captive audience, including yourselves, to sleep while viewing the finished product, try to keep your wedding video to less than 30 minutes (and consider something as brief as 15).

Use the same restraint when making a wedding album from your photos. While you may be tempted by the hundreds of proofs and dozens of contact sheets your photographer provides, most pros recommend that you limit the number of photos in your album to about 40 to 70. Editing your images to such a tight collection ensures that each will be the best of the best and that the overall effect won't be diluted by dozens of repetitive, ho-hum shots. As the great fashion editor Diana Vreeland once said, "Elegance is refusal." You don't need to have every look, gesture and detail represented, in other words—just the ones that capture your heart as well as a moment in time.

The beauty of a portrait of the bridal couple can be enhanced by such techniques as soft focus or sepia-toned printing (opposite).

HOW TO HIRE A PHOTOGRAPHER

DO YOUR HOMEWORK

Get referrals from friends, check out online portfolios and wedding-related Web sites, and scan local wedding magazines for images to get a sense of what you like. Also consider soliciting suggestions from one of your wedding vendors, such as your caterer, wedding planner or the owner of your bridal salon. Once you feel confident that you know what you like, schedule appointments with at least five or six photographers whose work appeals to you.

ZERO IN ON A CANDIDATE

Review the portfolio of each photographer with an eagle eye, and don't be afraid to ask for additional images. Request the full album from at least one wedding. That way you'll be able to judge by more than just the photographer's best shots. During the interview keep in mind that your wedding will be a long, emotionally intense day, and the manner in which photographers work varies as widely as their aesthetic. Choose a person whose temperament meshes well with yours.

CHECK THE CONTRACT

Once you've found someone within your budget whose work you love and with whom you feel a commonality of spirit, don't be afraid to pounce: Good photographers tend to be booked early. But before you sign on the dotted line, read the fine print. While the industry has no standard contract, the agreement you sign should clearly indicate the date of the ceremony, the hours the photographer and assistant(s) will work (as well as any overtime charges), the price and the cancellation policy. The contract should also address image ownership—under federal law photographers own the copyright to images they've shot unless they relinquish them, generally for a fee, which means you must rely on them to print your images and pay the amount they specify. If the photographer retains the rights, be sure to ask how long he or she will keep your digital files or film.

ABOVE: A couple poses for a formal photograph, which the photographer is shooting with a view camera.

KNOW WHAT THE FEE ENTAILS

The photographer's fee should be spelled out in detail because services vary widely. Some photographers charge a flat fee, which includes everything from time and film to a finished album. Others charge by the hour for their time; prints and an album are additional. Keep in mind that sometimes piecemeal packages can look cheaper upfront but are much more expensive in the end. To make sure you aren't unpleasantly surprised, ask your photographer to itemize the costs of his or her services, as well as of all prints and albums. A word to the wise: Most photographers discourage choosing a package that limits shots to a certain number. Film is cheap, and a photographer who is concentrating on the number of images he's shot isn't necessarily concentrating on what's happening around him. Finally, if you're booking a photographer well in advance, be certain that he or she will stand behind the quoted price, even if the rates go up before your ceremony.

BELOW: A photographer prepares to start shooting portraits of a bride, groom and their wedding party.

WEDDING ALBUMS

Just as wedding photography has evolved over the years, so have wedding albums. These options represent some of the many choices available for displaying your wedding-day images, from the sort that would look right at home next to your parents' wedding album to more handcrafted styles to bound volumes that take advantage of the latest printing technology to virtual albums for viewing online.

TRADITIONAL ALBUMS

The classic, custom-made album tends to be a stock size—10 x 10 inches is standard, though 12 x 12 and 8 x 10 are also common choices—and covered in durable leather or fabric, which can be embossed with information such as the couple's names and wedding date, and often features an inset photo. It generally contains anywhere from 40 to 70 white or black cardboard pages, often rounded and gilt-edged, with mats of varying sizes into which the photos are set, typically one or two per page. The pages are usually glued into the binding rather than sewn (sewn being the sturdier but costlier option). Though not particularly cutting-edge, these albums are relatively handsome and long-wearing and are available from a variety of sources. You should expect to pay anywhere from $300 to $1,000, not including the cost of prints, for a traditional album depending on the size, number of pages and other design features, if an album is not included in your photographer's package.

HANDCRAFTED ALBUMS

For an album that is less traditional and more distinctive, many photographers work directly with a hand binder, rather than an album company, which usually allows for more choices when it comes to size, materials and colors of everything from covers to endpapers. Photos are either mounted or printed directly onto heavyweight paper and, because they don't need to fit into mats, they can be nearly any size. Covers are typically made from high-quality fabrics such as Japanese silks and linens, though leather is also an option. With the former choice, couples can often opt for a matching slipcover. Bindings on these albums are handsewn rather than glued, giving the album the appearance of a beautiful art book. A 35-page, 12 x 12-inch, handsewn, bookbound album with a fabric cover costs about $500. (Mounting can run an additional $7 or so per photograph, depending on the binder.)

DIGITAL ALBUMS

One of the newest options, these sleek, contemporary-looking books rely on digital design and printing and resemble something you might display on a coffee table. A photographer will design each page on a computer, then print those layouts directly onto paper before sending them on to a bindery. (In some cases, the photographer will also give you a CD containing the images.) This style gives you even more leeway when it comes to creating a different look for each page—for example, some groupings of overlapping pictures that are visually tied together, or images that "bleed" to the edge of the page, as those in a magazine often do. Typically, digital albums are machine bound in plain but durable fabric. Although digitally designed albums can cost as much as other custom-made options, because they are designed on a computer, it's easier and less costly to create duplicate albums for parents and grandparents. An additional copy may cost 30 percent less than the price of the original album.

STORE-BOUGHT ALBUMS

If you're a bride on a budget, or you'd simply like to save money on additional albums for family and friends, consider buying a premade album and assembling the photos in it yourself. The key is to opt for one that's archival quality, meaning it uses acid-free paper that won't yellow or brown and that will keep your photos from discoloring and disintegrating over time. You can purchase lovely books—from leather-covered, handsewn styles to cloth-covered albums with ring binders and ribbon ties—from many department stores and stationers. (Prices range from as little as $30 to several hundred dollars, depending on the size of the album and the materials used.) Know, however, that mounting photos yourself into a store-bought album can be a time-consuming project. You may even want to consider hiring a scrapbooker.

OPPOSITE, CLOCKWISE FROM TOP: A bindery album, wedding journal and guestbook, each bound in cloth. Planner Rita Bloom puts a blank book, a camera and pens at each table so that guests can photograph themselves and write a few words; later, she binds everything into a single guestbook. Photo album with a photo of the bride and groom on the cover.

VIRTUAL ALBUMS

Some photographers have sites to which they upload their clients' photos so that clients and their guests can view and order prints online. If that's not an option, ask your photographer ahead of time if he can supply a CD containing digital images to be included in your package, which you can then upload to your own wedding Web site or to an online photo album service, such as kodakgallery.com, snapfish.com or shutterfly.com. (You may need to negotiate a separate fee with your photographer for this service.)

Of course, you can always create a virtual album using your own snapshots rather than professional images, in which case you may want to invest in a software program such as Adobe Photoshop or Microsoft Digital Image, which will allow you to manipulate images by cropping shots, eliminating red-eye and wrinkles and even lightening and clarifying dark and grainy images. Once your images are edited, use an online photo album service to create your own virtual wedding album at no cost. Simply upload your images, supply captions if you like, and the site will send out e-mails containing your link to friends and family for easy viewing. Visitors have the option of purchasing prints and can even leave notes in an online guest book. Many of these sites also allow you to create simple "hard copy" albums using uploaded photos. Though perhaps not elegant enough to serve as a primary album, they make good gifts for friends and family. A 10-page album costs $30 or so, with each additional page priced at about $2.

ROCK STEADY

ROB THOMAS AND MARISOL MALDONADO

The hit song "Smooth" that Matchbox Twenty frontman Rob Thomas wrote for Marisol Maldonado, the woman he would one day marry, includes the words "my Spanish Harlem Mona Lisa." Says Thomas, "She's actually from Queens, but 'my girl from Queens' doesn't work at all."

It might be the only detail Thomas was ever tempted to change about the model he met for 10 minutes backstage one night, then called every night for two weeks while on tour. He proposed a little more than two months later with an antique-style diamond ring, though as far as Maldonado was concerned, he needn't have waited nearly so long. "I left the night I met him and told my girlfriend, 'That's the guy I'm going to marry.'"

She did just that in a ceremony on the scenic grounds of the Santa Ynez, California, ranch belonging to Matchbox Twenty's manager. The couple's favorite song, Keith Richards's version of "The Nearness of You," played as Maldonado, wearing Vera Wang and carrying a nosegay of Black Beauty and garden roses interspersed with red pepperberries, walked down the petal-strewn aisle. The couple, who share matching tattoos of the Japanese character for loyalty, pledged to "trust what changes the future may bring," in a brief, nondenominational ceremony before slipping platinum bands—hers studded with diamonds—on each other's fingers. In a moment captured by photographer Yitzhak Dalal, they nuzzled noses as they walked back up the aisle.

At the reception, singer and friend Edwin McCain performed his hit "I'll Be" for the couple's first dance; later the new dance version of "Smooth" got the rest of the crowd up off their seats and dancing amid blossoming pink cherry trees and chandeliers lit by hundreds of candles provided by planner Sharon Sacks. She needn't have used all the matchboxes, symbolic though they may have been. Joked the groom's mother that night, "The room could be lit up by the electricity between Rob and Marisol."

ABOVE: The couple enjoys a quiet moment at the reception. **BELOW, FROM LEFT:** Thomas wore a bowtie for the ceremony as well as new gold earrings, a gift from the bride; Marisol tucked an antique crystal rosary into a secret pocket that Vera Wang made especially for it in the hem of her gown; the bride greets a flower-bedecked equine guest. **OPPOSITE:** Thomas, who wore a Gucci tuxedo, said his bride was a "sexy little number" in her duchesse satin gown.

THE WEDDING PARTY

At its essence, a wedding is the lifelong union of two people, spiritually as well as legally. But in a bigger sense, these rites are about more than just husband and wife. They are an affirmation of community, the joining of two families, and the gathering of all those people the bride and groom hold dear. Wedding guests serve as more than mere witnesses to this joyous yet sobering event; they are to some extent participants. And the love being celebrated on this day isn't just that between two people, but, as Walt Whitman wrote, "Love like the light, silently wrapping all."

One way a couple can acknowledge at least some of those who take part in the forging of this new community is by including them in the ceremony and reception through readings, toasts and other special roles, the most important of which are as members of the wedding party. The best man, the maid or matron of honor, the groomsmen and the bridesmaids all attend to the couple in ways both scripted by tradition and spontaneous. And because you will be relying on these people for practical as well as emotional support, deciding who will participate and what tasks they will undertake is important—your choices can have meaningful and lasting consequences.

For a young flower girl, the experience of a wedding—from wearing a wreath of flowers in her hair to swathing herself in the bride's gauzy veil—can be magical.

164

Generally speaking, the size and formality of your wedding determines the size of the wedding party. The old rule of thumb dictated that you should have one groomsman or usher for every 50 guests and one bridesmaid for every usher, though this guideline has certainly relaxed over the years. Indeed, some brides and grooms have no attendants at all, while others prefer to have more than the usual three or four each. Actress Felicity Huffman chose 11 bridesmaids for her nuptials, and at the wedding of TV's Star Jones and groom Al Reynolds, 12 stood up with the bride, including singer Natalie Cole and actress Vivica A. Fox. Yet when actor Josh Holloway and Yessica Kumula tied the knot in a simple ceremony on the beach in Kauai, the only people in attendance were a photographer, an officiant and a guitar player.

In other words, you should feel free to have the number of friends and family members you want to include, not the number you think you should. One trend that makes it easier for couples who want to avoid hurt feelings: asking

Members of the wedding party are there to pitch in, whether by making sure the groom has a few buddies with him as he heads to the ceremony, such as the groomsmen who attended the wedding of fashion designer Shoshanna Lonstein and her groom, Josh Gruss (above, left; Gruss pictured second from right), or, in the case of a bridesmaid, by helping a bride fasten her gown (above, right). Sometimes a bridesmaid will even offer a bride literal support (opposite).

Bridesmaids' dresses traditionally match each other (above), but they certainly don't have to. Those who took part in the wedding of actress Natasha Gregson Wagner (opposite) wore dresses created by the bride's friend, fashion designer Molly Stern. They all reflected the sophisticated, bohemian feel of the wedding but differed in style and color.

A bride adjusts her father's bowtie moments before the ceremony (above); actress Mariska Hargitay's young attendants (whom she referred to as "the parade of sweeties") crane to get a better look as the events of the wedding day unfold (opposite).

an uneven number of bridesmaids and groomsmen to serve as attendants, a break from tradition no longer considered improper. At actress Lela Rochon and director Antoine Fuqua's elegant wedding at Immanuel Presbyterian Church in Los Angeles, the attendants consisted of four bridesmaids and five groomsmen. As for the question of how the group then makes it back up the aisle, the answer is simple: One groomsman can escort two bridesmaids during the recessional, or vice versa. What's more, if a bride wants a man to be among her attendants or a groom wants a woman, that's now perfectly acceptable as well.

As you think about which friends and family members to choose for this duty, consider those who are closest to you, of course, but also those in your new family with whom you hope to build a relationship. It's always a nice gesture to ask a sister of your fiancé to be a bridesmaid, for example. If you or your groom have children from a previous marriage, you may want to have them play a role too, so that they feel included in the proceedings. Don't feel you have to assign them the traditional roles of junior bridesmaid, flower girl or ring bearer. When actor Matt LeBlanc and former model Melissa McKnight wed, the

best man was her 12-year-old son and the maid of honor her 9-year-old daughter. And Gena Lee Nolin had her 7-year-old son walk her down the aisle when she married professional hockey player Cale Hulse. Explains Hulse, "It was always *we*, not Gena and I. All three of us were getting married. That was our theme."

As you're making your selections remember that certain roles require certain duties. Since the best man usually makes the first toast at the reception, you'll want to tap someone who will feel comfortable taking on such a task. He also traditionally holds the bride's ring, helps to welcome guests, and makes sure the groom gets to the ceremony on time, so ideally you'll want someone who is organized, sociable and responsible. A maid or matron of honor is expected to do everything from help pick the bridesmaids' dresses to throw the bridal shower, so it might be impractical to choose someone who doesn't live nearby. (Though if your only sister or your very best friend lives on the other side of the world, you can certainly parcel out the traditional maid of honor tasks to others.) If you're planning a destination wedding or one that requires a heavy outlay of cash for dresses from the attendants, keep in mind the financial situations of those on your short list. Friends or relatives without much money to spend may be grateful rather than upset if you decide not to ask them. Or you could offer to help foot the bill. Either way, be sensitive to their circumstances.

No doubt you'll want to involve parents in the proceedings as well, particularly in ways that publicly honor them. Traditionally, a father walks his daughter down the aisle in Christian ceremonies, while both parents of the bride do so in Jewish ones. Nevertheless, it's acceptable to choose either or both parents no matter what your faith is. If your father is deceased, or if you'd merely like to make this

At the marriage of actors Taye Diggs and Idina Menzel, a multicultural ceremony on the beach outside the Round Hill Hotel in Jamaica, the bridesmaids wore skirts by Christiane Celle for Calypso and the groomsmen, including Diggs's brother Gabriel (far left), donned white shirts and trousers by John Varvatos.

ritual a family affair, a brother or brothers can do the honors, or they can take over for their father partway down the aisle, as actress Ashley Scott's did. "My brothers and I are very close," she says, "and I felt it wasn't fair to have just my dad walk with me." The father of the bride also usually dances with his daughter and makes a toast at the reception, while the father of the groom toasts the couple at the rehearsal dinner. (Mothers typically take a less active role.) One nice way to acknowledge all parents is to thank them formally at the reception. Or you may choose to do so at the ceremony with a unity candle. Rather than the bride and groom lighting a pillar candle with two tapers to symbolize the joining of two families, as is customary, tapers are given to parents as well. Be sure to ask your officiant about this tradition, as many Catholic and Jewish officiants don't allow it.

Finally, if you and your fiancé have young children in your families, you might want to have them participate as the flower girl, the ring bearer or junior bridesmaids (typically girls aged 9–14 who are too old to serve as flower girls though perhaps too young to be bridesmaids). If there are several children, you might consider additional flower girls and pages. Pages are young boys whose official duty is to carry the bride's train and whose unofficial ones are to behave impeccably and look absolutely adorable. And, like the rest of the wedding party, they're expected to celebrate with true love, enthusiasm and affection the two people who have invited them to take on a special role on this special day.

The bouquet toss is one time-honored way for a bride to share a moment with her bridesmaids (below). Though there is plenty of opportunity for more impromptu bonding at a wedding, too: Actress Alyson Hannigan (opposite, pictured in the center) shared a laugh with good friends January Jones (left) and actress Emma Caulfield during her reception, which took place at the Two Bunch Palms resort outside Palm Springs.

On such a momentous day, best friends and family can keep you calm by making you laugh.

DUTIES

Often those you invite to be your attendants will have had some experience with this role and therefore will know what's expected of them. But there's always the possibility that a bridesmaid or groomsman—or even the bride or groom—isn't clear about his or her duties and obligations. To avoid any confusion, review this list of who does (and pays for) what in the wedding party.

ABOVE: You can count on your maid of honor to make sure you look your best for the ceremony.

THE MAID OR MATRON OF HONOR

• Helps the bride shop for her gown and bridesmaids' attire if asked.

• If she lives in town, offers to run any wedding-related tasks for the bride, such as stuffing envelopes, buying stamps, mailing the invitations, dropping off the wedding gown to be pressed, helping to put together and drop off welcome baskets, etc.

• Organizes and hosts the bridal shower (unless it is impractical for her to do so, in which case she should make sure someone else takes on this task).

• Ensures out-of-town bridal attendants have all necessary information, including how to order their dresses, how to get to all wedding-related events, etc.

• Makes sure the bridesmaids know the time and place of any fittings, the bridal shower, the bridesmaids luncheon, the rehearsal, the rehearsal dinner and the ceremony.

• Organizes the bachelorette party, if there is one.

• Keeps the bride on schedule.

• Helps the bride dress the day of the wedding.

• Makes sure all bridesmaids have their bouquets and all mothers and grandmothers have their corsages, and that the bridesmaids all look presentable for their walk down the aisle.

• Holds onto the groom's ring before the ceremony.

• Arranges the bride's train and veil before the processional and recessional.

• Holds the bride's bouquet during the ceremony.

• Stands in the receiving line.

• Witnesses the signing of the marriage license.

• Makes sure the bride's hair, makeup and gown look photogenic throughout the day.

• Holds the bride's purse or makeup bag during the reception.

• Dances with ushers and single male guests.

• Takes care of the bride's gown and accessories after the reception.

THE BRIDESMAIDS

- Attend the bridal shower and bachelorette party, if there is one.

- Attend the rehearsal and rehearsal dinner.

- Assist the bride and the maid or matron of honor in running errands, particularly if the latter will be flying in for the ceremony.

- Stand in the receiving line.

- Dance with ushers and any single male guests who ask them.

- Help gather guests for the first dance, the cutting of the cake and the bouquet toss.

THE FATHER OF THE BRIDE

- Pays for the wedding, unless other arrangements have been agreed upon.

- Walks the bride down the aisle in Christian ceremonies (and joins his wife for this duty in Jewish ones) if the bride asks him to do so.

- Welcomes guests publicly at the reception, particularly the groom's family, and toasts the bride and groom.

- Dances with the bride following the first dance.

- Hosts the morning-after brunch, if there is one, for family, any out-of-towners and the wedding party.

THE FATHER OF THE GROOM

- Hosts the rehearsal dinner.

- Toasts the bride and groom at the rehearsal dinner.

- At the reception, publicly thanks the bride's family for hosting the wedding.

MOTHERS OF THE BRIDE AND GROOM

- Responsible for choosing their wedding-day attire, and the former often hosts the bridesmaids luncheon for the bride.

RIGHT, ABOVE AND BELOW: Joyce Azria's father, fashion designer Max Azria, walks his daughter down the aisle. Tennis legend Pete Sampras enjoys a dance with his mother, Georgia, at his reception.

along with their traditional vows, actress Sandra Bullock promised her groom, TV motorcycle mechanic Jesse James, that she would let him bring home stray dogs. James promised he would first get her okay.

And vows composed by the couples themselves can evoke tears as surely as they do laughter. James Brolin spoke from the heart as he stood with bride Barbra Streisand beneath their makeshift chuppah, announcing to his guests, "I'm so happy that you're all here to witness my deep love for this woman . . . . I can't tell you how lucky I am that this should have happened to me so late in life. . . . Every day, every night, every morning is a new adventure. . . . I love you, Barbra." Actor Robert Foxworth and his bride also wrote their own vows, keeping them secret from each other until the day of the wedding. The only rule: that each end with the line, "As we walk through life, side by side, hand in hand, heart to heart."

Perhaps you like the idea of nontraditional vows, but you'd rather not rely on words that you compose yourself. Consider reciting a poem or a traditional blessing that expresses how you feel. This selection from the *I Ching* is both simple and unusual: "When two people are at one in their inmost hearts/They shatter even the strength of iron or of bronze/And when two people understand each other in their inmost hearts/Their words are sweet and strong like the fragrance of orchids."

While the vows are by far the most important aspect of a wedding, the ceremony also gives you the chance to set your happiness to music, starting from its very first moments. Some brides see no need to try to improve upon the solemn, time-honored chords of "Here Comes the Bride" or the stately arpeggios of Pachelbel's "Canon in D." But others go for something a bit livelier. Actress Kathy Najimy eschewed a standard processional in favor of

At the lakeside ceremony of actors Alyson Hannigan and Alexis Denisof, which took place near Palm Springs, planner Rob Smith of Laurels Custom Flora & Events in Los Angeles hung trees with liquid silver, strands of Tibetan bells, white orchid garlands and thousands of white beads. Guests were given paper parasols with which to shade themselves.

"Fairy Tale of New York" by Irish punk band the Pogues. Talisa Soto opted for the folk-tune trills of Peruvian flute music, a nod to groom Benjamin Bratt's heritage. And actress Leah Remini chose Stevie Wonder's "Overjoyed" as the upbeat accompaniment to her walk down the aisle in Las Vegas. In addition to the processional, you may decide to have a favorite song or piece of music performed at your ceremony, whether the classic "Ave Maria" or something contemporary, such as Norah Jones's bluesy "Come Away With Me." Finally, you may opt to skip "The Wedding March" for a more novel recessional ranging from the gospel standard "Oh Happy Day" (Jessica Simpson's finale), to The Turtles' '60s pop classic, "Happy Together."

Readings and blessings allow a couple to add a bit of tradition as well as a personal note to the day. Both Pierce Brosnan and Toni Braxton decided on a traditional Biblical reading from I Corinthians, which includes the words, "If I have a faith that can move mountains, but have not love, I am nothing." Other popular selections: readings from Kahlil Gibran (Lisa Rinna's choice), and the Apache Wedding Blessing, which both Forest Whitaker and actress Annabeth Gish selected for their ceremonies and which reads in part, "Now you will feel no rain, for each of you will be a shelter to each other. . . . Now you are two bodies, but there is only one life before you."

Still some brides and grooms move beyond these familiar words, finding more unusual ways to convey both emotion and a sense of spirituality through spoken words. Olympic skater Kristi Yamaguchi's Hawaiian nuptials included Hawaiian wedding chants, one of which was said to call out to the spirits of ancestors and guardians to bear witness to the ceremony. Emma Thompson asked her groom's sister to read an obscure poem by Dorothy Wordsworth, sister of William, which includes the final lines, "'Likings' come and pass away; 'tis 'love' that remains till our latest day."

Don't forget the power of rituals, which can also add meaning to a ceremony, as well as honor your heritage.

Mira Sorvino and Christopher Backus, who wed in Capri, had an Anglican ceremony presided over by both the bride's childhood minister and the couple's current one, Susan Klein (above). Religious ceremonies include traditional elements, such as the prayer over the wine at Jewish ceremonies (opposite, top). For some, the most memorable moment is the ceremony's final pronouncement. Before Cindy Crawford and Rande Gerber's ceremony (opposite, bottom), the minister asked what words they needed to hear to feel married. Said Cindy, "I really wanted him to say 'I now present to you Mr. and Mrs. Gerber.'"

It seems there's hardly a time when a just-married couple isn't caught on camera kissing, whether when given permission to do so by their officiant after being legally joined in marriage (below) or when exiting the ceremony site (opposite).

Actress Tisha Campbell and her groom, Duane Martin, "jumped the broom," an African-African tradition meant to signify the sweeping away of evil spirits. American slaves used the custom to publicly acknowledge marriages that were not otherwise legally recognized, and it has thus evolved into a way to honor one's slave ancestors. Cindy Crawford's groom, Rande Gerber, wed barefoot on the beach, but he still managed to perform the Jewish tradition of breaking a glass beneath his foot—once he'd donned a pair of Birkenstocks. The ritual is said to be a sober reminder of the destruction of the Second Temple of Jerusalem and thus a warning against excessive joy.

Especially when weddings are interfaith celebrations, as so many are these days, an eclectic mix of ceremonial elements can serve to symbolize the blending of two different backgrounds. Actor Taye Diggs and bride Idina Menzel incorporated both Jewish and African-American traditions into their ceremony, including marrying under a chuppah, jumping the broom and breaking the glass. And when CNN medical correspondent Dr. Sanjay Gupta exchanged vows with his Christian bride, there were Hindu rites, such as one in which the couple circles a holy fire four times, as well as the reading of the Lord's Prayer.

Because this day is meant to celebrate community as much as it honors the bride and groom, many couples like to share such customs as the passing of a flame from candle to candle among the guests to signify the joining of friends and family in support of the newly married couple. Model Vendela Thommessen asked each guest to insert a flower into an archway of greenery at the head of the aisle. At the end of their backyard ceremony in Los Angeles, actress Elizabeth Perkins and her groom, cinematographer Julio Macat, released a balloon to which tags inscribed with family members' names were tied.

Of course, in addition to acknowledging loved ones, a ceremony is meant to celebrate love itself, an emotion that can't always be contained. Even the most well-planned ceremony is often interrupted by irrepressible outbursts. "Is it OK if we kiss?" Julia Roberts and Danny Moder kept asking, much to the delight of their guests, when they married on their ranch in Taos, New Mexico. And when Melanie Griffith wed Antonio Banderas, her 10-year-old son from a previous marriage yelled out before the ceremony was finished, "You may now kiss the bride!"

Not that anyone usually minds when a ceremony strays from the script like this. Barbra Streisand said of her wedding, which she acknowledged didn't quite go according to plan, "There is a saying: 'What comes from the heart, goes to the heart.'" Whether you choose to express your love and commitment through traditional rites or with something more personal, and whether things go off without a hitch or not, a ceremony filled with heartfelt emotion will be one that carries the day.

As actress Kimberly Williams and country singer Brad Paisley (opposite) walked back up the aisle of the Pepperdine University chapel, they were the center of attention. A couple finds a moment to take a more private stroll (above).

CHOOSING AN OFFICIANT

For a bride and groom who regularly attend the same house of worship, finding an officiant counts as one of the simpler tasks on their seemingly endless to-do list. Their priest, minister or rabbi—a person who both shares their religious beliefs and knows them well—is the obvious choice to perform this singularly important duty. And a couple who wants to legalize things with as little fanfare as possible can check with city hall or their local marriage license bureau and easily find a local judge, justice of the peace or court clerk who has legal authority to perform a by-the-book civil ceremony.

INTERFAITH AND INTERDENOMINATIONAL COUPLES

Things get a bit trickier, though, for couples of different faiths, those who may share religious beliefs but don't regularly attend a house of worship or those who want a ceremony that is not as cut-and-dried as a civil one but that steers clear of any overtly religious overtones. The first decision such couples need to make is whether they in fact want a traditional religious ceremony, an interfaith or interdenominational one, a nondenominational ceremony or a secular one. If you choose a traditional religious ceremony, know that there may be restrictions. Depending on the diocese, a priest may refuse to marry you in a place other than a house of worship. You can have a Catholic ceremony if one of you is not Catholic, but you both must attend Pre-Cana classes prior to the wedding. And some clergy cannot officiate at interdenominational ceremonies, so do some research online and with local congregations before assuming you can hire two people of different faiths to officiate.

NONCREEDAL CEREMONIES

One good resource for couples of different backgrounds who want a spiritual wedding but not necessarily one that follows the creed of any particular religious faith is the Unitarian Church, otherwise known as the Unitarian Universalist Association. Though this religious organization, whose congregants are committed to the idea of free religion and social justice, has Judeo-Christian roots, it is noncreedal.

Officiants from the American Ethical Union, a humanistic, religious and educational movement devoted to creating a more humane society, also perform interfaith marriages that, according to its Web site, "respect the individuality of each member of the couple as well as the ethical commitment of marriage." Both organizations are also good choices for couples looking for a nondenominational ceremony. For more information about the American Ethical Union, contact your local Ethical Culture Society or log onto www.aeu.org. The Unitarian Universalist Association Web site is www.uua.org.

ABOVE: An interfaith marriage that includes both a minister and a rabbi.

OPPOSITE, CLOCKWISE FROM TOP LEFT: In a standard Christian ceremony, the clergyperson can perform the ceremony with very little fanfare, as is often the case at a beachside wedding. In more formal ceremonies, the couple may choose to follow such conventional traditions as signing a church record book. Jewish couples are often wrapped together in a *talit*, or prayer shawl, as the rabbi offers a wedding blessing. In a typical Jewish ceremony the couple signs a marriage contract, usually elaborately decorated, known as a *ketubah* before being wed.

MORE ON OFFICIANTS

HIRING AN OFFICIANT

If you plan on a religious ceremony but don't have a regular clergyperson, one option is to ask the person who performed services at a house of worship you or your groom attended as a child. The advantage here is that he or she has had a relationship with you or your groom and with one of your families as well. But if that's not an option for you for whatever reason, you will no doubt be hiring a stranger, and you should probably begin your search not long after you become engaged. Start by asking friends and family members for suggestions, as well as using the Internet to search for sites listing names of officiants for hire in the place where you plan to wed.

Once you have a few names, plan to interview several of the candidates and be prepared to ask each some very specific questions. In the case of religious ceremonies, may a couple deviate from the script at all, incorporating self-written vows, for example, or must the wedding be performed in strict accordance with tradition? Ask, too, if you must attend any sort of premarital program before the officiant will marry you. If you are hiring an interfaith or nondenominational clergyperson, be sure to inquire how or whether that person will allude to God or specific religions, and make sure you are comfortable with his or her answer.

Perhaps most critically, since the words this person speaks at your ceremony will be important ones, make sure you understand and agree with an officiant's philosophy about marriage, and ask what, besides the prepared text, he or she intends to say during the ceremony. For instance, this person may like to remind people of the tough challenges marriage presents. If you find that a bit off-putting, look for someone else. Pay attention to the questions he or she asks you too. The person who is interested in getting to know a little about you will be more likely to conduct a service that isn't boilerplate. One bit of advice that, while it sounds obvious, is worth following: Make sure the person you decide on, particularly if he or she is not affiliated with a particular house of worship, has the legal power to marry you.

HAVING A FRIEND OFFICIATE

Finally, consider having a friend or family member perform the honors, an increasingly popular trend that appeals to couples who prefer that someone close to them perform the ceremony rather than a stranger. In California, Massachusetts and Alaska, anyone can apply for a one-day license that allows them to legally marry two people. Or have your officiant ordained on the Internet, as Julianne Moore and Sarah Michelle Gellar both did. Anyone who logs onto the Universal Life Church Web site (www.ulc.org) can become an officiant simply by filling out a form and paying a nominal fee. Legal requirements vary from state to state, however, and sometimes from city to city, so check with your marriage license bureau to find out whether you can marry this way in the place you plan to hold the ceremony.

OPPOSITE: In a typical double-ring Christian ceremony, the bride and groom exchange wedding bands after repeating vows read to them by their priest or pastor.

VENUES

Whether you plan to marry in a church or a synogogue, a ballroom or an outdoor garden, here are some inspiring venues for your dream ceremony.

ABOVE, FROM LEFT: A flower-filled ballroom. An outdoor ceremony, with a backdop of hills, in Napa Valley.

LEFT, FROM LEFT: Actress Mel Harris married Michael Toomey in an outdoor ceremony in a field of cut grass and flowering mustards. A ceremony takes place onstage, with a dramatic view outdoors.

BELOW, FROM LEFT: At a Jewish ceremony at The Breakers hotel in Palm Beach, Florida, the aisle is lined with flowers and culminates in a flower-bedecked chuppah. Benches set up for a beach wedding.

OPPOSITE, TOP: Actress Jamie-Lynn Sigler married her manager A.J. DiScala at the Brooklyn Botanic Garden in Brooklyn, New York.

BOTTOM ROW, FROM LEFT: A couple marries in a wooden frame built by the groom to symbolize a home. A traditional church ceremony. The forest surrounds an outdoor ceremony.

A RITE TO REMEMBER

GINA TORRES AND LAURENCE FISHBURNE

If music be the food of love, as Shakespeare once wrote, then actors Laurence Fishburne and his *Matrix* costar Gina Torres dished up a true gourmet feast at their autumn wedding in New York City. As Elton John, Keanu Reeves and other guests took their seats among the heather-scented gardens of Fort Tryon Park, a string quartet played musical selections ranging from Vivaldi's "Four Seasons" to Afro-Cuban jazz. A conch shell was blown to signal the start of the ceremony, which included performances of Bach's "Air on the G String," a Native American hymn, and a song that the maid of honor composed herself. "The wedding had to be a reflection of who we are," says Torres. "So the music was an integral part."

Bathed in the glow of hundreds of candle-filled lanterns hung from the trees, the couple had their hands joined with a binding cloth formed into a figure eight, an African custom. "It symbolizes the intertwining of lives," says Torres. The Reverend Bobby Klein then lit bundles of sage and waved them over the couple in a Native American ritual known as "smudging," said to cleanse a person or place of negative energy. The actress honored her own heritage by choosing *lechon asado*, a traditional Cuban pork dish, for the dinner menu.

Guests grazed on foie gras and caviar appetizers at a reception choreographed by event planner Jennifer Zabinski of the Wedding Library by Claudia Hanlin & Jennifer Zabinski, then dined at long banquet tables in a tent filled with hot-hued flowers by event designer Preston Bailey. Afterward came more music: Sinatra, '70s funk, and the Buena Vista Social Club, all following the first dance to the Mamas and the Papas' version of "Dream a Little Dream of Me." For Torres, the night itself seemed like a dream. "I was so profoundly happy. It was as if the smile was wrapped around my head twice, and the corners of my mouth met in the back," she said. "It felt like God was smiling down on us."

> **ABOVE:** The couple wed on a rose-covered platform overlooking the Hudson River. **BELOW, LEFT TO RIGHT:** The reception tent was adorned with flowers in the couple's favorite hues: orange, red and hot pink; escort cards were designed in the shape of gingko leaves and fastened to a tree meant to symbolize the tree of life; Torres's nine-foot-long mantilla-style veil was hand-beaded with about 3,000 crystals and glass beads. **OPPOSITE:** Torres wore a lace gown by Mira Mandich that she described as having "just enough slink," while Fishburne's Oswald Boateng tux featured a hot-pink lining.

THE
RECEPTION

The ring has been slipped on your finger, the vows said and sealed with a kiss and the final chords of the recessional have evanesced into memory. All that's left to do is to kick off your shiny new marriage in style, which is just what the wedding reception is meant to help you do. The word implies something passive—the receiving of guests' good wishes and congratulations—when in fact, this festive event is one you're meant to actively revel in with friends and family once the mostly solemn and sometimes nerve-wracking events of the ceremony have taken place.

If you'd grown up in your grandparents' time, your reception might have been thrown in a church basement or your parents' home with little more than cut-crystal cups of champagne punch and slices of wedding cake for your guests. In your parents' era, a catering or social hall with standard fare was more the norm. Now many couples go with something more distinctive, in keeping with their personal taste, their cultural traditions and the mood they'd like to convey on this day.

The first thing to bear in mind when planning your reception is that it is not only a big celebration, it's a big expense—figure that roughly 40 to 50 percent of your budget will be devoted to this aspect of your wedding, most of it going toward food and liquor. So it's wise to spend some time thinking about how best to spend your money. Because the setting will have a lot to do with the vibe and the formality of the party, you will most likely want to turn your attention to this detail of the event first.

Slim flutes of fizzy champagne held aloft are a wedding-day icon, a festive way for guests to toast the newlyweds—and each other.

Matt Lauer—along with his wife, Annette Roque Lauer—enjoyed the cocktail hour at the reception for fellow TV journalist Elizabeth Vargas and her husband, Marc Cohn. No reception would be complete without champagne served in flutes, like those at Kyle MacLachlan's wedding (opposite, top left) or in coupe-style glasses (opposite, bottom right). But consider offering signature cocktails as well, such as peach-flavored bellinis (opposite, top right), or even lemonade and fruit punch ladled from simple glass jars (opposite, bottom left) as a refreshing alternative.

Kristen & Patrick
July 14, 2001

Featuring:

"Harry's Bar Bellini
From Venice"

Made with Prosecco
and Peach juice

If you like the idea of an intimate celebration and your guest list is small, you may choose to hold your reception at one of your (or your parents') homes, as Julianne Moore and Bart Freundlich did after marrying in the garden of their New York town house, which they decorated with cast-iron urns of honeysuckle and clematis. Be aware that if you plan a large reception, you may not save money this way once you factor in the cost of tents, table and chair rentals, additional restroom facilities and the like. After all, Tori Spelling held her reception at her parents' home, and her wedding cost a reported $1 million.

If you still want to keep things casual but prefer to go farther afield, consider a celebration in a park or on the beach. Matt LeBlanc and his wife Melissa McKnight treated guests to performances by hula dancers, Samoan fire dancers and local musicians after they wed overlooking the sea on the Hawaiian island of Kauai. (The groom wore a lei over his open-necked, lavender shirt.) Rather be on the water than beside it? Actress Thandie Newton and her groom, Oliver Parker, cruised the Thames with their guests once they'd wed. Or maybe you have something grander in mind. Pierce Brosnan and Keely Shaye Smith threw their wedding gala in an 84-room, 13th-century castle in County Mayo, Ireland, the groom receiving guests in white tie and tails. Hotels are popular choices, too, from those featuring resplendent ballrooms and event managers who take care of every detail, to more laid-back venues. Actress Kate Hudson's guests danced to alt-country music at the Elk Mountain Lodge, a two-story log structure in a nature preserve near Aspen.

Clearly, you have a lot to think about, but booking the venue is only the first step in the process. What about the theme of the party you plan to throw there? You and your groom may want to look to your backgrounds for inspiration in choosing the kinds of rituals, food and music you want to incorporate into the occasion. Actor Dulé Hill, who

A wedding reception offers lots of opportunity for merriment, especially for the younger guests, who nearly always find a way to make their own fun (right). The grown-ups may also take a moment to bask in the emotions of the day and to reflect on its significance (right, above). One gathering point for guests of any age: a beautifully decorated dining table (opposite).

Once guests are seated, a bride often finds time to enjoy a quiet moment with her groom (above, left), though her first obligation is to make her way to each table to greet and converse with her guests (above, right). The ritual of guests sharing a meal together underscores the sense of community a wedding is meant to celebrate (opposite).

is of Jamaican descent, and his wife Nicole Lyn, who is half Jamaican and half Chinese, served a meal that reflected both of their cultures, including a traditional Jamaican rum-and-brandy fruitcake with marzipan icing called "black cake," and rum punch based on the groom's father's own recipe. Pete Sampras broke a plate at his wedding reception, which in his Greek culture is meant to bring good luck, while Marisol and Rob Thomas danced to a mariachi band in honor of her Latin background.

Such details represent wonderful ways to pay homage to your shared family traditions, yet you shouldn't feel limited to choices based on such criteria. The many details of a wedding reception can reflect your taste and personality as easily and appropriately as they do your heritage. For appetizers at their lavish Palm Beach wedding, Donald and Melania Trump served "beggar's purses," small pancake pouches filled with crème fraîche and glistening Beluga caviar, cinched with a chive bow and topped with a brush-stroke of gold leaf. Comedian Kevin James, on the other hand, offered guests McDonald's cheeseburgers as one of

the entrées at his post-nuptials fete, which took place at a California resort decked out to resemble a casino.

And, of course, food isn't the only aspect of your reception that you'll need to work out. Music is a wedding-reception tradition that goes a long way toward setting the mood as well as keeping guests entertained. Whether played by a band or a DJ, it can range from the rap selected by hip-hop artist Nas and his bride, R&B star Kelis, to the soft jazz performed by the trio hired for ABC newswoman Elizabeth Vargas's Park Avenue wedding, to the pulsing Latin techno that served as soundtrack to the nuptials of Jennifer Lopez and Marc Anthony. You can always mix things up if you like, too: Russell Crowe invited both the Australian Chamber Orchestra and an ABBA tribute band called Björn Again to perform at his reception, held at his 560-acre cattle ranch in the Australian bush.

And while everyone loves to hit the dance floor at a wedding reception, these days there are plenty of other ways you can ensure guests have a good time. Actress Katey Sagal and her groom, Kurt Sutter, hired palm readers to tell guests' fortunes, while actress Alyson Hannigan and groom Alexis Denisof had both a trampoline and a photo booth set up at their reception, the latter so that the couple could have a few charming reminders of their guests. Meanwhile, actress Kimberly Williams Paisley and singer Brad Paisley invited friends and family to celebrate the day after their ceremony at an outdoor hoedown, where a country band and an inflatable kids' castle kept things fun and laid-back.

Even carefully chosen favors can serve to delight your guests. At Catherine Zeta-Jones and Michael Douglas's wedding, guests received a Welsh "love spoon," a gift of affection from Zeta-Jones's native Wales. Singer Michelle Branch wed musician Teddy Landau on a tiny island off the western coast of Mexico and opted to use necklaces she'd made herself from fishing wire and seashells as favors. Kevin Costner and his bride Christine Baumgartner, whose nuptials took place at Costner's ranch in Aspen over a weekend that included swimming, canoeing and horseback-riding, gave guests tins of wildflower seeds, both to evoke the rustic setting of the event and to symbolize the start of something new.

Heartfelt (and sometimes humorous) toasts to the bride and groom represent one of the reception's main highlights—here ABC newswoman Elizabeth Vargas and her husband, songwriter Marc Cohn (above), react to a few well-chosen remarks. Nevertheless, little details can be memorable as well (opposite, clockwise from top left), from a flower tucked into a hem-stitched napkin or the pretty floral garland that rims an ice bucket to the script on a slice of a cake or the sheen of ivory-handled flatware resting on a silver tray.

During the first dance, all eyes are on the newlyweds as they glide across the floor. Actress Elizabeth Berkley and artist Greg Lauren (above), who met in a dance class, performed an elaborate routine choreographed to a medley of songs including Madonna's "Crazy for You" and "You're the One That I Want" from the musical *Grease*. But something as simple as an impromptu twirl (right) can make this ritual a pleasure for both the participants and the onlookers.

Four-day celebrations like Costner and Baumgartner's aren't unusual these days, particularly when they are part of a destination wedding, which gives couples even more of a chance to entertain their friends and get to know each other's relatives. Actress Elizabeth Berkley and artist Greg Lauren wed at a resort in Mexico, where the night before the ceremony, sofas were set up on the lawn and *Casablanca*, a favorite romantic movie, was screened for popcorn-munching guests. "Our joy came from making it personal," the actress says of the weekend-long wedding and reception festivities. "By the end, it truly felt like we were family."

That's one of the goals of a wedding reception, in fact: the bringing together of family and friends, not only to help you commemorate a milestone but to burnish and pay tribute to old relationships and to forge brand new ones that will, with luck, only grow deeper over the years. It's also a time during which rituals help to make the occasion that much more special. Toasts are made, songs may be sung, a father and a mother are invited to dance by their newly married children, cakes are cut, bouquets may be tossed and people are thanked, often in touching and meaningful ways that you rarely have the chance to repeat in such a public and festive setting.

What's more, the reception presents an opportunity to the bride and groom not just for celebration and commemoration but—once the toasts and thanks have been made—for reflection as well. Desiree Gruber, the bride of actor Kyle MacLachlan, recalls sitting at a table during her wedding reception in Miami Beach's elegant Biltmore Hotel. After the rack of lamb had been cleared from the tables and the swing and salsa bands had finished their last set, she took a moment to take stock of the evening. "It was three in the morning. The lights were brought down and the flowers were being moved for brunch later that day. I looked across the table at Kyle and at some of our best friends," she says, "and I thought, Lucky me."

The bride and groom feed each other a slice of wedding cake (above) to symbolize the idea of always providing for one another. Guests may not cut the cake at the reception, but they often cut the rug to tunes spun by a DJ (opposite, top left) or played by a band. It was local musicians' melodies that had Mira Sorvino dancing when she wed actor Christopher Backus on the island of Capri (opposite, bottom left). One group of guests treats the bride and groom to a song (opposite, top right). For some little guests, all the dancing, whatever the musical accompaniment, winds up being too much (opposite, bottom right).

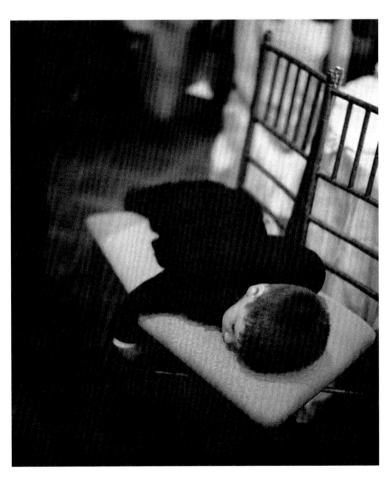

The grand finale: As the wedding photographer catches her final shots and this glorious day winds to a close, the only thing that remains to do is pause with your groom to savor the freshly-minted memories (opposite) before bidding your guests good-bye and heading off to your new life together (above).

VENUES

Perhaps more than any other element, the place where you hold your wedding reception will set the tone for the entire event. The difference in wedding venues is vast—from a public park to a private country club—and your choice will have a lot to do with your taste, your budget, the size of your guest list and how much effort you want to spend preparing the space. Gathering on the beach or in a park seems charming and simple enough, but once you've obtained a permit, arranged for a generator to allow for cooking (if the meal isn't prepared ahead of time) and lighting (if the party will last until after dark), and rented all the tables, linens and place settings, a hotel may prove the better option.

Full-service venues, such as hotels, country clubs, estates, catering halls and resorts, generally have event managers on staff to oversee all the fine points. The setting is usually tailor-made for a wedding, with good acoustics, a full kitchen, plenty of restrooms and public parking. And while the per-person charge may seem steep, because these venues come equipped with everything from linens to lighting, you won't have to worry about huge additional rental fees. When you factor in these extras, a full-service venue can save you an average of $30 per person. The drawback? They can sometimes seem a little impersonal unless you add a few memorable décor details of your own. Consider placing framed photos of your and your grooms' parents and grandparents on an antique table in the entryway, creating stunning centerpieces of silver urns filled with fresh fruit or hiring a top-tier band instead of a DJ. And make sure you arrange for a tasting before you book. Most full-service venues insist you use their in-house catering service.

Some venues, such as loft spaces and museums, are neither do-it-yourself nor full-service. They may require you to arrange for a caterer and rentals yet provide most other amenities. Whether using such a space—or even a full-service one—be sure to check if there are any limitations on décor. And museums in particular often charge a hefty insurance fee.

A local restaurant is a good choice for some couples because they no doubt have had a few meals there and the staff knows both the space and the menu well. What's more, as with a hotel or a private club, you won't have to worry about rentals. If you think you may want to hold your ceremony there as well, make sure there's room to do so, as some restaurants aren't set up for this sort of event. If you plan to hold your reception at home, factor in the money—and time—spent on renting such things as a tent, seating, trash removal services and, if you expect more than 50 guests, portable toilets. Have your heart set on celebrating outside? Make sure you have a covered back-up site in case of rain.

If you plan to hold your reception somewhere other than a private residence, ask the person in charge up front about such things as what the cancellation policy and overtime fees are, if a deposit is required and whether there are any hidden expenses, such as corkage fees for liquor you may want to bring in. Once you've found your spot and ironed out such details, you're ready to get the party started.

ABOVE: A wedding at The Central Park Boathouse in New York City.

OPPOSITE, CLOCKWISE FROM TOP LEFT: Appealing places for a reception include a country club's elegant ballroom, a charming country home, a beach by the sea, or an open-air tent.

FOOD

Because food and liquor represent one of the biggest chunks of any wedding budget, it's wise to give both elements a bit of thought. A buffet is generally less expensive than a sit-down meal because it doesn't require a large waitstaff to serve it. But if you opt for the former, plan on at least a couple of stations so that guests don't wait interminably for their food. Or have the first course served and the main course done buffet-style. Because guests won't all finish the first course at once, they won't then mob the buffet at the same time.

Most couples serve dinner at their reception, but breakfast, lunch, tea or cocktails and appetizers are also options and are usually less costly. It doesn't matter what type of food you serve (or when you serve it), but it is important that you offer enough of it so that guests don't leave hungry and that you don't skimp on quality. A clambake on the beach or appetizers of sushi and tapas can both be appropriate choices as long as they are made of the best ingredients and are served in abundance. Remember that the food is one aspect of the ceremony—and a big one—that shows your guests you have them in mind on your wedding day, so if you want to skimp on something, make it your dress or the number of limos, not the food. A bride who sashays around her reception in a designer gown while her guests nibble on wilted celery sticks stuffed with cream cheese won't be looked on too kindly.

In addition to the time of day, your setting will to some extent determine what you serve. You probably wouldn't offer guests foie gras on the beach, nor would your menu feature sirloin burgers at a fancy catering hall. And since the best food is what's in season, fresh corn salad in January is dubious as well. Take into account the number of guests you invite. Elaborate dishes that take a long time to plate and serve aren't ideal at a wedding with hundreds of guests in attendance. Instead of beef Wellington that would arrive at most tables soggy and cold, you're better off choosing something like lamb chops, which are easily prepared and can be served room temperature. Offer some variety, including a vegetarian option for guests who don't eat meat. But be aware that at many venues, you are required to use the on-site staff or a limited number of catering outfits, which will also affect the menu you choose.

Looking for ways to save money? Skip the dessert course and serve an assortment of cookies along with the wedding cake. Or instead of serving a salad and an appetizer, combine courses and serve a crab cake on a bed of greens. As for liquor, an open bar with a wide range of top-shelf liquors can up the total cost of the reception. The solution, however, is never, ever a cash bar. Instead, serve just wine, beer and perhaps a signature cocktail, such as a bellini or a cosmopolitan, along with soda and mixers. This choice can save you 50 percent over a traditional open bar.

LEFT: If your venue will provide them, three mini-entrées make a tasty main course (from top: lamb chops with baby beets, seared scallops with peppers and duck confit on greens).

OPPOSITE, TOP ROW, FROM LEFT: Squid topped with salmon roe and pea shoots. Tomato soup drizzled with crème fraîche. Seafood cocktails served in shot glasses.

MIDDLE ROW, FROM LEFT: Dumplings served with soy dipping sauce. Individual splits of champagne. A raspberry tartlet with champagne.

BOTTOM ROW, FROM LEFT: Shrimp canapés and blinis with caviar. Tiered mini-cakes topped with pastel icing. Beer and champagne cool in an iced-filled boat.

MUSIC

For many couples, the big decision when it comes to the music played at their reception isn't necessarily swing versus soul, but DJ versus live music. There are pros and cons to each, and you should weigh them carefully before you book. DJs are generally much cheaper than bands—several thousand dollars less, in some cases—and they provide a known quantity: the Top 40 hit you heard on the radio while you and your groom were courting will sound the same at your reception as it did then. A DJ's playlist is virtually endless, and he or she can switch from Sinatra to Cyndi Lauper without a pause, ensuring everyone from your grandparents to the flower girls will find something they can dance to.

But the same reason some people choose a DJ—the predictability—is why others choose to go with a live band. The latter may only play one or two types of music, but ideally it does so with a certain distinctive style and spontaneity. And while everyone may have heard "Somewhere Over the Rainbow," they might not have heard it done with the Latin flavor given it by a particular salsa band. There's also something about a band that announces the occasion as a particularly special one.

That doesn't mean that a band is always the better choice. Says Jung Lee, a partner in the N.Y.C. event-planning company Fête, "I'd rather have a phenomenal DJ who understands a party than a so-so band." If you want the best of both worlds, you can always choose to hire musicians for the cocktail hour and a DJ for the rest of the night or vice versa. But whatever type of entertainment you hire, you should keep a few things in mind:

SET A BUDGET

The standard duration of a set by either a band or a DJ is four hours, with overtime charges calculated by the half hour or hour (and generally set at a slightly higher rate than the main set's per-hour fee). Depending on the size of the band, you should be prepared to pay anywhere from $2,000 to $20,000, while a DJ will generally run about $750 to $2,500 (where you live and how long you book him or her for will affect the cost).

START YOUR SEARCH EARLY

If you are working with a wedding coordinator, find out if she has some trusted musical allies. Ask recently wed friends for recommendations, and keep your ears open at every wedding or event you attend. Most established bands have CDs of their music, and some even offer streaming audio online. But pros usually advise taking in a live set of any band you are seriously considering.

SET UP INTERVIEWS

When you've narrowed down your list of contenders, set up a meeting with each bandleader or DJ. Share your musical tastes—even bringing along a list of songs you've made as they've occurred to you while daydreaming or listening to the radio—as well as what kind of crowd will be attending so that your bandleader or DJ can tailor the musical selections accordingly.

LEFT: Grammy-winning musician Marc Cohn sang his ballad "One Safe Place" to his new wife, ABC newswoman Elizabeth Vargas.

PREPARE FOR THE WORST

Ask music vendors about backup equipment and talent in case of mechanical failure or illness, and make sure that you know the electricity requirements of your band or DJ and that your venue can accommodate them. If you're planning an outdoor wedding, ask for a dedicated sound-system generator.

RELINQUISH SOME CONTROL

Be aware that a talented bandleader or DJ needs some creative license. Don't hand either a song-by-song list and demand he stick to it. Often it's best if he plays what the crowd is responding to rather than what you want to hear.

NAIL DOWN SPECIFICS

Be sure to discuss the length of time your band or DJ will perform, whether there will be continuous music during the reception, cancellation policies, the first-dance song, tracks that must and must not be played, whether they will take requests from guests, and the amount of between-song banter, if any, that you'd like from the bandleader or DJ. You should also arrange ahead of time whether the band leader or a member of your party will make the important announcements or introductions. Finally, if you hire a band, be sure to provide the leader with lyrics and sheet music to any favorite songs the musicians don't know.

RIGHT, ABOVE AND BELOW: A swing band can keep the crowd dancing all night, while a jazz quartet makes perfect dinnertime music.

FAVORS

No guest will expect an elaborate keepsake from your wedding, but with a little creativity you can ensure they won't leave their favors behind on the table. How to go Jordan almonds tied up in mesh one better? By customizing the gifts to reflect the story of you and your groom. Actress Gena Lee Nolin and her groom Cale Hulse first met at a Starbucks, so they gave wedding guests gift cards to the coffee emporium. Billy Joel's bride Katie Lee, a professional cook, offered treats from her kitchen—rosemary biscotti—and Dulé Hill and his bride, who are both from Jamaica, gave guests CD's burned with his favorite reggae love songs. If you prefer something more traditional, a picture frame or a scented candle is both practical and pretty.

LEFT: Lavendar growing in a pretty pot is a table decoration you can send home with your guests.

BOTTOM ROW, FROM LEFT: Bottles of wine with commemorative labels. Personalized baskets with beach supplies. Travel candle with wedding motif.

OPPOSITE, TOP ROW, FROM LEFT: Elizabeth Berkley and Greg Lauren gave guests handmade bracelets at their Cabo San Lucas, Mexico, wedding. Prettily wrapped bulbs (pictured) or seed packets of the wedding's predominant flower. Heart- and flower-shaped cookies.

MIDDLE ROW, FROM LEFT: Suede baseballs in cream, tan and brown. Hershey's chocolate bar with personalized wrapper. I-Zone camera with leather notebook and pencils.

BOTTOM ROW, FROM LEFT: Kevin Costner and Christine Baumgartner gave cowboy hats to guests at their rehearsal dinner. Boxed heart- and flower-shaped soaps. Comfortable slippers to help guests "keep dancing the night away."

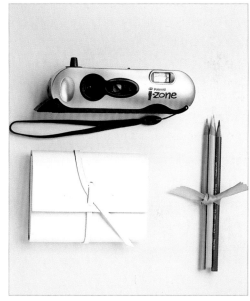

PLANNING A DESTINATION WEDDING

A wedding is meant to be romantic, and what could be more so than whisking friends and family away to an exotic location for an unforgettable weekend-long celebration? That's the idea behind a destination wedding, but if you're thinking of throwing one, know that planning it can be a challenging enterprise. Here are some tips on how to get hitched abroad without a hitch.

BE FLEXIBLE

In more remote locations, your choices in such things as catering, music and flowers will be limited. Don't have your heart set on a 12-tiered cake decorated with edible seed pearls if you plan to marry in Bora Bora.

THINK WEDDING-READY VENUE

To keep the budget reasonable, book a wedding location that has everything on site if possible. Setting up tents and bringing in rentals can often lead to logistical headaches hard to manage from afar and can also send the tab soaring.

BELOW, FROM LEFT: Chairs facing the reception tent at Kevin Costner's wedding to Christine Baumgartner. Writers Ilene Rosenzweig and Rick Marin celebrated their day in a restored 14th-century monastery in Santa Margherita Ligure, an Italian fishing village.

PREPARE FOR RED TAPE

If you plan to get married in a foreign locale, know that different countries have different requirements, including passports, birth certificates and, for some Catholic ceremonies, baptismal certificates. Certain countries prohibit interfaith marriages, and others require that you stay within their borders for a certain waiting period before your marriage is considered legal. What's more, paperwork may need to be translated into the language of the country to which you're traveling. Do your homework (starting with a call to the embassy or consulate of the country where you plan to wed) and allow plenty of time to get everything in order.

MAKE GUESTS FEEL WELCOME

If possible, provide transportation once they arrive at the airport. A limo service may be beyond your budget, but you can enlist relatives and friends to greet guests and bring them to the hotel. When guests first get to their rooms, make sure there's a welcome basket waiting. It can be simple (bottles of water and a snack) or elaborate (a scented candle, luxe toiletries, slippers), but be sure to include a personal note with each from you and your groom.

c. 5000 B.C. Distinctive forms of Northern and Southern Indian cultures emerge in Ontario lands

c. 1000 B.C. Introduction of pottery from the south

c. 500 B.C. Use of tobacco spreads northward

c. 500 A.D. Iroquois adopt cultivation of corn

1300 - 1400 Iroquois cultivate beans, squash, pumpkins and sunflowers

1500 - 1600 Algonquians remain hunters
Iroquois live in palisaded farming villages
Iroquois Five Nation confederacy takes shape as a "league of peace."

1534 Jacques Cartier sails the first French ship into the St. Lawrence

1535 Cartier encounters St. Lawrence Valley Iroquois

1608 Champlain begins lasting French occupation of the site of Quebec City
St. Lawrence Iroquois settlements have disappeared along the St. Lawrence

1615 Guided by Algonquians, French fur traders first travel to Georgian Bay

The Territory of Ontario

Centuries went into shaping Ontario's rich heritage. An actual Province of Ontario was only set up in 1867 as part of Canadian Confederation, but its direct ancestor, the Province of Upper Canada, appeared in 1791. At that time, two centuries ago, Upper Canada was first established by imperial Britain to meet the needs of settlers along the upper St. Lawrence and lower Great Lakes: settlers then chiefly composed of Loyalist migrants from a new United States, who had upheld the British side during the recent American Revolution. Thus began the political and governmental unit, the organized, distinct community which was to become Ontario. Still, long before there was any province at all, Ontario had seen much earlier beginnings in the days of New France; in 1615, at least, when French fur traders from their little post at Quebec on the St. Lawrence first

Overleaf. *Bon Echo Rock at Mazinaw Lake. This granite wall was formed as one huge slab of the Canadian Shield slipped down into the depths of what is now Mazinaw Lake. The section left standing is known as Bon Echo Rock. The Rock, extending as deep into the water as it does high into the air, has impressed many people. Among them were the Indians who painted pictographs on its face near the water line, as well as rock-climbers and tourists of much later ages.*

Timeline. *The timelines represent the time spanned by each chapter and the events which occured in them. The amount of space between entries in the timeline is not necessarily proportional to the number of years spanned.*

1. *The Trillium and the Coat of Arms of Ontario. The White Trillium is Ontario's official flower.*

2. *The Loyalists. In 1791 Upper Canada was first established by Britain to serve the Loyalist settlers who had come from the United States after the American Revolution. Thus began the political unit and organized community which was to become the province of Ontario.*

3. *Ontario's territory, as viewed from space.* EMG 1696.

1

2

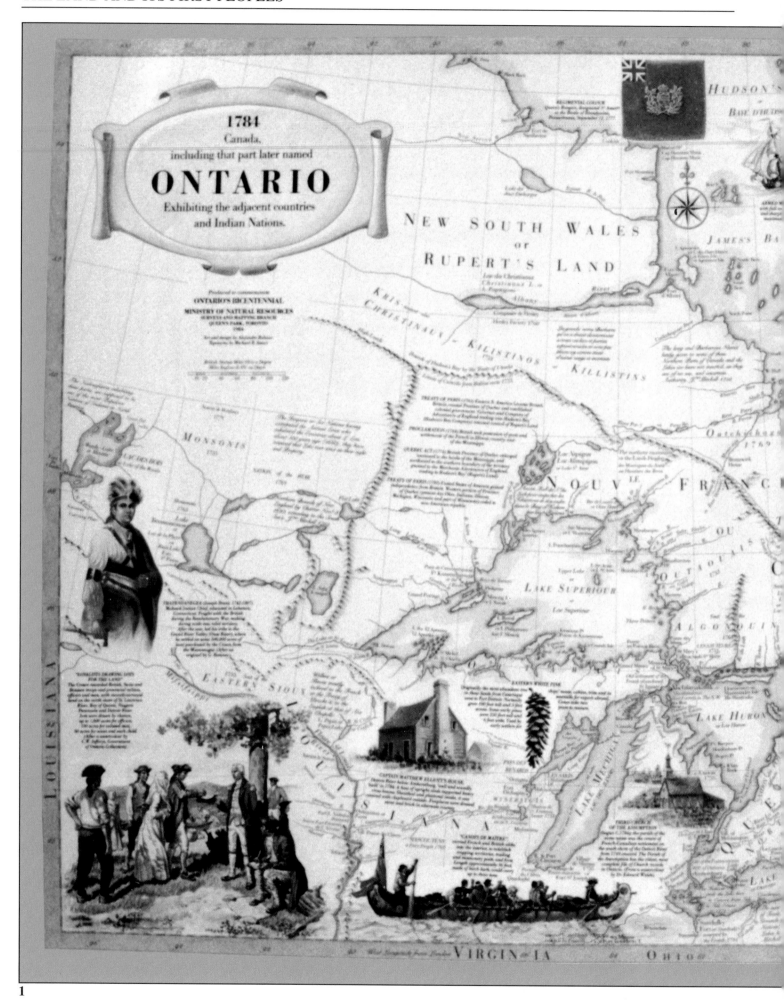

1

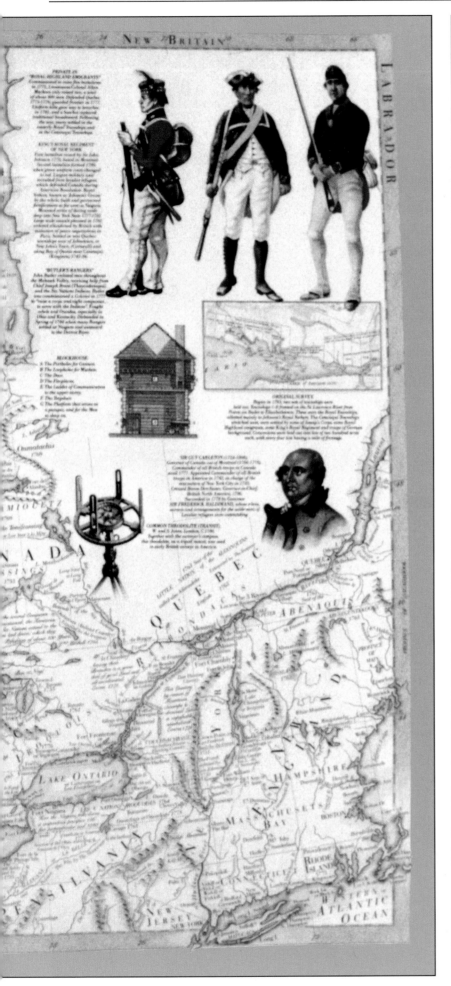

1. *The Ontario area in 1784. This map was produced in 1984 to celebrate the bicentennial of Ontario's settlement by Loyalists, following the American Revolution.*
2., 3. *Aerial Views of Lakeland and Rivers in Ontario.*

journeyed by way of the Ottawa River to reach Georgian Bay on Lake Huron, and thereby brought this great up-country realm of lakes and rivers into the written records of history.

And yet . . . across far more distant ages of a long pre-history, native peoples had already occupied and marked the Ontario domain in future Canada, making lasting contributions to its heritage. And far earlier still, before the first native peoples — migrants themselves — had emerged within the vast lakeland region near the core of the continent, basic forces of geography had decreed its natural forms and lines of access, its climate, vegetation and animal life, its resources stored in rock or soil, water or forest. Ontario's heritage runs back through centuries before 1791; but it still starts with the physical environment.

That physical world which was to be Ontario reached north to south for almost a thousand miles between bleak, subarctic coasts on Hudson Bay and fertile margin along Lake Erie, at Canada's southernmost limit. The northern portions of this giant land-mass stretched close to another thousand miles from east to west: from Lake Temiskaming (out of which the Ottawa River flowed southeasterly to meet the St. Lawrence) across to the Lake of the Woods, where

Evening, Lake Temagami. *Many areas of Ontario have captured the attention of artists with their beauty.* Painting by George Agnew Reid in 1941.

streams connected with the open western plains. Or else, along its southern bounds, this future Ontario spanned from the St. Lawrence not far above Montreal — on the water highway to the Atlantic and Europe — to the Detroit River set deep in the Great Lakes basin; and then on, up broad Lakes Huron and Superior, to smaller waterways that led to the Lake of the Woods, halfway across North America.

In sum, the territory of Ontario had as its main baseline the uniting St. Lawrence-Great Lakes water system, one of the world's finest natural communications routes. And though this territory contained two notably different physical sections, Northern and Southern Ontario, the two interpenetrated, and were bound together by essential paths of transport, as well as by joint historical developments. Northern Ontario indeed was vastly larger; but Southern Ontario would prove much more populous and economically dominant. Each of these sections calls for an introductory sketch.

1. *Lake Erie. The fertile shores of Lake Erie form both Ontario's and Canada's southernmost limit.* Philip John Bainbrigge (1817-1881), watercolour over pencil on wove paper c. 1836-1842.
2. *Sunset, Lake of the Woods. Many artists have endeavoured to capture the beauty of the Lake of the Woods area, near Ontario's western border.* Walter Joseph Phillips (1884-1963), colour woodcut, c. 1928.
3. *Lake Huron. Perhaps this is how Lake Huron looked to French fur traders when they first journeyed from their little post at Quebec, by way of the Ottawa River, to reach Georgian Bay on Lake Huron in 1615.* Philip John Bainbrigge, watercolour over pencil on wove paper, c. 1845.

1

2

3

1

2

1. *Mouth of the Nottawasaga River, Lake Huron. The Great Lakes both nurture Ontario, and, with the exception of Lake Michigan, mark its limits. Lakes Huron and Superior are the furthest west of those lakes.* Alexander Cavalié Mercer (1783-1868), watercolour over pencil on wove paper, 1824.

2. *Lake Superior. This watercolour by George Back entitled, "A Bay In Lake Superior Where We Were Detained By a High Wind" clearly shows the rugged northern terrain surrounding Lake Superior.*

3. *The mature hardwood trees in the forests of Northern Ontario often filter the light creating dark woods with little undergrowth. Over all, Northern Ontario is a major segment of the rugged, densely forested Canadian Shield.*

4. *This sombre Northern land can shine in sun or snow beneath brilliant skies.*

5. *Pine trees on the shore of a remote Northern Ontario lake at the end of a hot summer day.*

6. *The bark of the birch tree was often used by native people to construct canoes, and the trees themselves later served lumbering.*

3

4

5

6

1

2

3

1. *Typical of many in Northern Ontario Shield country, this bay has patches of open water mixed with floating mats of moss, surrounded by spruce trees.*
2. *A Beaver Lodge. Built in waters flooded by beavers, the lodge has an under-water entrance for protection.*
3. *A White-Tailed Deer Fawn. The lakes of Northern Ontario teemed with fish, the forest with deer and other animals taken by native peoples for food or clothing.*
4. *A commonly seen forest inhabitant of the Shield — the raccoon.*

4

1

2

The Geography of Ontario

Northern Ontario included a Hudson Bay Lowlands area of semi-barren tundra, scrub and struggling small trees; but over all, it was a major segment of the rugged, densely forested Canadian Precambrian Shield: that huge sweep of eroded, ancient rock that forms so much of northern Canada. Far-distant ice ages had ground away and rounded the Shield ranges; left thick glacial deposits of broken boulders and gravel, choked and changed drainage patterns into an intricate lace of riverways, lakes large or small, and peat-rich, swampy muskegs. The Shield country hence might seem difficult and daunting. It was full of blind channels, bogs and bugs, dark woods, looming granite walls and sombre heights; beyond which lay more endlessly rolling crests crowned with evergreens. Yet this same hard land could also sparkle in sun or snow beneath brilliant skies; and there was the glory of its rushing white waters, the mirror-calm of countless lakes, the cool scents of pine and balsam along its silent foreshores. Furthermore — on another level — the very intricacies of waterways could be solved and used for deft, free-roaming travel by the Indian art of the birch-bark canoe; while the lakes themselves teemed with fish, the forest in deer and other animals taken by native peoples for food or clothing — including the beaver, which ultimately became vital to the development of a powerful, white-directed fur trade from the seventeenth century onward.

Accordingly, the earliest resources of the northern Shield to be drawn on by humankind were those which were so generally available in a natural environment of woods, watercourses and abundant animal life. Nevertheless, the heavy tree-cover — hardly touched by the first peoples except for simple shelters and firewood — would come to serve large-scale lumbering: of pine, spruce, birch and more. Lumber operations spread in the later nineteenth century, as enlarging markets for wood brought increasing inroads by white

1. *Exposed Canadian Shield along Highway 7.*
2. *The Shield country is one of rocky, rolling crests crowned with evergreens.*
3. *Stamp Commemorating the Nickel Discovery at Sudbury in 1883. Ore bearing both nickel and copper was discovered here, and by 1887 mining for copper was underway. Nickel had little market value until the closing years of the century.*

Canada 32

nickel

Discovery at Sudbury 1883 / Sa découverte à Sudbury 1883

3

1

2

3

1. *Ontario offers spectacular sunrises and sunsets to the careful observer throughout the summer months.*

2. *The rushing white water of a typical Northern Ontario stream as it winds its way around granite boulders.*

3. *A Forest in the Winter. Though deciduous trees are bare in the winter, they still offer beautiful settings for skiers and hikers.*

4. *A View of Autumn Colours in the Underbrush of an Ontario Forest.*

4

1

1. *Although Northern Ontario as a whole did not lend itself to agriculture, it held localized farming pockets as well as great arable clay belts. These larger deposits were made up of soils left in the beds of ancient lakes: chiefly in the Little Clay Belt (New Liskeard-Haileybury) in the northeast, or the Great Clay Belt (Cochrane-Hearst) further west and north. In this aerial photo one can see some of the farming taking place around a community near Cochrane.* A22754-86.

2. *Dominion Nickel Mine, 1887.*

3. *Early Mine in Ontario, Marmora, Hastings County, c. 1870.* By Susanna Moodie (1803-1885).

4. *Cobalt Townsite Mine. This photo shows the mine buildings and the Temiskaming and Northern Ontario Railway (T & N.O.R.) which ran through them. Cobalt became a major centre of silver mining in the young twentieth century.*

2

3

4

"civilization." The term here is put in quotation marks, not necessarily in any derogatory sense, but because its values should consciously be checked, and never taken for granted. At any rate, for better or worse (and certainly affecting heritage), lumbering was to become a major concern within the Northern Ontario Shield, fostering companies and fortunes, together with towns, technology and jobs across the wilderness; although control of the companies and fortunes seemed more to settle in Southern Ontario, not to mention in the United States beyond.

Along with mounting outputs of timber, pulpwood and newsprint, the Shield's immense mineral and energy reserves also came widely into use, beginning in the later nineteenth century but soaring in volume and significance from the early twentieth forward. Copper and nickel around Sudbury, silver at Cobalt, gold at Timmins, Kirkland Lake, Hemlo and other sites, iron in Algoma or Atikokan, uranium at Elliot Lake: the successive list of finds and fields tells much of the modern history of the North. But with fortunes, jobs and new urban centres also went depletion, waste, pollution and human problems. Heritage does not just produce grand monuments and splendid achievements. Nevertheless, the hardy growth of multicultural mining and mill communities, the initial surface claims staked by prospectors that became deep-rock mazes of mine shafts and stopes, the local damsites that rose into giant hydro-electric power complexes from Sault Ste. Marie to Abitibi or Nipigon — all these left monuments as well in Northern Ontario's heritage.

Such a territory, however, was but marginally suitable for agriculture; much of it not all. The bare bones of some of the Earth's oldest rocks here lie on or close to the surface. Soils are mostly poor as well as thin; moisture in the cool-to-cold climate is usually sufficient by way of rain or snowfall; but the clearing of tree-cover without proper measures for reforestation may just produce raw wastelands in the wilderness. Granted, some localized farming pockets did appear in

1. *Mining Car on Tracks, 1877. Beginning in the later 19th century, the mineral and energy resources of the Canadian Shield came increasingly into use.*
2. *Work Begins, Sinking the Moffat Shaft, Bruce Mine, 1847. Mining in the Shield developed in the later nineteenth century but soared in volume from the early twentieth century forward. Bruce Mine was an early producer of copper, which also was discovered along with nickel in the Sudbury area when the railway was being built.*
3. *Pulp and Paper Industry. This stamp commemorates Canada's largest secondary industry. As the development of Northern Ontario went on, outputs of timber, pulpwood and newsprint grew, especially from the 1900s.*

1   2   3

1

1. *Indians in a Birch Bark Canoe. Northern Ontario waterways were widely used for travel, thanks to the Indian art of the birch-bark canoe.*
2. *Making the Native Bark Canoes. Note the typical outcropping of the Shield in the background.*
3. *Southern Farm in the Humber Valley, 1917. In the main, Southern Ontario plainly contrasts with Northern Ontario in its gentle landscapes and widely-settled countrysides.*
4. *One of the homesteads on the Canadian Shield in the later nineteenth century that had to contend with poorer soils and a shorter growing season, compared with the South.*

2

3

4

1

2

3

time near major places like Thunder Bay, the lake-shipping terminus at the head of Lake Superior, or busy Sault Ste. Marie, by the rapids between Superior and Huron. And there certainly were far larger deposits of arable soils left in the beds of vanished ancient lakes: chiefly in the Little Clay Belt (New Liskeard-Haileybury) of the northeast, or the Great Clay Belt (Cochrane-Hearst) further west and north. Still, short seasons limited most crops in the Clay Belts, as did their distance from major markets. In general, Northern Ontario's geography made it and kept it a region of great space and scant population outside its scattered towns and cities; a land of lavish resources — within firm limits — yet of hard dependence on external capital, markets, and overall direction.

Southern Ontario would stand in obvious geographic contrast in its milder outlines, widely-settled countrysides and massive urban-industrial developments. All the same, one has to note that the unrelenting Precambrian Shield pushed into it as well. South from Lake Nipissing, Shield terrain ran on through what is now Algonquin Park, through Muskoka-Haliburton, and then sent a granite thrust southeastward to reach the upper St. Lawrence between Brockville and Kingston: thereby setting those rocky gems, the Thousand Islands, in Canada's great river. Apart from this deep incursion of the Shield, however, Southern Ontario was largely a land of gentle slopes and well-tilled fields, where oaks, maples, elms, and beeches sheltered thriving farms. In the east, it was part of the long St. Lawrence Lowlands, here edged by the upper St. Lawrence and lower Ottawa Rivers. Westward, beyond the intervening tongue of Shield country, it spread out into the Great Lakes Plain, stretching to Ontario's southwestern tip at the Detroit River.

This lakeland plain, well watered and moderate-to-mild in climate, had two main surface levels. The lower level, along Lake Ontario to its head, would essentially become the province's central heartland: the site of its provincial capital and largest city, Toronto, and the focus of both key transport routes and heaviest population densities, in the "Golden Horseshoe" from Oshawa around to Hamilton and St. Catherines. A higher level of plain lay further to the west, beyond the long Niagara Escarpment which ran from the Niagara River, that

1. *Southern Ontario, as viewed from space.* EMG 1697.

2. *Rushing River, Lake of the Woods.* Walter Joseph Phillips (1884-1963), monochrome woodcut on wove paper, c. 1931.

3. *Glacier. During far-distant ice ages, glaciers like this ground away and rounded the Shield ranges. As they receded they left thick glacial deposits of boulders and gravel, choking and changing drainage patterns into a complexity of riverways, lakes, and muskeg.*

4. *Canadian Locomotives, 1836-1860. In the mid-19th century, railways with locomotives like these enabled timber to be brought down to new American markets.*

5. *Loading Logs on a Logging Sleigh in Northern Ontario with a "Jammer." The heavy tree cover of Northern Ontario would widely serve large-scale lumbering.*

Canada 32 — *Dorchester 0-4-0 type / Type Dorchester 0-4-0*
Canada 32 — *Toronto 4-4-0 type / Type Toronto 4-4-0*

4

5

1

2

3

1. *An early farm on the edge of the Canadian Shield.*
2. *Farm House and Barns Blanketed in Snow. Farming frontiers began to appear in the 1780s in Southern Ontario, but around the 1850s, the period of frontier agricultural expansion drew to a close in that area.*
3. *An old-growth forest of maples, once a common sight in Southern Ontario.*
4. *Within the networks of Ontario's waterways can be found some of the best recreational canoeing in the world — not to mention stunning autumn colours.*
5. *A Muskoka Sunset. The Muskoka-Haliburton area is one of the Southern Ontario districts to have the Shield terrain that is predominant in Northern Ontario.* Walter Joseph Phillips (1884-1963), colour woodcut on wove paper.

4

5

1. *A bird's-eye view of the Niagara River from Lake Erie to Lake Ontario.* W.R. Callington, Coloured lithograph.

2. *Autumn Leaves. Originally thickly forested, Southeastern Ontario contained large numbers of deciduous hardwoods, as well as many softwood evergreens towards the east.*

3. *Niagara Falls. Native Indians knew Toronto as an entry to a passage overland between the Lower and Upper Great Lakes that avoided the long travel path past Niagara Falls and on through Lakes Erie and St. Clair into Lake Huron.* James Erskine, oil painting, c. 1784.

1

2

3

linked Lakes Erie and Ontario, northward across to Georgian Bay on Lake Huron. The westerly, upland areas above the Escarpment thus formed a wide interlake peninsula, which was to provide some of the best croplands in Ontario, together with sizeable towns and cities too.

From this western peninsula through the central and eastern sectors, Southern Ontario had none the less originally been thickly forested; like the Shield, displaying major softwood evergreens, especially in the east; but generally containing large numbers of deciduous hardwoods, which further westward became plainly dominant. Furthermore, this tall Great-Lakes forest also featured sycamores, black walnuts and tulip trees in its warmer southwestern areas that amounted to extensions of the Carolinian woods. In short, here was luxuriant primeval timber country, which also held plentiful animal life, and certainly came early into the fur trade. Still further, it went on to yield a rich heritage in lumbering: an enterprise which by no means has wholly departed yet from Southern Ontario, especially in the Ottawa Valley, once home of magnificent white pine stands. Down the Ottawa and into the St. Lawrence, huge rafts of square-hewed timber were floated to Quebec for export to Britain, from the young nineteenth century onward. Oak, ash and many other woods were also cut for houses, ships and workplaces, all along the Great

1. *Beaver. The terrain of the Canadian Shield in Northern Ontario may have seemed difficult to early venturers, yet also it offered the beaver, which ultimately became vital to the development of a powerful, white-directed fur trade.* George Harlow White (1817-1887), pencil drawing, 1870s.
2. *Harrowing on Eaton Farm, Toronto, in 1922. Southern Ontario was and widely still is a land of gentle slopes and well-tilled fields.*
3. *Oak Wood on the Ottawa River in 1865. In this eastern area, Southern Ontario links with the long St. Lawrence Lowlands, here edged by the upper St. Lawrence and lower Ottawa Rivers.*

1

2   3

1

2

Lakes shores up to the forests of Georgian Bay. And from the mid-nineteenth century, railways, steam-driven mills and sawn lumber for American markets brought a whole new scope to timber operations; until, eventually, Southern Ontario's tree resources ran low, to be chiefly replaced by the Northern wood supplies.

But the lands of the South, when cleared of trees, of course, could broadly support a prosperous and enduring agriculture, whereas the North's could not. In fact, farming frontiers had appeared in the Southern Ontario region even while the fur trade still lasted there, and before the lumber trade had even started; at least from the days of Loyalist land settlement in the 1780s. Before then, too, fur-trade posts in the region had cultivated local fields, such as at Niagara. Yet again the native peoples were there first, in agriculture also. From pre-historic times some Indian groups, largely in the western Ontario peninsula south of Georgian Bay, had lived as village-dwellers raising crops of corn and beans, parts of which they traded to neighbouring hunting tribes for meat, skins and furs. Europeans emphatically did not introduce agriculture into Southern Ontario. Still, it spread widely once they settled in. Frontier farming expanded with the American pioneers who followed in the Loyalists' wake from the 1790s; and particularly with the sweeping British influx which went on through the earlier nineteenth century. Later inflows of varied European, then Asian, Caribbean or Latin American immigrants, would greatly add to the modern ethnic content of Ontario. But broadly speaking, the period of frontier agricultural expansion had come to a close around the 1850s; for by then most of the good arable lands of Southern Ontario had been taken up and put into crop-raising.

A boomtime followed in Ontario staple wheat produced for export, especially within the interlake peninsula. Over the later 1800s, however, mixed farming, specialized crops for processing, and raising foods for ever-growing nearby urban centres, became hallmarks of rural life in Southern Ontario. For what was powerfully under way was the rapid rise of towns and cities across that section. It was already closely knit and quite well populated. It had effective water communications, no major land barriers, and ready access to

1. *Snow near Niagara Falls, 1912. Despite this snow scene, Southern Ontario's western area has a climate that is usually much more moderate than that of Northern Ontario.*
2. *Thousand Islands, St. Lawrence River. The Precambrian Shield here thrusts south-eastward to reach the upper St. Lawrence between Brockville and Kingston: thus setting the Thousand Islands in this great river.* Elizabeth Simcoe (1766-1850), grey wash and watercolour over pencil.
3. *Typical woodlands of the transitional zone between Southern and Northern forest, at Brittania Bay on the Ottawa River, near Ottawa.*

3

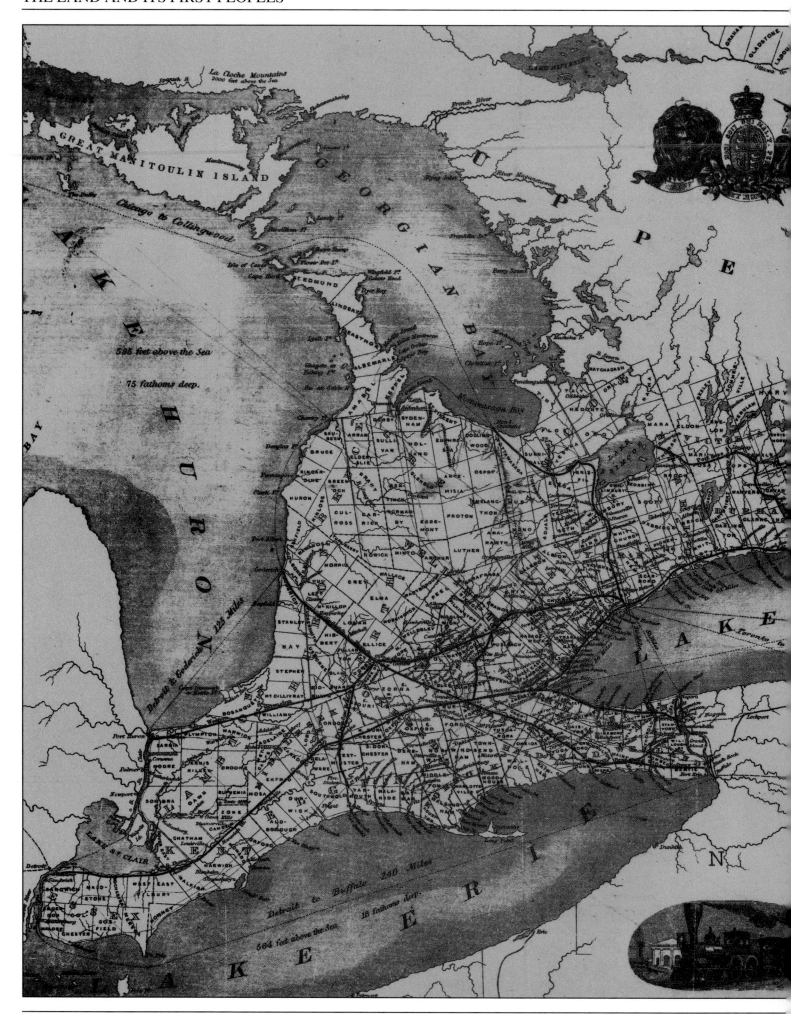

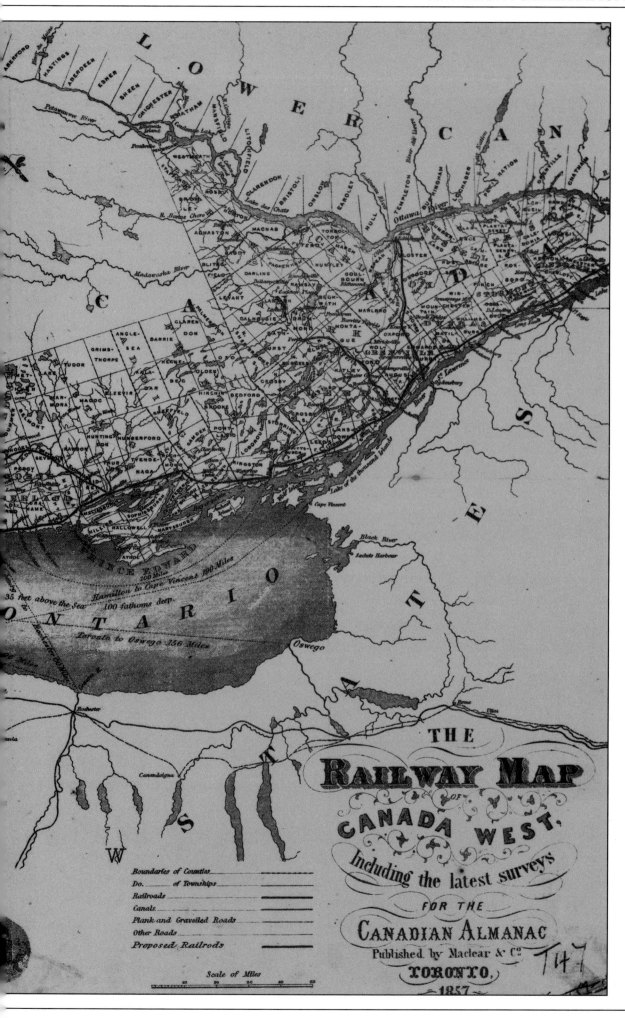

A Railway Map of "Canada West," 1857. The area's first railway boom began in the early 1850s but was over before the decade had ended. The railway then largely brought the industrial revolution to Upper Canada.

substantial markets across the Great Lakes basin; not to mention to Britain and Europe via the St. Lawrence, or to New York and the American seaboard via the Hudson River route. And so, based on fertile land and ample means of transit — which came to include canals, a network of rail lines, and then automobile highways — the Southern Ontario area grew big in economic power and urban places, steadily advancing through the nineteenth and twentieth centuries. Northern Ontario largely became a business hinterland for its cities, and in many respects, a great deal of Canada beyond.

Railways from the 1850s had fostered Southern Ontario towns and factory industry. Industry furthered city growth; first drawing on coal shipped easily across the Great Lakes, and next increasingly on hydro-electric energy brought from Niagara Falls, a superb natural power-house, or out of the Ottawa and St. Lawrence waters. Cities expanded widely and variously: from Ottawa, once the lumber village of Bytown, which became the political capital of federal Canada in 1867, to Hamilton, which rose as a heavy industrial city with railway building, and went on into basic steel production. Or there were Windsor and Oshawa, both shaped by twentieth-century automotive industry; or Kingston, Ontario's oldest port town, at the head of the St. Lawrence, and London, a well-to-do commercial and insurance centre in the prospering western peninsula. There are plainly too many other urban places to mark; except for Toronto, which had been founded as the town of York in 1793, and made seat of government for the province of Upper Canada set up in 1791.

In 1834, York was incorporated as the province's first city, under its former Indian name, Toronto. No doubt, this ruling place had already grown through government advantages; among them, the main provincial highway cut inland, Yonge Street, along which settlement and commerce spread. Still, Toronto also gained control of trade, traffic, industry and finance from its commanding crossroads

1. *Bush Clearing With Log-House. Farming frontiers arose in Southern Ontario in the 1780s while the fur trade still lasted there, and before the lumber trade had really started.* Engraving.

2. *Original stand of white pine, Algonquin Park. These pine are native to most of Ontario south of the 50th parallel, but are now very rare, thanks to lumbering. The trees could grow to heights of fifty-five metres and diameters of one and a half metres. Because the trunks grew so straight, they were often used for Royal Navy masts, and for the square timber trade.*

3. *J.R. Booth Company's lumber piles at Ottawa, c. 1873. From the mid-nineteenth century, railways, steam-driven mills and sawn lumber for American markets enlarged timber operations; until, eventually, Southern Ontario's tree resources ran low.*

4. *Timber Raft on Ottawa River. From the early 19th century onward, huge rafts of square hewed timber were floated down the Ottawa into the St. Lawrence, and to Quebec for export to Britain.*

1

2

3

4

1

2

1. *Factories of the McLaughlin Co. Ltd.; one of a series of plants utilized for the manufacture of motor cars. As Ontario cities expanded, many became noted for a particular industry. Both Windsor and Oshawa were shaped by the 20th-century automotive industry.*

2. *Universal Carriers for war service are completed in a final assembly plant, Ford Company of Canada, Windsor, 1942.*

3. *Queenston Heights Power House, Niagara Falls, Ontario, c. 1930. Industry in Southern Ontario towns first depended on energy from coal shipped across the Great Lakes, and later increasingly on hydro-electric energy from Niagara Falls.*

4. *Yonge Street, North from Adelaide, Toronto, c. 1885. In 1834, York was incorporated as the province's first city, Toronto. The city grew in part through having the main provincial highway cut inland, Yonge Steet, along which settlement and commerce rose steadily. Toronto also gained in control of traffic, industry and finance from holding a commanding crossroads position on the Great Lakes front.*

3

4

position on the Great Lakes front; Montreal to the east, Chicago to the west, New York to the south, and to the north behind it, the immense Ontario land-mass and its resources. Out of all this came the internationally important metropolitan city of the present — though Toronto had already been Ontario's own economic metropolis since about the mid-nineteenth century, and a national Canadian metropolis from at least the early twentieth. But much earlier beginnings could be traced for it, besides.

Native Indians in eras of pre-history certainly had known and resorted to the site of Toronto on a large and sheltered Lake Ontario bay. They knew it as a favoured landing-ground, the entry to a short-cut overland between the Lower and Upper Great Lakes, thereby avoiding the long travel path past Niagara Falls and through Lake Erie and St. Clair into Lake Huron. Instead, Toronto was the gateway to a passage by trail, lesser lakes and streams that reached direct to Georgian Bay on Huron. It was, in effect, an open gateway to distant realms of north and west; and its Indian name meant Place of Meeting. It is so still. Here, then, is a meaningful tie with the original moulders of Ontario's heritage, the first peoples — to whom we now can turn.

1. *Farm scene at Norwood, 1923. The fertile lands of Southern Ontario, when cleared of trees, could support substantially prosperous agriculture.*
2. *Field of Grain. Ontario farming experienced a boom in the mid-1800s, when wheat poured out for export. Over the later 1800s, however, mixed farming, specialized crops for processing, and raising foods for growing nearby urban centres, became hallmarks of rural life in Southern Ontario.*

1

2

1

2

1. *Algonquin Indian Encampment on the Ottawa River. The Algon-quins were mostly situated up the Ottawa and early became involved in the French fur trade.* Pastel by Alfred Worsley Holdstock (1820-1901).
2. *An arrowhead found on the shores of Mazinaw Lake during an archaeological dig. It seems that paleo-Indians first moved grad-ually north up the Ontario landmass, as giant ice sheets retreated, establishing a hunting culture that lasted for many centuries. Today it is revealed in finds of artifacts like these.*
3. *Noble Indien de la Nation Ottawa. The Ottawa were largely cen-tred on Manitoulin Island in Lake Huron around the time of French arrivals.* Hand-coloured lithograph.

3

1

2

Human Developments Prior to 1615

The writings of history record human activity in Ontario for close on four hundred years. The findings of archeology, drawn from the ground, report that human beings arrived here perhaps ten thousand years ago, amid the last, or latest, ice age. These "paleo-Indians" were the ancient predecessors of existing native peoples; though they were far removed themselves from their own ancestors, who most evidently had crossed from Siberia into Alaska by a vanished land-bridge over the Bering Sea, and in millennia thereafter had spread out through both Americas. In any case, the paleo-Indian venturers moved gradually north up the Ontario land-mass as the giant ice sheets retreated, establishing a hunting culture that lasted for thousands of years more. Today it is revealed in finds of worked stone tools, knives and dart heads use for taking game. There seems little need, however, to detail specific features of this or the succeeding early cultures classified by archeologists; except to note that differences certainly became apparent between a hunting-gathering existence in the harsher, colder north and in the warmer, better-endowed south. Hence in the period from about 5000 B.C., one may markedly distinguish between the Shield Archaic Culture and the Laurentian Archaic — as Northern and Southern Ontario asserted themselves even then.

Around 1000 B.C., the introduction of pottery, coming from the south, set another human mark. In fact, it identified the opening of the Woodland Culture period, which lasted on until European contacts began in the Ontario lands soon after 1600 A.D. It was within this Woodland period that the inhabitants of both north and south developed the language and culture patterns, the leagues, tribes or bands, which incoming Europeans were to meet and first write into history. And so an examination of the native peoples of Ontario, whose descendants form a vital part of its community today, may reasonably start here, in later centuries between 1000 and 1600 A.D., when the Indian nations and societies to be known in historic times had taken on their shape. But a primary point to be noted is that two great linguistic and cultural groups had also decisively emerged; the

1. *Jack Fish Bay, North Shore, Lake Superior. The Ojibwas were originally located around the shores of Lake Superior. Watercolour by J.H. Caddy.*
2. *These petroglyphs, or rock carvings, are found northeast of Peterborough. They are know as the kiromagewapkong, meaning "the rocks that teach" in Ojibwa and are revered by many native people in Ontario.*
3. *Chipewyan (Ojibwa) canoe. The Ojibwa canoe was narrow and flat-bottomed with low, flaring sides for hunting caribou and for travelling. Both stern and bow were partly decked, preventing water from entering the craft and both birch and spruce bark were used as sheathing.*
Overleaf Left. *Calling a moose. In winter, the Algonquian band split up into small family units to hunt for deer, elk and other game.*
Overleaf Right. *Spearing. In summer, the Algonquian band gathered at productive fishing sites.*

3

1

2

Algonquian-speaking peoples and the Iroquoians. The former were mostly northern in setting, migratory in life-style, and essentially dependent on hunting and fishing. The latter, who lived southward extending into what is now New York State, were settled village dwellers and crop-raisers, for whom hunting and fishing chiefly became just supplements.

Taking the Algonquian grouping first, one should immediately distinguish this far-reaching language term from one particular member-tribe, the Algonquins, who were largely situated up the Ottawa and early became involved in the French fur trade. Other major tribes would include the Nipissings, around the lake of that name, where Northern Ontario traditionally commences; the Ottawa, or Odawa, initially centred on Manitoulin Island in Lake Huron; the Ojibwas (often Europeanized to Chippewas) originally located along the shores of Lake Superior; and the Crees beyond them north to the treeline, from James Bay at the foot of Hudson Bay out to the western plains. Yet among these Algonquian peoples of the Shield, the tribe was generally a rather indefinite unit of common ancestry, belief and folklore, without political framework or controlling authority. The political and social reality far more rested in the band; a much smaller local unit with recognized ranges of territory, which its members roved annually to fill their needs of life. A band chief might be a celebrated hunter; but at least as important were the shamans, poorly translated as "medicine men," who were the people's spiritual interpreters and guides.

In winter, the Algonquian band split up into still smaller family units to hunt for deer, elk and other game; rejoining in the spring for

1. *Digging roots. While the men fished, the women gathered herbs and wild crops, and in more southerly areas tended some corn or other plantings. In the autumn the Algonquian bands harvested, or collected more wild foods, especially wild rice, before dividing again for long winter hunts.*
2. *Making Maple Syrup in an Indian Camp. The band rejoined in the spring for the tapping and boiling of maple syrup.*
3. *Among the Algonquian peoples were the Algonquins, the Nipissings, the Ottawa, (or Odawa,) the Ojibwas, (or Chippewas) and the Crees. They were largely migratory, living in bough shelters or small bark wigwams.*

The Algonkians Les Algonquins **Canada 8**

3

1

2

the tapping and boiling of maple syrup. In summer, the band also gathered at productive fishing sites, sometimes by weirs of stakes, brush and roots strung across the streams. Here while the men fished, the women gathered herbs and berries, and in more southerly areas tended some corn or other plantings: corn, for instance, had even reached the Ottawa on Manitoulin Island by about 1600. Then in the autumn the band harvested, or collected more wild foods, especially wild rice, before dividing for the long winter hunts again. Such was the Algonquian world: of roaming scarcely altered ancient woodlands; of living in bough shelters or small bark wigwams, and constantly questing for food while facing nature's threats of hunger — yet living, too, in close company with nature according to an age-old pattern; not willfully or heedlessly, but harmoniously and reverently.

If the Iroquoian groups were different, that did not necessarily hinder peaceful exchanges and co-existence with their Algonquian-speaking neighbours. Nonetheless, the Iroquoian peoples developed in their own way, largely by becoming reliant on field crops for up to four-fifths of their food supply. First to their lower Great Lakes lands came corn, perhaps spreading up from the Ohio and Illinois country as early as 500 A.D. Then came beans (whose high protein content cut down Iroquoian needs for animal foods) along with squash and pumpkins from around 1300 or 1400 A.D. And sunflowers, providing valuable oil from their seeds, arrived about the same time. Incidently, tobacco had appeared much earlier still, possibly around 500 B.C., to spread northward well past its actual growing range for ritual and social usages, as handsomely decorated stone and pottery pipes can testify. But Iroquoian tribes could and did grow tobacco, some to be traded to northern Algonquian peoples and beyond.

This crucial reliance on raising crops may in one sense have tied down the Iroquoians; but more importantly it promoted their

1. *Talon Falls and Red Granite Rocks Near Lake Nipissing. The Nipissing Indians were situated around the lake of that name.* Watercolour by Philip J. Bainbrigge, 1838.
2. *Pictographs, or rock paintings, are found scattered throughout much of Ontario and provide a lasting record of the presence of the native peoples. These are found along the base of a cliff in Bon Echo Provincial Park.*
3. *Maps of where the Algonquian Indians of the eastern woodlands and the Iroquoians lived.*

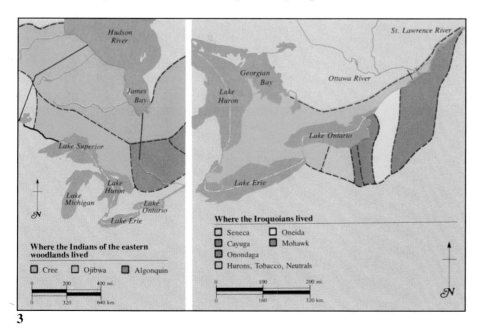

Where the Indians of the eastern woodlands lived
☐ Cree ☐ Ojibwa ☐ Algonquin

Where the Iroquoians lived
☐ Seneca ☐ Oneida
☐ Cayuga ☐ Mohawk
☐ Onondaga
☐ Hurons, Tobacco, Neutrals

3

freedom, organization and power. Within bounds, they were assured of a food supply. They could store it, trade off some of it, concentrate around the fields that produced it, and so construct a much more complex social and political life than the wandering Algonquians might ever know — thanks above all to their greater freedom from basic hunger. They still might have to shift village sites periodically, when fields but roughly cleared by stone axes, and tilled with wooden digging sticks, became worn-out or dense with weeds. Nevertheless, theirs was a settled existence, of a kind which further south in the Americas had led on powerful cities and rich empires long before the Europeans came; from the Mayas of Central America to the Incas of Peru, the Toltecs and Aztecs of Mexico. And who is to say what Ontario's own rising Iroquoian societies might have become — had not European interventions changed everything?

Be that as it may, the fact is that the Iroquoian-speaking peoples of Southern Ontario and adjoining areas built up both populous village communities and strong tribal units. As to the former, a village might have over two thousand residents living in large, wood-framed, bark-covered longhouses, each holding from ten to thirty families with apartment spaces and allocated fireplaces for them all: virtually an early example of the condominium. But these villagers with a fairly sure food stock from their croplands also could afford politics and war. They fought — evidently more over tribal honour or for vengeance against wrongs and killings than for material claims and gains — though human nature seems remarkably consistent. They had skilled warriors and war chiefs, long wicker shields and heavy war clubs. And from about 1500 A.D., when Iroquoian power was burgeoning, their villages were protected by triple palisades; tall, upright logs sunk side by side into the ground, with platforms for the defending bowmen and stone hurlers. Such fortified towns were even reported as "castles" by arriving Europeans.

The Iroquoians became expert in diplomacy, power-balances and hard-hitting forest raids. Yet their warlike strength did not lie so much in wilderness "stealth" or "ferocity" as Europeans would assert. It stemmed rather from effective political organization and commitment. Iroquoian tribal leaders had clear directing authority,

1. *The Iroquoians who developed in their own ways, distinct from their Algonquian-speaking neighbours.*
2. *Bad Boy, Qui-we-sain-shis, a Cree (Algonquian) Indian. The Crees were situated beyond the Ojibwas north to the tree line, and from James Bay at the foot of Hudson Bay out to the Western plains.* Watercolour over wove paper by William Armstrong (1822-1914).

Canada 10

The Iroquoians Les Iroquoiens

1

2

for it rested on a kind of democratic consensus and the knowing assent of tribal members. Policy questions were debated and resolved with persuasive oratory around council fires. Beyond that, the tribal chiefs were themselves elected; or more specifically, chosen by senior women, the female heads of families, who could also vote to remove an unsatisfactory chieftain. This points to the distinctive role of women in Iroquoian society. They were the gardener-cultivators of the essential food supply; while except for warfare, the men handled less vital concerns such as hunting and fishing. Moreover, family descent followed the female line in each longhouse, where men moved into their wives' homes under a family matriarch: age, too, had its recognition. And so, if the chiefs were male, they and both the tribal and familial structures were based on women. Were these Iroquoians pre-historic or post-modern?

In the Ontario region, the Iroquoians consisted mainly of the Petun, Neutral and Huron peoples, along with the Five Nations Iroquois, who were centred south of Lake Ontario but spread their influence (and at times their presence) well into Ontario lands. The Petun or Tobacco Nation, comprising two tribes, lived west of the Hurons on the Georgian Bay shores. The Neutrals or Attiwandirons, some ten tribes, held territory from the Hamilton-Niagara area to Lake Erie, on into the western peninsula. The name "Neutral" was actually applied by the arriving French, who then found them at peace between the warring Hurons and Five Nations. Yet theirs was surely an armed neutrality: they could call on 4,000 to 6,000 war- riors, maintained military alliances, and recurrently fought with old enemies across in Michigan. Less numerous were their Huron neigh- bours to the north, perhaps some 25,000 to the Neutrals' 40,000 around the start of the seventeenth century. Still, the Huron confed- eracy of four (later five) tribes was prosperous and prominent. For they were accomplished traders, enjoying a most valuable location.

South of Georgian Bay, the Hurons' fields and villages stretched to Lake Simcoe, villages that might hold up to 3,500 inhabitants. This was their bountiful home country, today still recognized as Huronia. But the Huron sphere reached further down to Lake Ontario; south via the overland Toronto trail from Lake Simcoe waters, or southeast

1. *Graphic symbolism of the Iroquoians.*
2. *The Huron Indians of Loreth [sic]. The Huron were one of the major early Iroquoian Indian groups in Ontario, though some of them were to move eastward into Quebec.* John Richard Coke Smyth (1808-1882), lithograph, c. 1838.

Canada 10

The Iroquoians   Les Iroquoiens

1

2

1

2

via the Kawartha Lakes and the Trent River. They no less traded northward with hunting tribes such as Ottawas and Nipissings, or the Algonquins on the Ottawa route that ran to the St. Lawrence. In sum, they held a powerful place at the junction between the wilderness resources of the Shield and the southern croplands, and on a through passage between the upper and lower Great Lakes. The French would come to appreciate the significance of that site. So would the Five Nations — less favourably so.

The latter also occupied a significant position below Lake Ontario, from the Hudson valley west to the Niagara country. Thus situated, they could control trade coming up the Hudson from the coast to the interior. They could tap, or block, the upper St. Lawrence route on the north above them, or thrust past Lake Ontario into central Great Lakes areas. They equally held fertile farmlands, with longer growing seasons than further north. The Mohawks ("keepers of the eastern door") were located along the Mohawk River that flowed into the Hudson, the Oneidas, Onondagas and Cayugas across the Finger Lakes district, and the Senecas ("keepers of the western door") from the Genessee Valley on towards Niagara. But in particular, these five peoples, who by 1600 probably included no more than 15,000 members, had joined together in a forceful partnership which in time proved better co-ordinated than that of the Hurons. This Iroquois confederacy apparently took shape in the 1500s as a "league of peace" among the Five Nations and against their external enemies. Headed by a council of fifty sachems, federal chiefs, it developed impressive political skill and capacity for united action. In truth, the Iroquois League of Five Nations (which became Six when the Tuscaroras entered it early in the 1700s) was to be a pivotal power in northeastern North America: a crucial force which European empires had always to contend with, and later in Ontario, a firm buttress, once the Six Nations Iroquois had settled here after the American Revolution.

1. A rather mythical view of Jacques Cartier on the St. Lawrence. When Cartier sailed up the "River of Canada" in 1535 he encountered the St. Lawrence Valley Iroquois, who had disappeared by the time Samuel de Champlain founded Quebec City in 1608. Chavane, engraving.

2. Champlain trading with Indians. This picture shows some of the items for which the Native Peoples were ready to trade. The metal goods, blankets, and glassware, represented kinds of technology which Indian cultures of stone, bone, wood and pottery did not know. Jefferys, oil on board.

3. This stamp commemorates Jacques Cartier's first voyage to Canada in April, 1534, in a stylized portrait based on a painting by Francois Riss. The clay tobacco pipe held by Cartier is of a type used at the time by Iroquoian-speaking peoples. The house depicted is the manor house at Limoelou, France, owned by Cartier during his last years. The larger shield on the stamp shows the ancient heraldic emblem of Saint-Malo — a guard dog rampant. The cross bearing the 16th century royal arms of France represents the one planted by Cartier to claim the new lands for the French state.

3

All in all, the long and masterful impact of the Five, or Six, Nations has meant that the very name "Iroquois" remains tied to them.

One still should go back to mention the vanished St. Lawrence Valley Iroquois, whom Jacques Cartier and his men had encountered in 1535, when the first French ship sailed up the long St. Lawrence waterway into America. Cartier then had found what were most evidently Iroquoian corn-farming villages, at the sites of modern Quebec and Montreal. Yet by the time the French under Samuel de Champlain began lasting occupation of the Quebec site in 1608, the St. Lawrence Iroquois settlements had disappeared all the way upriver, seemingly uprooted and erased. Native societies, however, had come and gone before. Life prior to the white man was hardly all unchanging peace and happiness. In spite of that, beaten tribes or peoples were most likely driven away or absorbed by the winners, not literally wiped out. Torture was a real, and ritual, part of Indian warfare; but beyond satisfying honour for both victors and vanquished, its use had limits. Many members of a defeated people, especially, though not entirely, its women and children, would be taken into a conquering group — which is a good reason why the Five Nations Iroquois repeatedly grew in size. And so in a wide upheaval the St. Lawrence Iroquois may have been dispersed to south and west or assimilated into other tribes. Nevertheless, a far wider upheaval was soon under way, a result of the arrival of the Europeans' fur trade.

The fur trade arose on the St. Lawrence after Jacques Cartier's voyages had opened the river to the French. Although they failed to establish a permanent base or colony on the great river till 1608, their ships began coming each summer to deal with the Indians for furs, chiefly downstream at Tadoussac, where commerce mounted steadily. The effect has been likened to that of a stone tossed into a lake, producing ever-spreading ripples. In Canada, the waves from the fur trade moved constantly onward, reaching and affecting native

1. *Champlain. This stamp was issued to commemorate the fact that Champlain began lasting occupation of the Quebec site in 1608.*
2. *Hudson's Bay Company Post. As the fur trade grew in importance, it brought ever-deeper and deeper penetration of Ontario by Europeans. The Hudson's Bay Company with its posts throughout Ontario, such as this one on Bear Island in Lake Temagami, became a leading factor in the advance of Europeans.*
3. *Harry J. Sims Co., Furriers. The fur industry was of immense importance in the operning of Ontario wilderness. Eventually even the establishment of private fur dealers like this on the Ottawa resulted.*
4. *Bark Canoe and Snowshoes Under Construction. The Europeans learned many skills from the Indian peoples, such as travel by canoe, snowshoe, and toboggan, without which they could not have penetrated the forest interiors.*

1

2

3

4

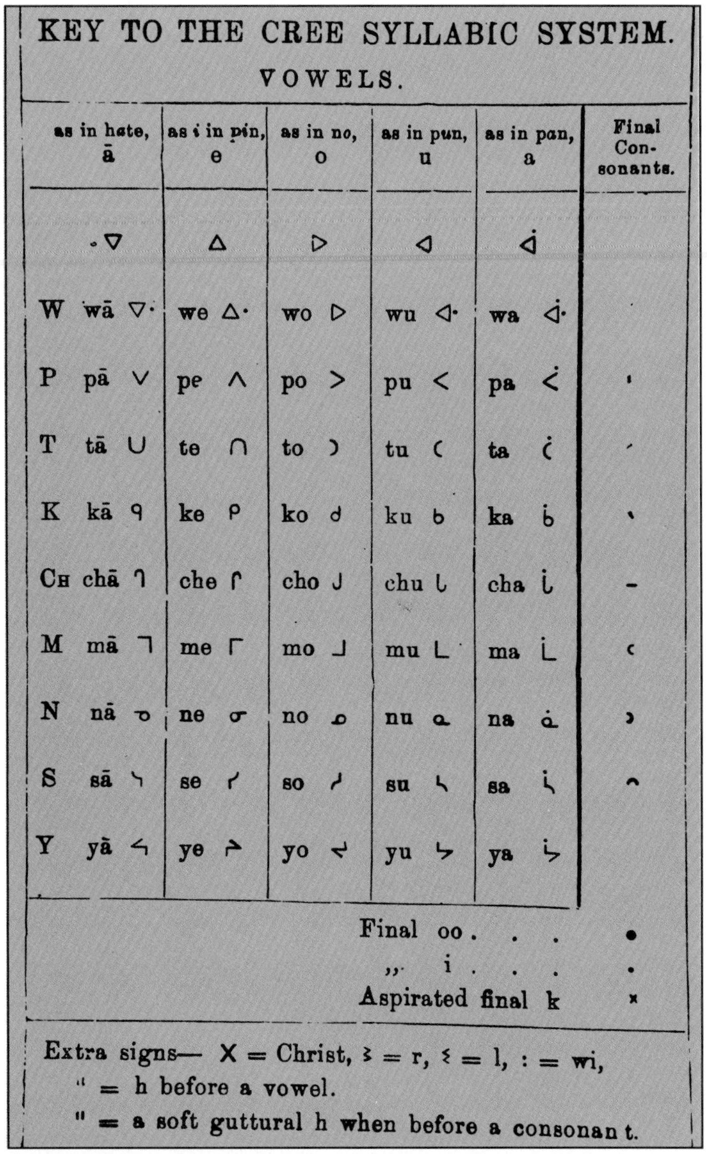

KEY TO THE CREE SYLLABIC SYSTEM.

VOWELS.

	as in hate, ā	as i in pin, e	as in no, o	as in pun, u	as in pan, a	Final Consonants.
	ᐁ	ᐃ	ᐅ	ᐊ	ᐋ	
W	wā ᐍ	we ᐏ	wo ᐓ	wu ᐗ	wa ᐚ	
P	pā ᐯ	pe ᐱ	po ᐳ	pu ᐸ	pa ᐹ	ᑊ
T	tā ᑌ	te ᑎ	to ᑐ	tu ᑕ	ta ᑖ	ᐟ
K	kā ᑫ	ke ᑭ	ko ᑯ	ku ᑲ	ka ᑳ	ᐠ
Ch	chā ᒉ	che ᒋ	cho ᒍ	chu ᒐ	cha ᒑ	ᐨ
M	mā ᒣ	me ᒥ	mo ᒧ	mu ᒪ	ma ᒫ	ᒼ
N	nā ᓀ	ne ᓂ	no ᓄ	nu ᓇ	na ᓈ	ᐣ
S	sā ᓭ	se ᓯ	so ᓱ	su ᓴ	sa ᓵ	ᐢ
Y	yā ᔦ	ye ᔨ	yo ᔪ	yu ᔭ	ya ᔮ	

Final oo . . . •
,, i . . . ·
Aspirated final k ×

Extra signs— X = Christ, ᕒ = r, ᓪ = l, : = wi,
" = h before a vowel.
" = a soft guttural h when before a consonant.

1

2

3

1. *Key to the Cree Syllabic System developed by James Evans.*
2. *Grey Owl. Grey Owl, who was not really an Indian but an Englishman named Archibald Belaney, did much to arouse sympathy for the native peoples in the 1920s.*
3. *James Evans, Methodist Missionary (1801-1846). Of English birth, he began teaching Indians at Rice Lake in 1828, then moved to the St. Clair River and later to the Lake Superior area. As Europeans settled in Ontario, they brought not only new technology to this land, but also a different way of life, including a new religion. Some were eager to introduce Christianity to the Indians. James Evans was one such man. He developed a written code for the Cree language, which could be used to write the Bible in the Cree native tongue.*

societies before they might even have seen a European, as trade goods were passed inland by exchanges from tribe to tribe. The metalware, the pots, knives, axes and awls, not to mention the blankets or the glass beads and other finery, represented kinds of technology which Indian cultures of stone, bone, wood and pottery did not know. Hence enlarging native demands for European products pulled the fur trade on: no less than rising European demands for prime beaver pelts (particularly suited for making felt hats) pushed the trade out to new resource areas further westward. Consequently, it invaded the Ontario region, as native groups first carried furs from there down the Ottawa and St. Lawrence to the French, and next brought the French back with them to the inland country.

The whole process developed strongly through the Indian peoples themselves. They were the vital suppliers and carriers in the emerging fur trade, and the consumers of its trade goods. They had the skill in wilderness transport by canoe, without which no European could then have penetrated the forest interiors. They also provided the snowshoe and toboggan for winter travel, along with the arts of hunting and surviving in a rigorous land. And where that land could usefully be cleared and planted, they gave well-adapted crops that would flourish and feed settlements: corn, squash, beans and more. In short, thanks to the Indian cultural heritage, Europeans could learn to live, move and thrive in the Ontario landmass, north or south. Altogether, it was the native peoples who enabled the newcomers to enter, who led them in and long sustained them, through their own ancient knowledge of the environment. Here lies a great debt, largely still unpaid. For these first peoples were also the first builders of Ontario.

There is one final gift they have offered: the clear recognition that humankind cannot live apart from the natural world around it, despite any illusions of unending material growth, technological progress, and the so-called "conquest" of nature. They keenly sensed, instead, that the devastation of nature through greed, neglect, or blind insistence on short-range returns, can simply bring about one's own destruction. This, then, was a vital heritage truth which the first peoples conveyed and which their descendants still embody. We surely should remember it today.

The horse-drawn sleigh was used as a practical vehicle to transport wood, baggage, sacks of grain, and sometimes passengers. In some rural areas it was used until the 1940s, to take children to school. These sleighs were equipped with two sticks on each side to secure the load and a deflector at the front to protect the occupants from snow and ice picked up and thrown by the trotting horse.

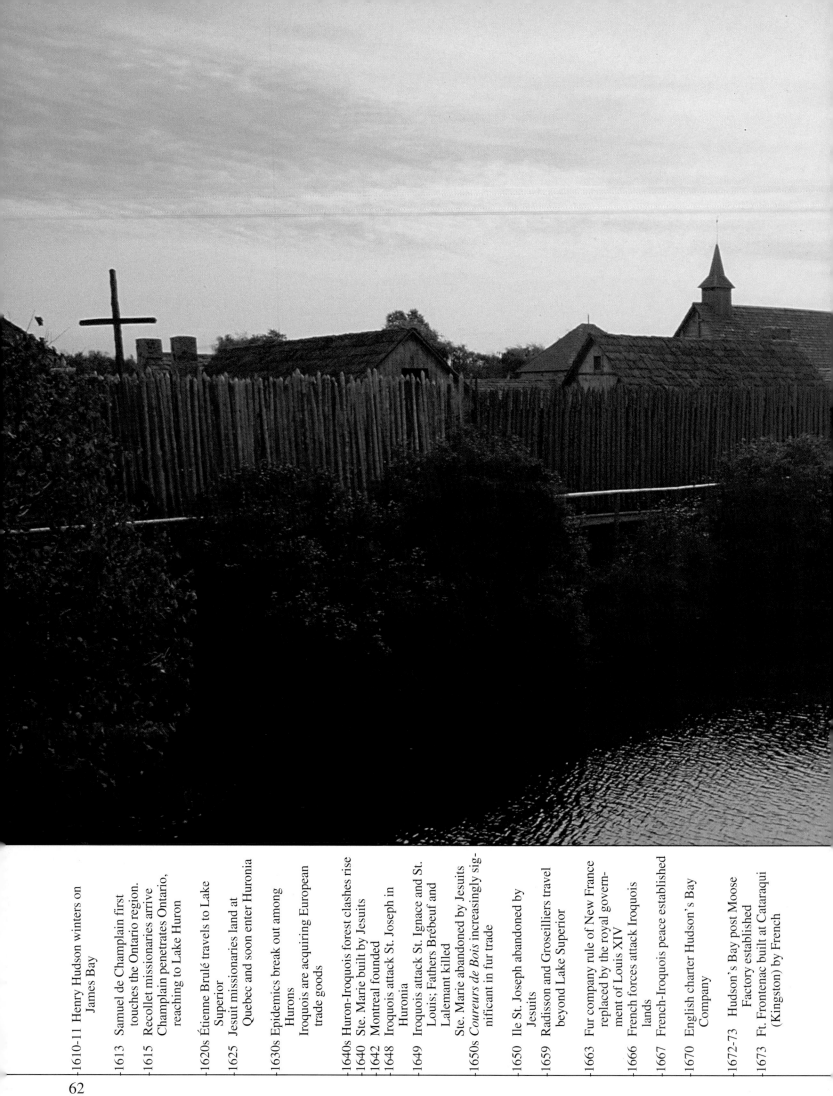

1610-11 Henry Hudson winters on James Bay

1613 Samuel de Champlain first touches the Ontario region.

1615 Recollet missionaries arrive Champlain penetrates Ontario, reaching to Lake Huron

1620s Étienne Brulé travels to Lake Superior

1625 Jesuit missionaries land at Quebec and soon enter Huronia

1630s Epidemics break out among Hurons
Iroquois are acquiring European trade goods

1640s Huron-Iroquois forest clashes rise

1640 Ste. Marie built by Jesuits

1642 Montreal founded

1648 Iroquois attack St. Joseph in Huronia

1649 Iroquois attack St. Ignace and St. Louis; Fathers Brébeuf and Lalemant killed
Ste. Marie abandoned by Jesuits

1650s Coureurs de Bois increasingly significant in fur trade

1650 Ile St. Joseph abandoned by Jesuits

1659 Radisson and Groseilliers travel beyond Lake Superior

1663 Fur company rule of New France replaced by the royal government of Louis XIV

1666 French forces attack Iroquois lands

1667 French-Iroquois peace established

1670 English charter Hudson's Bay Company

1672-73 Hudson's Bay post Moose Factory established

1673 Ft. Frontenac built at Cataraqui (Kingston) by French

Chapter Two
Faith, Furs and French Control:
1615-1760

1678 French post established at Niagara

1682 French establish own Hudson Bay Company

1689-97 English-French war
Many English forts in North America fall to the French
French win naval victory on Hudson Bay, Ontario
English maintain a foothold on James Bay

1689-1701 Heavy fighting between French and Five Nations Iroquois
French *Canadien* militia becomes increasingly important

1701 Peace established between French and Five Nations Iroquois

1701-2 Founding of Detroit by Cadillac

1702-13 English-French war; limited fighting in New France

1713 France recognizes Rupert's Land as belonging to Britain

1721 Small French fur post built at Toronto

1730s Jesuit mission established at Detroit

1740s French fur posts extend past Ontario, into the prairies

1749-51 French fort built at Toronto

1754 Fighting resumes between French and British in North America

1756 French capture Ft. Oswego in New York province

1758 British capture Ft. Frontenac

1759 British capture Ft. Niagara
Ft. Rouillé at Toronto abandoned by the French
British capture Quebec City

1760 Remaining French forces surrender at Montreal
Fall of New France

European Beginnings:
Explorers and Missionaries

On a day late in July, 1615, Samuel de Champlain stared out in wonder at the shimmering, open waters of Lake Huron, "the fresh-water sea" — as he termed it — set deep in a forest-continent. The French had come to the Great Lakes; had made enduring entry to Ontario. Already in 1613, Champlain, the master of the French fur-company base at Quebec, had first probed into Ontario's thickly wooded terrain, travelling up the Ottawa as far as Allumette Island in the upper river with an Indian guide and four French comrades. But there he had turned back, persuaded by the Algonquin chief, Tessouat, against continuing to the land of the Nipissings, since their Lake Nipissing was definitely not near the Northern Sea (Hudson Bay) as Champlain had been led to believe. Tessouat's words were true. Yet they also expressed the reluctance of native peoples to let the white man go past them and deal directly with tribes beyond. They might invite the European with his prized goods into their own territories, but did not want to lose the ability to pass on furs to him from more distant nations. In short, they wanted to keep a business-like grip on trade lines, as go-betweens or middlemen.

In 1615, however, the vigorous, venturesome and tirelessly inquiring Champlain resolved on an 800-mile journey to the country of the Hurons, already known for the beaver pelts they sent down the Ottawa to the St. Lawrence. Again Champlain took to the Ottawa way westward, along with two Frenchmen and ten Indian canoeists. This time he went on by the Mattawa, Lake Nipissing, and what would be named the French River to reach Lake Huron. Then he rounded Georgian Bay to the Huron lands; rich and garden-like he found them. Here was the real French entrance to Ontario; for the fur-trade partnership it launched led on to lasting European occupation, as the brief episode of 1613 had not.

Invited by the Hurons, Champlain had come to establish firm

Overleaf. *Ste. Marie among the Hurons at the River Wye.*
1. *The fur industry did much to shape the heritage of Ontario and remained a prominent Canadian enterprise for three and a half centuries.*
2. *Commemorative Stamp showing the Champlain Monument at Orillia.*

1

2

1

2

3

4

1. *Samuel de Champlain, 1557?-1635. In 1608 he founded Quebec City, and in 1613 first travelled from there up the St. Lawrence and the Ottawa to touch what was to become Ontario. But in 1615 he undertook an 800-mile journey into the land of the Hurons at the heart of the Great Lakes, established an alliance with them, and so began the French presence in Ontario.*

2. *Champlain Monument, Neapean Point, Ottawa. Champlain is shown holding an astrolabe, an early navigation instrument. He lost this in June, 1613 near Cobden in Renfrew County. An astrolabe, presumably Champlain's, was found near there in 1867.*

3. *Lake Nipissing near North Bay. In 1613, Champlain's first probe into Ontario, he went up the Ottawa as far as Allumette Island. There he was rightly persuaded by the Algonquian chief Tessouat that Lake Nipissing was not near the Northern Sea (Hudson Bay), that he sought, and he turned back.*

4. *The Ottawa River at Oiseau Rock. Photographed in 1906, this shows the vista as it probably looked to Champlain in 1613.*

1

1. *Junction of the Ottawa and St. Lawrence Rivers. Even before Champlain's journeys, the land of the Huron Indians was known for the beaver pelts which were sent down the Ottawa to the St. Lawrence.*

2. *The Jesuits Welcomed by the Recollets. Champlain first brought Christian Recollet friars from France in 1615. The Recollets, however, were not a strong missionary order. Consequently, in 1625, the Jesuits came to Quebec.* Drawn by C.W. Jefferys.

3. *An Encampment of Indians on Lake Huron. Champlain reached Lake Huron in 1615 by way of the Ottawa River, Mattawa River, Lake Nipissing, and the French River, the lasting French entrance to Ontario.* Painting by F.A. Verner.

4. *French Exploration. In the 17th century the French explored much of Ontario thanks to the help of Indian guides.*

5. *Champlain in Georgian Bay, c. 1615.* Watercolour by J.D. Kelly.

2

3

4

5

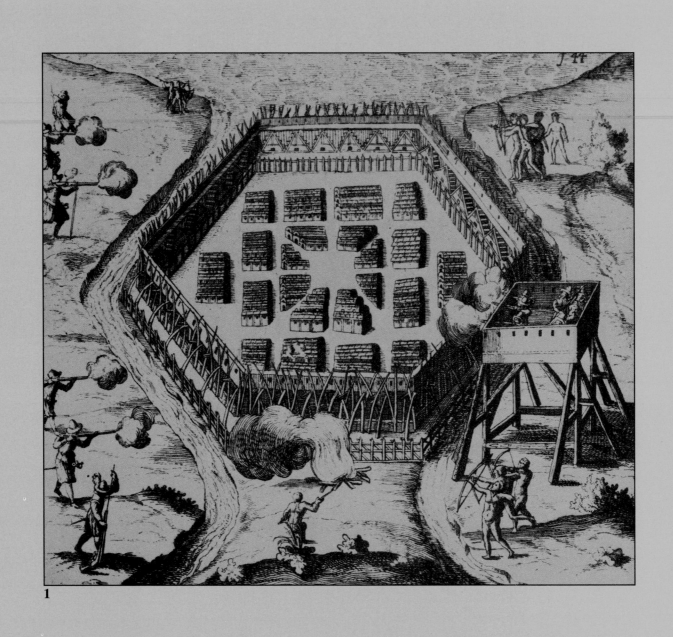

1

2

bonds with these important fur suppliers. He had earlier made necessary alliances with Algonquin and other groups on trade paths between Quebec and the interior; although this had brought him into conflict with the Five Nations Iroquois to the south, dangerous enemies of his own Indian friends. Now he was to join the Hurons, allies of the Algonquins, in another and larger strike at the powerful Iroquois: a veritable blood-binding of trade relationships, but no uncommon feature of the native alliance system. Through August, Champlain visited Huron villages like big Cahiagué near Lake Simcoe, observing, talking, planning. And his young interpreter, Étienne Brulé, who had been sent to live and learn with native peoples, was dispatched with twelve Huron warriors on a mission southward below the Iroquois country, to bring the Andastes as other Huron allies into the projected attack. Brulé was thus most likely the first European to travel down the Toronto trail and enter Lake Ontario from Toronto Bay — even if the Andastes he then called upon got to the battle site too late.

Meanwhile in September, Champlain and an eager Huron army had gone through the forests via the Trent River to Lake Ontario; and crossed it to reach what was probably an Onondaga Iroquois stronghold, defended by four stout palisades thirty feet high. The French commander duly applied proper European tactics to capture such a fortress, building a siege tower and moveable shelters for his men. But his Huron forces proved impatient and unmanageable. The planned assault in mid-October broke down in disorder. Champlain himself was wounded by arrows in the leg; not seriously, though at first he had to be carried out in the retreat, slung in a basket on a Huron's back. Returned to Huronia, the now recovered leader spent the winter there, and later went on to the Petuns and the Ottawas, Huron allies, before leaving for Quebec in May 1616.

In military terms, his had been a rather futile effort that goaded more than checked the Iroquois; yet it was most significant in other ways. It opened the central core of the Southern Ontario region to the French, from which came access over to Lake Erie as the Neutrals were visited — possibly first by Brulé, who also went northward to enter mighty Lake Superior in the early 1620s. Moreover,

1. *Attack on Onondaga Iroquois Stronghold. In September, 1615, Champlain and a Huron army attacked this fortress, which was defended by four palisades thirty feet high. The attack was unsuccessful, and Champlain himself was wounded.*
2. *Lake Superior at Nipigon River. Étienne Brulé has been claimed to be the first European to enter Lake Superior, in the early 1620s.* Watercolour by William Armstrong (1822-1914).

Huron-French political ties were confirmed, as was the role of Huronia as a major collecting-place or entrepôt for furs to be sent on down the Ottawa to Quebec. The Huron people, long established as traders in their favoured location at the margins of the Shield and the agricultural south, now became essential middlemen for a French St. Lawrence fur empire, dealing with a wide arc of hunting tribes north and west around the Great Lakes.

This rising fur empire of New France also strengthened its own crucial ties with Huronia by sending missionaries to spread Roman Catholicism and French cultural influence among the settled Huron-Iroquoian villagers — who indeed might offer a more effective mission field than could wandering Algonquian bands. In the earlier seventeenth century, when the great religious waves of the Protestant Reformation and Catholic Counter-Reformation were still sweeping much of Europe, there is no question that Catholic France sought earnestly to promote its faith in America, together with its own material wealth and national power. Champlain himself had gone to the Huron country with a keen desire to see Christian teachings carried there. He had already brought out four Recollet friars from France in 1614; and one of them, Father Le Caron, reached Huronia even before he did, to celebrate a first mass in future Ontario, with Champlain present, on August 12, 1615. The Recollets, however, were not a strong missionary order. Consequently, in 1625, the Jesuits came to Quebec: a far more powerful teaching and missionizing elite closely linked with the Papacy, who were to set their worldwide mark from Canada to Paraguay, India to Japan.

The full number of Jesuits who strove and often died as martyrs in early Ontario, Fathers Brébeuf, Lalemant, Daniel, Chabanel and others, cannot be covered here: any more than the lay brothers who assisted them, or the donnés who worked for them — labourers and craftsmen who gave their services freely. Yet a first and foremost example was Father Jean de Brébeuf, who arrived at the age of thirty-two in 1625. After five winter months of apprenticeship with a roving Algonquian band, he set out for Huronia, where he remained until recalled to Quebec in 1629, gaining a sure knowledge of Huron customs and language. He was back again in Huron lands by 1634,

Brulé at the mouth of the Humber River. He was most likely the first European to travel down the Toronto Passage from Georgian Bay and enter Lake Ontario from Toronto Bay.

1

2

3

serving and organizing new posts. And despite the indifference of many Hurons who wanted the European's goods and armed support but not his religion, or the outright hostility of others who held strongly to their own traditional beliefs and shaman guides, Brébeuf steadfastly kept on with the hard, frequently barren labours of conversion; right up to his own agonizing death by torture in 1649. Thus he became a towering Christian figure in early Ontario — who nearly three centuries later would be proclaimed as a Catholic patron saint of Canada by Pope Pius XII in 1940.

But while Jesuits like Brébeuf pursued the gruelling, uphill battles of care and conversion, their struggle was made much harder by outbreaks of killing epidemics among the Hurons during the 1630s. Sanitation was practically non-existent in the smoke and stench of a native longhouse — just as it was in the filth and garbage of crowded city streets in Europe of the day. Nevertheless, the epidemics were truly European imports, influenza, smallpox, dysentery and more, carried in unwittingly by the missionary groups who dwelled in Huron villages. Their Huron enemies accused them of evil, murderous sorcery. The French priests deplored such savage ignorance; but the fact was, they had introduced diseases to which Indian peoples had no inbuilt resistance. Europe, Asia and Africa had been open for many centuries to the interchange of infections along with people or trade; while the Americas had been isolated since the ancient disappearance of the Bering Sea land-bridge. And so the effects on the unexposed Hurons of the 1630s were disastrous — although, notably, their Five Nations foes were largely spared, because they did not have Europeans living in their midst. The Iroquois nations by now were dealing with the Dutch established southward down the Hudson, or soon the English in New England; but these traders kept close to their bases, and the well-knit Iroquois did not readily let intruders into their own lands. As a result, while the Five Nations were not drastically affected, the Huron population was nearly halved, reduced to

1. Contemporary artist's rendition of the death of Jesuit missionaries in Huronia, as martyrs during Iroquois attacks. Engraving.
2. The Martyr's Shrine, at Midland, dedicated to the memory of men like Brébeuf, Lalemant, Daniel, Chabanel, and Garnier.
3. Interior of the Martyr's Shrine, Midland.
4. Jean de Brébeuf (1593-1649). Brébeuf was one of the first three Jesuits to arrive in Canada in 1625. He went to work among the Hurons but was later seized by Iroquois and tortured to death.
5. Gabriel Lalemant. Father Lalemant was another of the early Jesuit missionaries in Ontario. He was later killed along with Father Jean de Brébeuf. Grégoire Huret, engraving.

4

5

1. *Ste. Marie among the Hurons. Begun by 1640, this large, stockaded site was to be the headquarters for an expanding French-Catholic domain, with it's missionaries distributed at some ten or more village stations.*

2. *Indian Village at St. Marie among the Hurons, which has been carefully restored and can be visited and viewed near present-day Midland.*

3. *Ste. Marie was the first European-built community in Ontario: in fact, in all of inland America north of Mexico. Ontario's first European farm, forge, school and hospital were all to be found here.*

4. *Ste. Marie included a timber Indian church as well as solid stone bastions to hold a garrison of French soldiers, sawn-timber dwellings, a barn, saw-pit and carpenter's shop.*

5. *A water system fed by aqueduct from the river Wye was also included in the construction of Ste. Marie.*

6. *H-shaped Stonework. Restoration of Ste. Marie among the Hurons. This stonework was probably the altar base of the original chapel.*

3

4

5

6

something like 12,000: a devastating and demoralizing sweep.

In its course, the French priests at times were bitterly harassed, even physically attacked. But in the 1640s the strains lessened as the epidemics lifted: conceivably the survivors had gained some immunities. Conceivably, too, the courage and compassion of the Jesuits had made some impression. And surely significant also, was the Hurons' sense that their own traditional beliefs and practices had failed to meet the terrible spirit-angers that had been unleashed. At any rate, Christian conversions now mounted, and mission posts increased. A new central mission, Ste. Marie, was already building by 1640 on the River Wye, near Georgian Bay and present-day Midland.

This large, stockaded site was to be the headquarters for an expanding French-Catholic domain, with its missionaries distributed at some ten or more village stations. Sainte-Marie among the Hurons thus rose as the first European-built community in Ontario: in fact, in all of inland America north of Mexico. It had solid stone bastions to hold a garrison of French soldiers, a timber Indian church complete with small steeple, sawn-timber dwellings, a barn, saw-pit and carpenter's shop, and a water system fed by aqueduct from the River Wye — all of which can again be visited and viewed in the carefully restored Ste. Marie of today. Here, too, lay Ontario's first European farm and forge, first school and hospital. By 1645, when the original fur-trade base at Quebec was growing into a small French colony of farm settlement, there were still only 250 white inhabitants in all of New France; and 58 of them, including 22 soldiers, were at Ste. Marie in Huronia. At Ste. Marie, moreover, were steadily enlarging numbers of Christian converts, both Hurons and Algonquins, housed in ample village space. A Jesuit-led, Catholic-Indian Ontario hence seemed to be emerging, somewhat akin to the strong Jesuit domain in Paraguay far south. Yet its life would be fleeting, and was already doomed: as a result of rising attacks from the Five Nations Iroquois, whose very threat brought more Hurons to look anxiously to the Christian fathers for help and comfort.

The deep-rooted Huron-Iroquois strife was seldom still for long. But in the 1640s their forest clashes grew worse; critically so because

Huronia in the 1640s.

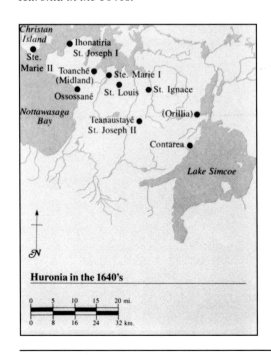

Huronia in the 1640's

of the impact of the fur trade. The Five Nations had themselves become deeply dependent on European trade goods from the Dutch or English — knives, axes, metalware, and soon the musket, which they began acquiring from about 1639. These Iroquois, however, had largely used up their own limited supplies of furs; and they were far from the hunting peoples of the north. They sought instead to divert furs southward from the St. Lawrence trade towards the Hudson River route. That led them not only to keep the upper St. Lawrence blocked, and raid the traffic down the Ottawa, but also to attack the Hurons with new force as the chief suppliers of the rival St. Lawrence trading system. In effect, it was a war between opposed middlemen, Iroquois and Huron; but to their traditional antagonisms, vital economic conflict and deadly European technology had now been added by the fur trade. Guns came in. By the late 1640s, the Iroquois had a clear superiority of perhaps 500 crude muskets to the Hurons' 120. The French had been urged by Jesuits to arm only Christian converts among the Hurons. And though this in some circumstances might have been an arguable policy, as it was, given the religious split in Huron ranks and the still sharp feelings among their anti-Christian elements, it only emphasized their division, and aided the Iroquois' lead in sheer morale as well as musketry.

Accordingly, the cycle of Five Nations' attacks mounted; from brief, testing forays as weaknesses were exposed, to relentless, all-out assaults upon a more and more demoralized Huron confederacy. On July 4, 1648, Iroquois raiders struck fiercely at the mission village of St. Joseph, towards the south of Huronia, killing Father Daniel and many others, and taking away 700 prisoners. On March 16, 1649, thrusting farther north, they seized St. Ignace and St. Louis, amid mass slaughter carrying off Fathers Brébeuf and Lalemant to horribly slow deaths by torture. Fortified Ste. Marie stood alone, as Iroquois war parties ravaged the countryside and Hurons fled away in terror. Father Paul Ragueneau, now the Jesuit superior, decided to abandon and burn Ste. Marie, to avoid further hopeless bloodshed. In May it was done, as Ragueneau and the remaining mission group moved their Indian converts to a supposedly safer site on Ile St. Joseph in Georgian Bay — or Christian Island. And after a dread winter of starvation and disease, this site also had to be abandoned. In June, 1650, the last remnants of the aspiring Jesuit enterprise of faith, some 60 French (including soldier-reinforcements who had arrived too late) with only about 300 surviving converts, set off on a long, sad journey down to Quebec. Huronia, and practically all Southern Ontario, were left to the rampaging Iroquois. It seemed that the European beginnings there had ended in total, tragic ruin.

1. *Martyrdom of Fathers Jean de Brébeuf and Gabriel Lalemant. On March 16, 1649, Iroquois raiders seized St. Ignace and St. Louis, and, amid mass slaughter, carried off Brébeuf and Lalemant to death by torture. Sainthood was conferred upon both in 1930 by the Roman Catholic Church.*

2. *Confiance Harbour, south-east point of Ile St. Joseph in Georgian Bay. After burning Ste. Marie, the remaining Jesuit mission group moved to a site on Ile St. Joseph in Georgian Bay (Christian Island). In June, 1650, this site was also abandoned.* By John J. Bigsby.

3. *Huron Chiefs at La Jeune Lorette. The Hurons who had escaped the Iroquois raids of 1648-1649 eventually settled close to Quebec City where their descendants inter-married with French Canadians. This picture by E. Chatfield was published in 1825. It shows Michel Tsioui, Teacheandale, Chief of Warriors (left), Stanislas Coska, Aharathaha, Second Chief of the Council (centre), and André Romain, Tsouhahissen, Chief of the Council (right).*

1

2

3

French Fur Empire

1. Coureur de Bois. *In the 1650s, after Huronia vanished, a new breed of Frenchmen rose in the fur trade. These* coureurs de bois *had begun with Brulé, and were now as much at home as the Indians in the wilderness.* Woodcut by Arthur Heming.

2. *Pierre-Esprit Radisson.* Coureur de bois *Radisson, along with his brother-in-law, Médard Chouart Des Groseilliers, pushed beyond Lake Superior in 1659, and learned of the fur resources around a great bay to the north—which later would bring about the Hudson Bay trade.* Drawn by Belier, c. 1885.

3. *Fox in an iron trap. The* coureur de bois *were armed with European technology, including guns and iron traps; easier and more efficient than traditional methods of trapping.*

4. Le Regiment de Carignan-Saliers. *This famous regiment was dispatched to New France by King Louis XIV and arrived in the spring of 1665. Until then, colonists had carried on their own defence; this regiment was the first regular military protection they enjoyed.*

It seemed still more so in the years that followed. The triumphant Five Nations turned to the Petuns and the Neutrals, shattering and dispersing them as organized tribes, in a determined effort to drive out the settled peoples and leave the Ontario region to the Iroquois or wandering hunters only. Yet once again let it be stressed that this kind of warfare did not kill off the original Ontario inhabitants. Many, including Hurons, were adopted by the Five Nations, replacing their own losses. Others escaped: eastward to the none-too-strong protection of Quebec, or west beyond the Great Lakes — where the Hurons, "Wendats" to themselves, became "Wyandots," as far as Oklahoma. Still, the full effect was to destroy the old tribal patterns across much of Ontario, leaving empty fields or deserted villages. And one ironic, ultimate result of this upheaval was that the very disappearance of fixed Indian societies, which might well have become largely French-speaking and Roman Catholic, also left the land that much more open to later incoming waves of European settlement which would primarily be English-speaking and Protestant in origin. Ontario today owes a lot that the Iroquois did not intend.

Furthermore, if the Five Nations had achieved the wide hunting ground they wanted, and the removal of the rival Huron middlemen, they also thereby led the way to the re-entrance of the French into Ontario, once the latter had rallied their own strength. In fact, the very absence of the Huron middlemen would draw the French back into the inland region to redevelop fur-trade links for themselves, sending them further onward to the tribes above and beyond the Great Lakes. Huronia had vanished. The long-range fur trade had not. There was a new breed of Frenchmen involved in it, the *coureurs de bois*, forest rovers who had begun with Brulé, and were now as much at home as Indians in the wilderness, yet had European technology (including guns and iron traps) readily at hand. From 1653 they went to live with the Ottawas north of the lakes, making

1

2

3

4

longer and longer canoe trips westward; then returning laden with prime beaver to run the Iroquois gauntlet down the Ottawa and St. Lawrence to Quebec. Two such daring adventurers, Pierre-Esprit Radisson, and his brother-in-law, Médard Chouart Des Groseilliers, pushed beyond Lake Superior in 1659, and learned of the rich fur resources around a great bay to the north — which later would bring about the opening of the Hudson Bay trade.

Nevertheless, the flow of western furs down to the colony of New France was intermittent, often just a trickle, as the Iroquois kept up a strangling commercial blockade; for they rightly saw that the French were their basic trade rivals, apart from any Indian suppliers, transporters or go-betweens. The Five Nations hence carried raids directly to the French themselves, particularly against Montreal, the bold, outlying settlement of New France, founded in 1642. A truce in the later 1650s helped the embattled colonists, as did growing French immigration and farming trade. But the renewal of war by 1660 left New France still in grave difficulties; until in 1663 its fur-company rule was ended and royal government took over, under the newly powerful French state of Louis XIV. The central bureaucracy in Paris sent out trained officials to direct the colony, along with far more immigrants and economic aid. But beyond these, they sent hardened regular troops to defeat the Iroquois. As a result, massed soldiers and colonial militia swept through the country of the Mohawks in 1665, the most aggressive of the Five Nations, burning crops, storehouses and whole villages. The badly shaken Iroquois sued for peace, achieved in 1667. Henceforth, for nearly twenty years the ways west were safely open to the French traders and entrepreneurs who fanned out across Ontario and beyond, vastly expanding the dominance of New France; with priests in company still — and a new Jesuit mission set at Sault Ste. Marie between Lakes Huron and Superior —

1. *La Salle at the mouth of the Mississippi. In 1682 by tracing the Mississippi to the Gulf of Mexico, he added enormously to French empire.* By J.N. Marchland.
2. *La Salle at Fort Frontenac, 1675. In July 1673, Governor Frontenac visited Cataraqui (Kingston), and ordered the construction of a wooden fort. The following year, Sieur de La Salle was granted seigneury at Cataraqui. He returned in 1675 and began work on a masonry stronghold, which he named Fort Frontenac in honour of the governor.* By J.D. Kelly.
3. *An imaginative reconstruction of La Salle's* Griffon. *The forty-five ton* Griffon, *equipped with five guns, was the first sailing ship to navigate the upper Great Lakes. Father Louis Hennepin, who accompanied La Salle, is shown standing on the quarter-deck.*
4. *Another fanciful picture, of the building of the* Griffon *on the Niagara River in 1679. The ship disappeared, however, on an early voyage soon after it was built. Several possible wrecks of the barque have been found; but no one can be certain.*

1

2

3

4

but paramountly seeking furs.

Moreover, now that the Iroquois no longer barred the upper St. Lawrence, French venturers moved directly by that route into the lower Great Lakes and the lands southwestward. The most audacious and ambitious of these entrepreneurs was Robert Cavalier de La Salle, who in 1682 would go on to trace the Mississippi to the Gulf of Mexico, and add enormously to French empire. Yet forceful La Salle also left historic impacts upon Ontario. On his recommendation, Fort Frontenac was erected in 1673 at Cataraqui, where Lake Ontario flowed into the St. Lawrence, a strategic point for collecting and protecting the fur cargoes to be sent on downstream, and for checking the Iroquois, never far away across the river. This fort at the future site of Kingston, was granted to La Salle as a seigneurial holding by his great patron in fur trade expansion; the royal governor of New France, Count Frontenac. It remained a primary base of French power in Ontario. But La Salle moved on further to establish another strategic post at Niagara in 1678, on the east-west river link between Lakes Erie and Ontario, and at a crossway point for travel north to the upper lakes or south to the Ohio country and the Mississippi lands.

In 1679 he built the *Griffon* on the Niagara River above the Falls, the first sailing ship to navigate the upper Great Lakes. With La Salle aboard, she voyaged to Michilimackinac Island, which had become a main western fur-trade rendezvous where Lakes Huron and Michigan met. On her return trip, however, laden with furs and after La Salle had left her, the *Griffon* disappeared. Several possible wrecks of the little barque have since been found; but no one can be certain. What is certain is that Great Lakes shipping traffic, so vital in Ontario's history, had now begun. Instead of light canoes that edged around the lakes, sailing craft with sizeable cargoes traversed the open waters, notably on Lake Ontario between Forts Frontenac and Niagara. Similarly on land: the Toronto trail and passage, that short-cut between the lower and upper lakes, was travelled by La Salle on some of his long-distance journeys, and by other French explorers, traders or mis-

Michilimackinac 15-20 miles distant. With La Salle aboard, the Griffon *voyaged to Michilimackinac Island, which became a main western fur-trade rendezvous where Lakes Huron and Michigan met.* By John J. Bigsby.

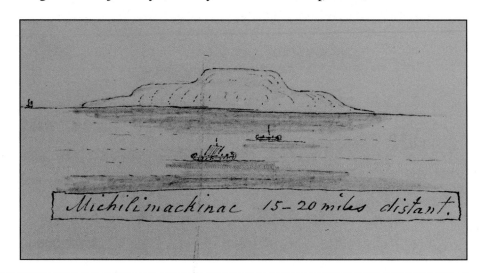

sionaries. If the fur trade was not settling the Ontario land-mass, it still was making its presence felt through routes and collecting points well known.

A Seneca village emerged at the Lake Ontario entrance to the Toronto trail: the Senecas, the westernmost of the Five Nations, now were colonizing the Ontario side of the lake. At this village, Teiaiagon, there might also be French traders, clerics or *bateaux* men en route between Cataraqui and Niagara; or even fur dealers up from the English base at Albany — for English merchants had replaced Dutch in the Hudson Valley trade, after England had seized the controlling town of New Amsterdam during the Anglo-Dutch war of 1664-7, renaming it New York. A growing English province of New York henceforth lay south of the Ontario region, an increasingly powerful presence that could back the Five Nations in the competition for furs, and which would send trade feelers into Ontario territory. Yet while these probing entries from the south went on, much more decided steps were taken by the English far to the north in the 1670s, on the coasts of Hudson and James Bays.

If the French had entered Southern Ontario terrain in 1613-15, the English had reached Northern Ontario margins in 1610-11, when Henry Hudson, searching for the Northwest Passage, had wintered on James Bay. Later expeditions confirmed that there was no open passage to the Pacific from the huge, cold bay that bore Hudson's name; but these expeditions did uncover its shorelines. And so, when the French *coureurs de bois* Radisson and Groseilliers, made renegades by harsh treatment from authorities in New France, went to England to propose that the vast fur wealth they claimed existed below Hudson Bay be tapped from the bay itself, they found financial backing for two ships to sail on an experimental voyage in 1668. The return cargo of furs in 1669 was very convincing. The next year the English Hudson's Bay Company received a royal charter in London,

A postage stamp commemorating the European discovery of Hudson Bay.

1

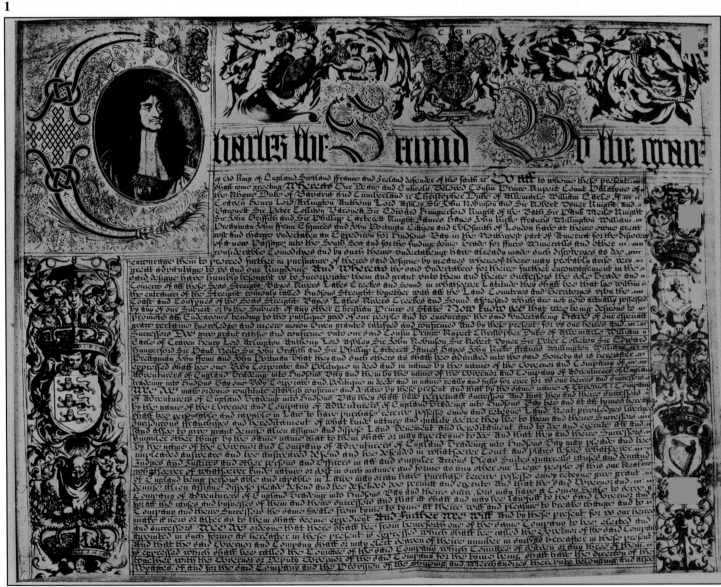

2

granting it rights of government, trade monopoly and land ownership in all the territories that drained into Hudson Bay. This charter of 1670 strongly stamped Ontario heritage; since by it most of Northern Ontario — not to mention much of Northern Quebec and the western plains out to the still-unknown Rockies — became part of the Bay Company's territory, Rupert's Land, named after Prince Rupert, the first governor of the company and cousin of reigning Charles II. Its trading posts went up along the shores: within Ontario areas, Moose Factory on the Moose River at the bottom of James Bay in 1672-3 (the second company post, the first being Rupert's House at Rupert River on the eastern, Quebec side of that Bay), and then Fort Albany and Fort Severn, each to have a long career in company hands.

The French grew anxious, however, about a northward drain of furs to the Hudson's Bay forts, away from their posts along the upper lakes: Kaministiquia at the head of Lake Superior, Michilimackinac, Sault Ste. Marie, or new posts on Lakes Nipigon and Abitibi. In 1682 they chartered their own Hudson Bay company — and by 1686 were openly assaulting the English forts, which lay in territory the French considered theirs; for they had not accepted England's claim to Hudson Bay, with all the lands that drained into it. In the meantime, far in the south, the Five Nations Iroquois also looked again to war: as they saw western furs flowing to Quebec with little benefit to themselves, as they sought more pelts to trade with the English behind them, and as they attacked tribes to the westward, seeking to bring them under Iroquois commercial control. They invaded the country of the Illinois in 1680. Within short years the French were drawn into a spreading conflict, to protect their own Indian allies and trade lines. But this time North American forest clashes became part of a still wider imperial contest, as a great Anglo-French war broke in Europe in 1689.

During the struggle, Forts Frontenac and Niagara came under heavy Iroquois attack. And in the north, around Hudson Bay, most of the English forts fell to French assaults; while on the Bay itself the thunder of warships gave France striking naval victory. Still, the English fur company won back and held a bare foothold. More influential in the long run, was the fighting south and east of Ontario

1. *Photo from c. 1866 of Indian homes at Moose Factory.*
2. *Hudson's Bay Company Charter. The Hudson's Bay Company received a royal charter in 1670, granting it rights to government, trade monopoly, and land ownership in all the territories that drained into Hudson Bay.*
3. *Henry Hudson. The English reached Northern Ontario in 1610-1611 when Henry Hudson, searching for the Northwest Passage, wintered on James Bay.* Woodcut.

3

1

2

3

1. *An early photo of a Hudson's Bay Company post at Lake Abitibi. The tents shown are Indian.* By D.L. Scott, 1906.

2. *Rupert's House. Rupert's House was the first post of the Hudson's Bay Company. It was established on the Rupert River on the eastern, Quebec side of James Bay.*

3. *H. B. Company post, Lake Temiskaming. After the establishment of the Hudson's Bay Company in 1670, it spread steadily and soon had posts across Rupert's Land, including much of present-day Northern Ontario.*

4. *Prince Rupert, the first Governor of the Hudson's Bay Company, and cousin of reigning Charles II.* Oil Painting.

5. *H. B. C. store interior at Lake Nipigon. Photo, c. 1890.*

6. *Moose Factory H. B. store. Moose Factory, on the Moose River at the bottom of James Bay, was established in 1672-1673 as the second trading post of the Hudson's Bay Company. This picture is of a much later building, of course.*

4

5

6

between the Iroquois and the forces of New France. There were border raids and counter-raids; a murderous Iroquois thrust at Lachine near Montreal in 1689; no less scorching, savage raids by the French and their Indian allies upon Schenectady on the New York frontier, or Salmon Falls in New England. But one growing factor was the seasoned *Canadien* militia, trained in the Indians' own art of guerilla warfare, who scoured Iroquois lands remorselessly. The Five Nations still fought on, until 1701; even though the European war of France, England and their allies had ended in 1697 in a largely stalemate peace. Nevertheless, the Iroquois were seriously hit by both war losses and disease, and by splits now in their own ranks between traditionalists and Christian converts. They had also been reduced to under 10,000, and had mostly pulled back from Ontario areas when they finally made peace. No longer could the Five Nations be an independent native power, outweighed as they were by the steady growth of the French or English populations and economies — although, whether neutral or leaning either to the French or English, they remained a power to be reckoned with.

1. *Fur post at Kaministiquia at the head of Lake Superior. After the chartering of the English Hudson's Bay Company, the French grew anxious about a drain of furs away from some of their far inland posts, such as Kaministiquia. In 1682 they chartered their own rival Hudson Bay Company or* Compagnie du Nord. *Kaministiquia was later the site of Fort William, which much later still joined with Port Arthur to become the city of Thunder Bay.* Watercolour painting by John Herbert Caddy.

2. *Destruction of Schenectady. The French and their Indian allies executed a savage raid on Schenectady in 1690 in the then colony of New York; a reflection of the Anglo-French conflict in Europe and North America.*

1

2

The Fall of New France

European war was actually resumed in 1702. It went on till 1713, when France, worsted in Europe far more than in America, was forced to recognize Rupert's Land, Nova Scotia and Newfoundland as belonging to England. Or rather, one now should say "Britain," since in 1704 England and Scotland had joined to form the United Kingdom of Great Britain. All of these developments would matter in the long run to Ontario; although it still remained a part of New France after 1713, and again had seen only limited fighting during this second great imperial war. Yet some closer events important for Ontario still occurred, such as the founding of Detroit in 1701-2 by Antoine Laumet de la Mothe Cadillac. Placed by Cadillac on what is now the American side of the Detroit River, this post nevertheless affected Ontario areas across the river as another rising European base in the growth of Great Lakes' life and commerce. And in quite another way, the years around 1700 also brought significant developments to native society, as bands of Algonquian Indians moved downward into much of Southern Ontario, replacing the weakened, retreating Iroquois who had earlier dispersed the original settled peoples. These newcomers, loosely to be called the Mississaugas, were members of the Ojibwa tribe originally from north of Lake Superior, who fought the Iroquois (according to their own oral traditions) and increasingly ranged the Southern Ontario forests. They took up a little planting at village or encampment sites, but lived essentially by migratory hunting, fishing and fur-trapping. They were here to meet white settlers when they finally came in — on lands which the Mississaugas had roamed for less than a century before these later immigrants arrived.

In any event, during the peace years after 1713, New France and its fur empire developed much further beyond the Ontario region, by way of trading growth southwestward from Detroit and Niagara, or to the northwest by a line of posts extended in the 1730s from Kaministiquia to the Rainy River, the Lake of the Woods and into the prairies. Other than that, a French post also appeared at Toronto itself, where the Seneca's Teiaiagon at the mouth of the Humber

Traders' house at Lake of the Woods. By the 1740s, the French line of posts extended even past the Lake of the Woods and on into the prairies.

1

1. *This photo of a monument to French Fort Rouillé was taken in the Exhibition Park at Toronto about 1893.*

2. *"They Travelled." This is a photo of a 1905 pageant of Ojibwa Indians at Grand River. The Ojibwa were originally from north of Lake Superior. From around 1700, Mississauga Indians, who were Ojibwa in origin, moved downward into Southern Ontario, replacing the weakened Iroquois there.*

3. *Fort Toronto or Fort Rouillé. This fort was built in 1750-1751 (on the grounds of the present Canadian National Exhibition). After Fort Niagara, a major French stronghold, was captured by the British in 1759, little Fort Rouillé was evacuated and burned by its own garrison.*

4. *Canada's earliest land industry. During the peace after 1713, New France developed its fur empire much further beyond the Ontario region. Eventually, the fur trade would reach far into the North West. By the 1890s, more than 35,000 dollars in furs were counted in a northern warehouse at Fort Chipweyan, where here Colin Fraser, a trader, sorts fox, beaver, mink and other valuable furs.*

2

3

4

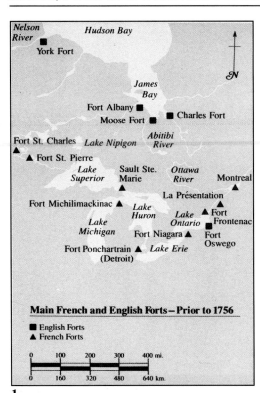

Main French and English Forts – Prior to 1756

■ English Forts
▲ French Forts

1

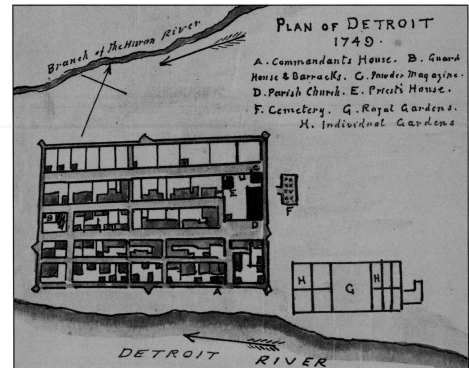

PLAN OF DETROIT 1749.

A. Commandants House. B. Guard House & Barracks. C. Powder Magazine. D. Parish Church. E. Priests House. F. Cemetery. G. Royal Gardens. H. Individual Gardens

2

3

4

River now had vanished. Erected in 1721, this new establishment was not much more than a log storehouse-shop surrounded by a palisade, intended to capture fur cargoes heading down to Lake Ontario and hopefully keep them from crossing to the English Hudson River route below the lake. Yet it led to an actual French fort, begun here in 1749, but moved to a better site east of the Humber in 1751 — in the present Canadian National Exhibition grounds in the city of Toronto. This Fort Rouillé, or Fort Toronto, was still small, being a mere outlier of the main French fortress at Niagara; but it had timber bastions and palisades, with four small cannons and a little garrison, plus some workers and *bateaux* transport men. Thus were Toronto's French beginnings.

These military foundations related, in fact, to a new French programme of building regularly garrisoned forts in the interior; partly to bolster Indian alliances in the face of the British fur competition spreading from the south, partly for actual armed defence of France's inland empire, should Anglo-French war break out again. And it had done so, in 1744-8; though the results were very indecisive. Accordingly, the government of New France laid out a chain of posts based on Niagara and Detroit, running southward into the Ohio country: a forward defensive zone for the French, but an area which traders and land-seekers from British colonies along the seaboard were already penetrating.

Toronto then was just a minor place in the French defensive chain, a link between Niagara and Fort Frontenac. More significantly at the time, French plans to strengthen Detroit as a supply centre for the western forts produced the first enduring farm settlement in Ontario made by French Canadians. A Jesuit mission, which gathered back scattered Hurons, Ottawas and other Indians had already been set up at Detroit in the 1730s. This "Assumption" mission was moved across the river to the Ontario side in 1748-9, while lands and aid were promised in all the French parishes back on the St. Lawrence to settlers who would come to the Detroit area. The first families to respond arrived in the summer of 1749; and were granted land near the Huron mission, in what became Assumption Parish. Other settlers joined them. By 1756, there were probably over 150 *Canadiens*

1. *French and English inland forts prior to 1756.*
2. *Plan of Detroit, 1749. Lands and aid were promised in all the French parishes on the St. Lawrence to settlers who would come to the Detroit area. The first families to respond arrived in the summer of 1749.*
3. *The British Fleet on Lake Ontario in 1756. This fleet was captured by Montcalm at Oswego. The French destroyed two of the vessels and incorporated the others into the French fleet after renaming them.* By Charles Henry Jeremy Snider (1879-1971), c. 1913.
4. *The French Fleet on Lake Ontario in 1756. The four French vessels were sunk by the British in 1758 when the British captured Fort Frontenac (at later Kingston).* By Charles Henry Jeremy Snider (1879-1971), c. 1913.

tilling fertile fields, feeding Detroit and posts beyond, spreading apple and pear orchards as well. And from this oldest, continuous white settlement in Ontario developed a Francophone presence in the Windsor and southwestern areas which remains today; with sure pride in a past that antedates anglophone Ontario.

By 1754, however, war had returned once more: the final, showdown struggle between the French and British empires in America which grew into the Seven Years War in Europe, officially dated there 1756 to 1763; although unofficial war had started two years earlier in America's Ohio country. Again the heaviest battles took place outside the Ontario region. Still, this time it saw wide and bloody fighting: clashes between war fleets on Lake Ontario, the French seizure of Fort Oswego in 1756, in New York province, across the lake from Fort Frontenac; the fall of Frontenac itself to the British in 1758, and then the next year their capture of Niagara. Fort Frontenac's loss really cut off the French fort chain to the west. The taking of Fort Niagara, by now a solid, stone-built stronghold, brought the evacuation and burning of weak Fort Rouillé at Toronto by its own garrison. But as British troops pushed on towards Montreal, Quebec was won in September, 1759, by the fleet and army under General James Wolfe, a victory which made final French defeat almost certain. Remaining French forces surrendered at Montreal in September, 1760. New France had fallen. Ontario itself was in British hands.

Out of this transfer by conquest would stem the later English-speaking province. In no way, however, does that imply that the slate of history was now wiped clean, that a century and more of French dominance across Ontario had not left substantial contributions on the record. There was the heroic design of the Jesuits, which had failed in practice but still shone bright in faith, the bold power of the Iroquois, unmaking yet remaking native life; the lasting life of the French Canadian settlement by the Detroit River. And there was the rise of commerce, transport routes and towns-to-be out of the fur trade — a future Kingston, Toronto, Thunder Bay and more. Beyond all these were human memories of courage, daring, tragedy and endurance; ever to be celebrated in Ontario's heritage.

1. The Castle or Chateau at Fort Niagara. The "Castle" was built from 1725-1749 by the French but was captured by the British in 1759.
2. The Capture of Fort Frontenac. Fort Frontenac fell to the British in 1758. Its loss cut off the French fort chain to the west.
3. The Marquis de Montcalm. Louis Joseph Montcalm was the French commander until his death in 1759. He led the forces that captured Fort Oswego from the British in 1756.
4. Surrender of Fort Niagara. After the fall of Fort Frontenac, Fort Niagara was also captured by the British under Sir William

1

2

3

4

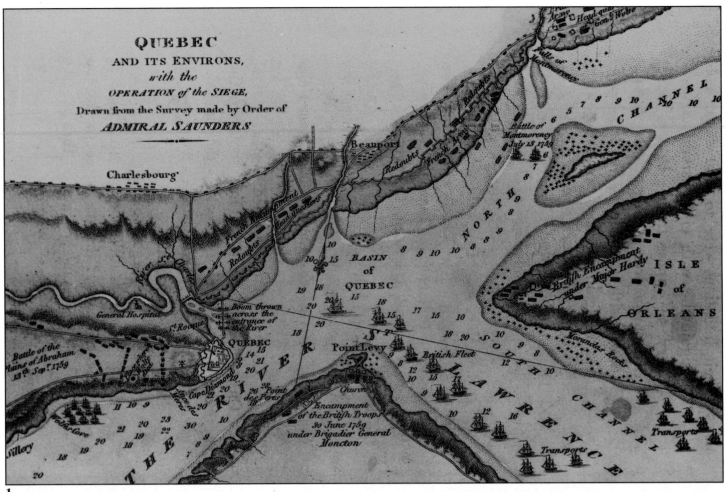

1

2

3

1. *Map of Quebec and Environs during the Siege of Quebec, which fell to the British in September, 1759.*
2. *A View of the Landing Place above the Town of Quebec. As inland British troops pushed down the St. Lawrence from Lake Ontario towards Montreal, Quebec itself was taken by the fleet and army under General James Wolfe, a victory which almost guaranteed final French defeat.* Engraving by Harvey Smyth.
3. *Entry of British troops into Montreal. The remaining French forces surrendered at Montreal in September, 1760. New France had fallen; Ontario itself was now in British hands.*

1760 Fall of New France

1760s British fur merchants and French Canadian *voyageurs* active in Ontario region
Montreal remains the fur centre of Canada, and enlarges its hold under British rule

1763 Peace established between France and Britain
Proclamation of 1763
Western Indians under Pontiac attempt resistance to British
Indians besiege Ft. Detroit
Michilimackinac and other posts taken by Indians

1764 In response, Ft. Erie built by British, who also begin building ships on nearby Navy Island

1765 Indians led by Pontiac make peace with Britain
Navy Hall built on western side of Niagara River (where Niagara-on-the-Lake will stand).

1768 Sir Guy Carleton becomes Governor of Quebec Province

1770s North West Company established in Montreal, to co-ordinate major fur interests

1774 J.B. Rousseau establishes local fur post at Toronto harbour
Quebec Act passed, adding Ontario region to an enlarged Quebec Province
Guy Johnson succeeds William Johnson as Indian Superintendent in New York Province

1775 American Revolution begins

1775-6 American rebel armies invade Quebec; Montreal falls; Quebec City holds out

1776 Colonel J. Butler organizes Butler's Rangers out of Ft. Niagara

Chapter Three
British Rule, American Revolution and Loyalism: 1760-1791

- 1777 Molly Brant moves to Niagara
  Loyalist refugees gather around Ft. Niagara

- 1778 Butler's Barracks built at Navy Hall
  Loyalist refugees also gather at Carleton Island and Oswegatchie (Ogdensburg)
  Sir Frederick Haldimand becomes Governor of Quebec

- 1780 Butler's Barracks and Navy Hall enlarged
  Loyalist refugees move to Sorel and Trois Rivières

- 1781 American-French victory at Yorktown
  American Revolutionary War over

- 1783 Treaty of Versailles signed
  Great Britain recognizes United States' independence
  800 Loyalist settlers live in "Township of Niagara"
  Large Loyalist migration into Ontario and Quebec begins

- 1784 Around 4000 Loyalists located along the upper St. Lawrence and Bay of Quinte
  Grand River Reserve established for Six Nations Iroquois

- 1785 Sir John Johnson first petitions for a British district in western Quebec

- 1786 Lord Dorchester (Carleton) returns as Quebec's governor

- 1787 Mohawk Chapel built at Brantford

- 1788 Four administrative districts created for Western Quebec (in future Upper Canada)

- 1789 Widespread crop failures hit Loyalist settlers

- 1791 Canada Act passed, giving political form to Upper Canada (future Ontario)

The New Province of Quebec

The Ontario region was largely under Britain's control even before the fall of New France in September, 1760. The British posts in Rupert's Land had not been challenged; British troops held Niagara, had destroyed Fort Frontenac, and in August took the last French positions on the upper St. Lawrence near what now is Prescott. Detroit surrendered in November. Except for the *Canadien* settlement across from it, and some French traders or clerics still in the forests, France effectively had left Ontario. Nevertheless, there was still the possibility that part or all of its territory might revert to France in the peace settlement, depending on military and diplomatic balances elsewhere. Certainly, occupying British Commanders realized that possibility, while many French Indian allies keenly hoped for it — though the Iroquois (now the Six Nations) stood divided between pro-French, neutral, and pro-British elements. When, however, peace at last was signed in Paris in February, 1763, the total weight of French defeats, especially in America, brought the loss of most of France's empire overseas, and confirmed British rule over all the farspread lands of Canada.

Following the peace settlement, the imperial British government in London put forth the Proclamation of 1763, to define and structure the vast holdings it had gained in America, above all including the St. Lawrence realm of New France. Here a new Province of Quebec was set up, mainly comprising just the French-populated lands of the lower and middle St. Lawrence Valley; not reaching east as far as the Labrador coasts, or north up to Rupert's Land. And to the west, this limited Quebec extended only to Lake Nipissing, though it included both banks of the lower Ottawa down to the St. Lawrence; thus incorporating a narrow strip of future Ontario in an essentially French-Canadian province. As for the vast west beyond Quebec's inland boundary, that was left for the present as Indian Country under British "Protection," and subject to treaty negotiations over land rights with its inhabitants.

Britain claimed suzerainty over this enormous area as transferred from France, roughly meaning control over its external relations, if

Overleaf. The Homeseekers. *Loyalists came chiefly to the Niagara area as individual families or small parties, without the collective movement carried out on the Upper St. Lawrence.*
Across. *The Toronto Purchase, 1788. The tract shown was obtained from the Mississauga Indians. The purchase was most likely negotiated by Sir John Johnson, as then Superintendent of Indian Affairs. It turned over an enormously valuable tract to European settlement and land ownership, but left various unresolved claims to Mississauga descendants.*

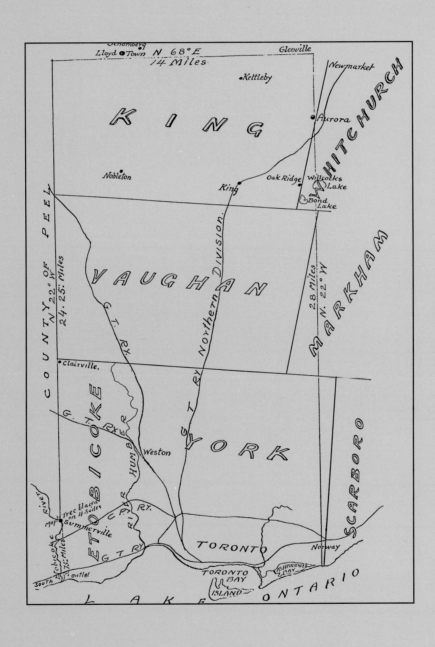

The Province of Quebec according to the Proclamation of 1763. The boundaries set up to define British holdings in North America mainly encompassed the French-populated lands of the lower and middle St. Lawrence Valley. The land west of the boundaries was left as Indian Country under British "protection."

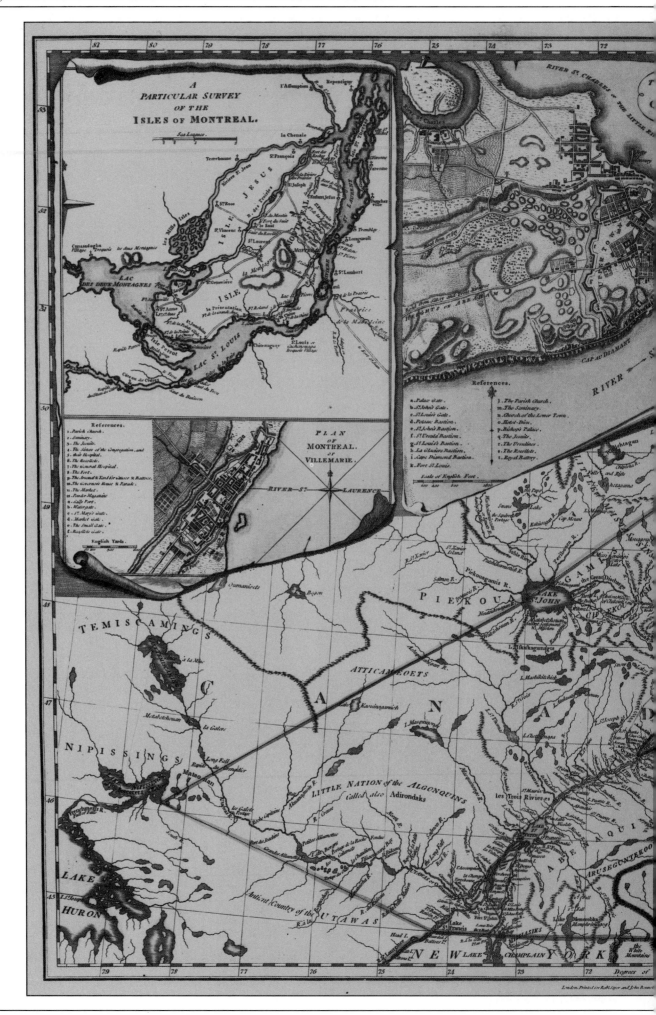

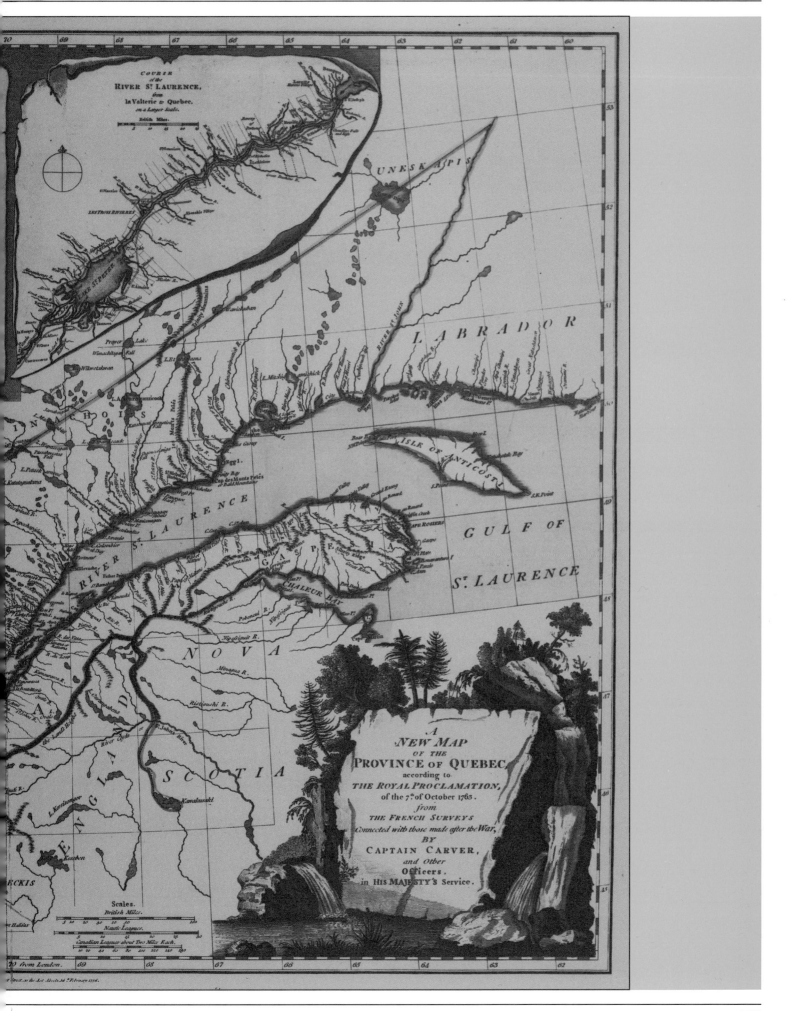

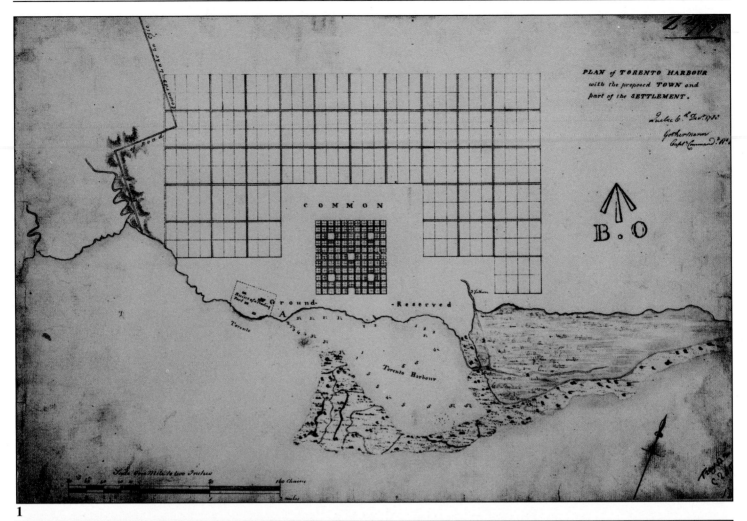

1

2

not necessarily its internal affairs. And Britain also recognized Indian land titles as the French had not; although the latter had made annual presents to meet native concerns over white intrusions. The British, rightly or wrongly, had traditionally regarded land as the very basis of law within England itself. They were thus prepared to make treaties to purchase Indian territory and set out native land reserves: in their own view, to "clear" Indian titles before white occupation. To native peoples who had concepts of continuing land use rather than outright land ownership, this might not prove good enough. But what could be said, is that the Proclamation policy of 1763, applied to Ontario or to lands beyond in future, at least sought to deal with undeniable native rights. Henceforth, at any rate, private land grabs already made or newly attempted in Indian territories were ordered null and void. Native claims were to be satisfied by official bargaining, due purchase and legal process; and whites were not even to enter the Indian lands unlicenced. The resulting bargains may still not have been fair — for example, how could anyone then judge the future value of the Mississaugas' cession of the Toronto waterfront? None the less, the agreements on treaty rights and reserves which this policy prescribed led on to native legal status and political means of betterment which simply had not existed under the French regime. The Proclamation scheme was surely partial; but far from negative.

Native rights, initially considered in the Proclamation of 1763, are very much an issue in Ontario and Canada today. Yet in that earlier time, more urgently important was the virtual closing of the Indian territory under the Proclamation policy, until violent unrest there could be met and conciliated. In the spring of 1763, a last-chance Indian resistance spread in the Detroit area, particularly led by the Ottawa chief and former French ally, Pontiac. The British-held fort was closely besieged from May to October. Michilimackinac and other lesser posts were taken by Indian forces. But gradually the rising fell apart among its tribal factions, until the masterful Pontiac himself was ready to make peace in 1765. Detroit had not fallen; and

1. *"Plan of Toronto Harbour with the proposed town," December 6, 1788. By the Proclamation of 1763, native lands were to be purchased by legal process and whites were not even allowed to enter the Indian lands unlicenced. The Toronto waterfront was purchased from the Mississaugas under such terms.*
2. *Pontiac in Council.* Wood engraving by Alfred Bobbett (c. 1824-1888/1889).
3. *Pontiac's medal. Pontiac, an Ottawa chief and former French ally, took up a final Indian resistance against the British in the spring of 1763, but made peace in 1765.*

3

the British had strengthened their links to it by erecting Fort Erie in 1764 as a supply centre on the Niagara River above the Falls; and building ships on nearby Navy Island to carry provisions onward to the Detroit River. Still, it was several more years before the Indians had been conciliated, and the Ontario region beyond the Province of Quebec was fully and freely opened to licenced traders and venturers.

British fur merchants, who had the market and money connections with London, came in partnership with French *bourgeois*, who knew the inland country and the trade — and were brought there by the canoe brigades of French Canadian *voyageurs*, who moved the cargoes of goods and furs. They swept across the Ontario region from the later 1760s: going well past it to the Mississippi lands or the northwestern plains, or then on north to compete with the Hudson's Bay Company posts; yet always tying this whole, immense network of outreaching trade lines back to Montreal, the fur metropolis of Canada. The main Great Lakes trading entrepôts, from Niagara up to Grand Portage on Lake Superior (which replaced Kaministiquia), were all linked back to Montreal. In that city during the 1770s, the hard-driving North West Company took shape: a group of principal fur merchants and partnerships who joined to pool their long-range transport costs and share the burdens of competing with a solidly incorporated Hudson's Bay Company. The Nor'Westers were to thrust right to Arctic shores in 1789, the Pacific by 1793. But Grand Portage was the key exchange point where their tough, fast-moving western brigades met the weighty canoes from the Montreal partners crammed with supplies; until in 1802 Fort William (at former Kaministiquia) became the great Ontario fur headquarters instead of Grand Portage. And from the age-old Ottawa route, or from the Toronto Passage, up to Sault Ste. Marie where the Nor'Westers cut the first canal past the river rapids, the life of the North West Company would constantly be interwoven with Ontario developments; till at length it was merged into the Hudson's Bay Company in 1821.

The Bay Company, of course, continued its own trade on the northern margins of Ontario — where Moose Factory, re-sited in 1730 and reconstructed in stone, became a major base at "The Bottom of the Bay." Moreover, lesser private traders were newly

1. *Fort Mackinack. This fort, whose name was shortened from Michilimackinac, was one of the "lesser" British posts taken by Indians forces during their brief western resistance which began in 1763.*
2. *The Wall and Block House of Fort Erie. Fort Erie was established by the British in 1764 as part of a move to back up Fort Detroit. It was to be a supply centre on the Niagara River, above the Falls. Fort Erie was later destroyed by the Americans in 1814.* Photo of the restored fort, July 14, 1949.
3. *Voyageurs on Lake Superior. The voyageurs moved cargoes of goods and furs across the Ontario region. They also journeyed far past this region to the northwestern plains and north, competing with the Hudson's Bay Company.* Oil by F. Hopkins.

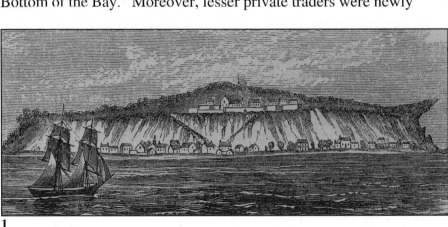

1

2

3

1

2

3

1. *Voyageurs Shooting Rapids. The outreaching network of canoe trade lines were tied back to Montreal, the fur metropolis of Canada.* Oil by Frances Anne Hopkins (1838-1919), 1879.

2. *Voyageurs travelling over a portage.*

3. *Crossing the Northern Ontario region.*

4. *Aerial view of reconstructed Fort William. In 1802, Fort William replaced Grand Portage as the chief Ontario fur headquarters for the North West Company.*

4

1

1. *North West Company house on Vaudreuil Street, Montreal, Quebec. In the 1770s, a group of fur merchants formed the North West Company in Montreal. In 1821, the company was merged into the older Hudson's Bay Company.*
2. *A North West canoe on the Mattawa River. The North-Westers reached Arctic waters in 1789 and the Pacific by 1793.*
3. *View of Grand Portage on Lake Superior. Grand Portage was the exchange point for the North West Company where western brigades met supply canoes from the Montreal partners, until replaced by Fort William.*

2

3

1

2

3

1. *Moose Factory, c. 1869: fur traders with their dogs in front of the Hudson's Bay post. Re-sited and reconstructed in stone in 1730, this long remained a major base at "The Bottom of the Bay" — James Bay.*
2. *A Hudson's Bay Company Fur Pack.*
3. *Arms of the Hudson's Bay Company.*
Watercolour, pen and black ink by Harry Jewell (1867/1868-1936), c. 1915.

active in Southern Ontario forests by the 1770s, once Indian unrest had passed; for though the grand, long-distance fur trade lay with the big companies, small enterprisers could still find sufficient furs to buy and sell in yet-unsettled Ontario wilds. Thus local fur merchants persisted in many areas until farm clearings finally spread and wildlife drew back. A local log fur-trading post then might become a general store for gathering settlers, and deal with farmers as well as trappers. One case in point is that of Jean-Baptiste Rousseau, a French-Canadian fur trader established at Toronto, who guided the ship of Upper Canada's first governor, John Graves Simcoe, into harbour on Simcoe's arrival at Toronto Bay in 1793. Rousseau had revived fur trading at the Toronto site, building a combined home and storehouse on the Humber at least by 1774. Later, this duly became a general store for the rising town of York — but its respected earliest citizen moved away to less crowded Ancaster in 1795, as York was getting too big.

All that indeed came later — on the other side of the great American Revolution, which was mounting by the 1770s and burst into open war in 1775. As the strains that led to violence grew between Great Britain and its American colonies, a largely wilderness Ontario was itself affected; indirectly, but inevitably. In 1774, the Quebec Act was passed by the imperial parliament, very much in response to looming American problems. It now brought Southern Ontario within the boundaries of a widely extended Province of Quebec. At the same time, the Act set up a distinctive kind of government for that province, which would no less affect Ontario-to-be. These matters do need some explaining here.

Back at the start of British rule, the Proclamation of 1763 had envisaged treating newly-acquired Quebec like other British colonies in America; that is, by establishing British laws and institutions, particularly meaning a representative system of government with an elected assembly, such as the Thirteen Colonies to the south long had known, and more recently, Nova Scotia. But Quebec did not turn out to be a province like the others. While a British merchant class grew powerful and prominent in the towns, especially in fur-trade Montreal, the mass of Quebec's people, strongly rural and agricultural,

Sir Guy Carleton, first Baron Dorchester (1724-1808). Carleton was Lieutenant-Governor of Quebec (1766), then Governor of Quebec (1768-1778), and Governor-in-Chief of British North America (1786-1796). As Governor of Quebec, Carleton sought to ensure peace and the loyalty of the French-Canadians by urging Britain to adopt a policy which would confirm the French character of Quebec. As a result the Quebec Act was passed in Britain in 1774.

stayed French and Catholic. And though the merchants demanded English laws, courts, and assembly as promised, the great number of French Canadians were indifferent or opposed; wanting their familiar French law and the seigneurial land system it upheld; accustomed to government by council from above; and beyond that, fearful lest their Roman Catholic Church lose its guiding role. Hence, the Proclamation plans remained unrealized; until Sir Guy Carleton, governor of Quebec since 1768, urged a totally different policy. Arguing that Quebec was overwhelmingly French and not likely to alter, he sought to ensure its peace and loyalty by confirming its French character, as the parliamentary act he proposed was meant to do. After some consideration the imperial government leaders took up Carleton's design, being increasingly aware themselves of discontent and disloyalty appearing in the Thirteen Colonies, and therefore hoping to make Quebec, at least, a secure bastion for Britain in America.

Accordingly, the Quebec Act was passed by the British parliament in 1774. It provided for English criminal law but French civil law, thereby maintaining the seigneurial system; for rule by governor and appointed council, with no assembly; and for legally-enforced tithes, or dues to be paid to the Catholic Church by its adherents, thus making Catholicism a state-recognized religion for the French Quebec society. Further than this, the Act extended the province's boundaries west to the junction of the Ohio and Mississippi, which not only took in much of Ontario, but also a great deal of territory beyond. This enlargement of Quebec province was partly intended to serve the major fur trade interests based within it at Montreal, partly to forestall westward expansion by the discontented Thirteen Colonies. Yet as a result, the Quebec Act was denounced in those colonies as restoring the old, hated French-Catholic power to their north, then giving it their west — a slight over-statement, but one which fed the fires of revolt and led in 1775-6 to an invasion of Quebec itself by American rebel armies. Montreal fell; Quebec City held out under Carleton, until the invaders withdrew defeated. But the Revolutionary War raged on: with profound consequences for Ontario.

Attack on Quebec by General Montgomery, Morning of December 31, 1775. The Quebec Act of 1774 was denounced by the Thirteen Colonies (later the United States of America) as restoring the old hated French-Catholic power to their north. This view led to an invasion of Quebec in 1775-1776 during which Montreal fell. However, Quebec City held out under Carleton until the American invaders withdrew.

Revolution and Loyalist Immigration

The guns of Revolution blazed along the eastern seaboard and into the midwestern interior; north to the Lake Champlain country, or down to the American south. The area which chiefly affected Ontario, however, stretched below Lake Ontario and the upper St. Lawrence, from Niagara eastward across the old Iroquois domain that had so often been involved in the Ontario story. In this area, the Iroquois Six Nations still had a pivotal place in the Revolution conflict: some striving to stay neutral; some, notably Oneidas who were persuaded by a New England missionary, taking to the rebel cause; others, especially Mohawks, backing the British side. The Mohawks for years had put their trust in Sir William Johnson, British Superintendent of Indian Affairs for New York province, who had led them and provincial troops in the capture of French Niagara in 1759. More important, this powerfully influential Irishman had taken as his consort Mary or Molly Brant, a most capable, intelligent and high-ranking Mohawk matron, whose brother, Joseph Brant, was a distinguished war chief of the Mohawks. Sir William Johnson died in 1774; but his nephew, Guy Johnson, succeeded him as Indian Superintendent; his son, John Johnson, as heir to Sir William's rich estates at Johnstown in the Mohawk Valley; while Molly and Joseph Brant remained commanding Iroquois allies of the British. Consequently, a major part of the Six Nations turned to war against the rebel Americans, who responded by laying waste Iroquois lands in northern New York. And not only Iroquois held to the British (and Johnson) connection but Highland Scottish and German settlers in the Mohawk Valley.

Fierce frontier warfare swept across this territory: crop, barn and cabin burnings, raids and massacres, as both sides spread death and vengeance; although Joseph Brant tried to restrain some of the slaughter. Sir John Johnson, his own lands seized, made his way up to Montreal to raise the King's Royal Regiment of New York, the Royal Yorkers, largely recruited from loyal Mohawk Valley settlers; and he and Guy Johnson took part in forays deep into the area. Molly Brant moved to Niagara in 1777, bringing her diplomatic talents and

1. *Joseph Brant (Thayendanegea) (1742-1807), Chief of the Six Nations. Brant, distinguished war chief of the Mohawks, commanded Iroquois allies of the British. A major part of the Six Nations fought along side the British against the Americans during the American Revolution.*
2. *Mary or Molly Brant. Undisputed leader of the Six Nations Matrons, Molly Brant was the consort of Indian Superintendent, Sir William Johnson and sister of Joseph Brant. She was a fervent loyalist and after the American Revolution, used her influence to gain lands from the British for the loyal Amerindians. This stamp was designed by Sara Tyson to show the three facets of Molly Brant's life: Iroquois, Loyalist, and European.*
3. *Captain John Brant (Ahyouwaighs) (1794-1832), Chief of the Six Nations. Son of Joseph Brant, John was chosen by his mother to succeed his father after the latter's death in 1807. John Brant continued in the Six Nations' tradition of supporting the British and participated in many of the major battles of the War of 1812.*
4. *Sir William Johnson (1715-1774), British Superintendent of Indian Affairs. Johnson was trusted by the Mohawks and took for his wife the high-ranking Mohawk, Molly Brant. He led both the Mohawks and British colonial troops in the capture of French Niagara in 1759.*

1

2

3

4

personal standing to the war out of Niagara. This was being waged most powerfully by Colonel John Butler, a Connecticut Loyalist who had commanded Indians at Niagara under Sir William Johnson, and had in 1776 organized Butler's Rangers from Loyalists who had been driven from their Mohawk Valley farms — where now they carried back grim retribution.

Dispossessed Loyalist families also flocked to the protection of Fort Niagara's guns and walls. The fort itself was set on the eastern or "American" side of the entrance to the Niagara River; Butler's Barracks, where Loyalist troops were based, went up in 1778 on the western or Ontario bank. A naval barracks (Navy Hall) had already stood here since 1765; and was enlarged during the Revolutionary War years, as winter quarters for the warship and crews that kept British command secure on Lake Ontario. But these Ontario-side beginnings were significantly extended by 1780, when farms started spreading along the shore to feed the refugee families and the fort. An agreement with the local Mississauga Indians covered this initial opening of an Ontario land tract. Its first survey made in 1783 showed over 800 Loyalist settlers already established in an Ontario-side "Township of Niagara."

Meanwhile, some other Loyalist refugees from northern New York journeyed by forest trails up to Carleton Island in the St. Lawrence, a new British naval base opposite the remains of old Fort Frontenac; or else they reached Oswegatchie (Ogdensburg) further down the river across from present Prescott. Loyalist regiments, too, were drawn back to base camps around Sorel and Trois Rivières in the later stages of the war. For the conflict was winding down by the early 1780s. France's entry as a major American ally, and the decisive American-French victory at Yorktown in 1781, spelled convincing defeat for a divided Britain sick of war, wiping out the varied successes won by British and Loyalist forces in other battles. After

1. Sir John Johnson (1742-1830). Son of Sir William Johnson, he became Superintendent of Indian Affairs in 1782. In 1776, he raised the Loyalist King's Royal Regiment of New York, or the "Royal Yorkers." After peace had been signed, Johnson was placed in charge of the final disposition of Loyalist regiments: including the first and second battalion of his Royal Yorkers. Because of his position, he also had the responsibility of resettling and reconciling the native allies of the British.
2. Colonel John Butler (?-1794). A Connecticut Loyalist, Butler served under Sir William Johnson in commanding Indians at Niagara. In 1776, he organized Butler's Rangers, from Loyalists who had been driven from their Mohawk Valley farms.
3. Badge of Butler's Rangers. This badge was found at Niagara-on-the-Lake.

1

2

3

1. *Navy Hall, 1893. This Hall was used for naval barracks and stores during the American Revolutionary War years. The Hall later briefly became Upper Canada's Parliament building in the 1790s.* Pencil drawing by F.H. Granger, 1893.

2. *Township of Niagara, 1792. An agreement with the Mississauga Indians first opened up this land to settlement. This first survey made in 1783 showed over 800 Loyalist settlers already established in a "Township of Niagara."*

1

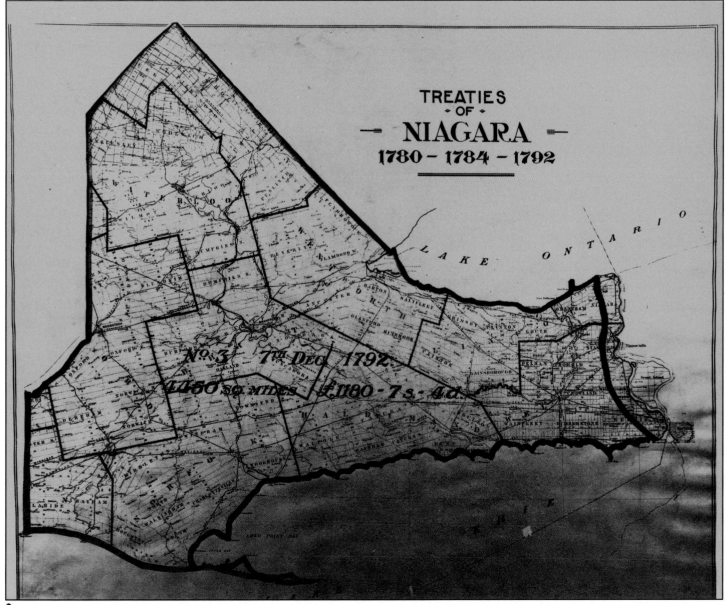

2

lengthy negotiations, the Treaty of Versailles was finally signed in September, 1783, as Great Britain acknowledged the independence of a Revolution-born United States, and a new boundary line was drawn along the upper St. Lawrence and through the Great Lakes. The peace thus left the Ontario region still wholly in British hands. But it also brought a mounting flow of Loyalist settlers into that territory, far surpassing the earlier wartime trickles. Farming districts, villages, even towns, would soon arise in the Ontario wilderness — thanks to the Loyalists who now came in, voting with their feet against the Revolution. Why they had rejected it, why they came, are critical questions in the building of Ontario, and for the mark they left upon it through time to follow.

Part of the answer lies in the very nature of the Revolutionary War. It was not just a struggle for American nationhood against an outside, "foreign" power; nor simply another great international conflict, even

1

1. *United Empire Loyalists Statue, Hamilton. This ten-cent stamp was issued in 1934 to commemorate the 150th anniversary of the coming of the Loyalists. The actual monument was unveiled on May 23, 1929; it first stood in front of the old City Hall and has since been moved to Prince's Square in Hamilton.*

2. *Carleton Island, ruins of fort, August, 1898. The British had set up a naval base on Carleton Island in the St. Lawrence, opposite the remains of the old Fort Frontenac, during the American Revolution. It was also used as a refuge by Loyalists who journeyed by trails up to the island, fleeing from northern New York.*

2

though the despotic kingdoms of France and Spain gladly lined up with American democracy to cut their old imperial rival, Britain, down to proper size. No, this was also an American civil war. Aside from the a-political or the undecided, waiting to see the way the cat would jump, here was a critical dispute between those who sought an outright, radical break with Britain, and those who might well agree reforms were needed, but did not want to drop the British ties and constitution deeply rooted in the colonies: or take to irresponsible visionaries and scheming rabble-rousers who would destroy established order and overthrow legal representative government, all for the sake of their own power and self-interest. Admittedly, this was the Loyalists' point of view, and biassed, no less than the other side's opinion of them as Tory reactionaries and renegades. But as Loyalists, they backed the Crown and Constitution they knew against unchartered republicanism, and the violence, mob-rule and harsh repression which they certainly experienced at its hands. Hence many Loyalists took up arms — to fight not so much for Britain as for the British America they represented — while many more than these men under arms shared the same outlook. They simply saw rebellion as treason. Just as Abraham Lincoln did in a later Civil War.

Moreover, many fairly recent immigrants, non-British in origin like the various German groups, or those with a non-English native tongue like the Gaelic-speaking Scots Highlanders, could and did become Loyalists: an order to support a lawful British America, which had given them lands, homes and security, against self-styled patriots who not only looked dangerously radical to these cautious newcomers, but might no less hold anti-foreign prejudices that today we would call racist. The Loyalists certainly included numerous old-stock English Americans, stemming back to early Virginia, Pennsylvania, or New England; but also they comprised Irish and Dutch, or French Huguenots (Protestants) and African ex-slaves, as well as German farmers, Highland clansmen, and still more. They were a contemporary cross-section of America, as typically American — if "British American" politically — as were their patriot-nationalist foes. And they equally contained a sizeable variety of religious as well as ethnic minorities: Quakers, Catholics, German

The Town of Sorel. Sorel was another base to which Loyalist troops withdrew at the close of the war. By J. Lambert (active 1775-1811).

Lutherans or small Protestant sects. For Loyalism was already multi-cultural in content, representing a diversity joined together under British laws and institutions; not the "one-nation" idea of a uniform Sovereign People which their revolutionary opponents strongly embodied. In this lay a vital difference between the new United States and Canada-to-be. Furthermore, unity in diversity, within one political framework, would come to be a mark of Ontario as well — put there initially by the Loyalists.

These Loyalists, besides, were a cross-section of the whole American social order. There were large land-owners among them, wealthy merchants, colonial officials and Anglican clergy, who all obviously held a stake in the Loyal cause because of their positions; which did not mean that they did not earnestly believe in it. There were as well substantial middle-class shopkeepers, workshop owners or prosperous farmers, conservative by temperament and conviction; and notably, too, many lower-class artisans, labourers and servants (in an age of hard work, where servants formed a major group) who were just as firmly fixed in Loyalist ranks, being particularly subject to "patriot" street-persecutions that scarcely won them over.

All the same, in the post-war emigration of Loyalists from a triumphant American republic to the remaining British colonies in North America, the greater numbers and the wider social spread went up the Atlantic coast by sea to the Maritime provinces of Nova Scotia, Prince Edward Island and New Brunswick: the last created by the very inflow of Loyalist settlers. More of the townspeople or upper-class and professional elements moved in this direction. It was indeed the most readily accessible from the populous, well-developed areas of the American seaboard, from which whole fleets of Loyalists sailed north out of the port of New York, held by Britain to the end. Some thirty thousand journeyed this way, compared to around seven thousand who went inland to the Ontario region. These inland settlers were chiefly frontier farmers from up-state New York and Pennsylvania; though some merchants and officials also came immediately or later, while more New Englanders, Southerners, or others from former Middle Colonies like New Jersey, would in time be added. But the point remains that the Loyalist inflow into the Ontario region was a

U.E. Loyalists Landing at the Site of Present-day Saint John, New Brunswick, 1783. The province of New Brunswick was really created by the flow of Loyalists into the Atlantic region. The Maritime provinces were the most accessible landing sites from the developed areas of the American seaboard. Print by John David Kelly (1862-1958), before 1935.

westward, pioneer migration which entered virtually unoccupied territory. That fact, and the large proportion of organized Loyalist soldiery who came in, gave this movement a specially strong impact. Truly, it brought Ontario out of the ancient forests.

At the peace, there was little use in going home for those Loyalist regiments stationed in Canada, or for the families that had joined them, when their former homes had been seized, and arrests, tarring-and-feathering or lynch mobs widely greeted recognized supporters of the losing cause. Much the same applied to Loyalists who had stayed home, and there gone through property confiscations and angry assaults. It is fair to add that, had the Loyalists won, persecutions might have followed on the other side. Still, despite American promises in the Treaty of 1783 to respect Loyalist rights, to give compensation for property taken or destroyed, and deal with claims for unpaid debts and illegal seizures, the state legislatures in the new republic paid scant attention to recommendations on these subjects made by a then-weak United States federal government. Consequently, if there was small reason for Loyalist troops to return home, there was little more for many resident Loyalists in the States still to stay and suffer. And so they left: not simply to escape, but with the resolution to go where they could find the King's justice, the British constitution, and new lands offering security and freedom. They moved northward and inland by river, lake and trail to settle in Ontario. The outcome was, that from the bitter upheaval of Revolution arose the heritage of Loyalism which would make and mould a province for generations to come.

Loyalists on the move near Halifax, Nova Scotia. Whole fleets of emigrants travelled from New York to the Maritimes. While some 30,000 journeyed this way, only about 7,000 went overland into the Ontario region, where they entered almost unoccupied territory. Watercolour by Robert Petley, c. 1835.

Map showing "British America by Treaty, 1783." This map includes the principal engagements of the American Revolution and the boundaries as settled in 1783, including those set for the "Rebel Colonies now the United States of America."

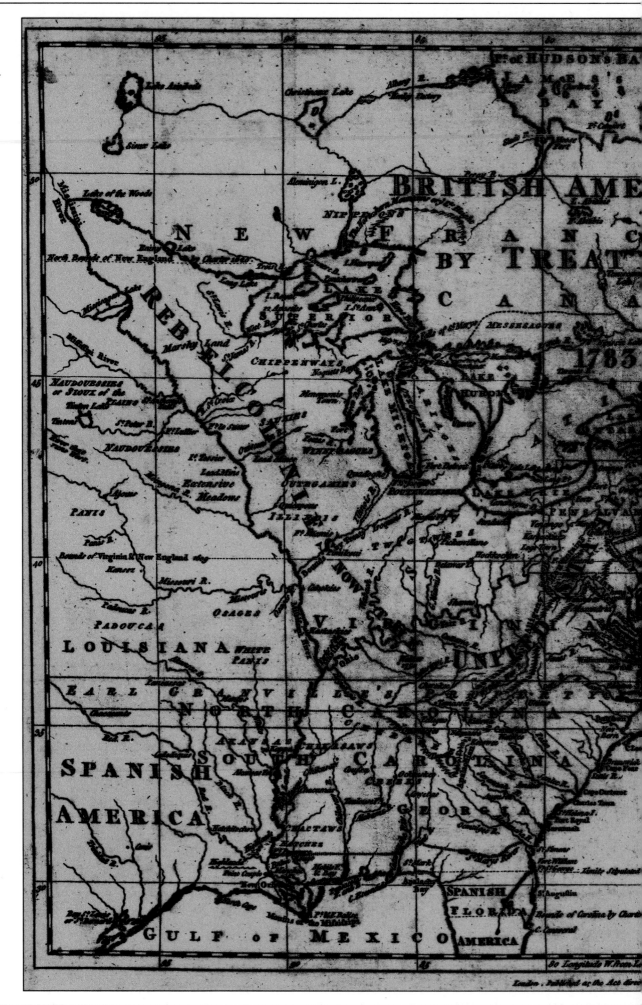

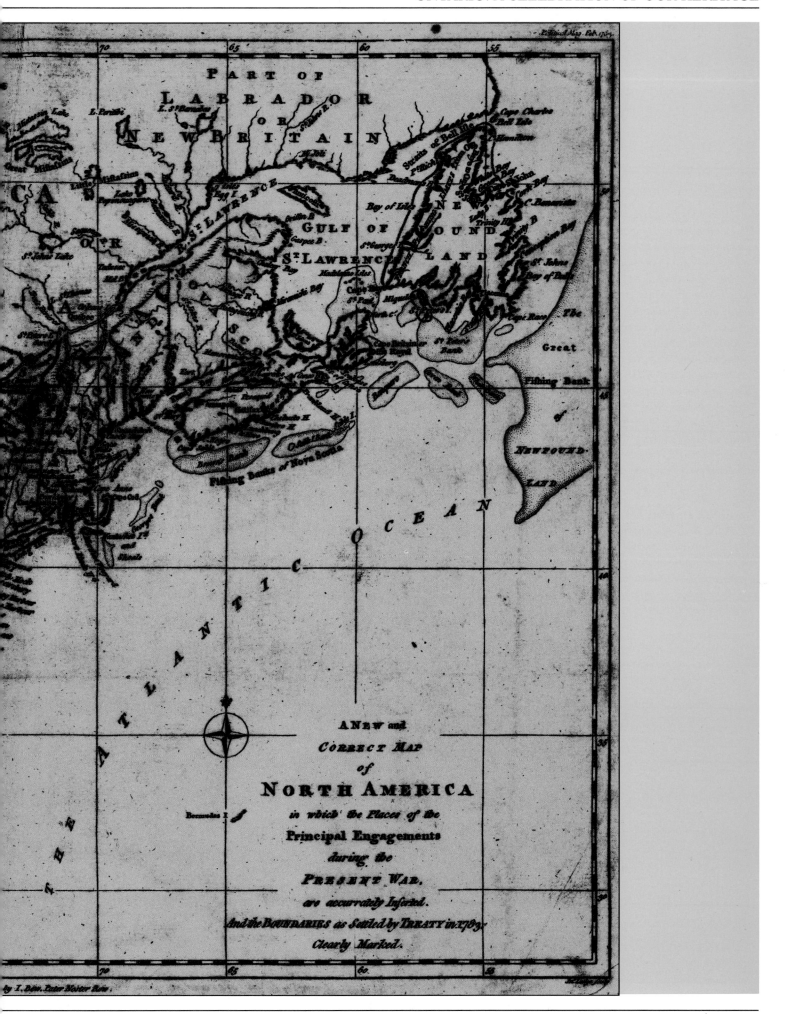

Loyalist Settlement and the Formation of Upper Canada

Rightly recognizing the debt owed the Loyalists who had sacrificed so much in blood, suffering and possessions, the British authorities moved in 1783-4 to provide lands and aid for those seeking to relocate in the huge, remaining territories of British North America. In the case of Ontario, or western Quebec as it still was, Loyalist settlement here could also strengthen Britain's hold along the inland American border. Accordingly, a whole set of necessary arrangements were efficiently organized under General Sir Frederick Haldimand who had succeeded Carleton in 1778 as governor of Quebec. Indian treaties were made to purchase large areas; lands were surveyed for actual grants to settlers; and plans particularly were worked out to give the Loyalist troops still at base camps in populated Quebec new farm lots to occupy well up the St. Lawrence, beyond the furthest French-Canadian seigneuries.

In the spring of 1784, long lines of *bateaux* thus went up-river, carrying Loyalist soldiers, their wives and families, baggage, food stocks and farm or building supplies. Flotillas would drop off along the way, to set the groups ashore at the chosen locations — according to an effective over-all scheme, which no doubt was the more effective because settlement was based on the regimental units, and their veteran comradeship and discipline made for orderly movements. As Haldimand had been instructed from London, the lands for these Loyalists had been surveyed in two blocks of townships laid out along the upper St. Lawrence, each township officially being a seigneury, as part of the Quebec French land system; but a royal seigneury, where the King himself was the seigneurial lord from whom the settlers would hold their farms.

The first five of the nine royal townships, running west from the end of the last French-Canadian seigneury of Longueuil, were allotted to Sir John Johnson's unit, the Royal Yorkers. They were located as the men of that regiment themselves requested, with Catholic Scots Highlanders set next to the French Catholics of Longueuil, then Scot Presbyterians, German Calvinists, German Lutherans, and

1. *General Sir Frederick Haldimand (1718-1791), Governor of Quebec. Although his military career prior to and including the American Revolution is noteworthy, Haldimand's chief legacy came from his role as colonial administrator. Of particular note is his resettlement of the disbanded Loyalist troops and the relocation of exiled Loyalist families during and immediately following the American Revolution.*
2. *An encampment of Loyalists at New Johnstown (later Cornwall) on the banks of the St. Lawrence River, June 6, 1784. After the Revolutionary War, British authorities provided land for those seeking to relocate. In the spring of 1784, many Loyalist soldiers and their families travelled up the river to take up this land.* Watercolour by James Peachey, 1785.
3. *Loyalists Drawing Lots For Their Lands, 1784. The British authorities in 1783-1784 sought to provide lands and aid for Loyalists in remaining British North American territories, to recognize the debts owed to a people who had sacrificed so much.* Pen and ink by Charles William Jefferys (1869-1951).

1

2

3

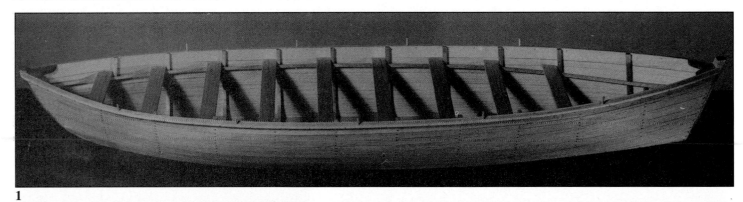

1

2

3

4

1. *Colonial bateau of 1776. This bateau is 30 feet long, has a beam of 6 feet, 6 inches and a draft of 2 feet, 10-1/2 inches. These vessels were principally built at Lachine, Quebec and were used by the Loyalists for transportation up the St. Lawrence from Montreal.*

2. *Loyalists camping beside the St. Lawrence. In the spring of 1784, many Loyalists travelled up the river to settle on their new lands.* Pen and ink by Charles William Jefferys, (1869-1951).

3. *A later bateau at the Hudson Bay Company post, Lake Temiskaming, 1897.*

4. *Arms Granted to Colonel Ebenezer Jessup, April 10, 1788. Jessup, brother of Major Edward Jessup, led the King's Loyal Americans.*

5. *Military Settlements of Upper Canada, c. 1820s. The amount of land allotted to these settlers depended on status or rank. The basic farm lot was 100 acres; however, more acres were assigned for family rights, and still more for higher official positions.*

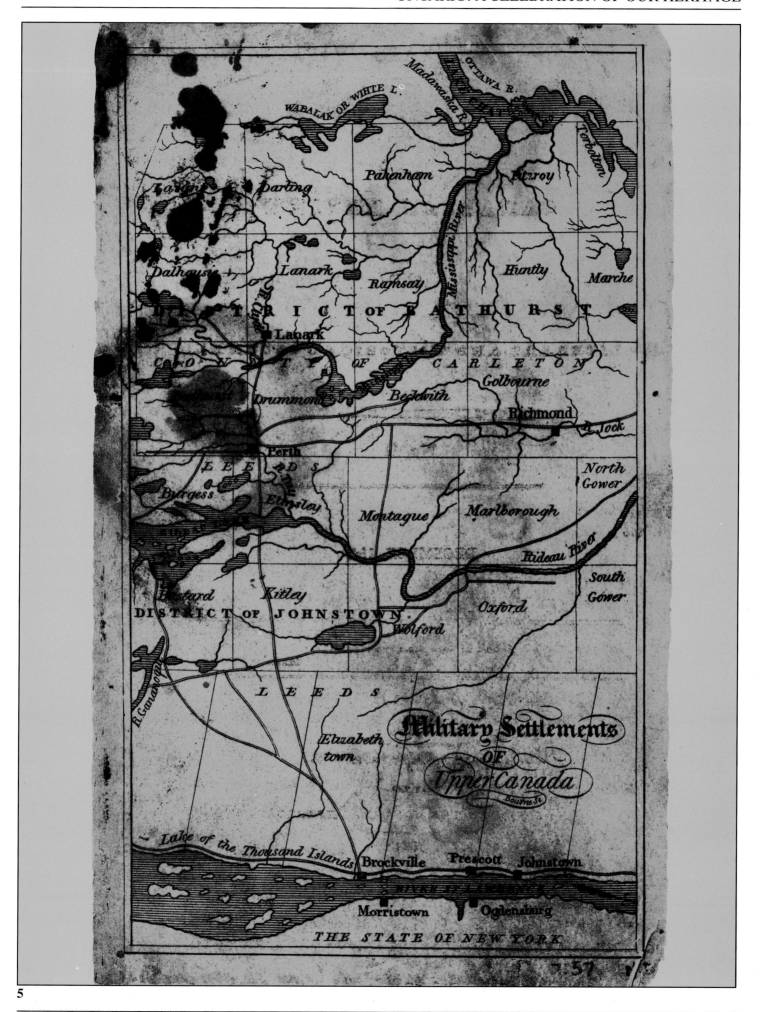

5

1

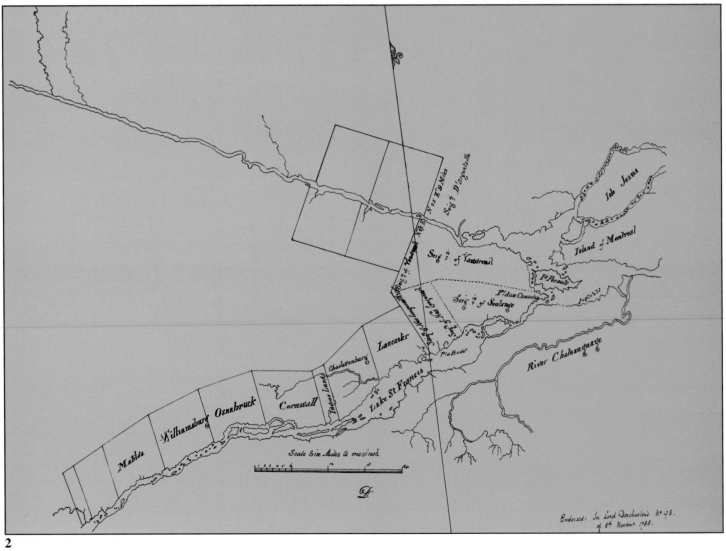

2

British Anglicans in that order. Nothing could more plainly convey the ethnic and religious variety of Ontario Loyalism. Jessup's Corps of Loyal Rangers came next: Major Jessup, a Connecticut Loyalist, would found the town of Prescott. Then, after a gap where the rough Precambrian Shield country came down to the St. Lawrence, there were five more townships, beginning at Cataraqui near the site of old Fort Frontenac, and continuing west to the Bay of Quinte on Lake Ontario. The first of these Cataraqui townships went to Loyalists under Captain Michael Grass, who led them out of New York port, around by sea and river, to what was to become the new town of Kingston. The townships beyond were occupied, in sequence, by more of Jessup's Corps, by the second battalion of Johnson's regiment, and by another group from New York city under Major Peter Van Alstine. The last of the Cataraqui townships (now Marysburg) was settled by disbanded British and German regular troops. In all, as Sir John Johnson who had been in charge of the operation, reported in July of 1784, nearly 3,800 people had been successfully located along the upper St. Lawrence front or the Bay of Quinte shores. Eastern Ontario still finds its roots in these Loyalist beginnings.

Furthermore, the pattern used in allotting lands to these settlers largely began land policy for the Ontario region, based on free grants from the Crown, but in amounts depending on status or rank. The head of a family would be given 100 acres, with 50 more for each family member, while a single man got just 50. And for the military Loyalists of the St. Lawrence, a private received 100 acres (with 50 again for each family member) and non-commissioned officers 200, while 500 to 700 acres went to junior commissioned officers, and 1,000 each to senior field officers. Essentially, then, the 100-acre farm lot was fairly basic, with more acres for family rights, and far more still for higher social position: altogether, a very eighteenth-century view on parcelling out inland America.

Meanwhile more land was certainly being taken up in the Niagara area, where Loyalists continued to arrive in individual families or small parties, without the collective movement made on the St. Lawrence. They came to Fort Niagara and the extending farms on the Ontario side; often travelling up through Pennsylvania or west across

1. *Prescott, from Ogdensburg Harbour, New York, 1840. Prescott was founded by Major Edward Jessup, leader of the Loyal Rangers and Connecticut Loyalists.* Engraving by William Henry Bartlett (1808-1854), 1840.
2. *Map of the Eastern Royal Townships, c. 1788. The five townships of Charlottenburg, Cornwall, Osnabruck, Williamsburg, and Matilda were allotted to Sir John Johnson's unit, the Royal Americans. Besides showing a plan of these townships, this map was also used to present a division line for Upper and Lower Canada, which is the line shown running through the seigneury of New Longueuil. The division, however, was fixed along the limits of the seigneury.*

New York by ox cart — when they were lucky — the men walking and guiding the oxen, the women in the carts watching the supplies (and small children) lest they bounce out in the slow, bumping progress over the trails. Other Loyalists even found their way to Lake Erie, and on to the shelter of Detroit, still in British keeping during and after the Revolution. Forts Detroit and Niagara, like several other British posts along the inland border, were now themselves actually on American soil, according to the peace treaty of 1783. Nevertheless, Britain felt good reason not to yield them yet.

The same peace had transferred the territories below the upper St. Lawrence and Great Lakes from British to American possession. But Indian peoples in that area, who had properly viewed themselves as British allies, not subjects, had been ignored in this white man's power-transfer that virtually handed them to the loving Americans: "sold to Congress," Brant had said. Britain's abandonment of the border posts as well — vital supply centres for the Indians, even for foodstuffs by now — could be a stark and final blow that well might turn the tribes in revenge against the British themselves. The latter, much aware of their own thin occupation along the border, wanted keenly to avoid that prospect. For now they held on to the posts, arguing that the Americans had not honoured the peace treaty through failing to meet the Loyalists' claims: a valid point, if not the crucial one.

In one area the British did strive to meet the debt they owed to their Indian allies, by setting up a reserve on the Grand River in 1784, for the Six Nations Iroquois who had lost their ancestral lands in New York State through fighting beside Britain in the Revolution. Land was purchased from the Mississaugas in an extensive tract along both sides of the Grand, which flowed down from the western Ontario peninsula into Lake Erie. Here about 2,000 of the Six Nations took up new homes and farms: Mohawks, Cayugas and Onondagas who had largely joined the British, but with some others, including Senecas and Tuscaroras. The Mohawks also obtained a reserve north of the Bay of Quinte, Tyendenaga. Yet this was small compared to the Grand River Reserve, where Joseph Brant had led the way, and long would dominate Iroquois councils. His sister,

1. *Scene on the Bay of Quinte. From Cataraqui west to the Bay of Quinte, more Loyalist townships were founded. By July, 1784, some 3,800 people had been successfully located along the shores of the upper St. Lawrence and the Bay of Quinte.*
2. *This simply-drawn later picture still graphically portrays the opening world of hard-won clearings and rough buildings in early Ontario settlements.*

1

2

1

2

1. *Mohawk Church, Brant's Ford (Brantford). The oldest surviving Anglican Church in Upper Canada, it was erected in 1787. It still houses the Queen Anne's Bible given to the "loyal Mohawks" in the early 18th century. The missionary Peter Jones was baptized in the church and Captain Brant was buried there. The Mohawks have traditionally been Anglican.*

2. *Brant's Residence. Joseph Brant led the way to the Grand River Indian Reserve and dominated in the Iroquois councils for years.*

3. *Council house, Tyendenaga Mohawk reserve, near Deseronto. Mohawks were given the Tyendinaga reserve, north of the Bay of Quinte, by the British authorities, although it was small compared to the main Six Nations Iroquois reserve on the Grand River.*

4. *First Page of an Address to the Earl of Dufferin from the Missionaries of the Church of England, August 25, 1874. This address welcomes the Earl and Lady Dufferin to "the Old Mohawk Church which is the oldest Protestant place of worship in the Province of Ontario." The missionaries had been sent to work with the Six Nations.*

3

To His Excellency
the Right Honorable Earl of Dufferin
K.P. K.C.B. Governor General
of the Dominion of Canada etc. etc. etc.

May it please Your Excellency.

We, the Missionaries of the Church of England to the Indians of the Six Nations under the auspices of the New England Company, one of the earliest Missionary organizations in Great Britain, whose beneficence has been extended to the Indians here for many years, most cordially welcome Your Excellency and Lady Dufferin to the Old Mohawk Church which is the oldest Protestant place of worship in the Province of Ontario.

As an Ecclesiastical edifice of such priority it will no doubt be an object of interest to Your Excellency, but its interest is greatly enhanced by the fact that, at the instance of the late celebrated Mohawk Chief Joseph

Molly Brant, who had gone to Kingston, also kept much of her influence. But the life of the Grand River Iroquois, still prominent today, mainly centred around Brant's Ford (now Brantford), and perhaps at the Mohawk Chapel erected nearby in 1787, a royal endowment from King George III which yet stands and houses the Queen Anne's Bible given to the "loyal Mohawks" early in the eighteenth century.

At all events, a world of settlement was taking shape in the Southern Ontario wilds, though putting the people on the land was only the start of the process. They had soils rich in untapped fertility. But there were the heavy trees to clear by axe, thick trunks to saw, slash to burn (often jointly with their neighbours); and then grain to sow amid the stumps, or vegetable plots to be tended by the women and children — not to mention building crude shanties, which later could shelter stock when the first log houses went up — while in the meantime living on fish, game and government provisions, until the harvests at last came in. The Loyalists had usually arrived with very little, through no fault of their own. They needed almost everything, from axes, hoes and seed grain to flour, kettles and gun powder. The government provided as it had to, not just tools, seeds, and rations for three years, but cows, saw and grist mills, and much water transport. This was one of the first times when Ontario conservatism aligned with something like government "socialism" — for the Loyalists' plainly practical reasons.

Yet if they necessarily shared state aid, they still found plenty of scope for individual action. Primarily pioneer farmers and families, they were sturdily reliant on their own skill, strength and will. Many of them had already cut farms out of wilderness, say twenty years before. The heartbreak was to have to do it all over again: the bright hope was that they knew how to do it. Naturally, the process itself was far from bright and easy. The Hungry Year of 1789 saw widespread crop failures and many hardships. Nevertheless, from their background of experience, their tough training and sheer determina-

Mohawk Village, on the Grand River Reserve, in its early years.

The Council House.   The Mohawk Church.

THE MOHAWK VILLAGE, GRAND RIVER, 1793.
(From a Drawing by Lieutenant Pilkington copied by Mrs Simcoe)

tion, the Loyalists won through. Cleared acres, expanding yields and developing communities steadily showed the gains made. On the St. Lawrence, New Johnstown (Cornwall to be) expressed the Johnson connection. On the Ontario shore at Niagara, where Colonel John Butler was now Indian Superintendent, the hamlet of Butlersbury emerged, to become the town of Newark, later Niagara-on-the-Lake. And at Kingston, where the Great Lakes flowed into the St. Lawrence, a key transhipment point as it had been in the days of Fort Frontenac, the first real commercial town in Ontario was coming into being. All this and more grew from Loyalist settlement, which was advancing still — towards obtaining the kind of legal and political system that befitted it.

The Loyalists might have been strongly pro-British and anti-republican. This did not mean they were less strongly committed to the institutions they had fought for. Once the earliest work of settling-in had been accomplished, they looked to gain local law courts supplying justice under familiar English law, and especially to have freehold tenure; that is, to own their lands fully, and not be seigneurial tenants even of a distant Gracious Majesty. As early as April, 1785, Sir John Johnson and a group of Loyalist officers petitioned the Crown, asking for a new district to be created in rising western Quebec which would have British laws and land tenure, still under the government of Quebec; while leaving the rest of the province to French laws and the seigneurial system as prescribed by the Quebec Act of 1774. Many other petitions followed. And Guy Carleton, now Lord Dorchester, who had returned as Quebec's governor in 1786 — but also had learned a lot about Loyalists from commanding their exodus from New York city at the end of the Revolution — himself warned that it was no longer sufficient just to maintain the Quebec Act system to suit the French Canadians. The Loyalists' wishes would also have to be met, if the great interior was to be held at all.

To do so in part, Dorchester increased Loyalist grants in 1787, giving 200 additional acres to heads of families who had already improved their lands, and 200 acres more, according to a register to be kept, for each Loyalist son on his coming of age or Loyalist

1. *Root or Stump Fence. Before the fertile soil of Southern Ontario could be used for farming, there was the back-breaking job of clearing trees, including stumps and roots. These could then be used roughly but effectively to contain livestock.*
2. *Rail fence, near Moira river. Clearing the land provided settlers with large quantities of timber, which could be used for fencing in different ways. The zig-zagging "snake" fence is one style which can still be seen today.*

1   2

daughter at her marriage. This, with the "Mark of Honour" also given, whereby those who had fought for the "Unity of Empire" might add the letters "U.E." after their names, would carry rights and distinctions of Loyalism on into the future. No less noteworthy, in July, 1788, Dorchester created four administrative districts in western Quebec. Named Luneburg, Mecklenburg, Nassau and Hesse, in reference to the British royal family's German connections, they ran east to west successively, from the French seigneurial limits of Longueuil on the St. Lawrence to the American border on the Detroit River. Each of these districts received its own Court of Common Pleas and Land Board, both much desired by the Loyalists. But this growing organization of the Ontario territory would soon lead on to provincehood.

The imperial government in London still had to deal with the broader problems of Quebec, so closely linked to the very coming of the Loyalists. Should it be one province or two? Should it have representative government? Was a new western province viable, or could there be a single representative system to contain two widely different societies that were strung out over many hundreds of miles? One compelling problem was the matter of taxation. In 1778, in the midst of the Revolution, the British parliament had (too late) renounced its power to tax the colonies, which had done so much to bring on the American explosion. Since then, Quebec's lack of a representative assembly to impose its own internal taxes had meant a constant drain on imperial revenues. Moreover, the powerful English merchants of Quebec were still pressing for the assembly first promised in 1763. It seemed altogether likely that representative rule would have to be adopted — but what of the Quebec Act guarantees to a solidly French-Catholic society, or what of that other society of English language, largely Protestant in faith and varied in cultural make-up, that was still growing fast in the Western Districts? The division of Quebec into two Canadian provinces looked like the only possible solution.

After extensive inquiries to Dorchester and advice returned from him or his officials, a draft bill to establish the new provinces of Upper and Lower Canada was sent from London in June, 1789: for the governor's comments on particulars, not principles. But given delays in slow Atlantic transport by sail, the reply came back too late for the bill to be

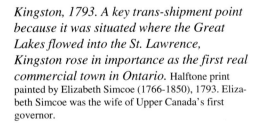

Kingston, 1793. A key trans-shipment point because it was situated where the Great Lakes flowed into the St. Lawrence, Kingston rose in importance as the first real commercial town in Ontario. Halftone print painted by Elizabeth Simcoe (1766-1850), 1793. Elizabeth Simcoe was the wife of Upper Canada's first governor.

brought before the parliamentary session of 1790. And so the Constitutional Act or Canada Act, that truly gave political form to Ontario, was not to be introduced and debated in parliament at London until the spring of 1791. It was passed there by the end of May, given royal assent in June, and finally went into effect on December 26, 1791 — the historic birthday of the Province of Upper Canada.

The Act itself did specify representative government with elected assemblies in both the Canadas, while retaining much of the Quebec Act for a mainly French Lower Canada; that is, French civil law, seigneurialism and the state-recognized Roman Catholic Church. As for a mostly English-speaking Upper Canada, it provided for the British law and land tenure which Loyalists had sought. Yet the detailed features of the Act concerning Upper Canada can be left for now, to take up the very basic matter of boundaries. By an Order-in-Council of August 21, 1791, the line between the two new Canadas was drawn down the Ottawa to the St. Lawrence; but not quite. A little tip of land west of the Ottawa near its mouth remained to Lower Canada as holding its furthest seigneury — a mark of what Loyalism had wanted to be free of, in its own making of Upper Canada.

Districts of Upper Canada, c. 1788. In July of 1788, Lord Dorchester created four districts in western Quebec, giving them the German names, Luneburg, Mecklenburg, Nassau and Hesse. The four men superimposed on the map are David Zeisberger of Hesse, William Moll-Berczy of Nassau, Friedrich A. von Riedesel of Mecklenburg, and Johann S. Schwerdtfeger of Luneburg, four notable Germans involved in Upper Canada's history before 1795.

Map of Upper and Lower Canada, 1798. This map was made soon after the Constitutional Act or Canada Act of 1791 in order to show the newly formed provinces of Upper and Lower Canada.

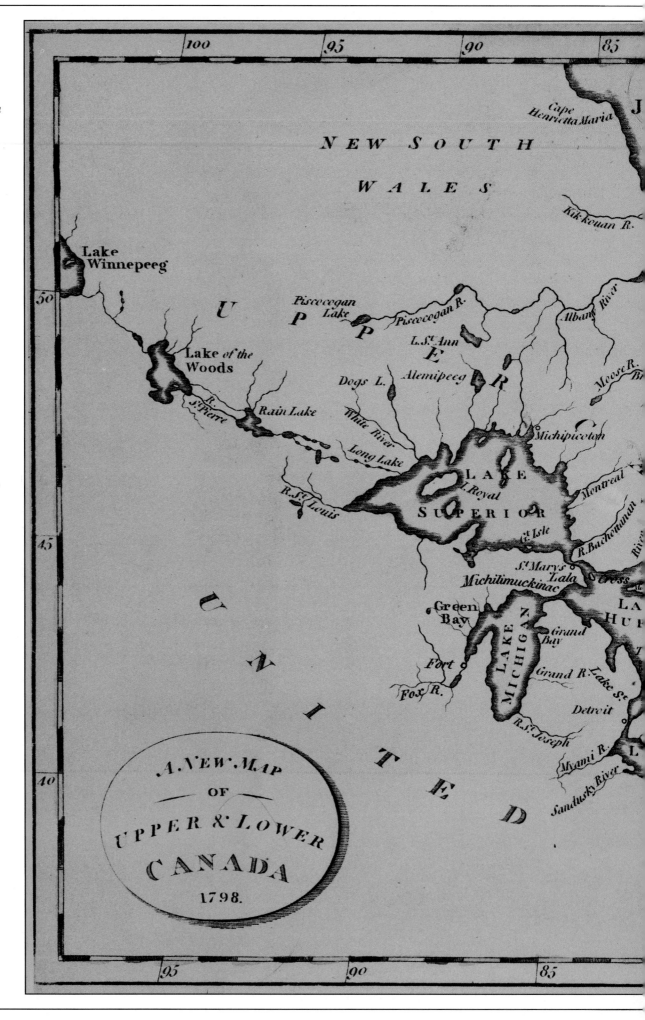

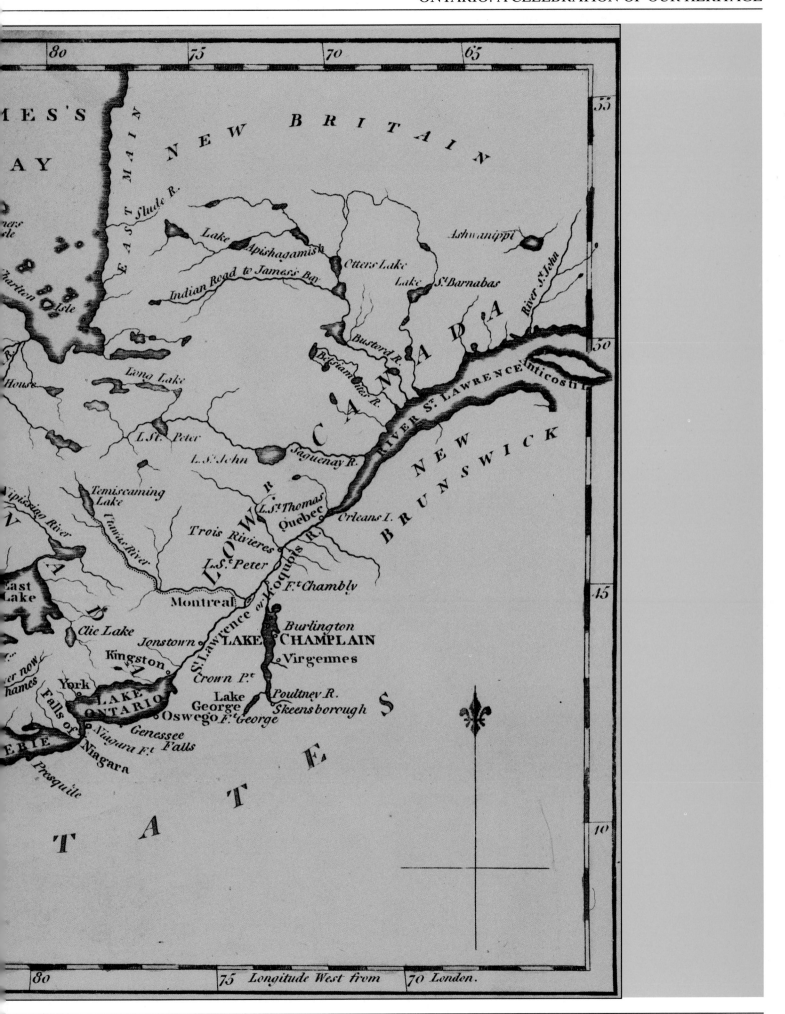

Chapter Four

The Building and Testing of Upper Canada: 1791-1814

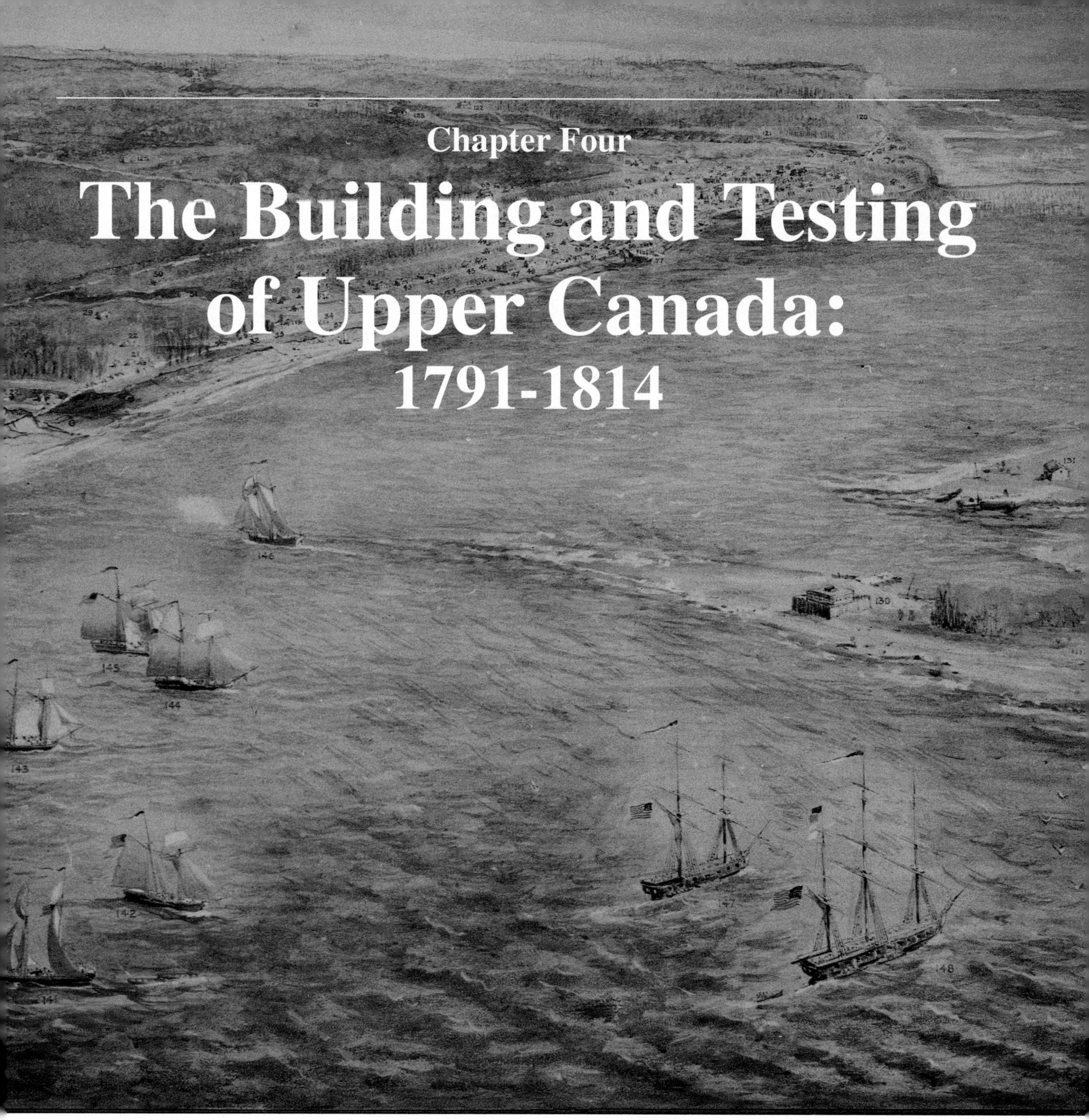

1811 Gen. Isaac Brock stationed in York
Battle of Tippecanoe

1812 Population of Upper Canada: c. 90,000
Population of Toronto: c. 700
June 18 - United States declares war: War of 1812 begins
July 17 - British capture Michilimackinac
August 16 - British capture Detroit
September 29 - Americans raid Gananoque, U.C.
October 13 - General Brock is killed; British win Battle of Queenston Heights, U.C.

1813 February 7 - Americans raid Brockville, U.C.
April 27 - Americans capture York, U.C.
May 15 - Captain James Yeo, Royal Navy, takes command of Lake naval forces
May 27 - Americans capture Fort George, U.C.
June 5-6 - British win Battle of Stoney Creek, U.C.
June 24 - British win Battle of Beaver Dams, U.C., after the heroic trek by Laura Secord informing them of Americans' positions
September 10 - Americans win Battle of Lake Erie
October 6 - Americans win Battle of Moraviantown, U.C.; Tecumseh is killed
November 11 - British win Battle of Crysler's Farm, U.C.
December 19 - British capture Fort Niagara, N.Y.

1814 July 5 - Americans win Battle of Chippewa, U.C.
July 25 - Battle of Lundy's Lane, U.C.; Americans withdraw
December 24 - Treaty of Ghent ends the war

The Shaping of Upper Canada

The founding Act of 1791 set the basic structure of Upper Canada for half a century, and began Ontario's parliamentary heritage by erecting a legislature of two houses. The upper house, the Legislative Council, would be appointed for life, to function much like Britain's powerful House of Lords in amending, passing or rejecting measures sent up from the lower chamber. It was, however, to have a minimum of only seven members to begin with; though this was in keeping with a population rising around 14,000 by 1791. The lower house, the Legislative Assembly, was a miniature colonial House of Commons that would devise laws and impose taxes, subject to the upper chamber's agreement. It was to be elected at least every four years, and initially to contain no less than sixteen members. They would be chosen in counties across the province by "forty-shilling free-

Overleaf. *Arrival of American fleet prior to the capture of York, 27 April 1813.* Watercolour by Owen Staples, c. 1914.
Below. *The Constitutional Act of 1791. This map shows the boundaries of Rupert's Land* (Terre de Rupert), *Upper Canada* (Haut-Canada) *and Lower Canada* (Bas-Canada) *as adopted for the Constitutional Act of 1791. It also has insets showing North America in 1791 (lower left) and the new governmental system (upper right).*

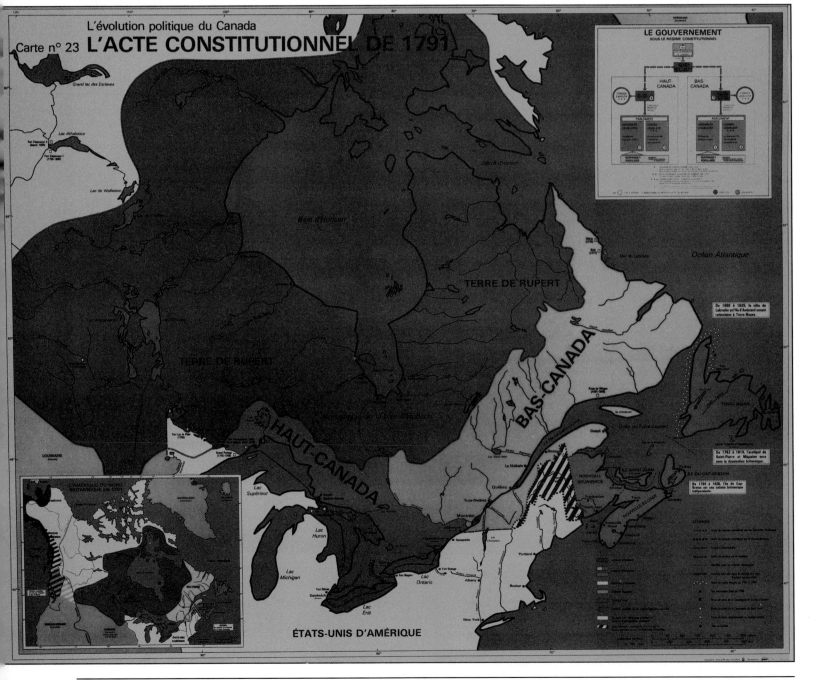

holders"; that is, by the owners of farm holdings that each were worth forty shillings, annually. This ancient franchise used in medieval English counties meant that a land-rich Upper Canada of family farms and not much landless population had a broad popular electorate from the start.

The Act as well had to deal with the executive powers of the Crown beyond the legislature. To exercise the King's authority, it provided a Lieutenant-Governor in each of the two Canadas, who was appointed by the imperial government in London and held wide sway over his province's political and administrative affairs. He could veto legislation or reserve it for imperial decision. He had local military command and sources of income independent of colonial parliamentary votes, plus control of immigration, the granting of Crown lands, and even more that kept him very much a ruling figure. To assist in administering the province, the Lieutenant-Governor also had his Executive Council, a traditional if ill-defined body of chief advisors and officials which was more taken for granted than spelled out in the Act of 1791. But since this appointed Council carried out the main government policies, it was to become the focus of an elite provincial power-group, and a Cabinet-to-be.

The whole Act which sought to transfer the revered British constitution to Canada was designed when Britain's own political

1., 3. *The Seal of Upper Canada, said to be designed by Governor John Graves Simcoe.*
2. *An open air gathering of members of the Upper Canada Legislative Assembly at Navy Hall, Niagara, 1792. One of the two houses of the legislature with the Legislative Council, the Legislative Assembly was a miniature colonial House of Commons. Initially, there were sixteen members who were elected at least every four years.* Oil on canvas by Charles Walter Simpson (1878-1942).

1

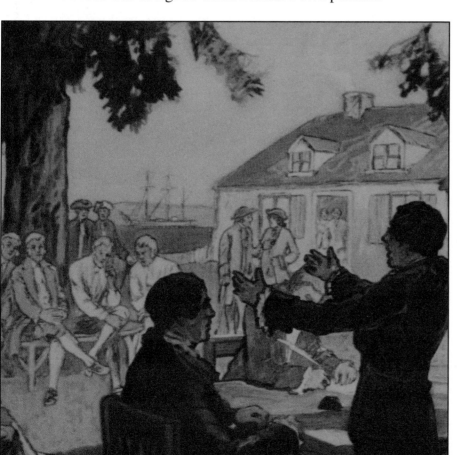

2

3

leadership was in a decidedly conservative phase, still reacting to the democratic revolutionary explosions in America, while uneasily watching the disorders of a new revolution on the rise in France. Accordingly, the Constitutional Act placed strong conservative checks upon Upper Canada: in the Lieutenant-Governor's broad ruling powers, in the solidly entrenched Legislative Council, which could toss out or replace bills sent up from an Assembly that might be all too full of hasty popular opinions, and generally, in the emphasis on established order that made "irresponsible" democratic views look suspect. Nevertheless, the Loyalists for whom the province had been made raised small objection. They were not at all submissive; but unchecked democracy to them darkly recalled republican excesses — rioting mobs, self-serving agitators, and ruinous anarchy. Hence there was slight attempt to question the conservative cast of early Upper Canadian government. Discords might develop between individuals in politics, or passing factions appear; still, no real consolidation of any opposition forces took shape. As a result, the political system that was laid down in 1791 served Upper Canada fairly well for some three decades to follow.

One other thing the Constitutional Act did was to strengthen public order and social control. It set up a state-endowed Anglican Church for Upper Canada by providing province-wide land grants to support a "Protestant clergy" — which then meant the ministers of

1. *First church built at Toronto. St. James' Anglican Church, as it was in 1816. The Constitutional Act set up a state-endowed Anglican Church for Upper Canada by providing land grants to support the Anglican clergy.*
2. *Portrait of Colonel John Graves Simcoe (1752-1806). Simcoe was an English soldier who was active throughout the American Revolutionary War during which he was made Commander of the Queen's Rangers. He became a member of the British Parliament in 1790 but left his seat vacant after he was commissioned Lieutenant-Governor of Upper Canada in September 1791. He arrived in Kingston, with his wife Elizabeth and their two children, in June of 1792.*

1

2

Anglicanism, the legally established faith in England. Chiefly Catholic Lower Canada already had state-enforced payment of tithes to its own priests. In largely Protestant Upper Canada, the social strength of organized religion was now to be assured by the Act's requiring that an amount equal to one seventh of all the Crown lands granted would henceforth be reserved to fund the Anglican Church. It was a weighty move that led to a host of future troubles; from the fact that Presbyterianism was just as much an established religion in the Scottish half of the United Kingdom but held no such Upper Canadian privileges, to the rise of discontented Methodist and other excluded Protestant sects, or to grievances that developed when unoccupied clergy-reserve lands seemed to block the spread of settlement. Still, in the early years of Upper Canada again, this part of the Act of 1791 raised no grave problems, since there was so much other wild land available for granting, and religious issues in a new land as yet were vague.

With the Constitutional Act passed by the summer of 1791, the British government went on to name the Lieutenant-Governor who would put Upper Canada into operation; although still under Lord Dorchester as Governor-in-Chief of both Canadas. That September, Colonel John Graves Simcoe was commissioned to direct the upper province, chosen over Dorchester's own preference, Sir John Johnson. Simcoe, an able English soldier who had fought in America right from 1775, and there commanded the Loyalist Queen's Rangers, had become a member of the British parliament in 1790. He had shared in the debates on the Constitutional Act, while to the authorities in London he urged his own ideas and interests in regard to serving in Upper Canada. Above all, he wanted to aid his "cherished soldiers," the Loyalists he had capably led throughout the conflict, earning their devotion, winning him distinction, wounds, and a period as prisoner of war. At times brusque or overbearing,

1. *The Queen's Rangers' Lodge Room at the Fort at York, 1795.* Print by W.J. Thomson.
2. *Robert Rogers, (1731-1795). Rogers was the founder of Roger's Rangers and the original Queen's Rangers.*
3. *A Light Infantry Man and "Huzzar" of the Queen's Rangers, c. 1780. The Queen's Rangers, a Loyalist unit, were raised in 1777, operated through the American Revolutionary War, and were commanded by John Graves Simcoe from 1777 to 1781. A second unit was recruited in England in 1791, also under Simcoe.*
4. *Sir Guy Carleton, Baron Dorchester. Guy Carleton, or Lord Dorchester, became the Governor in chief of both Canadas in 1786 and remained in that post until 1796.*
5. *Elizabeth Simcoe. Mrs. Simcoe produced a valuable record of Upper Canada in its earliest years through her diary and sketches.*

1

2

A Light Infantry Man & Huzzar of the Queen's Rangers.

3

4

5

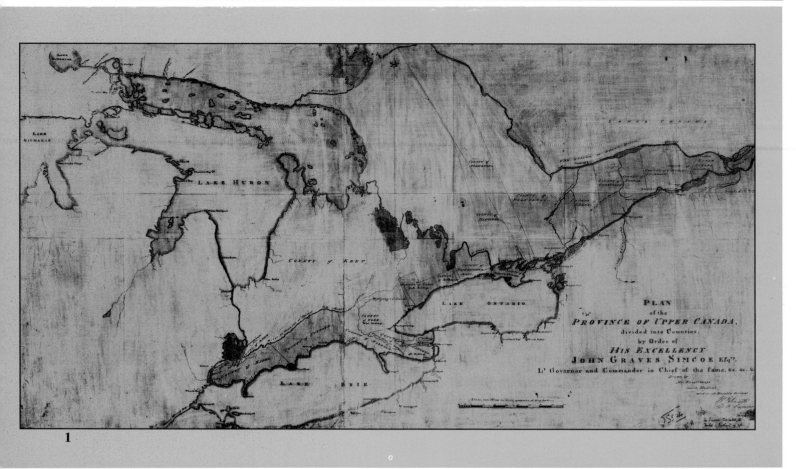

1

2

Simcoe might seem a hidebound, class-conscious Tory, sternly opposed to notions of equality or popular rule. Yet he was dynamic, warm-hearted, and bubbling with eager schemes for the province in his keeping, to make it a model of ordered British liberty and economic growth in order to show up the errors and shortcomings of the American experiment.

The new Lieutenant-Governor landed at Quebec in mid-November 1791, with his wife Elizabeth, plus two small children — and the lively, keen-minded Elizabeth Simcoe was to produce a vivid record of young Upper Canada in her published diary. But that infant province would not officially be proclaimed into life until late December, when the riverways were frozen over; nor could its governor be sworn in till his chief officials had arrived. Hence Simcoe spent the winter and spring in Lower Canada. There he consulted widely to

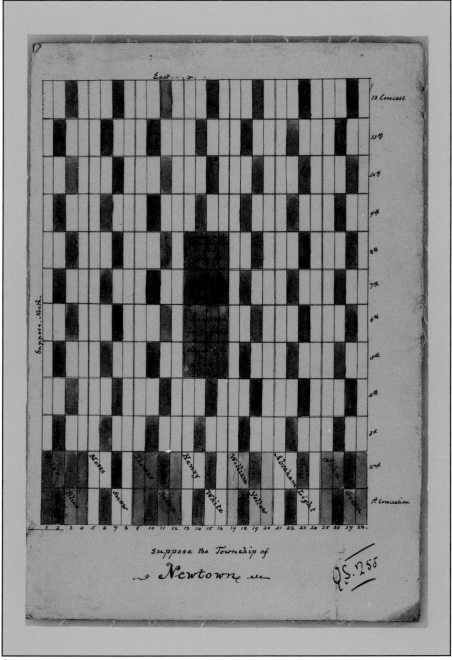

3

1. *Map of Upper Canada, drawn in 1793. The inscription on the map reads "PLAN of the PROVINCE OF UPPER CANADA, divided into Counties; by Order of HIS EXCELLENCY JOHN GRAVES SIMCOE Esqr., Lt. Governor and Commander in Chief of the same &c. &c. &c. Drawn by His Excellency's most obedient and most humble servant — [signed] W. Chewett, D.P. Surveyor."*

2. *An Upper Canada farm with partial improvements, from* The British Farmer's Guide to Ontario. *After Lieutenant-Governor Simcoe arrived in Quebec, he spent the winter there collecting information. In February 1792, he issued a proclamation promising 200-acre lots free to all who would settle in Upper Canada.*

3. *Crown and Clergy Reserves in Newtown. In February 1792, Simcoe issued a proclamation offering 200-acre lots free in Upper Canada to all who would settle and improve their grants, and take an oath of allegiance to the British Crown. As can be readily observed on this land survey drawn c. 1800, one-seventh of the land would be held back for clergy reserves and another seventh kept to produce government revenue; both these clergy and crown reserves would be distributed among the free-grant lots in a "checkerboard" design.*

collect information, and there in February, 1792, he issued a boldly promising proclamation of his own. It offered 200-acre lots free in Upper Canada to all who would settle and improve their grants, and take an oath of allegiance to the British crown. One seventh of the land, as surveyed into lots within townships, would be held back for clergy reserves, another seventh kept to produce government revenue; and both these clergy and crown reserves would be distributed among the free-grant lots in a kind of checkerboard design. News of this land policy, opening a huge store of fertile acres, spread into the United States, where speculators had locked up huge tracts to sell at their own prices. Simcoe believed, with some reason, that there were many passive Loyalists still left in the United States, and thus sought to draw them back to their "true" allegiance. But others there might also be drawn by the free-land offer, if they did not mind taking the oath. The result was that the governor did get his settlers, increasingly, though some of these Late Loyalists might turn out to be more late than loyal.

By June of 1792, Simcoe and family could go to Upper Canada, where at Kingston on July 8 he was sworn in before his Executive Council. That small group included Chief Justice William Osgoode, a notable London lawyer who was to set up English common-law practices for Upper Canada, William Jarvis, the Provincial Secretary, a Connecticut Loyalist and former Ranger officer, and Irish-born Peter Russell, Receiver General or treasurer, a professional British soldier who had become an efficient bureaucrat as well. Simcoe also appointed nine men to form the Legislative Council; among them,

1. *The Honourable Peter Russell (1773-1808). Russell was the Receiver General or treasurer in Simcoe's first Executive Council. He succeeded Simcoe in 1796 and became Chief Administrator of Upper Canada until a new governor was named in 1799.*
2. *The Honourable William Osgoode, (1754-1824). Osgoode was the first Chief Justice of Upper Canada.*
3. *A photo (c. 1923) of the building used for the First Legislature in 1792.*
4. *Lieutenant-Governor Simcoe opening the First Legislature in 1792. Simcoe was sworn in before his Executive Council in Kingston on July 8, 1792. Simcoe moved his seat of government to Newark (now Niagara-on-the-Lake) in that same month.*

1

2

3

4

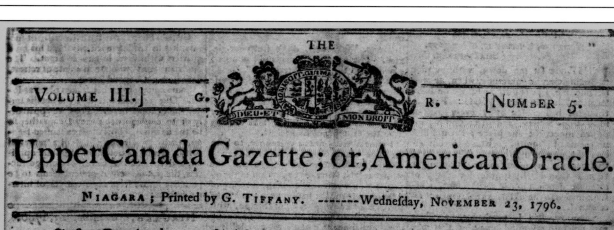

THE

Upper Canada Gazette; or, American Oracle.

NIAGARA; Printed by G. TIFFANY. -------Wednesday, NOVEMBER 23, 1796.

Volume III.] G. R. **[NUMBER 5.**

Just Received,
And for SALE at the
Printing-Office,
IN NIAGARA,
The following assortment of
BOOKS.
AMONG WHICH ARE,

QUARTO and School Bibles, Testaments, Prayer and Psalm Books, Cloud of Witn. Volney's Ruins, Willison's Balm of Gilead, Adventurer, by Hawksworth; Memoirs of Dumourier, Anson's Voyage. Harvey's Meditations, Morse's Universal Geography, 2 vol. Blackston's Commentaries, Johnson's Dictionary, Belknap's Answer to Pain; Bennet's Letters, Royal Captive, Life of the King of Prussia, 2 vol. 8vo. Moore's Journal 2 vol. 12mo. Franklin's Life with essays 2 vol. Burn's Poems, Cook's Life by Keppis, Lendrums American Revolution 2 vol. 12mo. Vicar of Wakefield, Moore's Travels 2 vol. Sheridan's Dictionary 2 vol. Buchan's Domestic Medecine, Scotland Delineated, Pelgrims Progress, Sherlock on Death, West on the Resurrection, Boston on the Covenant of Works, Rowe's devout exercise of the Heart, Oeconomy of Human Life, Gulliver's Travels, Washington's Letters 2 vol. Watt's Sermons 2 vol. Paley's Evidence, Rasselas Prince of Abissinia, Sorrows of Werter, Fool of quality 5 vol. Man of Feeling, Roderick Random 2 vol. Joseph Andrews, Man of the World, Idler by Johnson 2 vol. Eloisa 3 vol. Don Quixote 4 vol. History of the Devil, Citizen of the World 2 vol. Goldsmith's Essays, Confession of Faith, Religious Courtship, Robison Crusoe, Perigrine Pickle 4 vol. Watts and Dodridge's Life by Kippis, Logan's Sermons 2 vol. Paley's Philosophy, Junius's Letters, Arabian Knights Entertainment 2 vol. Lounger 2 vol. Brydonn's Tour, Afflicted Man's Companion, Boston's Four-fold State, Dodd's Thoughts, Dodridge's Sermons on Education, Kaim's Sketches 2 vol. Duncan's Logick—Johnson's Lives of the Poets 4 vol. Watts on the human Mind, Guardian, 2 vol. Rights of Women, Spirit of Laws 2 vol. Morse's Geography for the use of Schools—Gardiner's Life by Dodridge—Death of Abel—Marshal on Sanctification—Fordyce's Sermons 2 vol. Dodridge's rise and progress of religion. Poorman's help and young man's guide, General Songster, Akenside's Poems, Prideaux' Life of Mahomet, Lucky Idiot—Gacesby's Life, M'Alpine, Robison Crusoe abridged, Don Quixote, abridged, History of the American Rebellion, Esops Fables, Bunyan's Water of life, Complete Saviour, Solomon's Temple Spiritualized, Come and Welcome to Christ, War Atlas by Carey, Delolme on the Constitution of England—Ramsey's American war 2 vol. late edition, Lock's Memoirs, Infernal conference, Watt's Holy war, do. Greats, co. Heavenly Footman, Simon the Sorcerer, Erskine's Speeches, History of St. Tammany, Borlow's Hasty Pudding, Porcupine's Life, Pain on the Funding System, Burke's Letters, Seneca's Morals, New-year's Gift, Sentimental Journey, Doubtful Marriage, Embassy to China, Saint's Rest, Volney's Ruins, Farmer's Letters, Miss William's do. 4 vol. Vattel's Law of Nations—Cecelia, 3 vol. Rowe's Letters, Farmer's Friend, Hale's Contemplation 2 vol. Monitor, Family Instructor, Reign of Grace, Italian Nun, Letter on Courtship, Defence of Christianity—Student and Pastor, Political Fugative—Wilson on the Sacrament, do. on Meditation, Spiritual Letters, Mother's Catechism, Pain's Builder, do. Pocket Treasurer, President Washington's Messages, Watt's Miscellany, The Young Clerk's Magazine, Watt's Lyric Poems, Promptor, Saunder's Journal, Blair's Sermons, 3 vol. do. Lectures, 2 vol. Addison's Evidence, Brissot on Commerce, Love's Surveying, Watt's on the Passions, Willison's Afflicted Man, Principles of Politeness, Clark's Farriery, Pike's Arithmetic—The Hive, Inquisitor, The Complete Woman Cook,—Faithful Servant a sermon,—Columbas on the discovery of America,—Milton's Works, President Washington's Speeches, M'Ewen on the Types—Sky Lark, Tatler, 4 vol. Humphrey Clinker, Dodd's Beauties of History, Indian Cottage, Fairy Tales, History of a Reprobate, Story Teller, Journey to Jerusalem, Pelew Islands Dodd on Death, Vicar of Wakefield, Webster's 2d part, Gamuts and Books for the Vocal Music, Song Books and Pamphlets of various kinds, Children's gilt books and Primers,

An assortment of BLANK BOOKS,
—ALSO—
Gentlemen's Pocket-Books, Quills, &c. &c. &c.

N. B. THE above being a consignment, ready payment in cash will be expected.
November 2, 1796.

NOW preparing, and will in a few days be committed to the PRESS,

The Upper-Canada
CALENDAR:
FOR THE YEAR
1797.

Being a pocket almanack, containing, beside astronomical calculations, lists of the legislative, executive, and military officers, times and places of holding courts, &c. &c. *Being the first work of the kind ever attempted in this province.*

The publisher most respectfully solicits the assistence of every gentleman who possesses the means of promoting the design, by furnishing him with articles properly arranged, such particulars as may be in their power. Printing-office, Nov. 16.

For Sale,
Either together or in LOTS of
Ten Acres
each, and possession given immediately, SEVENTY ACRES of
WOOD LAND
In the neighborhood of the town of Newark, being a parallelogram; bounded on the south by a line, running due west, 37 chains and 50 links, close to Mr. M'FARLAND's north line; thence due north, 18 chains, and 80 links, along Mr. ARENT BRADT's land; thence due east, 37 chains, and 50 links; thence due south, 18 chain, and 80 links, to Mr. M'Farland's land, at the place of beginning. The terms to be known by *applying to the honorable*

PETER RUSSELL.
—WHO WILL ALSO DISPOSE OF BY—
Sale or Lease,
And give possession in October next, the REMAINDER OF HIS
LAND
In the township of Newark, consisting of about 130 Acres, fifty of them under good fences, on which there are a
Commodious Dwelling,
Coach house, stable, and other offices, all built within three years:—Terms to be known by applying as above.
Newark, October 18, 1796.

Advertisement.
DEEDS of bargain and sale, lease and release, mortgage, gift, transfer, exchange &c. of lands, houses &c. indentures, contracts, agreements, letters of attorney, wills settlements, memorials, petitions, and all kinds of instruments in writing required, will be drawn up and ingrossed on the shortest notice, and most reasonable terms, by a gentleman who has come to reside in this town, with the intention of giving his time and attention wholly to that line of business, and has supplied himself with the most approved forms, and legal instructions in conveyancing.—For further particulars apply at the office of As. M'DONELL, Esq.
November 16.

At private Sale.
TO be sold, one half share of those valuable Grist and Saw MILLS, with the whole of the two hundred acres on which the same stand, being in the well situated township of Ancaster, and Home district;—The terms of sale will be made known by applying to the Printer, Mr. James Willon of Newark, and to Richard Beatly, esq. Burlington Bay.
October 5, 1796.

Richard Cartwright, prominent Kingston Loyalist, Robert Hamilton, Niagara's top merchant, and Jacques Baby, a Detroit fur trader and leading member of its nearby French-Canadian community. Baby also served as Inspector General and sat in the Executive Council. But nothing then prevented individuals being members of both bodies, as Osgoode and Russell were. A struggling pioneer community had other tasks to fill its time, and few were qualified or ready for government duties. So the system was largely left to a small ruling clique, which gave generally acceptable service in these early years.

Simcoe moved on to Niagara before July was out, having besides set up counties in Upper Canada and called elections in them for the first Legislative Assembly. At Niagara, he and his family settled into Navy Hall in Newark on the Ontario side, the village which now became his seat of government. For though the chief Loyalist community, Kingston, already had some 400 residents, it seemed too far east of the province's centre, especially to a governor who also saw the western peninsula beyond as the future key to the Great Lakes heart of America. Then on September 17, 1792, Upper Canada's parliament met at Newark in a recently erected Freemason's Hall: with proper ceremony supplied by the Queen's Rangers, who had been freshly raised in England (but with some Loyalist veteran officers)

1. *Front Page of the* Upper Canada Gazette, *November 23, 1796. The first advertisement in the right-hand column of the paper was placed by Peter Russell.*
2. *Simcoe in Navy Hall, Newark, (Niagara). Simcoe moved with his family to Navy Hall in July 1792 and Newark became his seat of government.* Photolithograph J.D. Kelly, 1910.

2

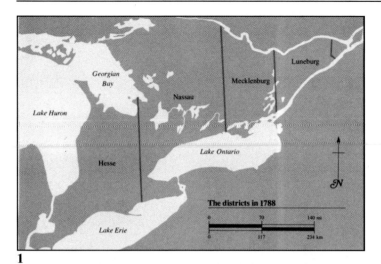

The districts in 1788

1

The districts in 1802

2

The districts in 1849

3

On Tuesday laft His Excellency went to the Council Chamber and gave his Affent to the following Acts:

✓ An Act for the better regulation of the Militia of this Province.

✓ An Act to eftablish a Court of Probate in this Province, and alfo a Surrogate Court in every diftrict thereof.

✓ An Act to confirm and make valid certain Marriages heretofore contracted in the Country, now comprized within the Province of Upper Canada, and to provide for the future folemnization of Marriages within the fame.

✓ An Act to provide for the appointment of Returning Officers for the feveral Counties within this Province.

✓ An Act to encourage the deftroying of Woolves and Bears in different parts of this Province.

✓ An Act to regulate the laying out, amending and keeping in repair the public Highways and Roads within this Province.

✓ An Act to prevent the further introduction of Slaves and to limit the term of Contracts for fervitude within this Province.

✓ An Act to provide for the nomination and appointment of Parifh and Town Officers throughout this Province.

✓ An Act to fix the times and places of holding the General Quarter Seffions of the Peace within the feveral Diftricts of this Province.

✓ An Act to eftablish a fund for paying the Salaries of the Officers of the Legiflative Council and Houfe of Affembly; & for defraying the Contingent Expences thereof.

✓ An Act to authorize the Lieutenant Governor to nominate and appoint certain Commiffioners for the purpofes therein mentioned.

✓ An Act to authorize and direct the levying and collecting of affefsments and rates in every Diftrict of this Province and to provide for the Payment of Wages to the Members of the Houfe of Affembly.

✓ An Act to eftablish a further fund for the Payment of the Salaries of the Officers of the Legiflative Council and Affembly, and for defraying the Contingent Expences thereof;—

After which his Excellency prorogued the Legiflature of this Province to the 26th day of next September, and made the following fpeech:

HONORABLE GENTLEMEN, and GENTLEMEN,

IT gives me great fatisfaction that by your unremitting diligence, the public bufinefs of the Seffion has been fo far transacted, that I am enabled to confult your

4

BY HIS EXCELLENCY
JOHN GRAVES SIMCOE, Efquire,
Lieutenant Governor and Colonel Commanding His Majefty's Forces in Upper Canada, &c. &c. &c.

PROCLAMATION.

 WHEREAS I have received Official Information from one of His Majefty's principal Secretaries of State, that the Perfons exercifing the Supreme Authority in France, did DECLARE WAR againft His Majefty on the firft Day of February laft, and have alfo received the King's commands to caufe the fame to be made as public as poffible in this Province.

PUBLIC NOTICE is hereby given thereof, to all His Majefty's faithful Subjects to the end that they may take care, on the one hand, to prevent any Mifchief which otherwife they might fuffer from the French, and on the other may do their utmoft in their feveral ftations to diftrefs, and annoy them by making captures of their fhips, and by deftroying their commerce; for which purpofe his Majefty has been pleafed to order Letters of Marque or Commiffions of Privateers to be granted in the ufual manner, and has alfo gracioufly fignified his intention of giving up to the owner of all armed fhips and veffels, his fhare of all French fhips and property, of which they may make prize.

Given under my Hand and Seal at Arms, at Navy Hall this fourteenth day of May, in the Year of our Lord One thoufand feven hundred and Ninety-three, and in the Thirty-third of his Majefty's Reign.

J. GRAVES SIMCOE.

By His Excellency's Command,
WM. JARVIS, Secretary.

GOD SAVE THE KING.

5

according to Simcoe's own suggestion, and brought out both to defend and help build the new loyal province. This first legislature put English civil law and jury trial into effect, renamed Upper Canada's four districts Eastern, Midland, Home and Western, while providing a court house and jail in each, and did some other useful organizing work before closing in October. It was just a beginning, but a solid one.

In the early months of 1793, the busy governor crossed the country westward to Detroit, and decided to build a military road to open it — Dundas Street, from the head of Lake Ontario to the Thames River, which the Rangers started building that summer. In fact, Simcoe conceived a network of roads with towns upon them, and envisioned a future capital city at the forks of the Thames, where London now stands, deep in the richly fertile western peninsula. For the present, however, he planned to put his capital at Toronto Bay on Lake Ontario. If Kingston was too far east, and subject to American attack each winter across the frozen St. Lawrence, Niagara was exposed year-round, being easily under American guns right at the border. But Toronto was not only the gateway to the Toronto Passage north to the Upper Lakes or the Ottawa route, but also had the wide (and never frozen) reaches of Lake Ontario between it and the United States. A British fleet based on Toronto, as the "naval arsenal" of the province, could keep the Lake secure. Simcoe without doubt thought in such strategic and defensive terms; yet not unreasonably, given growing strains along the American border and the still unsettled issue of the border posts. In any case, his views and his authority brought the founding of the town of York in July, 1793, later to become the city of Toronto, and remain Ontario's capital today. The Rangers built a garrison base at the entry to Toronto's roomy,

1. *The original four administrative districts of Hesse, Nassau, Mecklenburg, and Luneburg were renamed Western, Home, Midland, and Eastern in 1792.*
2. *By 1802, these four were subdivided because of increased population.*
3. *By 1849, there were nineteen different districts, counties being electoral units within them.*
4. *This list of the Acts passed by the new legislature of Upper Canada was published in the* Upper Canada Gazette *on July 11, 1793.*
5. *This proclamation, placed in the* Upper Canada Gazette *by Simcoe on May 16, 1793, reflects the way in which French-English relations in Europe had direct influence in Ontario. In the proclamation people are even encouraged to raid French ships because France had declared war on England.*
6. *Plan showing the original Castle Frank. Named after his young son, it became the home of Lieutenant-Governor Simcoe. It was Simcoe's views and authority that brought about the founding of the town of York in July 1793, later to become the City of Toronto, which still remains Ontario's capital today.*
7. *This monument in Queen's Park, Toronto, commemorates Simcoe as the first Lieutenant-Governor of Upper Canada.*

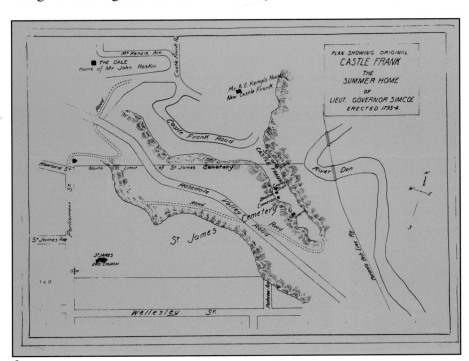

6

7

sheltered harbour, and worked on the York townsite, a dockyard and a sawmill. Meanwhile Simcoe travelled the Toronto Passage to Lake Huron, returning with new enthusiasms for the country he had crossed, and planning a main road north from York to open lands to settlement — which could also provide a route by road and river to the Upper Lakes, and naval control there. Thus came Yonge Street, two years later.

A more pressing issue also rose in 1793: conflict between the United States and the western Indian tribes south of the Great Lakes, which threatened to involve the British and certainly made the problem of the border forts far more acute and dangerous. Simcoe himself by no means wanted to see weak Upper Canada caught up in war. He had hoped instead that a united front by the western tribes could win American acceptance of a proposal to keep the territory between the Lakes and the Ohio river a neutral, Indian-held zone, thus protecting Upper Canada from American expansionism. The Indian front broke up, however, largely because Joseph Brant, at the head of the Six Nations, thought such a plan sadly unrealistic, and urged compromise with the increasingly powerful Americans. There was none; conferences failed. In 1794 a strong new American army launched a campaign against the western tribes, while Dorchester ordered Simcoe to build a fort in the Ohio country to guard its links with Detroit. That August, American troops came up to this still unfinished Fort Meigs, hot with victory, having just defeated the Indians decisively in the nearby Battle of Fallen Timbers. War was close; but cooler heads prevailed, and the Americans withdrew.

Moreover, Anglo-American negotiations had already begun in London in June 1794, where John Jay, United States Chief Justice, had led a mission. Jay's Treaty was signed in November. It brought a British agreement to give up the border posts by June 1, 1796, and American assent to settling the Loyalist claims at last. The Indians' rights were supposedly to be negotiated by the United States; but the defeated tribes got little in their Treaty of Greenville with the

1. *After the founding of York in July 1793, the Rangers built a garrison base at the entry to Toronto's harbour, and worked on the York townsite, a dockyard and a sawmill.*

2. *Plan of the Battle of the Fallen Timbers, 1794. This print, published in B.J. Lossing's* The Pictorial Field-Book of the War of 1812, *shows the battle in which the Americans decisively defeated the Indians.*

3. *Kingston was not chosen as the first capital of the young province in part because it was too far east. It also was subject to attack from the United States each winter across the frozen St. Lawrence, as can be seen by this photograph which includes the fort at Kingston and part of the St. Lawrence.* A27083-170.

4. *Niagara was not chosen to be the capital because it was exposed to American guns right at the border year-round. This photo shows the close proximity of Forts George (Canadian, built farther up-stream) and Niagara (American fort built nearer the Lake).* A18949-66.

5. *American Fort Niagara.* A26995-127.

6. *Canadian Fort George.* A26995-128.

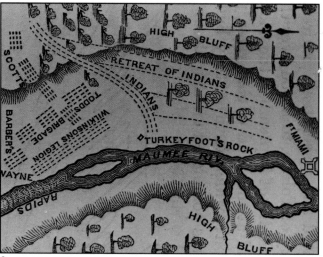

1

2

3

4

5

6

American republic in 1795, and gave up most of the Ohio country in the process. For Upper Canada, however, its own border perils had been lifted — for the present.

The emphasis now was on settlement and economic progress. More American Loyalists certainly entered the province to obtain new lands under the old Crown, while others came up from New Brunswick clearings, when their prospects looked less promising there. Many of these latecomers went to existing settled areas, but some opened a tract at Long Point on Lake Erie. As well, the abandonment of Fort Detroit brought Loyalists already settled on the American side over to the Ontario shore, where French-Canadian farm-dwellers had long been established. And at the Niagara River the evacuation of the old fort on the American bank brought its replacement by Fort George, begun by Simcoe, on the Canadian side at Newark. But far more widely significant, in the long-run, was the rise of non-Loyalist or Post-Loyalist American migration, as settlers came in mounting numbers just to get good lands free.

This movement commencing under Simcoe, and continuing long after, carried in ordinary American frontiersmen seeking farms. Yet also, some German settlers entered, led by William Berczy, land agent and talented artist, who brought them away from arrangements he did not like in up-state New York to the grant he was offered in 1794 by Simcoe in Markham township northeast of York. Berczy's men helped build the early town of York; and more than that, worked on Yonge Street, which the governor ordered the Queen's Rangers to cut northward through the forests in 1795. By April, 1796, Yonge Street was open (very roughly) for horses, foot and ox-cart travel to Holland Landing on waters entering Lake Simcoe. Settlement soon

1. *The Right Honourable Sir George Yonge, (1731-1812). Yonge Street was named after Yonge who sat in Parliament 1754-1796 and was Secretary for War 1782-1783 and 1783-1794.*

2. *Yonge Street was cut through the forests in a straight line northward from the early town of York. The clearing of land and settlement soon followed in its path.*

1

2

began to spread along this path.

Simcoe in 1796 also put the Rangers to raising parliament buildings at York (in brick), and instructed those officials still at Niagara to move to the new capital which was almost ready. They came unwillingly, from comfortable homes and gardens at Newark to a muddy, raw forest hamlet. Still, they came, because of the governor's compelling voice. Parliament, too, would meet at York in 1797; but by then Simcoe was gone. He had been worn down by constant activity, frustrated by Dorchester's chill opposition to his bright Upper Canadian dreams. And his health had suffered so much that doctors recommended a leave in England. He never came back, being ordered later to the Caribbean instead, to command British forces at San Domingo in the French Revolutionary War which now was raging around the world. Yet this first governor who left Upper Canada in the fall of 1796 had done a great deal in five vital, founding years.

Apart from setting the whole provincial system in motion, and putting his own strong imprint on it, he had actively invited farming settlement, encouraged trade and towns, established Toronto, laid out trunk roads; and as well, had reinforced the Loyalist Ontario heritage of order and conservatism — yet with a constant practical emphasis on economic growth. Furthermore, if any present-day critics tend to dismiss him as an old-guard Tory, let it be noted that it was largely Simcoe who pushed for, and in 1793 achieved, the effective ending of black slavery in Upper Canada as false to British freedom, though slavery was not to be abolished in the British empire generally until 1833, or in the popular, democratic United States until 1863.

The first parliament buildings, York, 1797-1813. Built by the Queen's Rangers in 1796, parliament first met in York (Toronto) in 1797. Simcoe also ordered all the officials to come from Niagara and, reluctantly, they did. The buildings were destroyed in the American raid during the War of 1812.

Immigration and American Influence

Simcoe was succeeded in Upper Canada by Peter Russell, his Receiver General and senior councillor, who directed the province as Administrator until a new governor was named in 1799. Russell diligently carried on his former master's work. He expanded York, and ordered a road cut west from it to connect with Dundas Street, and with the lakeshore path around to Niagara. He also contracted with Asa Danforth, an American, to open another route, the "Danforth Road," east to the Bay of Quinte, thus linking up with the Loyalist settlements that reached on to Kingston. This Lake Ontario front was filling in by now, mainly with Post-Loyalist Americans, who as well were taking up lands between the Niagara Loyalist area and the head of the lake.

Russell further tried to control land grants and speculation at a time when settlers were so widely moving in from the United States. Undoubtedly he and fellow councillors in government amassed large holdings of their own. Rather than some high-level conspiracy, however, this reflected Simcoe's own practice of making major grants to leading figures who then were to promote settlement. And it also reflected a society where land seemed nearly inexhaustible but money was scarce; so that high officials might be given additional acres instead of cash for government payments owed to them. Because of the shortfall in his salary, the Attorney-General, John White, in fact had to dig his own potatoes and chop his own firewood at York in 1798. Nevertheless, the government elite and their leading merchant allies did build up estates of high later value; decidedly including Peter Russell, who was a reliable but uninspired civil servant, except when it came to collecting property, where he shone. Yet while Russell remained a notable resident of York till his death in 1808, he largely became just one of the Executive Council group after General Peter Hunter took over as governor in 1799. Hunter, a Scottish soldier, was also named commander-in-chief of the forces in Canada. As a result, he was often away from his capital on military duties, which meant that the little core of resident councillors at York got even more into the habit of running things themselves. Hence the

1. *The body of this proclamation printed in the* Upper Canada Gazette, *October 12, 1796, reads as follows: "WHEREAS his most gracious majesty has been pleased to grant his royal leave of absence to his excellency major general SIMCOE, lieutenant governor, and commander in chief of this province, and to appoint me to administer the government of the said province, that all his majesty's officers and employments, I . . . issue this proclamation, authorizing the said officers,* to continue in their said offices and employments. . . ." *Simcoe never came back from this leave taken for health reasons, as he was ordered later to the Caribbean instead. In 1799 he was succeeded by Peter Russell.*

2. *The Reverend John Strachan, (1778-1867). Strachan came to Upper Canada in 1798 and began teaching school in Kingston before entering the Anglican ministry. He was the first Anglican bishop of Toronto from 1839 to 1867. Strachan, a champion of Conservatism, was also very influential politically.*

3. *Sir Francis Gore, (1769-1852). Gore was an English army officer and former Governor of Bermuda. He became Lieutenant-Governor of Upper Canada in 1806 and held that post to 1817. Gore, however, was absent from Upper Canada during the War of 1812, during which military authorities ran the province.*

4. *William Warren Baldwin, (1775-1844). Baldwin, both a doctor and a lawyer, became the champion of Reform in politics. He was an early Liberal who advocated the idea of "responsible government."*

By Authority.

By the honorable PETER RUSSELL, esquire, administering the government of his majesty's Province of Upper Canada, &c. &c. &c.

A PROCLAMATION.

WHEREAS his most gracious majesty has been pleased to grant his royal leave of absence to his excellency major general SIMCOE, lieutenant governor, and commander in chief of this province, and to appoint me to administer the government of the said province, that all his majesty's officers within the same should continue in their several offices and employments, I have thought fit by and with the advice of his majesty's council, to issue this proclamation, authorizing the said officers, *to continue in their said offices and employments*, of which all persons concerned are required to take notice and govern themselves accordingly.

GIVEN under my hand and seal at arms, at Niagara, this eleventh day of September, in the year of our Lord one thousand seven hundred and ninety-six, and of his majesty's reign, the thirty-sixth.

By his honor's command,
WM. JARVIS, sec.

1

2

3

4

future ruling oligarchy, the "Family Compact," might well be dated from here.

Governor Hunter, moreover, died suddenly while away at Quebec in 1805, and was replaced by Alexander Grant, another Scot, who had indeed served on the Executive Council from the very beginning. Yet Grant, too, as naval "Commodore of the western lakes," had often been absent; and his brief position as Administrator till 1806 did not change things much. Then Francis Gore became Lieutenant-Governor, an English army officer and former governor of Bermuda who held his Upper Canadian post till 1817. He went to England on leave in 1811, however, after which military authorities ran the province during the War of 1812-14. So Gore's return after the war was brief, and his absence over the critical war years may have lessened his reputation. None the less, in the pre-war period he showed himself shrewd and hard-working, if sometimes impatient and high-handed. And he was on his mettle in dealing with Thomas Thorpe, a rambunctious Irish judge appointed to Canada, who soon got himself elected to the Assembly. In 1807, Thorpe gathered a loose opposition around him there to denounce the government and the Scottish influence allegedly behind it — till Gore got his judgeship suspended, and the ex-judge sailed back to Britain. It might be tempting to see this and a few similar factional outbursts at the time as the birth of Reform; but in truth, it was less a clash of principles and policies than of Irish-Scottish animosities or personal feelings and interests. For some years yet, therefore, the government group continued securely to provide their not unworthy, not too efficient services; though serenely conscious of their own worth and scorning attacks from mere "troublemakers" like Thorpe.

But other early Irish or Scots immigrants stayed to make a name in Upper Canadian politics and society, such as William Allan, Aberdeenshire merchant, who settled at Niagara in the 1790s, but moved to York in 1800 to become its postmaster and customs col-

The Cairn raised by the Glengarry Highlanders, c. 1843. Four hundred Catholic Highlanders from a disbanded regiment, the Glengarry Fencibles, were located in Glengarry County with their families among their fellow Catholic clansmen, Highland Loyalists, who had arrived there twenty years earlier. Lithograph by Edward W. Battye (active 1817-1852).

necessarily took
emigration fina

Meanwhile, t
part of the whol
frontier was nov
northern flank l.
west might read
upper St. Lawre
some settlement
Lake Erie on to
Indian threats w
took the safer, of
freely available f
very low taxes; s
expenses from de
United States had
burdens had ever
stimulated mover

Frontiersmen d
great strain to tak
allegiance in whic
that not all Ameri
engrained nationa
and Patriots in the
non-political. And
among back-coun
in their hard work
they were left to fa
down in Upper Ca
equality and espec
tantism was also p

lector — and do still more as banker and capitalist later. Or there was William Warren Baldwin, born in Ireland near Cork, and an Edinburgh graduate in medicine, whose well-connected Anglo-Irish family took up property east of York in 1798. Baldwin moved into York itself in 1802, where he not only practiced medicine but became a lawyer also — and besides that, opened one of the first schools for boys in the town. With a first-class mind, boundless energy, and ample social grace, the urbane Doctor became the trusted lawyer of Elizabeth Russell, who had been left her brother Peter's large estate when he died an elderly bachelor. Doctor Baldwin married Elizabeth's niece: there was no hanky-panky here, but a sincere marriage within a small-town circle of families. Still, the upshot was to make Baldwin a prominent landowner himself. And all to the good, in easing his way when he subsequently became a champion of Reform in politics, a Liberal who would powerfully advocate a new idea — "responsible government."

An even more powerful future champion of Conservatism arrived when John Strachan, of the universities of Aberdeen and St. Andrews, came to Upper Canada in 1798 to take charge of the college projected for the province by Simcoe — but which would not actually be brought into being for several decades more. Hence Strachan began teaching school at Kingston, for the children of Richard Cartwright and other eminent Loyalists. Yet soon he entered the Anglican ministry (one might recall that many Scots then were Anglicans) and in 1803 was made the rector of Cornwall. At Cornwall, too, he ran a school which gained high repute, attracting the sons of leading families in Upper Canada. For whatever else Strachan was — fierily eloquent, sternly determined, stubbornly unbending — he was an excellent and dedicated teacher, who did a great deal for education in Ontario. More than that, his political (and Tory) influences on Upper Canada would be profound, almost from 1812 when he moved to York as rector, and onward through three decades to follow.

Of course, British immigrants well beyond describing here also arrived in this era between the Simcoe years and the War of 1812. But generally speaking, they were small in number. They tended to

Colonel Thomas Talbot, (1771-1853). Talbot was a member of the Legislative Council from 1822 to 1832. In 1803 he received a large tract of land on Lake Erie and established Port Talbot as his home and headquarters.

garrisons, but now it became the largest single religious element in the province.

Incoming Americans took lands up Yonge Street as well as along the Lake Ontario front. In Lake Erie areas, they went into the Thames Valley and to the Talbot Settlement. And besides largely filling a broad band along the Lower Lakes, around or behind original Loyalist areas, they also moved into the Ottawa valley, beginning large-scale timber operations there. Lumbering, of course, widely accompanied farm settlement, to supply timber for homes, farm buildings, bridges and more; so that sawmills soon followed tree-cutting. But on the Ottawa, the dense, tall pineries of that district invited the hewing of great "sticks" of red and white pine, that could be floated down the river for sale to mills at Montreal and Quebec, or — far more likely — be sent by sea from Quebec to the timber markets of Britain. Philemon Wright, who opened the Ottawa square-timber trade, came from Massachusetts in 1800 and established a small farm community at Hull on the Lower Canadian side of the river. In 1806, he took the first raft of heavy beams down the Ottawa. Lumbering soon spread on both sides of the river, aided especially by very favourable tariff rates from 1809 in Britain, which needed wood (especially for ships) from British North America, when Napoleon had cut off European sources. Consequently, the Ottawa area became a lumber empire for both the Canadas, an empire which flourished and spread greatly after 1815, but which began with American migration in the pre-war period.

Other settlers who moved from the United States were not ordinary frontier farmers, but came in distinctive religious groups, often known as the Plain Folk. These were small Protestant sects, many of them non-English-speaking, who stressed plainness and simplicity in religion as they did in dress and social custom. Mainly European immigrants, and generally pacifists in belief, they had faced a good

1. Floating timber down the Ottawa River. As well as occupying lands along Lake Ontario and Lake Erie, American settlers moved into the Ottawa valley and began large-scale timber operations there. The lumber was made into rafts to be sent down to Montreal and Quebec. They sometimes reached 300 metres and needed thirty to forty men to manage them. The job was often dangerous due to the many rapids on the Ottawa.
2. Residence of Philemon Wright near the cleft of the Chaudière Falls on the Ottawa, c. 1836-1842. Wright came from Massachusetts in 1800 and opened the Ottawa square timber trade. Watercolour by Philip John Bainbrigge (1817-1881).
3. Mill and tavern of Philemon Wright at Chaudière Falls, Hull, 1823. He first established a farm community at Hull on the Lower Canadian side of the Ottawa. By Henry DuVernet (active 1816-1842).
4. The Timber Slide, Hull, Lower Canada. "Slides" carried timber rafts down past rapids or falls. Engraving by J.P. Newell (active c. 1855-1878).

*Talbot Homestea
himself near futu
Talbot's aim was
land along the no
inland from there
Many early settle
American landsee
of British emigrat
Canada after 181.*

1   2

3

4

deal of antagonism in the Revolutionary United States, where, as often occurs in revolution, "those not with us were held to be against us." These devout, industrious people asked only to live in their own community of faith and work; but as they still felt harried in the republic, they looked northward to the Crown that had once protected them. Simcoe had initially made clear that Quakers — an old English-speaking "plain" group — would be welcomed and would not have to bear arms in Upper Canada. Thus Quakers did come to the Niagara and Quinte areas quite early, and established themselves up Yonge Street before 1810.

Much more numerous German-speaking Mennonites obtained lands in the Niagara peninsula; and above all, bought 60,000 acres in the upper Grand River Valley, to which they came increasingly from 1801. These lands had been part of the Six Nations reserve, but Joseph Brant brought the government to agree to sell them off — not simply to bring funds, but because he doubted that the Six Nations could hold so much land against white pressures. At any rate, the Mennonites made peaceable neighbours, as they moved north from Pennsylvania in their Conestoga covered-wagons (the real ancestors of the later "prairie schooners"), and opened Waterloo County, the first truly inland settlement in Upper Canada. And still others came to add to the Ontario mosaic. Mennonites and German Lutherans, who located in the townships north of York, arrived well equipped with cattle, goods and capital, so that they purchased fine-quality land, built grist mills, and made prosperous farms in one of the most

The Rockwood Academy founded by the Quakers. Quakers coming from the United States had established themselves in Upper Canada by 1810. They were pacifists and stressed plainness and simplicity in religion, dress, and social custom. The Rockwood Academy was established by Wm. Wetherald as a boarding school for boys, and still stands today.

successful settlements of the period.

As a result of this whole settling process, Upper Canada's population had risen to more than 90,000 by 1812, just some 700 of them in York. The roads, to be kept up by the residents along them according to law, were still incredibly rough by later standards. Yet they carried grain and foodstuffs out to markets, and store-goods inward for pioneer farms. Markets to start were small, mostly in flour, pork and peas for the military garrisons — even for American garrisons at border posts that had been given up. Some wheat went down the St. Lawrence, and supplies crossed both Lakes Ontario and Erie to new American settlements along their shores: since thanks to the Loyalists, Upper Canada had actually had a headstart. It was by now a thriving province, if still with a long way to go. But it could also face serious trouble: not just from the United States so near by, but also from the very kind of population it had recently acquired.

By 1812, the American-born made up about four-fifths of the province's white population, while only around a quarter of that large element were Loyalists in origin. It is true that the Post-Loyalist American majority felt no particular grievances against British rule, and were still not inclined to politics, being too busy on the land. Yet equally, if trouble came from within or without, there seemed no strong reason why they would hold on to British rule — oaths of allegiance or not. They were not disaffected; but they could be. In the event of an American war, they might at least refuse to serve or seek neutrality; at the most, join with United States forces to seize Upper Canada. Moreover, there appeared to be a widespread assumption among them that Upper Canada was destined to be absorbed into the United States; not now, but some day. No wonder provincial authorities grew anxious as relations with the United States began to deteriorate again. For at least from 1807, there were signs of a new war between Britain and the republic that could put young Upper Canada to its severest test.

1. A Quaker Meeting-House in Norwichville.
2. Four-Horse Settlers' Wagon. A legend about this "Conestoga" wagon (Conestoga was in Pennsylvania) says that it was driven by Abraham Weber, among a large party of German Mennonites from Lancaster County, Pennsylvania, to Waterloo County in Upper Canada, where Weber settled in 1807. These wagons were caulked and sealed for crossing rivers, when the wheels would be taken off, and they were poled across, or at times even propelled by wind and sail.

1

2

Main Events of the War of 1812

1812

June 18	United States declares war
July 17	British capture Michilimackinac
July 19	Americans defend Sackets Harbor, N.Y.
August 16	British capture Detroit
September 29	Americans raid Gananoque, U.C.
October 13	British win Battle of Queenston Heights, U.C.
November 9-10	Indecisive naval engagement off Kingston, U.C.

1813

January 22	British win Battle of Frenchtown, Mich.
February 7	Americans raid Brockville, U.C.
February 22	British attack Ogdensburg, N.Y.
April 27	Americans capture York, U.C., and withdraw.
May 15	Yeo takes command of British naval forces on the Lakes
May 27	Americans capture Fort George, U.C.
May 29	British attack Sackets Harbor, withdraw
June 1	H.M.S. *Shannon* captures U.S.S. *Chesapeake*
June 5-6	British win Battle of Stoney Creek, U.C.
June 24	British win Battle of Beaver Dams, U.C.
July 5	British raid Fort Schlosser, N.Y.
July 11	British raid Black Rock village, N.Y..
July 30	British raid Plattsburgh, N.Y.
September 10	Americans win Battle of Lake Erie
September 27	Americans capture Amherstburg, U.C.
October 6	Americans win Battle of Moraviantown, U.C.
October 26	British win Battle of Chateauguay, L.C.
November 11	British win Battle of Crysler's Farm, U.C.
December 10	Americans burn Newark and Queenston, U.C.
December 19	British capture Fort Niagara, N.Y.

1814

February 6	British raid Madrid, N.Y.
February 19-24	British raids on Salmon River, Malone, Four Corners, N.Y.
March 30	Americans occupy Odelltown, L.C.
May 6	British capture supplies at Oswego, N.Y.
May 15	Americans raid Long Point, U.C.
May 20-June 6	British blockade Sackets Harbor, N.Y.
May 30	British ambushed at Sandy Creek, N.Y.
July 5	Americans win Battle of Chippewa, U.C.
July 25	Battle of Lundy's Lane, U.C., Americans withdraw
August 14	Americans capture British schooner *Nancy*
August 15	British begin seige of American-held Fort Erie
August 24-25	British burn Washington, D.C.
September 3	British capture American schooner *Tigress*
September 5	British capture American schooner *Scorpion*
September 10	H.M.S. *St. Lawrence* launched at Kingston, U.C.
September 11	British defeated on Lake Champlain
September 12-15	British attack Baltimore, Md.
October 1	Americans lift blockade of Kingston, U.C.
October 20	H.M.S. *St. Lawrence* lies off Niagara
November 5	Americans blow up Fort Erie, retire
December 24	Treaty of Ghent ends the war

1815

January 8	Battle of New Orleans, La.

The War of 1812

War nearly began in 1807, when two warships, the British *Leopard* and American *Chesapeake*, clashed on the high seas over the right of search. In their all-out struggle, Britain and France had set up blockades against each other's seaborne commerce; and Britain claimed the right not only to search neutral ships for cargoes intended for the enemy but for deserters from the Royal Navy. Americans protested this interference with their shipping; by gunfire in the *Chesapeake's* case. And though war was averted this time, incidents continued, while resentment mounted in the United States. But it was in the west that resentments really boiled over, where Americans blamed British meddling for growing Indian resistance to American expansion. In truth, it was constant American pressures on land and rights that brought the western tribes to a last, desperate rising, under the Shawnee leader, the Prophet, and his brother, the great warrior, Tecumseh. At the Battle of Tippecanoe in 1811, United States troops crushed the rising. American western leaders, however, full of triumph, now demanded that the British be punished for their supposed conniving, and be driven out of the west once and for all. These "war hawks" in Congress looked to capture inland Canada while Britain

Action between H.M.S. Shannon *and the U.S. Frigate* Chesapeake, *off Boston Light House, June 1, 1813. In 1807, the* Chesapeake *was involved in a skirmish with the British ship* Leopard *over the right of search, nearly beginning a war. War was averted that time, but incidents continued, eventually leading to the War of 1812.*

Extract of a letter from a gentleman on board his Majesty's ship Leopard, dated Chesapeak Bay, June 25, 1807.

" We arrived here on the 21st inst. and, agreeably to the orders of the Hon. Vice Admiral Berkeley, (in the event of meeting the United States frigate Chesapeake, to search her for deserters, of whom we had information) the next morning, the signal was made from the Bellona to proceed to sea, which we did at 9 o'clock this morning; the Chesapeake was then passing the Bellona, about 3 miles within us—We stood to the S. E. with a wind at S. W. until eleven, when it shifted to E. which retarded the progress of the frigate, being obliged to beat—we kept on a wind under easy sail, until she got within two miles of us, when she shortened sail, and we bore down to her, we were about 13 or 14 miles from the land; when sufficiently close, the captain hailed, and said he had dispatches from the British commander in chief—the answer was, " send them on board, I shall heave too," which he did accordingly—I was sent on board with the Admiral's order, and a letter from captain Humphreys, saying, he hoped to be able to execute the Admiral's order in the most amicable manner; and,

1

2

3

4

was busy fighting Napoleon in Europe. Combining with seaboard and southern angers over the naval right of search, they brought the President, James Madison of Virginia, to declare war on June 18, 1812. As for Upper Canada, the war hawks and Madison's administration expected that thinly-settled province to fall easily, in a "mere matter of marching," to the vastly more populous and developed United States — when there were so few British troops to defend it, and so many American settlers living there. These expectations, however, left out three things in particular: the quality of seasoned British regulars *versus* scantily trained American troops, the abilities of General Isaac Brock in defending Upper Canada, and the power of Indians strongly committed to the British side.

There was only one British regiment in all Upper Canada before the war, the 41st, or some 1,600 men in total. Provincial militia chiefly existed on paper; for while militia laws required all fit men to bear arms when called (except religious objectors like Quakers), their training, aside from an annual muster-day, was virtually left till actual war began. Just the small regular contingent could really be counted on: for disciplined marches, skilled deployment on the battle-field, close, steady volleys, and, if need be, cool retreat without panic. This is not to write off all the militia, especially volunteers. They could learn, and did, to fight like veteran professionals; but it took time. Thus the firm core of Upper Canada's defence were the regulars, who bore the brunt of heavy fighting — poor men from English villages and town slums, Scottish crofts or Irish cabins, who, with often little credit, largely enabled Upper Canada to survive.

Then there was General Brock, a brilliant English officer who had fought in Europe, and for some time been stationed in the Canadas before being sent to York in October, 1811, as commander of the forces in Upper Canada and the Administrator of that province while Lieutenant-Governor Gore was absent on leave. Brock's posting was a sign of British alarm, as was the sending of a few reinforcements and more arms up-river. Yet not much more could be done when Britain was strained to its peak against Napoleon, and some of its troops already garrisoned in America had to be kept to protect Lower Canada and the St. Lawrence lifeline outward. Still, Brock did his

1. *This "Extract of a letter from a gentleman on board his Majesty's ship* Leopard, *dated Chesapeak [sic] Bay, June 25, 1807" was published in* The Upper Canada Gazette *on August 15, 1807. It discusses the action between the* Leopard *and the* Chesapeake.

2. *Battle of Tippecanoe. American pressure on Indian land and rights brought the western tribes to revolt under the Shawnee leader, the Prophet, and his brother, Tecumseh. At the Battle of Tippecanoe in 1811, United States troops crushed the rising.*

3. *The uniform of General Isaac Brock with the fatal bullet hole. Brock was sent to York in October, 1811, as commander of the forces in Upper Canada and Administrator of that province while Lieutenant-Governor Gore was absent on leave. No true likeness of Brock has been preserved as he apparently never sat for a portrait. Brock died during the Battle of Queenston Heights in 1812.*

4. *The Bust of Tecumseh. Tecumseh, a great Indian warrior, led his people through many battles.*

5. *This commemorative stamp was issued in honour of the 200th anniversary of Brock's birth.*

5

best to prepare defences. Still more, with his quick strategic grasp, professional knowledge and powerful personality, he was worth whole regiments himself. He saw his best defence in attack, to keep the enemy off balance in a war of movement, and meant to make the skills and experience of his few soldiers count — along with those of the Indians, the masters of forest war.

In a countryside where farms and bush clearings were hemmed by thick forest, where main roads were few and bad, the local trails still worse, only two means for a war of movement virtually existed: water transport along the Lakes (which the British "provincial marine" widely controlled) or Indian expertise in ranging through the wilderness. Indians as scouts provided swift military information; they could harry and disrupt enemy communications; hold down wide areas with sudden, bewildering thrusts that vanished into the trees. And they could sow panic, since Americans often carried a folk-memory of Indian cruelties, bred by generations of frontier warfare, in which they had practiced cruelties themselves. The native peoples in Upper Canada were British allies from long experience, largely established on reserves that seemed adequate as yet, while tended by an Indian superintendency under imperial control which also from long experience knew the military value of the Indian. And tribes in the nearby American territories who had lost so much to the United States, saw their last hope in Britain's cause. They were ready to stand beside the redcoats, if they would truly fight the hated blue-coats. Here was indeed a force worth many regiments, if they were shown that the British meant action. Brock did so, most convincingly.

Immediately on learning of the war made in Washington, he sent permission to the small British garrison at Fort St. Joseph, south of Sault Ste. Marie, to attack American Fort Michilimackinac at the entry to Lake Michigan. A mixed group of soldiers and fur traders surprised and seized the unprepared Michilimackinac, a key post.

1. Fort Mackinack. On learning of war in Washington, Brock soon attacked American Fort Michilimackinac at the entry to Lake Michigan. A force of soldiers and fur traders took the unprepared fort.
2. Detroit, Michigan in 1811. Through the use of effective psychological warfare, Brock and Tecumseh won the bloodless surrender of General William Hull and an American army of two thousand regulars and militia at Fort Detroit on August 15, 1812.

1

2

This prompt and daring strike brought the Indians of Michigan Territory and the Northwest in on the British side. Then Brock turned to Fort Detroit, where General William Hull had led an American army of two thousand regulars and militia. On July 12 Hull crossed the river to begin Upper Canada's first invasion. Yet after issuing a grand proclamation that promised the inhabitants freedom "from Tyranny and oppression," but death if they were found fighting beside Indians, Hull drew back to the fort: having failed to secure his shaky links southward into the United States, and alarmed by rumours that Indians under the dreaded Tecumseh were coming down from the north. Brock, meanwhile, had met the Legislative Assembly of Upper Canada; but did not get stronger militia laws from its representatives, who reflected the wary caution or even glum defeatism then widespread in the province. Now in early August, the British general made another swift move that was to bring new confidence. He sailed by lake right round to Detroit, taking forces from York, collecting more as he went, regulars, militia and Indians; and at Detroit, boldly demanded its surrender.

Brock would not have known the term, psychological warfare, but he knew how to practice it. He worked closely with the Indians led by Tecumseh — who on first meeting the tall and forceful General pronounced, "This is a Man." Brock used the Indians to cut Hull's communications and keep the Americans isolated, while warning darkly that he might not be able to control his allies if the fort held out. The Indians howled around it in the night; Brock paraded his soldiers on the opposite shore (adding more militia dressed in red coats to them), and opened up a brisk cannonade. On August 15, simply

Prize Brig Adams, *1812. The U.S.S.* Adams *was captured by the British at Detroit on August 16, 1812. The ship was renamed H.M.S.* Detroit *by its new owners (not to be confused with Barclay's flagship built a year later, which he also named the* Detroit.) *Then, in October 1812, the Americans took the ship back and burnt it the same day to avoid recapture.* Watercolour with pencil by Charles Henry Jeremy Snider (1879-1971), c. 1913.

beaten by bluff, Hull surrendered his whole army without firing a shot. And confidence rose in Upper Canada. One interesting sign of it was the popular ballad sung at inns and taverns, *Come All You Bold Canadians*, celebrating the bloodless and wholly unexpected victory at Detroit, while stressing the part that provincial militia took. This authentic voice of early Upper Canada glows with new pride — *"May the memory of this triumph go all the province round"* — and it is a very early occasion when the term "Canadians" was applied to the people of Ontario, when previously it had referred to *Canadiens*; that is, French Canadians.

Returning from Detroit, Brock now rushed to Niagara to meet a second American invasion. On the night of October 13, an army of several thousand that had been gathered around Fort Niagara crossed the river well above British Fort George, to seize the commanding heights behind the shore village of Queenston. Brock galloped the seven miles from Fort George to drive off the Americans before they became consolidated on Queenston Heights, leaving General Roger Sheaffe to bring up his main body of troops. This time, however, swift action proved fatal. Brock collected a small force to charge the heights, but was shot and killed as he was leading his men upwards. Yet Sheaffe, taking a longer way around, met the Americans on the heights, dislodged them and captured almost a thousand, for they had had no reinforcements — because the New York militia, refusing to serve outside their home state, would not cross the river.

General Brock had died in a hasty attack, after four months of a war that lasted over two more years. Was he the Saviour of Upper Canada, as he was once declared? At least no other individual could come as near that title. He had won daring successes at the start of a struggle that looked all but hopeless. He had ensured vital Indian support, taken two enemy armies, and by the end of 1812 there was no American invader left on Upper Canadian soil. Most of all, Brock had brought a new mood to the province's people that roused Loyalists to fight for the homes they had already given so much for, and led others not to assume British defeat or surrender. Hence those

1. *Tecumseh's tomahawk. Tecumseh himself presented this tomahawk to General Brock.*
2. *These three jars were presented to Brock by the Government of Upper Canada.*
3. *Contemporary view of the Battle of Queenston Heights, October 13, 1812. General Isaac Brock was killed in one of the early encounters. General Roger Sheaffe, with the main body of troops, met the Americans on the Heights and won the battle. Over 900 Americans were taken prisoner.*
4. *British troops charging at Queenston Heights, October 13, 1812.*

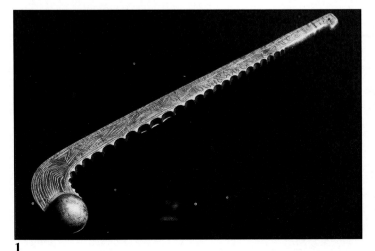

1

2

3

4

American settlers more inclined to disaffection, or at least to evading their militia duties, began to feel that failure to serve might bring the loss of their land grants, aside from the little matter of disavowing an oath of allegiance.

The problem of disaffection nonetheless continued; as did American attacks, which in 1813 brought the most dangerous days of all. Still, a heartened Upper Canada hold on. In April, when the shore ice had cleared, the Americans sent out the fleet they had been building to win control of Lake Ontario. Since Kingston, the main British naval base, seemed too strongly defended, they turned their ships loaded with soldiers to raid the capital town of York, a lesser naval dockyard. On April 27, 1,700 United States troops poured ashore, overwhelming a small British force of regulars, Indians and militia. General Sheaffe, who had succeeded Brock in both military and political command, retired towards Kingston with his few but vital regulars, ordering the garrison's magazine to be blown up as he did so. The blast killed some two hundred Americans who had swept into the fort. It did not make their comrades take kindly to York. During a week's occupation, not only were public stores and property destroyed, but there was private looting also, and the parliament buildings were burned down — not by any command, but the presumption was that Americans had done it. When the raiders sailed away, they left keen anti-American memories that long would affect the citizens of Toronto.

In May things got even worse. Fort George fell in a new American invasion, and the British retired to Burlington at the head of the lake, leaving the entire Niagara district open. Yet as would happen recurrently, lack of co-operation and strong leadership among American forces kept them from following up their gains. And on June 5, British regulars from Burlington surprised United States troops at

1. *The* Simcoe *off Kingston, September 10, 1812. The* Simcoe *was run aground by her Captain, James Richardson, as the American Fleet was intercepting her.*
2. *Sir Roger Hale Sheaffe, British general who succeeded Brock.*
3. *Monument to Sir Isaac Brock at Queenston. Brock died on October 13, 1812, in the Battle of Queenston Heights but not before he had made important contributions to the War of 1812. Brock had gained control of the northwest (Michilimackinac) from the Americans and had also forced General William Hull to surrender at Detroit. He worked closely with the Indians led by Tecumseh and contributed much to a new sense of confidence within Upper Canada.*
4. *Plan of the Fort at York. On April 27, 1813, 1700 United States troops raided outside the capital York, especially to destroy its naval dockyard. They quickly overwhelmed the small British forces, and General Sheaffe retired towards Kingston, blowing up the garrison's magazine as he did so. The explosion killed some 200 Americans, who had thrust into the fort. Their bitter comrades occupied York for a week, and much public and private destruction and looting occurred.*
5. *The Death of Brock at Queenston Heights* by C.W. Jefferys.

1

2

3

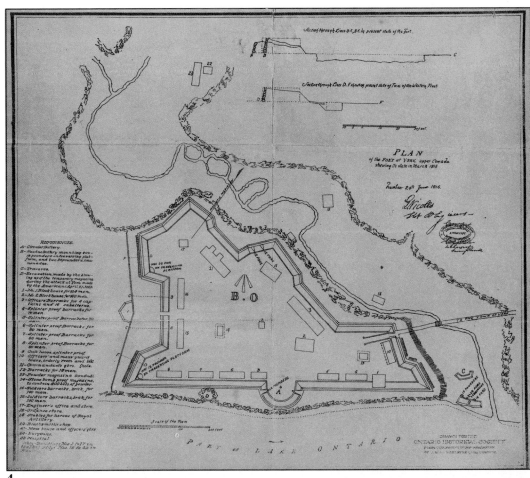

4

5

1

2

Laura Secord 1775-1868

To perpetuate the name and fame of Laura Secord who walked alone nearly 20 miles by a circuitous, difficult and perilous route through woods and swamps and over miry roads to warn a British oupost at De Cew's Falls of an intended attack and thereby enabled Lieut. Fitzgibbon on the 24th June 1813, with less than 50 men of H.M. 49th Regt., about 15 militiamen and small force of Six Nations and other Indians under Captains William Johnson Kerr and Dominique Ducharme to surprise and attack the enemy at Beechwoods (or Beaverdams), and after a short engagement, to capture Col. Boerstler of the U.S. Army and his entire force of 542 men with two field pieces.

3

4

Stoney Creek in a skilfull night attack, driving them back to the Niagara peninsula, where later that month some five hundred of them were captured at Beaver Dam by Indians. Laura Secord is rightly honoured for her hard and hazardous journey to inform the British commander, James Fitzgibbon, of the Americans' position at Beaver Dam. It does not lessen her own heroism to note that he already had been told, and only had to go to accept the surrender of a thoroughly demoralized enemy. The year thus ended in the Niagara area with the Americans even withdrawing from Fort George in December — after burning the town of Newark. That brought harsh retaliation, when a week later British troops took Fort Niagara, then ravaged the American shore to Buffalo, which they burned in turn.

Meanwhile, the British had greatly lost ground in the west: essentially because at the Battle of Put-in-Bay on Lake Erie in September, 1813, their fleet that had controlled the lake was totally destroyed by a new American fleet built with much bigger resources, including cannon cast in Pittsburgh. With water communications gone, British forces had to fall back into the western Ontario peninsula, where a larger, fresher United States army caught up with them at Moravian-town in October. Here Tecumseh fell, a grave loss to his people's cause. Yet the Americans under General William Henry Harrison failed again to follow up their advantage, retiring to Detroit, and leaving western Upper Canada mostly as a no-man's land of minor raiding till the end of the war. In the east, however, the Americans made a better strategic effort, to cut through the trunk of the province instead of hacking at branches, by crossing the upper St. Lawrence river below Prescott. But here they were soundly defeated in November at the Battle of Crysler's Farm, in which, as in other eastern Ontario engagements beyond recounting, a staunchly Loyalist militia played valuable roles.

The year 1814 saw the British regain the lead on Lake Ontario, especially after their naval commander, Sir James Yeo, successfully

1. Fort George. This is a view of Fort George taken from Old Fort Niagara before the American attack.
2. Battle of Fort George. After Fort George fell to the Americans in May 1813, the British retired to Burlington at the head of the lake, leaving the entire Niagara district open. The churches St. Mark's and St. Andrew's are shown as they were before the town of Newark was burnt down.
3. The text of the Laura Secord monument, Lundy's Lane, Niagara Falls.
4. Laura Secord Monument. This commemorates her dangerous journey of June 24, 1813, to warn British forces of American military plans.
5. Naval Battle on Lake Ontario, September 28, 1813. The American sloop General Pike *and the British sloop* Wolfe *are shown.*
6. William Henry Harrison, the American general who defeated retreating British forces in October, 1813, at Moraviantown on the Thames River. The death of Tecumseh here also hit the Indians hard. Yet the Americans under Harrison failed to follow up, soon retiring to Detroit.

5

6

blocked the American base of Oswego. Furthermore, although American troops by now were far better drilled than before, there was more hope of British reinforcements from overseas, while the provincial militia, especially the trained "flank companies" instituted by Brock, gave much better service in the field. The war in Upper Canada, in fact, settled into hardened fighting between two experienced foes, and centred mainly in the Niagara peninsula. Fort Erie fell to Americans well disciplined by Winfield Scott, a first-rate commander. British forces unwisely rushed a larger American army at the Battle of Chippewa, and found that American regulars could be first-class also. Then at Lundy's Lane on July 25, two sure, well-matched armies met in the war's hardest and most costly battle. By midnight, the Americans were too worn and battered to make another attack on the British who held the field, but who were too exhausted and hurt themselves to pursue as their enemies retired. It was the military climax. Thereafter, a British attempt in August failed to retake Fort Erie; but the Americans blew up the fort themselves in November, and withdrew to their own side of the river. The war was winding down, and Upper Canada would survive.

However, this survival was not without raids and forays elsewhere before the conflict ended; and above all, not without the persistent problem of disaffection producing drastic reactions. As the struggle went on, many settlers of American origins, but with not much politics, had necessarily done militia service. Once in, comradeship (and being shot at) had tended to make them view the invaders as just that — not as unneeded "liberators," but as enemies keeping them from their own families and farms. And so, out of the war, most would acquire a lasting identification with Upper Canada, the home and soil they had defended. But there were others of American origin who did maintain their republican and "patriot" convictions, who did still look for American victory, or who through personal interests, local

1. *Captain Sir James Lucas Yeo, (1782-1818). Yeo was commodore and Commander-in-Chief of the British naval force on the Great Lakes, 1813-1815. In this portrait he is shown with his coat-of-arms.*
2. *Crysler Farm Monument. The Americans were defeated at the Battle of Crysler's Farm in November 1813 after they had crossed the St. Lawrence river below Prescott.*
3. *Captain R.H. Barclay's flagship the* Detroit *on Lake Erie, 1813. The* Detroit *was built at Amherstburg in 1813 and was taken by the Americans September 10, at Put-in-Bay.*
4. *Commodore Perry's flagship the* Niagara, *Put-in-Bay, Lake Erie. The U.S.S.* Niagara *was built in 1813, sunk in 1825, and raised in 1919.*
5. *The* Sir Isaac Brock *on the Stocks at York (Toronto), April 1813. The* Sir Isaac Brock *was built in 1812-1813 but was burnt before completion in order to prevent her capture by the Americans who attacked York in April 1813.* By Charles Henry Jeremy Snider (1879-1971), c. 1913.

1

2

3

4

5

1. *The Storming of Fort Oswego, 1814. Sir James Yeo's successful blockade of Oswego was important to the British regaining the lead on Lake Ontario in 1814.*
2. *Yeo's Flagship the* St. Lawrence *on Lake Ontario, 1814. Launched on September 10, 1814, she was the largest wooden warship ever to sail on the Great Lakes. The* St. Lawrence *was over sixty metres long, had a crew of 1,000 and ultimately had 112 guns.*
3. *Lundy's Lane Monument. The Battle of Lundy's Lane near Niagara Falls was the war's hardest and most costly fight with both sides suffering more than 800 casualties. The Americans finally withdrew but the British were too exhausted to pursue them.*
4. *Ceremony of Re-interment of Eleven Soldiers from the Lundy's Lane Battle, c. 1900.*

jealousies or quarrels, both sympathized with and actively aided the cause of the United States.

In a province embittered by death and suffering, with barns and houses looted and burned by raiders, crops seized or destroyed, the response grew fierce against those who had co-operated with the attackers, or merely supported them by words. Accusations and arrests followed. In May, 1814, at Ancaster, nineteen men thus seized were put on trial for treason. Four were freed, fifteen convicted, and eight of them hanged. This "Bloody Assize" was the grimmest example; yet further, seventy individuals who had left the province were indicted, and an act of the Legislature permitted legal confiscation of the lands of those who had moved to the United States without government authority. Hence the war inevitably created a rift within Upper Canadian society, an issue of loyalty or treason which was the worse because it was loaded with suspicion and insinuation. To a great extent, the War of 1812 made Canadians out of Ontario settlers of various origins, Americans certainly included. But it also left a festering sore for the future.

Other results of the conflict were no less significant, among them the peace treaty itself. Signed at Ghent in Belgium in late December,

1

2

3

4

1814 (though not known in much of Upper Canada till the spring of 1815), the terms were practically a return to things as they were before the war, with borders as they had been, although boundary commissions were to look into some particular problems. The fact was that Britain, facing Napoleon's sudden return to power, chiefly wanted to put American distractions out of the way, while the Americans had made no gains and had had enough. And no one asked Upper Canada; though it was happy just to have come through the test, and still be complete.

Apart from such concerns, however, the province had gained economically as well as suffered from the war. Wartime damages were real, especially in much fought-over Niagara areas. Yet trade had grown with the demands of the military for supplies. Merchants, especially those with army contracts, had widely flourished; lumbering had enlarged, as had shipbuilding; and if local inhabitants had been killed or wounded in militia service, the mass of them had generally known high wartime demands for labour, crafts and crops. In sum, Upper Canada, materially, had come through well: to meet a new stage in its provincial existence.

1. *In 1814, Fort Erie, at the western end of the Niagara River, fell to American attack. A British attempt in August to retake the fort failed, but the Americans blew it up themselves in November, and withdrew to their own side of the river.*
2. *Ruins of Fort Erie, 1838.* Watercolour over wove paper by Philip John Bainbrigge (1817-1881).
3. *The Signing of the Treaty of Ghent. This settlement ending the War of 1812 was signed at Ghent, Belgium in late December 1814. The terms were practically a return to things as they were before the conflict.*

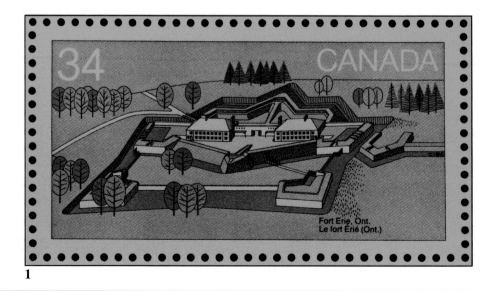

34 CANADA

Fort Erie, Ont.
Le fort Érié (Ont.)

1

2

3

Upper Canada Under the Family Compact

War damages in a rough-built pioneer society were fairly soon replaced, but the collapse of high wartime prices and demands left heavier impacts on Upper Canada for several years. As well, the world outside soon fell into a post-war trade depression, after the Napoleonic conflict finally ended in mid-1815. One brighter note was that transport costs fell sharply on the Atlantic, where there now was virtually a surplus of shipping. That meant that the poorer classes could hope to get to North America at prices they could afford, which depressed conditions in Britain urgently pushed them to leave. Still, the poor might want to leave in the bad times, yet not be able to scrape the funds together for food and passage. So they often had to wait for the opportunities of better times, unless they became part of some assisted emigration project. In any case, after 1815 a large-scale emigration movement gradually mounted in Great Britain, racked as it was by problems of adjusting to the spreading Industrial Revolution, to teeming, killing factory towns, declining village industries and poverty-stricken countrysides.

The resulting massive outflow, which ran on into the 1850s, grew slowly at first and still had peaks and lulls, depending on trade cycles generally. Yet the transatlantic flow affected Upper Canada throughout, in population and economic growth, in frontier farm expansion and town development. Furthermore, it overlaid pre-war American settlement, making the province far more British than it had been, as English, Welsh, Scots and Irish — Protestants from Ulster in the North, Catholics from the South — added to the variety of Upper Canada. Some Americans still arrived; but remembering wartime problems, both imperial and colonial authorities sought to discourage any big renewal of migration from the United States. By provincial order in October, 1815, Americans were not to be allowed

Overleaf. *Battle of Montgomery's Farm, December 7, 1837. As part of the Rebellion of 1837, some 800 hundred men gathered at Montgomery's Tavern on Yonge Street on the night of December 4-5. When reports of this spread, the militia was called out. They arrived on December 7 and scattered the remaining rebels. Had Mackenzie not wasted the two days he had, he could almost have surely taken the capital.*

1. *Allan "Glenpean" McMillan, 1828. McMillan, cousin of "Mulaggan" McMillan, was the co-leader of the 1802 emigration of McMillans from Scotland where they had been dispossessed of their land by sheep farmers. They settled in Glengarry County.*

2. *Emigrants on Board the* Cambridge, *July 1844. After 1815, a large-scale emigration movement mounted in Great Britain, racked as it was by problems due to the Industrial Revolution, teeming factory towns, and poverty-stricken countryside. Pen and ink by Titus Hibbert War (1810-1890), July 1844.*

3. *Three Emigrant Scenes,* The Illustrated London News, *May 10, 1851.*

Top: The emigration agents' office — the passage money paid.

Middle: Emigration vessel — between decks.

Bottom: Departure of the Nimrod *and* Athlone, *early steamships, with emigrants on board, for Liverpool. From there, the emigrants would sail to various destinations in North America including Quebec.*

1

2

MAY 10, 1851.] THE ILLUSTRATED LONDON NEWS. 387

THE EMIGRATION AGENTS' OFFICE.—THE PASSAGE MONEY PAID.

no less constant stream of well-clad, healthy, and comfortable-looking peasantry in our streets, induces me to send you the accompanying sketches and communications on that subject.

" Upon reference to notes and papers of my own, and to information afforded me by the emigration agents here, I am disposed to think that about the middle of May the great emigrational torrent ceases to flow from these shores. Looking backward for the last month, I find that, during the week ending April 11 the greatest rush for the season took place. The numbers who left Cork that week could not have fallen far short of 1500 souls, and this with the emigration

EMIGRATION VESSEL.—BETWEEN DECKS.

of the other ports of Limerick, Waterford, Dublin, and even of Belfast, will give us an approach to 5000 weekly leaving the country. Large as this number may appear, it is well known that it is considerably below the mark when the departures for Liverpool are included. One agent informed me that he himself had booked 600 emigrants in four days, and yet he is but one of the many agents who are to be met with not alone in the large towns and seaports, but even thickly scattered through each petty town and village throughout the country In England you can have but little conception of the sufferings of the poor Irish emigrant from the time he first announces his intention of leaving home

3

the oath of allegiance, and therefore, any more free land grants. Actually, not many American settlers would likely have come in any case, since the American frontier had now moved west into the prairies, past Upper Canada. The relatively few who still entered were largely business and professional men, or millers, storekeepers, and innkeepers. Henceforth the new farm families, lumber workers and town labourers would mainly stem from the British Isles, arriving by way of the St. Lawrence to land at Quebec, and proceed by river transport. Yet some who could manage it sailed to New York city (which drew faster and more frequent ships) and then went overland up to Lake Ontario.

In New York, the British consul James Buchanan, an Irish Protestant, did not want to see his countrymen from Northern Ireland settle in the United States without knowing the merits of British Upper Canada. By agreement with Governor Gore in 1816, he met emigrant vessels arriving at New York harbour and directed Ulster families on to the province, where they were given land in Cavan and Monaghan townships near Rice Lake and north of Port Hope (then Smiths Creek). More sizeable was the Perth Settlement of 1816-17, to the east in inland Lanark county. This in origin was a military scheme, to settle disbanded regular troops near the Rideau River that flows into the Ottawa, and form a barrier against any possible renewed American invasion. Free passage and land grants were provided, both to soldiers' families and poor Scottish settlers. But while many of the soldiers left their rather rough or swampy acres, the Scots endured, giving some success to this early government-aided migration. In fact, in 1820, a larger group of some two thousand unemployed Scottish hand-weavers and their families were similarly brought to the Rideau district. The British authorities also turned to Ireland, in order to try assisted emigration to ease its still worse problems of poverty. In 1823 Peter Robinson, an Upper Canadian Executive Councillor, voyaged to southern Ireland to collect worthy candidates; and some 600, almost all Roman Catholics, were settled between Perth and the Ottawa River. Two thousand more Irish were brought

1. *Notice to Emigrants. After 1815, a large-scale emigration movement mounted and ran into the 1850s. The transatlantic flow affected Upper Canada throughout, in population and economic growth, in frontier farm expansion and town development.*
2. *Emigrant Scenes in Ireland. These photos were published in* The Illustrated London News *on May 10, 1851.*

Top: Irish emigrants leaving home — the priest's blessing.

Bottom: Emigrants arrival at Cork — a scene on the quay.

1

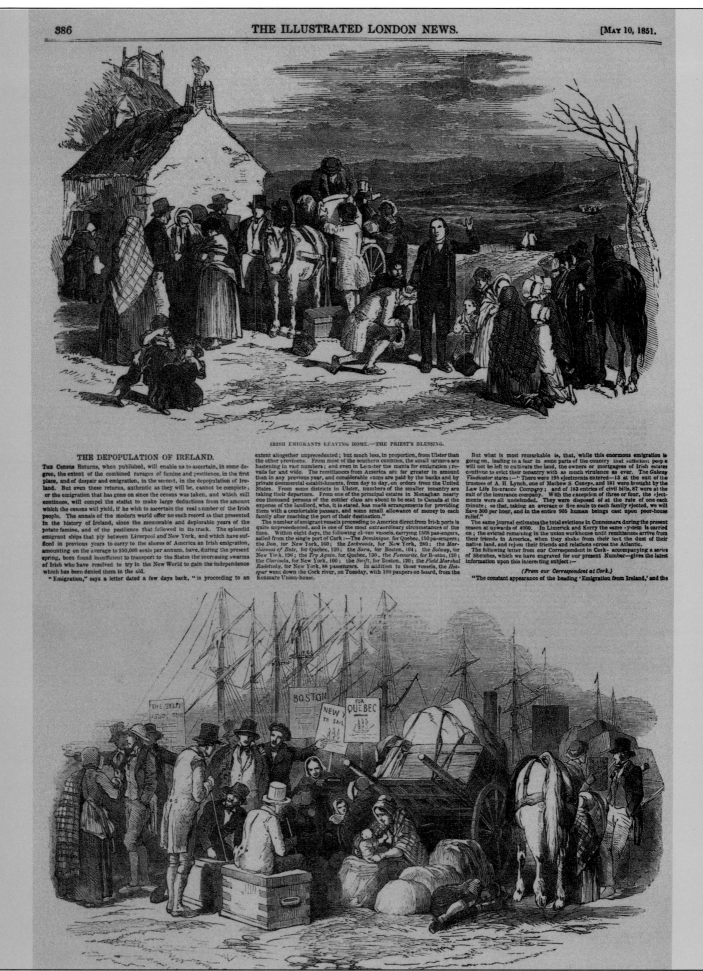

IRISH EMIGRANTS LEAVING HOME.—THE PRIEST'S BLESSING.

THE DEPOPULATION OF IRELAND.

THE Census Returns, when published, will enable us to ascertain, in some degree, the extent of the combined ravages of famine and pestilence, in the first place, and of despair and emigration, in the second, in the depopulation of Ireland. But even these returns, authentic as they will be, cannot be complete; or the emigration that has gone on since the census was taken, and which still continues, will compel the statist to make large deductions from the amount which the census will yield, if he wish to ascertain the real number of the Irish people. The annals of the modern world offer no such record as that presented in the history of Ireland, since the memorable and deplorable years of the potato famine, and of the pestilence that followed in its track. The splendid emigrant ships that ply between Liverpool and New York, and which have sufficed in previous years to carry to the shores of America an Irish emigration, amounting on the average to 250,000 souls per annum, have, during the present spring, been found insufficient to transport to the States the increasing swarms of Irish who have resolved to try in the New World to gain the independence which has been denied them in the old.

"Emigration," says a letter dated a few days back, "is proceeding to an extent altogether unprecedented; but much less, in proportion, from Ulster than the other provinces. From most of the southern counties, the small farmers are hastening in vast numbers; and even in Leinster the mania for emigration prevails far and wide. The remittances from America are far greater in amount than in any previous year, and considerable sums are paid by the banks and by private commercial establishments, from day to day, on orders from the United States. From some districts in Ulster, numbers of the smaller tenantry are taking their departure. From one of the principal estates in Monaghan nearly one thousand persons of the cottier class are about to be sent to Canada at the expense of the landlord, who, it is stated, has made arrangements for providing them with a comfortable passage, and some small allowance of money to each family after reaching the port of their destination."

The number of emigrant vessels proceeding to America direct from Irish ports is quite unprecedented, and is one of the most extraordinary circumstances of the time. Within eight days, the following eleven vessels, carrying 1568 passengers, sailed from the single port of Cork :—The Dominique, for Quebec, 150 passengers; the Don, for New York, 160; the Lockwoods, for New York, 280; the Marchioness of Bute, for Quebec, 120; the Sara, for Boston, 104; the Solway, for New York, 196; the Try Again, for Quebec, 130; the Favourite, for Boston, 120; the Clarisda, for New York, 100; the Swift, for Boston, 120; the Field Marshal Radetzsky, for New York, 88 passengers. In addition to those vessels, the Hotspur went down the Cork river, on Tuesday, with 100 paupers on board, from the Kenmare Union-house.

But what is most remarkable is, that, while this enormous emigration is going on, leading to a fear in some parts of the country that sufficient people will not be left to cultivate the land, the owners or mortgagees of Irish estates continue to evict their tenantry with as much virulence as ever. The Galway Vindicator states :— "There were 198 ejectments entered—13 at the suit of the trustees of A. H. Lynch, one of Mathew S. Coneys, and 181 were brought by the Law Life Insurance Company; and of 183 entries of civil bills, 87 were at the suit of the insurance company. With the exception of three or four, the ejectments were all undefended. They were disposed of at the rate of one each minute; so that, taking an average of five souls to each family ejected, we will have 300 per hour, and in the entire 905 human beings cast upon poor-house relief."

The same journal estimates the total evictions in Connemara during the present season at upwards of 4000. In Limerick and Kerry the same system is carried on; the evicted remaining in the union workhouse until remittances arrive from their friends in America, when they shake from their feet the dust of their native land, and rejoin their friends and relations across the Atlantic.

The following letter from our Correspondent in Cork- accompanying a series of Sketches, which we have engraved for our present Number—gives the latest information upon this interesting subject :—

(From our Correspondent at Cork.)

"The constant appearance of the heading 'Emigration from Ireland,' and the out by Peter Robinson in 1825. They were mostly located north of Rice Lake around Peterborough, named for him, in what became a very successful community.

Thereafter, there were no more large government schemes for assisted emigration, because they seemed to cost too much for whatever good they did. There still were various privately-assisted group projects, particularly when local parishes in Britain tried to ease the burdens of relief by paying the costs of moving their poor overseas; but on the whole, from the mid-1820s on, individual, unassisted emigration became the rule. Many people now were leaving to better themselves, not just because of poverty; and while assisted emigrants had largely come from hard-hit Scotland and Ireland, a lot of the unassisted came from better-off England. Moreover, these unassisted migrants also included middle-class business men, lawyers, physicians, teachers, and journalists, together with a significant number of half-pay army and navy officers retired from active service, who brought their capital, their education and leadership qualities to Upper Canada — where they built up landed property, became local magistrates, and spread more social control in new frontier areas.

Despite ups and downs in trade, economic growth generally continued as more immigrants came into the province. New urban centres took form; for instance, Hamilton was established as a village in 1816, the same year that Meyers Creek on the Bay of Quinte became Belleville, to honour Governor Gore's wife, Arabella. Farmers increasingly sold their wheat and flour to town merchants for export to Britain via Montreal; though the British markets also went up and down, according to the workings of protective imperial Corn Laws — "corn" being Anglo-Saxon for grain. Farmers sold quantities of potash for export as well; used in producing soaps and textiles and made from the ashes of great heaps of the hardwoods burned in clearing land, a sad end for a forest. And as transport rose in volume on main waterways, the steamboat appeared on Lake

1. *Dennis O'Brien, Irish Emigrant on Board the* Cambridge, *July 28, 1844. Pen and ink by Titus Hibbert Ware (1810-1890), July 28, 1844.*
2. *Peter Robinson (1785-1838), c. 1830. Representative of the east riding of York in the Provincial Parliament (1817-1830), he was later a member of the Legislative Council. In 1827, Robinson was appointed Commissioner of Crown Lands and held this position until his death. He was a brother of the powerful John Beverley Robinson, one of the chief government leaders in Upper Canada of that day.*

1   2

Overleaf. *View of Hamilton, c. 1852. In the early 19th century, economic growth continued as many British immigrants came into the province. Hamilton was one of the new urban centres, being founded in 1816.*

1. *Oldest House in Perth, which was settled around 1817 by disbanded troops. Such military settlements near the Rideau River were to form a barrier against possible renewed American invasion.*

2. *Belleville, 1899. A parade on Front Street honouring the visit of the Governor-General. In 1816, the town's name changed from Meyer's Creek to Belleville to honour Governor Gore's wife, Arabella.*

1

2

1. *Plaque on the old Bank of Upper Canada building in Toronto. The bank was charted in 1821 and was strongly backed by York business including the capital's wealthiest man, William Allen, who was the bank's president.*

2. *The Bank of Upper Canada, Toronto, 1872. The left portion of this structure which still stands on Adelaide St. E., was occupied by the bank c. 1830-1861, the extension to the right by the De La Salle Institute, a school which later occupied the entire building.*

Ontario in 1816. The paddlewheeler *Frontenac*, 170 feet long, with an engine imported from Britain, was built for a group of Kingston merchants, and ran between Kingston and Niagara until 1827. By that date the steamboat age was fully launched on Ontario lakes and rivers, speeding passenger travel especially.

Still, long-range commerce and expensive items like steamboats had to be financed, which led on to banking. A bank project launched at Kingston fell through in 1819, due more than somewhat to political wire-pulling by York interests, which in 1821 got their own Bank of Upper Canada chartered instead. Strongly backed by York business, with the capital's wealthiest man, William Allen, as president, the Bank had strong official ties as well; since a quarter of its stock was held by the government and four government directors sat on its board of fifteen. This, then, was a solid provincial institution (What else could it be?) that stayed powerful for many years ahead. But it also expressed the close relations between economic and social leaders at the capital town and the political ruling element centred there. Which brings us to that enduring power group which was soon to be termed the Family Compact.

The name itself, which came into popular use in the later 1820s, was exaggerated and inaccurate, but convenient. There was no compact of ruling families; families were not the real basis of the Compact's power. It was not a closed group, not deeply tyrannical or corrupt; it sincerely sought to give good government, and usually had considerable popular support. Yet this oligarchy unquestionably was privileged and prejudiced, chiefly against any suspected American democratic leanings. It could overreact accordingly; and the Compact did believe that its loyalty and dedication to service gave it an all-but permanent right to rule. In an inevitably popular North American society, these things could not go on forever. Yet in the Upper Canadian version of that society, shaped as it was by Loyalist conservatism, anti-American memories of the War of 1812, and firm pro-British convictions, there was room and approval for the Compact to last a good long time. But what was this Compact?

S.S. Frontenac. *The first steam-powered ship launched in Upper Canada, the* Frontenac *was a topsail schooner which had an engine, imported from Britain, for auxiliary power only. It measured 170 ft. The* Frontenac *was built for a group of Kingston merchants in 1816 and ran between Kingston and Niagara until 1827.* Sketch by Van Cleve.

Essentially, it was an elite group based in an Executive Council of nearly permanent officials (where Loyalist William Jarvis, for example, served as Provincial Secretary from 1791 till his death in 1817), but which also included leading Legislative Councillors and chief judges. This was, in sum, an inner circle of top officials and prime dignitaries, an overlapping group which also had spokesmen and supporters in the Legislative Assembly. But it was besides backed by minor local "compacts" across the province, mainly composed of appointed magistrates, district officials and large landowners. At the same time, business interests not just at York but throughout the province were widely aligned with the central Compact; for it was very much concerned with economic advances, as seen not only with respect to the Bank of Upper Canada, but soon also in big canal-building schemes or road and harbour developments. No doubt, the close links of government patronage with fat contracts or land grants were very real — just as they were in the democratic United States. But more than a network of places, jobs or favours held the Compact and its satellite groups together. Common beliefs and attitudes regarding loyalty, British principles and anti-American sentiments interconnected the whole system, which still was loose and full of individual differences: rather too primitive to qualify as a modern political party machine.

In a small society, family connection assuredly counted as well. Nevertheless, old family names were not the set admission to Compact roles. Ability, combined with "politically correct" views, mattered much more. Thus it was that the masterful John Strachan, of no family note, the Anglican rector of York, entered the Compact and rapidly rose to the fore, being named an Executive Councillor in 1818, and Legislative Councillor in 1820. Dr. Strachan had won some reputation for the right stance by striving boldly to maintain public order and British morale during the American raid on York in 1813. Yet he was further noted for his resolute defence of Anglican rights to the clergy reserves, his warm concern for education, and not least, for being the capable schoolmaster (now of the York Grammar School) who had already instructed many of the sons of Compact worthies. One of these whom he had earlier taught at Cornwall was a

William Jarvis (1756-1817). Jarvis was an officer in the Queen's Rangers under Lieutenant-Colonel Simcoe and served in the Revolutionary War. An early figure in the Family Compact, he was Provincial Secretary of Upper Canada from 1791 until his death.

brilliant favourite pupil, John Beverley Robinson. Son of the Virginia Loyalist, Christopher Robinson, who had died young, John Beverley had studied law until he joined the York militia to serve with Brock at both Detroit and Queenston Heights. His mind was outstanding, his record impeccable; and so he was made the acting Attorney-General of Upper Canada in 1813, replacing a war casualty. In 1818 he was named Attorney-General in his own right, and in 1821 was elected to the Assembly for York.

Accordingly, Robinson at thirty became the Compact's strongest voice in the elected house, where the Attorney-Generals and Solicitor-Generals regularly sat as the province's chief law officers. And more than that, this discerning, distinguished and upright Tory rose to be the leading member of the Compact's inner group. Nevertheless, neither Robinson, Strachan, nor any other prominent Compact member became an actual party head or wanted to be. To them, the true leader was the governor himself: to think otherwise would be illegal and disloyal. Yet since governors had often been absent or caught up in military affairs, and as they came and went while the officials stayed, then it was quite likely that much power would actually rest with the experienced top councillors. The governor still ruled in person, and had to be obeyed; but he might regularly be managed, unless he insisted on a position despite all his "advisors" said.

This was so with Sir Peregrine Maitland, Gore's successor as Lieutenant Governor in 1818, who did not leave until 1828. Maitland, one of Wellington's commanders at Waterloo in 1815, was by no means stupid or pliable. He was incisive and dutiful — and rigidly conservative. He thought a good deal like his Compact officials, thus relying

The Stately Home of John Beverley Robinson, c. 1860s. Robinson, by then long out of politics but still a leading judge, died in 1863.

on them to carry out his strict views: if anything, they might even want to tone some of them down. In effect, in the days of Maitland as those of Gore, a very Tory-minded imperial regime and its Tory governors in Upper Canada let the Compact grow and flourish. That did not mean that this provincial power elite had everything their own way; that they did not sometimes face instructions and policies transmitted from London through the governor which they might not like, and on occasions protested. But the basic ideas of London, the governors and the officials were in close accord. Hence government effectively by Compact continued on through the 1820s into the 30s; though it had to meet a growing set of challenges along the way.

The first of these challenges, the first that stirred considerable public feeling against the government, arose from the visit of Robert Gourlay to Upper Canada in 1817-19. Gourlay, a Scot, was the sort that one might choose as an ideal candidate for martyrdom: he eagerly sought to help people — and made enemies all around. Knowledgeable, intelligent, and zealous, his desires for sweeping reforms and human betterment were marred by arrogance, a quarrelsome, erratic temper, and a tendency to leap into print with bitter abuse of any who did not fully agree with him. Gourlay came to Upper Canada in the summer of 1817, to "put it right" in regard to efficient immigration and land settlement. Having good connections, he met leading people in government, and got approval for his plan to gather important statistics first. He thus issued an "Address to the Resident Landowners" with a questionnaire on conditions in each township, which township meetings were then called to discuss. When the replies came in, however, trouble began. They revealed a wide opinion that progress was being held back, not just by bad roads or distance from markets, but by thinly scattered settlement, resulting from the many tracts left undeveloped by absentee owners, or else retained in clergy, crown and school reserves. Also there was "a want of people," particularly those with capital and enterprise, thanks to inadequate emigration policies and the exclusion of Americans from further land settlement.

Gourlay's own temper had been stirred by what he had seen on a tour of the countryside — not helped by his failure to get himself a

Sir Peregrine Maitland (1777-1854). A veteran of Waterloo, Maitland served as Lieutenant-Governor from 1818 to 1828. He was decisive, diligent, and highly conservative.

personal land grant larger than the regulations permitted. In February, 1818, he published a second Address to Resident Landowners, a wordy, rambling onslaught on the colonial authorities which called for a legislative inquiry, meant to bring reform to the province. When that proposal had little effect, he issued a third and much more radical address urging a new series of townships meetings which would go right past a hopelessly bad provincial government (as he saw it), and collectively petition the Crown and Parliament in England for redress. These meetings, moreover, were to elect a set of "commissioners" to carry the petitions for reform to London. In sum, this suggested a popular democratic body, a kind of super-assembly. To the reviled and alarmed officials of Upper Canada, it also sounded like a fearsome revolutionary Convention, such as had taken over power in the great French eruption where the mob and the guillotine had run wild. But with no law against "seditious meetings" then on the books in Upper Canada, all Attorney-General Robinson could do to check Gourlay was to prosecute him for libel, to which his extreme accusations and personal abuse had certainly laid him open. Sympathetic juries, however, acquitted the totally outraged reformer — until in December of 1818, without the government having a hand in it, he was halled before a local court of magistrates in Niagara, and charged under the obsolete Seditions Act of 1804. That measure, which had really been aimed at supporters of the Irish Rebellion of 1798 who might then have entered the province, could in a purely legal sense be extended to Gourlay, even if, in all common sense, it was inapplicable. He was tried, and ordered from the province under the terms of the Act. He left in August 1819 — harshly banished and persecuted, whether he had invited that treatment or not.

In any event, the ferment raised by Gourlay rapidly died away. The new Assembly elected in 1820 (enlarged to forty members) had a few of his supporters, but scarcely held any reform party yet; while

The Entrance to the Home of Sir Peregrine Maitland.

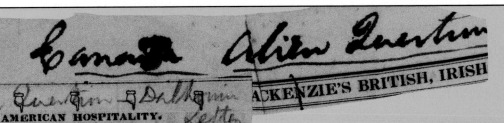

AMERICAN HOSPITALITY.

To Joseph Hume, Esq., M. P. for Kilkenny, London.

MONROE COUNTY PENITENTIARY, Nov. 5, 1839.

Sir :—If I had been told at any former period of my eventful life that the day would come in which I would deeply feel and be compelled to acknowledge the effects of American injustice and ingratitude; that I would be the victim of laws founded on political expediency, partially and vindictively executed; that fifty or sixty thousand persons would seek an alleviation of my sufferings from the authorities of the republic and seek it in vain; and that I would see the highest seats of the bench of civil and criminal justice prostituted to party purposes, without a hope of relief to the sufferers, I would have replied—"all this may be true of England, but of America, never!"

Among the millions of our countrymen who looked to America as a land of benevolence, mercy and justice; a land which would afford an example to the whole world of the happiness and friendship to be realized from democratic institutions, won by victorious patriots and administered in the spirit of the declaration of July 4th, 1776, few have been more enthusiastic, few more sanguine and confiding than myself. How far my hopes are likely to be soon realized, will appear from the sequel.

More than twelve years have elapsed since the late Robert Randall, Esq., a near relative of the celebrated statesman of Roanoke, and member of the Upper Canada Legislature for the country round Niagara Falls, placed in your hands a memorial to the English House of Commons signed by 15 to 20,000 persons, complaining that at the urgent request of George 4th, through his colonial secretary, Earl Bathurst, the Council and Assembly of Upper Canada had passed a bill to deprive of their freehold estates and civil rights, thousands of the inhabitants, because they were natives of the United States, unless they would solemnly swear to abjure for ever the land of their birth, in order to be made *subjects*, as far as holding and conveying of lands went, and in that province only—and that the judges of elections in Niagara and elsewhere had begun to turn from the polling places all Americans as strangers and aliens, while their titles to their farms were questioned in the courts.

This oath was to be kept on record and published, and the office holders of the colony well knew that few there were among the farmers who would submit to a condition so degrading, hence they looked forward to a rich harvest out of the people's property, and backed as they were by the military power and the machinery of law, expected to reduce them to the condition of serfs or drive them from the country.

The Americans had chosen a central committee, and had foolishly pitched upon Fothergill the king's printer one of their most inveterate enemies to take their complaints to England. As their sincere friend, as a warm admirer of the institutions of their native country, I consented to act as confidential secretary to the committee, persuaded them to keep their business perfectly secret, discard Fothergill and choose Randall. I sent printed copies of their memorial in every direction, received them back signed, drafted the agent's instructions, according to the views of the committee; and before it was known in Toronto that Mr. R. had been appointed, you had their memorial on the tables of parliament in London.

Your efforts and those of Mr. Warburton were successful; the secretary gave way, and the officials of the colony had scarce recovered from their consternation before Mr. R. returned with instructions from royalty to quash the bill, oath and record, and give the memorialists all they had asked.

You had the thanks of the legislature for defeating its measures, and I those of the committee. All parties acknowledged that justice had been done, and although I gained the lasting enmity of the family compact, I little thought that in the hour of exile, pain and privation, my reward from their countrymen would be a vindictive prosecution, an unjust trial, and close incarceration in an American bastile, with the gloomy winter prospect now before myself and family.

During the 18 months I remained in London, the agent of the Upper Canadians, you had opportunities of witnessing the sincerity with which I advocated popular rights. During an interview with a late prime minister of England, of three hours nearly, you heard me defend the generous, open hearted character of the American people against the doubts that were expressed on that subject; you heard me warn the government that if it came to blows they would find it an expensive, losing contest.

1

the large majority of the house so far looked readily to Governor Maitland and his officials. Still, Gourlay bequeathed long-term effects. Not only had he showed Upper Canadians that local grievances, especially over land, were province-wide and popular, but he had also left an enduring legend of a martyr for reform, to be used against government in years to come as proof of the tyranny and injustice of the Compact's rule. Yet starting in 1821, another, different issue came strongly to the fore, a question of the rights of non-loyalist American-born inhabitants of the province: the so-called "Alien Question" which brought a far greater popular challenge to the established powers, and did lead on to a Reform party in politics. It began with a petition against the election of Barnabas Bidwell, a non-Loyalist American in origin, as an Assembly member for Lennox and Addington.

Bidwell had been Attorney-General in Massachusetts before coming to Upper Canada in 1812, thereby escaping his trial for misuse of public funds when he had earlier been Treasurer of Berkshire County. The petition now raised against him (probably from friends of the defeated candidate) asked for his expulsion from the Assembly, both because of his bad character, and because as an official in the United States he would have taken oaths renouncing all British allegiance and therefore be an alien. He was expelled, by a majority of one, on the moral grounds. His son, Marshall Spring Bidwell, then stood for election in his place. Though American-born, there were no charges against him. But the returning officer rejected him as being an alien through his birth in the United States after the Revolution, whereupon the Assembly ruled that, in regard to allegiance, he indeed was eligible. The younger Bidwell was duly elected, to have an influential future career as a leading advocate of reform and speaker of the house. Yet the Alien Question was now an angry matter of debate: an issue of politics as well as legal status that lasted on till 1827.

Without getting into the full complexities of this issue, let it basically be noted that it involved legal rulings on naturalization (the process by which an alien became a British subject), plus the weight of non-Loyalist, American-born inhabitants of Upper Canada,

1. *Upper Canadian Alien Question. This article appeared in Mackenzie's* Gazette *in 1839. The "Alien Question" dealt with the process by which an alien became a British subject. It was an issue that lasted until 1827 and was especially heated concerning Americans, particularly due to powerful anti-American sentiments surviving since the War of 1812.*

2. *Hon. Marshall Spring Bidwell (1799-1872), 1829. American-born Bidwell was a member of the Legislative Assembly for Lennox and Addington (1825-1836) and served as Speaker in 1829 and 1835.*

2

especially in its western half, and the powerful anti-American currents that had flowed from the War of 1812. The imperial authorities and the Family Compact were keen to restrict American influences, and many Upper Canadians agreed with them, particularly in the eastern half of the province. But those who had come from the United States, who often had served in the provincial militia during the war, and at times held public posts since then, were not ready to be termed second-class citizens, much less aliens, according to some narrow legal rule. Furthermore, as well as filling posts or being elected to parliament, their own right to vote, or to hold lands, might seriously be at stake.

In reality, it did not go that far. The government was fully ready to maintain the land titles of the American-born, and would recognize their right to vote and take office, once the necessary legislation had been passed. But those in question were not willing to be granted what they believed they already had. The elections of 1824 for the first time produced a clear anti-government majority in the Assembly. There was political turmoil through several years thereafter; hot debates in the house, deadlocks between a Legislative Council seeking a very restricted law to establish the American-borns' rights, and a Legislative Assembly wanting a flat declaration that these same American-born were and always had been British subjects. There were appeals to Britain, bills, counter-bills, and disallowed bills. But at last — not until 1828 — an Assembly dominated by men who now could well be termed Reformers, Marshall Spring Bidwell among them, passed a fairly simple measure. It had to be accepted (with bad grace) by the provincial government because the Colonial Office in London itself had so advised. The Upper Canada Alien Act of 1828 thus declared that all were British subjects who had held provincial land grants or any public office, or who had come into the province before 1820, while those who had entered since then could be legally naturalized after seven year's residence. This settlement calmed the waters. Nonetheless, it was a plain defeat for the Compact's forces, and a victory for an emerging Reform movement, which henceforth could look to the American-born for decided support.

1. Election Poster of Robert Baldwin, 1828.
2. House of Colonel Samuel Strickland, Lakefield, Ontario, 1860s. Strickland came to Upper Canada in 1825 and left lively portrayals of frontier life there, as did his sisters Susanna Moodie and Catharine Parr Traill.
3. Celebrating the Incorporation of the City of Toronto, 1834. The population of the province's capital, York, had increased to nearly 10,000 by the year 1834 due mostly to overseas migration from Britain. Mssrs. Gooderham's and Worts' original windmill is shown in the picture, as is old St. James Church. Lithograph by Frederic Waistell Jopling (1859-1945), 1909, (75th anniversary of incorporation).

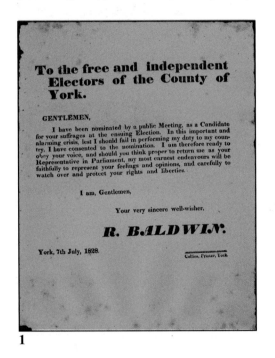

To the free and independent Electors of the County of York.

GENTLEMEN,

I have been nominated by a public Meeting, as a Candidate for your suffrages at the ensuing Election. In this important and alarming crisis, lest I should fail in performing my duty to my country, I have consented to the nomination. I am therefore ready to obey your voice, and should you think proper to return me as your Representative in Parliament, my most earnest endeavours will be faithfully to represent your feelings and opinions, and carefully to watch over and protect your rights and liberties.

I am, Gentlemen,

Your very sincere well-wisher,

R. BALDWIN.

York, 7th July, 1828.

Collins, Printer, York.

1

2

Celebrating Incorporation of Toronto 1834 formerly Muddy York

3

Growth Through Immigration

In the meantime, British immigration was mounting apace, to make the question of American settlers look less worrisome to the Conservative side. After depression years in 1825-26, the return of good times was reflected in growing immigrant arrivals on the St. Lawrence, which had averaged around 9,000 yearly in the earlier 20s, but rose to 16,000 in 1827. By 1830 annual landings at Quebec had reached 28,000. In 1834, nearly 31,000 landed there, the great bulk of them coming on to Upper Canada. These figures may look small by later Canadian standards; yet in terms of the numbers of inhabitants then, they were striking and influential. Thus Upper Canada's population increased to some 236,000 even by 1831, and ten years later would rise over 450,000, in growth mainly resulting from British immigration. The capital town of York itself advanced from some 1,500 in 1821 to become the city of Toronto in 1834 — the province's first incorporated city — with a population approaching 10,000: again very much a result of the overseas migration.

The new settlers undoubtedly swelled the towns, but they also pushed back the land frontiers. In the east, poor Catholic Irish with slight resources or farming skills went especially to the Ottawa Valley and into lumbering. Working, and fighting, with French Canadian *chêneurs* (originally "oak-cutters"), these Irish became the "shiners," who shared many a backwoods timber shanty or rowdy Valley brawl. Some Scottish farmers and families also settled up the Ottawa, as did English half-pay officers and merchants. In fact, it should be kept in mind that while one national element from Britain might stand out in a particular area of settlement, other stocks from the British Isles usually were close at hand, or were intermingled with the dominant group. On this basis, Scots, and later Irish, also

1. *Blythe, the Langton homestead, c. 1948. This homestead was originally developed by John Langton, who became a noted official as provincial Auditor-General.*

2. *Home of John A. Macdonald, 134 Earl Street, Kingston. Macdonald was born in Glasgow, Scotland and came to Kingston in 1820 with his parents among the many Scots who added markedly to the area.*

3. *Dunbar and Susanna Moodie on the steps of Moodie Cottage. Susanna Moodie came from England to Upper Canada in 1832. Her writings usually stressed the hardships of the frontier and served to prepare people wanting to emigrate to a new life.*

4. *Catharine Parr Traill (1802-1899), in her later years. Also arriving in Upper Canada in 1832, Traill was less critical than her sister, Susanna Moodie, of life there. In her book,* Backwoods of Canada, *she accepted the new reality facing her in a new, harder land.*

5. *Anne Langton (1804-1893), c. 1880s. Langton and her brother John (1808-1894), who both came to Upper Canada in the great wave in the early 1830s, also wrote vividly about their lives on the frontier farmlands near Peterborough.*

1

2

3

4

5

added markedly to the Kingston area — not forgetting a certain John A. Macdonald, born in Glasgow, who in 1820 came at the age of five with his parents to Kingston. That town, moreover, emerged as a centre of Scots Presbyterianism, as well as a military and naval base; and soon looked suitably Scottish in the stout grey limestone masonry it adopted instead of wood.

British settlers also filled in more of the Rideau Lake and Peterborough districts. In the latter area, in Douro Township, some remarkable upper-class English immigrants appeared, appropriately called "literary pioneers" for the writings they published on frontier life: Samuel Strickland and his sisters, Catharine Parr Traill and Susanna Moodie (who had married half-pay officers), or Anne Langton and her brother John. John Strickland came out in 1825, the others in the great wave of the early 30s; but they all left graphic, lively portrayals of the frontier world in Upper Canada — sometimes critical or discouraged by the drab, bleak isolation and endless toil of the backwoods — more often gleaming with hope at the bountiful natural realm and the rising human developments all around them. There were other such authors besides, but this little "gentry" group in one small fraction of an outstretched, unlearned pioneer community made most rewarding contributions to Ontario's heritage.

In central areas, immigrants spread farther up Yonge Street to Lake Simcoe, or north-west of York, where Ulster Irish settled in Mono and Yorkshire families in nearer Etobicoke. But it was in the fertile Western Ontario peninsula that farm frontiers most fully expanded. As immigrants poured into this south-west, and especially into Colonel Talbot's Lake Erie tract, he truly did a land-office business — in every sense, because he was entitled to receive 200 acres more for every 50-acre farm lot he settled. Over time, Talbot thus obtained a kingdom of half a million acres to direct, one that stretched for 130 miles from west of Long Point to the Detroit River, through Elgin, Kent and Essex Counties, and inland to cover much of Middlesex. Yet he served it well, building main roads and insisting that settlers clear and develop their lands. If not, they would be literally "rubbed out," their pencilled names erased from a map of the farms he had allotted, to be replaced by more worthy applicants. And the Talbot

1. Talbot and Back Road Junction. Named after Colonel Talbot, the Talbot roads in the early 19th century were among the best in the province. They ran from Fort Erie in the Niagara Peninsula to Sandwich (opposite Detroit). Watercolour by George Russell Dartnell (1798-1878).

2. Port Talbot, c. 1840. Colonel Talbot was entitled to receive 200 acres more land for every fifty-acre farm lot he settled. Over time, he obtained half of a million acres to direct. Talbot built the main roads and insisted that the settlers clear and develop their land or they would lose it.

3. Carling and Company Brewery at London in 1890s. The old building was burnt down on February 4, 1879 and then rebuilt. Chosen as the capital for the Western District, London even by 1827 could boast of having a court house, a tavern, a brewery, as well as a few frame shops and houses.

1

2

3

C. P. R. Depot—First House in GUELPH, Canada.

1

2

Roads were among the best in the province, running from Fort Erie in the Niagara Peninsula to Sandwich opposite Detroit.

In the land of the Talbot Settlement, Scots had particularly occupied Aldborough Township; English and Irish located more widely. As settled lands reached inland, London in Middlesex was chosen as the site of a new capital for the Western District. Simcoe's capital-to-be at last came into being, as in 1827 a court house, a tavern, a brewery, and a few frame shops and houses were erected. Yet by 1834 it was building in brick and was graced with "Eldon House," a fine mansion that still stands, erected by the District Treasurer, John Harris, a well-to-do English immigrant. In the western peninsula as well, there were other new towns rising, with many smaller farm settlements, such as that for the English poor charitably sent out in 1832 by the Earl of Egremont, which was established in Adelaide Township in Middlesex; though its settlers did include some with capital and farm equipment. And of course Scots and Irish also settled in Middlesex, or other southwestern areas outside the Talbot kingdom.

But the largest western settlement enterprise was that of the Canada Company, founded in London in 1824 through the drive and vision of John Galt, the Scottish novelist. When chartered in 1826, this corporation bought more than two million acres of dispersed Crown reserves from the provincial government, plus a solid 1,100,000 acres more which came to be known as the Huron Tract. The purchase money was to be paid in instalments to the government, while the Company made roads and improved the lands, then sold them to incoming settlers. The old free-grant policy, in fact, was running out; "free" lands (which did have registration and other fees) were tending now to be poorer in quality, or decidedly remote, as nearer, better lots were taken up by the immigrant inflow. Settlers who were able to pay, preferred to buy good lands, perhaps partly cleared, on roads with access to neighbours and markets; furthermore, such settlers often made the best farmers, having a valuable stake in their holdings. And so the Canada Company project was far from unrealistic in planning to develop and sell its properties;

1. *The Priory, First House in Guelph, c. 1908. This house, which was later used as a CPR depot, was built in 1827 by John Galt who founded the town of Guelph.*
2. *Street Scene, Goderich. The building of this port town was supervised by "Tiger" Dunlop. It was designed with a radial street plan with a civic park where the radiating roads met.*
3. *Court House, London, 1926. This building was erected in 1829 and was one of the province's first castle-like structures. It was said to be patterned after Malahide Castle, the family seat of Colonel Thomas Talbot in Ireland, because of his local influence.*
4. *Eldon House, London, 1967. This mansion was built by the Western District Treasurer, John Harris, in 1834.*

3

4

1

2

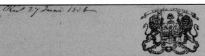

3

1. *Canada Company circular concerning land for settlement in Upper Canada, May 1, 1836.*
2. *John Galt (1779-1839). A well-known novelist, Galt founded the Canada Company in London in 1824.*
3. *Drainage Cut Construction by the Canada Company, Burwell Lake, Lambton County, c. 1871-1873.*
4. *Canada Company Coat of Arms. This company was founded in 1824 and was chartered in 1826, at which time it bought more than two million acres of dispersed Crown reserves from the provincial government.*
5. *Draft outline of the Huron Tract, 1829. In addition to Crown reserves, the Canada Company acquired 1,100,000 acres of land fronting on Lake Huron, which became known as the Huron Tract.*

4

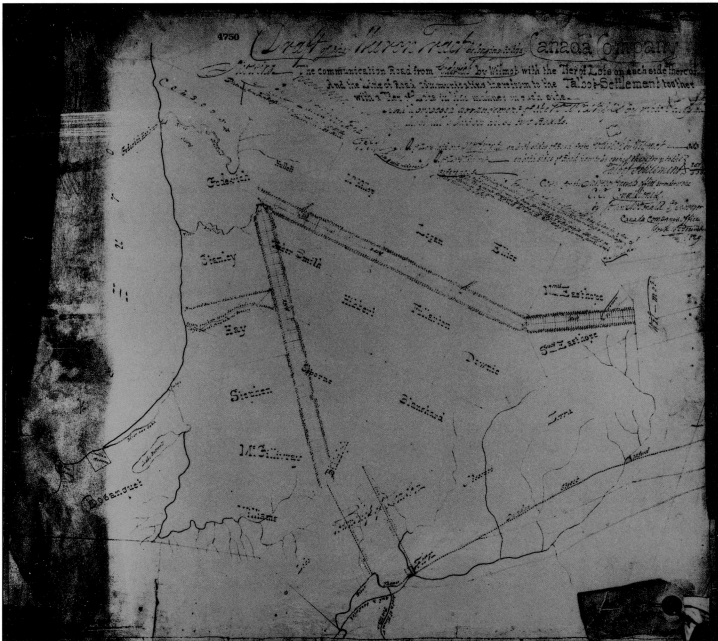

5

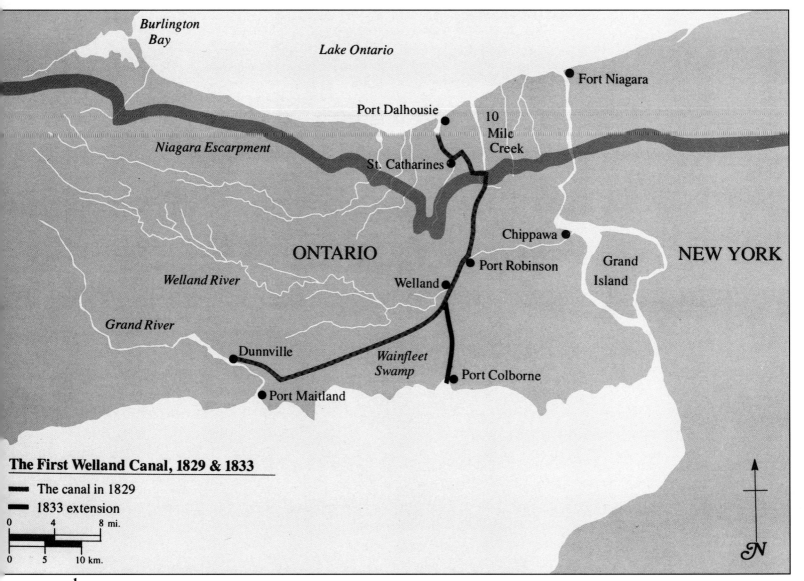

The First Welland Canal, 1829 & 1833

▬▬▬ The canal in 1829

▬▬▬ 1833 extension

0   4   8 mi.

0   5   10 km.

1

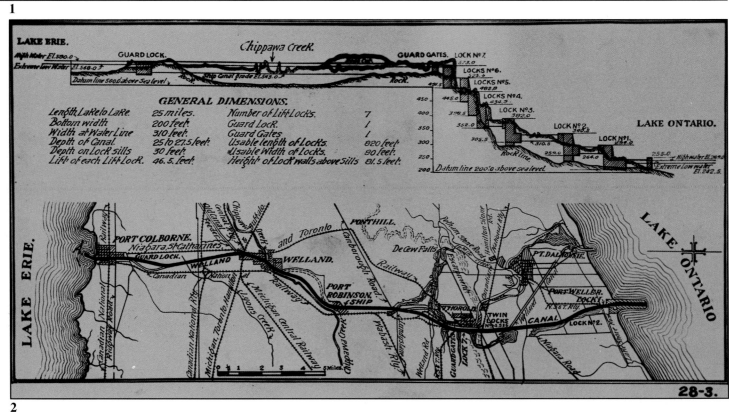

2

although profits to its investors might take longer in arriving than had been anticipated.

Above all, the Company laid out and settled its Huron Tract, a vast triangle of land that fronted on Lake Huron for sixty miles and ran back inland roughly to Guelph. That town of Guelph, with its interesting radial plan of streets, was founded in 1827 by John Galt as the superintendent of the Company, together with Dr. William "Tiger" Dunlop as its "warden of woods and forests," a former Scottish army surgeon who settled in the Huron Tract himself and worked hard to develop it. From Guelph, Galt built the Huron Road to Goderich on Lake Huron; and in 1828 Dunlop supervised the building of this new port town, which also had a radial street plan — instead of the typical Ontario square grid of streets — but this time, with an attractive civic park where the radiating roads met. More important, the Canada Company, by effective advertising in Britain and energetic work in Canada on roads, bridges and other improvements, drew thousands of Lowland Scots, English and Irish to the Huron Tract. The Company would later be accused by the dissatisfied with domineering over its settlers, and with having too close ties with the government; but its accomplishments are still there to see in Western Ontario today. It could be added, as well, that competition from the Canada Company, or from the sale of crown lands by public auction (a new policy adopted in 1826), brought the Anglican Church under Strachan's powerful leadership to promote a policy of land sales for its own clergy reserves. An imperial act of 1827 allowed them to be sold up to a maximum of 100,000 acres a year. The resulting successful sales of clergy lands increasingly removed them as economic barriers to settlement. After the 1820s, they really became more a political and religious issue, as funds from the sales accumulated to keep Anglicanism endowed and privileged.

By the mid 1830s — as British immigration rose to a peak — the farm frontiers of Upper Canada were broadening inland towards the

1. *Map of the First Welland Canal and its 1833 extension.*
2. *Map of the later Welland Canal showing route, dimensions, and elevation.*
3. *Stamp for William Hamilton Merritt. Issued on November 29, 1974, this stamp celebrated 150 years since the start of the construction on the Welland Canal.*
4. *Hon. William Hamilton Merritt (1793-1862), 1860. Merritt, a St. Catharines merchant-entrepreneur, was chiefly responsible for the initial building of the Welland Canal, which joins Port Dalhousie on Lake Ontario with Port Colborne on Lake Erie.*

3

4

rugged margins of the Shield; while up the Ottawa lumbering had entered the Shield itself. Large, unoccupied reaches of good farmland mostly remained just in the northern half of the western peninsula. And economic developments already heralded the rise of a more complex provincial society beyond the frontier stage. Along with new villages and towns fed by immigration, or expanding trade and enlarging business power, there came major projects that employed a host of immigrants. In late 1824, William Hamilton Merritt of St. Catharines, a merchant-entrepreneur, the son of a Loyalist, and a militia veteran from the War of 1812, began the Welland Canal to bypass Niagara Falls and provide unbroken navigation between Lakes Erie and Ontario. His Welland Canal Company ran into heavy engineering problems. It had to seek public loans that turned it into a private institution funded by the government (and taxpayer) in an all-too Canadian way. Nonetheless, when the canal opened in 1829, it was of tremendous benefit. It not only enabled Great Lakes shipping to move freely between the head of Lake Superior and the upper St. Lawrence, but also supplied a passage between Lake Ontario and the Erie Canal at Buffalo, which had been completed in 1825 and took barges from the Great Lakes down to the Hudson River — thus, for example, giving Toronto through water access right to New York City.

The Rideau Canal project was bigger, more costly and better engineered than the Welland, being a military design built under the Royal Engineers at imperial expense to connect the Ottawa River with Lake Ontario at Kingston. Begun in 1826 by Colonel John By of the Engineers, it aimed to provide a safe route inland, via the Ottawa and Rideau waterways, which could maintain connections between Montreal and the Great Lakes in the event of another American war. It is entirely wrong to think that a blissful peace descended on the Canadian-American border after 1814. Both sides continued worrying, with good cause, about a re-match, right down to the 1870s. In any event, Colonel By placed his base camp where the Rideau foamed into the Ottawa. Then, from "Bytown" he struck on southward towards Kingston, building massive stone locks along the way; not like the makeshift wooden walls of the original Welland

1. *Monument at the Site of Colonel By's House, Ottawa, June 1991.*
2. *Lock of the Welland Canal, Near Thorold, 1904. In the lock is the ship* Arthur of Toronto.
3. *A Statue of John By, Ottawa, June, 1991. There is no known accurate portrait of By, but many artists have tried to recreated his appearance for portraits and monuments. This statue is close to the site of his "Bytown" house which no longer stands.*
4. *Colonel By at the Building of the Rideau, 1826. The Rideau Canal project was bigger, more costly and better engineered than the Welland, being a military design built under the Royal Engineers at imperial expense to connect the Ottawa River with Lake Ontario at Kingston.*

1

2

3

4

1

1. *Locks of the Rideau Canal, Ottawa, c. 1870. The Rideau locks were built with stone as opposed to wood, which was used for the original Welland Canal.*
2. *A Map of the Rideau Waterway.*
3. *North Entrance to the Rideau Canal, Bytown (Ottawa), May 1845. This sketch was done from the Royal Engineer's office by Thomas Burrowes.*
4. *A Recreational Boat in the Locks, Ottawa, June 1991. Although the Rideau Canal was built for mainly military reasons, it never had to fulfil this purpose. It now remains a picturesque and much enjoyed holiday route.*

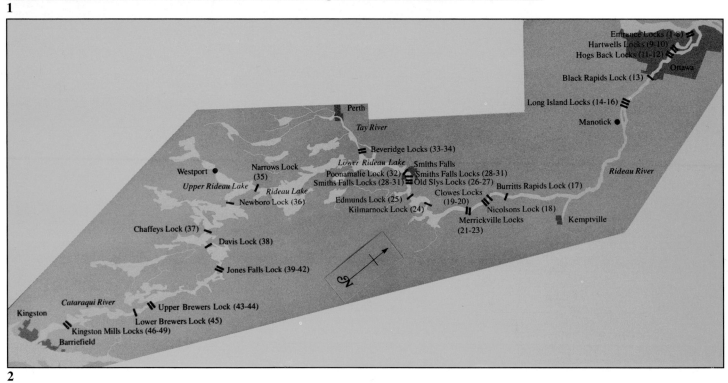

2

North Entrance of the Rideau Canal from the Ottawa River; taken from the Royal Eng. Office Bytown.

3

4

1

2

Canal, but triumphs of earlier nineteenth-century engineering. In the process of cutting channels and raising dams, however, far too many Irish labourers on the Rideau Canal died from the "ag-ue," mosquito-born malarial fever that bred in ponds and swamps en route. Nevertheless, by May of 1832, after gruelling pick-and-shovel work with only oxen and gunpowder to help, the most expensive military project in British North America was formally opened — while a massive new Fort Henry went up at Kingston to protect its entrance. The Rideau Canal, fortunately, never had to meet its military purposes: perhaps because it was there. But it long carried Ottawa lumber down to Kingston and American markets, or goods back to the interior; and it undoubtedly promoted Bytown as a lumber capital, not to mention fostering Kingston and several canal towns. Today it remains a picturesque holiday route, with handsome cut-stone walls and fortified blockhouses, recalling other memories of Ontario's heritage.

A developing, populating Upper Canada also took up social enterprises, particularly in the field of education. Even in earliest years, the province had sought to educate its young. While Simcoe's original hope for a university had proved premature, grammar schools — very loosely, small classical academies for chosen male pupils — had been erected in each district under the Act of 1806; and Dr. John Strachan thus came to head the York Grammar School in what was then the Home District. In 1816, elementary schools were added by an act of the legislature, that provided for teachers and established local trustees within the districts to supervise them. John Strachan pressed the early beginnings of public education. He went further, when in 1823 he was made president of the General Board of Education to direct provincial schools. Yet while Strachan and his supporters were concerned to check the spread of American biases through education — by cheap textbooks brought in from the United States, or untrained teachers entering from that highly assertive republic — the enemies of Strachan, who often were American in origin themselves, saw his purposes chiefly as aiming to keep a

1. Fort Henry, Guards and Cannon, July 6, 1957. First built across the harbour from Kingston during the War of 1812, the fort was strengthened by construction of the present massive redoubt in 1832-1836, which was done as part of a larger plan for defence of the entrance to the Rideau Canal.
2. The Fort Henry Guard. The fort was completely renovated between 1936 and 1938, and it is now preserved as a living museum of military history. The Fort Henry Guard, dressed in 1867 uniforms, carries out infantry and artillery drill for tourists and has won international recognition for its authenticity and precision of performance.
3. Stamp depicting Fort Henry. This stamp was issued as part of a series commemorating ten major Canadian forts.
4. Hopkins' School, One Early Seat of Learning, Kingston. In 1816, elementary schools were added to existing grammar schools by an act that provided salaries for teachers and established local trustees within the Districts of Upper Canada to select them.

3

4

46 CHRISTIAN GUARDIAN. DECEMBER 26,

*** The proceeds of this paper will be applied to the support of superannuated or worn-out Preachers of the M. E. Church in Canada; and of widows and orphans of those who have died in the work; and to the general spreading of the Gospel.

CHRISTIAN GUARDIAN.

YORK, SATURDAY, DECEMBER 26.

"*Honesty is the best policy.*"

"In necessary things, *Unity*.—In non-essentials, *Liberty*. In all things, *Charity*."

We were just preparing some observations on the recent policy of some injudicious friends of the Scotch Kirk, in connexion with certain dignitaries of the Church of England, when we received the following communication—from the pen of an able and experienced friend—in which this important subject is so comprehensively, candidly, and clearly brought before our readers, that we think it unnecessary to add any thing more, at the present time, than merely to express our increased conviction, that the latitude of Canada never was designed to wear the shackles of an ecclesiastical or literary despotism; that if our Government will be based upon the *affections* of an enlightened people—if *justice* have any place in its policy, and *prudence* rule in its councils—if the scourge of religious animosities is to be removed from our land, and the means of education will ever be brought within the grasp of the lower as well as the higher classes of the community—if our literary, religious, and various internal improvements, are to keep any kind of pace with those of our enterprising neighbours across the St. Lawrence, our Chief Magistrates must render themselves *worthy* of the endearing appellation of *Fathers*, and deal alike with all their equally deserving children—must imitate the example of the "Great God Our Saviour," and be no ***respecters of persons.***

[For the Christian Guardian.]

MESSRS. EDITORS:

It was with feelings of astonishment and regret that I read in the Kingston Religious Advocate of the 20th ult. the Report of a Committee of the General Assembly of the Church of Scotland on the Canada Petitions respecting the Clergy Reserves. I allude particularly to that part of the Report which professes to state the number of the adherents of the Scottish Kirk in Upper Canada. I believe it is *now* generally known to the public, that a small body of our fellow subjects in this Province professing to belong to the *Kirk*, or the Church of Scotland, have, for the last two or three years, been endeavoring to establish a claim to be a moity of an Established Church in this Colony, and to obtain one half of the Clergy Reserves.

In regard to the character of such a claim advanced by *any* body of Christians or Clergy, I believe it has been unequivocally declared by the public voice, both in and out of the House of Assembly, to be unfounded, impolitic, unjust, and destructive to the best interests of the country. That monopoly of patronage, exclusive privileges and power, and the system of priestly domination, so deservedly odious to the people of this country, and so warmly opposed by them, when claimed by the Episcopal Church, will lose none of its deformity and malignant qualities, when strengthened and increased by being extended to two bodies of Clergy instead of one.

Besides, on what principle of moral justice can the Clergy of the Kirk in Canada, claim exclusive power and privileges, and a liberal support from the public funds, any more than the Presbyterians, the Roman Catholics, the Methodists, or Baptists. A few years ago, our brethren of the Kirk could see the evil of partial laws and sectarian literary institutions as clearly as others; they felt the pressure and they cried out mightily against such things. I leave it to themselves to explain what weighty reasons produced such a change in their views as to induce them to abandon the cause of religious freedom, and to labor with so much zeal to build up the strong holds of bigotry and intolerance, which they once endeavoured to destroy. Their secession, it is true, has taken a little from the *numerical* strength of the liberal party, but nothing from the *moral* power of the righteous cause in which they are engaged. That will ultimately triumph, maugre the puny efforts of interested men to oppose its progress. Religious liberty is dear to the people of this country, and they will not tamely surrender their inherent rights; Public opinion has pronounced sentence of condemnation upon every system of intolerance, and it cannot be stayed in its victorious march, but sooner or later will prevail.

But it is very possible that these gentlemen of the Kirk see no injustice in appropriating for the exclusive advantage of a few, all those resources of the country which can be legitimately devoted to the purposes of religion and education, and leaving the body of the population destitute of the means of education, and, so far as public patronage goes, of the means of religious instruction. The exalted opinion which they may entertain of the excellence of their own communion, or of their own pre-eminent merits, arising from the prejudices of education, may make it appear but just and reasonable that *they*, should be clothed with superior power, and should possess peculiar and exclusive rights and privileges. Such probably being their feelings, we cannot so much blame them for striving to become, in conjunction with the Episcopal Church, the exclusive establishment, patronized and paid by the government of this country.

But though these considerations go to palliate the conduct of our Kirk friends in regard to the *end* they aim at, yet the ungenerous, not to say, iniquitous *means used*, admit of no such palliation. We can excuse them for wishing to be exalted over our heads and to have their feet placed upon our necks, but we cannot excuse and justify the duplicity and mis-representation used in order to obtain this pre-eminence. As to the character of the means used, we have a specimen in the Report before us. "With regard to Upper Canada, says the Report, it is established beyond all question by *these returns*, that of the whole body of the inhabitants of this province, supposed to average three hundred thousand and augmenting with great rapidity every year by new importations, *one half, at the lowest* estimate, are decidedly attached to the *doctrine* and *discipline* of the *Church of Scotland*." And in addition to this they go on to state, that the Seceders from Ireland and Scotland, and the Presbyterians from the United States, *are extremely* anxious to be connected with these 150,000! This precious information the committee profess to have received from their friends in this country. By giving us this information, they have exculpated themselves from the responsibility of this monstrous mis-representation, and have thrown the odium of it on their friends who are living amongst us.

This certainly equals any thing to be met with in the famous "Ecclesiastical Chart"—Half the population Scotch Presbyterians, and many others sighing to be connected with them! Why then is the connection not formed? Ask the independent Presbyteries of Upper Canada. I am only astonished that any respectable body of men in this Province, having the least regard for their character, would venture to forward to Great Britain a statement so palpably erroneous. Was it expected, like the "Ecclesiastical Chart," to effect its object before it could be controverted?—To attempt to disprove it, in this country where the facts are known, is quite superfluous, It is obvious to every one that the Kirk is amongst the least numerous of the different bodies of Christians into which the population of this country is divided. I will venture to affirm, without fear of successful contradiction, that they do not at most average more than one in fifteen or twenty. It does not even embrace much more than "one half" of Scotch Emigrants. I know Scotch settlements in this country nearly all Baptists, others Roman Catholics.

But facts, known to the committee themselves, ought to have convinced them of the great inaccuracy of the statements to which they were about to give currency by the sanction of their names. They know how small a number of Scotch Clergymen was employed in this Province. And could they for a moment believe that 150,000 of their communion, spread over an extent of country larger than Scotland, and these persons, as they stated, "zealously attached to the doctrines and discipline of the Kirk;" I say, could they believe, that so many of their brethren would live for years without the ministry of the Gospel, or be contented with the services of five or six ministers, while the Baptists & Methodists, who, according to their own and Dr. Strachan's division of the population, had no existence, employed more than 100 ministers? While at the same time so small was the demand for Church of Scotland Ministers, that their own schoolmasters, as they state, were taking orders in the Episcopal Church.

But, Messrs. Editors, had this display of numbers been only an idle boast, without any ulterior object in view—were it merely the effusion of national or sectarian vanity—I would most cheerfully let our brethren enjoy their imaginary superiority—But when I consider it as intended to influence the decision of the British Government on a question affecting the vital welfare of this Province, to mislead the Imperial Parliament, when legislating on a subject involving our religious rights, and liberties, and dearest interests; and finally, as designed to rivet upon the hands of the people of this colony the fetters of spiritual bondage; when I view these statements in this their true light, they assume a character of fearful importance, and I am constrained to consider them as an insidious & dangerous attack upon our rights and privileges. For suppose Dr. S. had succeeded in making the British Government believe that one half of us were church-men, and the authors of these statements, that the other half were "zealously attached" to the Church of Scotland, what would be the necessary result? Most certainly that we should have a double priest-hood established by law, and our civil, religious, and literary institutions so modelled as to suit this state of things, while our interests would be sacrificed, and our liberties prostrated.

When the Noble Lord who was the bearer of the documents furnished by the General Assembly, went to London, he went impressed with a belief that half the people in this Province were Scotch Presbyterians. He would of course endeavor to impress that opinion on the minds of His Majesty's Ministars, and on other members of Parliament.—Other Scotch Peers and Members of Parliament, receiving their information from the General Assembly, had the same opinion. What effect these things may have had, or are now having on the plans of the Government relative to Canada, I cannot precisely say, but this much we may be assured of, that it will be most unfavorable to the general interests and welfare of the Province.

But if the members of the Kirk in this Province have made these statements inadvertently, without any design to misrepresent, as I would wish to believe, to regain the public confidence, they are called upon, out of a regard to their own churches, as well as by the voice of an injured country, to disabuse His Majesty's Government and the British Parliament, by confessing the errors into which they have unintentionally led them. If the members of the Kirk will be advised by their best friends, they will retrace their steps, and again number themselves amongst the advocates of liberal principles and institutions. The dangers to our "civil and political as well as religious liberty," which would be the inevitable consequence of an exclusive religious establishment, are clearly and ably portrayed in the Scotch Pastoral letter, published at Montreal 1828, and it is much to be regretted that the same persons, who could express such truly Christian, manly, and liberal sentiments, as are contained in that letter, should join with the English Church to bring upon the country those evils which they then so feelingly deprecated. I should rejoice if our brethrren would apply to the rights and liberties of other denominations the sound and conclusive arguments which they adduce in defence of their own privileges.

I do not, Messrs. Editors, make these strictures in a spirit of hostility to the members of the Scotch Church in this Province, for I believe their claims to be as equitable and as just as those of the English Church; or rather that both are *equally* unfounded and unjust. On the grounds of Scripture, justice, and sound policy, I am alike opposed to the exclusive claims of *any* denomination of Christians. But I shall greatly rejoice to see the day, when, without legislative exclusion or partial patronage, every denomination of Evangelical Christians will be left to carry into efficient and universal opperation their benevolent plans for the instruction of *the whole* population of the Province.

As a contrast to the sectarian and selfish views and plans of many members of the Churches of England and Scotland in Canada—I wish, in conclusion, to notice the principles and proceedings of, what, in religious matters, is called "*the liberal party*."—This embraces at least nine-tenths of the population, including many intelligent and patriotic members of the English and Scotch Churches, Roman Catholics, nearly *all* of the Presbyterians, Methodists, Baptists, &c. One grand principle in which they all agree is this; viz. "*That liberty of conscience and worship is the unalienable birthright of every man as a member of the social body*"—And that consequently, "no civil disabilities should be imposed on any man on account of his religious opinions."—They contend that, in this Province, no particular form of Christianity is established by *law*, with exclusive and peculiar privileges, but that every peaceable and loyal subject has equal rights and is entitled to the enjoyment of equal privileges and immunities.

Their proceedings have been open, manly, disinterested, and magnanimons. They have petitioned *openly and publicly*, both to the Provincial and the Imperial Parliament, that the Clergy Reserves may be sold, and a fund formed from their proceeds to support a general system of educa-

1

narrow oligarchic and Anglican control over public learning.

The issue particularly came to a head in regard to the provincial university. Strachan set out to realize Simcoe's original project, and use lands reserved for educational purposes to support such an institution. In 1827 he went to Britain and secured a royal charter for a University of King's College, with properties just north of York for its estate. Still, that charter, fairly liberal for Britain of the day in allowing other than Anglicans to attend the university, seemed far from liberal to the mixed religious society within Upper Canada. For Anglican clergy would still control that institution, which therefore looked much like an instrument of conversion to non-Anglicans. Furthermore, Strachan's fudging of statistics to claim a lot more Anglicans in Upper Canada than there possibly could be, also made his return with the King's College Charter anything but a celebration. In truth, it took fifteen years still, before this state-backed provincial university finally got into operation.

At the same time, opposition to Anglican ascendancy rose increasingly from other Protestant bodies: Presbyterians, Baptists, and others; but especially the Methodists, the largest Protestant denomination in the province. Methodism had grown vigorously on the farming frontiers since pre-war American settlement days, gaining many British immigrants as well. And a separate Upper Canada Conference was established in 1828, which freed local Methodist bodies from American connections — and taints — so that this emotional, personal, and evangelistic faith stood firmly on its own against the disapproval of the more formal, authority-led churches. Particularly effective in upholding Methodism was Egerton Ryerson, a young minister of Loyalist background who in 1829 became editor of the new Methodist *Christian Guardian*. He tellingly attacked the Anglican hold on clergy reserves, the university and schools, standing for the removal of church privileges and for religious equality. Consequently, this first-rate controversialist soon made the Methodists valuable allies of political Reformers; although on other than religious issues, Ryerson would prove himself considerably more conservative in temperament.

In any event, Reform was clearly on the upsurge, as shown by the

1. *The* Christian Guardian, *December 26, 1829. Reactions of a gentleman to "the Report of a Committee of the General Assembly of the Church of Scotland on the Canada Petitions respecting the Clergy Reserves": astonishment and regret. Under Egerton Ryerson, the newspaper strongly attacked the Anglicans' hold on reserves and other privileges.*
2. *Rev. Dr. Adolphus Egerton Ryerson, (1803-1882), First Superintendent of Education. A minister of Loyalist background, Ryerson became editor of the Methodist* Christian Guardian *in 1829. He later was vitally involved in educational matters and is widely recognized as the builder of Ontario's public school system.*

2

1

2

3

elections of 1828 which returned a strong Reform majority to Assembly. Moreover, some party structure was beginning to develop: local Reform organizations to name candidates and fight elections, highly partisan Reform newspapers to keep popular grievances and demands before the voters, and a recognized set of leading party politicians. In response, a Tory-Conservative party similarly took gradual form on the other side, one which was wider than just the Compact government group, and had roots no less popular than those of the Reformers, both in the Assembly and among the voting public. As for the Reformers, one of their ablest leaders to emerge was Dr. John Rolph, member for Norfolk. Although an English immigrant, he made his mark defending the cause of the "alien" Americans — proving resourceful, eloquent and clever, if sometimes crafty and secretive as well. Another more moderate and socially prominent figure was the wealthy, Anglo-Irish Dr. William Warren Baldwin, who in 1829 put forth the idea of responsible government in a letter to the Duke of Wellington, then Prime Minister in England, proposing that, as in Great Britain, a colonial government should be removable if it lost the support of the people's elected representatives.

But most of all, there was William Lyon Mackenzie, a Scottish immigrant and at first a York shopkeeper. In 1824, he had founded the *Colonial Advocate* at Queenston, then later that year moved to York, where its sharply aggressive articles roused Reformers and stung Tories alike. In fact, the *Advocate* got so stinging (and plain slanderous) that in 1826 it was raided, foolishly, by young sprouts of the Family Compact, who tossed its type out into Toronto Bay. Thereby they made Mackenzie a new popular martyr, and won him substantial legal damages when he was going broke. And so this hotheaded, vindictive public critic — who equally was fearless in exposing privilege, favour, or injustice — rose by the 1830s to the role of a radical "people's champion." As a result, he moved a mounting mass of discords onward to rebellion; to change the world of Upper Canada itself.

1. *William Lyon Mackenzie (1795-1861). Mackenzie came to Upper Canada in 1820 from Scotland and launched his newspaper, the* Colonial Advocate, *in 1824. He became mayor of Toronto in 1834, but then spent thirteen years in exile in New York after his attempted rebellion near Toronto. He returned to Toronto in 1850 and became a member of the Legislature in 1851.*
2. *Dr. John Rolph (1793-1870). Rolph was a member of the Legislative Assembly for Middlesex (1824-1830), and for Norfolk (1836-1837 and 1851-1857). He conspired with Mackenzie and had to flee Canada. He returned to Toronto c. 1850 and became active in politics again.*
3. *Printing Office of W.L. Mackenzie, Toronto, 1840s. This building on the southeast corner of Front Street East and Frederick Street belonged to Dr. William Warren Baldwin before it became Mackenzie's printing office, and was the house in which Robert Baldwin was born.* Engraving by Toronto Engraving Co., c. 1879.

Rising Reform Movement and Rebellion

A new Lieutenant-Governor had replaced Maitland at the end of 1828. Sir John Colborne was another Napoleonic War veteran, yet more approachable, and determined not to be so dependent on his chief advisors. In fact, he put Archdeacon Strachan's nose out of joint by often not consulting him, while John Beverley Robinson was shifted from the Attorney-Generalship in 1830 and moved upstairs to be Chief Justice. Both Compact leaders kept their council seats and their extensive influence, Strachan, besides, as President of the University-to-be. But it did seem that they had been reined in, which did not hurt Colborne's popularity. Furthermore, people looked to the government to promote economic developments; and canal, harbour, and road construction well displayed its activities here. On the other hand, Reformers in the Assembly made a lot of airy speeches, including ones on responsible government, yet sounded the more irresponsible themselves in being mostly talk, no action. Accordingly, Tory-Conservatives won a majority at fresh elections held in 1830, in which Dr. Baldwin and his son Robert, a rising Reform lawyer, were both defeated in the people's shift to the right.

Marshall Spring Bidwell and William Lyon Mackenzie won seats, however; and as the former worked to shape a disciplined parliamentary opposition, the latter made himself the best-known Reform figure in Upper Canada. Expulsions largely did it. In 1831, by vote of a Tory-dominated Assembly, Mackenzie was expelled from that house for having libelled it in the scathing pages of his journal. But early in 1832 his own constituents for the county of York re-elected him in a landslide. The journal attacks, the expulsions and the re-elections went on, five times in all; only rendering Mackenzie still more a people's hero across the province. In 1833 he even took his mass of complaints to London, in order to make headway with the new Whig-Reform government that had finally replaced Tory rule in Britain, and which reformers in the colonies were eying more hopefully. Still riding the wave, Mackenzie was voted in as mayor of the new city of Toronto in March, 1834. And that October, he not only was triumphantly elected to a new Assembly, but also had considerable to do

Sir John Colborne (1778-1863). A competent Napoleonic War soldier, Colborne served as Lieutenant-Governor from 1829 to 1836.

with the wider victory of Reformers all across Upper Canada.

All the same, he still was not the party leader, and would not have done well at that job if it had then existed. Mackenzie was a one-man band; a matchless agitator and exposer of wrongs, but a wayward, carping commander who largely sowed dissension — as he did while Toronto's mayor. And the Reform party around him had its internal differences already. In 1833, Ryerson and Mackenzie had divided their ways, the former deeming Mackenzie's radical friends in England to be atheists and republicans, the latter branding Ryerson "a Jesuit in the garb of a Methodist preacher." Moreover, the main body of political Reformers was gravely stressed between radicals and moderates. The radicals, typified by Mackenzie himself, John Rolph and Dr. Charles Duncombe, member for Oxford County, pushed an elective, American-style constitution, particularly with an elected Legislative Council that would get rid of the barrier of an appointed upper house. The moderates well might include Bidwell, who shared many of Mackenzie's views yet was cooler and more balanced, and definitely included the influential Dr. Baldwin and Robert Baldwin. These two were out of parliament for the time; yet still very significant in voicing the opinions of a probable majority that looked to reform within the British parliamentary constitution — not to uproot it for an American system that had been first rejected by the original Loyalist founders of Upper Canada.

Now these differing Reform factions did share considerable common ground: in fighting the Anglican grasp on reserves and public education, in denouncing the government's links with the Welland Canal Company and the Canada Company, or its favouritism regarding land grants and official appointments. Nevertheless, the radicals clung to their sweeping constitutional reforms, deeming anything else partial and inadequate, while the moderates feared thus endangering the British tie and jumping into the arms of the United States. Instead, they thought with the Baldwins that a basic, sufficient remedy lay in the British principle of responsible government, whereby governments were held responsible to the people's representatives in parliament and resigned if they lost their parliamentary majority. All other wrongs could be put right by the people's

Dr. Charles Duncombe (1794-1867). One of the "radical" reformers, Duncombe headed a small rising in the London District during the Rebellion of 1837, but his followers dispersed when they heard that Sir Allan Napier MacNab and a column of militia were approaching. Duncombe fled to the United States and, though pardoned in 1843, never returned to Canada.

representatives, if this key principle were once recognized. But though radicals talked loosely of responsible rule, they still wanted to redraw the whole constitution, not just to apply Robert Baldwin's "great principle" of parliamentary cabinet government.

Hence the Reform party kept its dissensions even while it ramped through parliaments in 1835 and '36. Radical thrusts led moderates to pull back, Methodists to move towards conservatism. Radicals went on more fiercely, it seemed, as they grew more isolated, while Tory-Conservative forces rallied in reaction against them. In fact, this path would finally lead Mackenzie and some of his friends on to desperate violence, as they lost the battle for lawful support. Rebellion consequently came in 1837, when the radicals had been reduced to an out-of-power minority, who saw no other option left but force. And so William Lyon Mackenzie should personally be judged, not just for taking to arms, but for provoking a futile though far-damaging revolt. Yet first the radicalism that had seemed so ascendant in 1834 had to play out its fateful course.

In the Assembly, a committee on grievances steered by the tireless Mackenzie produced its huge, vehement (and faulty) *Seventh Report*, in 1835, condemning financial and land abuses, the reserves, and Compact patronage, while demanding the elective Legislative Council. Governor Colborne's own attempts at moderation had failed; but his abrupt dismissal of this *Report* to the Colonial Office as too inaccurate for comment led an alarmed and angry Colonial Secretary, Glenelg, to order his recall. Colborne's replacement, Sir Francis Bond Head, who arrived early in 1836, was scarcely a better choice. A minor Poor Law Commissioner, and another former British soldier, Head was hopefully greeted by some as a "tried reformer"; but though his breezy, erratic mind was willing to consider changes, his judgements were bad, his conceit unlimited, and the initial false hopes he raised were much more harmful in the long run. Indeed this rash, stubborn and obstreperous Sir Francis proved a lot like his chief antagonist, Mackenzie. They deserved each other — but at Upper Canada's cost.

The new governor seemingly started well by appointing Robert Baldwin, John Rolph and J.H. Dunn, a moderate, non-Compact

Robert Baldwin (1804-1858). A prominent leader of the moderate Reformers in Upper Canada, Baldwin was first elected to the Legislature in 1829. He became joint premier of United Canada with Louis LaFontaine in 1842-1843, and again in 1848-1851.

Conservative, to the Executive Council in February of 1836. Bond Head, however, soon rejected Baldwin's claim that this body should be wholly composed of Reformers since they held the majority in the Assembly. That claim might have put responsible government into practice then and there. But the imperious governor really meant to keep his officials under his own control, and so compelled the entire Council to resign as a lesson. Things at least were changing. The Assembly, led by its radical element, then retaliated strongly by refusing supplies — that is, to provide moneys for the government. Head in his turn made the next combatant move by dissolving parliament and calling new elections. They were held that summer, in a storm of angry emotions. The governor himself entered the campaign almost as a candidate, loudly appealing to the loyal majority against a scheming traitorous faction, and proclaiming, on behalf of faithful militia, "Let them come if they dare!" It was virtually an invitation to rebellion. Head and Mackenzie between them increasingly promoted violence.

As for the latter, he campaigned no less hotly; but was beaten in his own election for York County. Moreover, a Tory-Conservative majority swept in across Upper Canada; and while this surely reflected appeals to prejudice and emotion, on either side, it also suggested that Upper Canadians in general were very much concerned about the extremism and American leanings of radical Reformers. After allowing for Head's own bombastic nonsense, or the appeals made to recent British immigrants, who often just upheld the "old flag" that they knew, it still appears that the mass of Upper Canadians (including Ryerson and the Methodists) did not trust Mackenzie or his kind. At any rate, the defeated radical champion, along with John Rolph and his friends, were left in sullen frustration, to find other than constitutional ways to respond. The hard economic downturn that came in 1837 was by no means consciously seized for their advantage — but it undoubtedly helped their appeal to illegal force.

Upper Canada had gone on growing steadily in good years after 1833 with nearly 25,000 immigrants still entering at Quebec in 1836. Trade, shipping, banking and construction all rose further, and

Sir Francis Bond Head (1793-1875). Head replaced Colborne as Lieutenant-Governor in 1836 and remained in that office until 1838 — though already under recall to Britain. His waywardness and his interference in the election of 1836 convinced radical leaders that recourse to arms was justified.

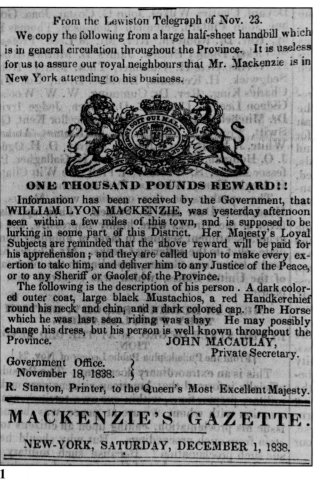

From the Lewiston Telegraph of Nov. 23.

We copy the following from a large half-sheet handbill which is in general circulation throughout the Province. It is useless for us to assure our royal neighbours that Mr. Mackenzie is in New York attending to his business.

ONE THOUSAND POUNDS REWARD!!

Information has been received by the Government, that WILLIAM LYON MACKENZIE, was yesterday afternoon seen within a few miles of this town, and is supposed to be lurking in some part of this District. Her Majesty's Loyal Subjects are reminded that the above reward will be paid for his apprehension; and they are called upon to make every exertion to take him, and deliver him to any Justice of the Peace, or to any Sheriff or Gaoler of the Province.

The following is the description of his person. A dark colored outer coat, large black Mustachios, a red Handkerchief round his neck and chin, and a dark colored cap. The Horse which he was last seen riding was a bay. He may possibly change his dress, but his person is well known throughout the Province. JOHN MACAULAY,
Private Secretary.

Government Office.
November 18, 1838.

R. Stanton, Printer, to the Queen's Most Excellent Majesty.

MACKENZIE'S GAZETTE.

NEW-YORK, SATURDAY, DECEMBER 1, 1838.

1

1. *Transcript of Wanted Notice from the* Lewiston Telegraph, *N.Y., November 23, 1838. Republished in Mackenzie's short-lived American journal,* Mackenzie's Gazette, *December 1, 1838, and offering a reward for his apprehension, the physical description is scarcely that of the original "Little Rebel"!*
2. *The March of the Rebels upon Toronto, December 1837. By the time the militia arrived at Montgomery's Tavern, many rebels had already drifted away in disillusion and doubt because Mackenzie failed to show effective leadership.* Pen and ink by C.W. Jefferys (1869-1951), c. 1912.
3. *Proclamation of Sir Francis Bond Head, December 7, 1837. This was issued immediately following the skirmish between the militia and the rebels near Montgomery's Tavern, as indicated by the date line.*

2

PROCLAMATION.

BY His Excellency SIR FRANCIS BOND HEAD, Baronet, Lieutenant Governor of Upper Canada, &c. &c.

To the Queen's Faithful Subjects in Upper Canada.

In a time of profound peace, while every one was quietly following his occupations, feeling secure under the protection of our Laws, a band of Rebels, instigated by a few malignant and disloyal men, has had the wickedness and audacity to assemble with Arms, and to attack and Murder the Queen's Subjects on the Highway—to Burn and Destroy their Property—to Rob the Public Mails—and to threaten to Plunder the Banks—and to Fire the City of Toronto.

Brave and Loyal People of Upper Canada, we have been long suffering from the acts and endeavours of concealed Traitors, but this is the first time that Rebellion has dared to shew itself openly in the land, in the absence of invasion by any Foreign Enemy.

Let every man do his duty now, and it will be the last time that we or our children shall see our lives or properties endangered, or the Authority of our Gracious Queen insulted by such treacherous and ungrateful men. MILITIA-MEN OF UPPER CANADA, no Country has ever shewn a finer example of Loyalty and Spirit than YOU have given upon this sudden call of Duty. Young and old of all ranks, are flocking to the Standard of their Country. What has taken place will enable our Queen to know Her Friends from Her Enemies—a public enemy is never so dangerous as a concealed Traitor—and now my friends let us complete well what is begun—let us not return to our rest till Treason and Traitors are revealed to the light of day, and rendered harmless throughout the land.

Be vigilant, patient and active—leave punishment to the Laws—our first object is, to arrest and secure all those who have been guilty of Rebellion, Murder and Robbery.—And to aid us in this, a Reward is hereby offered of

One Thousand Pounds,

to any one who will apprehend, and deliver up to Justice, WILLIAM LYON MACKENZE ; and FIVE HUNDRED POUNDS to any one who will apprehend, and deliver up to Justice, DAVID GIBSON—or SAMUEL LOUNT—or JESSE LLOYD—or SILAS FLETCHER—and the same reward and a free pardon will be given to any of their accomplices who will render this public service, except he or they shall have committed, in his own person, the crime of Murder or Arson.

And all, but the Leaders above-named, who have been seduced to join in this unnatural Rebellion, are hereby called to return to their duty to their Sovereign—to obey the Laws—and to live henceforward as good and faithful Subjects—and they will find the Government of their Queen as indulgent as it is just.

GOD SAVE THE QUEEN.

Thursday, 3 o'clock, P. M. 7th Dec.

☞ The Party of Rebels, under their Chief Leaders, is wholly dispersed, and flying before the Loyal Militia. The only thing that remains to be done, is to find them, and arrest them.

R. STANTON, Printer to the QUEEN'S Most Excellent Majesty.

3

farming had widely prospered. The lower reaches of Yonge Street were macadamized (layered with crushed gravel), while stage coaches bounced north to Holland Landing, or east and west along the Dundas and Danforth roads. There were even plans for building the new-fangled steam railways — until world depression spread from London and New York in 1837, driving markets, jobs and immigration severely downward. Farmers who had debts incurred in boom times were especially hard hit. Threatened with foreclosures, they understandably detested the bankers nestled close to the Compact in Toronto. All this now made eager audiences for Mackenzie as he toured the countryside above the capital that summer.

Burningly clear on wrongs, he was less clear on plans to end them, whether by new constitutions, American support, or a massive popular demonstration that somehow would bring the government to yield. Nevertheless, armed revolt was in the air, as stirred by Mackenzie's heady, glowing calls to freedom, pikes were forged, drills and "turkey shoots" were held. Secret meetings among radical leaders were also held in Toronto, where it was hoped the depression-hit workers might rise. Yet moderates like the Baldwins, or even Bidwell, stood aloof: not just because they believed an appeal to force would be self-defeating and ruinous, but also because Mackenzie and his group had publicly made plain that their ultimate goal for Upper Canada was to join the American union. John Rolph, cagey as ever, also seemed to stand aside; but he secretly worked hand-in-glove with Mackenzie.

In October, Governor Bond Head helpfully stirred the pot himself. In a grand gesture that showed how secure and content his own province was, he sent the regular troops off to Lower Canada, where a far larger rebellion had erupted, sprung from the historic clash of French and English in that domain. Mackenzie, however, seized gleefully on

1. *The Cutting-out of the* Caroline, *Navy Island, Niagara, December 29, 1837. Mackenzie proclaimed a provisional government for the State of Upper Canada on Navy Island, but the seizure of his supply ship* Caroline *by loyal forces led to the evacuation of the island by the Patriots and their American allies.*

2. *The Destruction of the* Caroline, *December 29, 1837. Allan MacNab ordered the raid which led to the capture and burning of the* Caroline. *The ship ran aground and broke up above Niagara Falls, but did not go over, as sometimes sensationally pictured.*

1

2

the fact that Upper Canada's seat of government now was all but undefended. And when late in November the news came that fighting had begun in Lower Canada, his call went out for "Brave Canadians" to rise and march upon Toronto. Overnight on December 4-5, some eight hundred men collected at Montgomery's Tavern on Yonge Street two miles above the city, farmers and hired hands, drawn mostly from older areas of American settlement around the highway. Meanwhile, alarm bells rang in Toronto, and militia were hastily called out. But Head had taken no steps for defence: if Mackenzie had made a determined thrust, instead of frittering away the next two days, he almost surely could have taken the capital. By December 7, 1837 it was too late. Militia had gathered to the city, including a steamer-load from Hamilton under Colonel Allan MacNab. That afternoon over a thousand men marched north from Toronto, with bands playing — and better, two small cannon. The rebel forces were already drifting away from Montgomery's in doubt and disillusion, as Mackenzie showed no effective leadership. The remnants of the would-be "Patriots" were quickly sent running, scattering into the countryside, while Mackenzie and some others escaped to the border, and safety in the United States. Within half an hour's skirmish, the Yonge Street Rising had been crushed, with one man killed.

John Rolph smartly took off over the border himself. Bidwell, who had had no part in the affair, was pushed by Head to leave, and did so, ending his own career in Upper Canada. Others were arrested, often wrongly, in a vengeful Tory hunt for culprits. But the most evident fact was the strong support that rallied to the government on every hand. Mackenzie simply had not led a strong popular movement for revolt, but just an unfortunate few hundred whom he had deluded to expect an easy triumph. Another abortive little rising in the Western District, headed by Dr. Duncombe, was settled near Brantford without a fight, the rebels melting away as the militia

Mrs. Samuel Lount Interceding with Governor Sir George Arthur. Mrs. Lount is shown here pleading for her husband's life, but vainly, as hearts were hardened, because of many casualties, against those held responsible for the rebellion.

neared. In one sense Bond Head had been right: he had not needed the regulars. Still, perhaps not even militia would have been required, if "Bone Head" had not virtually invited rebellion.

As for Mackenzie, what he had mainly produced was not the advance of Reform, but a fierce Tory reaction, when even "safe" moderates like the Baldwins had to wait for the storm to pass, while radicals were almost driven out of politics for a decade to follow. But above all (to give more cause for continued Tory fears and suspicions), the Mackenzie rebellion unleashed an angry, if unofficial war along the border. This brought new onslaughts from the United States that caused far, far more casualties and damage than the local, home-grown rebellion had ever done. At the start, a number of Canadian rebels were involved, those who had escaped to the republic as did Mackenzie himself — who at Buffalo then sought volunteers to join him in liberating Upper Canada. Very soon, however, the American volunteers bulked larger than Canadian rebels or "Patriots": partly in a belief that they would carry real American liberty to oppressed Canada, partly because of the free lands Mackenzie so readily promised his supporters, and partly because of American expansionism — now termed Manifest Destiny — which envisioned all of North America being brought under the Stars and Stripes.

And so the border warfare went on through 1838, some strains and dangers even into 1839. It all began at Navy Island, a bit of Canadian territory out in the Niagara River, where Mackenzie proclaimed a provisional government for the State of Upper Canada. But the seizure of his supply ship *Caroline* by loyal forces led to the island's evacuation by Patriots and their American allies, whereafter Mackenzie largely left the border battles to others, and for some months was

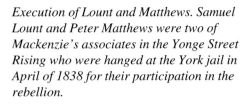

Execution of Lount and Matthews. Samuel Lount and Peter Matthews were two of Mackenzie's associates in the Yonge Street Rising who were hanged at the York jail in April of 1838 for their participation in the rebellion.

jailed instead for breaching the United States neutrality laws. The border troubles, however, simply spread, as more and more Americans took over: raids across the Detroit River in the early weeks of 1838, at Hickory Island on the upper St. Lawrence or Pelee Island in Lake Erie; the capture of the Canadian steamer *Sir Robert Peel* near Brockville in May, or the Short Hills invasion in the Niagara Peninsula by Americans in June. Then came the bloody Battle of the Windmill near Prescott in November, where the invaders held a massive stone windmill for four days until artillery from Kingston finally forced them out. The last main fight took place in December, 1838; the Battle of Windsor, in which American raiders caught were sometimes shot out of hand — a crime that could only be explained, not excused, by the fact that after a full year of ruffianism, terrorism, looting and open warfare, a harassed and worn Ontario militia had had a good deal too much.

In fact, Upper Canada in general had had too much, when its dead in the Windmill raid at Prescott exceeded British deaths at Queenston Heights in 1812. Hearts were hardened, despite pleas for mercy, when Samuel Lount and Peter Matthews, two of Mackenzie's associates in the Yonge Street Rising, were hanged at Toronto's jail in April, 1838. A new Lieutenant-Governor, Sir George Arthur, an experienced administrator who had replaced the eccentric Bond Head in March, refused to alter the lawful verdict reached by a jury on the two rebels, who on evidence were guilty. To have done otherwise, would have bitterly dismayed the mass of Upper Canadians fighting what the rebellion had let loose. Arthur first meant to establish firm authority — not like Head's shifting whims — and then apply moderation and conciliation, which he later did. In any case, far more correction and conciliation soon looked to be at hand when the Earl of Durham arrived at Quebec in May: as the Governor General and High Commissioner appointed by the imperial government to investigate the rebellions in the two Canadas, and recommend necessary changes in their governments.

1. *View of the Battle of Windmill Point, Below Prescott, November 13, 1838. In this bloody battle, invaders held a massive stone windmill for four days until artillery from Kingston finally forced them out.*
2. *Monument to Lount and Matthews, Toronto.*

1

2

1

Capt. Peter Matthews (cheerful) was a jolly, hale, cherry-cheeked farmer of Pickering, who lived on his own land, cultivated his own estate, and was the father of fifteen children, who beseeched the Sullivans, the Drapers, and the Robinsons in vain, for that mercy to their father, which they themselves must yet implore from a just God. Capt. M. had fought bravely for the king of England in the war of 1812, was a man of unstained reputation, well beloved by his neighbors, unassuming, and modest in his deportment, a baptist, unfriendly to high church ascendancy, a true patriot, and indignant at the treacherous fraudulent conduct of the detestable junto who, in 1837, governed Canada. I often got his vote, a seat in the legislature, and always his approbation.

Trial of Lount and Capt. Matthews.

☞ *Postcript, New-York, April* 20. Sir George Arthur, acting by special and direct orders from the Queen of England, in Council, has disregarded the petitions of 8,000 of the people of Upper Canada, and caused the brave and patriotic Colonel Lount and Capt. Matthews to be hung on the gallows, at Toronto—their bodies delivered over to the surgeons for dissection. They were both married men, with large families. Mr. Lount was a native of Pennsylvania; his father emigrated from England in company with the celebrated Dr. Joseph Priestley. He represented the county of Simcoe, in the Legislature of Upper Canada for several years; and a more honest, independent, and sincere man I never met with. Mr. Matthews was a farmer of Pickering, strong, bold, and resolute; deservedly the favorite of the country round. Some think that John G. Parker, from New Hampshire, will be hung; others, that he will be sent to Van Dieman's land.

General Theller, of Detroit, is ordered for execution. At Hamilton, on the 4th April, seven reformers, viz: Horatio Hills, Stephen Smith, Charles Walrath, Ephraim Cook, (Postmaster of Norwich), John Tufford, Nathan Town, and Peter Malcolm, were ordered to be hung, and their bodies dissected, on the 20th inst. John Montgomery, Esq., and Messrs. John Anderson and Morden are to be executed at Toronto, on the 24th inst. Four, at least, of these gentlemen are native born American citizens. All their personal and real property is confiscated to the use of the Queen; and their families thrown destitute upon the World. People of America, such cold blooded murders as these have seldom disgraced the last or present age, on this continent.

2

Durham, both a wealthy aristocrat and a determined Liberal, was joyfully hailed by Upper Canadian reformers. Still, it needs stressing that his mission was principally directed to the much wider, deeper-rooted rebellion in Lower Canada. He had been called to this task before news of the Yonge Street skirmish had even reached London; and he spent only days in July, 1838, in the western province, compared with five months in the eastern. Thus an old claim that Mackenzie's own localized rising at least brought Lord Durham out, is mostly mythical. Nonetheless, Durham did get knowledgeable advice on Upper Canada, from Robert Baldwin along with others; and the solutions he proposed were greatly to affect that province. They were set forth in the epoch-making *Report* he issued late in January, 1839, on his return to England, known in Canada by that spring. In regard to the upper province, his *Report* witheringly condemned its land and clergy reserve policies, its government favouritism and the narrow rule of the Family Compact; while also urging judicial reforms, efficient (elected) local government, and a lot more economic development. Yet past all this, Durham sought two crucial measures: responsible government and a union of the two Canadas. He already did believe in colonial self-government, though was probably affected here by Robert Baldwin's clear submission on the subject. Durham himself thought that maturing British colonies inevitably had to be set free to run their own internal or home affairs, and that imperial concerns, such as defence and external relations, were really not at issue. Responsible rule, however, in his mind tied in closely with his own idea of a Canadian union.

Lord Durham wanted to grant responsible rule to a combined Canada, one in which the "divisive" French Canadians could safely be outvoted. In fact, by wishful thinking he held that their old, outdated French society would surely be assimilated into the English-speaking majority within a union, once self-government and economic progress had been assured. And so the French would gradually become contented and absorbed into a broadly prosperous and strongly English Canada, steadily growing through British immigration. This confident view was willingly adopted by the imperial government in London keen to settle the embarrassing troubles in

1. *Notes Written by Mackenzie. These notes, labelled, "Trial of Lount and Matthews," describe Capt. Peter Matthews.*
2. Mackenzie's Gazette *April 17, 1838. This postscript appeared on the second page of the Prospectus of the* Gazette; *it reports the execution of Lount and Matthews despite the "petitions of 8,000 of the people of Upper Canada."*
3. *Sir George Arthur (1784-1854). Arthur, an experienced administrator, replaced the eccentric Head in March, 1838. He refused to alter the verdict reached on the two rebels. Arthur meant to establish firm authority, and then apply moderation and conciliation.*

3

British North America. In the fall of 1839, a new Governor-General was accordingly sent out to achieve a plan of union, and at least some of Durham's other recommendations: Charles Poulett Thomson.

Thomson, later Lord Sydenham, was of a new political breed; a capable businessman with a lot of management skills and cordial public appeal. Liberal in many respects — but decided, (and instructed) about keeping his own firm command, he set out both to win the projected Canadian union and to satisfy Upper Canada that it would not be swamped there by a more populous Lower Canada. In November, 1839, Thomson came on to the inland province, to spend several months in winning its political support for union. His portraits of the advantages to be won from a united St. Lawrence commercial system, with a new series of mainline canals and far bigger scope for economic development, seemed thoroughly convincing. Besides, his talk of responsible rule to Reformers, and of equal provincial representation to Tory-Conservatives — so that the western half of the intended union would not be overridden — did much to gain the eloquent Thomson the political backing that he needed in Upper Canada. And the Clergy Reserves Act he also promoted, to give Protestants other than Anglicans at least some share in the clergy funds, further helped his cause. Consequently, by the spring of 1840, the Governor General had gathered all the assent he needed in the upper province. That summer a Union Act was put through the British parliament, establishing a single Province of Canada.

The terms of this Union of the two former Canadas can be left for now. What matters here, is that the crucial Act of 1840, which went into effect in February of 1841, might well seem to have brought an end to original Upper Canada, the province set up seventy years before. Yet it did not. As one-half of the new United Province of Canada, as still a distinct and substantial community, Upper Canada endured. As a political unit it apparently had ended. But as a people, society and economy it remained: to grow through the Union period onward into the present province of Ontario.

Charles Poulett Thomson (1799-1841). Becoming Governor-General in the fall of 1839, Thomson was sent out by the imperial government to achieve union and settle problems in British North America. He received the title of Lord Sydenham for carrying the Union project through.

Main Events of the 1837 Rebellion Era

1834

March 27	York becomes City of Toronto. Mackenzie, already in Assembly, is mayor.
October	Reformers win Provincial election. Bidwell made Speaker of Assembly.

1835

Winter	Leading radicals in Assembly steer through the "Seventh Report on Grievances."

1836

January 23	Lt. Gov. Sir F.B. Head arrives to make changes. Appoints reformers Baldwin and Rolph to Executive Council, but they resign on March 4.
April 20	Head prorogues Assembly.
July	Rowdy, corrupt election. Tories win. Mackenzie and Bidwell lose seats.
Fall	Bad harvest and trade decline promote rural unrest.

1837

Winter	Head refuses to make Bidwell a judge. Tory Orangemen disrupt Reform meetings.
June-September	Mackenzie speaks to meetings in country north and west of Toronto.
July 31	Mackenzie's Central Committee adopts Declaration of Independence.
September	Head resigns through quarrels with Colonial Office but awaits arrival of successor.
October	Head sends troops to Lower Canada to help suppress Papineau Rebellion.
November	Mackenzie publishes a constitution for Upper Canada on the American model.
November 18	Mackenzie decides on *coup d'état* for December 7.
December 7	Skirmish on Yonge Street. Rebels dispersed. Mackenzie flees to Buffalo.
December 7-13	Duncombe gathers rebels at Scotland, near Brantford.
December 13	Mackenzie sets up provisional government on Navy Island in Niagara River.
December 14	Duncombe's men disperse as MacNab's militia approach.
December 29	U.S. steamer *Caroline* destroyed at Navy Island by loyal Canadians.

1838

January 14	Mackenzie leaves Navy Island and goes to Buffalo.
February 25	Canadian militia routs American Patriots on Fighting Island, Detroit River.
March 3	British troops & Canadian militia rout American Patriots on Pelee Island.
March 3	Sir George Arthur arrives in Toronto as Lt. Gov. Head leaves.
March 26	Peter Matthews & Samuel Lount tried at Toronto. Executed April 12.
May 29	Canadian steamer *Sir Robert Peel* burned in Thousand Islands by American raiders.
June	American raids on Short Hills, near Fort Erie, and St. John's, near Thorold. Patriots cross St. Clair River twice and loot. U.S. sloop loots Goderich.
July	Lord Durham arrives as Governor-in-Chief of the Canadas.
November 1	Durham returns to England to report.
November 11-16	Battle of Windmill, near Prescott. Von Schoultz and his invaders defeated.
November 16	Murder of militia captain, Edgeworth Ussher, at Chippawa.
November 21	U.S. proclamation: Americans crossing into Canada will not be protected.
November 26	Von Schoultz tried at Kingston, defended by a young lawyer, John A. Macdonald.
December 4	Battle of Windsor. Patriots and rebels cross from Detroit and are routed.
December 8	Execution of Von Schoultz and 10 others at Kingston over period to February 11.

1839

Jan.-Feb. 6	Joshua Doan and 5 others executed at London, U.C.
April	Many new incidents cause tension. British and U.S. ships fire on each other.
June 10	Americans sentence Mackenzie to 18 months in jail. Released May 10, 1840.
July 17	Rebel-Patriot plan to burn Cobourg foiled.
September	Canadian and American prisoners gathered at Kingston. 92 are sent to penal servitude in Van Diemen's Land (Tasmania).

1840

April	Top blown off Brock Monument at Queeston by Patriots.
September	Attempt to blow up locks of Welland Canal foiled.

1849

February 1	Mackenzie pardoned. By now some prisoners have returned from Van Diemen's Land.
March 18	Mackenzie returns to Toronto. Attempt made to lynch him.

1851

April	Mackenzie wins seat in Assembly as Member for Haldimand. Dies in Toronto, 1861.

Chapter Six

Union, Disunion and Confederation:
1841-1867

1852   Toronto Stock Exchange opened
1853   Separate School Bill passed
1854   Windsor becomes a village
        Liberal-Conservative coalition takes office under MacNab and Morin (later, John A. Macdonald and Cartier)
        Clergy reserves abolished
        Ottawa incorporated as a city
1855   Northern Railway opened, Toronto to Georgian Bay
        London becomes a city
1856   Grand Trunk Railway opened, Montreal to Toronto
        Bank of Toronto launched
1857   Brownite Liberals win election in Canada West
        Railway boom collapses
1858   Ottawa approved as permanent capital
        Windsor becomes a town
1859   Protectionist Galt tariff established
1860   First railway sleeping car built in Hamilton
1861   Population of Toronto: 44,000
        Population of Canada West: 1,400,000
        American Civil War begins
1862   Militia Bill controversy
        Moderate Liberal government under Sandfield Macdonald takes office
        Political deadlock increasingly develops
1864   Brown's proposal of Grit-Conservative coalition to work toward a Confederation is accepted
        "Great Coalition" takes power
        Charlottetown Conference approves idea of federal union
        Quebec Conference drafts Confederation scheme
1866   London Conference settles terms for British North America Act
1867   Bank of Commerce opened in Toronto
        British North America Act passed at Westminster

The Call for Responsible Rule

The Union Act proclaimed on February 10, 1841, kept much of the structure of the old Constitutional Act, applying it to one Province of Canada, not two. There was to be a single, appointed Executive Council, advising and serving a Governor-General; a single Legislative Council of not less than twenty members, still appointed for life; and a single Legislative Assembly of eighty-four, elected at least every four years, and now in full control of revenues, except for a "permanent civil list" that paid the salaries of judges and officials. But also — since this Assembly was based on equal representation of the two old Canadas — forty-two of its members would come from the English-speaking and mostly Protestant Upper Canadian half of the Union, now named Canada West; forty-two from the mainly Francophone and Catholic Lower Canadian half, now Canada East. Thus there would be two distinct blocks of representatives within one legislature. Furthermore, the eastern section would keep its French Law and Quebec Act rights; the western, its English Law and clergy reserves system. In short, two Canadas certainly persisted; and their sectional division was built right into the Union.

Perhaps it could not have been otherwise, given the widely different character and heritage of the two former provinces. Without question it would have been hard to get Upper Canada's assent to any union without equal representation, fearing as it did that its own population of some 450,000 would be hopelessly outweighed by the more than 650,000 within a much older Lower Canadian society. Yet as a result, the community of Upper Canada did stay very much alive inside the new United Province, where it held half the votes in what was actually a dual Canada. That is, there now were to be dual government posts, like the Attorney-General West and Attorney-General East to direct two legal systems; dual political parties, such as the western "Upper Canada Reform party" and an allied eastern, Lower Canadian one; two school and local government organizations, and separate crown land administrations for each section; plus a variety of government measures that applied only to one or the other of the two halves of the Union; for example, the "Upper Canada Game

Overleaf. *Fathers of Confederation at the key Quebec Conference of October, 1864, who drafted the basic plan for the federal union of the British North American colonies. The original of this famed painting by Robert Harris was destroyed during the fire at the Parliament buildings in Ottawa in 1916.*

Below. *City Hall, Kingston from the Lake, August, 1905. The domed City Hall was built when Kingston was chosen as the Union's capital in 1841 and still stands today.*

Laws." In other words, Upper Canada's own distinctive life and activities indeed went on through the Union period, to be continued unbroken when the new province of Ontario was set up at Confederation in 1867. During the Union years, moreover, the very name "Upper Canada" remained in popular and some official use, while "Canada West" tended more to be a geographic and postal description. Consequently we may, and will, use both terms ourselves. And we can begin by looking at conditions in Upper Canada or Canada West as they were when the Union was being erected around the start of the 1840s.

The depression that had helped bring on rebellion in 1837 had lingered for several years thereafter. British immigration, too, had stayed very low until 1840; for the post-rebellion disruptions and border fighting had added to the bad times in discouraging settlers. But by 1840 world trade was recovering; while border strains were mostly down to watchful patrolling, although they would not be carefully lifted till an Anglo-American Treaty of 1842 resolved outstanding issues. At the same time wheat and flour exports were flowing down the St. Lawrence again, in a mounting trade with Britain protected by the imperial Corn Laws; while the Ottawa timber industry was heading into a boom, as its broad-axe men reached up toward Lake Temiskaming. Hence with basic trades and transport thriving anew, with businessmen making fresh investments, and new imperial guarantees secured for building a chain of canals along the upper St. Lawrence, far brighter prospects once more attracted British immigrants in rising numbers. Over 44,000 of them arrived at Quebec in 1842. And that, of course, meant more growth in the towns and countryside of Canada West — without any heavy burden of social needs thus far, since these newcomers generally came well prepared and jobs were broadly available. In fact, labour again was in high demand for farms or timber camps, and soon increasingly for canal and urban construction as well.

As for urban places in Canada West, Toronto itself was gloomy when the Union first began in 1841, because it was no longer a seat of government. The capital for the United Province of Canada had

Farm House in Vaughan Township, York County. By the middle of the 19th century, many farms had well-fenced grain fields and pastures with substantial farmhouses, such as this one.

1

2

3

been transferred to Kingston, which built a splendidly classical and domed new stone City Hall to fit its status, even if the legislature would have to meet in the former General Hospital. Toronto, however — now with 14,000 residents — still grew because of its economic strength, attracting immigrants with enterprise like the young Scotsman, George Brown, in 1843, who the next year began his paper, the Toronto *Globe*, destined to be the most powerful journal in British North America. In any event, far more of the renewed immigrant stream still went to the countryside to continue extending the farm frontiers; until, by the end of the decade, there was little good wild land left to be taken up in the Southern Ontario region. In particular, the northern segment of the broad western peninsula was now filled in. This "Queen's Bush" largely became fertile cropland, as some of it had been in Huron Indian days. The Toronto *Globe* claimed rosily in 1848, "The backwoods now can scarcely be said to exist"; and if this was a bit excessive, it did hail the closing of a long age of frontier extensions. For farms were now coming up against the unyielding limits of the Shield, so that Upper Canadian growth thereafter largely became intensive rather than extensive.

The signs were more and more visible across the inlands of Canada West. Ragged bush clearings had turned into well-fenced grain fields and pastures. Orchards (which might include the McIntosh apple, sprung from an original tree in the eastern county of Dundas) were now set out along with barns and kitchen gardens around substantial farmhouses. The last-named, once squared-log cabins that had replaced the first rough shanties, were being replaced themselves by wooden frame-dwellings or in some parts by brick or stone. Concession roads thrust out where there had been narrow trails. And where "corduroys" had crossed low-lying areas — rough logs laid side by side across a swampy roadway — now there might be plank roads, sawn lumber nailed across long beams beneath, which gave a smooth, quick passage for wagons and buggies, or for mail delivery and newspapers, in communications that linked farm settlements together and to their nearby towns. Assuredly, all this must not be overrated; the degree of improvements varied greatly between older-settled, mainline areas and newer, outlying ones. Still the patterns of

1. *George Brown monument on Parliament Hill in Ottawa.*
2. *George Brown (1818-1880), c. 1870s. Born in Scotland, Brown emigrated with his parents to New York in 1837, from where he moved to Toronto in 1843. He founded the* Globe *there in 1844. In 1852, Brown became a member of the legislature and sat till 1867, but was lastingly more influential through the* Globe *than through his political career. A Father of Confederation, he came to favour a union of all the British provinces and, thus, the ending of the Union of 1841. Brown also opposed Roman Catholic separate schools because he felt they would adversely affect the public school system.*
3. *Alwington House, Kingston, June 6, 1926. The governor-general lived in Alwington while Kingston was capital of the United Province of Canada, 1841-1843.*

change were plainly there, consolidating the Upper Canadian community, bringing it out of primitive, frontier isolation even before the railways arrived. Furthermore, that process showed in other ways as well.

For one thing, there now was effective local government to serve a more populous and complex community: elective municipal institutions that took over from the old, simple sway of appointed district magistrates who had been charged with almost everything locally, and particularly with meeting four times a year in "Quarter Sessions." In 1841 instead, at the first Union parliament, a District Councils Act established locally-elected township and district councils in Canada West, under District Wardens still appointed by the central government. But in 1849, the Municipal Corporations Act put through by Robert Baldwin gave Upper Canada a complete scheme of democratic local self-government for both town and country — from cities to "police villages," and from counties and townships. The county, moreover, replaced the district as the chief rural unit of local government, thus becoming much more than just a parliamentary constituency. Much of this Baldwin Act still operates today, a landmark contribution from the past.

There was, besides, the development of public education, well past the hit-and-miss stage of earlier days in Upper Canada. The Common School Act of 1843 tied non-sectarian, public elementary schools in with the local government system, putting locally elected school trustees under the township and district councils, while the central government made grants to local school funds, and the trustees raised additional funding from property-holders and parents. Then the Act of 1846 went further by setting up regular school boards across Canada West, with a central Board of Education to advise its Chief Superintendent of Education — a post held by the redoubtable Dr. Egerton Ryerson from 1844 to 1876. Also of note was the opening of the provincial university of King's College at Toronto in 1843. John

George Brown. This stamp was issued on August 7, 1968 to commemorate the 150th anniversary of Brown's birth, November 29, 1818. Designed by Nickolay Sabolotny.

Strachan, now Anglican Bishop, had his cherished institution in operation at last. Yet by that time Methodist Victoria College was a going concern at Cobourg (under Ryerson as its principal from 1841, before he became Chief Superintendent), while Presbyterian Queen's had started up as well at Kingston in 1842. The emergence of these church-connected colleges forecast rivalries; but no less displayed Upper Canada's strong religious roots, and its obvious advance from frontier rawness towards higher education. Whatever else, this community was not just surviving, but steadily developing in its life and culture.

All, that is, except the old, original community of native people. The passing of the frontier world in Canada West meant that the Indians, too, virtually passed from sight and mind, as they were increasingly left to reserves in back townships. Their role as crucial military allies, their hunting and fighting skills which had won respect (and awe) through centuries, had almost ceased to matter since the War of 1812. Forest warfare had departed with the wilderness. In war or peace, white men's ways now ruled the settled countrysides, where Indians came to be regarded as picturesque, romantic or merely troublesome; but in any case, as sadly out of date, almost the worst thing to be said in an eagerly progressive North America. The native peoples also had to struggle to adapt to the alien world closing in on them; even to keep the reserved lands they still held in Upper Canada — which by 1836 had been mostly "cleared" of ancestral Indian titles, as one last large native reserve was set up on Manitoulin Island in Lake Huron. Indeed, the long established Grand River reserve of the closely-knit Six Nations itself faced frequent pressures from white land speculators.

The Indian peoples were still under the superintendence of the Indian Department and receiving regular treaty payments. Official policy also sought to Christianize and "civilize" the natives to fit

King's College, Toronto. First chartered by the British government in 1827, with John Strachan as its first president, Anglican King's College did not open in Queen's Park until 1843.

1

2

them in with white society — while inconsistently keeping them apart on reserves. None the less, unfamiliar settled life, culture shock and low esteem, never forgetting diseases and alcohol (the white man's gift, the Indian's retaliation being tobacco), all together wove a dark theme of native decline. It was least evident in northern areas where hunting and the fur trade still widely continued. Moreover, missionary efforts could bring other than spiritual help to the reserves, by fostering work practices, education and social stability there. It helped, too, when natives themselves took part as missionaries: such as Kahkewaquonaby or Peter Jones, a Mississauga who became an eloquent and able Methodist preacher and shared in converting thousands to Christianity. He also produced a history of the Ojibwa people, and carried his message of Indian need to Britain on into the 1840s, holding audiences spellbound — to leave his vivid personal contribution to Ontario's heritage.

That heritage, however, above all saw responsible government added to it during the 1840s; chiefly through the work of Robert Baldwin, the moderate Reform leader, his close lieutenant, Francis Hincks, and his great French-Canadian comrade, Louis-Hippolyte LaFontaine. The essential principle was Baldwin's: which would make Canada's government a cabinet responsible to the provincial Assembly, to stand or fall by the vote of its majority, thus assuring the control of the colony's own affairs by the representatives of its people. Baldwin obviously was not alone in this principle that he had acquired and developed from his father. It was based, of course, on the pattern of cabinet government practiced in Britain; Durham and others there had also advocated it for Canada. But Robert Baldwin's own contribution was to see clearly, and urge tirelessly, that responsible government meant responsible *party* government: that, if government was not in the hands of a majority party, one which stood united on its policies and programme, a governor could simply divide and rule — over a mixed set of leaders and factions that might give him a loose, overall majority in parliament, yet would not give the people a government truly built upon the party majority they had elected. But, first and foremost Baldwin had to gather a Reform party majority in the Union parliament, in its critical Assembly.

1. *Queen's University, Kingston, c. 1900-1910. This university under Presbyterian control was started up in Kingston in 1842.*
2. *The Methodists' Victoria College, Cobourg, c. 1847. Originally founded as Upper Canada Academy, Dr. Egerton Ryerson was its first principal from 1841 until he became Chief Superintendent of Education in 1844.*

It was Hincks who opened the way. This astute Irish Protestant Liberal, the editor of a young Toronto *Examiner* dedicated to the cause of responsible government, approached Louis LaFontaine, prominent among Lower Canadian French Liberals, to propose an alliance between the eastern and western groups. Such a combined front could effectively command a majority in parliament to win responsible rule; hence, at last enabling French Canadians as a body to join in running their own political affairs. It was LaFontaine who convinced his followers (ever suspicious of English plots and power) that this British responsible system could bring self-rule to them; and he faithfully held his group to the alliance with Baldwin and the Upper Canadian Reformers. Eventually, their combined votes did force cabinet and party government on the imperial authorities. The latter might be reluctant to see a colony run by its own cabinet leaders with the British governor reduced to not much more than arbiter or chairman; but they were equally reluctant to govern against that colony's wishes, after all the embarrassment and costly upsets of the 1830s.

The joint Baldwin-LaFontaine Reform demand for responsible rule began with the first parliament of the Union in 1841. It was called at Kingston in June by Governor-General Lord Sydenham — previously Charles Poulett Thomson before receiving his title for carrying the Union project through. Sydenham had already named Baldwin to his Executive Council, as undoubtedly the leading figure in Upper Canada Reform, more especially since the erstwhile radical element were in eclipse there. But just as the Assembly was about to meet, Baldwin sought to bring about the dismissal of Conservatives from the new Union's government — which now could well be termed the "ministry," since Sydenham was organizing it as an efficient set of departmental heads, or ministers. Baldwin asked instead for the admission of French Canadian Reformers to this ministry because of their strength in parliament. In brief, he was calling for an all one-party regime. But Sydenham, who intended to rule with majority but multi-party support, and be his own prime minister, refused Baldwin's bid; dismissing him instead. The Upper Canada Liberal might seem to have been swiftly outplayed. An overconfident

Rev. Peter Jones wearing the medal presented by King William IV. A Mississauga Indian, Jones became an eloquent Methodist preacher who shared in converting thousands to Christianity. He also produced a history of the Ojibwa, and in the 1840s spoke powerfully to audiences in Britain.

Sydenham thought so. Actually, however, Baldwin had strengthened his bonds with LaFontaine by pushing from the start for French entry to the Union ministry.

Sydenham did not see the outcome, dying that September as the result of a fall from his horse. Yet his successor did, Sir Charles Bagot, a veteran diplomat with a keen perception of realities. When Bagot met parliament in the following September, 1842, he had to face a solid Reform majority of French and English, and knew his government would be flatly defeated unless he remade it to bring in both Baldwin and the French Canadians, neither of whom would come in without the other. And so the governor yielded, wisely and gracefully. What has been called the first Baldwin-LaFontaine party ministry or cabinet took office: though it was not quite that, since Bagot still played a large part and had also kept one non-Reform, if non-partisan, minister. Nevertheless, this was a major step toward responsible rule — even if it was to be followed by a step back the next year. Elderly and ill, Bagot retired, to be succeeded by Sir Charles Metcalfe in March, 1843; a trained civil servant this time, but one who was wholly determined to yield no more authority. Quarrels grew between the stubborn governor-general and his equally stubborn Reform ministers; until in December the latter resigned, to be replaced by a weak caretaker government under the Conservative William Henry Draper, a polished, able Toronto lawyer of English immigrant origin — dubbed "Sweet William."

At first it seemed that Draper would have little chance, when Metcalfe dissolved the parliament and called new elections. But actually there was a swelling opinion in Canada West that the Reformers had pushed too hard, grown arrogant, even endangered the British tie. In this Upper Canadian community where Tory and Conservative sentiments could easily be called up, old memories of war and rebellion urged public caution. At any rate, Reform was defeated in

Medal presented to Rev. Peter Jones by King William IV in 1832.

1

2

3

Canada West in the elections of 1844, though it still held Canada East: thereby giving Draper a bare overall majority in the Assembly. The irony was that in the next few years while "Sweet William" struggled to keep his narrow parliamentary lead, he was all but practicing responsible government himself. More than that, Draper was really directing a party (Conservative) cabinet and handling government appointments, since Metcalfe had fallen gravely ill — with fatal cancer — and left things wholly to the one man he could trust, his deft and devoted chief minister.

Nevertheless, changes were still advancing. Canada West Reform was recovering, and Baldwin and Hincks had never given up. In Britain, too, new Whig-Liberal ministers dedicated to free trade took office late in 1846; and being opposed to protective tariff structures like the Corn Laws or timber duties, they were prepared to grant responsible government to advanced colonies, which did not seem to need political constraints if they were no longer to be kept under economic controls. Accordingly, Lord Elgin arrived as Governor General in January, 1847, to recognize and carry out responsible rule. This judicious and broad-minded, but firm and patient governor was admirably suited to his tasks. While Draper still held a slim majority, Elgin gave him all proper support as his responsible cabinet leader. But early in 1848 new elections were held, and this time Reform swept both sections of Canada. After parliament met, the beaten Conservative ministers resigned. Elgin then asked Baldwin and LaFontaine to form the first all-Reform cabinet. It took office in March, with LaFontaine and Baldwin as co-premiers — in that order, because the former had the larger following. Be that as it may, Baldwin's principle had been accepted and triumphantly confirmed — though serious tests still lay ahead for the hopeful Reform party government.

The new LaFontaine-Baldwin ministry moved to take up waiting issues, particularly that of compensation for damages done during the Lower Canadian Rebellion of 1837-8. Compensation had already been paid in 1845 for Upper Canadian Rebellion losses, but those had really been limited to a relatively few loyal sufferers from the small local uprising there. In the far more extensive Lower Canadian

1. *Opening of the first Union Parliament, Kingston, 1841. This painting depicts the arrival of Governor-General Lord Sydenham, in official dress for the occasion.* Oil on canvas by Charles Walter Simpson (1878-1942), c. 1925-1926.
2. *Sir Francis Hincks (1807-1885), (also in official or "court" dress, during his later years as Cabinet member.) Photo c. 1870. Editor of the Toronto* Examiner *and dedicated to the cause of responsible government, it was Hincks who largely opened the way for that cause in Union politics.*
3. *Wikwemikong Indian Reserve on Manitoulin Island, 1856. Set up on Manitoulin in 1836, this area remained one of the major Indian holdings left in Upper Canada.* Watercolour by William Armstrong (1822-1914), 1908.

1

2

3

case, however, damages were not only far larger, but there was the question of whether some of the compensation might actually be going to French-Canadian sympathizers with the revolt. Racism now combined with partyism as Anglo-Tories raised a cry, "No payment for treason." And so the Reform government's Rebellion Losses Bill for Canada East ran into heavy weather, both in parliament and without. The storm centre was Montreal, Canada's commercial metropolis, which had also been made its capital in 1844, when Kingston was held to be too small and outlying for that role. In the spring of 1849 riots broke out in Montreal, once Lord Elgin gave royal assent there to the Losses Bill. He did so in a clear application of responsible rule; that is by approving a bill that had been passed by parliament and advised by his responsible cabinet. But many Tory-Conservatives in Montreal, who had not yet given up the notion of a British governor who would protect his "true" friends against semi-republicans, fiercely exploded in outrage. The Parliament Building went up in flames on April 25. Mobs stoned Elgin in the streets, or attacked the Reform ministers' houses, while lesser outbreaks spread to Bytown, Hamilton and Toronto. Still, the Governor-General rejected any use of military force, resolutely sitting out three days of violence till Tories cooled into sulky gloom, and order was restored.

In Canada West, Tory feelings were largely taken out on burning straw-filled dummies of Lord Elgin — or in Toronto, those of Robert Baldwin and old William Lyon Mackenzie also, who had been pardoned and had now returned to Canada from exile. Yet the real majority feelings for Elgin, Baldwin and the government quickly rallied across Canada, pouring in petitions of support. In point of fact, the Baldwin concept had been put to trial, and not found wanting. And through it, Ontario had gained self-government for the centuries ahead.

1. William Henry Draper. Photographed here in his old age, Draper was a shrewd and experienced politician who headed a Conservative Union government from 1843-1848, and later was a leading judge.
2. Sir Charles Theophilus Metcalfe (1785-1846). Governor-General from 1843-1845, Metcalfe fought hard against the growing Reform movement until he fell fatally ill with cancer.
3. The river steamer Lord Sydenham *arrives at Montreal on April 27, 1841, the first steamer after long months of winter freeze-up.*

ELECTORS BEWARE!!

THE late "Reform Alliance Society" now sailing under new Colours, with the title of the "Constitutional Reform Society," lately put forth a Document in the Columns of the Correspondent & Advocate, addressed to "their brother Reformers in Upper Canada. This Document was afterwards sent forth in PAMPHLET shape, to distant parts of the Province. Now mark the base conduct pursued on this occasion !! The PAMPHLET contains a most ATROCIOUS PARAGRAPH in allusion to the Lieutenant Governor, which DID NOT make its appearance in the Correspondent & Advocate. The PAMPHLET was sent by thousands ABROAD, where it was no doubt hoped it would escape detection, and at the same time work upon the passions and prejudices of the unwary, into whose hands it might fall.

ELECTORS Beware! be on your guard against REVOLUTIONISTS in the garb of REFORMERS.

The atrocious Paragraph in the Pamphlet is this—speaking of the Lieutenant Governor it says :—

" He betrays the chilling belief, that as the U.
" E. Loyalists shed the blood of their friends &
" kindred to prevent the United States from ac-
" quiring their Independence, they will now e-
" ven in their old age stain our country with our
" blood, to prevent our retaining what Governor
" Simcoe announced to them as the reward of
" their suffering Loyalty !!"

Signed by—   T. D. MORRISON M. P. P. Mayor,
       PRESIDENT,
JOHN McINTOSH M. P. P.
       VICE-PRESIDENT,
J. E. TIMS, M. D } SECRETARIES.
T. PARSONS }

ELECTORS! Will any honest, candid, reasonable man among you, justify, or in any way uphold such diabolical language being applied to the King's Representative ? Can you conceive any thing more atrocious !!! Or can you believe that a greater prostitution was ever made of the official signature of a Member of Parliament—the Mayor of a City—and the President of a Society, calling themselves REFORMERS !!! Does it not rather look like the language of angry, disappointed, discontented men, who would play upon your passions, to goad you on to *Revolution !!!*

Beware of these men, and of all like them! are they worthy of your confidence! give your answer at the Hustings !!

A CONSTITUTIONALIST.

1

2

3

BURNING OF THE PARLIAMENT HOUSE BUILDINGS IN MONTREAL.

The Tories of Canada have at length unmasked themselves before the world. The garment of loyalty under which they have concealed their deformity, has been cast off by their own hands, and they stand revealed as the enemies of social order, the enemies of British connexion—the enemies of constitutional liberty—the abettors of mobs, and the destroyers of property. We know there are many exceptions to this description, but we challenge any man to show that this is not now their legitimate character as a party. We could not have conceived it possible that men moving in a respectable rank in life would do such things, if we had not heard assassination defended by magistrates in Toronto, and did not know that burning and rioting had become the favourite pastime of the Tories of Montreal.

The intelligence of the signing the Rebellion Losses Bill by Lord Elgin reached Toronto on Wednesday evening, by telegraph. On Thursday morning came the astounding news that the Parliament Houses had been burnt down by a mob. Circumstances have been added, such as that Lord Elgin was personally insulted, which formed no part of our telegraphic despatch, and are only backed by the apocryphal authority of Tory journals, This intelligence has been received by these journals in a manner most discreditable to them. The *Patriot* took the lead on Thursday morning, in using the language of menace. He calls on all "Conservatives to do nothing rashly—to think well before they act : and above all things to act unitedly." What did he mean by *acting* after the Bill had finally passed the Legislature ? Resistance unquestionably to the law. He makes a mock talk of appealing to the Queen, and the Imperial Parliament, although he admits it is too late. He gloats over the alleged pelting of Lord Elgin, giving it in Italics. He pities him,—styles him an enemy of his countrymen,—recommends the Tory members of Parliament, to resign their seats, and winds up with asking the ludicrous question, "Is our loyalty to be contemned or not ?"

The *Colonist* is more rabid—although the intelligence of the Montreal disturbances was known in Toronto when he wrote. He speaks of the burning of the Parliament Houses—their valuable libraries and public records, like one who is quite pleased with what he styles *the result*—talks of the Bill as outraging *morality and decency*, and holds the Governor General and his Councillors as answerable for all the consequences. A slight qualifier of *regret* follows over these "occurrences," but he is immediately consoled by the reflection that they are but a "consequence" of the measures of the government. Then follows a plain hint that enough had not been done.

"Nor do we conceive, from present appearances, that the evil consequences have as yet fully developed themselves. The nature and full extent of them, will be exhibited from day to day, while the people are labouring under the effects of the gross insult that has been offered to their better feelings and judgments."

He see-saws along, hoping and expecting—talking of no good resulting from wild exhi-

4

1. *A Tory attack on the "Constitutional Reform Society." Despite gains by the Reform Party, in the early 1840s, there was a growing feeling in Upper Canada that the Reformers had pushed too hard, even endangered the British tie. Consequently, they were defeated in the 1844 elections in Canada West; but still held Canada East.*
2. *James Bruce, 8th Earl of Elgin, (1811-1863). Arriving as governor-general in January, 1847, Lord Elgin was instructed to recognize and carry out responsible rule. In 1848, he invited the formation of the first all-Reform cabinet, reflecting its sweep in the elections earlier that same year.*
3. *Sir Charles Metcalfe opening Parliament, Montreal, 1844 or 1845. In 1844, Montreal was made capital as Kingston was judged too small and outlying.* Oil by Andrew Morris, 1845.
4. *Burning of the Houses of Assembly, Montreal, April 25, 1849. In the spring of 1849, riots broke out in Montreal because of the compensation being given for losses due to the Lower Canadian Rebellion of 1837-1838. Lord Elgin was acting in the spirit of responsible rule when he gave royal assent to the Rebellion Losses Bill, but Tory-Conservatives exploded in outrage.*
5. *Burning of the Parliament Buildings in Montreal as reported in the* Globe, *April 28, 1849.*
6. *Remains of the Houses of Assembly. This engraving appeared in* The Illustrated London News *on May 19, 1849.* Wood engraving by Martin Somerville (active 1839-1856), 1849.

Discontents with the Union of the Canadas

The violence of 1849 had other roots outside politics in renewed, severe depression and in social problems that came with a grim flight from famine in Ireland, which soared in 1847. To take this second first, a disastrous potato blight that had destroyed Ireland's basic food crop brought thousands to flee overseas away from ruin and starvation. Of close to 90,000 immigrants to Canada in 1847, some 70,000 were Irish, who largely arrived destitute, malnourished and often racked with killing diseases like typhus and cholera. Though this outflow of suffering Irish continued for some years, the worst year was its first. Afterwards, stricter regulations on the passage by ship and better Canadian health provisions, reduced both the flow and the death rate, until by the fifties British immigration in general was again reasonably sound and manageable at under 40,000 yearly. Before then, however, thousands of newly-arrived Irish had perished. Those who avoided the mass graveyards at St. Lawrence quarantine camps might still collapse and die as they struggled pitifully westward into Upper Canada, and especially at the "immigrant sheds" of Kingston or Toronto. Local authorities, churches, charities and individuals, strove urgently to provide food, shelter or hospital care. But the needs and burdens were great for a still small society that certainly was no welfare state as yet. Hence this was a harshly tragic story that left many of the surviving Famine Irish impoverished, unskilled, and at the bottom of the social ladder — until in rising later generations, the memory of the terrible migration became a sad, proud part of their family heritage in Ontario.

The diseases that spread from the Irish influx, its heavy health and welfare charges, its jobless, beaten or incapable, were still just part of the problems that accompanied the economic slump from 1847 to

Boulder commemorating the victims of "ship fever." This monument was placed near the entrance of Victoria Bridge in Montreal, a city where many British immigrants arrived in Canada. Those especially devastated by "fever," actually diseases such as typhus and cholera, were Irish settlers leaving their homeland because of the great potato famine of 1847. The Victoria Bridge, built across the St. Lawrence for the new Grand Trunk railway in the late 1850s, had many Irish construction workers.

1849. In 1847 both the staple grain and timber trades fell sharply as world prices collapsed. In 1848 the expensive chain of St. Lawrence canals was finished, providing a nine-foot seaway from Montreal through to Lake Ontario; yet they stayed half empty, while their construction jobs were gone and their debts remained. And in 1849 business bankruptcies multiplied in and around Montreal, where canal expectations had proved false. Some of the resulting bitterness surely came out in the Rebellion Losses riots. But it was far more powerfully expressed by those Anglo-Tory business leaders in Montreal who signed an Annexation Manifesto in October, 1849, calling for union with the United States. In their view, they had been deserted both by the British governor and by an imperial government that had callously dropped its protective duties on colonial wheat and timber for the sake of free trade — leaving only "ruin and decay" in Canada, and the only answer to join the American republic. So their desperate Manifesto proclaimed.

Canada West, however, scarcely agreed with this dark, eastern Montreal defeatism, which also wrongly blamed British free trade for what was a world depression. Both western Conservatives and Reformers strongly rejected the very idea of annexation. They were confident also that their fertile lands and thick forests would again send plentiful grain and timber outward when prices had recovered, free trade or not. And while they hoped for the success of the St. Lawrence canals, they already had the American Erie Canal as another outlet to markets and the sea. Annexationism, in fact, was practically swamped in both halves of Canada within a few months; even in Montreal, where Tory loyalty strengthened as trade began to revive by 1850, and then swelled towards a great new boom. Still, a few right-wing Tories and some left-wing Liberals played with the notion for a year or so, while more moderate Conservatives in Canada West sought a newer programme, to remove any stain of annexationism or of past resistance to responsible government from their own party. Thus the Conservative British American League of 1849-50, centred in Kingston and Toronto, spoke out for a Canadian protective tariff and a federal union of the British North American colonies: two premature ideas, at that time, but not so within ten years.

Ontario Heritage Foundation Plaque to King's College, Toronto.

Other new currents were rising in Upper Canada Reform, where radicalism was re-emerging, to challenge the Baldwin-Hincks moderate leadership. That regime had been busy through 1849 establishing municipal self-government, changing Anglican King's College into a secular, provincial University of Toronto (to Strachan's outrage), and a good deal more. Yet to the radicals these were only halfway measures. They wanted to go much further: to use responsible rule to make fundamental changes; that is, to achieve a purely democratic and elective, written constitution. Those who pressed such basic, purifying doctrines became called "Clear Grits." They included both veteran radicals like Mackenzie and John Rolph (also recently back from exile) and young idealists like William McDougall, who wanted to turn Canada into "a common-sense democracy," and who in May of 1850 launched the Toronto *North American* as organ of an expanding Clear Grit movement. Baldwin and the moderate Reform majority, however, stood by the British cabinet and parliamentary model they had worked so hard to gain, rejecting an American congressional system that looked far less flexible, much more open to corruption, and which as well had been deeply split by its own North-South sectional rivalries. A popular force on the ministry's side was the Toronto *Globe*, under its owner-editor, George Brown. Brown's forceful paper had grown powerful while championing Baldwin and responsible government in the 1840s struggle. The *Globe* now heavily blasted the *North American* and the Clear Grits — their delusions of directly electing everyone from governor or judge to local sheriff's officer, the sheer envy and lust for power that had led them to try to take over the Reform party — as the *Globe* saw it.

1. Hon. Augustin-Norbert Morin 1803-1865. Morin was a member of the Legislative Assembly 1830-1855 and in 1851 took over the Reform ministry of Baldwin and Lafontaine as co-premier with Francis Hincks. He also later served as Judge of the Superior Court of Lower Canada.
2. Roman Catholic Convent and School, c. 1880-1900. Separate schools for both Protestant and Catholic religious minorities were provided in Upper Canada from the 1840s. The Common School Act of 1850 enlarged the rights of Roman Catholics partly because of an increasing Catholic minority. It began a heated issue, which continued even to present-day Ontario — where in 1984 the Catholic separate schools were granted public funding on through their final, senior grades.

1

2

Nevertheless, Grit radicalism made some headway through 1850-51, drawing support in rural Upper Canada, particularly in the farming western peninsula. This support was less roused by the Clear Grits' sweeping political schemes than by their emphasis on cheap, simple government without privilege — serving honest farmers, not city moneybags and lawyers — and especially by their talk of secularizing the clergy reserves, to apply the clergy lands and funds to secular state purposes like education. The Reform ministers themselves hoped to get rid of the reserves. George Brown certainly did. Besides, he was a Free Church Presbyterian, the church which had split in Scotland in the 1840s from the state-established Presbyterian main body; and thus he was an ardent "voluntaryist," a foe of all church-state connections. Yet imperial legal assent was still needed before dealing with the reserves (they were part of the original British Constitutional Act of 1791), while the Lower Canadian Reformers, as French Catholics, feared any sort of assault on official church links with the state. Accordingly, impatient farmers of Canada West more hopefully looked to the Grits, whose own following grew as the Reform Cabinet seemingly hung back from settling the question.

Clear Grit strength in parliament, in fact, was able to defeat Baldwin on an Upper Canadian vote in June, 1851, and bring him to resign from office. The vote was temporary, inconclusive, and on a minor issue; but Ontario's father of responsible rule was sick of ungrateful harassment, worn out and ready for private life. For similar reasons, after battling the Lower Canadian radicals called *Rouges*, his partner LaFontaine retired a few months later. Their two chief lieutenants, Hincks and Augustin-Norbert Morin, took over the ministry as co-premiers; and soon were headed into railway building, a new golden quest that drowned a lot of political unrest in its happy visions of wealth and progress. But first Hincks, the realist, handled his Clear Grit problem by taking two leading Grit politicians, old Rolph and younger Malcolm Cameron, into the Canada West half of the ministry. There they were largely neutralized, just as Hincks

Front page of The Globe, *March 4, 1864. Begun twenty years before by George Brown,* The Globe *was used to voice Brown's opinions and support the Reform movement.*

intended. George Brown and his *Globe*, however, now went loudly into opposition themselves, charging that Hincks had betrayed Baldwin's own integrity just to keep power, while the Grits had pocketed their pure principles to get it. By the end of 1851, when the Hincks-Morin government faced trial by general elections, Brown ran for parliament as an independent Liberal, and was elected for the far western county of Kent. He was only one man still; but he in turn was gaining wider western support for his own anti-state-church stand on the reserves — and also for his opposition to state-supported Catholic separate schools.

Separate schools, for either a local Catholic or Protestant religious minority, had been provided in Upper Canada from the 1840s. But the Common School Act of 1850 had enlarged separate school rights specifically for Roman Catholics, chiefly as a result of the growing Roman Catholic minority within Canada West that stemmed from heavy Irish Catholic immigration. To ardent voluntaryists like Brown, however — numerous in what was still the overwhelming Protestant majority in Upper Canada — state support for any particular church was basically wrong; at least as wrong for Catholic schools as it was for Anglican clergy reserves. It cut into the non-denominational public school system and broke down common citizenship. It harmed religion itself, by inevitably bringing it into political dealings. And it entangled the state in sectarian jealousies and prejudices. On the other side, of course, to Catholics, it was no less basically a matter of faith: they held that education could not be severed from the Church's care. The opposed arguments were practically unanswerable. The best to be hoped for were acceptable bargains. Yet Brown for years fought against what he saw as ever-recurring Catholic demands for more. At any rate, he won increasing companions among Upper Canadian Reformers in parliament when he got there in 1852: not only for his anti-state-church and separate-schools positions, but for his slashing attacks on the Hincks government's failure of principle, its lavish railway spending and mounting signs of corruption — things the Clear Grits now found

Parliament House, Quebec City. After the burning of the Parliament building in Montreal in 1849, the Union capital moved to Toronto through 1851, and then to Quebec City until 1854. This shuttling continued until 1866 when Parliament moved to Ottawa.

difficult to talk about, because they had indeed been taken into camp as "Hincksite"government supporters.

Parliament that year met in Quebec; which requires some explaining. When Montreal had disgraced itself by burning down the parliament building in 1849, the capital was shifted. First it went to Toronto through 1851, then to Quebec to stay through 1854, in what was meant as a temporary arrangement but really showed the strength of sectional division in the Union. This costly shuttling between the two former capitals of the old Canadas continued even after Ottawa was approved as a permanent seat of government in 1858, since new buildings would not be ready there till 1866. Yet the fact that Toronto again served as a capital for some periods of the Union did not notably affect the growth of that main Upper Canadian city as much as it might have in the past. Its development was rapid in the 1850s for other reasons, in a time when both town and country prospered greatly across Canada West in good years that ran until late 1857.

World trade climbed from 1850; the St. Lawrence canals were full. The Ottawa Valley's square timber streamed overseas to Britain, despite the loss of the old preferential duties; and now its sawn lumber was also finding ever-rising demands in the United States. Furthermore, Upper Canadian wheat poured into busy British markets; since even with the Corn Laws gone it could compete, thanks largely to the rich fertility of recently-opened soils in the western peninsula. In fact, a veritable wheat boom rose in Canada West — the Manitoba of that day. Still further, coarser grains and other farm products went to the fast-populating United States. Then the Reciprocity Treaty of 1854 provided free trade in natural products between British North America and the republic, much expanding the already flourishing commerce in lumber and farm goods that flowed southward from Upper Canada. And in this high tide of prosperity, the

Stacked Ontario wheat at harvest time. Wheat from Upper Canada poured into British markets during the boom of the 1850s. The rich fertility of recently opened soils in the western peninsula made Canada West into the Manitoba of that day.

1

2

railway — widely promoted, but scarcely built during the 1840s — did more still to provide jobs, develop towns and industry or encourage banking and finance across Canada West.

Now that trade and capital were readily available in the good times, rail construction spread rapidly. The Northern Railway, begun in 1851, was completed from Toronto up to Collingwood on Georgian Bay by 1855, renewing the old Toronto Passage in iron track, and linking the city with the shipping, lumber and mining resources of a vast upper Great Lakes hinterland. The Great Western, pushed by Hamilton enterprise, ran from Niagara Falls via Hamilton to Windsor opposite Detroit by 1855; and was extended that year from Hamilton to Toronto. Hence it gave Toronto rail access west to London, Detroit and beyond, or south to New York City, since the Great Western met American railroads at the Niagara River, crossed by an amazing new suspension bridge. Among other lines, two ran south from the Ottawa to the upper St. Lawrence, mainly to carry lumber to American markets. But largest of all was the Grand Trunk Railway, a huge transprovincial route across both Canadas, and the Hincks government's chief railway concern, since the Grand Trunk's bonds were guaranteed by the province, while it received a good deal more public aid as well. The core-section of the Grand Trunk, from Montreal to Toronto, was opened in 1856. The western section on to Sarnia at the foot of Lake Huron took till 1859, by which time the buoyant railway boom was over. It left masses of debt behind (especially the Grand Trunk's), plus a seamy political record of influence and scandals; but equally, it transformed communications across the land, and brought whole new levels in industry and technology. For the railway really marked the onset of the Industrial Revolution in Canada West. And that particularly affected the growth of its urban centres.

Toronto was a leading beneficiary as a main focus of the new rail routes, and of the wholesaling, banking and factory enterprises they

1. *Hewing Square Timber. With world trade climbing from 1850, square timber from the Ottawa Valley again poured freely out to Britain, despite the loss of old preferential timber duties.*
2. *Sawn Lumber, McLachlin Brothers Lumber Company. Shown here is the main lumber yard in Arnprior mills Numbers Three and Four. In the 1850s, there was a rising market for sawn lumber in the United States, aided by the Reciprocity Treaty of 1854.*
3. *Desjardins Canal train wreck, near Hamilton, March 12, 1857, one of Ontario's first railway disasters. A passenger train went off the tracks while crossing the bridge, killing fifty-nine people.* Lithograph by J. Sage and Sons.

3

1

2

3

1. *Suspension Bridge, Niagara Falls, 1859. This very early photo by William England catches a train crossing the 1268-foot-long bridge.*
2. *Niagara Suspension Bridge, Niagara Falls. The first suspension bridge across the Niagara River was actually built in 1848, but was shortly rebuilt and opened to rail traffic in 1855.*
3. *Portal of St. Clair Tunnel, c. 1890s. This tunnel connecting Sarnia and Port Huron was part of the Grand Trunk line. The western section of the line from Toronto to Sarnia was not completed until 1859, by which time the railway boom was over.*
4. *Construction on the Grand Trunk Railway. Rail construction spread rapidly in the 1850s, since trade and capital were readily available during this period.*
5. *Great Western Railway station at Toronto. The Great Western ran from Niagara Falls to Windsor via Hamilton by 1855; and in that year was extended from Hamilton to Toronto.*
6. *Locomotive No. 774, Grand Trunk Railway.*

4

5

6

fostered. The Toronto Stock Exchange appeared there in 1852, largely to serve big wholesale merchants; the Bank of Toronto in 1856 and the Bank of Commerce in 1867, to challenge the power of the leading Bank of Montreal. The city's population rose from 30,000 to 44,000 between 1851 and 1861. Beyond that, it erected stately new buildings in the glow of rail prosperity which still remain heritage treasures today; among them, St. Lawrence Hall, Osgoode Hall (in its present classical form), University College at the University of Toronto, and St. James Cathedral. But Hamilton, a city by 1846, especially developed as a rail-industrial centre, the home of the Great Western shops (where the first railway sleeping car was built for the visit of Edward, Prince of Wales, in 1860) and of iron moulding and machine-making. Further down the Great Western rails, London became a city in 1855; while Windsor, made a village in 1854, was incorporated only four years later as a town, thanks to the railway. At the other end of Upper Canada, the thriving lumber centre, Bytown, became the city of Ottawa in 1854: now directly served by rail, and with steam saw-mills and woodworking plants collecting there. Altogether, urban places expanded vigorously over the 1850s, while the population of Canada West as a whole increased from some 950,000 in 1851 to almost 1,400,000 by 1861.

That population growth raised new problems. Already in 1851 Canada West had passed Canada East in numbers, 952,000 to 890,000, mostly in consequence of British immigration. And as the Upper Canadian lead steadily extended, so more Upper Canadians questioned the principle of equal representation in the Union, contending that the larger western population should have its true weight recognized — by representation according to population. This, then, would overcome "French dominance" of the Union: the alleged fact that a close-knit French Canadian block did not just control an equal Lower Canada, but also barred any action on the Upper Canadian

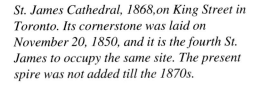

St. James Cathedral, 1868, on King Street in Toronto. Its cornerstone was laid on November 20, 1850, and it is the fourth St. James to occupy the same site. The present spire was not added till the 1870s.

clergy reserves, drew more out of the public revenues than did Upper Canada, which supplied the larger input, and, above all, forced ever-increasing Catholic separate-school provisions on the western section. Any one of these charges could well be argued. Except that, whether a distinct, state-backed Catholic school system should have existed in Upper Canada or not — either as a matter of justice or practicality — it undoubtedly was not something Upper Canada that would have given itself. It came about within the Union largely through the support that was provided to the western Catholic minority by eastern French Catholic votes, which thus carried the separate school bills. Here, then, was a potent cause of sectional discord: and it inspired hot western demands for "rep by pop" to end this unchecked eastern domination.

The Upper Canada Separate School Bill of 1853 was a particular source of western indignation. It was bitterly fought by George Brown in parliament at Quebec, to the accompaniment of anti-Protestant rioting in that city and Montreal (by Irish Catholics rather than French Canadians). Also in parliament in 1853, a bill came up to enlarge membership in the Union's Assembly from 84 to 130: a measure needed to meet the increasing growth in both sections, yet allotting them 65 members each to maintain the principle of equal representation. Brown tried an amendment to change the basis to representation by population. But though he failed here, as on the Separate School Bill, he widened his own power and following in Canada West, while the Clear Grits grew more and more dismayed by their association with a "French dominated" ministry which was widely marked by railway scandals also.

Accordingly, split by sectionalism, hit by charges of waste and corruption, the Hincks-Morin Reform government broke up after confused elections in the summer of 1854. That September, a strong Liberal-Conservative Coalition took office instead, the MacNab-Morin ministry. To some extent this marked a shift to the right. Radicals like the Clear Grits went into angry opposition; Tories and

Model of Great Western Railway Sleeping Car No. 1, c. 1869. In 1860, the first railway sleeping car was built in the Great Western shops for the visit of Edward, the Prince of Wales.

1

2

3

1. *Bank of Toronto, Church and Wellington Streets, 1868. This bank was started in Toronto in 1856.*
2. *Bank of Montreal, Yonge and Front Streets, 1868. The building was constructed in 1845 and served the bank until its office was moved in 1884-1885.*
3. *Bank of Commerce, 1868. Looking south along the east side of Yonge Street. The building on the corner is the bank and to its right is the American Express Company.*
4. *University College, Toronto, c. 1875. This handsome structure was opened in 1859 and was designed by F. W. Cumberland and W. G. Storm.*
5. *Osgoode Hall, the provincial law courts as rebuilt in Toronto in the glow of rail prosperity, and still standing today.*
6. *Library of University College, pre-1890. This building was gutted by a fire in 1890, but restored.*

4

5

6

Conservatives entered power; while the incoming western co-premier, Sir Allan MacNab, himself was leader of the Upper Canada Tories, and earlier had been a fire-eating militia colonel during rebellion and border warfare days. Nevertheless, in other ways this Coalition of 1854 was more significantly a centre-of-the-road formation, one which joined the railway-minded Hincksite moderates with Upper Canadian Conservatives who were no less concerned to keep the Union going and to develop its railways and economic life. As for the mass of Lower Canadian Liberals who stayed on with Morin's own half of the ministry, they now appeared more centrally conservative themselves in seeking to preserve French Canada's position in the Union, or its Catholic interests in particular — becoming called the *Bleus* in distinction from the small but forceful radical element still left in opposition in Canada East, known as the *Rouges*.

Moreover, increasingly active within this new ruling combination of Conservatism, Hincksite Liberalism and *Bleu-isme* was the new Attorney-General West, John A. Macdonald. A friendly, good-humoured, but wonderfully shrewd judge of people and power, this Kingston Conservative had first been in Draper's government in the forties, then worked to help reshape his Upper Canada party to fit the politics of responsible rule. He was also highly effective in making and re-making the Liberal-Conservative Coalition of 1854, so that it held office for most the rest of the Union period, and eventually became a Liberal-Conservative party led by John A. Macdonald. Even by 1856 Sir Allen MacNab was out, leaving the right-wing Tories high and dry, as Macdonald became co-premier. By 1857, John A. also had found his own great Lower Canadian partner, George Etienne Cartier, who became leader of what now could be called the *Bleu* Conservatives of Canada East. Indeed, Macdonald-Cartier or Cartier-Macdonald governments would do much to keep the Union running, in spite of the mounting forces of disunion, especially in evident Canada West. And that brings us back to George Brown.

From the moment that the old Reform regime had finally collapsed in 1854, Brown had been at work trying to rebuild the Upper Canada

Sir Allan Napier MacNab (1798-1862). Tory MacNab was knighted in 1838 for his service in fighting against the rebels in 1837-1838, and was co-premier of the Union, 1854-1856.

Reform party. One rooted issue at least was removed when the new Liberal-Conservative ministry abolished the clergy reserves in 1854, applying their funds to Canada West municipalities. Another separate school bill in 1855, however, only fired up western fury — passed as it was at the very end of the last parliamentary session at Quebec, when most of the western members had already left for home. Consequently, the Clear Grits gained renewed support in rural Upper Canada as they denounced the Union as hopelessly in French hands, and even called for its dissolution — an early western separatist surge in Ontario. Brown, however, was now working to win over the Grits, while as a prominent member of the Toronto business community, he had a larger sense of the economic worth of the Union, its linking railways, commerce, and united St. Lawrence route out to the sea. Hence he sought to maintain the Union's benefits, but also to re-make it, through gaining representation by population. Then it would become a "true" union, he claimed, with no dividing line between equal sectional bocks in politics; while once it had a due majority of seats, Canada West would no longer be coerced by French power. Here was a compelling popular appeal, that even drew former Grit enemies toward Brown. Furthermore, he and the *Globe* added another powerful call, to open up the British North West, the farspread Hudson Bay Company territories beyond the Great Lakes, and annex them to Canada. This shining prospect, pushed in 1856, appealed both to land hunger among Clear Grit farmers, and to urban business interests in Canada West, seeking broad new areas for their trade, transport and financial enterprises.

Consequently, in January, 1857, a Reform Convention held in Toronto managed to re-unite the Upper Canada party, by combining Clear Grit numbers in the western constituencies with Brownite leadership centred in Toronto, and bringing back some disenchanted Hincksite moderates also. The new party programme adopted rested

1. Sir John Alexander Macdonald (1815-1891), c. 1880. A Conservative lawyer from Kingston, Macdonald was first elected to the legislature in 1844. He went on to become co-premier of the Union by 1856, and was knighted in 1867 for his efforts in bringing about Confederation.
2. Sir George Etienne Cartier (1814-1873), c. 1860s. Leader of the Conservatives in Canada East, Cartier joined forces with John A. Macdonald. The Macdonald-Cartier or Cartier-Macdonald governments did much to keep the Union running into the 1860s, despite growing forces of disunion.

1

2

1

2

basically on "rep by pop" and North West annexation; yet it did not include the old Grit stand-by, an elective, American style constitution. For Brown, a convincing and commanding leader, was deliberately moving away from the old political arguments he had had with original Grittism. The remade party that he (primarily) put together might still be dubbed "The Grits"; but actually he was guiding it towards a respectable, middle-class British Victorian liberalism, away from sweeping American populism or radical democracy. More than that, Brown had also constructed a formidable Upper Canadian Reform front to challenge the reigning Liberal-Conservatives. The elections held late in 1857 showed his success, as Brownite Grit-Liberals swept Upper Canada.

But meanwhile, Cartier's *Bleus* had carried Lower Canada, in a virtual stand-off. The resulting sectional friction, the strains of disunion, showed themselves when parliament next met at Toronto in 1858 in fierce debates over separate schools, rep by pop, and much more. Finally, in a context of manoeuvre and counter-manoeuvre, Macdonald and Cartier resigned. Brown and the Lower Canadian *Rouge*, Antoine-Aimé Dorion found themselves in power for brief days in early August. They were on fast-shifting sands; however, the Brown-Dorion cabinet in turn had to resign, beaten in a sudden Assembly vote. A Cartier-Macdonald ministry quickly replaced it, through a notorious use of loopholes in the law that has come down in history as the "Double Shuffle." Thus the old guard came safely back, and the Brownite Grit-Liberals were left outside, fuming angrily. Yet decidedly constructive ideas would emerge from this seeming political dead-end.

1. *Law offices of John A. Macdonald, Kingston.*
2. *"Bellevue," home of Macdonald during the late 1840s, Kingston, now a national historic site.*
3. *Sir Antoine-Aimé Dorion (1818-1891). After Macdonald and Cartier resigned in 1858, the Liberals Dorion and George Brown found themselves in power. However, their hold on office was brief as they were beaten in an Assembly vote a few days later. They were quickly replaced by a Macdonald-Cartier ministry by use of loopholes in the law — the "Double Shuffle."*

3

Confederation Achieved

For one thing, the renewed Cartier-Macdonald ministry made approaches to the other British North American governments in September, 1858, to see if there was any interest in a conference to discuss a general federation of the colonies, as a broader way beyond the troubles in the Union of the Canadas. There was small response; the idea was still premature. None the less it had plainly been proposed as official Conservative cabinet policy, an alternative to the existing Canadian union and its sectional problems which could be raised again if those problems grew still worse. Also, Alexander Galt, the Lower Canadian Conservative now Minister of Finance, brought up another idea which was no longer premature: a tariff with duties raised to 20 and 25 per cent, rates that definitely were protective. This high Galt tariff approved in March, 1859, was without doubt an effort to increase revenues in order to meet the heavy public deficit due to railway expenditures. Despite official lip-service to free trade, however, it also worked to shield emerging Canadian industries. Thus began a long Conservative connection with protectionism (until our most recent years); although Reformers like Brown held on to the classic liberal free-trade doctrines. And since industrial interests were scarcely as strong as commercial in Upper Canada thus far, many of its chief businessmen would agree with Brown and his earnestly free-trade *Globe*.

Something further: the Reformers themselves met in November of 1859 at another party convention in Toronto, and took up the idea of federal union; but this time, one just between the two Canadas, a dual federation. They also hoped for a general federation in the future; but felt it was a distraction now, when the sectional troubles of the Canadian union were urgent and pressing. Settle them first — then later look to bring in the Maritime provinces also, or new ones in the vast North West. The immediate task, it seemed, was to resolve the split in the present United Province: by giving distinctly sectional and local matters (such as schools, lands, and social or cultural concerns) to a government for each of the two Canadas, while allotting broad and common matters (such as canals and public works, tariffs and

1. *Sir Alexander Tilloch Galt (1817-1893), c. 1878. Son of John Galt, Alexander was a member of the Legislative Assembly (1849-1850 and 1853-1872) and Minister of Finance (1858-1862 and 1864-1866). After Confederation, Galt was first federal Minister of Finance. Much interested in the railroads, he was especially concerned with the Grand Trunk Railway.*

2. *A veteran moderate Reformer, John Sandfield Macdonald (1812-1872) was co-premier of United Canada from 1862 to 1864.*

3. *Sir Etienne Paschal Taché (1795-1865). In 1841, Taché became a member of Parliament and was Commissioner of Public Works from 1848 to 1849. He served as Speaker of the Legislative Council from 1856 to 1857. In 1864, he and John A. Macdonald led the last, brief Conservative ministry in the old Union. More important, he then headed the Great Coalition ministry that strove for Confederation in 1864, as a kind of non-partisan umpire over the main party champions in that ministry, John A. Macdonald, Brown and Cartier.*

4. *William McDougall (1822-1905), c. 1870. McDougall ran the newspaper* North American *which was absorbed by the* Globe *in 1855. He became a close Liberal associate of Brown's and sat in the Great Coalition ministry of 1864.*

1

2

3

4

debt, and major economic policies) to a general government or "joint authority" for both halves of the Union. This federation project, which hence would leave the dividing issues of sectionalism to provincial regimes, was resoundingly approved by the more than 500 delegates in St. Lawrence Hall — brought there by railways. After that, the Reform Convention scheme was to be set before the next session of parliament in 1860.

It met at Quebec, to which the capital had now been returned, and where it would stay till the Ottawa buildings were ready. George Brown put the Reform Convention plan to the Assembly in April. In May it was defeated, by mainly Conservative and French Canadian votes. That might be expected at this stage. More serious was the fact that Brown had not held all his own Reformers, since a significant number from the eastern end of Upper Canada, closely linked to the St. Lawrence and Montreal, still hoped to make the existing Union work with far lesser changes. Most powerful among them was John Sandfield Macdonald of Cornwall, who might have become party leader if Brown had not; a distinguished "old Reformer" and a former minister from the 1840s, though now more evidently moderate than reforming. At any rate, the dual federation plan was laid aside for the time being, as Brown went back to trying to restore his party's unity.

Rep by pop returned as the prime Grit-Liberal demand, especially after the census of 1861 revealed that Canada West's lead over Canada East was now more than 300,000. Western indignation soared over these "300,000 unrepresented people" in Upper Canada, even drawing some loyal Tory-Conservative supporters as well. Nevertheless, elections in the summer of 1861 still kept the Cartier-Macdonald regime in power — just barely. Among other factors, Brown's own lengthy absence played a critical part. He had been seriously ill, missing the entire parliamentary session of 1861; and his too-confident Grit lieutenants had overplayed their hand. Moreover, John A. Macdonald had astutely made rep by pop an open question for his Upper Canada Conservatives during the elections, meaning that they could endorse it even if their government had not — thus letting off considerable steam in local Tory ridings. Within months,

1. *St. Lawrence Hall, Toronto. Built during the prosperity of the 1850s, St. Lawrence Hall was the place where more than 500 Reformers met in the Convention of 1859, and adopted a federation project to re-make the union of the two Canadas.*
2. *Parliament Buildings, Ottawa, c. 1904. Ottawa was approved as the seat of government in 1858 but the buildings were not ready until 1866. This picture shows the original centre block which burned in the fire of 1916 and was replaced by the present one.*

1

2

however, the weak Conservative regime fell over a very different issue: the Militia Bill of 1862.

This was a response to the tremendous Civil War in the United States that had broken out in April, 1861. Canada was inevitably concerned as a close neighbour; and numbers of Upper Canadians would serve in the armies of the anti-slavery North. Still, there was also good cause to fear highhanded American ways, or new border troubles with an embattled and heavily armed republic. Accordingly, the Militia Bill was drafted, to give due provincial support to British regular forces being poured back into Canada to keep it secure. But the bill appeared too sweeping and costly both to many French Canadians and western farming Grits; and was hence defeated in the house in May, 1862, bringing down the Conservative ministry with it. In its place, a Sandfield Macdonald-Louis Sicotte Liberal government took office, promising a more moderate militia bill. In fact, the ministry's whole position was moderate, rejecting any structural changes. It sought instead to make the Union work by the "double majority" principle, whereby legislation essentially concerning either Canada East or Canada West would need a majority vote within that particular section to pass. Unfortunately, the principle was impractical and simply failed when applied. The very problem of the Union was that governments could not keep a sure majority in both Canadas, not when Grit Liberalism dominated the West and French Conservatism the East.

Interior of the original Senate Chamber, Ottawa.

And so the Sandfield Macdonald middle-road government could not find a middle road any more — as was most obvious when it even passed another Upper Canadian separate school bill in 1863 by Canada East votes in the face of an opposed Canada West majority. George Brown, now back in parliament, strove to reshape and redirect this stumbling Liberal regime. Thus it was a reconstructed Sandfield Macdonald-Dorion ministry which tried new elections in mid-1863. Once more, however, these settled nothing: the Brownite Grits decisively won in Upper Canada, the Cartier Conservatives in Lower. No one could win a majority over all. In March, 1864, the Sandfield Macdonald cabinet finally gave up its struggling and resigned. Another shaky Conservative ministry under John A. Macdonald and Etienne Taché came in, then in June, was beaten in turn. After two elections and four governments in three years, the Province of Canada was hopelessy deadlocked: deep in sectional disunion with no evident way out.

But then a way was opened. As gloom spread, and worried politicians grew ready to consider solutions beyond narrow party bounds, George Brown deliberately offered to support a new ministry that would take up structural changes and create a federal union. He proposed to bring Grit strength to a coalition with Conservatives — yet for the vital purpose of removing the problems that had trapped Canada. Brown's boldly constructive approach brought quick reply from John A. Macdonald, Cartier and Galt, who opened negotiations with him. Together they agreed to form a government; committed, first, to seeking a general confederation of all the British North American provinces, the Conservatives' preference, but if that failed, then the Reformers' federation of the two Canadas. To this plan Brown's side could willingly agree, since they did not wish to oppose a broader federation if they could get it; only to be sure the smaller federal union would be achieved if a general one proved unreachable. Furthermore, representation in the new federal system would be based on population.

And so Brown and two leading Upper Canada Liberals now joined the ministry with John A. Macdonald and Cartier: the ardent William McDougall, who had been Brown's close associate ever since his

Sir Oliver Mowat (1820-1903). Mowat, a Kingston lawyer and Toronto alderman, entered Parliament in 1859 and sat in the Great Coalition ministry that won Confederation. He would go on to become premier of Ontario for twenty-four years.

CONVENTION AT CHARLOTTETOWN, PRINCE EDWARD ISLAND,
OF DELEGATES FROM THE LEGISLATURES OF CANADA, NEW BRUNSWICK, NOVA SCOTIA, AND PRINCE EDWARD ISLAND,
TO TAKE INTO CONSIDERATION THE UNION OF THE BRITISH NORTH AMERICAN COLONIES, - SEPTEMBER 1, 1864.

1

2

North American had been absorbed by the *Globe* in 1855, and the quietly capable Oliver Mowat, a Kingston lawyer and Toronto alderman before entering parliament, and now a personal friend of Brown. This new ministry, the powerful "Great Coalition" that would bring about Confederation, entered office on June 22, 1864; and at once began to plan that grand design, to lay before a conference with the Maritime provinces called at Charlottetown in September.

By this time, too, the economic picture had much improved for British North America in general, thanks to booming wartime markets in the United States and broad world trade recovery. As for Upper Canada specifically, the years that followed the collapse of the railway boom late in 1857 were hard. But things had picked up in the earlier sixties, as lumber and foodstuffs poured into the American North to meet the demands of a Civil War that continued into 1865, all under the Reciprocity Treaty with the republic which would last until 1866. Consequently, the drive for Confederation was launched in an economic mood that was still anxious yet hopefully aspiring at the same time. And popular expectations rose widely across Upper Canada when the Charlottetown Conference of September, 1864, brought an agreement in principle for a projected federation of the colonies, while the Quebec Conference in October worked out the full scheme in detail. This Quebec scheme then went to the legislatures of the several provinces to gain their approval. But by the time it came before the parliament of the Canadian Union in February, 1865, new trouble was looming. Not in Canada, where the published Confederation Debates still reveal the thorough parliamentary examination that ended in a decisive assent; but rather in the Maritimes, where an initial enthusiasm was sharply overtaken by doubts and second thoughts.

Nevertheless, Upper Canada remained warmly in favour of a plan that would deal with its sectional grievances, give it just representation in a strong federal union that would bring in the wide northwestern territories — and return it to provincehood once again. Any Ontario voices opposed to Confederation were consequently few. Without doubt also, Ontario's hopes for a strong new union, and its own anti-American memories, were reinforced by the Fenian Raid upon its soil in June of 1866.

1. *Delegates at the Charlottetown Conference, September 1, 1864. Here delegates from the Canadas, New Brunswick, Nova Scotia, and Prince Edward Island agreed in principle to a projected federation of the colonies.*

2. *Fathers of Confederation at the final London Conference in 1866. Six delegates from Canada and four each from Nova Scotia and New Brunswick met in London to draft an amended version of the Quebec plan, which was then enacted into law by the Imperial Parliament.*

The Fenians represented an Irish-American movement (or fantasy) which sought somehow to free Ireland from British rule by seizing Canada. Largely Civil War veterans, over 600 of them invaded at Fort Erie, crossing from Buffalo; and they only retired again after the violent little Battle of Ridgeway. Once more this was unofficial border war, though American authorities arrested Fenians on their return. Yet the dead of the Queen's Own Rifles, young University of Toronto under-graduates, were not helped by the fact that the United States had unofficially allowed this latest replay of 1812 or 1838 to take place.

At length, far to the east, New Brunswick and Nova Scotia came round to Confederation; for reasons which are, however, outside our scope here. And so the London Conference met late in 1866 to draft a final version of the Quebec plan, which was then to be enacted into law by the imperial parliament. Meanwhile in 1866, the Union's parliament met for the last time (but the first time in Ottawa) and drew up constitu-tional arrangements for the "new" provinces of Quebec and Ontario, to be incorporated in the imperial Confederation Bill. The resulting Ontario provincial structure (with its own responsible government of premier, cabinet and elected legislative assembly) can best be looked at in more detail during the second volume of this study, covering the post-Confed-eration period. Suffice it now to say that the Bill which established both the new federal Dominion of Canada and the banner Province of Ontario was passed at Westminster in March, 1867, as the British North America Act; and (as all Canadians must know) came into being on July 1 of that year.

Confederation had been born. Ontario (old Upper Canada) had been re-born at the same time. The two processes can hardly be separated; moreover, Ontario leadership and mass support had had a great deal to do with creating the new federal Canada. John A. Macdonald and George Brown stand out in particular as its chief architects from Upper Canada. Macdonald's negotiating skills, broad statesmanship and insight had carried him to the fore in the great Confederation conferences. Brown's initiative, drive and strong sense of purpose had set the whole Confederation process under way. He actually left the cabinet late in 1865, his ruling purpose achieved; while Macdonald went on to be Canada's first prime minister. And though Macdonald Conservatism

1. *Aerial view of the Parliament buildings, Ottawa, c. 1920. In 1866, the Union govern-ment met for the last time, but its first time in Ottawa. The government that year drew up constitutional arrangements for the "new" provinces of Ontario and Quebec, to be incorporated into the Confederation Bill.*
2. *The East Block, Parliament Hill, Ottawa, June 1991. This building, completed in 1865, was the centre of Canada's govern-ment for eighty years. It housed the offices of the Privy Council, the Prime Minister, and until 1942, those of the governor-general. In 1981, Public Works Canada completed the restoration of the historic chambers and the renovation of offices for parliamentarians.*

1

2

BY THE QUEEN.
A PROCLAMATION
For Uniting the Provinces of Canada, Nova Scotia, and New Brunswick into One Dominion under the Name of CANADA.

VICTORIA R.

WHEREAS by an Act of Parliament passed on the Twenty-ninth Day of March One thousand eight hundred and sixty-seven, in the Thirtieth Year of Our Reign, intituled " An Act for the Union of Canada, Nova Scotia, and New Brunswick, and the " Government thereof, and for Purposes connected therewith," after divers Recitals, it is enacted, that " it shall be lawful for the Queen, by and with the Advice of Her Majesty's most Honorable " Privy Council, to declare by Proclamation that on and after a Day therein appointed, not being " more than Six Months after the passing of this Act, the Provinces of Canada, Nova Scotia, and " New Brunswick shall form and be One Dominion under the Name of Canada, and on and after " that Day those Three Provinces shall form and be One Dominion under that Name accordingly :" And it is thereby further enacted, that " such Persons shall be first summoned to the Senate as " the Queen, by Warrant under Her Majesty's Royal Sign Manual, thinks fit to approve, and " their Names shall be inserted in the Queen's Proclamation of Union :" We therefore, by and with the Advice of Our Privy Council, have thought fit to issue this Our Royal Proclamation, and We do Ordain, Declare, and Command, that on and after the First Day of July One thousand eight hundred and sixty-seven the Provinces of Canada, Nova Scotia, and New Brunswick shall form and be One Dominion under the Name of Canada. And We do further Ordain and Declare, that the Persons whose Names are herein inserted and set forth are the Persons of whom We have, by Warrant under Our Royal Sign Manual, thought fit to approve as the Persons who shall be first summoned to the Senate of Canada.

FOR THE PROVINCE OF ONTARIO.	FOR THE PROVINCE OF QUEBEC.	FOR THE PROVINCE OF NOVA SCOTIA.	FOR THE PROVINCE OF NEW BRUNSWICK.
JOHN HAMILTON,	JAMES LESLIE,	EDWARD KENNY,	AMOS EDWIN BOTSFORD,
RODERICK MATHESON,	ASA BELKNAP FOSTER,	JONATHAN M'CULLY,	EDWARD BARRON CHANDLER,
JOHN ROSS,	JOSEPH NOËL BOSSÉ,	THOMAS D. ARCHIBALD,	JOHN ROBERTSON,
SAMUEL MILLS,	LOUIS A. OLIVIER,	ROBERT B. DICKEY,	ROBERT LEONARD HAZEN,
BENJAMIN SEYMOUR,	JACQUE OLIVIER BUREAU,	JOHN H. ANDERSON,	WILLIAM HUNTER ODELL,
WALTER HAMILTON DICKSON,	CHARLES MALHIOT,	JOHN HOLMES,	DAVID WARK,
JAMES SHAW,	LOUIS RENAUD,	JOHN W. RITCHIE,	WILLIAM HENRY STEEVES,
ADAM JOHNSTON FERGUSON BLAIR,	LUC LETELLIER DE ST. JUST,	BENJAMIN WIER,	WILLIAM TODD,
ALEXANDER CAMPBELL,	ULRIC JOSEPH TESSIER,	JOHN LOCKE,	JOHN FERGUSON,
DAVID CHRISTIE,	JOHN HAMILTON,	CALEB R. BILL,	ROBERT DUNCAN WILMOT,
JAMES COX AIKINS,	CHARLES CORMIER,	JOHN BOURINOT,	ABNER REID M'CLELAN,
DAVID REESOR,	ANTOINE JUCHEREAU DUCHESNAY,	WILLIAM MILLER.	PETER MITCHELL.
ELIJAH LEONARD,	DAVID EDWARD PRICE,		
WILLIAM MACMASTER,	ELZEAR H. J. DUCHESNAY,		
ASA ALLWORTH BURNHAM,	LEANDRE DUMOUCHEL,		
JOHN SIMPSON,	LOUIS LACOSTE,		
JAMES SKEAD,	JOSEPH F. ARMAND,		
DAVID LEWIS MACPHERSON,	CHARLES WILSON,		
GEORGE CRAWFORD,	WILLIAM HENRY CHAFFERS,		
DONALD MACDONALD,	JEAN BAPTISTE GUÉVREMONT,		
OLIVER BLAKE,	JAMES FERRIER,		
BILLA FLINT,	Sir NARCISSE FORTUNAT BELLEAU, Knight,		
WALTER M'CREA,	THOMAS RYAN,		
GEORGE WILLIAM ALLAN.	JOHN SEWELL SANBORN.		

Given at Our Court at Windsor Castle, this Twenty-second Day of May, in the Year of our Lord One thousand eight hundred and sixty-seven, and in the Thirtieth Year of Our Reign.

God save the Queen.

LONDON: Printed by GEORGE EDWARD EYRE and WILLIAM SPOTTISWOODE, Printers to the Queen's most Excellent Majesty. 1867.

1

3

1. *Proclamation of Confederation, May 22, 1867.*
2. *1867 Prospectus of the* Globe *Newspaper, December 31, 1866.*
"The year 1867 will probably be the most eventful year in the history of the British North American Provinces," this article proclaims. It goes on to say that the Globe *will secure its prominence among newspapers by use of the telegraph and "able correspondents" in bringing news from London in regard to the Confederation Act.*
3. *Confederation Medal. This medal was struck by the Canadian government in 1867. The obverse (top) shows Queen Victoria's head, the reverse (bottom) is an allegory: Britain gives the charter of Confederation to Ontario (with sheaf of grain and sickle), Quebec (with a paddle and* fleur de lis*), Nova Scotia (holding a mining spade), and New Brunswick (with a timber axe).*

2

CONFEDERATION DAY.

The Dominion of Canada.

HISTORICAL NOTES

HOW CONFEDERATION HAS BEEN BROUGHT ABOUT.

STATISTICS OF THE UNITED PROVINCES.

Extent, Population, Trade and Resources of the Dominion.

With the first dawn of this gladsome midsummer morn, we hail the birthday of a new nationality. A united British America, with its four millions of people, takes its place this day among the nations of the world. Stamped with a familiar name, which in the past has borne a record sufficiently honourable to entitle it to be perpetuated with a more comprehensive import, the DOMINION OF CANADA, on this First day of July, in the year of grace, eighteen hundred and sixty-seven, enters on a new career of national existence. Old things have passed away. The history of old Canada, with its contracted bounds, and limited divisions of Upper and Lower, East and West, has been completed, and this day a new volume is opened, New Brunswick and Nova Scotia uniting with Ontario and Quebec to make the history of a greater Canada, already extending from the ocean to the head waters of the great lakes, and destined ere long to embrace the larger half of this North American continent from the Atlantic to the Pacific.

Let us gratefully acknowledge the hand of the Almighty Disposer of Events in bringing about this result, pregnant with so important an influence on the condition and destinies of the inhabitants of these Provinces, and of the teeming millions who in ages to come will people the Dominion of Canada from ocean to ocean, and give it its character in the annals of time. Let us acknowledge, too, the sagacity, the patriotism, the forgetfulness of selfish and partisan considerations, on the part of our statesmen, to which under Providence are due the inception of the project of a British American Confederation and the carrying it to a successful issue. Without much patient labour, a disposition to make mutual concessions, and an earnest large-minded willingness

years ago. In the duties, therefore, of the present, and in the hopes and aspirations which gild our future, there is room and scope ample enough for the purest patriotism and the loftiest ambition. Let us hope that Canadians—using the word in its new and large acceptation—will worthily fulfil the duties which Providence has confided to them.

From the commencement of the movement until its auspicious consummation to-day, THE GLOBE has been ever its zealous and persevering advocate. We have striven to meet objections, to remove obstacles, to smooth down asperities. We have endeavoured to combat its opponents, and to shield it from the injury it might have received from injudicious supporters, who were foolish enough to try to make it subserve their paltry personal and party interests. As a not uninfluential organ of public opinion, we may be pardoned for claiming that THE GLOBE has contributed, in some degree at least, to the successful result over which we this day rejoice. And now, standing at the point of transition between the old and the new, on this day when the Dominion of Canada starts upon its career, we may, with peculiar propriety, look back on the past, at what has been accomplished, and forward to the future, whose history has yet to be acted and written. We propose, therefore, to devote to-day a large portion of our space to laying before our readers at one glance, and in as brief compass as possible, the most essential information with reference to the new Confederacy—its extent and population, its trade and resources, its wealth developed and undeveloped, and the prospects in store for it—with, at the same time, a rapid sketch of the history of its component parts, and of the negotiations and proceedings which have resulted in their Union. And before proceeding to the other points, we shall commence with this brief historical sketch, as the first in order of time.

HISTORICAL SKETCH.

The discovery of Canada is generally attributed to Jacques Cartier, of Saint Malo, in France. There is a sort of legendary story, however, which makes the Spaniards prior discoverers, and derives from them the name of our new Dominion. It is said that the Spaniards were the first Europeans who visited the country, but that finding no gold in it—not having penetrated as far as Madoc—they speedily retraced their steps. When the French came afterwards, the Indians so frequently

division of the French army under Gen. Bougainville proceeded still higher up the river, to prevent the English troops from landing. During the night the British ships dropped silently down the river with the current, and at four o'clock on the morning of the 13th, the troops began to land at the point since known as Wolfe's Cove. By eight o'clock, the British had ascended the Heights. The Marquis de Montcalm, with more bravery than prudence, without waiting to concentrate his army, drew up his disposable forces in front of the British, and the battle of the Plains of Abraham, which decided the fate of Canada, was gallantly fought by the contending forces. Great valour was displayed by the commanders and the troops on both sides, but the fortune of war was on the side of the English, and the control of the destinies of Canada passed into the hands of the British race. General Wolfe died in the moment of victory, at the age of thirty-five, having won for his country what has been justly termed "the brightest diadem in the Crown of England." The brave Montcalm died of his wounds a few days afterwards. On the 18th September, Quebec capitulated to General Murray, who succeeded General Wolfe in command. In the west also fortune favoured the English troops. The fort of Niagara was taken by Sir William Johnston, and those at Ticonderaga and Crown Point, by General Amherst ; and the three British Generals having formed a junction, invested Montreal, where the French forces made a stand under the Governor-General, M. de Vaudreuil. On the 8th September, 1760, De Vaudreuil, finding further resistance hopeless, capitulated, surrendering Montreal and all the French fortresses in Canada to Great Britain. By the treaty of 1763, France formally ceded all its northern possessions in America to England.

A letter from Governor Murray to the Lords of Trade and Plantations, gives an interesting account of the state of the Province in 1765, five years after the Conquest. The towns of Quebec and Montreal then contained about 14,700 inhabitants. Exclusive of Quebec and Montreal, there were 110 parishes, containing 9,722 houses, and 54,575 Christian souls. The population occupied of arable land, 955,755 arpents—an arpent being somewhat less than an English acre. In the year 1765, they sowed 180,-300 minots of grain—a minot being somewhat greater than an English bushel—and possessed 12,546 oxen, 22,724 cows, 15,039 young horned cattle, 27,064 sheep, 28,976 swine, and 13,757 horses. The Indians within the Province, how-

stimulate them to act worthily Canadian name.

The system of separate Govern for Upper and Lower Canada con for precisely half a century, from till 1841, when the two Provinces united under one Government and lature. Unfortunately, the terms Union, establishing an equality of sentation between the two Pro were such that very soon the inhab of the Upper and more progressiv vince felt themselves in the gallin tion of not having that share i government and legislation of the co to which their numbers, intelligen wealth entitled them. Their effo obtain justice were successfully re through a long course of years, by jority in the Legislature, which wa tained by the defection from the Canada ranks of a minority, chiefly on enjoying the sweets of office ; ur last, the working of the Union beca tolerable - nay, impossible - and we enter on a new system, under which Province shall have the entire m ment of its own local affairs, and share in the administration of mat general concern. We must than acknowledge, however, that in sp our political difficulties, Canada has great progress during the last quart century. The settlement of the coun made rapid advances : canals hav opened to render available our unec chain of water communication ; gre ways have been constructed ; our n resources have been partially deve our lumber has been turned to go vantage ; and our population, th immigration and natural increas been augmented in an almost unexe ratio. And now, when our section ficulties are removed—when we pre the world a united front, and full dence may be reposed in the stab our institutions—may we not ho our progress in future years will b more wonderful than anything th yet been witnessed in our history ?

NOVA SCOTIA was first discov 1497 by John Cabot, or his son Seb who conducted an exploring expedi the New World, under a commissio Henry VII. of England. It wa however, till a hundred years late an attempt—under French ausp was made to colonize it. In 1603, Monts obtained from Henri IV. of a commission constituting him Go of all the countries of America, 40° to 46° north, including Nov tia, then called Acadia. De equipped four ships, and sailed fo

PUBLISHED EVERY MORNING NOS. 26 & 28 KING STREET EAST.

"THE SUBJECT WHO IS TRULY LOYAL TO THE (

VOL. XXIV., NO. 156

TO

Globe.

ISTRATE WILL NEITHER ADVISE NOR SUBMIT TO ARBITRARY MEASURES.—Junius." { **SIX DOLLARS PER ANNUM;**
SINGLE NUMBERS 8c.

MONDAY, JULY 1, 1867. **WHOLE NO. 5385**

ly increasing until now it numbers a quarter of a million.

the history of NEWFOUNDLAND and CE EDWARD ISLAND, which have not consented to enter the Dominion of da, we shall only allude with the st brevity. The former island was vered by Cabot in 1497, and called m "Baccalaos," the name given to h in the native language. During succeeding century, though the eignty of the island was claimed by nd, ships from various countries d the prosecution of its fisheries; was not till the year 1610 that an pt was made to form an actual ment in the country. In that year, Guy, a merchant of Bristol, with gentlemen, received from James I. arter entitling them to settle the , and to make such arrangements uld secure to England the exclusive ment of the fisheries along its coasts 6, Dr. William Vaughan settled a h colony in the southern part of l. In 1621, Sir George Calvert, after-Lord Baltimore, founded a Roman olic colony, which he called Avalon. e latter part of the century, France ted with England the possession of oundland; but by the treaty of ht, Placentia and all other parts of sland which had been occupied by rench, were ceded to Great Britain. soil and climate of Newfoundland unsuited for agriculture, its pro-has not been so great as that of other British American colonies, highly favoured in those respects; as the centre of an immense fishing , it has become the cradle of a hardy ring population, whom we trust we ere long have the satisfaction of ming into the British American ederation. PRINCE EDWARD ISLAND iscovered by Cabot in 1497, on the June (St. John's day) and received him the name of St. John's Island, it continued to bear until 1799, when, Act of its Legislature, it was changed Prince Edward," in honour of the of Kent, then Commander of the h forces in America. In 1758, when overeignty of the island was trans-d from France to England, its popu-n was about 10,000. In 1768, it re-d a separate Government, having ously been attached to Nova Scotia. progress of the colony has been se-ly retarded by an unfortunate sys-of land-tenure which dates from its settlement, and its population now, a growth of a hundred years, scarce-ceeds that of some of our larger r Canadian counties. It has, how-a Lieutenant Governor a Cabinet

and Mr. John A. Macdonald succeded in getting together a Cabinet, to which the Reform party felt it their duty to give the strongest possible opposition. On the re-assembling of Parliament, after minis-ters had returned from their elections, the Government found themselves in much the same predicament as the Macdonald-Dorion Administration had been at the commencement of the session; but with this difference, that whereas the latter had a majority of one or two, the former were in a minority of about the same proportions. They struggled on for a few weeks, during which period Mr. Brown's Constitutional Committee sat with closed doors. It was composed of leading members of the House on both sides of politics, and a very free inter-change of opinion took place. In the course of the discussions it appeared pro-bable that a union of parties might be ef-fected for the purpose of grappling with the constitutional difficulties pointed out the 14th of June, the Committee presented their report, which stated that "a strong " feeling was found to exist among the " members of the Committee in favour " of changes in the direction of a Fede-" rative system, applied either to Canada " alone or to the whole British North " American Provinces and such progress " has been made as to warrant the Com-" mittee in recommending that the sub-" ject be again referred to a Committee " at the next session of Parliament." This report had been adopted in the Committee by a vote of 12 to 3 the nays being Hon. John A. Macdonald, Hon. John S Macdonald, and Mr. Sco-ble. By the force of events, the question was put in the way of settlement, sooner than had been contemplated by the com-mittee, when they recommended their re-appointment in the following session. Affairs were brought to a crisis on the evening of the very day on which the committee had presented their report, by a vote of censure on the Administration being carried by a majority of two. At-tempts were made by them to detach some members of the Opposition; but they failed, and a dissolution of Parlia-ment appeared to be imminent, although a general election had taken place in the previous year. The opportunity seemed a favourable one for attempting a solution of the constitutional difficulty, and over-tures by Mr. Brown, on behalf of the Re-form party, were met by Mr. John A Macdonald, with a greater cordiality than could have been anticipated, judging from his vote a few days before against the re-port of the Committee. The result of the negotiations was the formation of a Coalition-Government, pledged to seek

Union were almost unanimously adopted; but no steps were taken to carry the principle into practical effect, as regarded that Island. The little Island of Prince Edward repudiated the action of its delegates at the Quebec Conference, and did not, like New Brunswick, take a wiser second thought. It has chosen for the present to remain out of the Union—to its own loss we should fancy, rather than that of Confederacy.

Arrangements were made early in June, 1866, for the assembly in London of a Conference of Delegates from the several Provinces, to determine the precise terms of the Bill giving effect to the Union of British America, to be submitted for adoption by the Imperial Parliament. Delegates were duly appointed by the Governments of Canada, Nova Scotia, and New Brunswick, and an agreement was made that they should all sail for Eng-from the Lower Provinces on their part, fulfilled this agreement, but they had to wait several months for the arrival of the Canadians, and the Conference was not organized till the 4th December. In con-sequence of this delay, the Confederation measure, instead of being carried through the Imperial Parliament, in 1866, as it might have been, was not submitted to that body till the session of 1867.

The Imperial Parliament assembled on the 5th of February. On the 7th, the Bill for the Confederation of the Pro-vinces was introduced by the then Colo-nial Secretary, the Earl of Carnarvon. On the 19th, it had its second reading; on the 22nd passed through Committee of the Whole, and on the 26th February was read a third time. Having been immedi-ately taken down to the House of Com-mons, it was moved to a second reading in that body, on the 28th February; and, after an interesting debate, in the course of which there was scarcely any opposition given to the measure except by Mr. Bright, who made a somewhat carping, ill-natured anti-Colonial speech, the motion was agreed to without a divi-sion. It passed through Committee on the 4th March. Mr. Aytoun, the member for Kirkcaldy, spoke against the proposed guarantee for an Intercolonial Railroad loan, but did not on this occasion press to a vote an amendment hostile to that guarantee, of which he had given notice. On the 8th March, it was read a third time, and finally passed by the House of Commons without a debate. On the 12th, certain amendments which had been made by the Commons were agreed to by the Lords; and on the 28th March it received the Royal assent, and became a law of the empire.

isthmus connects it at its south-eastern extremity with Nova Scotia. On the east, its coasts are washed by the waters of the Gulf of St. Lawrence, and on the south by those of the Bay of Fundy. Its area is 27,105 square miles.

Nova Scotia, previous to 1770, comprehended also Prince Ed-ward Island, and the territory which now forms the Province of New Bruns-wick. In that year, Prince Edward Is-land was separated from Nova Scotia, and in 1783, New Brunswick and the Island of Cape Breton were also separated. In the year 1820, however, Cape Breton was re-annexed. Nova Scotia lies within the latitudes of 43° and 46° north, and the longitudes of 61° and 67° west. It is about 320 miles long (from east to west) with an average breadth of 70 miles. Its greatest width is about 100 miles. The coast of Nova Scotia being everywhere indented by arms of the sea, no part of it is more than 20 miles dis-tant from salt water. Its area, including Cape Breton, is 18,660 square miles.

The area of the four Provinces, consti-tuting the new Dominion, may therefore be stated as follows:—

	Square Miles.
Ontario,	121,260
Quebec,	210,020
New Brunswick,	27,105
Nova Scotia,	18,660
Total,	377,045

The Province of Ontario, exceeds, in its dimensions, those of Great Britain and and Ireland, which are 119,924 square miles. The Province of Quebec has an area almost equal to that of France, which is 211,852 square miles. Nova Scotia is as large as the kingdom of Greece, and New Brunswick is equal in extent to Denmark and Switzerland combined.

If we add the area of Prince Edward Island, 2,100 square miles; that of New-foundland, 40,200 square miles; that of British Columbia, 200,000 square miles; and that of the Hudson's Bay and North West Territories, 2,750,000 square miles —we will have as the total area of the countries which will probably at no distant day be included in the Dominion of Canada, the enormous extent of 3,389,-345 square miles—nearly three times the extent of territory embraced in the Em-pire of China, with its four hundred millions of inhabitants—and greater by 400,000 square miles than the whole territory of the United States.

POPULATION.

According to the census taken in 1861,

would rule in Ottawa, Brownite Grit Liberalism would come to hold Ontario: apt outcomes to the work of both these leaders in the Union years. But more important still for Ontario's heritage, was its own prime role in the achieving of a Canadian nation. That nation had come into its own in 1867, when Confederation took effect. And the driving presence of Ontario, now its strongest province, would continue to build and mould the Canadian federal union through all the post-Confederation years that lay ahead.

Overleaf. *Confederation Day,* The Globe, *July 1, 1867.*
1. *London Conference, 1866. Issued on May 26, 1966 and designed by Paul Pederson, this stamp marks the 100th anniversary of the London Conference.*
2. *Stamp Issued to Commemorate the Parliament Buildings, Ottawa.*
3. *Dominion Day poster, Richmond Hill (1872). An advertisement for the festivities, showing popular ways of celebrating in the late 19th century: athletics, parades and fireworks.*

1

2

- 1867 July 1: British North America Act takes effect
        Population of Ontario: 1,500,000
- 1867-71 Liberal-Conservative coalition government rules new Province of Ontario under John Sandfield Macdonald

- 1870s Silver Islet mines in production in Thunder Bay
- 1872 Liberal Oliver Mowat becomes Premier
- 1874-96 Largely years of world recession or depression
- 1876 Re-organization of the public school system in Ontario

- 1880s Multiplying factories and fast-expanding city working-class Electric city lights and trolley cars come into use in the province
- 1884 Ontario-Manitoba boundary dispute settled
- 1885 Canadian Pacific railway completed; copper and nickel finds on the route bring development of Sudbury
- 1888 Secret ballot and vote without property qualifications in Ontario

- 1900-13 World economic boom
- 1902 Construction starts on provincial railway to tap the Ontario North (Temiskaming and Northern Ontario)
- 1904 Silver boom develops at Cobalt on the T.N.O.
- 1905 Under Whitney, Conservatives come to provincial power, ending 34-year Liberal rule
- 1906 Provincial hydro-power commission established

- 1914-18 World War I
- 1917 Women given provincial vote
- 1918 Women given federal vote
- 1919 United Farmers of Ontario led by Drury hold power until 1923

Chapter Seven

Ontario from Confederation to Our Own Time:

A Glance Ahead

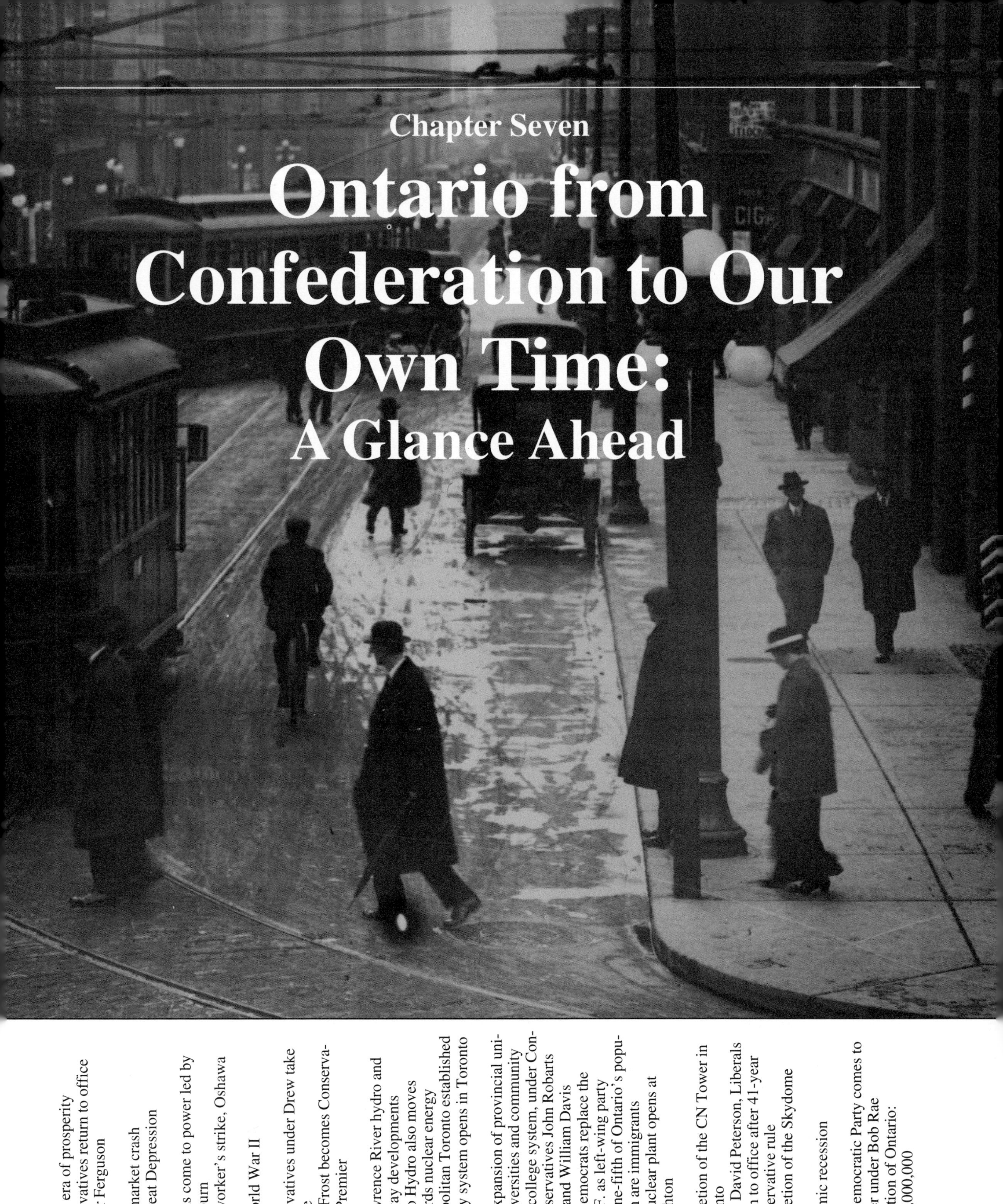

1920s Mostly era of prosperity
1923 Conservatives return to office under Ferguson

1929 Stock market crash
1930s The Great Depression

1934 Liberals come to power led by Hepburn
1937 Auto-worker's strike, Oshawa

1939-45 World War II

1943 Conservatives under Drew take office

1949 Leslie Frost becomes Conservative Premier

1950s St. Lawrence River hydro and Seaway developments
Ontario Hydro also moves towards nuclear energy

1954 Metropolitan Toronto established
Subway system opens in Toronto

1960s-70s Expansion of provincial universities and community college system, under Conservatives John Robarts and William Davis
1961 New Democrats replace the C.C.F. as left-wing party
Over one-fifth of Ontario's population are immigrants

1962 First nuclear plant opens at Rolphton

1976 Completion of the CN Tower in Toronto

1985 Led by David Peterson, Liberals return to office after 41-year Conservative rule

1989 Completion of the Skydome

1990s Economic recession

1990 New Democratic Party comes to power under Bob Rae
1991 Population of Ontario: c. 10,000,000

A Liberal Era: 1872-1905

To carry Ontario's ever-widening story forward from Confederation to our own day will properly require a second volume on the same scale as this first one. Nevertheless, it is both possible and useful to close the present book with a brief survey of the years still to be covered by the succeeding volume. These years will extend, of course, from the launching of the new province of Ontario within the Canadian federal union of 1867 up to the two-hundredth anniversary of the old, original province of Upper Canada that had been erected back in 1791. And in order to survey this whole post-Confederation period, we may conveniently divide it here into three main eras: from 1867 down to 1905, from 1905 to 1949, after the Second World War; and finally, from 1949 to the present time.

Each of these three broad eras was largely marked by its own particular political patterns; but without question, there was a lot more to any and all of them than politics alone. To give just a few leading examples, Ontario's huge northland at last was opened up to major resource development and settlement; while the population of the entire province, swelled in part by new and varied streams of immigration, rose sweepingly from around a million and a half in 1867 to close on ten million by 1991. Furthermore, a once-rural, staid and simple farming province — although with some significant industrial and urban beginnings — now became increasingly transformed into an industrialized and urbanized community of big business, big labour and high production, of teeming cities and advanced technology, complex social services and massive provincial government. That brings us back to politics again; yet we may proceed from there to look at each of the three main eras in turn: always keeping in mind that such a brief, general view can only present the basic outlines of the province's history from 1867 onward; for instance, saying little until the volume to follow of its role throughout in federal-provincial relations.

At any rate, it might next be said that the opening era in post-Confederation Ontario was mostly dominated by Liberalism, especially

Overleaf. *Downtown Toronto, c. 1914.*
1. *Barley harvest, near Fisherville, Haldimand County, c. 1906. Ontario became increasingly transformed into a heavily industrialized and urbanized community after Confederation.*
2. *Apartment Buildings, Toronto, July 24, 1991. Ontario's population rose from about one and a half million in 1867 to close to ten million by 1991 due mostly to varied streams of immigration.*
3. *Certificate of the County of Peel Public Schools, 1885. The Education Department Act of 1876 unified the educational system from the provincial university to elementary schools under a Minister of Education and a growing bureaucracy.*
4. *Interior of Consumers' Gas Company, c. 1911. Even by then, Ontario was very much business-directed.*

1

2

3

4

as led by Oliver Mowat, who served as provincial premier from 1872 to 1896, and whose party heirs then held on to office until 1905 in a remarkable span of Liberal rule. True, in the earliest few years after Confederation, from 1867 to 1871, a coalition of both Liberals and Conservatives governed the newly created province under its first premier, John Sandfield Macdonald: a long-time Reform rival of George Brown, the chief builder of Ontario's widely popular Grit Liberal party. Sandfield, moreover, was essentially the choice of John A. Macdonald, a shrewd first prime minister of the young federal Dominion of Canada, who was only too glad to see a firm enemy of Brown — his own greatest rival, though once his vital partner in achieving Confederation — nicely established in Toronto in charge of the Dominion's most powerful member-province. Despite his productive work as Ontario premier, Sandfield, however, could not long withstand a mounting series of Liberal attacks on his coalition regime. And so, at the end of 1871, Edward Blake took power instead at the head of an all-Liberal provincial cabinet; but the next year was himself replaced by an older master-politician, and a Liberal Father of Confederation brought back from the senior judicial post of Vice-Chancellor: Oliver Mowat.

Mowat, a veteran party associate of George Brown (who did not re-enter active political life himself) was an earnest Victorian Liberal full of Grit principle, and smart politics besides. By highly skilful managing, and cautious yet keen judgement, he kept tight control of the province for more than two decades; winning over its Catholic minority through fair-minded treatment of their separate schools, holding the Protestant majority despite the anger of more fervent Orangemen and Tories; and even fending off agrarian discontents, as farmers felt their rural world declining in its weight. Opponents simply could not make lasting headway; although the forces of Conservatism — including John A. Macdonald, a Kingston man like Oliver Mowat — railed long and loud against this "Little Tyrant." But a continuing majority of Ontario voters instead saw the Tyrant as their own staunch champion of Provincial Rights. An accomplished courtroom lawyer, Mowat indeed won landmark cases involving disputed federal and provincial claims under the new Canadian

1. North West Angle of Lake of the Woods, October-November, 1872. This picture was taken by the North American Boundary Commission, 1872-1875. The provincial boundary finally was settled at Lake of the Woods instead of the head of Lake Superior as the federal government had sought.
2. Monument to John Sandfield Macdonald, Queen's Park, Toronto. From 1867 to 1871, the new province of Ontario was governed by a coalition government of Liberals and Conservatives under J.S. Macdonald.
3. Monument to John A. Macdonald, Queen's Park. First prime minister of the Dominion of Canada, he would be active into the 1890s.
4. Monument to George Brown, Queen's Park. Brown did not enter parliamentary life after Confederation, but kept politically involved through his newspaper, the Globe.
5. Monument to Oliver Mowat, Queen's Park. Mowat led the Liberals in the post-Confederation era and was premier for twenty-four years, from 1872 to 1896. The Liberal regime shaped by Mowat lasted until 1905.

1

2

3

4

5

1

2

constitution. Of all these issues, the most notable for the Ontario acclaim it brought him was the vexed question of the province's western boundary — which in 1884 was finally confirmed at its existing limit on the Lake of the Woods; not back at the head of Lake Superior, as John A. and his allies had steadily insisted.

Quite aside from thus upholding Ontario's concerns (and property) against the dark designs of federal authority in Ottawa, Mowat's administration also gave the citizens a good deal of what they wanted from their provincial government. On one hand, his regime enlarged the scope of the individual and furthered popular democracy: as in the Education Act of 1876, which re-organized the whole public system from elementary school to university under a strong new ministry of education, or through enacting the secret ballot and giving the vote without property qualifications by 1888. On the other hand the government also carried factory regulations and workmen's compensation laws, plus a valuable set of measures which laid the basis for state-provided social welfare. In short, the Liberal government kept abreast of a changing Ontario, in which pioneer self-reliance or farm home-care (both often grossly inadequate) were now inevitably giving way to the collective needs of rising cities and industrial life, of disadvantaged workers and dependent poor.

In spite of a long depression which, with ups and downs, gripped world trade from about 1874 to 1896, Ontario's economic growth generally surged forward throughout these years. It did experience some bad times or boom phases of its own. But in particular, the 1880s brought it multiplying factories and a fast-expanding city working-class, in the spreading age of steam, smoke and iron. Railways played an intimate part, as well. More and more lines were built, to serve Ontario factory towns and tie them to the resources and markets of a transcontinental Canadian dominion. In 1885, the Canadian Pacific was completed, from Montreal and Ottawa across northern Ontario and the Canadian West, right to Vancouver. By the next year, rails up from Toronto had linked into the C.P.R. near

1. *Interior of a steam-driven plant for generating electricity. The 1880s brought multiplying factories and a fast-expanding city working-class. Note the new electric lights inside the plant.*
2. *Part of the Big Fill, Construction on the National Transcontinental Railway, Dryden area, Northern Ontario. The National Transcontinental was built at the federal tax-payer's expense and leased to the Grand Trunk.*
3. *Men at Work on the National Transcontinental. It ran from Quebec City through mid-northern Quebec and Ontario, and linked with the Grand Trunk Pacific that reached on to the West Coast.*
4. *Men Leaving for Work on the Canadian Northern Railway.*

3

4

1

1. *Confederation Life Building on Richmond Street, West, Toronto, 1890s. This building is still standing today, but now hemmed in by skyscrapers.*
2. *Medallion of the Knights of Labour. The Knights first entered Canada in Hamilton in 1881. They sought to organize large masses of workers without regard to skills or gender.*
3. *Bird's Eye View of Toronto, 1886. The population of Toronto more than doubled between 1881 and 1891, increasing from 86,000 to 181,000, forming 8.6 per cent of the province's population.*

2

3

North Bay. Hamilton rose much further as an iron-working, then steel-making city. Toronto developed a richly varied range of manufacturing, from large agricultural machinery to clothing, from publishing to electrical goods. Ottawa grew with great lumber or pulp and paper plants; and many other smaller factory centres prospered as well. One broad result was great new industrial wealth and powerful corporations; another, newly active, mass labour unions, although many of these did not survive the economic downturns of the nineties. In any event, by the end of Mowat's rule, when he retired undefeated in 1896, he had seen the face and very nature of his sedate Victorian Ontario already enormously altered.

Meanwhile, the northern expanses of the province were also being increasingly opened up to change. In fact, the economic penetration of the North, by more than the wilderness fur trade, had started even before Confederation. Thus lumbering had gone on advancing along the upper Ottawa from the 1850s, ever probing northward to fresh stands of timber; while on the Great Lakes margins, it gradually spread around Georgian Bay to the north coast of Lake Huron, later onward to Lake Superior. Moreover, mining reached Huron's north shore by the early fifties, when the copper deposits of Bruce Mines were brought into production there. And by the seventies deep, if localized, silver veins at Silver Islet, outside Thunder Bay on Lake Superior, were yielding wonderfully high returns. Nevertheless, the vast inlands behind the shorelines of the Upper Lakes could not really yet be tapped; nor the rugged wilds that stretched on westward to the prairies — not until railways made them accessible to masses of workers and heavy equipment, and enabled the commodities of forest and mine to flow out in bulk to markets. Then the Canadian Pacific opened the way in the 1880s, while Canadian Northern in the nineties and other lines that followed, continued to promote a developing Ontario North: cleary visible as a great new empire in its right by the time the twentieth century had begun.

Around Sudbury on the C.P.R., large copper finds first made when that line went through, grew far more valuable for their abundant nickel content, because nickel became a critical component of

1. *The Algoma Iron Works (left) and the Sulphite Pulp Mill (right), Sault Ste. Marie, c. 1900. These industries were two of the many enterprises Francis Clergue set up in Sault Ste. Marie, inspiring a boom there. Basing a resource empire on the town, he experienced brilliant success and total collapse in quick succession.*
2. *The Grain Fleet. As part of the advances felt in the North, both Port Arthur and Fort William became busy Lakehead wheat ports.*

1

2

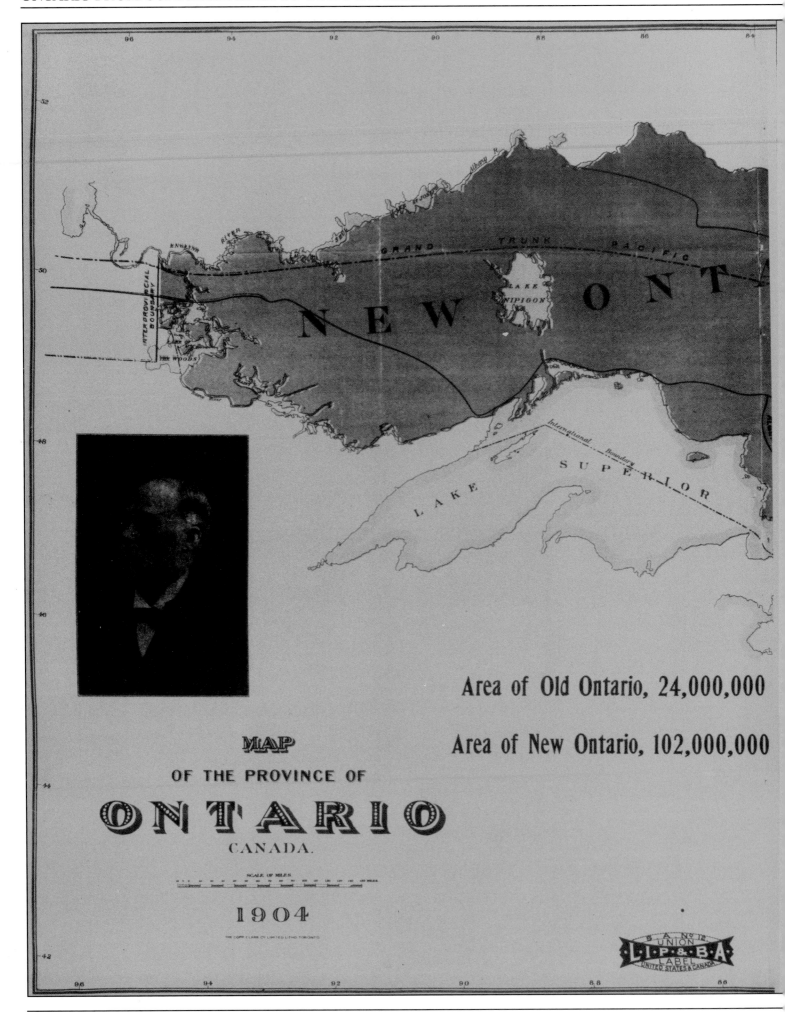

Area of Old Ontario, 24,000,000

Area of New Ontario, 102,000,000

MAP

OF THE PROVINCE OF

ONTARIO

CANADA.

SCALE OF MILES

1904

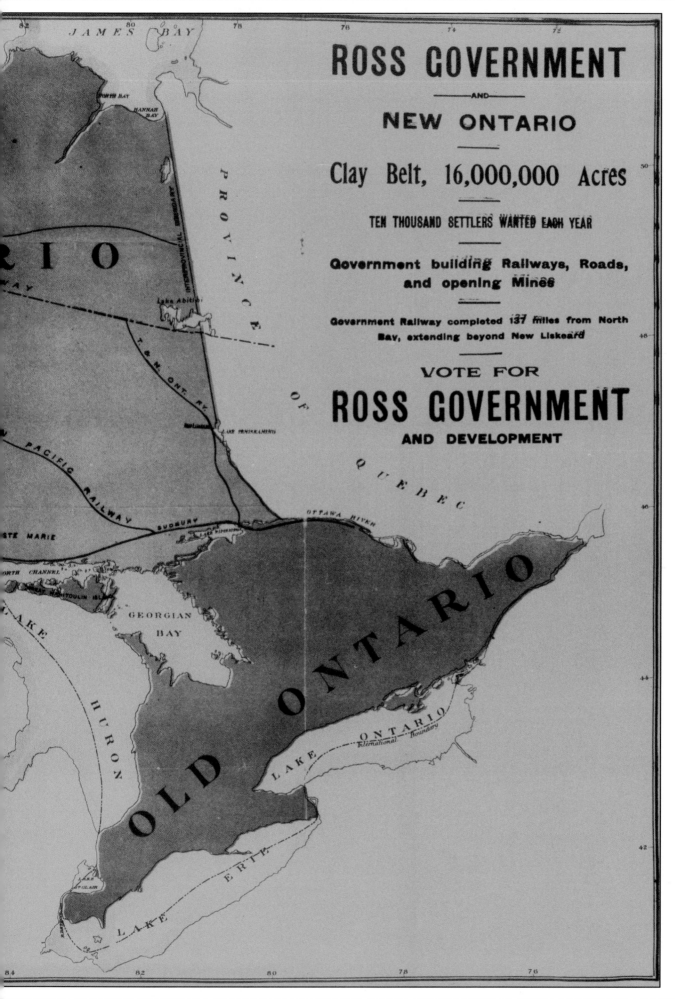

Map of the Province of Ontario, 1904. "New Ontario" covered the fast advancing Northern Ontario resource empire of that day.

1

2

3

modern technology, from naval armour plate to automobiles. At Sault Ste. Marie, which was both on a C.P.R. branch line and a major Great Lakes water-passage, hydro-electric power along with iron mines, pulp mills and steel plants, produced a potent new industrial complex. And whether at the busy Lakehead grain ports of Port Arthur and Fort William, in the silver mines which boomed from 1904 at Cobalt, or in the gold fields which soon arose near Timmins, the young century brought dazzling advances to the North, to "New Ontario." This was an area of enlarging land settlements, as well as aspiring towns and big, Southern-controlled resource industries. It gained strong economic importance; but far less political weight — and so remained an uncertain region of discontents, then and recurrently since.

Northern development assuredly attracted Mowat's Liberal successors in government; first Arthur Hardy, then George Ross, who had initially made his name as an efficient Minister of Education. Ross especially was caught up with the North, and in 1902 began building the province's own railway line (to become the Ontario Northland) out of North Bay up to Cochrane, a line which finally would reach James Bay at Moosenee and open wide north-eastern districts. But Premier Ross, in spite of his northern enthusiasms and activities, soon lost ground politically to resurgent Conservative forces under James Pliny Whitney. Perhaps Ross had grown too sure of power, after long decades of Liberal rule. He indeed failed to mend his political fences with Mowat's former care, although the charges of corruption brought against his government were much overdone. In any case, Ontario was now ready for a change. And the boldly capable, but very practical Whitney — a dynamic Conservative from old Loyalist Eastern Ontario — seemed to offer both businesslike policies and enduring ideals to meet the young twentieth century. He swept to victory in the election of 1905. Ontario's initial Liberal age was over.

1. *Sir James Pliny Whitney (1843-1914), c. early 1900s. A lawyer from Morrisburg and Member for Dundas County from 1888 until his death in 1914, Whitney became leader of the provincial Conservative party in 1896. He and his Conservatives swept the election of 1905, carrying Ontario into the 20th century and leaving the Liberals behind.*
2. *Sir George William Ross (1841-1914). Successor to Mowat and Hardy as Premier of Ontario (1896-1905), Ross' defeat in 1905 was the end of thirty-four years of Liberal rule in Ontario. Ross had earlier served as Ontario's Minister of Education (1883-1899). From 1907, he was a member of the Canadian Senate.*
3. *View of Cochrane, 1914. In 1902, Premier Ross began building the province's own northern railway line, to reach Cochrane from North Bay. The town was founded in 1908 and named for Frank Cochrane, Minister of Lands, Forests and Mines (1905-1908) under Premier Whitney.*

Prosperity, Depression, and War: 1905-1949

The next main era, from 1905 to 1949, largely saw the Conservative party in office in Ontario, from Whitney's premiership forward. Yet after the First World War and into the 1920s, a United Farmers' government took charge of the province, while during the Great Depression of the 1930s, and onward into the Second World War, the Liberal party came back to power; not to yield to Conservatives again till 1944. Hence no one political party commanded this whole period. Instead, it was all the more shaped by broader forces: by general Canadian and international prosperity during the young twentieth century; by renewed flush times in the 1920s, followed by ruinous depression in the thirties — and beyond that, by both the grave demands and tragic losses of two huge conflicts, World War I, 1914-18, and World War II, 1939-45. But we will start with the pre-war years from 1905 to 1914.

The province flourished mightily in these golden years — borne along by world good times, the rapid rise of the Canadian West (and thus its markets for manufacturers), by the continuing development of Ontario's North, and by the flow of immigrants from Europe, which fed both northern towns and resource industries and the expanding factories and services of the urban South. British immigration remained by far the largest; but now, also, Finns, Hungarians, and Slavs came to Sudbury mines or the northern rail and lumber camps, while Jewish, Italian, Greek and other workers gathered in Southern Ontario cities, and especially in the metropolis of Toronto. In sum, the multicultural character of modern Ontario, which would later widen from European to Asian, Caribbean, Latin American and African arrivals, now laid strong foundations in the community. At the same time, too, the jobs were there for newcomers in the opening twentieth century, an era of busy construction and confident demand. Skyscrapers climbed, particularly in Toronto; electric street railways spread. Trunk sewers, extending public health services — paved streets, major bridges and highways for the emerging world of the automobile — all marked a far more expansive age for urban society;

1. *Toronto's First Electric Railway. Small electric trolley cars appeared in Toronto in 1885 to take passengers to the Toronto Industrial Exhibition (later the Canadian National Exhibition). The train pictured ran from the south end of Strachan Avenue to the Exhibition Grounds.*

2. *Immigrant Children, York Public School, 1923. Fourteen nationalities are represented in this group of children. Front row (L-R): Russian, Danish, Bulgarian, "Canadian", Chinese, Jewish, Polish, Italian, Austrian, Syrian. Back row (L-R): Chinese, English, Scottish, Negro, Swiss. Ontario's population has repeatedly grown through overseas immigration; first from Britain and continental Europe, but then increasingly from other continents as well.*

3. *Toronto, c. 1925. The skyscrapers in Toronto had their start with the ten-storey Temple Building in 1895, the fifteen-floor Canadian Pacific Building in 1913, and the twenty-floor Royal Bank of 1915. This aerial view of downtown was taken by the Royal Canadian Air Force.*

1

2

3

while in the countryside, large agricultural machinery and specialized crops, telephones, better roads and rural electrification, no less marked a very different day from that of isolated pioneer homesteads, or even from tranquil Victorian farms.

The Conservative government of James Whitney very effectively served this bustling, ever-changing province by bringing it plentiful supplies of electric energy. Electricity was already providing city lights in the 1880s, driving the trolley cars which replaced horse-drawn street cars during the nineties; while in the new century, it furnished an ever-growing range of power for cleaner, more efficient factories, for elevators in city business towers or machinery on country farms. Accordingly, the Whitney regime made a truly historic move when it sought to check the hold of private power corporations over the vast hydro-electric energies supplies of Niagara Falls, and so in 1906 established a provincial hydro-power commission to buy, distribute, and sell electricity at cost to the municipalities and plants of Ontario. Over the years that followed, "Ontario Hydro" would supply cheap energy, build great dams and generating stations from Niagara to Northern Ontario, and so vitally aid Ontario's industrial economy in keeping its prices competitive. But perhaps, too, over time, Hydro by its very size and influence raised problems of its own; notably when from the 1950s it moved into the costly new field of nuclear energy as well. Still, no one could doubt that this provincial power authority first created by the Whitney government had enormous impact on Ontario heritage. And, it might be added, his Conservative, business-oriented Ontario cabinet then felt little difficulty in promoting "public-utility socialism" for good business reasons.

Problems of space prevent more mention of Whitney's ready hands-on dealings with provincial economic growth, from northern colonization schemes to railway and municipal regulation; though

1. *Alexander Graham Bell (1847-1922). In 1874, Bell invented the telephone in his father's home in Brantford.* This painting was done from a portrait by L.P. Panneton.
2. *Toronto's First Commercial Telephone, 1879. In 1876 the world's first long distance call went between Brantford and Paris, Ontario. Canada's first telephone exchange opened in Hamilton in 1878; by 1881 Toronto had 400 telephone subscribers.*

1

2

1

2

1. *H.R. Williams Machinery Company Ltd., Toronto, c. 1913.*
2. *Chippewa Power Station, under construction at Niagara, 1904. In 1906, the Whitney regime established a provincial hydro-power commission, "Ontario Hydro", to buy, distribute, and sell electricity at cost to the consumers of Ontario.*

apart from a new workmens' compensation act of 1914, he showed much less interest in social concerns. Whitney died in 1914, however, just a month after the First World War had broken out in Europe. Thereafter his ministry was led by William Hearst, a Northerner, who was conscientious and determined but lacked Whitney's flair. Still, Hearst had to face the gruelling demands of the war years, and on balance met them pretty successfully. Close to a tenth of Ontario's population served in the Canadian forces, and 68,000 of them were casualties before the fighting ended late in 1918. Women went into nursing service or auxiliary units, both in Canada and overseas. Their active, vital role in these services, not to mention in replacing male workers on the homefront, did much to defeat long-drawn arguments and antiquated prejudices over giving women the vote. In 1917 an Ontario bill at last awarded them the provincial franchise; although this was not federally completed, on equal terms with men, till 1918. As for the men of Ontario who fought in the war, some joined Canadian and British naval forces, or notably the new air service, the Royal Flying Corps; but most by far enlisted in the Canadian army that went through the blood and horror of trench warfare in France. From Ypres and the Somme to Vimy Ridge and Arras, they shared fully in the proud and costly record of Canada's military effort during 1914-18.

At the same time, Ontario made great economic efforts as well. An abundantly-producing North poured forth lumber, nickel, steel, copper, and chemicals, all basic supplies for war — along with the gold that helped to pay for it. Southern war factories turned out ships, guns and munitions, trucks and military vehicles that much expanded the automotive industry, or aircraft frames and engines, and a great deal more. Machine technology, hydro-electric power, large-scale management and unionism all made big steps forward in the province under the demands of war. But when it all was over, there were harsh problems of readjustment: closing war plants, yet the need of jobs for returning soldiers; eager hopes of a bright new day of peace, but bitter, pent-up memories of wartime strains. The Hearst government could not cope with the resulting tangle of exasperation and unrest. In 1919 it fell from power — to be replaced by something entirely

1. Sir William Howard Hearst. Hearst served as Minister of Lands, Forests and Mines under James Whitney and went on to succeed him as premier in 1914. He held this position until the next election in 1919.
2. Toronto-Built JN4's, 1917. Ontarians who enlisted in World War I could join the Royal Flying Corps. Others joined Canadian and British naval forces; however, most enlisted in the Canadian army.
2. Recruitment Poster of World War I. During the war, conscription came to be necessary because of heavy casualties. The French-speaking population mainly opposed it, seeing it as an Anglo-imperialist move to override the Francophone minority.

1

2

1

1. *Departure of Volunteers, Streetsville, July 14, 1915. These were part of the large number of Ontarians who flocked to enlist after Prime Minister Borden backed Britain's declaration of war. Two months after the declaration, the First Canadian Contingent of 31,000 men was aboard ships bound for Britain.*

2. *Poster Advertising a Suffrage Meeting, 1917. The role women played in World War I, as well as in replacing male workers on the home front, did a lot to defeat arguments and prejudices over giving them the franchise. In 1917, an Ontario bill awarded women the provincial vote.*

3. *Camp Borden, Simcoe County, 1916. A huge airfield, Camp Borden grew during the First World War as a pilot training camp.*

4. *Recruiting Office, Acton, c. 1914-1918. On this building are displayed many recruiting posters from the First World War. Over 242,000 men from Ontario, nearly a tenth of the province's population, served in armed service; 68,000 of these were dead wounded or missing by the time the war had ended.*

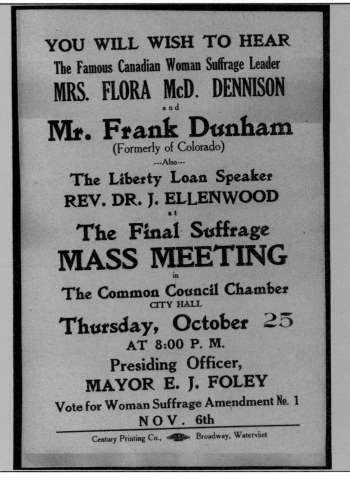

YOU WILL WISH TO HEAR

The Famous Canadian Woman Suffrage Leader

MRS. FLORA McD. DENNISON

and

Mr. Frank Dunham

(Formerly of Colorado)

---Also---

The Liberty Loan Speaker

REV. DR. J. ELLENWOOD

at

The Final Suffrage

MASS MEETING

in

The Common Council Chamber

CITY HALL

Thursday, October 25

AT 8:00 P. M.

Presiding Officer,

MAYOR E. J. FOLEY

Vote for Woman Suffrage Amendment No. 1

NOV. 6th

Century Printing Co., Broadway, Watervliet

2

3

4

1

2

THE NEW ONTARIO CABINET PHOTOGRAPHED ON THE FIRST OCCASION ON WHICH THE MEMBERS ALL MET TOGETHER.

Left to right: Manning Doherty, Minister of Agriculture; Harry Mills, Minister of Mines; Walter R. Rollo, Minister of Health and Labor; H. C. Nixon, Provincial Secretary; F. C. Biggs, Minister of Public Works; E. C. Drury, Premier and President of the Council; W. E. Raney, K.C., Attorney-General; Peter Smith, Provincial Treasurer; Lieut.-Col. D. Carmichael, D.S.O., M.C., Minister without Portfolio; R. H. Grant, Minister of Education; Beniah Bowman, Minister of Lands and Forests. This picture is of unusual and historic interest because of the fact that it was taken especially for The Star Weekly in the office of the Secretary of the United Farmers of Ontario, at 130 King street east, on the first occasion the entire Cabinet met together. As soon as the photograph was taken the newly-chosen Ministers went to Government House to be invested.

3

different, the United Farmers of Ontario.

The Farmers represented the protests of a rural Ontario which since at least the 1890s had felt itself losing power and significance, and now made a concerted try in politics to restore the interests of agricultural society. But the U.F.O., more a movement than a party, suddenly found itself in office because it reached a voting public considerably fed up with the two old parties — and more than that, because it also made an effective political alliance with labour, a growing force in the ever-bigger towns. Under Ernest Drury, who proved a determined leader, the unexpected U.F.O. victors set up a pretty competent cabinet and tried to pursue an extensive programme of reforms. But excess of zeal and cross-purposes in the movement, coupled with post-war recession and unemployment, meant that keen idealism did not get very far. In 1923 the province swung back to the Conservatives, electing them to power under Howard Ferguson, a masterful and perceptive leader from Kemptville near Ottawa, who had served well in Hearst's government.

Times were good again: and Ferguson ended prohibition — begun in wartime, renewed under the U.F.O. — instead establishing regulated sales under a government Liquor Control Board of Ontario. Whether carried along by booze, jazz or world prosperity, the booming twenties now spread sunnily across Ontario, while Ferguson had little trouble keeping on in office through 1929, building big new hydro projects, or highways for an affluent day of multiplying cars and summer cottages, of rising suburbs and golf or country clubs. But then the Great Depression struck: to be faced by George Henry, now the Conservative premier of Ontario, since Ferguson had well chosen to retire in 1930, by becoming Canadian High Commissioner to Britain.

The thirties brought grim Depression years in Ontario, as world trade dried up, businesses collapsed and jobs disappeared. Unemployment rose over twelve per cent. Thousands were on direct relief, of about $4. a week for a family's food; municipalities went broke, and job lines or bread lines were everywhere. Things still were not as bad as in the prairie West, hard hit as it was by drought and heavily based on wheat-raising. Ontario had a more diversified and balanced

1. Ernest Charles Drury. A Simcoe County farmer, Drury was co-founder and first president of the United Farmers of Ontario set up in 1914. He became premier in 1919 as head of this group and held the office until 1923.

2. George Howard Ferguson. Ferguson succeeded Hearst as leader of the Conservative party which regained power in the 1923 election. Ferguson was premier until 1930 when he was appointed High Commissioner to Britain and turned over his position to George Henry.

3. Drury and his U.F.O. Cabinet. In 1919, the United Farmers of Ontario found itself in office largely because of a public protest vote against the two old parties. Led by Drury, the new ministry tried to pursue a programme of reforms.

1

2

economy; its own crop yields stayed fair, while some mining areas in its North even expanded, because the price of gold rose high. Nevertheless, conditions were quite bad enough, what with the province's manufacturing cut far back, revenues steadily falling, deficits constantly mounting, and the jobless suffering acutely. Yet the Henry government's efforts to meet the crisis were either inadequate or simply futile. Hence they lost the elections of 1934 to a revived Liberal party led by Mitchell Hepburn, a well-off St. Thomas onion farmer and federal Liberal member, who now brought his breezy energy and bustling self-assurance into Ontario politics.

Hepburn as premier at least produced a shower of activities, cutting government costs, extending both welfare and minimum wages, securing safely pasteurized milk. But mainly he appeared encouragingly busy, while the Depression gradually began to lift of its own accord. Then in 1937 the Liberal premier fought a giant auto-workers' strike at General Motors plants in the car-building city of Oshawa. The strike was largely the product of a continental drive for mass unionism, shaped by the powerful American-based C.I.O., the Committee for Industrial Organization. But at the same time a small but tightly-organized Communist Party was working to penetrate labour movements in Canada, while the Depression had given birth to Canada's own democratic-socialist party — not communist — the C.C.F., or Co-operative Commonwealth Federation. Consequently, many Canadians, and especially big business interests (with whom Hepburn had strong links), feared foreign American intervention in Canadian factories; not to mention C.C.F. socialist influences over union labour, and worst of all, Communist incitements to violence or even revolution. Hepburn reacted, and overreacted, by raising a special mounted police force to defeat the Bolshevik threat — nicknamed "Hepburn's Hussars." Still, the strike ended in a peaceful compromise settlement, although the warlike premier claimed a telling victory. He was also growing more erratic, and was feuding increasingly with the Liberal Prime Minister, Mackenzie King in Ottawa, once his own federal leader. Yet such provincial matters were soon greatly overshadowed by the outbreak of the Second World War in Europe in 1939.

1. *Model T, Moon River, Muskoka, 1922. Ferguson had little trouble staying in office until 1929, building hydro projects and highways for an affluent day of multiplying cars and summer cottages.*
2. *Campsite for Motorists, 1924. As the motor car became more popular, services for the motorists also increased.*

1

1. *George Stewart Henry. Henry succeeded Howard Ferguson in 1930 and became inescapably linked with the Great Depression. He had seemed well-equipped to take over as premier and had served as Minister of Agriculture under Hearst and Minister of Highways under Ferguson. However, in 1934, Henry and his party lost to the Liberals under Mitchell Hepburn.*
2. *Mitchell Frederick Hepburn. Hepburn was elected to Ottawa for the Liberal party in 1926 and held his seat there even after taking over the headship of the provincial Liberals in 1930. He became premier in 1934 and kept this position until 1942.*
3. *George Alexander Drew. A veteran of World War I and leader of the Ontario Conservatives since 1938, Drew became premier in 1943. He held office until 1948, when he left to head the federal Conservative Opposition in Ottawa.*

2

3

In this new struggle, Ontarians again went overseas; in greatest numbers with the Army to fight Nazi and Fascist forces in Sicily, Italy, France, the Low Countries and in Germany itself. But this time, proportionately far more of them went into the Royal Canadian Navy and the Royal Canadian Air Force — while some, too, were sent to serve with British warships or bombing squadrons. From Dieppe and Ortona to Normandy, Holland or the Rhineland, from the Atlantic to the Arctic, the Mediterranean and Pacific, Ontario's servicemen performed gallantly and at hard cost. And women also served in greater numbers than in the First World War; not only in the vital nursing units, but in much bigger auxiliary forces at home and overseas. Furthermore, Ontario's economic effort was far larger and more advanced besides. The province particularly became an immense airbase for training Commonwealth as well as Canadian flyers; and aircraft from trainers to Lancaster bombers poured out of Ontario plants. Shipbuilding, artillery, truck and tank production equally climbed. Above all, so did electronic industries, precision-made instruments, and chemical synthetics like polymer rubber. Hence when the war ended in 1945, a new "high-tech" Ontario had already been born.

Meanwhile, in 1943, the province's Liberal regime had fallen. For Hepburn had carried a political and constitutional feud with Prime Minister King to absurd lengths, especially in wartime — claiming, and believing, that his own was the stand of patriotism, but actually looking abusive, divisive and unpatriotic amid a vast war for very survival. Thus in 1943 the Conservatives under George Drew came back to office at Toronto; Drew being no less anti-King than Hepburn, but considerably smarter and better controlled about it. Premier Drew, however, gave way to his federal ambitions in 1948, resigning at Queen's Park to head the Conservative forces in Ottawa. The Ontario government soon went to his prudent and clearsighted Provincial Treasurer, "The Silver Fox," Leslie Frost from Lindsay. And Frost's accession as premier effectively marked a whole new era for Ontario, when Tory rulers would command that province right through the fifties into the eighties.

1. *North View of the Chippewa Power Station at Niagara, 1913.*
2. *Chippewa Power Station, the Forebay, Looking South, 1917. Despite expansion in hydro-electric power supplies, there were still shortages due to increasing demands, including rural electrification. In 1926 the government and Ontario Hydro thus made contracts to lease surplus power from Quebec companies.*

1

2

1

Post-war immigrants from the Netherlands. After World War II, many new settlers came to Canada from a ravaged Europe.
1. *This family of seventeen, the Rhebergen's, emigrated from the Netherlands to Canada in June, 1948. They first moved to Holland Marsh, Ontario, and later settled in Smithfield as farmers.*
2. *Antoinette Koene, née Burgman, immigrated in 1952 by airplane rather than by the much more common mode of transport, boat. Although the flight was to Montreal, her destination was Oshawa, but she later settled in Bowmanville, Ontario.*
3. *The De Roos family ready to leave the Netherlands to come to Ontario by a cross-Atlantic liner in 1957.*

3

After World War II to Our Own Days: 1949-1991

The Frost Conservative ministry took over (or really continued on) from Drew in a time of glowing post-war prosperity. Of course, there were down-spells; but by and large, the good times rolled through the sixties and seventies in Ontario; in spite of growing worries over inflation, American and world competition, technological unemployment in outdated enterprises, or insufficiently trained workers, and more. Without forgetting the dark spots, it would still be broadly true to say that no serious recession was felt in the province until the early 1980s, and no very grave one until the opening nineties. In short, Tory times mostly turned out to be good times — whether the Conservative governments truly deserved the credit they then gained or not. In any event, the province advanced mightily over these years. The results appeared in much-expanded population, mostly urban or suburban and in Southern Ontario still, but also in a far more complicated and multicultural society. For even by 1961, over a fifth of Ontario's residents had reached there from outside Canada. The largest group still remained of British origins; yet other minorities were of mounting weight — whether Italians and Portuguese, the post-war settlers from the Netherlands, Germany, Central and Eastern Europe, or later migrants from the Middle East, Southeast Asia, the West Indies and Latin America — on down to the most recent arrivals from Hong Kong. Here then, was a very different community from that of the original frontier province of Upper Canada.

And this Ontario of the latest decades went on enlarging its basic energy sources and resource industries: with the giant St. Lawrence River hydro-electric developments of the 1950s, or with new nuclear plants, the first one being opened at Rolphton up the Ottawa River in 1962. Equally, far more Northern nickel now came from the Sudbury Basin, plus iron from Atikokan, uranium for nuclear power from Elliot Lake, or gold from the discoveries made at Hemlo by the early eighties. Moreover, continued industrial growth in the South

Junction of Highways 401 and 400, Toronto, July 24, 1991. During his time in office, Premier Leslie Frost financed the construction of many highways including Highway 401, the "holiday highway" 400, the Trans-Canada Highway, and the Burlington Skyway.

produced big new automotive complexes in and around Windsor and Oshawa; but also at Oakville and elsewhere, as automobiles loomed ever higher among Ontario's manufactured products. High-tech industry — directed to computers, robot-controlled machinery, aircraft, telecommunications and aero-space satellites — no less brought striking developments and high-level expertise. But still larger economic changes came in a growing shift from manufacturing to service industry. That is, beyond the blue-collar making of goods, the white-collar servicing of society became considerably more important. And in this area women gained particularly in what was, to a large extent, a shift from brawn and muscle-power to information, expertise and skills. At any rate, the service sector grew powerfully in a flourishing Ontario of great office buildings and high-rise apartment blocks, of widespread suburban living, shopping malls, and teeming highway traffic.

Transport services far past the earlier days of rail and steamboat routes were now multiplied by bus, highway truck and airline — or in metropolitan Toronto, by the subway system opened in 1954. Learning, information and communications services were equally marked by the rapid expansion of the province's universities and community colleges from the 1960s — or surely, too, by the completion of the world's tallest free-standing structure, the CN Tower in Toronto in 1976, a monumental spire for the gospel of television. And recreational services, decidedly significant in this time of spreading wealth and leisure, were further expressed in Toronto's Skydome opened in 1989, a huge monument itself to a multi-billion dollar sports industry based on expert athletic skills. Yet beyond all these, there were the government services no less expected in the modern Ontario society and economy: from health and old-age care to welfare for children, the disabled and disadvantaged, or state protection for workers, the unemployed, and various social groups faced with racial or other sorts of prejudice. The list as given here still is incomplete. But one general fact remains, that the Ontario government from Frost's day onward was especially concerned with providing public services to meet the needs of a constantly growing province; be they for more highways, colleges or hospitals, for state

1. *Leslie Miscampbell Frost. Lindsay lawyer and First World War army veteran, Frost entered the Ontario Legislature in 1937, and was named Provincial Treasurer and Mines Minister in the Drew cabinet in 1943. In 1949, he was chosen Conservative party leader and became premier in his own right, till he retired undefeated in 1961.*

2. *John Parmenter Robarts. A Second World War naval veteran, he joined the legislature for London in 1951, and became Minister of Education in the Frost Conservative cabinet in 1959. In 1961 he replaced Frost as premier, remaining in that post until his own retirement in 1971.*

3. *William Grenville Davis, 1989. Bill Davis was first elected for Peel in 1959, and served as Minister of Education (1962-1971) and Minister of University Affairs (1964-1971). In 1971, he was elected leader of the Conservative party, replacing John Robarts in power. He remained premier until 1985 when he retired.*

4. *David Robert Peterson. A London lawyer, he was elected to the Legislature in 1975 and was chosen as Liberal party leader in 1982. He became premier in 1985 after defeating the Conservatives under Frank Miller, but was himself defeated, along with his government, in 1990.*

1

2

3

4

assistance to young and old, the employed or the unemployable — and all because the people wanted it (while often reacting against the costs), so that popular democratic governments tried to provide these services — Conservative governments certainly included.

Consequently, under Leslie Frost, the province underwrote costly hydro schemes, highway networks, expressways and subways; and established Metropolitan Toronto in 1954 to bring the whole sprawling Toronto urban region within one super-municipality. The Frost ministry also enlarged grants given to private welfare agencies, supported health insurance, launched new schools and universities, and enacted an Ontario Code of Human Rights against racial or religious discrimination in work and housing. But social-service activities went still further under Frost's successor, John Robarts, a high-powered London lawyer who replaced his former cabinet leader as premier in 1961. With Robarts in charge, and emphasizing a "big-business" managerial approach to big government, the Ontario administration grew even larger. At the same time, it added still more universities and colleges, better old-age pensions, minimum wages and municipal grants, while funding separate schools on up to grade ten. Above all, through federal agreement, it went forward to full public health insurance. These were large social advances, but expensive even in good times. They raised problems of mounting deficits, which Robarts had by no means answered when he retired from politics in 1971 and his capable Minister of Education, William Davis, succeeded him as head of the Conservative regime.

Davis, a blandly amiable lawyer from Brampton near Toronto, was much more shrewd, determined and responsive than his easy-going manner might convey. At any rate, he very successfully held power till 1985, and left while fully in control of Ontario still. During his time of office Davis also showed a new awareness of environmental issues, steadily rising in Ontario consciousness. Besides a ministry of the

York University, July 24, 1991. Under Frost's ministry, there was an expansion of the province's universities and community colleges. One of the first of these was York University in Toronto. The sculpture shown is titled, "Sticky Wicket" and was done by a campus sculptor, who later donated it to the university.

environment, he set up a housing ministry, in an era of spiralling home costs and many other living problems. And he appointed the first women members to the provincial cabinet, consolidated the public educational system, then extended Catholic separate-school funding on through the senior grades of high school. But further, this careful premier drew back from Robarts' big-management, bureaucratic style, returning the cabinet more to its responsible ministers, and slowing down schemes for regional government bodies, often not locally popular. Still, cabinet attempts to balance social demands with economic resources did not solve the problems of massing provincial budget deficits. Nonetheless, Premier Davis faced no serious political rivals in his own day. The Liberals in opposition had not yet found really influential new leaders or policies since the Hepburn era. In fact, their own rivalry with another contending force, the New Democratic Party, largely meant that the striving Liberals and a hopeful N.D.P. cancelled each other out, again leaving the field to long-entrenched Conservatives.

The N.D.P. were the socialist heirs of the Depression-born C.C.F. — which certainly had held a significant place in the Ontario legislature from the 1940s, and had even briefly then become the Official Opposition, as second-largest party. Then in 1961, the broader-based New Democrats, with powerful links to labour-union numbers, had taken over from the old C.C.F.; while in 1975 the N.D.P. advanced to be the province's Official Opposition instead of the Liberals. But once more, neither opposition party made lasting inroads — until Bill Davis had left the premiership in 1985. Davis' successor, his Treasurer, Frank Miller, was worthy but unimpressive, representing a small-town Ontario that no longer carried political clout. Thus in the provincial elections of 1985 the Liberal leader, David Peterson, another likeable London lawyer, won the largest block of seats, as Ontario finally turned away from the long Conservative dominance. But notably, Peterson was largely able to form a working minority government through an accord with the N.D.P., which had also expanded its Assembly following. The new leader of that party, the young and able Bob Rae, thus enabled a different pattern in politics to begin; by making an agreement to support the Liberal Peterson

The C.N. Tower, Toronto, July 24, 1991. The Tower was completed in 1976, and was the tallest free-standing structure in the world.

1. *The SkyDome, Toronto, July 24, 1991. The SkyDome stadium was completed in 1989 for the high-powered, high-priced sports industry and its patrons.*
2. *The Skywalk. This walkway was built to connect Union Station with the SkyDome for patrons travelling into downtown Toronto by VIA rail, GO train, or subway transit.*

ministry in office for a specified period, in return for its pursuing mutually agreed areas of reform.

The Peterson ministry did perform to public satisfaction, as shown by its winning an outright majority in the agreeable summer elections of 1987. But now it stood on its own; and soon began to look far less agreeable as scandals arose (not major, but damaging) while the Liberal government appeared both too complacent and indecisive for its own good. Accordingly, in September, 1990, an ill-advised attempt to win another pleasant summer election of people-meeting and barbecues, instead brought disastrous defeat to the Peterson regime. In its place, the first N.D.P. government in Ontario came into office, headed by a vigorous Bob Rae. In some respects, this was another rejection of old-party rule like the United Farmers' sweep of 1919: a popular verdict that those in power should never get too snugly sure of their places — as true for bygone Family Compact Tories as for modern Peterson Liberals. The N.D.P., however, had deeper and more solidly organized support than the brief U.F.O. movement had ever known: although by 1991, especially after a highly expensive deficit budget brought in to offset recession, it was in no way clear how well the Rae ministry might fare in days to come.

Still, by 1991, two centuries after the Constitutional Act of 1791 had first brought Upper Canada into being, some other things were clear in its successor province of Ontario. Ontario's own heritage, laid down before Confederation, and reaching back to its first peoples in ages far more distant, had not only been strongly rooted and firmly shaped; but had been strengthened all the more since the province had become part of the Canadian federal union in 1867. Its pre-Confederation story — told in these foregoing pages from Indian inhabitants to fur traders, Loyalists or frontier farmers, and from war, rebellion and responsible rule to railways, sectionalism and federal nationhood — had surely been as rewarding as it was exciting and challenging throughout. What would follow after the dividing date of 1867 was no less rewarding, if greatly more varied and complex: as the brief outlines given in this concluding chapter should indicate. But it will take a whole second volume after 1867 to present the full variety and scope of that still-continuing story of heritage.

1

2

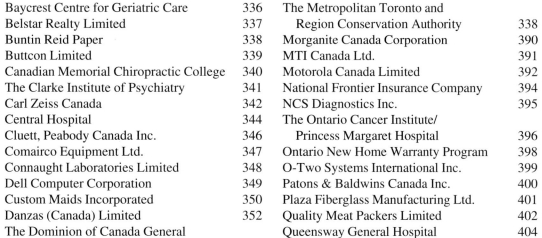

Chapter Eight

Partners in Progress

Piet J. Koene

Baycrest Centre for Geriatric Care

Over seventy years ago, Baycrest Centre for Geriatric Care began a tradition of providing the highest quality long-term care possible for the elderly and their families. Throughout its history, the Centre has grown, developed and modified its services according to the needs of the community, earning a reputation in providing both institutional and community programs and services designed to meet the varying health and social needs of older adults.

The Centre began in 1918 as the Toronto Jewish Old Folks Home in a small house on Cecil Street in the Kensington Market area of Toronto. It was an ambitious undertaking for the Ezras Noshim Society, a group of women who cooked, sewed and did the housework for frail, elderly individuals.

Today, located on eighteen acres in north Toronto, Baycrest Centre provides institutional and ambulatory care, community outreach, and caregiver support programs through a chronic hospital, home for the aged, day care service for seniors, a seniors apartment residence and a community centre for older adults. In addition, the Rotman Research Institute of Baycrest Centre is devoted to studying brain function in both normal aging and in the presence of illness such as stroke and Alzheimers. Baycrest Centre is also a teaching institution fully affiliated with the University of Toronto.

Baycrest will continue to change as the face of society changes. More and more, older adults want to remain in their homes for as long as possible. Baycrest will continue to provide institutional care for people who cannot avoid or postpone institutionalization, but it will also continue to find the ways and means to care for people in their homes.

One of the longest-running of Baycrest's community services is Baycrest Day Care Services for Seniors, providing support to older adults and their families. The Samuel Lunenfeld Special Day Care program, established in 1987, was developed for people with cognitive impairments.

Other community programs include a day treatment centre; clinics such as dentistry, chiropody, ophthalmology and neurology; and, a psychiatric day hospital designed to provide services to older adults in the community suffering mild to severe depression. The goal of community programs such as these is to assist the elderly in attaining and maintaining optimum physical and psycho-social functioning in order that they may remain living in the community.

With society's growing and changing elderly population, Baycrest's challenge is to enrich the quality of their lives through its programs, its research into the needs of older adults, its education of professionals, students and families, and its emphasis on healthier aging. At the same time, Baycrest will strive to continue with the spirit, determination and compassion of the women of the Ezras Noshim Society who began the tradition of caring for and responding to the needs of the elderly, and who laid the groundwork for the Baycrest Centre for Geriatric Care that exists today.

Located in Toronto, the Baycrest Centre for Geriatric Care provides many services for the elderly and their families, including extensive health and social services through individual one-on-one care.

Belstar Realty Limited

1

The largest private Realtor in Metropolitan Toronto, Belstar Realty Limited was incorporated in 1978 under the guidance and leadership of the late Pasquale ("Pat") Fidei. The company began with a handful of people in a modest 1,000 square feet office. A strong reputation was quickly established in the field of new homes sales. In the first year, Belstar sold 265 homes in Woodbridge and ten months later, these homes were occupied.

By 1979, there were 16 salespeople working for Belstar; one year later, the number had increased to thirty-five, with a further increase in 1981 to fifty salespeople. In 1982, the sales staff doubled to 100. A new head office consisting of 8,000 square feet was established in North York. This phenomenal growth has yet to cease; today, Belstar Realty employs close to 200 people.

Belstar opened its first branch office in Thornhill in April, 1981, and its second in Woodbridge in June, 1982. Due to their success, they had to relocate to larger premises in Richmond Hill and Woodbridge. Meanwhile, the New Homes Division had grown to ser-

vice eleven builders. This rapid expansion led the relocating of the division from the head office to its own offices in Woodbridge.

Belstar Realty, known in the industry as the "Star Performers," is made up of a dynamic, co-operative, competitive and hard working force of individuals working together like one big family. However, as in all families wherein tragedies occur, Belstar as well, has suffered a heavy loss. On October 12, 1985, Pat Fidei died suddenly at the young age of thirty-nine.

The unlimited ambition and creative insight so much a part of the founder's character continued to flourish through his successor, Elena Fidei. Ms. Fidei's steely determination to realize all of her husband's dreams inspired the birth of the Industrial, Commercial and Investment Division. The event marked the culmination of Belstar as a full service real estate agency. A Mississauga branch was opened in 1987 to service the west part of greater Toronto.

Following a Hong Kong selling experience in 1990, Belstar entered an exciting new venture by opening its first fully operational foreign

office in Taipei, Taiwan. The Taipei office assists prospective immigrants with their move to Canada and provides services for all their real estate needs.

Belstar has recently relocated its head office and the Richmond Hill branch to newly built offices in Richmond Hill. The former head office in North York will continue to house the resale staff as well as provide ample space for the Industrial, Commercial and Investment Division.

Similar in its makeup to the people of Ontario, Belstar Realty is a cultural mosaic. Its staff, with their diverse ethnic backgrounds, are able to easily relate to the client's needs. With this rich blend of nationalities and an infrastructure based on the creative insight and entrepreneurial spirit of its founder whose ideals have continued to be instilled within the company, Belstar Realty Limited is ensured of continuing success.

1. *Pasquale ("Pat") Fidei, Founder of Belstar Realty.*
2. *Belstar Realty's head office in Richmond Hill, Ontario.*

2

Buntin Reid Paper

When Alexander Buntin began a small printing company in Toronto in 1856, few people would have envisioned the company into which it has grown today. Buntin Reid Paper, now owned by Domtar Inc., has become one of the most versatile of Canada's fine paper merchants, and occupies over 235,000 square feet in Mississauga and carries a large selection of different paper grades.

Born in Scotland in 1822, Alexander Buntin had his future planned and knew what he wanted when he immigrated to Canada at the age of 25. After beginning companies in Hamilton, Ontario and Montreal, Quebec, he founded Buntin Brothers & Co. on Yonge St. in Toronto with his brother James Buntin. The growth of the young company was steady and practical, and in 1858 John Young Reid joined, later to become a partner. By 1889 the expanding business was ready to move to larger premises on Wellington Street, where it stayed until the great Toronto fire of 1904, which caused heavy losses to The Buntin Reid Company.

Although the company had engaged in the manufacturing of stationery, blank books and writing inks before the fire, Buntin Reid devoted itself entirely to fine paper at its new location on Colborne St. Alexander Buntin, Jr., who had joined the company prior to his father's death in 1891, carried on in partnership with John Reid until the latter retired in 1899. After Alexander Buntin, Jr., passed away in 1922, neither a Buntin nor a Reid was associated with the company any longer.

Newly incorporated in 1923, the company was faced with a new period in Canadian industrial expansion, with floors, counters and walls becoming battlegrounds for display space; organized direct mail was beginning, and advertising was becoming an accepted corollary of modern business procedure. The demand for paper grew steadily, and Buntin Reid Paper Company Limited expanded accordingly. It survived and grew during the depression years, and in 1931 the company moved to Peter Street. In the early 1950s new warehouses and divisions opened in London and Ottawa to serve their respective areas. In 1962 Buntin Reid moved to King Street, and in 1972 the company was purchased by Domtar Inc.

Domtar Inc. began as the Dominion Tar & Chemical Company with the establishment of a coal tar distillation plant at Sydney, Nova Scotia, and was incorporated in 1929. Throughout the 1950s and onwards it acquired new interests. It is now a resource-based corporation serving customers worldwide with a broad range of pulp and paper products, packaging and construction materials manufactured in Canada and the United States.

With its broad selection of different grades and its large inventory, Buntin Reid Paper, at its present location in Mississauga since 1982 and the warehouses in Ottawa and London, has become widely known at "The Paper House" and continues to serve its customers mainly in Ontario.

1. Alexander Buntin, Sr.; 3. John Young Reid; co-founders of Buntin Reid Paper. 2. The company's original location, at 61 Yonge St. in Toronto, Ontario.

1

2

3

Buttcon Limited

1

From general contracting and project management to construction management and design build, Buttcon Limited has the experience and skills to handle the most challenging project. Founded in 1979 by Michael Butt, Buttcon has the resources to apply innovative, practical solutions with equal efficiency to institutional, commercial and industrial construction in both the public and private sectors.

Following his graduation from the University of Toronto with a degree in Civil Engineering, Michael Butt spent eight years overseas with a British company as managing director. After several years as a partner in another construction company, he sold his share in 1979. Immediately following this, Butt, along with two other minor partners, began Buttcon Limited in Rexdale, Ontario. The company is now owned by Michael Butt and a number of its employees.

In the early days of the company most of the projects were relatively small. Buttcon handled small factory additions, and office renovations were not uncommon. The first large project started in 1979 was The Society for Goodwill building at the corner of Adelaide and Jarvis Streets, a new three-storey office and showroom structure.

Involved in construction only in Southern Ontario, Buttcon Limited keeps a healthy balance between the work obtained through negotiated and competitive bidding and that of lump-sum and management projects. Buttcon has also started a separate development company, Buttcon Development Corporation, to own a share of some of the developments. This was primarily set up to accommodate clients coming to Buttcon with projects and inviting Buttcon to participate as part owner.

Buttcon Limited has been associated with the construction of many prominent projects. In 1991 Buttcon completed the design and build contract for the new Aurora Civic Centre. Novatel on The Esplanade in downtown Toronto, which opened in 1987, was one of the larger undertakings. The Esplanade area was originally the city's waterfront, with the old dockside site dating back to the 1800s. Butt recalls that "it was a very interesting project. The excavation unearthed old wharfs, many bottles and a case of flintlock muskets complete with bayonets weighing about fifteen pounds each."

Buttcon has also done restoration and renovation work. The company devised a number of innovative construction techniques to transform an old factory on John Street in Toronto into an updated nine-storey office building. Buttcon renovated the Monitor Building at the corner of King and Jarvis Streets in Toronto; the old five-storey structure required a dramatic transformation into a modern office-retail building.

Each year has been a year of growth for Buttcon Limited. Butt attributes the company's success to the reputation it has gained amongst its clients and their consultants. The company's approach in dealing with its customers and their problems is straightforward, honest and co-operative. With a specialized team of professionals, carefully selected to provide the ideal combination of skills and experience, and close co-operation with owners, subcontractors and suppliers, a project moves smoothly and quickly.

Having successfully completed more than 200 industrial, commercial, institutional and residential projects, Butt emphasizes that "Buttcon meets its schedules and commitments, while living up to the stiffest standards of workmanship and construction quality. Every project has added to Buttcon's reputation."

1. *Michael Butt, the Founder and President of Buttcon Limited.* **2.** *Novatel on The Esplanade in downtown Toronto, was one of Buttcon's larger undertakings, and was opened in 1987.*

2

Canadian Memorial Chiropractic College

Built by chiropractors for chiropractors, the Canadian Memorial Chiropractic College is the only chiropractic college in Canada. A privately funded education institution, the College offers a four year professional program leading to the Doctor of Chiropractic Diploma. The primary purpose of the College is to educate the future chiropractors of Canada and thereby ensure a vibrant and growing chiropractic profession.

Chiropractors have been providing health care to Canadians for almost one hundred years. Chiropractic is a primary contact, health care profession whose philosophy is based on the relationship between the nervous system and the musculo-skeletal system. Chiropractors utilize manual manipulation of the spine and extremities, exercise, nutrition, and other therapies involved in a wellness model of patient care aimed at enhancing health.

The history of the College began in 1943 when the Dominion Council of Canadian Chiropractors found it important to establish a Canadian College. The Dominion Council, now the Canadian Chiropractic Association, understood the importance of an educational institution to the profession. They appreciated that no profession could continue to grow without the support of a continuous supply of well qualified graduates or without ongoing research. A founding committee was formed, and on September 18, 1945, the fiftieth anniversary of the first chiropractic adjustment, the College opened its doors.

What was formerly the old Medonia Hotel on Bloor Street in downtown Toronto became the academic home to the College's first class of ninety-seven men and women. Two years later, when additional space was required, the three storey Henderson Building was constructed to the rear of the renovated hotel.

In April, 1959, part of the College's land was expropriated by the City of Toronto for subway expansion. Excavation soon began, and at one point a portion of the Henderson Building was suspended in mid-air, resulting in considerable structural damage. The court case, which lasted until 1968, awarded partial damages to the College.

The Canadian Memorial Chiropractic College grew into one of the leading institutions of the profession, which came to command the respect and admiration of the community. The College's move in 1968 to a newly constructed campus on Bayview Avenue further enhanced the College's academic and clinical image.

The first off-campus, out-patient clinic was opened on Parliament Street in Toronto's "Cabbagetown" area in 1976. The Clinic served the College in two ways: ensuring a positive chiropractic profile in the community, and providing a logistical solution to the ever increasing number of interns needing a place to develop their clinical expertise. Presently, the College operates three outpatient clinics in Toronto, located on the Bayview Avenue campus, on Dundas Street West at Bloor Street, and on Eglinton Avenue West near the Allan Expressway.

Today, the Canadian Memorial Chiropractic College, which has an enrolment of approximately 600 students, continues to improve its rating as a primary-contact, healthcare, professional, educational institution. Fulfilling its responsibilities to the profession by providing both excellent research and well qualified graduates, the College remains committed to the development of graduates who possess the necessary knowledge, skills and attributes to practice chiropractic care effectively and safely.

1. The original location of the Canadian Memorial Chiropractic College, in what was formerly the old Medonia Hotel on Bloor Street, in downtown Toronto.
2. *The College today, located on Bayview Avenue.*

1

2

The Clarke Institute of Psychiatry

1

Part research lab, part hospital and part university campus, The Clarke Institute of Psychiatry has facilities for psychiatric research, education, diagnosis and treatment. Operating as a hospital and resource centre for clinicians, educators and investigators in the mental health field, all of The Clarke's activities are directed to the conjoint aims of advancing knowledge and caring for patients. The Clarke operates as a public hospital with its own Board of Trustees and, although funded by the Ontario Ministry of Health, it is not part of the Ontario psychiatric hospital system.

The Clarke is named in honour of Dr. Charles Kirk Clarke, the first professor of psychiatry at the University of Toronto and often considered the father of Canadian psychiatry. His efforts led to the opening of the first psychiatric out-patient clinic in Toronto in 1909, and eventually to the founding of the Toronto Psychiatric Hospital, The Clarke's predecessor, in 1925, one year after Dr. Clarke's death.

Specializing in the development of new and innovative treatment approaches, The Clarke plans and provides programs with the highest level of academic and clinical standards, and with a sensitivity to the needs of the province.

The Clarke's basic treatment approach includes a full program of psychiatric rehabilitation. A Continuing Care Division for the chronically disabled matches treatment to each stage of the illness. A Day Centre provides a variety of skill training programs for patients living at home, while an innovative home treatment program uses home visits as an alternative to hospital admissions.

The Forensic Division at The Clarke conducts research and treatment for problems of sexual violence and impulse control, and also operates the Metropolitan Toronto Forensic Service (METFORS).

For children, The Clarke operates a Child and Family Studies Centre. A day treatment program for children includes schooling and supportive therapies. A separate facility on Yonge Street, the Family Court Clinic, provides care and counselling for children of divorce, abused children and young offenders.

The Institute also operates a range of outpatient and inpatient services. These include a Mood Disorders program, specialty clinics for anxiety disorders, cognitive therapy, deafness, speech pathology, assessment, and an Emergency Department and Crisis Unit.

These services represent only a portion of the activities at The Clarke; others include a cross-cultural psychiatry training program, consulting services on Baffin Island on the mental health of native people, programs in culture, community and health, and research into the biochemical, molecular and neuroendocrinological bases of psychiatric illness. A new Positron Emission Tomography Facility provides sophisticated new brain imaging technology.

Its close ties with the University of Toronto permit The Clarke to provide undergraduate and graduate medical education, and training of students in seven other health disciplines. As research is a primary mandate of the Institute, research activities occur throughout The Clarke.

Located on College Street close to downtown Toronto, the Clarke Institute of Psychiatry provides, promotes and enhances psychiatric research, education, and clinical care as mutually enhancing activities. Serving as a centre of expertise and learning, The Clarke continues to be a provincial resource striving to provide leadership to investigators, educators and clinicians in the mental health field.

1. *Dr. Charles Kirk Clarke (1857-1924), considered the founder of Canadian psychiatry.*
2. *The Clarke Institute of Psychiatry celebrated its 25th anniversary in 1991.*

2

Carl Zeiss Canada

The origin of the optics and precision mechanics industry lies in centuries of co-operation between scientists and artisans. Optical engineering is one of the most exact technologies known to man, and progress in this field requires ever increasing accuracy and precision. It is in this demanding environment that the firm of Carl Zeiss has become famous as "The Great Name in Optics," the master at shaping glass to supremely close tolerances and producer of instruments of marvellous ingenuity and quality.

Carl Zeiss has always been at the forefront of technology, and today designs and manufactures a wide array of precise optical, electronic, and mechanical devices and components for science, medicine, industry and the quality conscious consumer. They range from individual lenses used in the creation of microelectronic components small enough to fit on a finger tip and complex enough to serve as the heart of a computer, to measuring machines large enough to accommodate an automobile body and accurate enough to measure it to the millionths of an inch.

Carl Zeiss, a master precision mechanic and optician, founded an optical workshop in 1846 in Jena, Germany to produce high quality

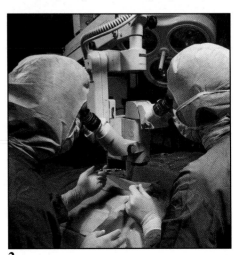

microscopes and other laboratory equipment for the University of Jena. The enterprise prospered and quickly became renown throughout Europe for its quality work.

Optical manufacturing at that time, however, was based on trial and error, depending largely on the skill of the mechanic. In 1866, Dr. Ernst Abbe, a young university mathematician and physicist, joined Carl Zeiss. After several years of exhaustive calculations, he developed a precise mathematical theory of optics. His theory of microscopic image representation created a solid base for developments in engineering optics, and led to the invention of optical instruments with hitherto unthinkable performance characteristics.

The days of trial and error were over, but the glass available for microscope lenses remained less than ideal. This problem was resolved in 1884 when the chemist Dr. Otto Schott joined Zeiss and Abbe to create the Schott Glassworks. Schott put the manufacturing of optical glass on the same scientific basis as Abbe had put the production of microscopes. It was this exceptional team of Carl Zeiss, the precision mechanic; Ernst Abbe, the theoretical physicist; and Otto Schott, the glass chemist, that made possible the modern era of microscopy.

When Carl Zeiss died in 1888, his principal partner, Dr. Abbe, inherited a company that was already world famous for its precision products. An unusual combination of scientist, businessman and far-sighted social reformer, he deeded his entire holdings, one year after the death of Carl Zeiss, to the Carl-Zeiss-Stiftung (foundation), an institution he created as the sole owner of the enterprise.

The foundation is unique both in

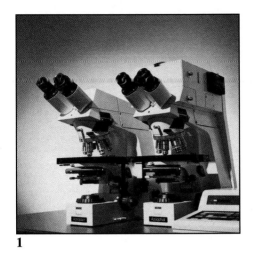

1. *Zeiss is a world-leader in microscope design and innovations for use in biological and material sciences applications, medicine, education, and industrial quality control and production. The product line includes light microscopes, photomicroscopes, laserscan and electron microscopes, photometers, and integrated microscope systems.*
2. *Micro-surgery became practical in the 1950s when Carl Zeiss introduced the first commercial operation microscope. Today Zeiss remains in the forefront of operation microscope design with models for procedures ranging from delicate eye surgery (shown here) to the latest in laser techniques.*

terms of corporate structure and for pioneering many modern social benefits for its employees. The charter of the Carl Zeiss Foundation guaranteed the employees far reaching benefits and, in many ways, became the pioneer and standard for modern social legislation.

All business activities of the foundation are carried out by two independent companies, Carl Zeiss and Schott Glaswerke, which have no shareholders, partners, or state associates. All profits are used to finance the growth of the companies, employee benefit programs, and for the support of scientific and cultural activities. The foundation is believed to be the only organization in the world in which there is no external financial control or influence.

Due to this solid scientific, social and economic basis, Carl Zeiss has survived some severe crises. The foundation companies in Jena were partly destroyed during World War II and Jena was occupied by American troops. Before Jena was integrated into the Soviet occupation zone and its holdings were expropriated, American troops transferred the management of the foundation to the western sector. The foundation relocated to Oberkochen, West Germany, and on August 1, 1946, a new optical works was established.

Today, the Carl Zeiss Foundation is a worldwide organization with over 31,000 employees and includes companies and agents in over 100 countries on six continents. Of that total, Carl Zeiss, which also has its headquarters in Oberkochen, Germany, is a $1 billion enterprise and has over 15,000 employees.

Carl Zeiss companies in North America, including Carl Zeiss Canada, serve the largest market for Zeiss precision instruments and consumer products. Carl Zeiss products were well known in North America even before the turn of the century, with a number of American firms acting as dealers or agents. In 1919, Carl Zeiss formed its own company with headquarters in New York City. By the end of the 1930s, thousands of Zeiss microscopes, binoculars and other Zeiss products had been sold in North America.

As the age of high technology grew, Carl Zeiss expanded rapidly around the world to fill the increased demand for its precision products. Carl Zeiss Canada, headquartered in the Toronto suburb of Don Mills, was established in 1963 to market Zeiss products in Canada.

Carl Zeiss products are the result of complex research and development processes within the company and at universities and research institutes, combined with intensive consultation with users. Zeiss prod-

1

ucts in turn contribute to scientific progress throughout the world. This highly productive and synergistic collaboration between science and industry is reflected in the reputation of Zeiss products as being in the forefront of technical innovation and performance. Over thirty per cent of current instrument sales are products that have been on the market for less than three years.

In the consumer area, Zeiss binoculars, eyeglasses, sunglasses, camera lenses, riflescopes and planetarium projects have made Carl Zeiss products well known throughout Canada. Zeiss instruments are of inestimable benefit to medicine and scientific research. In industry, thousands of enterprises rely on Zeiss products in the areas of research, measurement, microelectronics and for surveying and mapping.

Today, Carl Zeiss has achieved a level of performance which ensures it a leading position in world markets in many important fields, while fulfilling its social obligations to workforce and society alike. As the source of new impetus and ideas in optics, precision engineering and electronics which reverberate throughout the world, Carl Zeiss will continue to meet and master new challenges in the future.

1. *The largest, most precise and smoothest X-ray mirrors ever made were produced by Carl Zeiss for use on board the "ROSAT" X-ray observatory satellite. Placed in orbit in 1990, the system has exceeded all expectations, providing unprecedented resolution and sensitivity.*
2. *Zeiss coordinate measuring machines play a key role in improving productivity and quality control in the automotive, aeronautical, computer, defence, and energy industries. Carl Zeiss is the world's largest supplier of CMMs with systems for major industries to compact models for small to mid-range machinery and metalworking shops.*

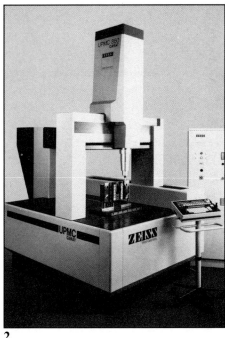

2

Central Hospital

Central Hospital began as a dream of two Hungarian doctors. Doctors Paul and John Rekai, recognizing the urgent need in Toronto for a hospital with a multilingual staff, introduced the multilingual, multicultural concept to Canadian hospital services. Since the founding of Central Hospital in 1957, hospitals across Canada have followed in its path in their efforts to meet the communication needs of patients who are unable to speak English.

The Rekais were raised in Budapest, Hungary, by a Hungarian father and Austrian mother in a bilingual ambience which enabled them to learn English rapidly as a third language. After post-graduate studies, they joined the medical and surgical staffs at hospitals in Budapest where Dr. Paul also served in administrative capacities. Later, both of them served at other hospitals across Europe. Their extensive experience would enable them to begin a hospital in Canada.

The two doctors, along with their families, immigrated to Canada in 1950. After serving their internships, in 1951 they opened their own practices on St. Clair Avenue West in Toronto.

The post-war tide of immigration created gigantic problems for Toronto's overcrowded hospitals, with many of the patients speaking little or no English. After only three years in practice in Toronto, they decided to open a small hospital to address those needs.

Taking the initiative, they acquired an old residence of the Canadian National Institute for the Blind at 331 Sherbourne Street. The building required extensive and costly alterations, along with the purchase of modern equipment, and all at the expense of the Rekais themselves. Dr. Paul Rekai recalls that it "was difficult to finance a

1

hospital," but with help from Hungarian friends and from a bank, they were able to continue working towards the establishment of the hospital.

At that time, licenses to operate a private hospital were already being discouraged by the Ontario Department of Health. Greatly impressed by the ability, determination and integrity of the applicants, and seeing the urgent need in Toronto for a hospital with a multilingual staff, the Department made an exception in the Rekai case. On May 15, 1957, the "impossible dream" of Drs. Paul and John Rekai became a reality, when Central Hospital, a thirty-two bed facility, opened its doors to patients from around the world.

From its beginnings, Central Hospital was unique in many ways. The Rekais focused public attention on the lack of services in languages other than English, and they pioneered methods which are now widely used in handling patients with language difficulties. These methods included training programs for staff members in correct interpretation and translation proce-

dures, as well as awareness of cultural differences in approach to health care, food preferences, traditions and customs. Also, new doctors, at the time, had difficulty obtaining appointments to the staff of a downtown hospital. However, Central Hospital operated, since its inception, as an open hospital, granting privileges to all competent practitioners in good standing within the limitations of their training and experience.

1. Central Hospital's original building.
2. Dr. John Rekai, 1914-1978, co-founder of Central Hospital.

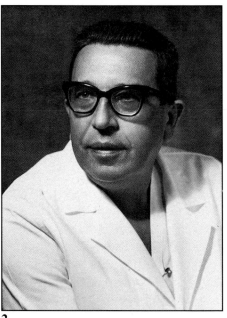

2

In 1961 Central opened a forty bed addition. Two years later the Hospital became accredited by the Canadian Council on Hospital Accreditation — a unique accomplishment for any hospital at the time and particularly so for a private hospital. Until 1965, all capital costs were provided by the Doctors Rekai, without receiving any assistance from public donations or government grants.

To realize their dream of a modern 175 bed facility, the doctors were ready to hand the private hospital over to a public corporation at depreciated cost. In October, 1965, a Public Hospital charter was granted, and plans began immediately for the construction of a new building. On September 21, 1969, the new facilities opened, offering its multilingual services in an expanded and modern environment.

The next major expansion of the hospital was in 1975, when a multi-specialty, out-patient consultation service was organized by Dr. Paul, located next to the hospital. Central Clinic was fully integrated with the hospital and functions as its extension, enabling the hospital to provide total health care services to the community in a much more efficient manner. Central Clinic is now owned and operated by Central

1. *Central Hospital today, located on Sherbourne Street in downtown Toronto.*
2. *Dr. Paul Rekai, co-founder of Central Hospital, Toronto's multi-cultural hospital, and founder of Central Clinic and Rekai Centre.*

Hospital Foundation.

In 1978, Dr. John Rekai passed away. For him, Central Hospital had meant everything. Never having worked for awards or rewards, both Drs. Paul and John Rekai were acknowledged for their dedication in helping others and leading the medical profession at Central Hospital. They were awarded the Civic Award of Merit from the City of Toronto in 1973. Dr. Paul Rekai was appointed to the Order of Canada in 1973, and Dr. John Rekai in 1977. Subsequently, Dr. Paul was recognized as one of the three Citizens of the Year in Metropolitan Toronto in 1986, elected a Life Member of the Ontario Medical Association in 1987, and in May 1989 was awarded Senior Membership in the Canadian Medical Association. On May 31, 1990, he was presented with the Ontario Senior Achievement Award in recognition of outstanding contributions to the citizens of Ontario. Dr. Paul has also been active in the community, always finding time to help Hungarian institutions, temporal and spiritual. In addition, he has been closely associated with the musical world, organizing the Canadian Opera Company's and Roy Thomson Hall's medical services.

In 1988, Central Hospital celebrated the opening of the Drs. Paul and John Rekai Centre, another

dream of Dr. Paul Rekai, being the first multilingual, multicultural, non-profit, nursing home in Canada, and the first hospital-affiliated nursing home in the City of Toronto. Services are provided in thirty languages to the Centre's 125 residents, with full detail given to their cultural background, ranging from international menus to recreation events and spiritual values. The Rekai Centre completed the health care complex, incorporating the basic multi-cultural principles of the active care Central Hospital and the multi-specialty Central Clinic.

Today, Central Hospital provides services in forty-one languages and dialects. From the beginning, the hospital has focused on providing quality interpreters who are culturally familiar and provide accurate translations. Central has concentrated on being culturally sensitive in all aspects of a patient's visit, whether it be eating or drinking, concerning pain, mourning and bereavement, or admittance.

The Central Hospital complex will always be a cornerstone in the multicultural life of the people of Toronto. Its motto, "A small spark has become a flame," is a reminder that Central is no longer only a spark; it is now a flaming torch of service to all those who are in need of it. When it began, it was only a dream. Today it is a flaming reality.

Cluett, Peabody Canada Inc.

Beginning as a manufacturer of men's shirt collars in Troy, New York, over 120 years ago, Cluett, Peabody has also become a major contributor to men's fashion in Canada. Better known as The Arrow Company, the company has manufactured and marketed its quality products in Canada for over eighty years.

Attempting to establish itself in the competitive American market, the company was, under the leadership of Frederick F. Peabody, able to achieve its goal of making Arrow a household name. Peabody, who had become partners with the Cluett family in 1913, began a pivotal advertising campaign in 1915. Using illustrations by the commercial artist J.C. Leyendecker, the "Arrow collar man" was launched. This idealized male figure caught the imagination of the public and for years was the symbol of glamour for North American men.

Cluett Peabody Canada Inc. was established in 1911 when the company began manufacturing in St. John's, Quebec. The Arrow Company, Canada, started in 1920 when Cluett acquired a collar and shirt manufacturing plant from Williams, Greene and Rome Company in Kitchener, Ontario.

After World War I fashion changed significantly, and The Arrow Company responded quickly with major innovations in the clothing industry. Men who had worn uniforms with soft collars were unwilling to go back to the starched styles of prewar days, insisting that comfort be more important than stiff formality. The Arrow Company, in response to these consumer demands, developed the Arrow shirt, with an attached collar and buttons.

The firm further influenced the men's fashion market by addressing the problem of shirt

1

shrinkage. In 1928, Sanford L. Cluett, Vice President in charge of research, patented a revolutionary mechanical process to reduce the shrinkage of cotton fabric. This unique process was licensed to cotton finishers around the world under the trademark "Sanforized." To further underscore this innovation, the company devised the slogan, "A new shirt free if one ever shrinks out of fit." The new Arrow shirt would not shrink, was tailored to fit the lines of the body, and had a permanent collar and buttons. To make the public aware that it was a shirt manufacturer and no longer solely a maker of collars, the company devised the copy line "Only Arrow Shirts have the famous Arrow Collar."

The Arrow Company, Canada, has enjoyed steady growth throughout its history. The Arrow trademark can now be found on many new products such as

sportshirts, casual shirts and underwear. Philip C. Turner, who first joined the company in 1962, assumed the presidency in 1986. Under his direction the company continues to expand and diversify its products. In addition to Arrow branded shirts and sportswear, the company also markets the American designer line Colours by Alexander Julian and has become a significant supplier of store label products to many of Canada's finest stores.

Today, Arrow is the largest branded shirt manufacturer, employing approximately 500 people. The firm has attained its present position by anticipating and reacting to changes in style, business methods and marketing trends. For Arrow, the business goal that has guided its progress throughout its history has been "to provide a quality product at competitive prices."

2

1., 2. *The "Arrow Collar Man," developed early in this century, became an important symbol of glamour for North American men.*

Comairco Equipment Ltd.

1

2

A compressed air equipment company established in 1972, Comairco Equipment Limited represents quality and service, in equipment and in people. With a well-qualified staff on hand to assist customers when buying or renting air compressors and compressor related equipment, and by supporting customers with efficient and reliable service, Comairco has found a steadily growing base of customers to be the best sales force a company could have.

The history of Comairco has been a story of continuous growth. Comairco started in 1972 with one office and seven employees. When Ed Murphy and Roland Nadeau were presented with the option to purchase the company in 1978, they seized the opportunity. In 1984 Comairco merged with another company to expand into Quebec. A Winnipeg sales and service office was opened in 1989 to serve Manitoba and Saskatchewan. And in 1990 Comairco acquired a controlling interest in Pump & Compressors, located in Buffalo and Rochester, New York.

From the original 4,000 square feet of office space, the company has now expanded to over 40,000. The number of employees has also grown, to approximately eighty-five at present, many of whom are bilingual.

Comairco is committed to total service. The company sells and services air compressors and associated equipment to all who use it. A separate company, employee-owned by Comairco's staff, handles the rental aspect. Although Comairco's main thrust is its industrial accounts, it has a broad range of customers; the company today has over 4,000 accounts.

With a tremendous size range of equipment for a variety of users, Comairco supplies compressor related equipment, including contractor tools, industrial tools and special consumer application tools. Representing only selected manufacturers, Comairco is recognized as the largest dealer in North America of Sullair products, a supplier based in Michigan City, Indiana.

By emphasizing quality — in service, equipment and people — Comairco has built an excellent reputation, which it intends to maintain in the years to come. "Our goal is to be in a position to provide the best service possible through the quality of our suppliers and the quality of our people," Ed Murphy emphasizes. "The way to do this is to continually upgrade our employees and to carry sufficient inventories to meet all customer requirements."

Murphy likes to point out that "We believe in team play . . .. The whole company works together." With a total dedication to customer service, the staff are all very familiar with the products and are specialists with the equipment. There is continual upgrading of skills through a comprehensive training program. The employees also show a dedication and loyalty to the company; of the original seven employees, six are still with Comairco today.

Although originally largely focused on industrial needs, recently Comairco has also expanded into the construction and mining sectors. *Comairco Equipment Ltée. représente en effet la qualité et le service en équipement et en personnel.*

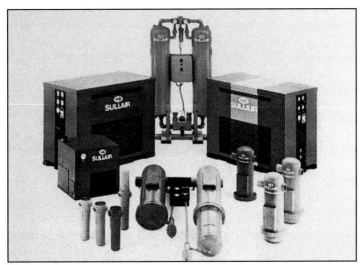

3

1. Ed Murphy and 2. Roland Nadeau, co-Founders of Comairco Equipment Ltd. 3. Comairco supplies compressor related equipment, including contractor tools, industrial tools and special consumer application tools.

Connaught Laboratories Limited

From its successful development of vaccines for diseases such as diphtheria, smallpox, typhoid, tetanus, meningitis, polio, influenza, measles and tuberculosis, to its current research into a treatment for AIDS, Connaught Laboratories Limited has demonstrated its leadership role in the preventive health care needs of Canada and the world for almost eighty years.

Today, Connaught is recognized as Canada's leading biotechnological research firm and North America's largest vaccine manufacturer.

The company's origins date back to 1913 when John Fitzgerald, a young University of Toronto physician, and William Fenton, his technician, became alarmed at the rising death rate from diphtheria and began production of horse-serum diphtheria antitoxin. Early in 1914 the University permitted Fitzgerald to start an official production facility, The Antitoxin Laboratory, in the basement of its Medical Building.

Later, these operations were moved to a twenty-two hectare site north of Toronto, and the facility became The Connaught Antitoxin Laboratories and University Farm. By the end of World War I, the facility was producing diphtheria, small pox, typhoid, tetanus, meningitis and rabies preparations for home and abroad.

In 1921, researchers Frederick Banting, Bert Collip, John Macleod

and Banting's student assistant Charles Best discovered the hormone insulin at the University of Toronto. Subsequently, Connaught became the first manufacturer of insulin in the world. In the 1950s, Connaught assisted first Dr. Jonas Salk and then Dr. Albert Sabin in their efforts to develop polio vaccines.

The World Health Organization, in their global smallpox eradication program which began in 1966, chose Connaught as one of the two World Smallpox Vaccine Centres. By 1977, doctors had diagnosed the world's last recorded case of smallpox.

Connaught has also been a leader in the worldwide assault on tetanus, diphtheria, pertussis, polio, measles and tuberculosis, providing more than 350 million vaccine doses annually.

The company remained part of the University of Toronto until 1972, when it was bought by the Canada Development Corporation. In 1978 Connaught Laboratories Inc. was established in the United States with the purchase of laboratory facilities in Swiftwater, Pennsylvania. This purchase increased Connaught's manufacturing capacity to nearly 900,000 square feet and its staff to more than 1,300 employees.

Connaught joined the Pasteur Mérieux group of companies in 1989, making it a part of the world's largest manufacturer of vaccines for human use operating in every corner of the globe. As a member of the Pasteur Mérieux group, Connaught continues to represent Ontario and Canada to the world as a leader in preventive medicines.

The union of Connaught and Institut Mérieux was a major event in the biologicals industry. For more than three generations,

1

Institut Mérieux has been dedicated to basic research and is renowned for its expertise in the biological sciences. Together, the two organizations have achieved synergies in research and manufacturing that would not have been possible on their own. The fusion of these world leaders in the biologicals industry promises dramatic advances in the eradication of human disease.

Throughout its history, Connaught has been perceptive of the needs of society and creative in its response to them. That tradition continues today.

1. A Connaught research scientist working on a cell culture.
2. Connaught's original research farm building, still in use today at the company's North York location.
3. Connaught scientists conducting a quality control maintenance inspection of a viral vaccine production fermentor.

2

3

Dell Computer Corporation

Having grown rapidly through its innovative and personal relationship with the people who use computers, Dell Computer Corporation has become the largest direct-to-end-user manufacturer of personal computers in Canada. The company designs, manufactures, sells, services and supports a complete range of high-performance industry-standard personal computers.

Now one of the top five personal computer manufacturers in North America, Dell Computer Corporation of Austin, Texas was founded in May, 1984, by Michael S. Dell, who remains the corporation's Chairman and Chief Executive Officer. Because of the worldwide acceptance of its products, the company soon opened subsidiaries in England, Canada, Germany, Sweden, Italy, Spain, the Benelux countries, France, Finland and Ireland, with a combined total of over 1,800 employees. International sales are now thirty-three per cent of total revenues.

Dell Canada was incorporated in May, 1988 and has since opened branch offices in Halifax, Montreal, Ottawa and Calgary.

Because of expanding sales, Dell Canada's head office and manufacturing facility was moved to a larger building in the summer of 1990 located in Richmond Hill, Ontario.

Each subsidiary, including Dell Canada, replicates the Dell operation in Austin, Texas, developing and servicing its own markets by employing the same one-to-one direct-to-the-customer strategy that made Dell successful in the United States. This strategy provides superior service and support and allows customers to purchase a total system, built to their specifications and needs, directly from the manufacturer. Each international operation is responsible for its own assembly, marketing, technical support and customer service.

Dell's personal computers are based on high-performance and industry-standard microprocessors and operating systems. By optimizing standard technologies in products that feature enhanced performance and improved operating speeds, Dell has earned worldwide industry recognition for technical excellence. The company's products have received

many prestigious awards for quality, reliability, compatibility, price/performance ratio and the company's high level of expertise in service and technical support.

Dell Canada's customers range from individuals to small, medium and large businesses and it derives a substantial percentage of sales from major corporations, governmental entities and educational institutions. The company's customer support services are provided though an industry-leading, bilingual, twelve-hour per day, toll-free telephone service department and free, on-site service for one year. The information from this daily contact with the end-user makes Dell highly responsive to the dynamic requirements of the marketplace.

Dell Computer Corporation's operating strategy and the price/performance benefits of its products enable the company to compete with personal computer manufacturers many times its size. Dell now possesses the people and resources to accomplish its goal to be the best direct response computer manufacturer in the world, with the highest possible level of customer satisfaction.

The central offices and manufacturing facilities of Dell Computer Corporation in Richmond Hill, Ontario.

Custom Maids Incorporated

In the spring of 1978 Des Breau was unemployed and looking for work. Starting an apartment cleaning service in the building where he and his wife Dana lived, Breau would design, print and distribute flyers throughout the building and then wait for customers to call. This simple but effective routine quickly became a success. Breau soon realized that this combination of a direct mail approach offering a wide range of housecleaning services held a great appeal for many busy homes. Today, Custom Maids Incorporated provides services to its customers in Toronto and also in the California communities of San Francisco, Oakland and Berkeley.

For the first two years Breau worked by himself, all the while accumulating more information about this new industry. In the fall of 1980, he asked his wife Dana and his brother Andre to join the business. With Andre and Dana alongside, Des Breau decided to take full advantage of his innovative approach to this relatively open field, and the three partners incorporated the business in January, 1981.

The gamble paid off. With no initial capital to work with, both brothers spent the next year delivering brochures door-to-door every night and then joining Dana at the office during the day to handle the telephone calls that would follow. Growth was slow but consistent during 1981. Dana at first handled many of the cleaning jobs herself, but soon new employees were added to the staff every month. By the end of 1981, Dana was able to relinquish her cleaning mop in exchange for the position of chief administrator for the twenty cleaning people they now employed.

By the end of 1982, that figure had doubled. A year later, the

number of employees had nearly doubled again, with seventy cleaners employed, and the forecast for 1984 promising that it would be the best year yet. At this point growth was rapid. The company moved into new corporate offices on Eglinton Avenue in Toronto, computerized all office and scheduling operations, and decided to launch the most aggressive advertising campaign its now considerable resources would allow.

A market research firm was hired to develop a demographic profile of a typical "maid service user" using Custom Maids' client files, which numbered in the thousands. From this research a complete mailing list was developed, consisting of 400,000 Metropolitan Toronto

From left to right: Andre Breau, Vice President of Operations; Dana Anderson-Breau, President; and Des Breau, Vice President of Administration.

households. Upon completion, Custom Maids commenced their mail campaign. As Andre recalls: "Our telephone rang off the hook. We went from three telephone lines to seven and our office staff went from three people to six just to handle the influx of calls."

Utilizing all the revenue that this campaign generated, the company placed all its resources into other forms of advertising. Custom Maids' advertising appeared on billboards in every Toronto subway station, on the Toronto Transit buses and it could be heard on various Toronto radio stations. As Des Breau explained, "We wanted to wage a campaign that would ensure the highest possible awareness level for Custom Maids in Toronto to ensure our longevity in the Toronto marketplace."

And that is exactly what they did. By the end of 1984 the company had popularized its logo in Toronto and had etched a permanent place for themselves in the ever-growing maid-service industry. Dana recalls that "By the end of 1984, advertising companies were coming to us. We received calls from radio stations, billboard companies, product manufacturers who wanted to do promotions with us, magazines, newspapers, even television stations." By 1985 Des and Andre had appeared on the John Gilbert radio program; Andre had appeared on CTV's national television program Canada A.M.; and the company was written up in local Toronto newspapers, magazines and the national *Financial Post.*

In 1985, with revenues soaring and 150 full-time housecleaners on staff, Custom Maids began looking for out-of-town expansion. Montreal, the only other Canadian city large enough, was ruled out because of language difficulties. Therefore, they hired a research company to find the company another market that would fit its demographic profile. In September, 1985, Custom Maids went international with the opening of its first U.S. office in San Francisco.

The Breaus have duplicated their success in San Francisco and now service Oakland and Berkeley also. Today, Des and Dana maintain a home in San Francisco while Andre oversees the Toronto operation.

While the past few years have seen a proliferation of maid service companies selling franchises all over Canada and the United States, the Breaus have not chosen that route for themselves. "When you cannot rely on a constant flow of cash from the sale of franchises,

1

you've got to be good," Des explains. "From the beginning we have generated all our profits from cleaning revenues alone. If we let down on our quality, our revenues will go down. From day one, our overriding objective of quality over quantity has worked for us and we're not about to change that formula by selling franchises and losing our sense of control."

Although impressive financial figures have prompted recent buy-out offers from a large Canadian-based company and an offer by a major American company to take the operation in the direction of a national franchise, there are no plans to accept either

of these offers. However, a new market for Custom Maids is being considered as the next logical step in its growth.

1991 marks the tenth anniversary of the incorporation of Custom Maids. Now well-established and a leading contender in the competitive maid-service industry, Custom Maids Incorporated remains committed to Ontario as it looks to the future with plans for further growth and expansion.

1. *A Custom Maid's advertisement on a Toronto Transit bus.*
2. *The corporate offices of Custom Maids Incorporated in Toronto, Ontario.*

2

Danzas (Canada) Limited

1

2

Experts in both domestic and international freight transportation, Danzas Limited recently celebrated its 175th anniversary in 1990. With its central headquarters located in Basle, Switzerland, Danzas Limited specializes in logistics management; for example, Danzas Limited is the first company to ever declare that it was importing an entire McDonald's restaurant into the Soviet Union, moving six transport trailers with twenty-four tons of equipment for more than 2,500 kilometres through the winter snows to Moscow in 1989. As part of this worldwide transportation network of more than 14,000 employees located in thirty-four countries, Danzas (Canada) Limited offers a full range of professional, international freight forwarding services.

On June 18, 1815, on the Field of Waterloo, not only was the future of many nations decided, it was also the historic day that decided

the future of Marie Mathias Nicolas Louis Danzas, a lieutenant in the 13th regiment of "Chasseurs à Cheval." Deciding to return to his family's home in the Alsace region of France, he acquired an interest in a transportation company and laid the foundations of one of the world's largest forwarding groups.

After taking up the reins of management, in 1840 he changed the company's name to Maison de Commission et d'Expédition Danzas et L'Evêque à Saint-Louis. In 1855 a merger between transport companies led to the foundation of the firm Danzas, Ouzelet & Cie, and the establishment of the first Danzas branch in Switzerland.

After the turmoil of the Franco-Prussian War, the company moved its headquarters in 1870 to Basle, Switzerland, where the head office is still located today at the same location. In 1903 the company was incorporated and became Danzas & Co. Ltd., continuing an already long tradition of transport innovation.

Expanding first through Europe and then worldwide, Danzas companies introduced one of the first rail consolidation services, express

deliveries, ocean and air services and, eventually, electronic control and "just-in-time" stock deliveries.

Danzas (Canada) Limited was incorporated in 1975 and initially served as a sales delegation with small sales offices in Montreal and Toronto. The primary thrust of the company was selling export services from Europe to Canada. When Danzas Limited began looking for someone to manage the Canadian company, and not finding a Canadian adequately suited already working for Danzas, the company chose H.J. Kuhn, who had experience with Danzas in Switzerland, Japan and North America.

1. Marie Mathias Nicolas Louis Danzas laid the foundations of Danzas Limited, one of the largest forwarding groups in the world.
2. H.J. Kuhn, President of Danzas (Canada) Limited.
3. Danzas (Canada) Limited's central offices overlooking Pearson International Airport in Toronto, Ontario.

3

Kuhn remains as the President of Danzas (Canada) Limited today.

Kuhn arrived in Canada, and in May, 1978, Danzas (Canada) Limited became operational with eleven employees in Toronto and Montreal. Soon realizing the need for expansion in this highly competitive business, the company began to develop other market trends and broaden its scope of activities, such as export traffic.

In 1983 Danzas opened branch offices first in Winnipeg, needed to service large volume accounts in that city that were dealing with Danzas Brazil, and Calgary. By 1984, the Vancouver office completed a network of 100 employees serving all of Canada's major industrial centres. In 1989, through a merger of Danzas and Northern Air Freight in the United States, the company expanded its North American capabilities linking United States business with Canada and with the worldwide transportation resources critical to their success. The North American network now comprises more than fifty offices and 1000 employees.

In Canada and around the world, 700 Danzas offices provide customers with door-to-door transportation services and total logistics management. Close contact between Danzas and its clients generate feedback which frequently suggest unexplored areas for expansion.

Customers rely on Danzas to select the right combination of transportation resources to carry their freight. Danzas offers many standardized and customized services to meet the requirements for each industry sector, such as multimodal transportation arrangements to suit the needs of every exporter and importer; specialization in moving heavy and oversized shipments with expertise in planning and executing entire projects — recently Danzas (Canada) Limited moved an entire copper mine operation into the South American Andes mountains from Canada; customs clearance services to facilitate timely delivery; and consulting services for warehousing, distribution, packing, documentation, letter of credit negotiations and other international banking needs.

Danzas Canada has experienced dynamic development with substantial growth every year. With over 150 employees now servicing all of Canada's major industrial centres, Danzas (Canada) Limited is one of the transportation industry's largest purchasers of air and ocean cargo space. Kuhn points out that most decision making takes place in each area locally, and not from the central office, allowing for the flexibility needed to succeed. Knowing that Danzas (Canada) Limited is part of a much larger network, builds confidence in its customers.

Efficiency, flexibility and purchasing power will be vital factors for successful shippers in the 1990s. As part of one of the world's largest freight forwarders and customs brokers, Danzas (Canada) Limited applies these factors to find competitive advantages for its customers.

Supporting customers with worldwide telecommunications, electronic data systems, customs brokerage, banking, foreign exchange expertise, warehousing and distribution services, Danzas serves shippers anywhere in the world. Having acquired a well-deserved reputation, Danzas (Canada) Limited's progressive, innovative marketing techniques and use of modern technology will ensure that they maintain their competitive edge in the future.

1. *Customers rely on Danzas to select the right combination of transportation resources to carry their freight.*
2. *Danzas Limited is the first company ever to declare that it was importing an entire McDonald's restaurant into the Soviet Union.*

1

2

The Dominion of Canada General Insurance Company

At 4:30 p.m., on May 31, 1985, "Black Friday," the lights went out in Barrie, Ontario. Few realized that a tornado had brought down a main hydro transmission line forty kilometres south of the city. Within half an hour, the twister reached Barrie after leaving a trail of destruction and death behind it; shopping malls, barns and homes were laid to waste. When the tornado hit Barrie, a huge, black cloud twisted and sucked up trees, poles, cars, roofs and whole houses, leaving eight dead, sixty seriously injured, 800 homeless and 120 million dollars of losses.

At the end of the first week, all insureds had been contacted. After most of the claims had been settled, The Dominion had processed 1150 claims with losses of $3,710,280. The Dominion, and the insurance industry as a whole, had done their job. Amid the devastation and the sorrow, insurance provided the people of Barrie and neighbouring communities with hope — and the essential funds to rebuild and start again.

The story of The Dominion of Canada General Insurance Company runs parallel with the history of Canada. It is a story of people working to achieve personal success while providing their fellow Canadians with insurance services vital to their businesses, their homes and their lives. It is the story of a company that grew over a period of more than one hundred years, with Canada, and for Canada. Formed by George Gooderham and Sir John A. Macdonald, it was the first wholly Canadian casualty insurance com-

1. *The Right Honourable Sir John A. Macdonald, Prime Minister of Canada, 1867-1873 and 1878-1891; and President of the company, 1887-1891.*
2. *George Gooderham, co-founder and President, 1891-1905.*

pany. It was founded when the new nation of Canada was large, healthy, strong and twenty years old, when a railroad spanned the country and the pioneer was turning townsman.

George Gooderham was the son of William Gooderham, who, together with James Worts, had founded the venerable Gooderham & Worts Distillery in Toronto. When William Gooderham died in 1881, George Gooderham took over as President. At the time he was also President of the Bank of Toronto and the Canada Permanent Mortgage Corporation. He saw great opportunities ahead for an insurance company designed to serve this growing nation; it would be truly interwoven with the growth of Canada.

Sir John A. Macdonald, as Canada's first Prime Minister, had a particular interest in the building of our new nation, and wanted a transcontinental economy based on

1

2

an east-west axis. He had confidence in George Gooderham's new business venture, believing that the new company would serve the country's best interests, and he agreed to be President of the company.

Originally, the company was to be incorporated under the name "The Manufacturers' Life and Accident Insurance Company," but it was recommended that two companies be formed, one for accident insurance and one for life insurance. Therefore, on June 23, 1887, Bill No. 125 was passed in Canada's Parliament and The Manufacturers' Accident Insurance Company, the precursor of what is now known across Canada as The Dominion of Canada General Insurance Company, was incorporated. The company shares its birthday with The Manufacturers' Life Insurance Company, now a friendly competitor.

When the company commenced business at 38 King Street East, Toronto on November 5, 1887, Toronto had a population of 181,000. The company's first President was Sir John A. Macdonald, and its Vice President was George Gooderham. By early 1890, the Head Office was moved to the Traders Bank Building at the corner of Yonge and Colborne Streets. The rent at this new location was $600 a year, which included taxes, heating and cleaning. At the same time, a typist received eighteen dollars a month and a policy-writer five cents per policy.

When Sir John A. Macdonald died in 1891, George Gooderham was appointed President of the company. The company applied to and was granted by Parliament permission to amend the Act of Incorporation, enabling the company to transact guarantee bond insurance and to change the company's name to "The Manufacturers' Guarantee and Accident Insurance Company."

The Dominion's Toronto Head Office Staff, 1904.

In 1895 there was a feeling of confidence in the Canadian air, and Prime Minister Sir Wilfrid Laurier proclaimed: "The twentieth century will be Canada's." In 1896 the company engaged in a new concept and opened a permanent branch office in Montreal. In the same year expanding business required larger quarters and the Head Office was moved to the McKinnon Building, at the corner of Jordan and Melinda Streets in Toronto. Two years later, in 1898, the company received permission to change the company name to "The Dominion of Canada Guarantee and Accident Insurance Company."

In 1905 George Gooderham died and was succeeded as President by his son, Col. Albert E. Gooderham. The company's first branch office in Western Canada was established in Calgary in 1907. The company prospered in Western Canada, and another branch was soon opened in Winnipeg. In 1910 Col. Albert Gooderham was appointed Chairman of the Board and J.E. Roberts became President. It was during this period that new and

innovative products, including plate glass and burglary insurance, were added to the company's line of business.

The company celebrated its twenty-fifth anniversary by opening a branch office in Vancouver. In 1914 automobile insurance was included in the company's policies, and, one year later, fire insurance was also included. When J.E. Roberts died in 1916, Col. Albert E. Gooderham was re-appointed President. He continued to strictly adhere to the principle laid down by his father: "We are building for the future, not the immediate present." To this principle of building slowly but surely, the company owes much of its growth and success.

During World War I, Col. Gooderham, Colonel of the 10th Royal Grenadiers regiment, co-operated as fully as possible with the government towards the war effort. For example, he provided funds to build a huge complex of laboratories, named the Connaught Laboratories, on the outskirts of Toronto to help produce an anti-toxin to combat tetanus poisoning in wounded soldiers.

In 1921 the company opened a new branch in Ottawa. A year later, celebrating its thirty-fifth anniversary, the company moved to the new Dominion building at 26-28 Adelaide Street East in Toronto. The anniversary brochure proclaimed that "Fairness and promptness in making settlements are a firm policy of the company as attested by the record that 96 per cent of all claims are settled within one day of receipt of proof." Two years later, the company was authorized to engage in the life insurance business.

The Casualty Company of Canada, which was transacting general insurance business in all the provinces of Canada, was acquired in 1926. In 1927 electrical machinery and inland transportation insurance were added to the company's list of products. In 1927 the company changed its name once again, to The Dominion of Canada General Insurance Company.

In 1935, a few months before his death, Col. Albert Gooderham was granted Knighthood in recognition of the extensive public service performed by both himself and his wife Mary. He was succeeded as President by his brother, George H. Gooderham. In that year the company had over 20,000 accident policyholders in every province in Canada, in Newfoundland, England and the West Indies; its policies were written in three languages, English, French and Spanish.

The post-war years were years of unbridled optimism and the company prospered. In 1951 Harry W. Falconer was elected President, succeeding Edward D. Gooderham, who had been President from 1943 to 1950. Falconer passed away a few months after being elected,

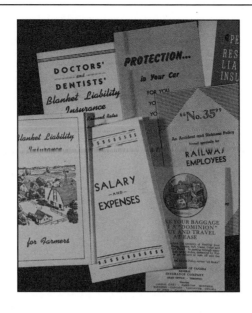

The Company's product range is illustrated by marketing brochures produced between 1941 and 1949.

and Henry Stephen Gooderham was appointed President, renewing the continuity of a member of the Gooderham family occupying the Chief Executive position.

In 1961 the company applied for and received a listing on the Toronto Stock Exchange. A new Head Office building was officially opened in 1962, with Henry S. Gooderham stating, "During the past seventy-five years, Canada has developed from a young Dominion to become one of the leading trading nations of the world, and our company, fully owned by Canadians, providing complete insurance coverage for Canadians, has kept pace with that growth." The scene was set for the company to enter the fourth quarter of its first century — a period of twenty-five years in which the annual written premiums for The Dominion would increase more than twenty-fold.

In 1969 the Board of Directors voted to join with The Empire Life Insurance Company as wholly-owned subsidiaries of a new holding company, E-L Financial Corporation. With a long history of association between the Gooderham's and the Jackman's, who controlled The Empire Life

Insurance Company, the move made good financial sense for both companies. While preserving their independent character, the combined organization would result in a stronger entity. Henry R. Jackman, Chairman of the Board of The Empire Life, became President of E-L Financial and Henry Gooderham became Chairman. Although E-L Financial's interests have expanded, the operating independence of each of the component parts has been a cardinal principle.

In 1969 Henry Gooderham retired as President and was appointed Chairman of the Board, a position he held till his retirement in 1972, when he was succeeded by his son Peter S. Gooderham. A decision was made by The Dominion's Board of Directors to open the position of President to all employees and H. Norman Hanly was elected President. In 1972 Kenneth G. Hutchison was elected President, overseeing the company till 1978.

One of the more significant corporate decisions of the seventies was to establish a presence in the Maritime Provinces. A branch office was established in Halifax and a service office in Charlottetown. Both quickly proved successful and The Dominion became a truly national company, from sea to sea. The driving force behind this expansion was Frederick G. Elliott, President from 1978 to 1981.

The company has long been involved in the process of automation, and has been an industry leader in the adoption of new and improved methods. By the 1950s, the old manual computing systems had been mechanized into a new punch card system. By 1960 the company began the transition to electronic computerization. Today, high speed electronic communication links every office from the Atlantic to the Pacific, paralleling Sir John A. Macdonald's early vision.

1

In keeping with its commitment to the people of Canada, the company established The Dominion Foundation in 1978. Funds are maintained and distributed by the Foundation, which supports a variety of Canadian activities including the arts, education, charitable agencies and institutions, and research projects across Canada.

During the late seventies the company enjoyed productive and profitable times, but soon the world economy weakened and severe recession hit the country. The company's fortunes followed those of the industry with large underwriting losses. Donald A. Waugh, who began his career with the company as a Claims Supervisor in the Montreal office in 1956, was elected President in 1981. He prepared the company to take its place in the forefront of today's competitive insurance industry. The company retained its strong financial position, and 1983 and 1984 were two of the most successful years in the company's history.

Several new branches were opened in Ontario in the 1980s. The company opened offices in London in 1980, in Hamilton in 1984, and in Willowdale, serving Central and Northern Ontario, in 1984. By 1985, in addition to the Head Office, The Dominion had a total of twenty-nine offices, including ten full service branch offices.

In 1985 The Dominion purchased The Canadian Indemnity Company,

a company strong in Western Canada where The Dominion wanted a stronger presence. By 1986 the establishment of a single Head Office organization was completed. Also in 1986, The Dominion sold the American operations of The Canadian Indemnity Company, enabling The Dominion to focus all of its energies and resources in Canada.

With the purchase of The Canadian Indemnity Company placing The Dominion in the top ten insurance companies in Canada, the hopes of the founding fathers had been achieved. George Gooderham's early promise to "place the company in the first rank of Canadian insurance companies" had been kept. The Dominion continues to seek out new opportunities to develop into the best, the most effective, and the most profitable operation in the Canadian general insurance field.

As an example of its progressive position in the Canadian insurance industry, in 1990 The Board of Directors of The Dominion

appointed a President and Chief Executive Officer from the financial sector — one of the first insurance companies to do so. Rowland W. Fleming, an experienced senior banker, filled the position of President and Chief Executive Officer on September 1, 1990.

On March 12, 1991, a Letter of Intent was signed whereby The Dominion of Canada General Insurance Company agreed to purchase the Canadian operations of SAFECO Corporation. This acquisition will put The Dominion in the top level of general insurance companies in Canada.

Rowland Fleming emphasizes that "The Dominion of Canada General Insurance Company not only has a strong Canadian heritage which it can be proud of and build upon, but also maintains an innovative and progressive attitude for the future growth of the Company . . .," thus reflecting the motto set forth by George Gooderham, "to build for the future, not the immediate present."

2

1. *The Dominion's logo, which is also the Canadian Coat of Arms, reflects how the history of the company is closely integrated with the history of Canada.*
2. *Rowland W. Fleming, the company's current President and Chief Executive Officer.*

DUCA Community Credit Union Limited

One of the most successful Dutch immigrant organizations, DUCA Community Credit Union Limited has come to represent a quality style of financial services. DUCA's style is based on a sense of community and a real commitment to address the needs of its individual members. This style is what gives DUCA its own personality and vision.

The Dutch Canadian Toronto Credit Union Ltd. received its charter on May 5, 1954, with a mere $236 in assets and a mandate to provide Dutch Canadians with a more responsive means of saving and borrowing. Joining the Ontario Credit Union League, DUCA's first office was located on Danforth Ave. in Toronto. The initial limit on loans was set at $200.

The first year was exceedingly difficult for DUCA. With only $300 in shares, there was not even enough funds to cover the office costs and expenses, and DUCA considered closing the office. However, drawing its strength from a small group of dedicated people, by December DUCA was in the black again. By May, 1955, shares totalled more than $1,000 and the first loan was extended.

DUCA continued to grow and one year later shares amounted to over $17,000. The organization could proudly proclaim that "The Dutch Canadian Toronto Credit Union Ltd. has caught on with the Dutch people." Within five years, the number of shareholders had grown to 450.

Expansion in 1962 entailed the purchase of an adding machine at a cost of $230! When DUCA reached 1,000 members, it hired its first full-time employee. *The DUCA Post*, the organization's newsletter, was launched in 1963. One year later there was a staff of four full-time employees and a membership of over 3250.

Always a community organization, DUCA hosted many social events, such as the Tulip Festival, Annual Picnic, Orange Ball, car rallies and children's parties. DUCA was, from its beginning, a unique organization with a dual role, meeting the social and financial needs of its people. In 1969, for the first time, the invitation to attend the Annual Meeting was printed in English in *The DUCA Post*. It was evident that the Credit Union was successfully combining steady and rapid growth, financially and culturally, while remaining faithful to their original community.

To accommodate its steady growth, DUCA moved into a building on Shaftesbury Ave. In 1970 the Credit Union replaced its old bookkeeping machine and bought an office computer. One year later, the name was changed to DUCA (Toronto) Credit Union Limited. In 1972 DUCA needed to move once again, this time to Yonge Street in Willowdale. The first employee of non-Dutch descent was hired in 1976, and DUCA also opened its first branch office in Scarborough.

After changing its name to DUCA Community Credit Union Limited in 1978, the Credit Union changed its base of operations further north on Yonge Street. In 1984 DUCA entered the top ten and became the ninth largest credit union in Ontario.

Today, with a membership of over 31,000 and with offices throughout Metropolitan Toronto and the surrounding region, DUCA is ranked as the fastest growing and the fourth largest credit union in Ontario. DUCA's distinctive personality will all but ensure that the astounding growth and success of the past thirty-five years will continue far into the future.

1. *The 1972 DUCA Annual Meeting.*
2. *DUCA's head office and main branch in North York, Ontario.*

1

2

The ECE Group Ltd.

Mechanical and electrical engineers dedicated to excellence in engineering, The ECE Group Ltd. has been involved in the design of systems for a wide range of well-known commercial, institutional and special purpose buildings. With offices in Toronto, Calgary and Baltimore, Maryland, the firm provides integrated mechanical, electrical, communication and associated engineering services to meet the specific challenges of demanding clients.

The ECE Group Limited began in 1955 when a partnership between Gerry Granek and Jack Chisvin was formed. Although at that point there were two proprietorships operating as one partnership, to the outside world it was a single firm, Chisvin and Granek Associates. Located on Yorkville Street in downtown Toronto, the firm began with five employees.

The first major project undertaken by the partnership was Toronto's O'Keefe Centre, the most modern theatre in the world at the time. The firm quickly grew, moving first to Yonge Street and later to Bathurst Street, adding an office in Montreal in 1958.

In the early 1960s the partnership accepted the challenges of Commerce Court, a large office complex in downtown Toronto. Critical to

1

the business community of Canada, the Commerce Court complex was "ahead of its time," in the application of innovative and inventive building systems. Gerry Granek pioneered a revolutionary ventilation system which, in case of fire, would remove the smoke directly out of the building rather than spreading it throughout the structure.

In 1966 The ECE Group Ltd. moved to its present location in Don Mills, Ontario. After briefly considering becoming a public company under the name Environmental Consulting Engineering, it was finally decided to

keep the firm private, and in 1970 The ECE Group was formed. To better service western Canada, a Calgary office was opened in 1972. In 1980, The ECE Group Ltd. was incorporated.

Every project has added to The ECE Group's creative and innovative capabilities. Many advances in the state-of-the-art building technology were developed by The ECE Group. The Atrium on Bay, for example, in downtown Toronto, requires only one-half the energy consumption as that of a building constructed ten years earlier. A revolutionary heating and cooling system frees the usage of the floor to the exterior walls with considerable savings in useable space.

Canada's Wonderland, located north of Toronto, is a 130 hectare entertainment site which confirmed the firm's ability to tackle any project. Wonderland's man made mountain is much more than a centrepiece, it is an important functional part of the park's mechanical system.

The list of projects with which The ECE Group has been associated is almost endless. The National Gallery of Canada and the National Arts Centre in Ottawa, Osgoode Hall Law School at York University, Hamilton's McMaster Health Sciences Centre and the Metropolitan Toronto Reference Library are only a few of the firm's achievements. The ECE Group has also been associated with many buildings across the United States and in Asia.

Today, with approximately 120 employees, The ECE Group Ltd. continues to respond to social and community needs in the creation of unique, enjoyable and safe environments. The ECE Group Ltd.'s works, withstanding the test of time from coast to coast, are a tribute to the firm's success.

1. Toronto's Eaton Centre, just one of the firm's many achievements.
2. Gerry Granek and Jack Chisvin, co-founders of The ECE Group Ltd.

2

Electrolux Canada

1

With a wide array of home cleaning systems available to the discerning consumer, Electrolux Canada has become one of the most respected household names in the cleaning industry.

The Electrolux tradition began in Sweden at the beginning of the twentieth century, when the company was founded by industrialist Axel L. Wenner-Gren. Through determination and hard work, he improved and marketed a new domestic motorized canister vacuum cleaner. This revolutionary new household product spread rapidly throughout Europe and was introduced into Canada on November 24, 1931, in Toronto, Ontario.

In January 1932, Axel Wenner-Gren and Russell Y. Graul, manager of the company's first Canadian branch in Toronto, held a sales meeting for fifteen dealers. The new company quickly grew, and in March 1932 competed successfully with and outperformed its neighbouring Electrolux Company in the United States, winning the North American Sales Cup. In 1934 the company opened its first Canadian manufacturing facility, in Montreal, Quebec.

Electrolux was quickly becoming a household word, offering the consumer an efficient, quality vacuum cleaner. Although the times were economically depressed, a new Electrolux growth record was set in 1935 with a 500 per cent increase in sales! More and more homes were being converted into Electrolux homes. In 1947 Electrolux purchased the 100,000 square feet Ford Motor Plant in Montreal, thereby increasing the production levels required to meet the high demand for Electrolux quality products.

Product development was also a priority and continued to progress. In 1955 Electrolux designed the first automatic cord winder for selected models. Soon after, the first, fully automatic cleaner was introduced. In 1960 a three brush polisher and shampooer model was marketed, completing the Electrolux home care system. Electrolux pioneered and introduced the power nozzle during the 1960s, enabling the consumer to clean carpets even more efficiently.

Expansion throughout the company was an ongoing activity. In 1964, hopes for a new and more modern plant materialized with the opening of the Pointe Claire, Quebec manufacturing facility. Production capacity was at its fullest in 1968 as the factory rolled out more than 100,000 major units. A major expansion was needed in 1972 and the plant's capacity was increased. The Brockville, Ontario plant, acquired in 1974, began producing shampooer/polishers to meet the constant demand for this invaluable product. In July 1989, the company introduced a line of state-of-the-art water purification systems, meeting the consumers' demand for quality drinking water.

Electrolux has continued to change and evolve, but one thing has remained constant: the dedication to quality service provided

2

through its direct sales force across Canada.

Today, Electrolux Canada, with stores across Canada, remains a highly respected household name which the consumer has learned to associate with quality. With its outstanding products and a dedicated team of professionals providing superior service, Electrolux is assured of continuing success well into the future.

1. *Alex L. Wenner-Gren founded Electrolux in Sweden at the beginning of the 20th Century.*
2. *Electrolux Canada opened its first factory on Basin Street in Montreal, Quebec, in 1934.*
3. *The Electrolux advantage, then and now, is its direct contact with customers.*

3

Embury Company

1

One of the first continuous coil anodizing firms in the world and presently the only coil anodizer in Canada, Embury Company produces custom metal building materials for use in the construction trade.

The company began in 1952 when Lloyd Embury, being unemployed at that point, was asked to repair a storefront. Although he did not have the necessary tools, he was able to borrow what he needed to complete the job. Having learned the metal working trade previously by working for other companies, he decided to continue working as an independent contractor. He began with a metalworking shop located in his garage and continued repairing storefronts in Toronto, Ontario.

Embury soon acquired his first employee and also began working for glass companies. Supplying more and more custom metal work, he worked with anodized aluminum and stainless steel, the same two materials that comprise the bulk of Embury Company's products today.

As Embury Company continued to grow, it acquired more employees, and within four years Embury had six employees. Although in those early years of the company installation of the product was part of the work, today Embury Company is a supplier only, leaving the installation work to others.

Embury Company underwent a major expansion in the early 1970s, when the company acquired a custom anodizing plant in Orillia, Ontario. Anodized aluminum has a protective layer of oxidized aluminum on the surface of the product, achieved through a rapid method process rather than letting the oxidization occur naturally over a greater period of time.

Selling anodized aluminum sheet metal across Canada and the United States, Embury began adding more and more colour to its custom built products. Colours, such as black, bronze and gold, are chosen carefully for their ability to withstand fading over long periods of exposure to the elements.

Today, the dual aspect of the firm's activities — coil anodizing for some of the world's largest metal fabricators and a long history of custom metal fabrication for a multitude of clients — provides a unique product assurance and single source responsibility, leading to wider and better application of metal products for architectural use.

Although Embury has some standard products, each product is still custom made for each specific building. One major product that Embury produces is Emburite, a preformed composite building panel. Only one-quarter inch thick, the panel is comprised of two outer skins of aluminum alloy laminated to a high density rigid polyvinylchloride light-weight core using a neoprene based adhesive. Other Embury products include continuous coil anodizing, extrusion bending and stretch bending, aluminum sheet metal fabrication, insulated panels, stainless steel, and metal forming, galvanized back panels.

Today, Embury Company owns and operates two plants in the greater Toronto area. Lloyd Embury attributes the success of the company to innovation. He points out that in many way Embury has been a leader in the industry. Many of the machines were invented and patented by Embury. With over forty-five employees, Embury Company continues to develop under the direction of its founder, Lloyd Embury.

1. *Lloyd Embury, Founder and President of Embury Company.*
2. *Embury Company's central manufacturing facilities and offices in Downsview, Ontario.*

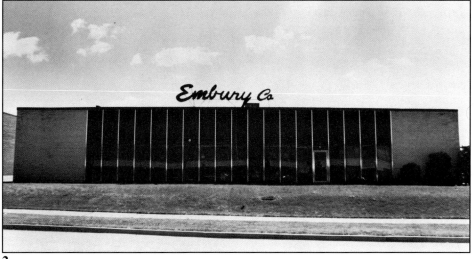

2

Export Packers Company Limited

1

To understand Export Packers Company Limited, one must examine its history, and its history is essentially the story of Max Rubenstein, the Chairman of the Board. In 1926, his father, Herschel Rubenstein, borrowed fifty dollars to pay for the first month's rent and began a small Kosher retail poultry store, with living quarters for himself and his family above the store.

When Max Rubenstein was fifteen, his father asked him to look at the bookkeeper's accounts. Although they were in disarray, Max corrected them in a single night. The following day his father put him to work full time.

One year later, in 1937, Max Rubenstein hired three salesmen to solicit the hotel, restaurant, and retail butcher shop businesses, and Export Packers was founded.

The firm's first poultry plant, in Brussels, Ontario, enabled Export to sufficiently expand its poultry inventory to service the chain stores while still maintaining its market share of the restaurant and butcher trades. As poultry supply became a problem for the entire industry, Export Packers was one of the first companies to import poultry from the United States. The company became and still is one of the largest poultry importers in Canada.

By the mid-1940's, the company expanded into the egg processing business. The Manning Avenue poultry plant in Toronto was acquired and a section of it converted to the production of liquid eggs. Later, powdered eggs were imported from Europe. In 1955, the United Farmers Co-operative building located on Adelaide Street was purchased. The majority of this structure was used for cold storage of poultry and a portion of the building was converted to the first mechanical egg breaking operation in Canada. This was followed by the acquisition of a creamery and egg grading operation in Dublin, Ontario.

In 1978, Export Packers moved its egg processing operations to a new 90,000 square foot facility in Winnipeg, Manitoba. This fully automated plant, designed by Jeff Rubenstein, Max's eldest son, utilizes state-of-the-art equipment and allows Export to process in excess of 1.5 million shell eggs per day. In this ultra-modern facility which is federally inspected and U.S.D.A. certified, eggs are processed into liquid, frozen, or dried egg whites, yolks, or whole eggs. These processed eggs are, in turn, sold to the baking, dairy, food processing industries, specialty food processors, and the hospitality trade.

1. Max Rubenstein founded Export Packers Company Limited, a privately-owned Canadian company that is a major exporter of food products and biochemical products to four continents. 2. A 1926 photo of Max Rubenstein's family: (left to right) Fay, Rose, Herschel (his father, who laid the foundations of Export Packers by beginning a small Kosher retail poultry store in 1926), Toby, Edith (his mother), and Max himself.

2

In addition to being the major processed egg supplier for the Canadian market, Export Packers has increased its sales in the Far East, Europe, the United States and Central and South America, distinguishing the firm as Canada's largest exporter of processed egg products..

In its Science and Technology Centre adjoining the egg processing plant, Export Packers maintains a full research staff and laboratories to research, develop and produce biochemical products, new product types and production methods.

In 1986 the Canadian Government awarded Export Packers the Gold Medal in the Canada Awards for Excellence in Technology Transfer for its production of Lysozyme. Lysozyme is an enzyme extracted from egg whites and is used by the pharmaceutical industry as an anti-viral agent in the treatment of shingles, hepatitis and herpes, and by the food industry, as a preservative. Export Packers is now the world's largest single producer of Lysozyme.

Over the past half century, this small Toronto-based food wholesaler has evolved into a significant component of the Canadian food processing, wholesaling and biotechnology industries. Export Packers is now a major exporter of food and biochemical products to four continents and supplies the following distinct product groups: frozen meat, poultry, and seafood; egg products; biochemical products; and frozen juice concentrates. Frozen meats, poultry and seafood are distributed to prominent Canadian and United States wholesalers under Export Packers' trademark, "Family Delight," as well as other labels.

A privately-owned Canadian company with its corporate headquarters located in Brampton, Ontario, Export today employs 160 people in Brampton and Winnipeg and maintains trading offices in western Canada and the United States. Officers of the company include Max Rubenstein's two sons: Jeff, who is President and Chief Executive Officer, and David, who holds the position of Vice President, Seafood Operations.

The company received the Manitoba Export Award in 1986 as a premier exporter of agricultural commodities and also, in the same year, received Honourable Mention in the Canada Export Awards. Since 1987, Export Packers Company Limited has been ranked by *The Financial Post "500"* as one of the leading corporations in Canada, based on consolidated sales and assets.

Export Packers is committed to the research and development of biochemical products derived from eggs and other food sources. The company believes, for example, that eventually more eggs will be broken for science than for food. Today, while the food portion of the business is expected to expand further, Export Packers Company Limited continues to move into the biotechnical research area to complement its food commodities. With this unique blend of high-tech research related to food

1

processing, and emphasis on both the domestic and foreign markets, Export Packers is well positioned to continue its pattern of growth and leadership within the industry.

1. *Jeff Rubenstein, President and Chief Executive Officer.*
2. *Export Packers' fully automated egg processing plant in Winnipeg, Manitoba processes in excess of 1.5 million eggs per day. Adjoining this ultra-modern facility is the company's Science and Technology Centre, where Export Packers maintains a full research staff and laboratories to research, develop, and produce biochemical products, new product types and production methods.*

2

Fairway Cartage & Express Ltd.

Having begun as a two truck operation, Fairway Cartage & Express Ltd. expanded rapidly and is now a prominent carrier in all of Ontario. By encouraging customer feedback and responding quickly with new and innovative services, Fairway has mushroomed in size since its first day of business on December 1, 1975.

Established by Angelo Demangos, Fairway has from its inception identified a need for and has provided three distinct types of service: rush, same-day and next-day throughout Ontario. Fairway was one of the first carriers to provide expedited service for its customers who needed immediate

delivery. In the early days Demangos and Vice President Marie Deveau were the company's entire staff. Demangos recalls that "there was plenty of hard work. We dispatched, loaded and unloaded trucks, billed, did the accounts . . . the whole show."

In 1983 Fairway successfully obtained a class "C" licence to service the entire province of Ontario, the first such licence to be granted to a trucking company in twenty-five years. In 1984 Fairway was also the first company in over eight years to acquire a licence to service Pearson International Airport.

Fairway's enthusiastic staff of 175 is one of the company's best forms of advertising. An employee profit sharing program was established in 1985 and has proven very successful.

Fairway began to diversify in 1986 by entering into the warehouse and distribution business. Fairway, as a distribution partner, structures its services to provide a quality link to their customers. By tailoring a service to fit the partner's specific needs, Fairway helps them reduce the overall cost of distributing their goods.

In 1987 Fairway Cartage designed its own customized com-

puter software program, the first for the transportation sector. Rating, billing, accounting and dispatch are now all fully computerized.

Fairway Cartage is also very involved in the community. The company helps sponsor the Special Olympics for the handicapped and donates drivers and vehicles to many charities on a consistent basis. A highlight each year is the children's Christmas party which Fairway sponsors for the families of its staff. Fairway's annual adult Christmas party for staff and customers attracts over 1,000 people.

Today, Fairway Cartage & Express Ltd. operates a modern fleet of more than 175 pieces of equipment. Through its affiliated companies and divisions, Fairway is able to respond quickly and efficiently to its customers' needs, ensuring that it will continue as a strong regional carrier and remain in the forefront of the trucking industry.

1. *Angelo Demangos, Founder and President of Fairway Cartage & Express Ltd.*
2. *Fairway's central headquarters in Rexdale, Ontario.*
3. *Santa arrives via Fairway's Flatbed division to the company's annual children's Christmas party.*

G.G.S. Plastic Engineering Inc.

Shaping the quality standard of injection molding, G.G.S. Plastic Engineering Inc. is a foremost manufacturer of intricate, precision plastic components. The company's steady, continued growth has been built on a foundation of exercising total control over every stage of its service, from the initial design to creating original molds in its on-site tooling facility, to the final production of a high quality product.

Inspired by Gabriel Martinovic, and joined by his son Goyko Martinovic and a third partner, on May 3, 1979, G.G.S. Tool & Die Ltd. was founded. The third partner left the company soon thereafter with only Gabriel and Goyko remaining. Very quickly they directed G.G.S. towards a specialty in the construction of molds for plastic injection applications, and expanded from an initial two employees to ten.

Having become very efficient mold makers, the company embarked on a major expansion in 1986 into the actual injection molding of plastic parts. G.G.S. acquired seven injection molding machines, quadrupled its workforce to forty employees, and began molding plastic parts, primarily for the automotive trade.

From 1986 to the present the company has become recognized as being a foremost injection molder in the automotive industry, specializing in insert moulding, the process of molding plastic around metal inserts. In 1989, G.G.S. received a major contract for the Ford Motor Company to supply fifty per cent of Ford's seatbelt slip tongue requirement. The contract doubled G.G.S.'s production volume and workforce. During 1989 to 1991, G.G.S. was instrumental in developing a plastic door lock housing for the same automotive manufac-

turer, changing what was primarily a metal product into a plastic application.

G.G.S. prides itself on its ability to produce precise, and, at times, complicated plastic components, evidenced by its area of expertise, insert molding. The company has also achieved an enviable standard of excellence in the molding of non-insert plastic parts, which can be produced in a wide range of materials and colours. Seat belt tongues, hood and trunk releases, and many hidden, internal components are only a few of the many products that G.G.S. Plastic Engineering has manufactured over the years.

At the heart of G.G.S. is a philosophy that believes the only way to produce a truly, high quality product is to have the resources to take responsibility for every stage in its development. In this respect, G.G.S.

has an established, integrated tooling facility on-site, staffed by many of the industry's most experienced and respected moldmakers. G.G.S.'s ability to create quality components is a combination of the latest technology, accumulated knowledge and the expertise of dedicated technicians, all supported by a pro-active mold and machinery maintenance program.

Today, with approximately 100 employees and twenty injection molding machines at its facilities in Brampton, Ontario, G.G.S. Plastic Engineering Inc. is shaping its own future by building on the company's reputation for quality. G.G.S. has the resources, the expertise and experience to do more than continue to simply satisfy the needs of its customers for quality plastic components. Its objective is to surpass them.

1

3

2

1. *Inspired by Gabriel Martinovic and his son Goyko, G.G.S. Plastic Engineering Inc. was founded on May 3, 1979.*
2. *The central offices of the company, located in Brampton, Ontario.*
3. *G.G.S. has approximately 100 employees and twenty injection molding machines at its central manufacturing facilities in Brampton.*

Gore & Storrie Limited
Consulting Engineers

When two civil engineers, William Gore and William Storrie, formed a partnership in 1919 with Dr. George Nasmith, a bacteriologist and public health specialist, the new company, Gore, Nasmith & Storrie, combined two disciplines within a single firm. While this was an unusual combination in those days, it now looks like an astute recognition of the expertise that would be required for dealing with the environmental issues that face society today.

When this partnership was formed in 1919, the company was a pioneer in the consulting engineering profession, since at that time the whole of Canada boasted only twenty other consulting engineering firms. Today there are more than 1,600. Thanks to its early and distinctive specialization, Gore & Storrie Limited (as the firm became named upon its incorporation in 1954) is now Canada's largest consulting engineering firm practising exclusively in the environmental field.

Wholly owned by its employees, the company is renowned for its innovative process and design capabilities in both municipal and industrial wastewater treatment, water supply systems, sewerage and storm drainage systems, water resources, air pollution control, building services, hazardous and solid waste management, energy management, and environmental planning. Expansion in the past few years has led the company into international waters, with municipal and industrial wastewater treatment design assignments in the United States, China, England, France, Belgium, Germany and Holland, as well as municipal water treatment design projects in the United States and Tanzania.

In the early 1920s, through the pioneering efforts of Dr. Nasmith, the company was involved in North America's earliest experiments with activated sludge for sewage treatment plants. The activated sludge process is a biological treatment process, whereby wastewater is mixed in aeration tanks with micro-organisms that consume the organic waste. The process was employed in Canada long before the United States adopted it, and the North Toronto plant — the company's original sewage treatment assignment in Toronto, built in 1927 — was one of the earliest plants on this continent to use the activated sludge process.

A major Toronto area assignment commencing in 1929 was the design of the R.C. Harris Water Purification Plant — a plant that has been dubbed "the queen of water filtration plants." Originally constructed in 1932, this plant has been a landmark in the Beaches area of Toronto for decades. Today, it is most exalted for its splendid *Art Deco* architecture. The man responsible for that was Gore, Nasmith & Storrie's in-house architect Thomas C. Pomphrey.

In contrast to that richness initiated in the early thirties, these days were the beginning of the Great Depression. By 1931, however, the company began winning enough assignments to keep it busy and solvent — particularly in the development of Leaside. Now a prosperous neighbourhood in Metropolitan Toronto, Leaside was then a separate municipality, heavily in debt and unable to sell land for development

Metropolitan Toronto's largest water filtration facility, the R.C. Harris Plant, was designed by Gore & Storrie, constructed in the 1930s, and enlarged in 1954. A grand and gracious monument to public service, this venerable plant is now extolled for its splendid Art Deco *architecture — created by Gore and Storrie in-house architect, Thomas C. Pomphrey in 1929. Today, Gore and Storrie designs water treatment plants that are high-tech, innovative award winners.*

because it was without services. The banks stepped in and guaranteed debentures for development, one street at a time, and thereby Leaside developed incrementally until Word War II, with Gore, Nasmith & Storrie designing and developing the sewer system.

West of the city, in 1931, the company installed the first piece of watermain in what was then called Toronto Township, now Mississauga, connecting it to the Port Credit system along Lakeshore Road. This project provided work for many depression-time unemployed, as all the trenches were dug entirely by hand.

Projects were not limited to Toronto even in the company's early years. During the 1920s and 1930s, the number of clientele for both sewage and waterworks projects grew across Ontario in towns such as Belleville, Trenton, Ajax and Pickering — and even as far afield as Calgary, where the firm designed and supervised construction of the Glenmore Dam, reservoir, and water treatment facilities, which serve the city to this day.

Also during the 1930s, extensive discussions began with the City of Toronto for establishing a main sewage treatment plant. These were the earliest conceptional seeds of the now venerable Metropolitan Toronto Main Treatment Plant — the largest activated sludge wastewater treatment facility in Canada. The plant was constructed in 1943, and Gore & Storrie has had major involvement with its development ever since. Initially, the plant provided only

Metropolitan Toronto's Main Treatment Plant is the largest activated sludge wastewater treatment plant in Canada. The plant serves a population of about 1.75 million. The sludge handling facility incorporates the world's largest thermal sludge conditioning installation currently in operation. Gore & Storrie Limited has been involved with the plant's design, construction administration and commissioning since it was first built.

primary treatment, but in the late 1950s, construction began on secondary treatment facilities, and expansions and upgrades to keep pace with Toronto's population explosion have been virtually continuous ever since.

With the dawning of environmental consciousness and concerns in the 1980s, a constant stream of ever-more sophisticated upgrades have been required to meet not only population increases, but also increasingly stringent municipal and industrial pollution control legislation. The older this plant becomes, and the more state-of-the-art it is required to be, the greater the degree of engineering ingenuity required to keep it operating within compliance.

In 1991, Gore & Storrie won a major Award of Excellence for an ingenious sludge dewatering, transportation, and incineration upgrade at the Main Treatment Plant. This triple retrofit doubled dewatering efficiency, halved incineration fuel requirements, and dramatically reduced odours and spillage. This upgrade was accomplished not only within the severe space constraints of this decades-old plant, but with no

disruption to daily operations.

Gore & Storrie has won several national awards for its water and wastewater treatment facility designs. These include the 1986 Schreyer Award — the highest honour awarded by the Canadian consulting engineering fraternity — for its patented hybrid anaerobic (HYAN®) treatment process. The HYAN process treats high-strength wastes while generating significant amounts of fuel gas.

Other notable award-winning projects are: Lorne Park, west of Toronto, North America's first major underground water purification plant with parkland on top; and a closed-loop sludge destruction system with energy recovery that eliminates the need for supplementary fuels at the Lakeview Pollution Control Plant in Mississauga.

Dedicated to safeguarding the environment through excellence in engineering and science, Gore & Storrie continues to specialize in its original environmental disciplines, pioneering innovative designs and processes, and maintaining the practice according to the traditions established by its founders.

Green Forest Lumber Corporation

1

One of North America's leading softwood lumber and waferboard wholesale distribution companies, Green Forest Lumber Corporation supplies retailers with the lumber needed to satisfy their needs. John T. Sereny, President and Chief Executive Officer, stresses that his goal was to build a lumber distribution company based on product quality, fair market prices and fast delivery; today, with over 25,000 truckloads of lumber being delivered annually, one must agree that he has succeeded.

The company was incorporated in 1957, and in 1960 Sereny began to work for the firm as a lumber trader. When the original owner did not see much future in the business, Sereny borrowed $5,000 and purchased the company. At that point there were only two people with the company, Sereny himself, who acted as the softwood lumber trader, and his secretary. Originally the business was strictly back-to-back sales, with the lumber purchased from mills and delivered to customers in Ontario and Quebec.

In 1970 Green Forest Lumber acquired the Chapleau Lumber Company Limited which had a saw-mill and timber licence in the Chapleau, Ontario region. To further achieve its goals, the company opened its first lumber distribution centre in Midhurst, Ontario in 1973. This lumber distribution centre allowed the company to purchase in larger quantities to obtain the best prices, and to stock inventory to quickly supply customers. In order to increase sales to U.S. customers, a new distribution centre was opened in Fort Erie, Ontario in 1978. The Midhurst distribution centre was relocated to Windsor, Ontario, in 1979 and the company's newest distribution centre was opened in Huntersville, North Carolina in 1988.

Also in 1988, the construction of a new sawmill was begun for Chapleau Forest Products Limited, the successor to Chapleau Lumber Company. Today the Chapleau facility is one of the most modern sawmills in eastern Canada supplying approximately ten per cent of all the lumber that Green Forest Lumber sells. As a major employer in a town of 3,000, the company feels it has a moral obligation to enrich the life of the people of Chapleau; therefore, it is involved in community activities and sponsors numerous amateur sports.

Today, with over 240 employees and with offices in Toronto, Chicago, LaSarre, Quebec and Charlotte, North Carolina, Green Forest Lumber sells primarily softwood, i.e. spruce, pine and fir and waferboard. John Sereny, who has been the guiding force from the beginning, believes that employees are the strength of the company. Today's management team consists of some of the brightest young minds in the forest industry.

Although Green Forest Lumber Corporation markets its product in Japan as well as in Europe and has its largest market in the United States, Sereny points out that the company has made the choice to remain in Ontario, where the company first began, and where it continues to grow.

1. *John T. Sereny, President of Green Forest Lumber Corporation.*
2. *Materials handling equipment in one of Green Forest's distribution centres: lumber and waferboard arrive by rail, they are unloaded by forklift, inventoried, and, when needed, placed onto trucks for distribution to retailers.*

2

The Hardie Corporation

Well-established, reliable, and extremely service-conscious, The Hardie Corporation has over the years come to enjoy a reputation as Canada's top manufacturer and distributor of institutional textiles. Servicing over 6,000 accounts from coast to coast, The Hardie Corporation is recognized as the leading Canadian company providing a wide range of industrial textile products for the health care, hospitality, and laundry and dry cleaning industries.

When the company was founded on April 2, 1924, by George Alexander Hardie, it was located on King Street East in Toronto and distributed industrial wipers and mill-ends to commercial laundries and industrial accounts. The real success story of this Canadian enterprise began a few years later, when Hardie moved away from its original product line and started with the converting of textiles.

Later, the company also began supplying cottons for padding and covers for flatwork ironers and presses in hospital laundries, commercial laundries and linen rental operations. Enjoying tremendous success in this area, the company then went a step further, and began producing textiles for the hospitality, health care, laundry and dry cleaning industries.

Now located in Mississauga, The Hardie Corporation has always been regarded as true innovators in the textile industry, both for their significant advances in the manufacturing process and for their innumerable improvements in product durability. The examples are many: Hardie extended the longevity of bedsheets by putting a two-inch hem at both the top and bottom; Hardie eliminated the rolling of pillow cases on the flatwork ironer by using a flat seam in their construction; and, Hardie introduced green linen in hospital operating rooms to reduce eye strain.

Whereas most companies specialize in laundry, hospitality or health care markets, The Hardie Corporation is unique in that they operate as a distributor and manufacturer for all these sectors. The majority of Hardie's customers are located in Ontario, but with the company's national network, the company also has customers in the Maritimes, Quebec and the western provinces. Hotels, motels, restaurants, laundries, hospitals and

1

nursing homes comprise the bulk of Hardie's customers. The company is now looking to expand in the United States and international markets.

With over sixty-five years of innovation and achievement behind it, The Hardie Corporation is heading into the future with the same pride and determination that has distinguished it in the past. Through the years the company has maintained the dedication, dependability, and integrity that proved so instrumental to its initial success. The most G. A. Hardie ever asked of his people was they "do an honest job and make a sincere effort." They did. And they still do today.

2

1. *Alfred Billes, who became President and Chief Executive Officer in 1990.*
2. *The Hardie Boys — providing leadership for The Hardie Corporation from 1924 to 1990. George Alexander Hardie (centre), who founded the company, and his sons, Paul (left) and Gene (right).*

Hillsborough Resources Limited

Now the largest publicly traded mining and engineering contractor in Canada, Hillsborough Resources chose to establish its engineering, administrative, marketing and central shop resources in Brampton, Ontario.

A location near Toronto was selected to fulfill the requirements that a successful mining contractor should be centrally positioned in Canada without being exclusively committed to any specific areas or minerals, be close to the largest concentration of customers, and have ready access to superb transportation.

Canadian Mine Development, now a division of Hillsborough Resources Limited, was formed in 1984 by five veteran mining executives who had worked effectively and harmoniously together for many years supervising the engineering, administrative, and field work for a very large mining contractor. They grasped an opportunity to acquire both work and equipment under advantageous conditions and established their own enterprise early in 1984.

The five founders were George Vooro, an experienced mining executive skilled in the art of hard rock mining and who is now the controlling shareholder and Chief Executive Officer; Archibald McCutcheon, an experienced mining administrator who is now retired; Kenneth A. Hawrelak, a chartered accountant, wise to the ways of mining industry financial controls; Joseph I. Tatak, a mining engineer with a three dimensional vision and special talent for the design of mining operations combining productivity and safety; and Eli Eliev, an experienced hands-on project development executive.

Canadian Mine Development received positive client response almost immediately, and since its formation in 1984 more than fifty mine contracting projects have been completed satisfactorily. In 1987, two significant changes were implemented. On February 26, 1987, the enterprise successfully made the transition to publicly-owned status and its shares began trading on the Toronto Stock Exchange under the name Hillsborough Resources Limited. That same year, the company began acquiring claims for subsequent exploration and, therefore, established the groundwork for its now very successful mineral resources division.

The mine engineering and contracting division has successfully completed mining projects in almost all of the provinces and territories in Canada and its range of mineral experience encompasses gold, lead, zinc, silver, uranium, potash, asbestos, coal and graphite.

The mineral resources division of Hillsborough was created to develop synergies arising from the expertise generated by contracting operations. To date, investments have been made in two projects located in the Rocky Mountain Trench and a large number of mineralized properties and projects have been examined across Canada.

Mt. Hundere, in the Yukon, is the first producing property in which Hillsborough has an equity interest. Production commenced in the summer of 1991 and is scheduled to operate at an annual rate of 550,000 tonnes beginning in 1992.

Mt. Hundere is expected to contribute significantly to Hillsborough during the life of the mine. Also, the mineral resources division is actively investigating several other properties, both in Canada and in other countries, and the future prospects continue to be highly optimistic.

The magic of mining is that wealth which has lain hidden for millions of years is being mobilized for the benefit of all Canadians. Hillsborough Resources Limited is proud to be one of the leaders which makes this happen.

The central office of Hillsborough Resources Limited, located in Brampton, Ontario.

Honeywell Limited

Over 100 years ago, Honeywell laid the foundation for its future success when it developed and marketed the world's first environmental control for the home. In Canada for over sixty years, Honeywell has always pursued development of a distinctively Canadian character and responsible participation in the Canadian economy. Honeywell's products span the Canadian economy, playing a major application role in virtually all of Canada's key economic sectors of growth.

Honeywell was founded as a controls company in 1885 in Minneapolis, Minnesota, when the company developed the first commercially successful room temperature control. Forty-five years later, in 1930, the company moved to develop its business multinationally. It incorporated in Toronto its first manufacturing and marketing affiliate outside of the United States.

Under the able direction of Tom McDonald, the company's first general manager, the Canadian enterprise quickly grew. Manufacturing began in 1932, with the assembly of temperature controls. The first full Honeywell office outside Ontario opened in Montreal in 1937, which was followed by another in Calgary and a third in Vancouver.

When a relatively minor firm, Small Electric Motors Company in Leaside, a Toronto suburb, closed following the end of the World War II, Honeywell decided to purchase the plant. It was here for the first time that the company entered the manufacturing field on a significant scale. The first product manufactured completely in Canada was the 56 Aquastat, so designated because 56 The Kingsway had been the address of Tom McDonald's home. The number "56" has another signif-icance as well, because it was in 1956 that the name of the company was changed from Minneapolis-Honeywell Regulator Limited to Honeywell Controls Limited.

Today, the company's largest Canadian manufacturing facility, located in Scarborough, is recognized among the company's worldwide affiliates as a "Manufacturing Centre of Excellence," and employees on the production floor are challenged by an increased emphasis on training and education.

The evolution from branch plant to "Centre of Excellence" began in 1984, when Honeywell management in operations around the world responded to increased global competition with foresight and strategic planning. Worldwide manufacturing facilities were streamlined and rationalized to achieve economies of scale, and maximize productivity. The completed process involved the rationalization of fifty different products to the current focus on five core product mandates: valves and actuators, fan and limit controls, products for electrical energy conservation, and indoor air quality products.

The move has placed the Canadian Honeywell operation in a unique position to serve the global marketplace. Last year, as much as eighty per cent of the products man-ufactured in the Scarborough facility were exported to the United States, Europe and Asia through the company's distribution network of worldwide affiliates.

The company has prepared for the challenge of global competition with a multi-million dollar commitment to invest in new product development, computerized technology and training on the factory floor. The latest achievement is the plantwide integration of an on-line computer system that links all areas of the manufacturing facility together in an information network and tracks production through all processes of manufacturing.

Today, Honeywell provides control products, systems and services for energy management and environmental control, for process control management in manufacturing and natural resource industries, and for security applications in homes, buildings and financial institutions.

Control technology began with a Honeywell invention. It grew with Honeywell innovations. And today it remains the core of Honeywell's business, as it provides the controls that enable people around the world to live better and more productively.

Honeywell Limited's Canadian corporate headquarters are located in North York, Ontario.

The Hospital for Sick Children

On March 13, 1970, a pleasant looking man with a fringe of white hair edged around the cashier's counter of the Hospital and opened a canvas travel bag, pulling out more than five thousand dollars in crumpled and musty bills "for the poor kids." In 1937, in the box for donations at the door of the Hospital, a large diamond was found wrapped in cotton batting. Officials speculated that perhaps it was from the engagement ring of a mother whose child had been saved by the Hospital in the polio epidemic and who gave the gem in gratitude.

These unexpected gestures of thanks are indicative of how The Hospital for Sick Children, known affectionately for generations as "Sick Kids," has found a special place in the hearts and minds of all who are associated with it. Having earned a world-wide reputation for the standards of excellence it has set in the treatment of the young, its history is a heartwarming story of human dedication and medical progress, pioneering new research and new levels of proficiency.

The Hospital for Sick Children, now the largest paediatric hospital in North America, was founded in the spring of 1875. Elizabeth McMaster and a group of friends opened The Hospital for Sick Children in a small downtown Toronto house that had eleven rooms which they rented for $320 a year. In the first year forty-four patients were admitted and sixty-seven others were treated in out-patient clinics. Under John Ross Robertson's direction, publisher of the *Evening Telegram* and Chairman of the Hospital's Board of Trustees, the Hospital opened its first brand new building, on College Street at Elizabeth in 1892.

A few years later, in 1908, the Hospital installed the first milk pas-

1

teurization plant in Canada, with staff leading the fight in Canada for compulsory pasteurization. Pablum, a precooked baby cereal, was developed at Sick Kids in 1930. In 1953 the Research Institute was established. Through the 1980s, advances in genetics have led to the identification and cloning of a number of genes responsible for causing hereditary diseases such as Duchenne muscular dystrophy and cystic fibrosis. Today, more than 800 staff, including senior scientists, physicians and students, are engaged in more than 400 research projects in seventy-five fields.

The Hospital also pioneered renowned surgical developments such as the Salter operation to repair dislocation of the hip and the Mustard operation to correct a heart defect that often was fatal. In the 1960s, the Hospital opened one of the first intensive care units in North America devoted exclusively to the care of critically ill newborn and premature babies.

Early in the 1990s a brand new patient care centre will be opened, with all new operating rooms, two intensive care units, and emergency department. Most patients will have

their own rooms with a private washroom and a sofa-bed for a parent.

Today, in all of its many roles, as a teaching hospital for the University of Toronto, as a research institute, and as a treatment hospital for children from Toronto and from around the world, The Hospital for Sick Children continues with the same spirit and compassion that first led Elizabeth McMaster to establish a hospital dedicated entirely to the care of children.

1. *A free outpatient clinic draws mother and child to The Hospital for Sick Children in 1915.* **2.** *Then as now, snacktime is popular with young patients.*

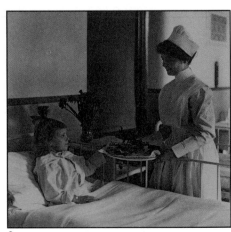

2

International Tele-Film Enterprises Ltd.

Committed to providing top quality video programs for its customers, International Tele-Film Enterprises Ltd. is a Canadian owned and operated, award-winning distribution company that has been an industry leader for thirty years. This innovative organization is the largest privately-owned, non-theatrical film distribution company in Canada, with unique access to the Canadian and international markets.

Murray L. Sweigman, a pioneer in the Canadian film industry, drew on his vast experience in all facets of the film and video industry to form International Tele-Film in 1961. Formed originally to distribute feature films, specials and series to the television market, the company has gained vast experience in this media for both network and syndication sales.

With its head office in Toronto and branch offices in Montreal and Vancouver, the company offers bilingual services in French and English. International Tele-Film is now one of the most comprehensive marketing and distribution organizations in television and video training programs; its well-established customer base is the largest in Canada. The company represents a wide range of Canadian and foreign producers, both domestically and internationally.

International Tele-Film works

1

with three distinct groups of customers: the television market, in which the company started; the educational market, with which the company began working in 1967; and, since 1969, the corporate training market. For the television market, the company distributes feature films, classic motion pictures, series and documentaries to an all-encompassing market, including, among others, television networks, independent stations, closed circuit television and cable stations. The company's educational products are marketed to educational institutions, libraries, governments, non-profit organizations, and health and law enforcement agencies. The company's corporate customers range from small businesses to large companies, who are provided with films and videos concerning areas such as sales training, and all areas of management skills.

Having a vast supply of products in stock at all times for viewing and evaluation purposes, International Tele-Film is able to supply its customers with the majority of their needs almost immediately. If the company does not have a certain product in stock, it is usually able to promptly procure it from the producer. The company's state-of-the-art computer network provides unparalleled customer service, ensuring that all clients and suppliers receive prompt, reliable, and efficient attention.

The experienced and responsive professionals that comprise International Tele-Film provide unsurpassed service to customers throughout North America and around the world. Stuart Grant, President, points out that from the beginning there was a vision for growth; there was a foresight to see what future markets would be like and to anticipate them. It is this entrepreneurial spirit that has allowed the company to progress as it did, and it will allow International Tele-Film Enterprises Ltd. to continue to grow and expand in the future.

1. *Murray L. Sweigman, Founder of International Tele-Film Enterprises Ltd.* 2. *Steven Sweigman, Vice President of Operations.* 3. *Stuart Grant, President.* 4. *Randi Perry, Vice President of Marketing.*

2

3

4

I S S Equipment Company Limited

Guy Raekelboom, President of I S S Equipment Company Limited — the fastest growing conveyor company in Canada, started his long career at the age of thirteen working in "The Laugh In the Dark," the spook house at the Canadian National Exhibition. Working sixteen hour days, seven days a week for the duration of the CNE, he quickly learned the work ethic that has stayed with him for his entire life.

After a short and inglorious military career, he briefly attended university, finally went through various careers from chemist to racing car driver, and ended up as a hippie and antiwar protester in the Middle East, preaching love and peace to Palestinians and Israelis while working on a communal farm in the desert. This mission being a failure, he then spent several months accompanied by a dog in the Greek Islands and the French Côte d'Azur begging coins from tourists.

Returning to Canada in 1971, he started a brand new career as an installer with a conveyor company. Within a few months he was service and installation manager, and eventually part owner of the company. Not happy with how this company was run, Raekelboom decided to start his own in 1975.

In the early years of I S S Equipment, it was literally a one man company. Raekelboom would sell a job, return to his small shop in Brampton, Ontario, and single-handedly design and manufacture the conveyor system. It is with pride and good humour that Raekelboom talks about the early days when one winter he could not afford heat and literally worked with his overcoat on, always complaining to any visitors that "the landlord has let our heating system break down again."

One of his favourite stories is about a potential customer who wanted to see his manufacturing facilities. Raekelboom took him to the back of one of the larger conveyor companies. He knew there would be no name sign, and then proceeded to give the customer a guided tour of the manufacturing area, hoping that no one would question him about what he was doing there. He received the order.

It is this spirit of determination, innovation, and plain hard work that has characterized I S S Equipment and has laid the foundation for the future growth of the company under the leadership of Raekelboom.

In 1979 I S S Equipment Company Limited was incorporated, and, after having only part-time help for several years, was able to hire several employees to work full-time in the shop and in sales. In 1982, outgrowing the industrial unit in which it was located, the company expanded into the neighbouring unit. Outgrowing also this double unit, I S S expanded into a third unit.

I S S soon began to experience accelerated growth, doubling in size during several consecutive years. To accommodate this growth, in 1987 the company relocated to its present 40,000 square feet facility in Brampton. Currently, I S S has sixty employees.

I S S Equipment Company has many distinctive conveyor designs. Able to manufacture unique systems more economically than its larger competitors, the company prides itself that one of its major selling points is, in fact, the price of the units.

One well-recognized conveyor system manufactured by I S S Equipment is the parcel pick up conveyor found in A & P supermarkets across Ontario.

I S S sells through industrial dealers across Canada and the United States; however, with larger jobs or turnkey systems, I S S will deal directly with the end user. The company is now manufacturing its own control systems, including software as well as hardware.

As designers, manufacturers, and installers of package handling conveyors, I S S Equipment offers a broad array of conveyor systems. With its conveyors successfully operating in a wide variety of industries, including automotive, manufacturing and warehousing, I S S Equipment Company Limited can look forward to a future of growth.

Guy Raekelboom, Founder and President of I S S Equipment Company Limited. I S S Equipment, the fastest growing conveyor company in Canada, designs, manufactures and installs a broad array of conveyor systems.

Italian Canadian Benevolent Corporation
Villa Colombo • Columbus Centre

A few file folders with little in them, a bank book showing a balance of a few hundred dollars, a tiny office, and a big vision; such was the beginning of the Italian Canadian Benevolent Corporation. Twenty years later, the dream of the few has become a vast array of much needed services. Remaining always "proudly Canadian and fiercely Italian," the Italian Canadian Benevolent Corporation is a marvellous testimonial to the spirit of the Italian Canadian community which today enriches the social and cultural patrimony of our country.

In 1971, as the Italian Canadian community was reaching a certain level of success and integration in Toronto, a group of good-willed community-spirited individuals banded together to form a charitable, non-profit organization. With its mandate the creation of social services for the community, the first project of the Corporation was to develop a home for Italian seniors. After purchasing land at Lawrence and Dufferin Streets in 1974, the Villa Colombo Home for the Aged opened its doors in 1976 to 188 residents. With an expansion in 1986, Villa Colombo is now home to 268 residents and caters to many other seniors through its day care program.

The adjoining property was purchased in 1978 with the help of the provincial government, and by 1980 the Columbus Centre opened: to be of service to everyone, to showcase a lifestyle based on family and heritage, and to share that lifestyle with the rest of society. The Columbus Centre has become an established focal point, a social, cultural and recreational centre visited by thousands of people for the large selection of services and activities it offers. Pal Di Iulio, Executive Director of the Italian Canadian Benevolent Corporation, explains that "Columbus Centre has become a piazza, a bridge to ourselves and to the greater community."

At the request of the provincial government, the Corporation had been operating a pilot project, the Parent Relief Program, which provided weekend respite care to developmentally or physically handicapped children and their families at Villa Colombo. In 1980, this program was moved to new and larger quarters at Columbus Centre.

Caboto Terrace, a senior citizens' apartment complex, was developed by the Corporation in 1983. Located adjacent to the Columbus Centre, Caboto Terrace is home to more than 300 independent residents.

In 1985 the provincial government once again asked the Corporation to sponsor group homes and a day program for the developmentally handicapped. In response, Vita Community Living Services was born and now provides twenty-four hour care for twenty-five adults through its three group homes. Just as important, Vita operates a day program for approximately seventy people and there are additional homes planned for the near future.

Through a substantial endowment from Joseph D. Carrier, part of the Columbus Centre was designated the Joseph D. Carrier Art Gallery. Opened in 1987, the Gallery encourages artistic development and appreciation in the Italian Canadian community and the northwest quadrant of Metropolitan Toronto.

In 1991 the Corporation opened its fifth major project, Casa Del Zotto. Located on the same campus as the Columbus Centre, it is home to 250 self-sufficient and handicapped seniors who are aided by an attendant care program.

With a commitment to effective communication and sharing through the quarterly publication *Lifestyle* and active caring, the Italian Canadian Benevolent Corporation now offers a wide range of social, cultural, educational and health services to the wider community in the spirit of multiculturalism. The Corporation has become an example and a symbol of the co-operation between the volunteer sector and governments in how to contribute and make a positive difference in this world. It has come a long way from the statement made by its dynamic President and catalyst for community development, Anthony Fusco, who in 1974 stated "Our job is to leave this corner of the world a little better than we found it."

A few aspects of the dynamic Columbus Centre lifestyle. The Centre is a proud contribution of the Italian Canadian community to the multicultural spirit of Metropolitan Toronto.

ITT Canada Limited

One of Canada's most impressive business conglomerates, ITT Canada Limited is a diversified product and service company engaged in the manufacture and distribution of automotive parts, electronic components and fluid handling equipment, and in the provision of financial, insurance and hotel management services. With 4,200 employees, ITT Canada carries on business at over fifty locations in nine provinces.

Wholly owned by ITT Corporation in New York, ITT's Canadian operations began in 1946 when a ITT subsidiary acquired a 90,000 square foot facility in Montreal. Known as the Federal Electric Manufacturing Company Limited, the company began to build radio, telephone, telegraph and instrument landing-systems equipment. In 1954 responsibility for the Canadian operation was transferred to ITT's United Kingdom based Standard Telephone and Cables Limited.

Management responsibility returned to North America in 1961, when the corporate name of the Canadian subsidiary was changed to ITT Canada Limited.

An era of growth for ITT Canada took place during ITT Corporation's acquisition drive of the 1960s and early 1970s. In almost all cases of acquisitions in the United States and Europe, there was a corresponding branch plant in Canada.

As ITT's Canadian presence became solidified, the work of establishing a strong national identity for the company began. A staff office was opened in 1967 in Toronto to coordinate ITT's activities in Canada. Thomas H. Savage, CBE, Chairman and President of ITT Canada Limited, points out that ITT Canada began

to manage the full range of corporate activities from Toronto, while the individual operating units of ITT in Canada are now managed as autonomous organizations in their own industry sector.

ITT Canada is also very active in the community. The company is a member of the Business Council on National Issues, and Savage is a member of its Policy Committee. He is also the Business Co-Chairperson of the Canadian Labour Market and Productivity Centre. In addition, the company also contributes to health care, drug awareness and education programs across Canada.

Today, ITT Canada is a complex amalgamation of companies operating at over fifty locations across Canada. ITT Canada has six companies in the automotive industry, six in fluid technology, four in hotel management services, three in electronic components, two in the insurance business, and one each in the commercial finance, defense and natural resources fields.

Almost all of ITT's operating units in Canada are consolidated within ITT Canada Limited and work under the auspices of ITT

Industries of Canada Ltd. and Abbey Life Insurance Company of Canada. ITT Corporation also operates the ITT Hartford Insurance Group in Canada as a separate subsidiary and ITT Felec Services Inc., an ITT company in Winnipeg, Manitoba which manages the early warning radar stations in the Arctic for the United States Air Force. ITT Canada provides support services to these subsidiaries.

With almost $700 million in annual revenue, including ITT Hartford and ITT Felec Services Canada, the large and complex organization known as ITT Canada now ranks among the top 150 Canadian industrial companies, and continues to be recognized as a leader in trade and commerce.

Directors and officers of the board of ITT Industries of Canada Ltd. and ITT Canada Limited: (seated left to right) Louis Guolla, Q.C.; Marcel Piché, O.C., Q.C., LL.L.; M.C. Woodward Jr.; T.H. Savage, CBE; John H. McChord Jr. (retired); the Hon. S.R. Basford, P.C., Q.C.; (standing left to right) Serge Bourque; Ronald P. Jaeggin; Gerald B. Fedchun; John W.C. Macfarlane, Q.C.; Frederick Musinka; R.G. Eisner; R.W. Beicke.

Longo Brothers Fruit Markets Inc.

When Tom Longo complained to the supervisor at the supermarket where he worked in 1954 that the mushrooms were of poor quality and should not be sold at full price, he was curtly told that he was paid to work, and not to think. He promptly quit. Joe Longo, working for the same supermarket chain, also left his job and joined his brother to start on their own.

They were able to open their first store, Broadway Fruit Market, on the corner of Yonge and Broadway Streets in Toronto in 1956, and concentrated primarily on selling produce. From the beginning it was a family-oriented business, and all eight employees at the first store were family members. In 1965 a third brother, Gus Longo, also became a full partner.

When the lease expired at the Yonge St. location in 1962 they were forced to move and re-located themselves at the corner of Woodbine Avenue and Mortimer Drive. By now the company was also selling groceries and some meat products, and it soon expanded by opening a second location in Malton in 1967. In 1971 they sold the Woodbine store, and soon opened a new store in Burlington in 1972. When their Malton store was

1

expropriated in 1980, they moved to another location in Malton.

Throughout the 1980s Longo Brothers Fruit Markets has grown rapidly. In 1982 they opened a new store in Oakville; in 1986 they moved to a new location in Burlington; in 1987 they expanded into Markham; and in 1990 they opened yet another store, in Thornhill. In 1991 they expect to expand the Malton location and also open a sixth store in Vaughan.

One important reason for its growth has been the emphasis that the Longo Brothers has always placed on freshness. Although they look for the best price, the quality and freshness of the product is the most important. As their slogan declares, "Where anything fresher

is still growing." Another important reason has been the emphasis on hands-on management. Gus and Joe Longo Jr., son of Tom Longo, still personally buy the produce every day for all the stores, ensuring that it is the best; in the summertime they buy directly from the farmers. The quality of its 600 staff members is another significant reason for the stores' success.

Longo Brothers Fruit Markets Inc. also places much emphasis on community minded activities. As Anthony Longo, one of the sons remarks, they "believe that it is important to be active in community activities and put an investment back into the communities where they are located." They actively support local cultural societies, minor hockey leagues, local fund-raising and food drives. In recognition of this community involvement a street in Mississauga was recently named in their honour, Longo Circle in Malton.

Longo Brothers Fruit Markets Inc., today a well-stocked supermarket offering a full range of products, continues to be a successful family-owned and family-oriented business. From its simple beginnings to the present, Longo Brothers Fruit Markets Inc., has placed the same emphasis on quality, and has consistently been met with success.

1. *The Markham location of Longo Brothers Fruit Markets Inc. today.*
2. *Broadway Fruit Market on the corners of Yonge and Broadway Streets in Toronto, the first location of Longo Brothers Fruit Markets Inc.*

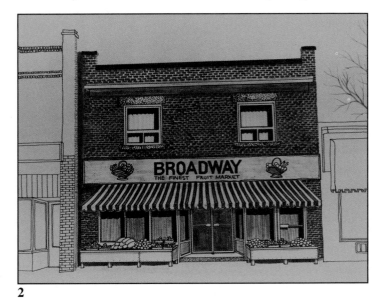

2

J.D. Smith and Sons Limited

Since 1919, J.D. Smith and Sons Limited, a third generation trucking company, has concentrated on providing consistent service in the distribution of products. Through years of dedicated hard work, J.D. Smith and Sons has grown to become one of the best known transportation and distribution companies in Ontario, and now enjoys unequalled delivery capability developed through special working relationships with all the major food chains. Professional distribution, contract trucking, refrigerated transportation, storage, warehousing and cross-docking operations from a single source, along with its dedication to dependability and reliability, have ensured the continued success of J.D. Smith and Sons.

In 1919, John Dudley Smith, a steamfitter by trade, started a small cartage and delivery service in partnership with his brother-in-law. The company, known at first as Bennett and Smith, operated out of J.D. Smith's residence on Arlington St. in Toronto, and provided timely and effective food delivery for the grocery trade. Several of the company's early customers still remain today as accounts of J.D. Smith & Sons.

Jack Smith, son of J.D. Smith, joined the company in 1943 and a second truck was added. In 1947, Douglas Smith, Jack Smith's brother, finished highschool and joined the company, which then became a three truck operation. At this point the partnership with Bennett ended, and there were three Smith's and three trucks.

The next major expansion of J.D. Smith and Sons was the purchase of New Toronto Cartage in 1952, along with its accounts and five trucks. The company began to rent a warehouse on Nashville Ave. and added several more trucks. J.D.

1

Smith soon retired and left the operation of the company to his sons.

By 1960 J.D. Smith and Sons had added a second warehouse on Caledonia Road and operated approximately 25 vehicles. In 1975 J.D. Smith and Sons added a refrigeration division when the company acquired Gladstone Cartage, along with its fleet of refrigerated trucks.

Jack Smith retired from the company in 1985, but Douglas Smith's three children are now also involved in the company. Scott Smith is Sales Manager, Brian Smith is Operations Manager, while Susan Smith is Administration Manager.

Over the years J.D. Smith and Sons has added more warehousing, and today it has over 260,000 square feet of warehousing capabilities. The company's fleet of vehicles, about half of which are under contract to other companies, has also grown, and now has approximately seventy tractors, 100 straight trucks and over 150 trailers. "Growth is important, of course, but the quality of our existing services is more important," emphasizes Douglas Smith. With more than 250 employees, J.D.

Smith and Sons will continue with carefully controlled growth, concentrating on the company's valued reputation of reliability.

Although J.D. Smith and Sons is one of the largest haulers of wholesale grocery products in Ontario, the company also services other industries, such as the pharmaceutical, steel, plumbing supply and office furniture businesses. Most of the company's cartage is local to

1. John Dudley Smith, Founder, J.D. Smith and Sons Limited.
2. Douglas S. Smith, son of the Founder and current President.

2

the Toronto region. Douglas Smith points out that "the bulk of our business — eighty to eighty-five per cent — is within ten miles of Toronto. We have licences for Ontario, Quebec and the United States which secures our growth potential for the future."

One major aspect of the company's trucking operation which anticipates significant expansion is the contract trucking service. Contract trucking enables customers to acquire independent cartage capability without the costs and responsibilities associated with fleet start-up and operation. J.D. Smith and Sons supplies and manages the equipment and drivers, while minimizing the uncontrollable costs associated with small or medium sized fleet operations.

Although trucking is still the major component of J.D. Smith and Sons, its warehousing and distribution services are continually growing. The company offers four distinct services: distribution, cross-dock operation, refrigerated service, and storage and warehousing.

J.D. Smith and Sons works closely with all the major food chains in the distribution aspect of the company. Delivering to the major chains on a daily basis, the company, in addition to prompt pick-up and delivery, offers its unique computerized pallet interchange system to monitor and protect each client's investment in pallets.

The cross-dock operation of J.D. Smith and Sons is capable of handling any size load shipped by rail or truck, and to break it down for delivery according to the customer's specifications. The company's refrigerated service provides reliable and safe delivery in its well-maintained refrigerated vehicles.

Modern storage and warehouse facilities provide 260,000 square feet of clean, heated and sprinkler-equipped warehouse space with bulk and rack storage capacity and private rail facilities. The state-of-the-art computerized inventory control permits clients to access stock balances, critical minimums, transfers and vital documentation.

J.D. Smith and Sons has also been actively involved with the community. Always trying to promote a family atmosphere, the company offers a Christmas party and a safety banquet each year. Douglas Smith was President of the Toronto Trucking Association, and was also President and Director of the Ontario Trucking Association.

From the beginning, J.D. Smith and Sons has concentrated on a tight control of costs and prices. Whether through more efficient operations, better distribution areas, or ensuring that their trucks are in top condition, the company is always working on keeping costs to a minimum. Its progressive stance has also meant the introduction of employee profit sharing. Douglas Smith attributes the company's suc-

1

cess to its innovation, good service and good management. Although not the biggest, they have provided a quality service that has sold itself.

The company's ability to grow and adapt to meet the changing needs of the industry has enabled J.D. Smith and Sons to maintain their level of service excellence. With over seventy years of experience in providing prompt pick-up and delivery, J.D. Smith and Sons Limited will continue to build on the Toronto region's healthy market for warehousing, distribution and contract truck services.

1. *J.D. Smith and Sons Limited was one of the first trucking companies to computerize its entire operation, including the warehouse and truck maintenance.*
2. *J.D. Smith and Sons Limited's fleet of more than 300 vehicles deliver goods in the greater Toronto area and throughout Ontario.*
3. *The next generation of the Smith family is already involved with the company that their grandfather founded: (clockwise) Susan Smith, Brian Smith, and Scott Smith.*

2

3

J.J. Muggs Gourmet Grille

An innovative Toronto based restaurant company, J.J. Muggs Gourmet Grille is regarded as an industry leader in casual dining. Starting with its Bloor Street West location, the Mug Restaurant introduced the public to the "definitive" eatery: an innovative menu combining traditional fare with creative flare, and an extensive selection of large portions of great quality food enjoyed with personable, efficient service.

Ted Nikolaou, the founder of J.J. Muggs, is proud to say that his restaurants are still among the most beautiful and comfortable around today. All four locations reflect the J.J. Muggs philosophy of developing and operating restaurants at the highest possible standards.

Nikolaou emigrated from Greece to Canada with his family in 1955. Being the eldest child in the family, he needed to help with the family finances and soon was employed as a shoeshine boy in downtown Toronto. Maintaining a strong work ethic, he boasts that since that time he has never had a day when he was unemployed. After working at several other jobs in Toronto, at the young age of nineteen he had saved sufficient money to buy Rex Grille in 1960. Successfully operating the twenty-two seat restaurant located at Lakeshore and Mimico for ten years, he then sold it to allow himself the opportunity to begin the J.J. Muggs tradition.

The success story of J.J. Muggs began in 1971, when the Mug Restaurant and Eatery opened on Bloor Street West. The "Mug," as it was known then, quickly became one of Toronto's most popular gathering places, an eatery style restaurant offering large portions, low prices and plenty of variety. In a city with an ever-growing population of theme or specialized eating spots, the 120 seat Mug was an oasis in a

1

crowded desert, and an instant success. The Mug's concept was enduring — high quality food, excellent service and great value.

The first large scale Mug opened in the Eaton Centre in 1982. The concept included spacious surroundings and a decor featuring leaded stained-glass windows, decorative brass railings, a giant spiral stairway leading to an entire upstairs level of dining, and a beautiful concave stained-glass dome adorning the ceiling. Guests cannot help but feel the warmth and inti-

macy of the restaurant.

In 1985 the Woodbine Centre location overwhelmed guests with a greenhouse atrium, seven levels of dining, a mezzanine overlooking a spectacular convex stained-glass dome and a completely open kitchen. A new name was also introduced, J.J. Muggs Gourmet Grille.

In 1987 the Bloor Street location was expanded and refurbished. When it reopened as J.J. Muggs, it had been refitted with Italian marble columns and floors, neon accents, stylish artwork and more

2

1. *J.J. Muggs Gourmet Grille's President and his wife, Ted and Joan Nikolaou, cutting the cake at the opening of the Woodbine Centre J.J. Muggs in 1985.*
2. *Starting with the Bloor Street West location in Toronto, the public was first introduced to the "definitive" eatery in 1972.*

1

2

comfortable surroundings. The dark mirrored glass highlighted by a large green awning identifies the restaurant and augments the spectre of the entire Bloor Street annex.

Recently the newest location was unveiled, J.J. Muggs Erin Mills Town Centre. Located in Mississauga, this spectacular showpiece of marble, granite and quarry cast stone has three floors of dining, two backlit illuminated marble bars and a kitchen which is completely open to the dining room.

While J.J. Muggs boasts decorative and spacious surroundings, with both intimate and party-style seating, its true pride lies in culinary imagination. With an emphasis on excitement and a concern for convenience, J.J. Muggs is open daily for breakfast, lunch, dinner and late night snacks. From classical to modern cookery, the menu crosses multi-cultural borders to include Italian, Greek, Mexican, Jewish, Eastern, French and, of course, North American dishes. Nikolaou points out, "Because of the wide range of clientele, the menu must have something for everyone." Children are also welcome, receiving special attention with a colouring book menu.

The J.J. Muggs catering division has been operating since the early 1980s, and has grown so rapidly that an entirely new catering facility was built to accommodate the rapidly growing list of clientele.

To ensure a successful event, catering representatives assist in developing the proper menu for each client, whether it be selections from the catering menu or special requests to fill individual requirements.

Realizing that the location of each restaurant is very important to the eventual success of the establishment, Nikolaou personally undertakes a critical approach to site selection, carefully applying criteria to ensure a successful location. In many other areas of management there is this same hands-on approach. For example, Nikolaou works closely with the professional interior designers to create J.J. Muggs' unique atmosphere. In addition, Nikolaou credits the entire J.J. Muggs team, and in particular his Operations Manager, Tony Palermo, with the smooth operation of the restaurants.

Looking back over the twenty years of development of his restaurant enterprises, Nikolaou also acknowledges the support he has received from his family. As he warmly comments, "It takes a special kind of family to give the support needed for the type of hard work required for this business. Without the encouragement of Joan [Mrs. Nikolaou] and my children, Steven and Lisa, all this would not have been possible." Steven has also joined in the business and manages one of the restaurants.

Today, the excitement is just beginning at J.J. Muggs Gourmet Grille. With an ever-changing concept, new ideas are only limited by the people that create them. With the finest food available, this multi-purpose dining establishment looks forward to continued growth and success.

1. *The first large scale J.J. Muggs opened in Toronto's Eaton Centre in 1982.*
2. *In 1985, the Woodbine Centre location, also in Toronto, overwhelmed guests with a greenhouse atrium, seven levels of dining, a mezzanine overlooking a spectacular convex stained-glass dome and a completely open kitchen.*
3. *Located in Mississauga, Ontario, the newest J.J. Muggs was recently opened in the Erin Mills Town Centre.*

3

Loomis & Toles Company Limited

Loomis & Toles originated in 1946 as the brainchild of Clare Loomis and Paige Toles. After graduating from the Ontario College of Art, they opened an art supply outlet on Grenville Street in Toronto. Several years later, the company was taken over by the M. Grumbacher Company, while retaining the Loomis & Toles name. Within a few years, the company settled at the now familiar Adelaide Street location.

The company continued to grow as numerous products became available and its reputation spread. The store expanded into space obtained from the printing company located adjacent to Loomis & Toles. New products and services emerged, such as housebranding and delivery, initially by bicycle and later by truck, and specialty staff were hired.

Towards the late 1960s, Loomis & Toles pioneered the introduction of darkroom cameras for artwork production and became a dealer for a new product called Letraset. Letraset revolutionized the commercial art field and soon Loomis & Toles was the largest Letraset dealer in Canada.

In 1973 Letraset International purchased Loomis & Toles from private owners and shortly thereafter both companies were purchased by Esselte, a large Swedish conglomerate. Loomis & Toles continued to grow, expanding to the Eglinton and Brentcliffe location in 1976. Then, in 1982, Loomis & Toles purchased the Thomas R. Fisher company, a chain of art supply stores with branches in Halifax, Fredericton, Ottawa and Montreal. In 1988 the company opened a third store at Sheppard Avenue West in Downsview, Ontario, which also houses its head office and warehouse.

1

In 1991 Loomis & Toles launched its first mail order catalogue in recognition of the growing craft and fine arts market. In addition, to accommodate the evolving needs of the commercial artist, the company added state-of-the-art products to support the computer technology of the 1990s.

Today, Loomis & Toles Company Limited is a multi-million dollar company with seven branches across the Maritimes, Quebec and Ontario, as well as a network of wholesalers across the country. Building on its forty-five year reputation for quality and service, Loomis & Toles maintains its role as a leader in the industry by responding to the needs of its customers and by continuing to offer a wider range of products and services to more people through more channels.

1. Paul Marshall, Product Manager from Agfa Canada Inc., demonstrates the latest in computer graphics technology to Carole-Ann Miller, President & General Manager of Loomis & Toles Company Limited, and Craig Anderson, Sales Representative.
2. The familiar Adelaide Street locations of Loomis & Toles.

2

McCarthy Milling Limited

McCarthy Milling Limited has uniquely added to the history of our province. Not only did William Lyon Mackenzie seek refuge at the site, but the mill was also one of the last turbine operated mills in Ontario.

In 1825 William J. Comfort built a dam, along with a saw and grist mill, on the Credit River below Streetsville. It was here that William Lyon MacKenzie took refuge in 1837, when escaping after the fight at Montgomery's tavern in Toronto. In 1843 several members of the Barber family bought the mill and converted it to a woollen mill. In 1852 they built a new, four story stone mill which still stands today. By the mid 1860s the mill was one of the most respected textiles companies in Canada, being the largest in the area with 100 employees and producing 1000 yards of cloth a day.

In 1916 Frederick H.B. Mercer and his Toronto Milling Company converted the mill, removing the textile machinery and installing flour milling equipment. Following several more changes of ownership, W.H. McCarthy purchased the mill, incorporating it in June 1931 as the McCarthy Milling Company Limited.

In the 1930s the mill began to

1

grind hard spring wheat for household baking and Ontario winter wheat for pastries, offering such popular brands as High Loaf, Cavalier and Planet. In 1946 the company changed hands again, being bought out by J.J. Page. In the 1960s the mill had one of the three remaining flywheel and water turbine systems in Ontario still in operation. Using water power, the mill was able to produce 1,200 one-hundred pound bags of flour a day, and employed 50 people.

C.L. Rogers, who bought control of the mill in 1960, began an ongoing modernization of the mill's equipment, increasing efficiency and capacity to remain competitive in the highly competitive modern milling industry. In May, 1974 a massive flood tore out the western

1. *"The Mill and a house in Streetsville," May 14, 1922, as photographed by John Boyd.*
2. *1877 view of the Toronto Woollen Mills, now owned by McCarthy Milling Limited. The centre two buildings remain today.*

2

embankment, leaving the dam and spillway high and dry in the middle of the river. Therefore, it was decided to convert the entire operation to electricity, and in 1975 the dam was lowered and the Credit River allowed to return to its original channel.

George Weston Limited, one of Canada's major public companies, bought McCarthy Milling Limited in June, 1972. Its ongoing concern with quality, efficiency and service to the public soon was reflected in McCarthy Milling Limited. During 1991, an agreement was reached for ADM Milling Co. of Leawood, Kansas, United States, to purchase the assets of McCarthy Milling from George Weston Limited.

McCarthy Milling Limited is also involved in community events. It helps to sponsor the local bread and honey festival annually as well as several charities. The street on which the mill is located is named after the Barber family, one of the previous owners of the milling company.

After more than a century and a half of milling grist, textile and flour, powered throughout most of its history by the Credit River, and operating continuously since 1916, McCarthy Milling Limited today manages a modern hard-wheat flour mill, serving customers throughout Ontario, Quebec and the Maritimes.

Marshall Ventilated Mattress Co. Ltd.

In 1899 James Marshall knew he had a great idea. He just wanted to sleep on it a while. Setting the future course for the mattress industry in North America and around the world, his Canadian invention, the pocket coil, became the worldwide standard for mattress construction. Today, Marshall Ventilated Mattress Co. Ltd. is still the first choice for reliability and workmanship. Its lines of mattresses, boxsprings and frames reflect the latest in design, technology, utility and fashion.

Engineer James Marshall invented the world's first spring-filled mattress in 1899. His wife had wanted a more comfortable mattress than the traditional stuffed mattress. In response, he developed the world's first innerspring mattress, also called the pocket coil. After making the inner core by hand, a massive honeycomb of pocket coils, he finished it with substantial padding and cover to create the mattress.

Marshall designed a pre-compressed coil spring sewn inside a fabric pocket, which provided uplifting support on its own. When fitted together, the coils became an independent suspension system that contoured to each person's form and provided unsurpassed comfort. Since then, consumers worldwide have benefited from Marshall's design and his legacy to future gen-

erations of bedding makers extended beyond his original patent; he also handed down a spirit of innovation that has led to advancements in innerspring mattress design ever since.

After obtaining a patent for the Marshall Pocket Coil Mattress in 1900, he began mass manufacturing of the mattress under the Marshall trade name, Regal Pocket Coil, on Lombard Street in Toronto. North America, tired of the traditional mattresses filled with wool or other materials, quickly embraced the new concept. Within less than ten years, he was licensing franchises for the production of the pocket coil mattress. To illustrate the extent of his penetration into the market, it is noteworthy that Canadian Pacific Railways began using Marshall products in all its steamship and railway lines.

Although able to convince North Americans of the merits of the new style of mattress, Europeans were more resistant. Displaying the innovation which has characterized the Marshall Company throughout its history, he convinced the famous English shipping company, The Cunard "White Star" Lines (which had its origins in the Canadian Maritimes), to use the Marshall mattress on all its cross-Atlantic voyages. Thereby, he was able eventually to introduce the Marshall mattress first into England,

and years later throughout all of Europe.

In the early 1920s, with the Canadian economy in a depression, James Marshall lost control of his company to L.A. Young Industries, originally a Toronto-based wire maker and a major supplier to Marshall Company. Although the parent company had relocated to Detroit, Michigan, it not only maintained Marshall Company in Toronto but also expanded the mattress company, adding several more production facilities.

Chrysler Corporation, which was using Marshall products in its cars, later acquired the company. When in the early 1960s Chrysler experienced financial difficulties, it sought to concentrate on its main industry, and divested itself of non-related subsidiaries such as Marshall Mattress.

Harry Warner, who previously already had substantial successful experience in the bedding industry as the owner of the Inner Spring Mattress Company, purchased Marshall Mattress in 1965. In the latter

1. *The original Marshall Pocket Coil Mattress patent, obtained by James Marshall in 1900.*
2. *A 1948 Marshall sewing room, located in the company's factory in Leaside, Ontario.*

1970s his two sons Bradley and Marc Warner joined him in the company. When their father passed away in 1981, they assumed control. In 1987 Bradley Warner and his wife, Sharan, acquired complete ownership of Marshall Mattress.

Carrying on the company's innovative tradition, Sharan and Bradley Warner have continued to enhance the operation of Marshall Ventilated Mattress Co. Ltd. The company has improved the method of handcrafted mattress making by marrying traditional techniques with modern technology and still retaining the original quality of the pocket-coil mattress design. Marshall's combined approach adds to the product's quality, its comfort and its durability.

Marshall mattresses and box springs must be constructed following a series of critical operations by skilled workers who take pride in their work. Each step in the manufacturing process is carefully scrutinized. Before any product leaves the factory, it undergoes a meticulous final examination. Only after having passed through such quality control does a mattress receive its approval for sale and accompanying warranty. A standard for the industry, the comprehensive warranty backs the integrity of the labour and materials that go into every Marshall product.

By focusing on the pocket coil mattress, the company is able to place its entire history and tradition behind its central product. Bradley Warner emphasizes that the pocket coil mattress remains the most popular type of mattress around the world. It has never grown obsolete, it is the most comfortable of all designs, and Marshall Mattress was the original producer.

With a hands-on approach to management, the Warners personally design the look and style of the company's products. Sharan Warner operates Marshall's manufacturing facility as General Manager. In addition, the Warners

work in close contact with the company's dealers.

Marshall markets its products through exclusive Canadian dealers, such as the Hudson's Bay Company, Art Shoppe, Ridpath's, Cannonball Bed Shoppes, and Smitty's Fine Furniture. Marshall Mattress also operates a growing contract bedding supply division for hotels, hospitals and institutions. Marshall mattresses can be found not only in private homes and fine hotels across Canada, but also around the world in our Canadian embassies.

Clearly, what James Marshall first slept on, millions have since

discovered. It is craft, not technology, that sets a bed apart. And it is devotion to craftsmanship that sets Marshall Ventilated Mattress Co. Ltd. apart. At its best, bedmaking is an art, and the resultant product a very personalized item to be sold. And like all art, it requires a delicate balance of aesthetics and expertise. The skilled craftsmen of Marshall have mastered this balance, a balance which has withstood the test of time.

A full page on Marshall Mattress in the April 30, 1932, edition of the Halifax Herald.

McCormick Canada Inc.

When W.J. Gorman and D.J. Dyson forged a partnership with $750 in capital and set up business in an old carpentry shop at the corner of Carling and Talbot Streets in London, Ontario in 1883, few people would have envisioned that this small company would grow into one of the major divisions of a nationwide leader in the food industry. But grow it did, and today it forms the Club House Division of McCormick Canada Inc., a company whose continuing creative responses to its markets figure largely in its success.

The Canadian operations of Club House began in London, Ontario in 1883 under the name Gorman, Dyson & Company. Its original products were coffee, turpentine, liquid ammonia and sewing machine oil; within two years, spices, extracts and baking powder were added to the product line. Partnership changes resulted in renaming the company Gorman, Eckert & Company in 1890, and the business expanded to include Spanish olives. By 1900, the company had established itself as the largest olive packer in the British empire. In 1959 Gorman, Eckert & Co. Ltd., became a subsidiary of McCormick & Company Inc., based in Baltimore, Maryland, and the world's largest seasonings and

flavourings firm. In 1969, the name was changed to Club House Foods Ltd., reflecting the major brand name, Club House.

But Club House Foods is only half the story behind McCormick Canada Inc., which was formed on June 1, 1989, through the consolidation with Stange Canada Inc. Canadian operations of Stange began as a joint-venture under the name Stange Pemberton in Toronto in 1952. Stange Co. Ltd. in the United States began in 1905 and had developed a leadership position in seasoning technology and a reputation as the "Silent Partner in Famous Foods." The new Canadian company was the first operation outside the United States. In 1963, the

Canadian division became known as Stange Canada Ltd. and business grew steadily through joint-ventures, acquisitions and an expanded customer base. The McCormick/Stange Flavour Division was formed in 1981 when McCormick & Co. purchased all Stange operations, including Stange Canada.

Today, McCormick Canada Inc. is a national leader in the spice, seasoning, flavouring and specialty food industry, with its head office in London, Ontario. It has manufacturing, sales and distribution centres in Montreal, Edmonton, Toronto, London and Calgary. The Club House Division serves retail grocery and food service customers with products such as spices, seasonings, salad dressings, sauces, gravy mixes, Spanish olives and food colourings. The Stange Division serves the fast food industry and industrial customers across Canada with custom seasonings, flavours and ingredients.

The company's versatility and willingness to adapt are easily traced throughout its history and the evolution of its products. These characteristics provide the foundation for McCormick Canada Inc. to continue as a leader in the food industry.

1. *The facilities of the Stange Division of McCormick Canada Inc. in Mississauga, Ontario.*
2. *The Club House facilities of McCormick Canada Inc. in London, Ontario.*

McIntyre & Dodd Marketing Inc.

Dedicated to providing new ideas in marketing communications, McIntyre & Dodd Marketing Inc., with headquarters in Toronto and a branch in the United Kingdom, is a diversified, innovative direct marketing company. Since its inception in 1949, the company has been committed to providing efficient and innovative ways to deliver consumer promotions. McIntyre & Dodd Marketing was responsible for successfully launching Canada's first co-op envelope, the *Carole Martin* co-op envelope and Canada's first Free Standing Coupon Insert the *Shop & Save*. Both continue to be Canada's first choice for coupon and print advertising distribution.

O.E. McIntyre, born in St. Thomas, Ontario, started the company in New York, primarily as a circulation promotion service for several large magazines, such as *Time, Life,* and *Reader's Digest*. His two sons, Randall and Angus, joined the company immediately after university and were involved with the business for their entire careers.

Angus McIntyre moved to Montreal in 1949 and launched O.E. McIntyre Ltd. in Canada. Making direct mail a serious marketing tool, McIntyre was the first in Canada to have a national database maintained by computer. The company established a position of leadership very early in its forma-

tion by successfully generating extensive mailings through computerized database management.

By 1964 the company had expanded to Toronto and had become a fully autonomous company, independent of its American counterpart. During that time, O.E. McIntyre began its order fulfilment service. Major book clubs began to entrust their order fulfilment requirements to O.E. McIntyre. This grew to become the largest book fulfilment service in Canada. Subsequently, the services expanded to include other audio visual products such as records, cassettes and videos.

O.E. McIntyre introduced Canada to the co-op direct mail envelope in 1973. The *Carole Martin* co-op envelope made direct mail, a traditionally expensive means of communication, practical and efficient by combining messages of many advertisers in a single envelope, thereby sharing the cost of distribution. The first two participants in the envelope are, in fact, clients still today.

The Carole Martin program has grown to the point that now more than thirty million co-op envelopes are distributed across Canada each year. The integral contents of the co-op envelope include packaged goods coupons and samples, mail order merchandise offers, and direct response offers for magazine subscriptions and catalogues.

The name Carole Martin is also associated with a line of gifts, clothing, and houseware products that are sold directly to the consumer through the mail.

In 1978 Bill Dodd joined O.E. McIntyre in Toronto to head "McIntyre & Dodd Marketing," initially a division of O.E. McIntyre. Bill Dodd was responsible for the introduction of the first Canadian Free Standing Coupon Insert, *Shop & Save*, a media success story in itself. Launched in 1980, it has since proven to be the most commonly used method of coupon distribution. Filled with coupons and consumer offers, over thirty-five million *Shop & Save* inserts are delivered via newspaper annually.

In 1985 the company head office moved from Montreal to Toronto and subsequently changed its name to McIntyre & Dodd Marketing Inc., when Bill Dodd became a major shareholder.

With a history of growth in the dynamic field of direct marketing in Canada, the McIntyre & Dodd team of professionals have an in-depth understanding of couponing and promotional advertising. Today, the entire production process, including concept, creative, colour separations, print, and distribution is all done under one roof. As Canada's largest promotional marketing company, McIntyre & Dodd Marketing Inc. can look forward to a future of global opportunities.

1. *O.E. McIntyre, the founder of McIntyre & Dodd Marketing Inc.*
2. *Bill Dodd, Chairman and Chief Executive Officer.*
3. *Angus McIntyre, Vice Chairman.*

The Metropolitan Toronto and Region Conservation Authority

Exemplifying the accomplishments that can be achieved through a provincial and municipal partnership, The Metropolitan Toronto and Region Conservation Authority, since its formation in 1957, has carried out a comprehensive program of water management to prevent loss of life and promote conservation land management. The Authority's jurisdiction covers the watershed of nine river systems, from their headwaters to Lake Ontario, and from Mississauga and Brampton east to Ajax and Uxbridge.

The Authority, with one-third of Ontario's population within its area, acts in the community's interest through advocating and implementing watershed management programs that: maintain and improve the quality of the region's lands and waters; contribute to public safety from flooding and erosion; provide for the acquisition of conservation and hazard lands; and enhance the quality and variety of life in the community by using its lands for inter-regional outdoor recreation, heritage preservation and conservation education.

The Conservation Authorities Act, passed in 1946, provided the means by which the Province of Ontario and the municipalities on Ontario watersheds could join together as a conservation authority to undertake

1

programs for natural resource management. In 1957 four existing Conservation Authorities, Etobicoke-Mimico, Humber, Don, and Rouge-Duffin-Highland-Petticoat, agreed to the establishment of one central authority, The Metropolitan Toronto and Region Conservation Authority.

The impetus for co-operation was the disastrous flood following Hurricane Hazel in October 1954, which dramatized the devastating effects of floods. This disaster, combined with postwar urbanization and the formation of The Municipality of Metropolitan Toronto, led the province and the municipalities to determine that the public would be better served with one conservation authority having jurisdiction over the entire regional watershed.

The new Authority had jurisdiction over nine river systems and covered more than 2,500 square kilometres, an area inhabited by more than a tenth of Canada's population. The backbone of the Authority's program was flood control and water management, just as it is today.

Through the development of a sound flood control and water management system, the Authority was able to substantially reduce the effects of flooding and erosion. At the same time, it could pursue its policy of creating conservation areas for public use on lands acquired for flood control and water conservation. Hand in hand with this activity was the growth of outdoor conservation education programs embracing both student and adult learning, reforestation, fish and wildlife conservation, land management and historic sites preservation.

The early achievements of the Authority were little short of spectacular. Accomplishments were realized in every aspect of the conservation of renewable natural resources. Major flood control projects were undertaken. A modern flood warning system was established. Conservation areas became an important part of community life, as established areas such as Heart Lake, Boyd and

1. Flood control is at the heart of the Authority's work.
2. Conservation areas provide for active and passive recreation.

2

Albion Hills were further developed and new ones were opened. The importance of reforestation to the overall conservation effort remained a prime consideration of the Authority. Fish and wildlife conservation programs were given high priority.

The Authority's Historic Sites Advisory Board, in an effort to involve the public, planned and built several facilities. Perhaps best known to the general public of all the Authority projects, Black Creek Pioneer Village, officially opened in 1967. The nineteenth century crossroads village boasted seventeen authentic buildings in a living community that became a major tourist attraction.

In 1961 The Metropolitan Toronto and Region Conservation Foundation was created. Known today as The Conservation Foundation of Greater Toronto, it gives opportunities for other foundations, businesses, industry and individuals to participate directly in conservation work through donations of money and property. The efforts of the Foundation have had a profound effect on the capability of the Authority to provide benefits for the people of the region and to attain its conservation goals.

In 1970 the Authority accepted the challenge of implementing the Metropolitan Toronto and Region Waterfront Development Plan. The Plan had as its goal the creation of a handsome waterfront along Lake Ontario, providing access and water-oriented recreational opportunities to the public. The first major facilities developed as a result of the plan were Petticoat Creek Conservation Area and Bluffers Park, both of which opened in 1975.

The other work of the Authority has also continued, including the construction of flood control dams, such as the G. Ross Lord dam on the Don River in northwest Metropolitan Toronto. By the beginning of 1977, the Authority had acquired in excess of 10,000 hectares of land and fourteen Conservation Areas had been opened.

In 1988, the Authority was the first agency in Canada to make the conservation of greenspace its goal and to develop objectives to attain that goal. Since then, conservation of greenspace has become the focus of much public attention. Greenspace comprises the headwaters of the rivers, the river valleys and the Lakefront. It is important because it allows the land to perform its natural functions, while providing people with the opportunity to experience and enjoy the natural environment.

The Authority's conservation vision for the twenty-first century is outlined in a document entitled The Greenspace Strategy for the Greater Toronto Region. It urges greater co-operation between the Authority, the province and the municipalities in managing the regional watershed. It also advocates protection of the watershed's headwaters in the Oak Ridges Moraine Complex through proper land planning, land acquisition and private land stewardship. Under the Strategy, the Authority will continue to create more public access to the Lake Ontario shoreline and establish environmentally compatible recreational facilities in the conservation areas.

Today, with the support of the province and the member municipalities, including The Municipality of Metropolitan Toronto, the Regional Municipalities of Durham, Peel, and York, and the Townships of Adjala and Mono, The Metropolitan Toronto and Region Conservation Authority continues its work of resource management, waterfront planning, water management, heritage and conservation education and the creation of recreational facilities.

The residents of Metropolitan Toronto region may well take pride in the accomplishments of their Conservation Authority over the past years. With an impressive number of tangible accomplishments, and a new public awareness of the need for and the meaning of resource management, one has only to look back at what was done yesterday for the possibilities of resource management in the future.

1. *In the spring of 1990 the Boy Scouts of Canada planted 40,000 trees on Authority property.*
2. *Black Creek Pioneer Village, officially opened in 1967, had its beginnings as a pioneer program in 1954 with The Humber Valley Conservation Authority.*

1

2

Morganite Canada Corporation

From the nosecones of rockets to the small carbon brushes of electrical motors; from foundry furnaces to the substrates needed in the manufacture of computer boards, Morganite Canada Corporation, the largest supplier of carbon and ceramic products in Canada, provides Canadian industry with the specialized products that it requires. Although the company began in 1942, it was recently restructured, and now Morganite Canada Corporation is the holding company for three subsidiaries: National Electrical Carbon Canada, Morganite Thermal Ceramics, and Thermal Ceramics, each with its head office located in the greater Toronto area.

Their customers come from a diverse range of companies. Steel mills, the pulp and paper industry, non-ferrous casting foundries, the Canadian Mint, furnace and heat-treating customers, and transit authorities across Canada are all supplied by Morganite Canada. Each subsidiary of Morganite Canada manufactures specialized products. National Electrical Carbon Canada produces carbon and related technical ceramics materials and components for electrical and mechanical applications. Morganite Thermal Ceramics supplies its customers with furnaces, crucibles and accessories for the non-ferrous metal industry. Thermal Ceramics manufactures ceramic fibre refractory insulating materials for iron, steel, non-ferrous metals, petrochemical and fire insulating applications, in the form of bulk fibre, blanket and vacuum formed shapes and insulating firebrick.

On a global scale, Morganite Canada belongs to the Morgan Group of companies. The Morgan Group spans the world with over 140 companies operating in 35 countries and selling into over 124 countries. It is comprised of five divisions: carbon, technical ceramics, thermal ceramics, specialty chemicals, and electronics, the first three of which are represented in Canada. Its products are found in a diverse range of applications, such as in space satellites, oil drilling rigs, nuclear particle accelerators, artificial hip joints, telecommunications equipment, the transportation industry and household appliances.

From its worldwide head office in Windsor, Great Britain, the Morgan Group operates a very decentralized management structure. The individual companies have a high degree of independence and the accountability for performance is within each country. Although worldwide it has more than 11,000 employees, each individual company will range from 100 to approximately 500 people, with much emphasis placed on hiring nationals. Its research and development is centrally located in the United Kingdom at Morgan Materials Technology Limited, but its effects are felt in each of the companies, including in Morganite Canada Corporation, resulting in new

1

and innovative products being produced.

Because there are few industries or markets in which Morgan products do not make a significant contribution, the opportunities for growth have never been greater. With its main objective to maximize customer satisfaction, Morganite Canada Corporation is a company for now and the future, with materials and products which will help revolutionize tomorrow.

1. *The Executive Board Members of Morganite Canada Corporation; from left to right, W.E. Macfarlane, J.A. Stewart, D.J. McFadden and centre front is D.S. Kahle.* **Below:** *Products from the five divisions that comprise the Morgan Group;* **2.** *Special purpose foundryware;* **3.** *Carbon current collectors for electric traction units;* **4.** *Flexible printed circuits for military and commercial applications;* **5.** *A selection of ceramic components for thermal, mechanical and electrical applications;* **6.** *A selection of Morgan's automotive chemicals.*

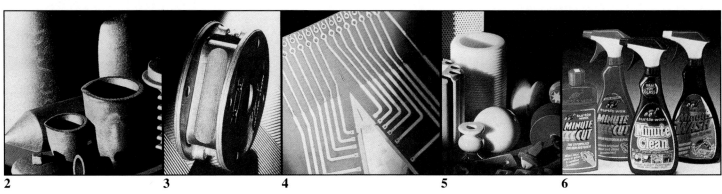

2 3 4 5 6

MTI Canada Ltd.

MTI Canada Ltd. is the Canadian sales and service facility for the Mitutoyo Corporation of Japan, the largest manufacturer of precision measurement and calibration instruments in the world.

Mitutoyo was originally founded in 1934 by Yehan Numata, principally as a means to provide funds to further the teaching of the Buddhist religion. He chose to pioneer the production of micrometers in Japan, and, two years later, he succeeded. Sales were slow at first, but after surviving World War Two, the company began a rapid pattern of growth. From its humble beginnings as a small shop producing the first Japanese micrometers, Mitutoyo at present comprises a network of twenty-seven facilities incorporating research and development, manufacturing, sales, and technical service, located in Japan and seventeen other nations; plus a vast framework of distributors in more than eighty different countries throughout the world.

The "Mitu" of Mitutoyo stands for three, and the "Toyo" signifies abundance, based on the ideals of becoming a perfect man, successful in business, and contributing to world peace. The corporate motto is "Good Environment — Good People — Good Techniques."

MTI Canada formally came into existence in October, 1973, and opened for business in rented space in Montreal on January 1, 1974, under the leadership of Shigeru Yamamoto, President. A distribution network was established throughout Canada, to promote the sale of a wide range of instruments for linear dimensional measurement, including micrometers, calipers, dial indicators, gauge blocks, optical gauging equipment and many other gauges.

As business expanded, so did the need for office and warehouse space. In 1978 MTI Canada began the construction of its first building in Mississauga, Ontario. In 1982 the building was enlarged, and in 1988 a second building was erected, also in Mississauga, and is the present site of the main office, warehouse, and principal Metrology Centre for MTI Canada. Satellite offices and metrology centres are also located in Montreal and Vancouver.

From an initial five or six employees, MTI Canada staff now number a total of sixty-eight. The product line has also expanded to include laser, circular geometry, surface finish and coordinate measurement systems, with ancillary computers and software. Over the years, many digimatic gauges and data processors were developed to meet the needs of industry's statistical process control requirements. It is anticipated that, in the near future, the original building will become the location for the manufacture of Mitutoyo optical gauging equipment.

As the demand for quality processing becomes increasingly strident and urgent, MTI Canada has devoted itself to the marketing of precision measuring instruments. And in keeping with the founder's dream of furthering the teaching of Buddhism, the company has

1

recently established a Numata Chair at the University of Toronto, Mississauga Campus.

The company aims to remain a leader in the development and manufacturing of precision measuring and calibration instruments designed to meet or exceed the demands of industry around the world; however, as Noel Ryan, President and C.E.O. of MTI Canada comments, "the company's ultimate measurement is customer satisfaction."

1. The MTI Canada team. 2. The central offices, warehouse and principal Metrology Centre of MTI Canada.

2

Motorola Canada Limited

One of the world's leading providers of two way radio communication, electronic equipment, systems, components and service for worldwide markets, Motorola Inc. is a diversified, technology company. Its history is one of strong and consistent growth. Since the development of the first commercially manufactured car radio in 1930, the name Motorola has been synonymous with electronics leadership, particulary in the field of communications. Fifty years later, the company maintains that leadership position, no where more so than in Canada as Motorola Canada Limited.

Underlying the corporate belief that quality and innovative products help to create a better world, is Motorola's legacy of technological achievements which have truly improved modern times. Although most widely known for its communications technology such as two-way radios, pagers, cellular

telephones and systems, which is, in fact, the largest segment of Motorola Canada Limited, Motorola's product range also includes semi-conductors, aerospace electronics, automotive and industrial electronics equipment, computers, data communications, and information processing and handling equipment.

Among Motorola's innovative contributions to the electronic industry are the first commercially manufactured car radio in 1930; the first hand-carried portable FM transceiver in 1942; the first two way radio equipment for Earth-Mars communication in 1964; and the first cellular hand-held portable telephone demonstration in 1973 — to name only a few of its significant "firsts."

Motorola Inc., based in Schaumburg, near Chicago, Illinois, first entered the Canadian market in 1944 by distributing mobile radio sets on a franchise basis through a

Canadian based company, Rogers Majestic, which was licensed to build and sell Motorola products. To more effectively market and ultimately to manufacture Motorola products, The Canadian Motorola Electronics Company was established in 1957 as a licensee operation with its head office in Toronto and sales offices in Montreal, Winnipeg, Edmonton and Vancouver.

The person Motorola chose to launch and head up the Canadian company was Reginald McLaren Brophy, who had both fostered and served the electronics industry for over fifty years prior to his appointment as President of the company. Canadian Motorola was Brophy's fifth successful career. Brophy had served two other electronics companies in Canada and the National Broadcasting Corporation in New York, in addition to his career as a Canadian public servant. Known across Canada as a radio pioneer, he had also been President of the Radio Manufacturers Association of Canada. He realized that electronics was "our technology which the future will use to achieve new knowledge, new experience, new affluence and perhaps even wisdom beyond today's imagination."

Brophy organized Canadian Motorola during the latter months of 1957 to manufacture, market and service Motorola industrial and commercial products and systems in Canada. The manufacture of some lines of two-way radios in Canada first began in 1959. Full production was accomplished by 1960.

During his ten years as President, Brophy oversaw the company as it grew from fifty-seven people to 500, increased the volume of equipment sold tenfold, and moved into the new facility at Steeles and

Reginald McLaren Brophy, 1902-1971. Known across Canada as a radio pioneer, he both fostered and served the electronics industry, and was Motorola Canada Limited's first President, beginning the Canadian operations in 1957.

Woodbine Avenues in Willowdale. A wide range of new Motorola products were introduced, and Canadian Motorola became entrenched as the acknowledged leader in its major field, the design and manufacture of VHF and UHF communications. By 1967, Canadian Motorola was filling more of Canada's communication needs than all of its competitors combined.

In 1969 the company name was changed to Motorola Canada Limited, and has since continued to expand. Motorola Canada has also grown through the acquisition of other companies. One recent addition to the Motorola family was MDI, Mobile Data International, of Richmond, B.C., which expanded Motorola's involvement in two-way radio data communications.

In 1988 the Communications Division of Motorola Canada was proud to be the official sponsor of radio communication for the XV Olympic winter games in Calgary, Alberta. In its sponsorship role, Motorola designed and supplied an extensive two-way radio communications system for inter-venue and intra-venue operations.

Although it is a wholly-owned subsidiary of Motorola Inc. in the United States, Motorola Canada Limited is largely autonomous and strongly nationalistic, providing Canadians with opportunities to learn, to train and to practice their professions in a highly-technical environment. With an extremely high ratio of skilled workers, Motorola is dependent on the intellectual resources of its people and the loyalty of its dealer network. It believes that its people are the key to quality and productivity, so people come first at Motorola.

The company has also a strong history of community involvement, from monetary and equipment donations to local health and charitable organizations, to technical support for special events such as the 1984 historical visits of Pope

1

John Paul II and Queen Elizabeth II. The Reginald M. Brophy Scholarship underlines Motorola's dedication to higher learning by providing a university scholarship to qualifying children of company employees.

The divisional structure of Motorola Canada allows the company to focus its resources on its customers, ensuring that the organization remains flexible and responsive. Few companies the size of Motorola Canada can claim so few management layers between the customer and senior management. The divisions share information and resources, taking advantage of access to the wealth of Motorola research and development, technologies, manufacturing and marketing expertise that reside in other areas of the company. In

1. On January 15, 1987, the Motorola corporation embarked on a worldwide program to achieve the level of quality known as Six Sigma, a statistical term which represents a 99.9997 per cent perfect product. In recognition of its achievements, Motorola was awarded the first Malcom Baldrige National Quality Award in 1988 by United States President Ronald Reagan.
2. Motorola Canada Limited's head offices in North York, Ontario.

total, the seven divisions have more than 2,500 employees in Canada.

Viewing quality, innovation and responsive customer service as the three cornerstones of its success, Motorola Canada Limited has become a leader in people, in ideas, and in technology. In the future, Motorola Canada will continue to grow as a leader as it has grown in the past, with single mindedness and vision, entrepreneurship and corporate strategy, and, above all, dedication to quality, technology, and its valued customers.

2

National Frontier Insurance Company

Although many said it was impossible, a small insurer operating out of North Bay in Northern Ontario has not only survived but has actually flourished. Developing not out of a desire to own or build an insurance empire, but rather to fill a need, the initial objective of Northern Frontier General Insurance Company (later to become National Frontier Insurance Company) was simple and modest: to provide a stable and competitive market for members of the Northern Ontario Tourist Outfitters Association. National Frontier has since grown into an all lines insurer serving brokers across Ontario.

In the mid 1970s, most insurance companies were reluctant to insure the hundreds of remote fishing and hunting establishments dotting the wilderness of Northern Ontario. The Northern Ontario Tourist Outfitters Association was asked to find a solution to its members' insurance problems.

In 1979 a prospectus for a new insurance company was prepared and sent to the Association's 800 members. Within three months, over one million dollars of share capital had been subscribed by 150 shareholders from Northern Ontario.

Northern Frontier General Insurance Company was incorporated in June, 1979, and received its license in October of that same year, the first insurer to be licensed in Ontario in over twenty years, and the first stock insurance company with a head office in Northern Ontario.

The young company was able to capitalize early on two market niches, one geographic and one a product niche. "As the only regional company, we immediately had the loyalty and support of Northern Ontario brokers," points out David Liddle, the company's first President. "Our connection with the tourism industry allowed us to develop a profitable commercial portfolio at a time when other companies openly ridiculed us for writing such 'risky' business."

In those early years Northern Frontier grew by developing personal relationships with its brokers and by emphasizing its flexibility, its northern perspective and knowledge, and its commitment to superior service. The company's premium volume, $1.6 million in 1980, more than doubled in 1981 and had more than tripled by 1982. In 1983, it hit $8.6 million.

The early 1980s were unfavourable years for acquiring the equity financing required for further growth, so the original shareholders agreed that the best strategy for the future of the company would be to sell to a larger institution with a broader financial base. In March, 1985, Northern Frontier was acquired by the Optimum Group, a Canadian firm of actuaries headed by Gilles Blondeau and Henri Joli-Coeur. Northern Frontier fitted perfectly into the Optimum Group's mission of developing a national network of regional companies, each capitalizing on local strengths but benefitting from the actuarial, reinsurance and financial resources of the parent company.

In 1989 the operation of Upper Canada Insurance Company, a sister company, was merged with Northern Frontier, resulting in the addition of a Toronto office and a mandate to write commercial business in the Golden Horseshoe region of Ontario. In 1990 the name was changed to National Frontier Insurance Company, reflecting a new beginning for the enlarged corporation, as well as its affiliation to National Insurance Group, the general insurance arm of the Optimum Group.

In its second decade, National Frontier Insurance Company now provides all lines insurance protection, and serves approximately 150 insurance brokers across Ontario. With a staff of sixty and annual premiums of $23 million, National Frontier will continue to grow and prosper in the Ontario marketplace.

David Liddle, Vice President and Chief Operating Officer of National Frontier Insurance Company, alongside the company's original name and logo.

NCS Diagnostics Inc.

1

NCS Diagnostics has just marked its tenth anniversary. As a manufacturer and distributor of products for use in medical and clinical laboratories NCS Diagnostics, once a small, unknown company, competing for a position among corporate giants in the health care industry, is now a company with a respected name in the field, its products to be found in laboratories throughout the world.

Walter Schmidt, President and founder of the company, has brought the new organization to the fore in the industry. Through vision, optimism, and sheer tenacious energy, he has led his team through almost insurmountable obstacles to its position today.

When Schmidt founded NCS Diagnostics in 1980, most medical diagnostic products were manufactured in the United States and the United Kingdom. His intent was to develop a company that would produce Canadian products in the medical diagnostic field that contained some level of uniqueness.

Research and development — the key to success and backbone of the company has enabled NCS to introduce many unique and innovative products represented by Canadian, U.S. and international patents which are proudly displayed in the NCS Boardroom. The company also interfaces between the academic and industrial sides of the medical industry, utilizing the information gained to develop new product offerings.

NCS is a leader in the development and manufacture of microtransport systems. These unique products, under the trade name of KultSure, are used to collect human specimens for transport to a laboratory for testing. The specially designed containers, filled with one of several types of media, form a transport system that will not only ensure the integrity of the specimen, but also protect the safety of laboratory personnel who receive and test potentially hazardous material. New collection and transport systems have been recently introduced which offer patented media and containers that now can provide transportation of micro-organisms that previously have been considered too fragile to exist outside the body and would have been very difficult to transport to a laboratory for testing.

NCS also manufactures a comprehensive line of serology screening tests for infectious diseases such as Syphilis, Mononucleosis, Rheumatoid Arthritis, Strep, Staph, and Lupus, to name a few.

In addition to its own manufactured products, NCS offers many which are sourced from recognized international companies and marketed in Canada by the NCS' team of sales professionals, all of whom are highly trained Registered Technologists.

The NCS head office, with fifty employees, is located in Mississauga and houses in a 25,000 square feet facility, administrative offices, sales and marketing. Research and development, quality control and manufacturing operate from a fully equipped laboratory and clean room. The warehouse/distribution area provides a refrigeration capacity of 5000 cubic feet of storage.

A wholly owned subsidiary, NCS Diagnostics Corporation, is located in Niagara Falls, New York, employing six people. Providing a centre for assembly/manufacturing/distribution servicing the United States and destinations throughout the world.

Schmidt states that the goal of NCS Diagnostics is to become the first choice supplier to the medical diagnostic marketplace. This goal is well on its way to being achieved by providing state-of-the-art NCS brand products, together with complimentary niche products sourced from high tech manufacturers with whom NCS works very closely not only in distribution but development and improvement of products, adapting their suitability to meet Canadian market needs.

1. *F. Walter Schmidt, President; founded NCS Diagnostics in 1980.*
2. *Walter Schmidt and the NCS Research and Development Team.*

2

The Ontario Cancer Institute / Princess Margaret Hospital

With its discoveries and programs influencing cancer research and patient care around the world, the Ontario Cancer Institute/Princess Margaret Hospital has been a world leader in many key areas of clinical and basic cancer research for more than thirty years. The contribution of the staff to the understanding, diagnosis and treatment of cancer is extensive. These developments are the result of a belief that clinical and scientific staff should work together to understand the basic processes of carcinogenesis, to develop new ways of treating cancer, and to provide the best care possible for patients and their families.

When the Hospital opened in 1958, the Honourable Leslie M. Frost, Q.C., then Premier of Ontario, said: "It will combine under one roof both research and clinical approaches to the problem of cancer. The investigator and the therapist will be constantly aware of each other's activities and problems. They will work together to their very considerable mutual advantage . . . .. This institute is a hospital of hope."

Since the doors opened, clinical staff have focused on diagnosing cancer, and caring for patients using radiation therapy, chemotherapy and hormonal therapy. In the research divisions, OCI/PMH scientists have been leaders in cell and molecular biology, immunology, radiobiology, imaging and almost all key areas of biological research.

Through the unique collaboration among professionals in clinical and research disciplines, new treatments, plus new equipment for diagnosing and treating patients, have been developed. The following are but a few highlights to

give a sense of the broad scope of the achievements in biology, physics, treatment, diagnosis and education.

Research in the 1960s by Dr. E.A. McCulloch and Dr. J. Till on the origin of blood cells provided definitive evidence that one pluripotential stem cell gives rise to all blood cells. The special quantitative spleen colony assay developed at the Ontario Cancer Institute was an international breakthrough that led to studies not possible before. It has led to studies and understanding of diseases such as leukemia and other blood disorders.

Some of the initial studies establishing that Hodgkin's Disease can be cured by radiation therapy were performed at OCI/PMH by Dr. Vera Peters in the 1960s. The con-

cepts developed remain the basis of international treatment approaches.

In the 1980s the receptor on human T lymphocytes was cloned for the first time by Dr. Tak Mak in an OCI/PMH research laboratory. This critical breakthrough in immunology research has had, and will continue to have, a major impact on immunology research around the world.

The Clinical Physics Division pioneered the use of computers in radiation therapy planning and developed techniques which have influenced planning throughout the world. Preservation of the voice through radiation therapy was pioneered at OCI/PMH. The pathology and research staff made important contributions to the international classification standards for

*The new OCI/PMH will be the core of an extensive and comprehensive cancer care system with an environment and infrastructure that promote the integration of clinical and research staff to develop new approaches to diagnosis and treatment.
The front view of a model of the new OCI/PMH is pictured here.*

Hodgkin's and non-Hodgkin's lymphomas. Discovery of a regulatory difference between normal and leukemic stem cells in the 1960s began a new physiological understanding of chemotherapy.

In the 1980s, one mechanism for the apparent ability of tumour cells to become resistant to drugs was elucidated. This discovery by Dr. Victor Ling has opened the door for numerous studies at OCI/PMH and laboratories around the world into ways to overcome this common clinical problem.

The first bone marrow transplant unit in Canada now performs more than fifty bone marrow transplants every year for patients with acute myeloblastic leukemia and aplastic anaemia.

Since the OCI/PMH opened, staff have played a pivotal role in the development of new radiation therapy machines and improvements on previous designs. Special teaching programs for patients receiving different types of

The back view of a model of the new OCI/PMH, which is scheduled to open in 1995.

treatment have been developed by staff in many departments. These programs are an integral part of their treatment and allow many patients to continue their treatment and recovery at home.

The OCI/PMH is also the largest centre in Canada for training radiation and medical oncologists. The research divisions, in conjunction with the University of Toronto, established a graduate student program in 1959, the Department of Medical Biophysics, based at OCI/PMH. The School for Radiation Therapy is also a leading Canadian centre for training radiation therapy technologists. Graduates of all these programs are now staffing hospitals and research centres around the world. They have been influential in developing and setting standards of care across the country.

A new pathology laboratory that provides diagnostic tests on the leading edge of research was opened in late 1988. The Interface

Lab will be used by pathologists to do more refined cancer studies, and by clinicians and basic researchers to evaluate new discoveries related to cancer and its control.

Through the years OCI/PMH staff have received many international awards and honours for excellence in patient care and research. For example, five staff have won Gairdner Awards; and the Gold Medal from the American Society of Therapeutic Radiology and Oncology has been awarded to PMH physicians three times. In 1991, Dr. Victor Ling won the highly prestigious General Motors Kettering Prize and the Dr. Josef Steiner Award, and in doing so became the first Canadian to win either of these international awards for cancer research.

During 1995 the new OCI/PMH will open its doors on University Avenue. When those doors open, it will reveal much more than just a new building. It will reveal a centre which will be the heart and core of an extensive and comprehensive cancer care system with an environment and infrastructure that promote the integration of clinical and research staff to develop new approaches to diagnosis and treatment. A unique linkage and integration with the provincial cancer centres will allow OCI/PMH to reach out to patients across Ontario. Also, at several levels the OCI/PMH and Mt. Sinai Hospital will be physically linked to facilitate mutual access to equipment and integration for programs that will be shared by the two centres.

Although it will be a new hospital in a new location, the commitment to patient care, teaching, and to leadership in research are values and traditions that will be carried into the future — a future which has its foundations in the achievements of the past, which gains its foresight from the dedicated and enlightened staff of the present, and is inspired by the new challenges that still lie ahead.

Ontario New Home Warranty Program

The only mandatory new home warranty program in Canada, and one of only a few such programs in the world, the Ontario New Home Warranty program provides new home buyers in Ontario with substantial warranty protection. A non-profit corporation, it administers the Ontario New Home Warranties Plan Act by registering builders, enroling new homes and resolving disputes between the builder and buyer.

The Program had its beginnings in 1972, when the industry group, the Housing and Urban Development Association of Canada, responded to a growing public concern over the quality of new homes. The Association met with representatives of the federal government, provincial governments and consumer groups that were lobbying both the industry and the governments. They all agreed that each province would establish a warranty program. That original industry program became the seed of what now exists today in Ontario.

In 1976 the provincial government passed the Ontario New Home Warranties Plan Act, making the voluntary warranty program in Ontario mandatory, and the industry's warranty arm was named to administer it. Since then, the Association has been renamed the Canadian Home Builder's Association, and the program was renamed the Ontario

New Home Warranty Program.

Managed by a Board of Directors that includes representation from the building industry, mortgage insurers, mortgage lenders, the provincial government, the housing industry, the Consumer's Association of Canada and from municipalities, the Program provides a balanced approach to the administration of the Act: to protect consumers' interests while encouraging a healthy industry through technical support and assistance to builders. Reporting annually to the Ontario Legislature, the Program works to make certain that all builders register with the Program and enrol the new homes that they offer for sale, as required by the Act.

With offices across Ontario, the Program provides information about builders and home buying to consumers. Its major publication directed at potential new home buyers, *Home Buyer's Guide to After Sales Service*, is an annual guidebook which lists every registered builder and includes ratings of the after-sales service of many of them. It also publishes a quarterly newsletter called *The Link*, dealing with warranty issues and customer service tips. In addition, training for the homebuilding industry is provided through technical publications, videos, seminars and workshops which teach good construction practice and better purchaser relations.

The Program is paid for by the fees that builders and vendors pay to register with the Program and to enrol the new homes that they sell. The basic warranty protection that the Program provides is for one year for most items, such as defects in workmanship and materials, two years for some items, such as electrical, plumbing and heating, and seven years for major structural defects. If the builder does not correct the problems, the Program will help resolve the dispute.

1

From the commencement of operations in 1976, the emphasis has been on resolving home buyer's complaints and paying claims. Currently, the emphasis is being redirected to work more closely with builders encouraging the prevention of defects, while continuing in the role of conciliator when disputes arise.

Although the techniques and procedures will change somewhat, the goal remains the same — to continue to provide Ontario's new home buyers with the most comprehensive warranty protection in the world.

1. *Ernest W. Assaly, Founding Chairman of the Ontario New Home Warranty Program.* 2. *Reginald T. Ryan, Chairman of the Program's Board of Directors.*
3. *J.B.S. Rose, President and Registrar of the Program.*

2

3

O-Two Systems International Inc.

The first sign of trouble was at 8:15 a.m., September 26, 1990, when a boy collapsed in the school gymnasium. Shortly thereafter, others complained of nausea, headaches and dizziness. Soon, the front lawn of Glenhaven Senior Public School in Mississauga was turned into a makeshift hospital, with firefighters and ambulance staff treating students and staff members for suspected carbon monoxide poisoning before sending them to area hospitals. Much of the equipment that the emergency personnel used, such as the oxygen and resuscitator kits, was manufactured by O-Two Systems International Inc. Specializing in pre-hospital emergency equipment, O-Two Systems produces over 1000 products, including oxygen therapy equipment, first aid supplies and kits, eye, head, face and hand protection, stretchers, breathing and resuscitation apparatus, ambulance, rescue and firefighting supplies, and diagnostic and monitoring equipment.

O-Two Systems began in 1971 when Steve Flynn, a respiratory therapist at the Henderson Hospital in Hamilton, saw the need for a better resuscitation valve. Deciding that a better product was possible, he started to make an improved resuscitation device and soon launched the Flynn valve. This same valve, with some slight modifications, is still in use today and was used at the Glenhaven Senior Public School emergency.

Joe Lassaline owner of the company since 1982, expanded the manufacturing and the distribution of O-Two products. Currently, O-Two Systems has offices in Mississauga, Calgary, Vancouver and Halifax, although all the manufacturing occurs in Mississauga. sixty per cent of its sales are outside of Canada, with the largest portion sold in the United States.

O-Two Systems' products can be found, among other places, in hospitals, emergency services and the military. Each fire department and ambulance in Ontario carries some of O-Two System's products. Both the Canadian and American military are important customers of O-Two Systems, taking the company's products on their missions, including to the Middle East during the Iraq-Kuwait crisis.

O-Two Systems International Inc. also concentrates on research and development. One new and innovative product is a unique, patented, one step primary burn management/heat stress relieving fire protection kit which contains a dressing that is self-cooling, non-adhering, and designed to be used on all types of burns. It can also extinguish small fires. The company hopes to see products such as these and others marketed through department stores for household use.

With its unique devices helping to provide life-saving care in twenty-six countries around the world, O-Two Systems International Inc. continues to grow and expand, always improving its product line. As long as there are medical emergencies, there will be a need of O-Two Systems International Inc.'s products.

Carbon Monoxide poisoning at Glenhaven Senior Public School, September 26, 1990.
1. *Firefighters and ambulance personnel use oxygen kits manufactured by O-Two Systems to treat the students and staff.*
2. *A grade 7 student receiving oxygen from a fellow student using the Flynn Valve-Mask Resuscitator, manufactured by O-Two Systems.*

1

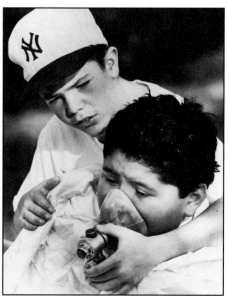

2

Patons & Baldwins Canada Inc.

The craft of handknitting can be traced back in history for over 2,000 years. In Canada, knitting has become a genuine folk art with a truly practical purpose — providing clothing that fill our needs of warmth and style. Patons & Baldwins Canada Inc. has filled the needs of Canadian knitters throughout this century, supplying yarn, ideas and pattern books.

James Baldwin of Halifax, England, and John Paton of Alloa, Scotland, never met one another. In their own lifetimes, and through three generations of both families, they were the greatest of commercial rivals. They built two empires that competed with one another in Britain's developing textile industry.

Baldwin established a wool washing and cloth fulling concern, expanding it later to include carding, dyeing and worsted spinning operations. Paton founded his Scottish firm in 1813, a machine spinning operation that was later expanded to include a dye works. Both became large firms and expanded quickly throughout the century, their growth fuelled by the great resurgence of knitting as a leisure-time pursuit in Victorian England.

Even before their merger in 1920, both countries had interest in the Canadian market. John Paton, Son & Co., had a warehouse in Montreal and a general agency in Vancouver. It also had an active business selling yarn through the Eaton's catalogue, which dated from the turn of the century. Baldwins also had a clientele in the overseas market, including in the Dominions.

The new company quickly turned its eyes towards Canada, where knitting had been introduced by the early French and British settlers needing substantial clothing against the harsh winter climate. Patons & Baldwins selected Vancouver for its base of operations, but because of Vancouver's distance from other major Canadian population centres, the company soon began to look for a more centrally-located base. In 1928 it acquired Aked and Company Ltd., a firm that had been producing fancy handknitting yarns in its Toronto factory since 1918.

By 1931 the demand for Patons & Baldwins' products necessitated larger premises, and a new Toronto mill was constructed which the company still occupies today. The isolation of the mill was a matter of concern, being located in the countryside, but today the site is considered to be almost downtown Toronto.

Patons & Baldwins Canada was incorporated in 1963. Although it continues to sell some of its British yarns here today, the greatest part of its business and continuing success now comes from producing quality yarns and patterns for Canadians. Patons & Baldwins Canada Inc.'s finely tuned design department knows how to capture the Canadian imagination, and the company's products have made an indelible impression on the minds and memories of Canadian knitters.

1

1. Jock White, President of Patons & Baldwins Canada Inc., 1968-1989, receiving, on behalf of the company, the Towers' 1988 Supplier of the Year award. 2. The Toronto mill of Patons & Baldwins, built in 1931, where the company is still located today. When the mill was built in 1931, concern was expressed over its rural location; today, the site is close to Toronto's downtown district.

2

Plaza Fiberglass Manufacturing Ltd.

The success story of Plaza Fiberglass was an inspiring history of one individual and the people who worked with him — people who were both inspired and trained by him in the field of fiberglass automobile component manufacturing. A pioneer in his field, one of Adam Citron's particular talents was to be so inventive that he could find what was missing in the market and fill the void, producing something that no one else did. Expanding in the direction that the need dictated, Citron founded several related companies, all leading to his crowning achievement, the successful development of Plaza Fiberglass.

Plaza Fiberglass and the innovative products it produced was the brainchild of Citron, who started in business shortly after arriving as an immigrant in Canada in the early 1950s. The company, which started with a few employees in 1960, grew to employ as many as 400 people at the time its Chief Executive Officer became the victim of cancer. After a courageous fight to overcome this devastating disease, cancer took Adam Citron's life one year later on November 14, 1985. His wife, Sabina Citron, recalls, "The employees felt a very great loss. It was as if they had lost a father, for that is what he truly was to the company."

His unerring business abilities and his innovative products made Plaza Fiberglass a successful supplier to the major automotive manufacturing companies. He was always improving on the company's products; the company's major product, fiberglass hoods for trucks, was Citron's own invention.

Working as a supplier for many years for major truck companies, Citron's efforts were crowned with success in 1975, when Plaza Fiber-

Adam Citron, a pioneer in his field, founded Plaza Fiberglass, an innovative company which supplied vehicle parts and prototypes to many major truck and automotive manufacturers.

glass was able to secure, among other contracts, a five year contract to supply molded fiberglass rooftop assemblies for International Harvester Company's line of trucks. Citron not only designed the rooftop assembly, he also designed the container in which to transport them.

Plaza Fiberglass supplied automotive body parts and prototypes to such companies as Ford Corporation of United States; produced body parts for General Motors buses; and manufactured truck hoods and other parts for International Harvester and its successor Navistar, for White Company and its successors Volvo G.M. and Volvo Sweden, as well as for Mack Truck, Chrysler and others.

Never tiring of venturing into a related field, Citron founded Citron Automotive in 1982. Located on Citron Court in Concord, it was a modern steel-stamping plant, sup-

plying metal parts for light-duty trucks and cars.

The entire lifestory of Adam Citron was a struggle against tremendous odds, which he overcame beyond his wildest expectations before succumbing to cancer. He belonged to a generation whose work ethic was a matter of pride, and the fruit of his labour, as well as his contribution to society, constituted rewards in themselves.

Adam Citron was a true entrepreneur in the best tradition of Canada. He had an abiding love for this country which provided him with the ability to innovate without hindrance. Always thankful for the opportunities that his new country had given him, Adam Citron wanted to be more than merely a successful businessperson. He wanted to serve society and give back to Canada generously — which is what he did, and many times over.

Quality Meat Packers Limited

1

2

W hen Nathan "Nick" Schwartz began supplying neighbourhood butcher shops with pork, few people would have imagined that it would grow into the international meat processing business that it is today. Supplying customers in Canada, United States, Japan, Europe, South America, Asia and the Caribbean, Quality Meat Packers Limited, which celebrates its sixtieth anniversary in 1991, now employs more than seven hundred people which process over 20,000 hog carcasses weekly.

Nick Schwartz, who had operated a meat business in his native Russia with his father, immigrated to Canada in 1923. He soon opened his first store in Toronto on St. Clair and Dufferin Streets. Needing larger facilities, Schwartz soon began leasing additional premises and, eventually, had eight stores in Toronto and one in Brantford under the name Pure Food Meat Markets.

Pure Food Meat Markets achieved a very high profile in the independent retail business, providing a good choice of products and cuts while emphasizing personal service for its clientele. Bacon, for example, was sliced right in the store for the customer and custom cuts were the order of the day.

But already by 1930 Nick Schwartz decided that his butcher shops could operate more successfully with a secure source of pork. He became a partner with a small supplier, from whom he soon bought the company, and Quality Meat Packers Limited was established. The Depression was a difficult time in which to start a business, but by 1931, 250 animals per week were being processed and distributed to the company's retail outlets. The demand quickly spread to other independent butchers and restaurants as people wanted to purchase from a small independent source rather than the large packinghouse.

Business flourished and the company soon moved to larger premises on First Avenue in Toronto. The added space allowed for expansion of activities as well as volume,

1. *The late Nathan Schwartz, Founder of Quality Meat Packers. From small beginnings, with a firm respect for hard work and strong principles, he launched what is today a solid international business.*
2. *Rose Schwartz worked with her husband in his first Pure Food Store and saw him grow to hand over a strong business to his family.*
3. *Pure Food Meat Market, 517 Bloor Street West, was one of eight stores in the Toronto area and home of the popular Poppy brand.*
4. *Looking back to times when service was always one to one and a good roast cost twenty cents a pound.*

3

4

and Quality Meat Packers became involved in the pork processing business, offering bacon, hams, wieners and other cuts under the "Poppy" brand name. The company grew steadily through the 1940s and 1950s, processing over 1,000 hogs per week by the late 1950s.

In 1960 Quality Meat Packers purchased the municipally-owned and operated Toronto Civic Abattoir located on Tecumseth Street. This location still is the site of the company's head office, distribution centre and largest production facility. In the same year, Quality Meat Packers also founded Toronto Abattoirs Limited as a custom slaughterer and by-product renderer and distributor. The company also became federally inspected, allowing for the export of its products to other provinces and countries.

A shift in marketing strategy was necessary. The last Pure Food Meat Market store was sold in the late 1960s and a more global outlook was adopted. New products and market opportunities were developed. In 1972 the company began selling boneless pork cuts to the Japanese market and that initial container load deal has now grown to over six million pounds per year.

Quality Meat Packers has developed a strong export business for fresh and frozen meats in the United States. The domestic market

1

was also simultaneously strengthened. The company became a major supplier of fresh primal cuts to butcher shops and chain stores across Southern Ontario.

As the company began outgrowing its downtown location, it purchased a modern processing facility on Milliken Blvd. in Scarborough in 1980. This new facility, known as the Milliken Division, processes sausages, burgers, portion controlled chops, boneless pork cuts, and also provides custom boning and trimming services. This plant, as well as other major modifications in the existing processing department, paved the way for major thrust into the processed meat business under the "Town Club" and "Country Manor" labels.

In 1987 the company moved the bacon slicing operation to its new Lenworth Division, which slices millions of pounds of bacon per year. This move permitted the company to increase its chilling capacity by twenty per cent, allowing it to keep pace with the increasing customer demand for Town Club products.

Quality Meat Packers Limited is pursuing steady growth in the meat business, with more aggressive mar-

keting of branded products both at home and abroad, and introducing products with specific nutritional value, new deli meats, and new fresh pork products.

Frank Schwartz, son of the founder and current President of the company, believes that Quality Meat Packers has maintained its competitive edge by focusing on the company's strengths of excellent service and consistent attention to quality. He stresses that the company has always been a family business. His son David is now Vice President of Sales. Frank Schwartz points out that "we have always strived to maintain our focus as a family business dedicated to providing the best possible service to our customers. Personalized attention and the objective to supply exactly what the customer wants is of the utmost importance to all of us here, whether it be to a chain store in Toronto or to a customer in Japan."

2

1. *The Milliken Plant in Scarborough Ontario; 35,000 square feet of spotless and efficient meat processing.*
2. *Frank Schwartz, President, worked in the store as a youngster and today heads a company that employs over 700 people.*
3. *David Schwartz, Vice President of Marketing and Sales, third generation and growing from strength.*

3

Queensway General Hospital

"I remember . . . a dark and windy day in October 1954 when a small group of doctors from the Toronto Western Hospital tramped through the mud of a potato field in Etobicoke. After some discussion, we agreed that this dismal place, so remote and so far from human habitation and public transport, was no place to build a hospital. Fortunately, nobody listened to us." Fortunate indeed, that nobody listened to those words, as recalled by Dr. F.A. Jaffe, former Director of Laboratory Medicine, because for over thirty-five years, the Queensway General Hospital has specialized in the delivery of caring, effective, up-to-date health care as an active, thriving community hospital.

Over the years, Etobicoke's first hospital has built and sustained a meaningful relationship with the residents of Etobicoke and eastern Mississauga by being, first and foremost, a family hospital. The cornerstone of the 429 bed hospital's success has been its ability to continually meet the needs of a growing, cosmopolitan community through the delivery of appropriate, quality health care. In the late 1940s, it became clear to many that a general hospital was needed to serve the area between Toronto and Oakville. The proposal for a hospital was received with enthusiasm by both industry and the local community. On November 9, 1951, the Lakeshore Hospital Association was incorporated. The name "Queensway" was later chosen following a 1952 contest among Lakeshore-Etobicoke school children, which was won by nine-year old Joan Smith, who later would become a nurse and work in the hospital that she had named.

With a charter, a name, a site and a plan, the Association set about to raise the $2 million needed from the private sector to build the hospital. In August 1956, the 131 bed facility admitted its first patients.

The need for additional space is a never ending concern for a busy hospital. Expansions occurred frequently throughout Queensway's history, with a major expansion taking place in the early 1960s when the hospital, responding to the dramatic growth in the area and an increased demand for its acute care services, was enlarged to house 309 beds.

The community surrounding the hospital has significantly changed over the years, as its population has come to include more elderly. Naturally, Queensway focused on ways to adapt its role to accommodate this change and, in response to emerging needs, the hospital entered into a innovative joint venture with a private entrepreneur to construct and administer a 120 bed chronic care wing. Opened on December 11, 1984, the George St. Leger McCall Wing represents a unique example of cooperation between a public hospital and the private health care sector, the first of its kind in Canada.

With the establishment, in 1990,

of The Goodhealth Centre, a referral and resource service for seniors and their caregivers, Queensway continues to expand its programs to meet health care requirements of its elderly neighbours. Queensway is also committed to the development of partnerships to increase accessibility to health care resources through involvement in the Westcare group of hospitals, and the Regional Geriatric Program for Southwest Metropolitan Toronto.

In 1986, Queensway began formally assessing the suitability of facilities and programs as the hospital prepared to meet the challenges posed by the 1990s and the next century. The optimum role for Queensway was determined to be a comprehensive Health Care Centre. In order to fulfil this function, the existing facility will be improved through renovations. The vital functions of Labour & Delivery, Day Surgery, and Critical Care will be regenerated; existing ambulatory support services and the Emergency Department will be enhanced; and others, such as disease prevention and mental health day programs, will be introduced.

Etobicoke's first hospital is now preparing to carry its proud tradition of leadership in community-oriented treatment well into the future. Building on thirty-five years of quality health care, and through the hospital's innovative and visionary approach to the future, "The Torch" of Queensway General Hospital will continue to burn brightly for many more years.

Etobicoke's first hospital has built and sustained a meaningful relationship with the residents of Etobicoke and eastern Mississauga, Ontario. Queensway Hospital is now preparing to carry its proud tradition of leadership in community-oriented treatment well into the future.

R.L. Polk & Company Ltd.

1

Ralph Lane Polk was selling patent medicine door-to-door when he encountered an enumerator who was gathering names and addresses for a city directory. The city directory service so impressed Polk that he applied for work with the publisher at a wage of two dollars a day. After working in a number of American cities, a twenty-one year old Ralph Polk arrived in Detroit, Michigan in 1870 with nothing more than courage and a vision. A stern and frugal man, he was also a superb salesman.

His auspicious decision to enter directory publishing on his own would eventually establish R.L. Polk & Co. as a leader in information services. Today, the company employs almost 7,000 people in the United States, Canada, Australia, England, West Germany and Barbados.

In 1956 R.L. Polk & Company expanded into Canada with the purchase of Annuaires Marcotte Ltd., city directory publishers for Quebec City and several smaller communi-

ties in Quebec. Its name was soon changed to R.L. Polk & Company (Canada) Ltd., which became the holding company for all of R.L. Polk's Canadian operations. The company quickly established itself as a major force in Canadian city directory publishing. In 1957 it acquired B.C. Directories Ltd. of Vancouver, which published twenty-one city directories in British Columbia. Henderson Directories, Ltd., of Winnipeg, Manitoba was purchased in 1960. The Motor List Company of Toronto, which included motor vehicle statistics, list compilation and direct mail, was added to R.L. Polk in 1961.

By the mid-1960s, the City Directory, Marketing Services and Statistical Operations were all very committed to data processing, enhancing R.L. Polk's products and creating an influx of new business. To accommodate their rapid growth, a new building was constructed on Bartley Drive in Toronto. With two subsequent additions, the 100,000 square foot complex serves as Canadian headquarters for the City Directory, Statistical Services and Marketing Services Division.

In 1967, the company acquired Might Directories, a long respected name in Toronto's printing trade as a publisher of directories as well as

a producer of advertising and marketing materials. R.L. Polk's Motor Vehicle Registrations Division in Canada has the responsibility to obtain title and registration information from all Canadian provinces.

Throughout the 1980s the Canadian operation became more closely linked with R.L. Polk & Company in the United States. Each division operates in conjunction with its American counterpart, permitting an interchange of techniques, experience and expertise in compilation, production and marketing. This organizational structure has proven beneficial to enhancing and improving Polk's products and services to its Canadian clients.

At present, the Bartley Drive plant and offices are being substantially remodelled, indicating R.L. Polk's commitment to its business endeavours in Ontario and all of Canada. With nearly 700 employees in Canada, R.L. Polk & Company Ltd. continues to be a diversified leader of information services with an outlook toward substantial growth in the future.

1. *Ralph Lane Polk, Founder and President, 1870-1923, of R.L. Polk & Company.*
2. *R.L. Polk's Canadian facility in Toronto, Ontario.*

2

R.G. Mitchell Family Books Inc.

A family retail and wholesale business offering distinctly Christian books and other products suitable for every member of the family, R.G. Mitchell Family Books Inc. now distributes products for over forty publishing houses and companies. Originally known as the Home Evangel Book Shop, R.G. Mitchell Family Books has continued to expand, growing from a small corner bookstore to its present location and size of close to 40,000 square feet in the Toronto suburb of Willowdale, in addition to two other retail stores in Kitchener and St. Catharines, Ontario.

Although raised in a Christian setting, R. Gordon Mitchell, the founder of R.G. Mitchell Family Books, did not personally become a Christian until as a young man, while studying business administration in Toronto, he was confronted with the clear message of salvation under the ministry of the late Dr. H.A. Ironside. That evening in his room he read in his Bible I John 1:9, *"If we confess our sins, He is faithful and just to forgive us our sins, and to cleanse us from all unrighteousness."* As he recalls, "I thought, I believe this is it! If I am forgiven of my sins, I *must* be a child of God. Without a second thought, I dropped to my knees and confessed. As I did, I became aware that Christ bore the punishment for *my* sins. That night I received Him into my heart by faith." This incident set the course for the remainder of Mitchell's life and business. It was not long until he and two other Church friends went out preaching in what was known as The Gospel Van.

After finishing his studies, Mitchell had planned to go to Ottawa the following Monday, but decided to stay in Toronto for one more weekend. That Saturday he was offered a position with a business in Toronto, and, unable to refuse, he began working immediately. Several years later, in 1934, when the opportunity arose to become a partner in a small Christian bookstore known as Home Evangel Book Shop, he accepted.

Mitchell and his partner divided the work between the two of them. While his partner travelled across Canada, selling to Christian book dealers and acting as an agent for a small number of publishers, Mitchell remained in the store and assumed the administrative duties. Five years later, Mitchell purchased the entire business from his partner.

Along with the business also came the need for Mitchell himself to begin travelling throughout most of Canada. For twenty years he personally made the trips annually without a break, six weeks in Western Canada and two weeks in Eastern Canada.

Supplying bookdealers with products from a variety of publishers, Mitchell soon realized that much time and expense would be saved if he were able to provide the books from a central location in Toronto. Soon, dealers were given the choice of buying products out of Mitchell's warehouse in Toronto or directly from the British and American publishers that he represented. Slowly, more and more of what he

1

sold was shipped from Toronto.

In order to provide better service to his customers, Mitchell also began producing a catalogue and made it available to retail bookstores throughout Canada. This was the first catalogue of its kind offered in Canada. The idea was very successful and soon other suppliers were offering catalogues also.

By 1954, with Mitchell being an exclusive dealer for several British and American publishers, he realized there was a greater need to emphasize the wholesale aspect of the business. The original location on Church Street in Toronto, an old, three storey structure, was filled to capacity and the company needed to relocate. Choosing a location on Waterman Avenue that provided what appeared to be ample space, he signed a ten year lease. Although the rent was more than quadruple the previous rent,

2

1. *Soon after becoming a Christian, R. Gordon Mitchell, the founder of R.G. Mitchell Family Books, went out preaching in what was known as The Gospel Van.*
2. *The original Home Evangel Book Shop.*

the business prospered and was able to absorb the extra expense.

After being on Waterman Avenue for seven years, the company was once again operating at full capacity. Upon successfully renegotiating the lease, Mitchell was able to purchase land and erect a building on Hobson Ave., the first location which the business did not rent. Although the building had 12,000 square feet, 5,000 more than the previous location, it was not long before Mitchell needed to enlarge the building by an additional 5,500 square feet.

While on Hobson Avenue, the business began to become a family enterprise. Mitchell's son Peter soon joined the company. After briefly working as a travelling salesman, he took charge of the financial end of the business and became Vice President. Keith Cheshire, Mitchell's son-in-law, also began working for the company, and was soon Vice President as well. Now these two men carry the responsibility of the business, although R.G. Mitchell retains an office and is available for advise and consultation.

After twelve years on Hobson Avenue, the expanding company had outgrown its location again. Mitchell recalls that one day Keith Cheshire came to his office exclaiming, "If we get one more skid of books today, it will have to sit outside, for we'll never get it in the door!" Deciding to purchase two acres of vacant property on Gordon Baker Road in Willowdale in 1973, the company erected a building of 30,600 square feet, constructed to match the specific needs of the growing company.

All the while the business was becoming more modern and efficient. Already on Hobson Avenue, the warehouse was completely mechanized with a conveyor system for the movement of merchandise with the minimum amount of labour. In the office, a computer system, which has been upgraded several times since then, handled invoicing, inventory, accounts receivable etc. The company also began to have a telephone salesperson, realizing that it was unworkable to have representatives travelling to all the remote regions of the country.

In the early 1980s, concerned about the availability of Christian products in the Toronto region, the company decided to open a retail store which represented, in addition to the company's own products, all evangelical publishers. After reviewing the possibilities, Mitchell expanded the warehouse by 7,000 square feet and located the retail bookstore at the same site on Gordon Baker Road, with parking for over 100 cars. In 1986 another retail bookstore was purchased in Kitchener, Ontario, which was followed by a third bookstore in St. Catharines, Ontario, in 1988.

Although the business required much of R. Gordon Mitchell's time, he has also managed to assist many others through the years. He has served as an advisor, member and President of many boards for a wide range of organizations, including the Christian Booksellers Association International and North York General Hospital.

Today, with over ninety employees, R.G. Mitchell Family Books Inc. is still committed to products that are not only appropriate and valuable for this life, but also point the way to eternal life. After more than fifty-seven years of distributing Christian books, music, recordings, greeting cards, church school curriculum, Bibles, religious novelties, plaques and framed pictures, R.G. Mitchell Family Books is proud that its product lines remain true to the Bible and can be relied upon as good for every member of the family.

1. R.G. Mitchell Family Books' central warehouse and retail bookstore in Toronto, Ontario.
2. The R.G. Mitchell family portrait: (back row, left to right) Kimberly Mitchell, Peter Mitchell, Rachelle Cheshire, Keith Cheshire; (front row, left to right) Nicholas Mitchell, Christopher Mitchell, Doreen Mitchell, R. Gordon Mitchell, Gertrude Mitchell, Gwenda Cheshire, Ryan Cheshire, Justin Cheshire.

1

2

Richmond Tile & Terrazzo Ltd.

1

One may admire the fine tile or marble flooring in certain commercial buildings, and perhaps one may be caused to reflect on the fine craftsmanship behind the design and installation of such classic yet elegant flooring. As in other sectors of design and construction, certain companies provide the particular expertise and skill required to supply the quality flooring which may be both admired and walked on by countless thousands of people for generations. One such company is Richmond Tile & Terrazzo Ltd. Servicing the commercial and industrial contractor segment of the construction industry, Richmond Tile & Terrazzo specializes in the installation of many types of flooring materials.

After many years of experience working together for another construction firm, Angelo Bonomo and Melvyn Merker felt it was time to begin their own business. In June, 1978, Richmond Tile & Terrazzo Ltd. opened its first office, located on Toryork Drive in North York, Ontario.

With Merker's administrative capabilities and Bonomo's skills as a craftsman, the company immediately began to grow. From the original nine employees, the company has progressed to its cur-

rent size, employing approximately eighty-five tradesmen. After outgrowing several offices, the company moved to is present location in Weston, Ontario.

Within the 15,000 square feet building, Richmond Tile has been able to construct a marble-finishing shop. Complete with the latest technological advancements in machinery, the facility is able to custom-cut, finish and polish the marble for the exterior of buildings, lobbies and custom-made furniture.

One of the most important factors that contributed to the growth and recognition of the company occurred when it was awarded the Metro YMCA project in Metropolitan Toronto. A very complex and intricate job, the work established the company's reputation within the construction industry. The company has also done work at such prominent locations as The Hospital for Sick Children, the Marriott Hotel and the Scotia Plaza in Toronto.

Each material which Richmond Tile installs has its own specific characteristics. Tile, a premade finished material, is installed without any further finishing. Terrazzo material is mixed, poured, trowelled and ground on site by skilled tradesmen. Marble is purchased in either slabs or tiles, and then installed to suit; only the amount of marble needed for each installation is imported.

Today, the company also installs carpet and resilient flooring. In addition, the company has moved into other facets of the construction industry. Through a subsidiary company, drywall and specialized contracting services are now provided.

Richmond Tile & Terrazzo Ltd. feels that its success is the result of the co-ordinated efforts of the management team on the administration side, and the skilled tradesmen who carry out the actual work in the field. Although one may have a supply of quality product and have the most advanced machinery for the construction or installation of such product, Mel Merker, President of Richmond Tile, states "It is still the people in the company that make the primary difference in the quality of workmanship." And ultimately, it is the company's people, both on the field and in the office, that provide the type of customer satisfaction that has allowed Richmond Tile & Terrazzo Ltd. the type of long-term relationship with the general contractors which has earned the firm its reputation over the years, ensuring that the company will continue in the forefront of this specialized sector of the construction industry.

1. *Melvyn R. Merker, President (left) and Angelo Bonomo, Vice President (standing), co-Founders of Richmond Tile & Terrazzo Limited.*
2. *The Richmond staff: (standing, from left to right), I.F. Marques, Deborah Rideout, Anthony Filazzola, Dale Ward; (sitting, from left to right), Therese Crowe, Sheila Sawyer, Tammy Whitt, Steve Stafford.*

2

Ste-Alco Inc.

1

Staircases, railings, structural and decorative work; the C N Tower, Royal Bank Plaza, Sherway Gardens and the Mississauga Library; Ste-Alco has worked with all of them. Founded in 1965 by Erwin Fritze, Ste-Alco Inc. has grown from a small, steel fabricating company into one of the major competitors in its field.

Erwin Fritze, born in 1919 in Germany, immigrated to Canada and began working for several companies, including a steel company, where he gained much of the necessary knowledge to begin his own firm. Originally located on Lenworth Dr. in Mississauga, the company began with the founder and two other employees. Ste-Alco soon outgrew its first location and

moved to a 12,000 square feet location on Mattawa Ave. In 1989 the company moved once again, this time to its present location on Cardiff Blvd, also in Mississauga, an 18,000 square feet facility with storage area, allowing them a little more space in which to work and grow.

Working with steel and aluminum, the company began by concentrating on smaller items and projects, such as in schools and residential jobs. The work was also further afield, with the company many times having clients in locations as far away as Sudbury and Ottawa. Today, the projects are much larger in scale and are located mainly in the Toronto area. Also, the company now works largely with steel; however, there are highly specialized employees working with other metals, such as stainless steel, brass and aluminum.

The company's work begins with its draftsmen creating detailed plans for each project. After the raw materials are purchased, much of the work is then performed very similarly to an assembly line process. The materials are cut to size for each configuration, formed, assembled, welded, and then finished. Very little of the work is repetitious, because each job has been uniquely designed. The last step is the actual physical installation of the work at the job site.

Much of Ste-Alco's work can be found in office towers, hospitals and shopping centres. Many times the company's work is concealed, such as its structural and elevator shaft work, and not visible to the casual viewer; occasionally, it is highly visible, such as at Sherway Gardens, where all the brass, aluminum and steel railings and bridges were manufactured by Ste-Alco. Much of the company's work can also be found in restaurants, such as at the revolving restaurant in the C N Tower, where Ste-Alco did all the stainless steel work.

With forty-eight employees, Ste-Alco Inc. today is a major competitor in the steel fabricating field. Erwin Fritze's sons, Richard and Paul, have now assumed managerial positions, with Erwin Fritze involved mainly in a consultative role for the company. Celebrating its twenty-fifth anniversary in 1990, Ste-Alco Inc. continues to be a leader in the highly competitive field of steel fabricating.

1. Erwin Fritze, Founder of Ste-Alco Inc.
2. The steel railings, brass planter supports, and brass features at the columns were designed and produced by Ste-Alco Inc. for Sherway Gardens Shopping Plaza in Etobicoke, Ontario.
3. The main feature staircase, with stainless steel handrails, steel stairs, and steel balustrade railing were custom manufactured for the Toronto Sun Building.

2

3

Ryka Blow Molds Ltd.

There are few products today that we utilize in our daily activities that do not originate out of a mold of some description. Mold making and tool and die craftsmanship can be traced back to early civilization. Today, it is a diverse industry experiencing a revolution through the combination of human resource skills and high technology. Ryka Blow Molds Ltd. is considered a leader in the unique specialization of mold making for the plastics industry. Its expertise is devoted to the field of blow molded plastic products ranging from sophisticated packaging concepts to automotive and industrial component parts, to recreational and safety products, and enjoyable, safe toys for our younger generation.

Ryka Blow Molds Ltd. was founded by Michael Ryan in 1972. The company's mandate was to specialize in the blow molding sector of the plastics industry. It was evident that future growth in technology within the plastics industry would necessitate specialization as it has in many endeavours like engineering, medicine, law, accounting and business management.

From the outset, Ryka Blow Molds Ltd. was export oriented. Its first mold order was for a major plastics processor in the United States. Today the company exports over seventy per cent of its capacity to the United States, as well as Europe, New Zealand, Australia and South America.

In the late 1970s Ryka Blow Molds recognized the beginning of a revolution in automated machining technology. New sophisticated equipment was being introduced world wide that would result in accelerated, close tolerance machining techniques. This new wave of expertise was also developed to help solve a world wide shortage of skilled craftspeople. Canada, and especially the Province of Ontario, to this day live with a growing shortage of skilled craftspeople necessary to compete in a world class manufacturing forum.

Ryka Blow Molds Ltd. accepted the challenge by establishing a new facility consisting of 28,000 square feet, situated minutes from the Toronto airport, in late 1979. Following extensive research for two years, the company introduced its first automated CNC machine

(Computerized Numerical Control) in February of 1982. In June of the same year, the company also introduced a computer assisted design system (CAD) to complement its journey into new technology.

Since that first step, Ryka Blow Molds Ltd. has continued to expand each year with additional state of the art equipment and continues to be recognized as a leader in the industry. Today, every segment of Ryka's operations, from scheduling, engineering, mold manufacturer, accounting and shipping, is totally computerized.

Sophistication in computerized machinery does not diminish the need for quality human resources, nor does it reduce the number of people required to produce an accurate mold; rather, it complements the skills of human

1. *Generating a computer listing of all the dimensions of a product, a Coordinate Measuring Machine is used for quality control to ensure the dimensional stability of all Ryka's products before they are shipped.*
2. *An electrical discharge machine (EDM) completes the finish of a mold's cavities.*

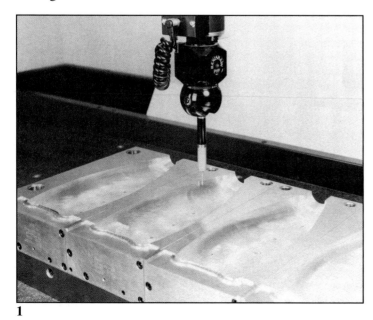

1

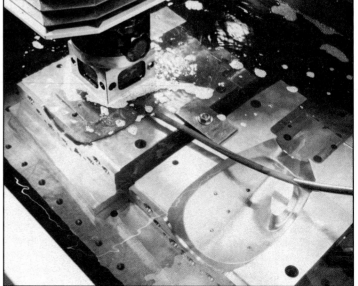

2

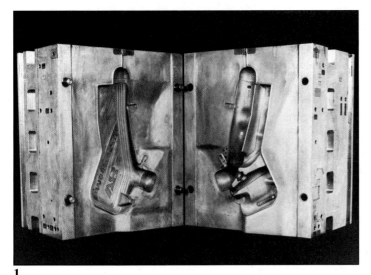

1

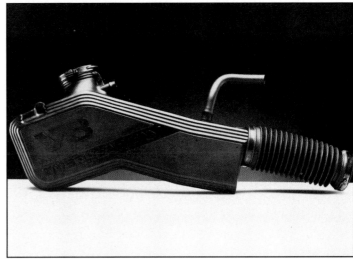

2

resources and allows for a high degree of efficiency and accuracy. Michael Ryan points out that Ryka personnel are a key element in its effort to provide quality products and dependable service within a world class manufacturing environment.

Because of the lack of skilled tradespeople in Canada, many of Ryka's employees come from foreign countries. To offset this shortage, Ryka initiated an in-house apprenticeship program in 1974. The first graduate apprentice from this program remains in a senior mold making position with the company today. In connection with the apprenticeship program, Ryka Blow Molds Ltd. attempts to

bring an awareness of the career opportunities within the industry to the youth of our province and throughout Canada.

Within Ryka there are also training facilities to further develop the skills of its personnel in keeping with the introduction of new technology. By providing long-term employment — two of the three original employees are still with the company — Ryka creates the continuity necessary to re-invest in its human resources. As a result, Ryka presently employs fifty-four highly skilled people in engineering, manufacturing, and after sales processing consultation. The growth in personnel represents an eighty-five

per cent increase over the total number of people employed by Ryka at the outset of its expansion program in 1980.

The wide range of products in present and future markets utilizing the blow molding process stimulate the talents of Ryka's engineering and manufacturing personnel. Product design today is taking on a new and challenging perspective. New formulations in plastic resins necessitate fresh technology in mold making. Consumer awareness in recycling with plastics is leading to the next phase of development that will challenge our industry through the turn of the century and beyond. Today, Ryka Blow Molds Ltd. continues to follow the original mandate of 1972: to grow and promote its activities as specialists in our chosen field, and to promote Canadian mold making technology with world class manufacturing facilities.

3

1. The two halves of a mold that will produce an all-plastic resonator for a 1991 automobile. With this and many other products, Ryka was involved from the design concept to the final product.
2. The all-plastic resonator.
3. Michael Ryan, Founder and President of Ryka Blow Molds Ltd., a company devoted to the field of blow molded plastic products and considered a leader in the unique specialization of mold making for the plastics industry.

St. Michael's Hospital

In 1892, the Sisters of St. Joseph answered the needs of a community being hard hit by a diphtheria epidemic by founding St. Michael's Hospital. What was "Notre Dame des Anges," an old Baptist church serving as a boarding house for working women, became, almost overnight, a twenty-six bed hospital with a staff compliment of six doctors and four graduate nurses.

St. Michael's Hospital has grown steadily over the past almost 100 years, just as the city is serves has grown. With growth and progress have come changes — changes in the surrounding community, and changes in the way health care is delivered to the public.

Today, St. Michael's Hospital has 700 beds, employs more than 3,000 people, serves 20,000 patients per year and offers a full range of health care services. It provides community-based health care in 129 out-patient clinics in twenty-two different locations across the city; it is one of Canada's finest teaching hospitals, training doctors and nursing staff; and it has a reputation for excellence in medical research. The hospital and its dedicated staff are responsible for the research and development of

1. *St. Michael's Hospital in 1938, at the corner of Bond and Shuter Streets in Toronto, Ontario.*
2. *St. Michael's Hospital today, at the corner of Queen and Bond Streets in Toronto, Ontario.*

many life-saving procedures and technologies, including the world's first sciatic nerve transplant and innovations in space medicine.

It's all a far cry from 1892 and the Notre Dame des Anges. All except for one very important principle which has remained a constant over the course of the century: the Hospital's commitment to providing compassionate, quality health care to people in need.

It is this commitment that has made St. Michael's Hospital an integral part of the community, and a leader in meeting the changing needs of a changing community. From one-

of-a-kind outpatient clinics for multiple sclerosis and haemophilia, to a downtown detoxification centre, to shelters for battered women, refugees and street kids, to Casey House, the first and only AIDS hospice in Canada, St. Michael's Hospital has demonstrated leadership in identifying and meeting new health care challenges.

And there are more challenges to meet. Balancing the increasing, and increasingly diverse, needs of the community with dwindling health care resources is the most important challenge hospitals face today.

To this end, St. Michael's Hospital has become part of the Fontbonne Health System which was created in 1990 to integrate St. Michael's Hospital with St. Joseph's Health Centre. Owned and operated by the Sisters of St. Joseph, the Fontbonne Health System combines the strengths of these two institutions in the areas of patient care, teaching and research to further the Sister's mission of care and compassion.

As St. Michael's enters its centennial year, it continues to recognize its special role in the delivery of health care, a role which is firmly established in the past and present, and which will evolve to meet new horizons in the future within the Fontbonne Health System.

St. Joseph's Health Centre

For seventy years, the dedicated team at St. Joseph's Health Centre has provided high quality health care with caring hands extended to the growing community of Sunnyside in Toronto's west end. The third largest hospital in Metropolitan Toronto, St. Joseph's Health Centre continually demonstrates both care and compassion when delivering health care to patients, while providing a full spectrum of active, chronic, and rehabilitative care to all ages.

From its origins as an orphanage to its present integration into the Fontbonne Health System, St. Joseph's has been building on change. Founded by the Sisters of St. Joseph in 1921, a Catholic religious order that had already established orphanages, homes for the aged, and St. Michael's Hospital in Toronto, St. Joseph's Health Centre has adapted well to changes in its surrounding community.

One such recent adaption occurred in 1980, when St. Joseph's Hospital, a 534 bed acute care hospital, merged with Our Lady of Mercy Hospital, a 297 bed long term care facility, thereby creating St. Joseph's Health Centre. The caring team at St. Joseph's continually strives to ensure that the services and programs offered are consistent with community needs and with the mission of the Sisters of St. Joseph.

Functioning also as a teaching hospital affiliated with the University of Toronto, St. Joseph's offers a broad range of primary and secondary level programs as well as selected tertiary programs. Major areas of concentration include: general, medical and surgical services, mental health services, rehabilitation services, long term care services, obstetrical and paediatric services, family support services,

1

health promotion and illness prevention services.

As an institution with strong roots in the community, St. Joseph's operates a number of outreach programs, such as the Pre-natal Screening Program, the Detoxification Unit, the Women's Health Centre, the Respiratory Ambulatory Home Care Program, and the Community Health Centre, one of the largest ambulatory programs in the City of Toronto.

Maintaining and improving the health care services that St. Joseph's provides has led the Health Centre to seek new avenues of development. One such avenue was the decision by the Sisters of St. Joseph in 1990 to integrate the resources of St. Joseph's Health Centre with its sister hospital, St. Michael's, into the Fontbonne Health System. As both are exemplary health care facilities, the new

relationship promises to further enhance and strengthen the Catholic presence in health care, education and research, and to make more effective use of funds so that each institution can better respond to the health care needs of the communities that they now serve.

Today, St. Joseph's Health Centre continues to fulfill its mandate as a community hospital dedicated to quality care. Through their dedication and commitment to health care, the Sisters of St. Joseph have laid a strong foundation upon which St. Joseph's continues to build its ambitious and exciting vision for the future within the Fontbonne Health System.

1. *St. Joseph's Health Centre in Toronto continues to address the needs of its diverse population into the 21st century, maintaining a broad range of both inpatient and outpatient services.*

2. *In 1921, St. Joseph's Health Centre found its beginnings in converted buildings which were formerly part of the Sacred Heart Orphanage.*

2

Samuel, Son & Co., Limited

Samuel, Son & Co., Limited has grown from a small warehouse operation to a large steel, stainless steel and aluminum service centre of national scope. Spanning five generations as a family owned and operated business, the company and its principals have enjoyed a close relationship with the province of Ontario.

Known as M. & L. Samuel, the company was founded by Mark and Lewis Samuel in 1855. After selling gas chandeliers in Toronto for a brief while, the company soon developed into commission and wholesale merchants in metal and hardware, with offices in Toronto and Liverpool, England. Mark Samuel settled in Liverpool and sent most of the products to Canada where there were very few metal plants. There was also some eastward trade as some Canadian customers were able to pay only with non-perishables such as hides, tallow and beeswax, which could be shipped to and sold in England. It was good arrangement, resulting in low prices and good, fast, and efficient service for the customer, while building a reputation for honesty, service and quality.

The growth of the company parallels the growth of industry in Canada in many ways. It grew from the distribution of hardware and metals, imported from Europe and principally England, to the distribution of Canadian-made products, with the growth of steel mills here in Canada. When the need for manufacturing arose later, the company started manufacturing also.

As the company continued to grow, it took on Alfred Benjamin as a partner in 1880, and the firm became known as M. & L. Samuel, Benjamin & Company. Lewis Samuel passed away in 1888, but his son Sigmund, born in 1867, was available to carry the company forward. In 1899 the company did away with shelf hardware, which allowed them to concentrate better on metals and heavy hardware. Some of the pig iron and steel that they imported was for such early Canadian companies as the Masseys and Sam McLaughlin's. The company also introduced the first broad flange beams into Canada, which were able to withstand much greater loads.

By 1912 Sigmund Samuel was a fifty per cent partner, while the other fifty per cent belonged to the Benjamins. Moving back and forth between England and Toronto, he managed the company quite successfully, as well as being involved in other endeavours. During the First World War he bought a collection of almost four hundred pieces of Greek and Italian vases for the Royal Ontario Museum, giving it one of the finest collections of ancient Greek and Italian art in North America. After a visit to Israel, he helped start trade in oranges between the two countries, receiving the first two cases of Jaffa oranges shipped to Canada.

In 1929 the company was ready to change locations in Toronto again, moving to the corner of Spadina and Fleet Streets. This was the company's third home. After originally renting at Front and Wellington St., a location known then and still today as the "Coffin Block," they had built a new brick

The changing faces of Samuel, Son & Co., Limited.
1. Lewis Samuel, who helped found the company in 1855.
2. Sigmund Samuel, who continued to manage and develop the company.
3. Ernest Samuel, who continues today to direct and expand the company.

1

2

3

1

2

warehouse and office building at King and Spadina which they also outgrew. When Frank Benjamin decided to retire in 1931, Sigmund Samuel became the sole proprietor of the firm, and immediately changed its name to Samuel, Son & Company. The company soon closed down the London office, becoming more and more a service centre in metals produced in North America.

As the company became more involved domestically, Sigmund Samuel also became more involved in Toronto. He helped acquire a Chinese library for the Royal Ontario Museum. Later, he also donated his lifetime collection of Canadiana, and then helped to construct the building where it eventually was to be located, the Canadiana Gallery. He was also involved in the Toronto Western Hospital and the University of Toronto, which named one of its libraries in his honour. For his involvement in the affairs of Toronto, he received the City's Award of Merit medal in 1958. Continuing in this same tradition, the family also recently made possible the opening of the Samuel European Galleries at the Royal Ontario Museum.

When the city of Toronto expropriated the Fleet St. location in the late 1950s to build a ramp for the Gardener Expressway, the company moved to its present location on Dixie Rd. in Mississauga. Ernest L. Samuel, a grandson of Sigmund, designed the Mississauga facility, and then became President of the company in May, 1962. As the company continues to expand, the 365,000 square feet Mississauga facility remains as its flagship location, with the corporate head office and administrative central offices situated there.

In 1985 three of its manufacturing divisions were combined to form Samuel Manu-Tech Inc., a public company on the Toronto Stock Exchange which focuses on manufacturing. Samuel, Son & Co., Limited, continues as the majority shareholder in Samuel Manu-Tech Inc. The company develops and sells its technology and products worldwide, such as its metal pickling technology and stainless steel pipe and tubing.

The distribution side, Samuel, Son & Co., Limited, continues to be a private company. Its computer system allows it to have one of the most sophisticated costing and operating systems in the industry, with instant access to inventory, costing, order status, and customer profiles on a national basis for all its divisions. Just-in-time deliveries are not a problem with its massive warehousing capabilities throughout Canada and the U.S. and a huge truck fleet.

The company finds its role as the middle man between the mills and manufacturers. Its state-of-the-art equipment allows it to produce almost any size, gauge, grade or type of metal product needed, ranging from aluminum aircraft alloys, galvanized sheet, stainless plate and rolled bars to virtually any carbon steel, aluminum or stainless steel product.

Beginning as a family business that was customer orientated, the company continues to be family owned and operated, dedicated to its customers, and involved in community affairs. Mark C. Samuel, son of Ernest Samuel, and Vice President of the company, points out that this is a company that has demonstrated throughout its history that people truly are the strength of the firm. This commitment to its personnel has fostered a strong loyalty among its employees, and encourages long-term employment with the company.

Samuel, Son & Co., Limited, today a large steel, stainless steel, and aluminum service centre of national scope, continues to be committed to the best products, equipment, systems and people in the industry. It has a history it can be proud of and a strong future to look forward to.

1. *An early location in Toronto, Ontario for a company that continued to grow.*
2. *The present location for Samuel, Son & Co., Limited in Mississauga, Ontario.*

Sharp Electronics of Canada Ltd.

Microwave ovens, computers, photocopiers, electronic cash registers, televisions, video cassette recorders, compact disc players, calculators and a commitment to the changing times best describe Sharp Electronics. It is a company in touch with society, a company committed to people, and a company which believes that the development of original technology is a corporate responsibility that a manufacturer must assume. While it works to bring technology and people as close together as possible, it also focuses uncompromisingly on the goal of achieving harmony between people and high technology.

In 1912 a small metal working business was set up by Tokuji Hayakawa in Tokyo, Japan. By 1970 that small business had developed into the world famous Sharp Corporation, which derived its name and trademark from the Ever-Sharp Pencil that Tokuji Hayakawa himself invented in 1915. Throughout its history, Sharp Corporation has been at the leading edge of the development of electronics, dedicated to the continuous search for new horizons in this highly technological field. The company was heavily involved already in 1925 in the assembly and marketing of crystal radio sets, and by 1951 it was developing an

1

1. Sharp Electronics of Canada Ltd., Mississauga, Ontario.
2. The name of Sharp Corporation and its trademark are derived from the Ever-Sharp Pencil invented by founder Tokuji Hayakawa.

2

experimental television set. Within two years it was mass-producing televisions, to coincide with Japan's first TV broadcasts. A mere seven years later it was also mass-producing colour television sets. Microwave ovens were added to the product list in 1962. The company began the production of the world's first all transistor-diode electronic desk-top calculator in 1964, and in 1973 Sharp began the world's first mass-production of liquid crystal display (LCD) units and incorporated them into the electronic calculator. Recently, it has passed the 300 million electronic calculator production milestone.

In 1974 Sharp Corporation established Sharp Electronics of Canada, and the company has been introducing new products into the daily lives of Canadians continually ever since. Sharp has brought to Canada the first micro-computerized cassette tape deck, the super-thin card-size calculators with sensor touch, electronic translators, voice-synthesized clocks, cash registers, solar powered calculators, sound-equipped video cameras, personal computer television sets and many other products.

Not only does Sharp produce and deliver household products, it also provides many products for industry. It has developed inte-

grated electronic communications systems which use existing telephone lines. It is at the top of the U.S. market in the total number of facsimile units marketed. Currently, Sharp has the smallest and lightest portable computer on the market, reflecting the recent expansion of its line of electronic organizers and laptop/notebook computers. The company has developed inexpensive plain paper facsimile machines, high-quality colour copiers, state-of-the-art scanners and many other products that are essential to today's business community.

Sharp is also heavily involved in the development of advanced electronic technology. It is the world's largest producer of laser diodes, which are used as the laser pickup in compact disc players. Sharp is taking the initiative in forging new technological frontiers in the area of optoelectronics, where optics and electronics are merged. Optoelectronics exploits the unusual properties of light that allow it to communicate, store, transform and process large amounts of information flawlessly at high speeds. Sharp also works in the field of Very Large-Scale Integration (VLSI) of electronic circuits, which can hold 20 million electronic components on eleven square millimetres of silicone. The company continues to conduct extensive experimental research of the "High Vision" satellite broadcasting system in order to achieve a clearer, more dynamic picture. Sharp has also developed traffic/weather information control systems for bridges, such as the one installed on the world's longest road/railway suspension bridge, Japan's 37.3 kilometre long Seto Ohashi Bridge.

Sharp has been playing a major role in the development of LCD technology for the 1990s, with a "three to four year advantage in the quality of LCD device," according to Mark Yoshida, Sharp Canada's senior Vice President of engineering. The premiere LCD product is the XV-100 projector, an advanced motion picture technology to create big screen ultimate home theatre entertainment, capable of adjusting the image from 20 to 100 inches with a built-in lens. Sharp Electronics of Canada's President Doug Koshima points out that "because of our extensive research and development it will take the others longer to catch up." Sharp is also developing other LCD products, including portable televisions and personal computers that have enhanced graphics capabilities.

In order to develop new product concepts better suited for our modern lifestyle, Sharp has established Creative Lifestyle Focus Centers to study everyday life. Located in Japan, United States and in West Germany, these Centers analyze, from all possible aspects, the relationship between products and lifestyle in many different cultural settings. In this way Sharp designers are able to design user-friendly products with human-engineered ease of operation.

Sharp products are manufactured in 23 countries at 31 different plants, and are enjoyed by people in 135 countries around the world. The Sharp trademark has become accepted as a local brand in every country that it appears, because of its constant efforts at internationalization through technological transfers and policies of conducting local manufacturing in a manner most mutually beneficial to all those involved.

Sharp Electronics of Canada has 210 employees and is divided into two sales and marketing divisions: its Business Products division and Consumer Electronics division. Although its head office and central warehouse are located in Mississauga, Ontario, Sharp has five branch offices and 2700 authorized dealers across Canada. Always interested in assimilating itself with the local community, Sharp Electronics of Canada helps sponsor area sports clubs, community projects and cultural activities.

With its many products used by Canadians throughout the country, Sharp Electronics has become an established household name that can be relied on and trusted. It is to maintain this customer confidence that Sharp Electronics of Canada Ltd. continues to be committed to the principle of serving society with new products that serve the daily needs of its associates and consumers.

1. *The 2.5 metre LCD projection system provides the home with dynamic movie-theatre realism.*
2. *Sharp's electronic organizers have become essential tools for today's busy executives.*
3. *Sharp manufactures innovative consumer electronic products such as this new portable audio product.*
4. *Sharp plays a major role in the development of LCD technology including one of the world's first LCD colour laptop computers.*

1

2

3

4

Simmons Canada Inc.

Who ensured that athletes at the 1988 Calgary Olympics had a comfortable night's rest? Simmons, Canada's number one mattress manufacturer! Every Olympian and, in fact, the entire Olympic village slept on a Simmons Maxipedic* mattress and box spring.

The company has a long and proud history as a leader in the Canadian furniture industry. Its Beautyrest* mattress is the number one seller in the country, and its Hide-A-Bed* convertible sofa has become the household word for that most versatile piece of furniture. These products are found in homes, hotels, motels and resorts across the country and around the world.

In 1991, Simmons marks its one hundredth year in Canada. Throughout its history, the company has introduced many innovations to the furniture industry. For example, it was the first to produce queen and king size mattresses in Canada, and the first to introduce the pricing of mattresses by size, a practice that has become standard in the industry.

The pillow-top mattress was another enhancement to sleeping comfort. But the most significant innovation was the Contour-Flex* pocket coil system, the unique coil construction of the Beautyrest mattress. It's a patented design that enables the mattress to conform to

1

the body's contours, providing superior support and comfort.

Today known as Simmons Canada Inc., the company was purchased in June, 1990, from the United States parent in a management-led buyout. The purchase was completed in conjunction with financial partners CIBC/Wood Gundy Capital, Manvest Ltd., Thornmark Capital, and Kenrick Capital.

The Canadian company began as J.H. Sherrard Manufacturing Co. Limited, founded in Montreal in 1891. It was incorporated under Dominion Charter granted "to collect, purify, manufacture and deal in feathers and down feathers and down goods and bedding of all descriptions throughout the Dominion of Canada." The business grew rapidly, with plants added in Montreal in 1894, Toronto in 1900, Winnipeg in 1904, and Vancouver in 1913.

In 1919 Simmons Co. of the United States purchased a number of

small bedding firms in Canada and incorporated the business as Simmons Limited. Firms included Alaska Bedding (Montreal, Winnipeg, Calgary and Vancouver), The Ideal Bedding Company Limited (Toronto), Hutchings Company Limited (Saint John, New Brunswick), and George Gale & Sons Limited (Waterville, Quebec).

The Canadian operation ran with great autonomy, and underwent a major period of expansion during the 1960's. The U.S. company was also expanding at this time, both in the U.S. and internationally with opera-

THE DYNAMICS OF COMFORT
Beautyrest

SIMMONS

3

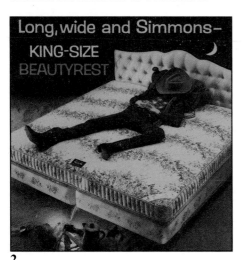

1. *An early bedding delivery truck. In those days, springs, mattresses and pillows were delivered unwrapped.*
2. *A successful advertisement campaign from the late 1950s.*
3. *The Contour-Flex "Orbs" campaign was a finalist at the thirtieth annual CLIO awards honouring advertising excellence worldwide.*

2

1

2

tions in England, France, Belgium, Australia, Venezuela, Japan, Puerto Rico and Mexico.

As sales in Canada grew and technology advanced, modern new facilities were required. A new plant replaced the existing one in Vancouver in 1956, the Toronto plant was replaced by a new factory in Brampton in 1964, the Calgary plant was opened in 1966, and the Mississauga head offices in 1976. The old Montreal facility was replaced by a modern plant in Cornwall in 1987 and an updated showroom and sales office opened in Montreal.

For a number of years, the company was involved in superior quality furniture production. It owned the Elora Furniture Company Limited, a wood furniture factory from 1965 to 1986, and an upholstered furniture factory in Elora, Ontario, from 1967 to 1989. In 1973, it acquired the Andrew Malcolm Furniture Company Limited, producing fine wood furniture at Kincardine and Listowel, Ontario, until 1978 and 1990, respectively.

Today, the focus of Simmons' manufacturing is on quality bedding products for the home and for the hospitality industry, markets in which it enjoys a commanding market leader position. The company also markets a full line of upholstered products including Hide-A Bed convertible sofas, leather sofas and chairs, as well as a complete line of case goods furniture for the hospitality and nursing home industry. Its

products are known for their high quality of materials and craftsmanship, and have won awards for their superior quality standards; for example, in January of 1990 Sears Canada Inc. named Simmons the first Sears Quality Certified Manufacturer of mattresses.

Pat Thody, who began as a salesman for the company in Victoria, British Columbia in 1971, and today is President and Chief Executive Officer, points out that the primary reason for Simmons' success is its people and their ideas. Widely recognized as a company with innovative concepts, Simmons

Canada Inc. has never strayed from the ideal of quality products which have been critical to its success. It is because of this commitment to excellence and value that Simmons continues to maintain leadership in the bedding industry in Canada.

*T.M. Simmons I.P. Inc.
  Registered User Simmons Canada Inc.

1. *An early manufacturing plant interior.*
2. *The "Open Wide And Say Ahhh . . ."
Hide-A-Bed convertible sofa campaign.*
3. *Hidy and Howdy with chaperon at the 1988 Olympic Games in Calgary, Alberta. As an official supplier, Simmons provided over 10,000 pieces of bedding.*

SIMMONS*

Official Supplier of Beds to Calgary 1988 Olympic Winter Games
Fournisseur officiel de lits aux Jeux Olympiques d'hiver de Calgary de 1988

3

SPAR Aerospace Limited

"To dare to reach beyond tomorrow, to extend the reach of the human mind." With these words, John D. MacNaughton, President and Chief Executive Officer, describes the mission of SPAR Aerospace Limited. Canadian shareholder-owned, SPAR Aerospace is known throughout Canada and the world as the company which developed the Canadarm, the space shuttle arm which has already successfully deployed and rescued numerous satellites. But SPAR Aerospace is much more than the Canadarm, it is an advanced technology company actively engaged in the design, development, manufacture and servicing of systems for the space, robotics, communications, electro-optics and aviation markets.

In 1967, SPAR was the Special Products and Applied Research division of de Havilland Aircraft of Canada Limited, producing advanced technology but very little for immediate use. When de Havilland Aircraft displayed interest in selling the SPAR division, Larry Clark, Vice President of Administration and Planning, offered to buy it in August 1967. Thus, SPAR Aerospace Limited began on October 27, 1967, with Larry Clark as its President.

With a staff of more than 300, the company's first year was largely spent in the repair and manufacture of aerospace products. In 1969 SPAR decided to acquire the financially troubled York Gears Limited, and it soon received a multi-million dollar contract from General Electric for a helicopter jet-engine gearbox. In the mid 1970s SPAR acquired the satellite design and manufacture capability from RCA, and the space-electronics manufacturing assets from Northern Telecom Limited, thereby doubling SPAR's size.

In the late 1970s SPAR opened the Remote Manipulator System division, the division which eventually would construct the Canadarm. In 1981 it delivered the first of three of the arms, and the project was a complete success. The Canadarm, in addition to rescuing crippled satellites and other activities, has recently successfully deployed the Hubble Telescope.

Throughout the 1980s, SPAR Aerospace Limited has been heavily involved in the development of communications systems. In May, 1982, it was chosen to produce two communications satellites for Brazil. Much of the success of gaining the bid was attributed to the training that Canada offered Brazil. In 1984 SPAR won the contract

Artist's view of the Mobile Servicing System, Canada's Contribution to the International Space Station, Freedom.

from China for 30 earth stations, and again success in winning the bid was attributed to the training and technology that were offered.

The Satellite & Communications Systems Division has also received many other contracts. It will develop and manufacture the communications antennas for the international space station Freedom. SPAR is the prime contractor for the Anik E communications satellites being built for Telesat Canada, which are designed to carry television, facsimile, modem, and other sophisticated business data traffic. Transport Canada has awarded SPAR the contract for an advanced system for air traffic control communications.

In December, 1990, the Canadian-based Telesat Mobile Inc. and the American Mobile Satellite Corporation granted SPAR the contract for the communications payload of the world's most powerful and technologically advanced mobile communications satellites. The MSAT satellites will establish an integrated North American mobile communications system providing voice, fax, positioning and data communications to mobile users on land, sea and in the air.

In the international high technology marketplace, SPAR is also a leading player. In its first breakthrough in the Japanese market, SPAR recently was awarded a contract by Toshiba to provide engineering support for the Japanese contribution to Freedom. SPAR is also involved in the construction of a satellite communications system for the Republic of Sierra Leone, and Mexico awarded SPAR the contract for three large networks of satellite telecommunications.

In the area of satellite remote sensing systems, SPAR is also a world leader. On January 26, 1990, SPAR signed the contract with the Canadian Space Agency for Phase One of the Radarsat remote-sensing satellite program. It is a Canadian led, international project scheduled to launch in 1994. What makes it unique is its Synthetic Aperture Radar, a powerful microwave instrument that records data day and night, through clear or cloudy skies, a capability which current satellites do not have. This vital force in the protection and management of our environment will observe the High Arctic each day, most of Canada every three days, and all of the earth every twenty-four days, enhancing Canada's claim to Arctic sovereignty.

Building on the experience gained from developing the Canadarm, SPAR is the prime contractor for Freedom's Mobile Servicing System, Canada's main contribution to the international space station. Weighing 4,800 kilograms, it will have a payload capacity of 100,000 kilograms. A separate smaller robot, the Special Purpose Dextrous Manipulator will have two smaller arms for more delicate jobs. With cameras installed to give close-up views, it will be an extension of the astronauts' own senses. This smaller robot will be

Larry D. Clarke, Chairman of the Board (left) and John D. MacNaughton, President and Chief Executive Officer.

voice controlled and will literally be able to see and touch.

Not only is SPAR involved in satellites and communications, it is also an important contender in the development of defence systems. SPAR has delivered two AN/SAR-8 Infra-red Search and Target Designation Systems to the United States Navy for testing. The system, a joint development program of the Canadian and U.S. Navies, it is the most advanced naval infra-red surveillance system in the world. Its ability to identify and track incoming targets at low levels will greatly enhance ship survival in the case of airborne attack.

In October, 1990, the newly-formed Applied Systems Group of SPAR acquired certain assets of Ottawa-based Leigh Instruments Ltd., along with the accompanying federal government contracts. The Applied Systems Group, based in Kanata and Carleton Place, Ontario, has already received an important contract from McDonnell Douglas Corporation of Saint Louis, Missouri, for the development of a Deployable Flight Incident Recorder Set for the F/A-18 aircraft.

From its humble beginnings, SPAR Aerospace Limited has grown into one of the largest technological groups in the private sector in Canada with more than 2000 employees, 600 of which are engineers and technicians. Twenty per cent of SPAR's engineering activities are dedicated to research and development, including co-operative programs with several Canadian universities. Whether it is developing innovative ideas such as the retubing arm for Ontario's Hydro nuclear reactors and robots to strengthen mine tunnels before the workers enter, or being involved in the design and manufacture of space, aeronautics, defence and communications systems, SPAR Aerospace Limited continues to dare to reach beyond tomorrow.

Stage West All-Suite Hotel & Theatre Restaurant

The slogan for Stage West is "We're Dramatically Different," and indeed, this unique facility is the only one of its kind in Ontario. Combine famous TV, screen and stage stars with a gourmet buffet and entertaining live plays and you have Stage west Theatre Restaurant.

Add an all-suite hotel, a giant water slide and aquatic centre, a fitness facility and you have Stage West All-Suite Hotel, and all just ten minutes from Toronto International Airport.

Although dinner theatre is common in the United States, the concept only recently became popular in Canada and much of the credit for its popularity can be attributed to Stage West co-founders Eugene and Howard Pechet. In 1973 Howard Pechet was an energetic, 24 year old university graduate looking for a challenge. His father, hotelier Eugene Pechet, was building the Mayfield Inn in Edmonton, and was open to new ideas. After a trip to the United States to investigate dinner

1

theatre, the Pechets opened the first Stage West on January 21, 1975 in the Mayfield Inn. After some initial difficult times, the concept of a dinner theatre and hotel combined took hold. Stage West, Edmonton has been an overwhelming success ever since. Stage West soon appeared in Regina, Winnipeg, Calgary, and opened in Mississauga in 1986 on Dixie Road.

Stage West has an unbeatable formula. Guests indulge in an elaborate buffet and are then entertained by internationally known stars. They specialize in classic, lighthearted performances such as *Tribute*, *Chapter Two*, and *Move Over Mrs. Markham*. Stage West also often presents Canadian debuts of Broadway plays. The combination of good stars and good food ensures that Stage West will continue to be one of the most popular and successful entertainment concepts available.

The theatre's clientele ranges from blue collar to tourist, to business executives. The theatre was complimented by the addition of a magnificent 224 all-suite hotel which opened in September 1990.

Daniel J. Royer, co-founder of Relax Inns, is President of Stage West Mississauga. He attributes much of the success of the hotel to the existence of the theatre, pointing out that many people stay at the hotel after attending the theatre, and corporate guests enjoy access to all of the facilities in one complex. No other facility offers so much, making Stage West an enjoyable experience that is "Dramatically Different."

1. *Inside the popular Stage West Theatre Restaurant.* **2.** *Stage West Hotel & Theatre Restaurant, located in Mississauga, Ontario.*

2

Stone & Webster Canada Limited

The Stone & Webster organization is the outgrowth of a partnership formed in 1889 by Charles A. Stone and Edwin S. Webster, graduates of the first electrical engineering class of the Massachusetts Institute of Technology. Stone & Webster first entered Canada in 1907 and was active here for many years on projects such as Toronto's Hospital for Sick Children, Ontario Hydro's change from 25 to 60 cycle frequency, and the first catalytic heavy water plant to be placed in operation, in Trail, British Columbia.

A small office was established in Toronto in 1945 with activities being co-ordinated by Leonard L. Youell, who later became Vice President, General Manager and a Director of Stone & Webster Canada Limited.

In January 1950, Stone & Webster, Inc. President Whitney Stone and Vice President Philip Scott made a visit to some ongoing Canadian projects. Accompanied at times by prominent Canadian industrialists, they also visited oil and gas fields, met with the Prime Minister and the Minister of Lands and Mines, and attended a formal party for 100 leading Ontario executives and public officials. Returning to New York, they agreed that the business climate was conducive to finalizing plans for a Canadian company.

Because of their common interest in equestrian affairs, Stone and a Toronto entrepreneur, John W. McKee, had become personal friends. With the decision to establish a Canadian company, McKee agreed to organize a Board of Directors and serve as its first Chairman. Stone & Webster Canada Limited was incorporated on July 7, 1950 — an event marked by a dinner attended by

1

2

1. *The Richard L. Hearn Generating Station, which Stone & Webster originally designed and constructed in the 1950s and later expanded.*
2. *Charles A. Stone and Edwin S. Webster, founders of Stone & Webster, Inc.*

many prominent business leaders.

The first job carried out in Canada after incorporation of the company was a new oil refinery at Corunna for Canadian Oil Refineries Limited. The editors of *World Petroleum* magazine selected this refinery as the "outstanding event of the oil industry in Canada" in 1952.

A relationship between Stone & Webster and Ontario Hydro, begun in 1934, continued into the 1950s with the design and construction of the Richard L. Hearn Generating Station and its later expansion from 400 to 1200 megawatts, and with the provision of consulting services in connection with the first four units of its Lakeview Generating Station. This relationship continues into the 1990s through the company's substantial involvement in the rehabilitation and modernization of both the Lakeview and Lambton Generating Stations.

One project carried out between 1953 and 1955 was to gain special

attention by launching Stone & Webster into a specialized area where it had previously touched only the fringes. The assignment was to supervise the design and construction of a Toronto brewery for one of the oldest and best-known companies in the business, Molson Breweries.

Glenn H. Curtis became President in 1961. It was in the early 1960s that a corporate decision was made to offer the company's services to all industrial sectors rather than specialize in power and petrochemicals. This was a period of major growth for Stone & Webster, adding such companies as Dow Chemical, Union Carbide and Imperial Oil to its list of clients. It also marked the company's entry into the steel industry, and its involvement in such landmarks as the McLaughlin Planetarium and the John P. Robarts Research Library for the University of Toronto.

Certainly the largest project undertaken in Canada at this time

Stone & Webster supervised design and construction of Molson's Toronto Brewery.

was the design and construction of a major petrochemical plant for Gulf Oil Canada Limited at Varennes, Quebec. This 250 million pounds/year ethylene plant, started up in 1969, was expanded a few years later to 500 million pounds/year.

In 1966 the company undertook to double the size and completely modernize the Walkerville Distillery of Hiram Walker & Sons Limited, the company's first major undertaking in that field. In 1967, The Algoma Steel Corporation, Limited awarded Stone & Webster a contract for the construction of all major expansion and renovation work at its Sault Ste. Marie mill, beginning a relationship which has lasted over twenty years.

Diversification remained a keynote in the 1970s under the

direction of Jacques J.H. Pley, who became President in 1971. Marketing efforts were directed to the international scene and much attention was focused on gasoline additives and Stone & Webster's experience in the fermentation field was applied to the "gasohol" industry.

Energy conservation and improved production of existing plants had become the trend in the mid-1970s, and became an important field for Stone & Webster. Major improvement and expansion work was carried out for Shell Canada Limited at various refineries as well as for Du Pont Canada Inc. at its Maitland Works.

Having outgrown its headquarters several times, in 1975 the company became one of the first tenants in the Yonge-Eglinton Centre. An office was also opened in Calgary in order to participate in the major energy related projects planned in that province.

Stone & Webster was retained to provide engineering and design of the ski-jumping complex for the 1980 Winter Olympic Games in Lake Placid, as well as the substantial training facilities at Thunder Bay. The company's expertise in such facilities centred on Vice President Karl Martitsch, a former member of the Austrian National Ski Team. It was later responsible for design of the ski-jumping complex at Calgary Olympic Park for the 1988 Winter Olympic Games.

In 1980 an office was established in Halifax with the primary focus being to participate in the offshore oil and gas industry. Stone & Webster Engineering Limited of the United Kingdom, an affiliated company which had been active in the offshore industry in Europe and the Middle East since 1970, provided extensive training to Canadian engineers.

Throughout its forty-year history, the company has been dedicated to the philosophy of the enhancement of the technical capabilities of the engineering community in Canada. Transfer of technology from affiliated companies has included thermal power (in the early 1970s) and offshore technology; however, its greatest contribution has been to the nuclear power industry. The transfer of special expertise in the area of pipe stress analysis and piping systems permitted the hiring of an average of fifty new graduates annually from Canadian universities over a ten-year period, ensuring them an excellent "head-start" in their professional careers.

The company's strong process engineering capability and its credentials in the upgrading of operating process plants have resulted in work being carried out for every major petroleum refiner in the country. Much of the recent work carried out for these and other process industries clients relates to environmental concerns and the concerted effort being made by all to comply with environmental legislation.

At Texaco Canada Inc.'s Nanticoke Refinery, now Esso, Stone & Webster carried out a major modernization encompassing several energy conservation and clean products improvement projects. Similar modernization and upgrading work has also been carried out for Petro-Canada Products at its Lake Ontario Refinery and for Esso Petroleum Canada at various refinery locations.

Stone & Webster has always "kept up with the times," evidenced by its ability to diversify to meet the needs of its clients. In the 1990s and beyond, the company looks forward to continuing to play an important role in a constantly changing technological environment as well as maintaining its longstanding tradition of quality work.

From left to right: Robert C. Wiesel, Executive Vice President; Theodore J. Doyle, Executive Vice President; Albert E. Garred, President and Chief Executive Officer of Stone & Webster Canada Limited.

Summit Ford

1

2

As one of the top ten Ford dealerships in Canada, Summit Ford is proud of the reputation that it has earned. Known as a friendly family business by all who have worked with Summit, Scott Vickers, President of Summit Ford, is determined not only to keep but also enhance Summit's image.

Les Vickers, Scott Vickers' father, began working for car dealerships in 1960. Unhappy with the situation in which he found himself, he was planning to leave his position as sales manager. While in the process of leaving, he was approached by a representative of Ford, inquiring whether Les Vickers would like a Ford dealership of his own. When Les Vickers answered affirmatively, the Ford representative offered him a dealership in Woodbridge, Ontario.

After arranging the financing with Ford, in January, 1968, Les

Vickers became President of Summit Ford. When Summit ordered its first 100 cars, the agency had sixteen employees. Working hard, the dealership grew quickly. Les Vickers' sons were soon employed after schooldays and on weekends, doing janitorial duties and cleaning the cars.

In 1970 Les Vickers made a bold move and purchased the property on which the dealership is currently located, in Etobicoke. Scott Vickers likes to point out the foresight which his father had when he purchased this property. At that point there was only farmland in the whole area. When Summit opened at its new location in 1972, Scott Vickers recalls overhearing predictions that the dealership would not be able to last, not even for six months. However, strategically situated today in the midst of thriving new development, Summit has not only survived, but excelled in its service to this community.

In 1978 Scott Vickers began to work full-time for Summit Ford, becoming involved in the leasing section. By 1982, when his father was interested in selling the dealership, Scott Vickers was ready to offer to purchase Summit. Although Ford at first was reluctant to authorize the purchase, having other applicants and feeling that Scott Vickers was rather young at twenty-seven to manage a dealer-

ship with annual sales of over forty-five million dollars, Ford eventually agreed, and after two years the deal was arranged. In November, 1984, Scott Vickers became President of Summit Ford.

Scott Vickers explains that the dealership has three interconnected philosophies that form the pillars for its success. First, the employees must enjoy their work. Many of Summit's employees have been with the dealership on a long-term basis; several, like the general manager, have been with Summit from the beginning. Second, the dealership must be profitable to continue. And, third, the agency must completely satisfy the customers. Many of Summit's clients are now repeat customers, expressing confidence and satisfaction with Summit.

Today, with ninety-five employees, Summit Ford is still dedicated to being a family style business. Having won the President's Inner Circle, the highest honour Ford bestows on its dealers, five out of six years recently, Summit Ford can look forward to a future of further growth and success.

1. *Scott Vickers, President of Summit Ford.*
2. *In 1970 Les Vickers (Scott Vickers' father) made a bold move and purchased the property on which the dealership is currently located in Etobicoke, Ontario. When the dealership was constructed, there was no development nearby.*
3. *Summit Ford today.*

3

Takara Belmont Company Canada Ltd.

As part of an international group of companies that supply an estimated ninety-five per cent of the special chairs needed in barber shops and beauty salons around the world, Takara Belmont Company Canada manufactures products for distribution in Canada and throughout the world.

Takara Belmont was founded in 1921 by Hidenobu Yoshikawa in Japan to manufacture equipment for barber shops and beauty salons. In the 1950s the company expanded its operations to establish manufacturing centres in the United States, Europe and South America. The company opened its Canadian manufacturing facility in 1966. In the 1960s, Takara Belmont drew on its advanced hydraulic technology to commence the manufacture of dental chairs, a move leading to the development of a wide range of products for the medical and dental professions.

Anticipating advances in dental techniques, the company's international network of facilities maintains close contact with practising professionals through which

1

its 300 engineers plan and perfect systems to meet virtually any equipment need. As a result, Takara Belmont offers a comprehensive line of dental operatory systems, including specialty units for pedodontic and orthodontic practice. All components, from the advanced x-ray, lighting, and dental consoles to the totally automated chairs, represent the optimum in professional convenience and patient comfort. In Canada and the United States, Takara Belmont's self-contained dental operatory was patented in 1979.

Ergonomically designed to minimize fatigue, all of the company's products reflect an emphasis on quality and durability. Quality is built in by meticulous design to harmonize the equipment with the people who use it — the customer and the professional.

Today, the Takara Belmont worldwide network embraces distributors in eighty countries and subsidiaries and factories in seven other countries. Annual sales are now over $600 million.

Takara Belmont Company Canada has more than forty employees at its 28,000 square feet facility in Mississauga, Ontario. As part of the international network of Takara Belmont, the Canadian division manufactures products for the barber shop, beauty salon and dental divisions.

1. *Takara Belmont's manufacturing facility located in Mississauga, Ontario.*
2. *The company's programmable, totally electronic barber chairs feature the latest in design and comfort.*

2

Tippet-Richardson Limited

For over sixty years Tippet-Richardson Limited has been moving more Canadian families and corporations than any other company. Its founding goal in 1927 was to provide high quality residential and commercial services; today, this commitment to service is an integral part of each of Tippet-Richardson's specialized divisions.

The company began as a residential moving service, a new and hazardous proposition. The two partners, C.F. Basil Tippet, President and C.A. Richardson, Vice President, had been partners in a previous business venture, and they started Tippet-Richardson with a rented warehouse and one van, operating on the highways as an independent operator. The company moved furniture to the United States, Ontario and Quebec; because there was as yet no

Canadian highway to Western Canada, they travelled west through the United States to make deliveries to Western Canada.

In 1929 the company became an agent of Allied Van Lines, Inc. in the United States. Two years later, they also became an agent for the independent Canadian company, Allied Van Lines Limited. But times were difficult and by 1934 the two partners had lost all the money they had invested. Tippet, who attributed it largely due to inexperience, reimbursed Richardson for his original investment, and the latter resigned in 1936.

At approximately the same time, the expansion of the company really commenced. Since then, Tippet-Richardson has been able to do more business each year than the previous year. During the depression years the

employees had to work long hours and received low salaries, but the company managed to survive. In 1944 H. Russell Naylor and W.W. Naylor became Vice Presidents of the company. The first experimental trips to Western Canada were made in 1947 over the new Highway #11 as soon as it was opened between Northern Ontario and Manitoba.

The company soon began to expand to more locations, and in 1952 it moved into Hamilton by purchasing control of McDougall the Mover Limited. In 1954 Tippet-Richardson opened a branch in Ottawa and built a new warehouse in Downsview, Ontario. C.F.B. Tippet passed away in 1959, and as a result H.R. Naylor became President of Tippet-Richardson. The same year saw the company moving into Stratford and Waterloo, Ontario.

Two years later, through the purchase of existing operations of Fox Cartage and Storage Limited, the company moved into Trenton, North Bay and Pembroke, Ontario.

In 1971 H.R. Naylor retired as President but remained as Chairman, and Peter Naylor assumed the responsibilities of President. H.R. Naylor, after more than fifty years of service with Tippet-Richardson and its affiliated companies, passed away in 1976, and Bruce Naylor became Vice President. 1981 marked the company's move into the United States, with the opening of an office in San Jose, California. The following year the head office was moved to East Don Roadway, its present location. In 1986 Tippet-Richardson named Peter Naylor as Chairman of the Board and Bruce Naylor became President.

Today, Tippet-Richardson Limited is a highly diversified service organization that has over 775 employees in sixteen offices across Canada, including nine throughout Ontario, and also an office in San Jose, California. It operates a fleet of 360 vehicles. The company is still a major player in the residential moving sector, but it has also diversified its services, which include household goods moving and storage for local and long distance throughout North America; international household goods moving; specialized moving facilities for sensitive equipment; computer refurbishing; trade show transportation and co-ordination; office relocation; public warehousing and distribution; systems furniture installation; furniture refurbishing; and records management services. A major area of growth for the company in the last twenty-five year and which has grown rather quickly in the last fifteen years has been its off-site records storage and management service, storing at present over one million cartons of records in its facilities.

Looking back at the company's history and recognizing the success achieved by Tippet-Richardson already by the 1950s, Basil Tippet once wrote that "The progress of Tippet-Richardson has been largely from the efforts of our older employees, the gentlemen with the longest beards, in present positions of senior responsibilities." In reflecting on this comment, Bruce Naylor, the current President and Chief Executive Officer of Tippet-Richardson remarks, ". . . the success of the company today does not relate so much to beard length, but does still relate to people — people with the qualities of dedication and innovation, qualities found in people of varying ages — and beard lengths!"

For over sixty years, Tippet-Richardson's fleet of vehicles has moved more Canadian families and corporations than any other company.

Top Grade Machining Ltd.

First, learn about the customer's needs; second, build a high quality mold; and third, follow it up with expert assistance. Using this blueprint for a successful business operation, Top Grade Machining Ltd. has continued to grow and expand for over twenty-five years, while always producing top grade injection molds. These injection molds are then used by industry to produce a wide range of plastic products through a process involving the injection by high pressure of the heated plastic material into the cavity between the two halves of the mold. The molds that Top Grade manufactures are used in a variety of medical, packaging, commercial, automotive, and other industrial applications, wherever injection molding is needed.

Joseph Slobodnik, who received his training in the Republic of Slovenia before immigrating to Canada in 1960, began the company in Downsview as a part-time business in 1964. In 1965 the company, now requiring his full-time attention, moved to Weston, and it was incorporated in 1966. From the beginning, Top Grade Machining has enjoyed continuous growth and by 1975 it needed to move again to larger premises, this time to Mississauga. In 1979 the company moved to its present location, still within Mississauga, and recently it

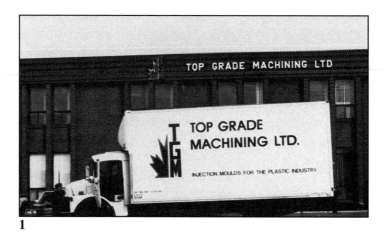

1

has expanded to 26,000 square feet of production space.

Much of the growth in recent years is attributable to increased productivity through the increasingly important role that computers and technology have played within the company. In 1983 the first 3-axis CNC (Computer Numerical Control) machining centre was purchased; a mere six months later, the company also obtained a microcomputer-based 3-D CAM (Computer Aided Manufacturing) system. Later, a CAD (Computed Aided Design) drafting system was also purchased. Prior to automated techniques, each mold tool was still produced manually and individually, but with CAD/CAM technology the turn-around time has been cut in half. "Top Grade wouldn't be able to manage the work load without CAD/CAM," points out Slobodnik.

Although this state-of-the-art equipment is essential to the continued success of the company, it still only complements, but does not replace, the company's loyal and able employees. Without people such as his wife Doreen and a few faithful employees, all who have been with the company almost from the beginning, Joe Slobodnik emphasizes that Top Grade could not have succeeded.

With approximately sixty per cent of its high quality, reliable molds exported to the United States, Mexico, Venezuela, New Zealand, and as far away as Indonesia, Top Grade Machining continues to ride a wave of success due to hard work, good people, and good customers. With more than twenty five years of injection mold manufacturing experience, Top Grade Machining knows what it takes to design and build the finest molds.

1. The company's present location in Mississauga.
2. Joseph Slobodnik, President and Founder of Top Grade Machining Ltd.
3. Joseph Slobodnik, Jr., working with the CAD/CAM system.

2

3

The Toronto School of Business Inc.

1

In today's fast changing business world, it is the well-trained, skilled employee who will be first in line for the best job opportunities. The Toronto School of Business has prepared more than 100,000 men and women for new and meaningful careers. The Toronto School of Business, proud of its reputation for exceptional graduates, has grown from its small beginnings to being the largest chain of private career training schools in Canada, with twenty-seven campuses coast to coast across Canada.

The school was founded as a private business college in 1976 by Allan N. Ebedes, a chartered accountant, in Toronto. While working as an accountant, he continually noticed that there was a lack of knowledge and understanding of basic bookkeeping. Realizing that there was a need for formal classes, he began to offer instruction in the evenings.

The School opened its first campus at Yonge and Finch Streets. At this point, all the instructors were only teaching part-time, offering evening and Saturday morning classes. As the demand for more courses grew, the School began to offer typing as well as bookkeeping courses. From there, it was a natural progression to also offer word processing classes.

With the success of his schools becoming well known, Ebedes was approached with the unique idea of opening a School in Scarborough as a franchise, patterned after the original two Schools. As the Schools were essentially a people-orientated business, they needed personal attention. An owner on site rather than just a manager would give the personal attention and care the institution needed. The Scarborough School was opened on this basis, setting the pattern for the opening of many more Schools across Canada.

In 1983 a fourth School was opened in St. John's, Newfoundland, operating under the name of CompuCollege School of Business, which set a precedent for all the other Schools outside of Ontario.

Today, the School has a comprehensive curriculum offering training for many different careers. Specializing in training men and women for business and computer-related careers, the curriculum is constantly being updated to take into account the needs of an ever-changing business world. Most of the diploma programs can be completed in as little as six months by way of full-time study. Morning, evening or week-end courses are offered and attendance can be full or part-time.

The Toronto School of Business Inc. has developed a unique methodology of course design and delivery, called a modular curriculum. A modular curriculum requires students to complete one fundamentals course per program and allows students to concentrate on just one course at a time, enabling the Schools to accept newly enroled students on a monthly basis throughout the year.

An important component of all programs is the mandatory two week job placement workshop. It includes video-taped practice interviews, information on effective resume preparation, the best methods of getting interviews, and how to find jobs not advertised.

Today, proud to have prepared thousands of men and women for satisfying successful careers, and with an excellent job placement rate, The Toronto School of Business continues to prepare men and women for new and meaningful careers.

2

1. *Allan N. Ebedes, B.Com., M.B.A., C.A., the founder and current President of The Toronto Schools of Business Inc.*
2. *With small class sizes, students are assured of individual attention, using state of the art equipment.*

Trans-Northern Pipelines Inc.

Trans-Northern Pipelines Inc. operates the longest and largest refined petroleum products pipeline system in eastern Canada, stretching from Montreal, Quebec to Nanticoke, in southern Ontario. The

travel on the lakes and storage facilities. To be able to meet the need, the same capacity in lake tankers and additional rail vehicles would require a much greater tonnage of steel than would the construction of

tions were installed and the capacity of portions of the line increased to approximately 60,000 barrels per day. By 1956, with four further pumping facilities, the capacity of the entire line increased

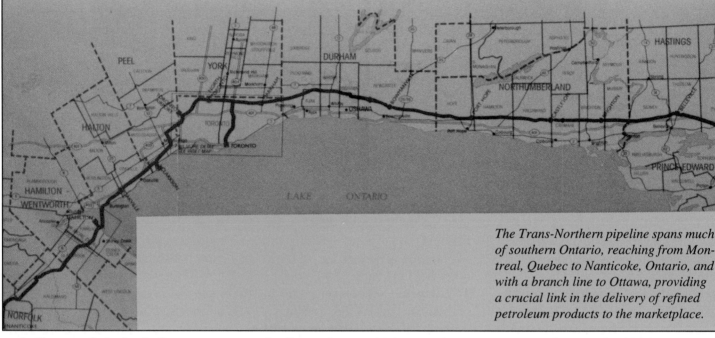

The Trans-Northern pipeline spans much of southern Ontario, reaching from Montreal, Quebec to Nanticoke, Ontario, and with a branch line to Ottawa, providing a crucial link in the delivery of refined petroleum products to the marketplace.

main line parallels the St. Lawrence Seaway and the north and west shores of Lake Ontario.

Incorporated as Trans-Northern Pipe Line Company by Special Act of the Parliament of Canada which received Royal Assent on April 30, 1949, the company was formed for the purpose of constructing and operating a pipe line system to provide year-round transportation and delivery of refined petroleum products from refineries located in Montreal, Quebec to marketing terminals located along the system.

Before the pipeline, railway tank cars, supplemented by lake and river tankers during the period of open navigation, supplied the area. A complete inventory of products was required at marine terminals for the winter months when canals and harbours were impassable. Demand for petroleum products kept increasing in the post World War II era, along with increased tanker

a pipeline, a factor which was of paramount importance in obtaining the initial allocation of the necessary steel plate for the rolling of pipe from government authorities.

It was essential that operation of the pipeline commence at the earliest possible date because postponement would have resulted in a shortage of petroleum products in some areas. In May, 1952, after several years of engineering, planning, surveying, and acquiring the right-of-way, construction of the project commenced and was completed in October of that same year. In addition to the main Montreal to Hamilton line, a branch line was also constructed to serve the Ottawa area.

With four main pumping stations located at intervals along the line, 40,000 barrels per day began to flow in November, 1952. By 1953, forecasts of demand indicated that the capacity would be inadequate, and therefore additional booster pump sta-

to approximately 80,000 barrels per day.

Initially, the pipeline moved product only for the three companies which originally formed Trans-Northern: McColl-Frontenac Oil Company, British American Oil Company, Ltd., and Shell Oil Company of Canada, Ltd. In 1955, Petrofina Canada became a shipper, followed by BP Canada Ltd. in 1960, Imperial Oil Ltd. and Sun Oil Company in 1963, and later Spur (Murphy), Ultramar, Petro-Canada and Ryfas, thereby making the pipeline a mode of transportation for all major marketers in the area served by Trans-Northern.

With the advent of the National Oil Policy and the restriction of movement of products refined offshore to west of the Ottawa Valley, the company was forced to significantly revise its mode of operation. In November, 1963, fifty-three miles of pipeline east of Kingston, Ontario

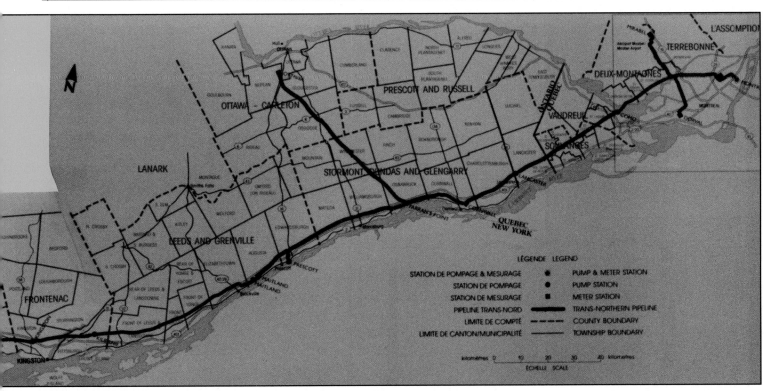

were taken out of service, along with a number of booster stations. Product movement westward from Montreal terminated at Ottawa and Maitland, Ontario, while the Toronto area refineries moved western Canada's products eastward as far as Kingston.

The company has also continued to modernize its equipment and facilities. In 1968 Trans-Northern replaced part of its Ottawa branch line, which was originally constructed with second-hand pipe, and has continued to update other lines. Facilities were constructed to serve Montreal's Dorval Airport and Toronto International Airport in 1969 and 1971. In 1975 the company provided facilities at the new Mirabel Airport outside of Montreal. In 1978, an extension westward of the main pipeline was completed, which brought the pipeline to the Imperial Oil refinery at Nanticoke, Ontario.

Facilities that had been mothballed in 1963 remained so until they were reactivated in 1972 and 1973 to accommodate movements from the Toronto area refineries to the Ottawa region during the national energy emergency. Following discussions with a task force formed to consider the maintenance of supply to the

Montreal market, that portion of the pipeline remained open. Starting in 1975, a significant part of the Ottawa market was also supplied from Toronto area refineries.

In late 1982 the company was requested by industry to reverse the flow of the pipeline from Farran's Point, Ontario to Montreal to enable product movement from Toronto area refineries eastward to Montreal. In February, 1983, the reversal of the system all the way to Montreal was completed, and product started to flow eastward to Montreal. The section of the line from Montreal to Farran's Point is now bi-directional, making the system a more valuable link between the two refinery centres of Montreal and Toronto.

The planning, scheduling and operating techniques involved in the movement of petroleum products are complex, each product having its own unique characteristics. Mixing of the products is kept to a minimum by operating at rates of flow which, with due regard for the different properties of each product, will maintain turbulence in the products as they move through the pipeline. Scheduled movements through the system are revised,

sometimes daily, due to fluctuations in supply and demand, mechanical and power failures, or other seasonal factors.

When the company began, it was under the jurisdiction of the Board of Transport Commissioners, with very light, almost non-existent regulation. In 1959, with the formation of the National Energy Board, regulation grew steadily until today, when virtually every aspect of the company's operation is regulated. All capital expenditures must be approved by the National Energy Board; through tariff procedures all operating costs are authorized, and earnings levels are also set by the National Energy Board.

Today, being the safest and most economical system of transportation for oil and petroleum products, underground pipelines remain vital to our way of life. With approximately 120 employees, Trans-Northern Pipelines Inc. continues to operate as the link between the refining areas, placing the company in a very favourable position for the future. Regardless of the source of crude or the point of refining, the Trans-Northern pipeline system will continue to serve as the vital link with the marketplace.

Tri-Tel Associates Ltd.

1

Distributers of electronic components and consumer products across Canada, Tri-Tel Associates Ltd. has developed into a premier distributorship with a difference. Willing to spend the necessary time and expense to learn what the end buyer wants and needs in a product, Tri-Tel has cultivated a unique relationship with the consumer.

Tri-Tel Associates was founded in 1961 by Eric Boyden, Joe McCormick and Ralph B. Finkle. Their previous employer, Canadian Marconi Co., was planning to close the import division of the company. Seizing the opportunity, the three employees formed a partnership and were able to purchase the import division.

The company was first located on Sheppard Avenue West in Toronto, in a small, second-floor office and warehouse. With Boyden's electronic engineering background, Finkle's experience as general manager, and McCormick's abilities in sales, they were able to successfully launch the new company.

Tri-Tel began as importers and distributors of electronic components and high-fidelity stereo equipment. One of the original equipment lines with which the company began, Stantion Mag-

netics Inc., is still with Tri-Tel today. Because of expanding sales, the company relocated in 1965 to a 10,000 square feet facility in Downsview, Ontario.

As the company was beginning to grow and establish itself, Joe McCormick, the sales manager, was unexpectedly killed in 1969 in a airplane crash while returning from a sales trip to Montreal. When Finkle's son, Ralph W. Finkle, was asked to fill the position as a sales manager, he accepted.

As a result of a business trip by Ralph Finkle, Jr., to Japan, Tri-Tel became the Canadian distributor of Maxell Ltd. products in 1975. Today, Tri-Tel Associates Ltd. is still the exclusive Canadian dealer of Maxell audio and video cassettes.

Growing sales once again forced the company to seek larger facilities, and in 1976 the company moved to its present site, in Willowdale, Ontario. When Boyden and Finkle, Sr., retired in 1980, Ralph Finkle, Jr., was able to purchase the company. Three years later, he formed a partnership with Hank Gruenstein, the company's sales manager. Today, Finkle, Jr., is President of Tri-Tel Associates Ltd., while Gruenstein serves as Vice President.

The company has also recently

developed its own line of hardware products, Pro-Power Tools. Built in Taiwan and distributed by Tri-Tel through industrial stores, they are targeted primarily for the tradesman and specialized worker.

However, Tri-Tel's central focus remains its electronics products. Finkle points out that although the consumer does not buy directly from Tri-Tel, the company views the consumer as its own customer. In order to provide the desired product to retail stores, Tri-Tel needs to be in constant contact with the consumer. Through a frequent-buyer program, surveys, sweepstakes and other promotional ideas, Tri-Tel has secured for itself a loyal base of customers for the products it distributes.

Today, Tri-Tel Associates Ltd. has become the exclusive Canadian distributer for a wide range of electronic manufacturers. With its unique knowledge of and relationship with the consumer, Tri-Tel has assured itself of continual growth in the future.

1. *Ralph B. Finkle, (father of Ralph W. Finkle, Jr., the current President), founded Tri-Tel Associates Limited in 1961 with two other associates.*
2. *Tri-Tel Associates' central offices in Willowdale, Ontario.*

2

Valdi Foods (1987) Inc.

1

With knowledgeable and friendly staff, good management and clean stores, Valdi Foods offers value: the ability to buy quality products that the consumer wants and needs, at the best possible price. The leading, limited assortment, box store format in Canada, Valdi provides its customers with excellent value on non-perishable, brand name grocery, and health and beauty aid products. Operating within Steinberg Inc.'s multi-format food retailing strategy, Valdi currently has a total of 100 stores in operation — eighty-four in Ontario and sixteen in Quebec.

The limited assortment box store concept was originally developed in Europe, and involved small stores with a very limited number of non-perishable items at substantially discounted prices as compared to traditional supermarket operators. The facilities were generally very austere, with wooden shelving or warehouse style racking; all designed to support the lowest cost operation to enable an adequate return at a discount retail pricing level.

Steinberg Inc.'s entry into the box store format was undertaken in the fall of 1978 with current Valdi Foods President and General Manager, Harry Lutgens, as one of the original founders, and Morris Ladenheim, who took an early retirement several years ago. Having worked for Steinberg Inc. for fifteen years, Lutgens was asked to start the new operation in Ontario. Lutgens led the Valdi team throughout the entire history of the chain, from the initial staff of two, located in a 300 square feet office, to Valdi's present size of more than 1500 employees.

The Valdi banner was coined to represent Value and Discount, the two themes that continue to be dominant in marketing today. Valdi was the first box store to operate in the Canadian market, with two stores opening in Metropolitan Toronto on October 18, 1978. In rapid succession, stores were opened in Mississauga, two in Hamilton, and one in Burlington. By the summer of 1979 there were six stores in operation, resulting in a constant flow of positive customer feedback.

The Valdi version of the box store concept was positively received by customers, as a clean, easy to shop retail food store with very low prices. Initial tests were positive and expansion was undertaken, along with a warehouse dedicated to supporting the emerging retail format. In August, 1979, three stores were opened on the same day in London, Ontario.

Valdi was making a very serious statement about its plans for the future of the business, and the industry was taking notice. Customer feedback encouraged them to expand even further. Expansion in the Ontario market proceeded rapidly, with a total of sixty-six stores in operation by July, 1985. Valdi has continued to grow in both Ontario and Quebec, and several new sites are currently under development.

Valdi continues to enjoy a loyal customer base that is sensitive to the cost of food and very well aware of the value and convenience that Valdi provides. Valdi Foods has been successful in the past, and plans to continue to enjoy success and growth in the future by properly executing its innovative retailing concept, while offering real value to its customers.

1. *Harry Lutgens began Valdi Foods in Ontario, opening the first two stores in Metropolitan Toronto on October 18, 1978.*
2. *The Kingston store, one of the 100 sstores that Valdi Foods currently operates across Ontario and Quebec, opened on August 27, 1980.*

2

The War Amputations of Canada

Recognized by the public as the organization that helps people recover their lost keys, The War Amputations of Canada has had as its hallmark for over seventy years the unique philosophy of amputees helping other amputees. The Key Tag Service is but one of many programs that the organization has set up to help it achieve its goals.

Founded by national charter in 1920 as The Amputations Association of The Great War, a fraternal society was envisioned that would be able to provide direction for its members while also seeing to their needs. Counselling, self-help and practical assistance were emphasized.

The organization's first President was Lieutenant Colonel Sidney Lambert, an army padre who had lost his leg in action in France during World War I. He saw the need for an organization that would assist amputees. During his tenure, he laid the groundwork for each ensuing generation of amputees and shaped the philosophy that, with courage and determination, amputees could succeed in life.

It was during his stay in Toronto's old College Street Veteran's Hospital that he first conceived of the idea of a national association to help solve the problems of all "men and women who have lost a limb or limbs or complete eyesight whilst giving their service to Canada, the British Empire, and the Allies in the Great War."

He helped galvanize his comrades in the early years. Later, he spearheaded a drive to set up a sheltered workshop where war amputees could work for competitive wages, while providing a service that would generate funds for the organization. The name of the association was changed to The War Amputations of Canada, and as disabled veterans returned from World War II, the organization provided information, fellowship and employment opportunities to all of its members.

In 1946 the Key Tag Service was launched as a means of providing employment for war amputees. Since then the service has grown into a computerized program that returns approximately 30,000 sets of lost keys annually, but always is dedicated to providing employment for Canadian amputees and people with other disabilities.

The Civilian Liaison Program began in 1953 in order that war amputees could share their knowledge with others who are missing limbs from causes other than war. Later, the program was divided into two, one for adults and a separate program for children.

H. Clifford Chadderton, who lost his right leg during World War II, became the Chief Executive Officer of the organization in 1965. The War Amps had been there to assist him in rebuilding his life as an amputee, and, in return, for more than twenty-five years he has tirelessly served the needs of Canadian amputees, both young and old.

With Chadderton at the helm, the organization grew dramatically and has become known around the world for its innovative programs and ideas. Realizing that war amputees were being well served by existing programs and that in the future their needs would decrease, he turned the organization's attention to child amputees and in 1975 started the Child Amputee (CHAMP) Program. More than 1600 youngsters are now enroled in

Padre Sidney Lambert, who founded The Amputations Association after World War I and who guided the organization for over fifty years, and H. Clifford Chadderton, OC, O.Ont., DCL, who benefitted from Padre Lambert's efforts and who has been Chief Executive Officer since 1965. Together they epitomize the history, traditions and strengths of The War Amputations of Canada.

CHAMP, and the program is as unique as the children enroled in it. The organization tries to reach all amputee children and their families as soon after an amputation as possible, providing special prostheses, education and counselling to help the children cope with their amputations.

The War Amps sponsors regional CHAMP Seminars annually across Canada, bringing together child amputees to meet their peers and learn about artificial limbs and new developments. The organization has produced many award-winning films, which are available free of charge, concerning prosthetics and encouraging amputees of all ages to live their lives to the fullest. To be a good example, Chadderton learned how to downhill ski at the age of sixty-six.

Maintaining a very high profile in the veterans' community, Chadderton is called upon regularly by the media to comment on veterans' issues. His efforts have meant that The War Amps has been granted consultative status at the United Nations as a Non-Governmental Organization, a singular achievement for any organization of its kind in the world. Chadderton also helped form The War Amps Thalidomide Task Force in 1987, providing assistance to Canada's thalidomide "babies," now-grown-up victims of a disastrous anti-nausea medication prescribed to their pregnant mothers in the early 1960s.

The War Amputations of Canada also has many other programs. It publishes a journal, *Amputation*, that provides up-to-date information on new artificial limbs and devices for amputees. The organization's Safety Walk program encourages parents to take their children on a walk to inspect potentially dangerous sites in their neighbourhood. PLAYSAFE, a project aimed at cautioning Canadian youngsters of the dangers while at play, is a kids-to-kids

Two youngsters who are members of the Child Amputee (CHAMP) program and who represent a new generation of amputees benefitting from the association's programs; one uses an artificial arm, and the other, an artificial leg.

approach to child safety awareness. Matching Mothers, initiated in 1984, matches parents whose children have similar amputations from similar causes for support, counselling and information. The association also provides financial assistance for artificial limbs and specialty limbs and devices not covered by government or private health plans.

The Fred Tilston, VC Super Sheltered Workshop is a specialized computer training workshop that provides excellent employment opportunities for amputees. Courses are individually tailored for each student in the different facets of computer work, classroom and practical experience. Founded in 1984, the Workshop was subsequently dedicated to Fred Tilston, who lost both legs and one eye as a result of

injuries sustained in combat during World War II and who was awarded the Victoria Cross, the Commonwealth's highest gallantry medal.

The organization is also laying the groundwork to change The War Amputations of Canada into the Canadian Amputees Foundation when the time is right to do so. When the war amputees will no longer be able to run the affairs of the association, the new Foundation will continue the organization's important work, ensuring that Canada's amputees will be well-cared for in the future. For many years to come, however, The War Amputations of Canada will continue to provide many valuable services to its members, to other disabled persons, and to the Canadian public.

Wedlock Paper Converters Limited

When you go grocery shopping at your local supermarket, buying item after item from your shopping list, have you ever wondered where the packaging materials came from for each one of those products? There is a good chance that, if it is a paper container, it may have come from Wedlock Paper Converters Limited. A completely independent Canadian and family owned company, it has been providing quality packaging materials to customers throughout Canada and the United States for more than half a century.

Wedlock Paper Converters Limited was founded as Wedlock Paper Bag Company Limited by Louis Merritt Wedlock, who, after working for other companies, decided to test his entrepreneurial spirit in 1932. Evidently, he succeeded quite well. The company's small factory and office were originally located on Duchess Street in Toronto, where it manufactured grocery bags, candy bags, notion and millinery bags, corset bags, bottle bags and shoe bags.

Due to the keen ability of the founder, the company grew quickly and was able to purchase Purity Fibre Products Company Limited in 1936, makers of paper plates and disposable fibre cutlery. The two companies soon moved to larger premises on King Street West later

that year, continuing to thrive and succeed.

In 1949 the company was forced once again to search for larger premises, deciding to enlarge the building with an addition rather than moving. It was here at the corner of King and Dufferin Streets that the company became a well-known landmark in the area, with its conspicuous signs and the company's logo emblazoned over the door: Wedlock's Better Built Bags.

When the founder passed away in 1955, control passed to his son Alan J. Wedlock. The company soon changed its product line, halting its stock bag production and producing more custom bag and packaging directed mainly toward the food industry. In 1959 the company moved once again, locating itself in newly built facilities on Stanfield Road in Mississauga. All stock manufactured items were discontinued except those which Purity Fibre Products continued to manufacture. After a change in name, the Purity Fibre and Foil Products was soon amalgamated with Wedlock Pager Bag Company Limited into Wedlock Paper Converters Limited in 1967.

In recent years the company has discontinued the manufacturing of paper plates, concentrating rather on the production of a wide range

of bags and overwraps, printed, coated and laminated materials, while employing various printing processes. The company is a major supplier of quality packaging materials to most large national food product manufacturers, including sugar refineries, flour mills, cookie manufacturers, coffee packers and pet food manufacturers throughout Canada and the United States.

The next generation of Wedlock's has already moved into the company. Sean M. Wedlock is Executive Vice President and General Manager, while Marcus C. Wedlock is Vice President of Manufacturing and Production Manager. Both are sons of Alan Wedlock.

Wedlock Paper Converters Limited continues to grow and prosper, and it now occupies 75,000 square feet and employs 90 people. The company proudly remains a solidly owned and managed Canadian company, providing quality packaging materials to markets throughout Canada and the United States.

1. Louis Merritt Wedlock founded Wedlock Paper Converters Limited in 1932.
2. Alan J. Wedlock, son of the Founder and current President.
The next generation of Wedlock's:
3. Sean M. Wedlock, Executive Vice President.
4. Marcus C. Wedlock, Vice President of Manufacturing.

1

2

3

4

Weil Company Limited

1

Although it can't teach you to cook, it can make your life in the kitchen easier and far less time-consuming. What is this marvellous tool? It is a blender, food mixer, meat grinder, ice crusher, slicer, shredder, peanut-butter maker, milkshake maker, dough and cake mixer, and much more. It is Cuisinart®. This revolutionary device has changed the life of cooks throughout Canada and around the world, and it has also changed the history of Weil Company Limited.

Founded in 1954 by Edward Weil, Weil Company began by importing housewares and hardware from Europe and distributing them wholesale to the area hardware stores and ethnic gift shops. In the early years Edward Weil was the sole salesman, selling for three days a week, packing one day, and delivering one day, with the bulk of his merchandise warehoused in the basement of his home. Soon after his two sons were born, his wife requested that he find alternate warehouse space. In 1960 he hired his first employee and opened an office and warehouse in a small office building in mid-town Toronto. By 1968 the company had outgrown the facilities and moved to an 18,000 square feet warehouse in Downsview. The following year he built a new office and purchased the building next door, increasing the warehousing space to 28,000 square feet.

Against fierce competition by other firms, Weil Company received the sole Canadian distribution rights for Cuisinart® in 1975. Invented by the French and introduced to the United States by Carl Sontheimer in 1971, this one product that makes the basic blender utterly obsolete also completely changed the structure of Weil Company. The first 300 units he obtained were sold out in two days. Able to sell over 50,000 units per year in Canada alone, sales jumped from $3,000,000 to $15,000,000 in less than two years, and soon the company opened the new electrical appliance division.

The company continued to grow and in 1981 Weil Company started Multichef® for the company's own line of electrical appliances. Edward Weil's sons Steven and Allan joined the company fulltime. Allan is now the General Manager, while Steven is the Operations Manager. In 1983 Weil Company entered the coffee market, and is now one of the major cappuccino/expresso distributors in Canada. The company opened a major new showroom in Montreal in 1983. Presently, negotiations are underway for a new warehouse of over 80,000 square feet.

Edward Weil points out that a major part of the company's success is the thirty-seven service depots, which can service all of Weil Company's machines from coast to coast. The company continues to remain at the forefront of the marketplace by developing new and improved products. It has just released a completely new method of cooking, a convection, jet-stream oven, in direct competition to the microwave oven.

One of the few private Canadian distributors which has not been bought out by a larger company, Weil Company Limited currently has approximately forty employees and in addition has a demonstration force in department stores and supermarkets. Through hard work, honesty, and servicing its customers to their complete satisfaction, Weil Company Limited continues to hold a name in the housewares market of the highest standing possible.

1. *The founder and President of Weil Company Limited, Edward Weil.*
2. *The company's facilities in Mississauga, Ontario.*

2

West Park Hospital

With over eighty-five years of service to the community, West Park Hospital is dedicated to providing the best possible quality of life for residents and patients requiring highly specialized and complex care. Today, building on the strong foundation of expertise gained over years of experience, West Park Hospital specializes in continuing care, geriatrics, respirology, amputee and neurological rehabilitation, as well as transitional living for disabled persons.

Originally a farm on the banks of the Humber River in Toronto, Ontario, the hospital site was purchased by Sir William Gage, founder of the National Sanatorium Association. One of the first Canadian facilities devoted exclusively to the treatment of advanced cases of tuberculosis, the thirty-bed Toronto Hospital for the Consumptive Poor opened in 1904.

In 1924 the name was changed to the Toronto Hospital, Weston, and the facility became the largest sanatarium in Canada, accommodating 650 patients at one point. In the 1940s, advanced surgical techniques pioneered at the hospital and the discovery of

antibiotics helped bring tuberculosis under control. As the demand for tuberculosis beds decreased, emphasis shifted to providing the latest equipment, techniques and facilities required to meet new challenges in continuing care and rehabilitation.

With a substantial grant from the National Sanatorium Association and with government funding, West Park Hospital, as it became known in 1976, opened a new facility in 1979. The most recent addition to the hospital campus was in 1986 with the opening of the twenty-four suite Gage Transitional Living Centre.

A major landscaping project, completed in 1988, created an eleven hectare, outdoor environment for social, recreational and rehabilitation activities. The innovative design features wheelchair height garden beds, extra-wide walkways and gently sloping ramps with adequate space for two-way wheelchair traffic. This project was recognized for its unique design considerations with a Premier's Award for Accessibility and a Regional Citation Award from the Canadian Society of Landscape Architects.

The hospital campus also encompasses a prosthetics and

orthotics training facility with Computer Aided Design/Computer Aided Manufacturing (CAD/CAM) equipment for on-site design and manufacture of custom prostheses. Another piece of state-of-the-art assessment and diagnostic equipment at West Park is the Computerized Driving Assessment Module (CDAM) for the testing of disabled and elderly persons.

Affiliated with recognized teaching institutions such as the University of Toronto and George Brown College, West Park's specialized programs are in keeping with the reality of continuing care and rehabilitation hospitals in the 1990s. Today, with a staff of over 700, West Park Hospital is dedicated to an inter-disciplinary approach to excellence in continuing care and rehabilitation.

1. *Fresh air, rest and an extremely nutritious diet were the mainstays of tuberculosis treatment in 1910. Patients enjoy a sunny summer's day in front of the Toronto Hospital's King Edward Building (left) and Administration Building (right).*
2. *One of four buildings on the campus, West Park Hospital's Main Building was officially opened in 1979 and currently houses over seventy per cent of the hospital's 423 patient-care beds.*

1

2

W.G. McKay Limited

1

When he was twenty-six years of age, Winfield George McKay was "Chief Clerk" for the customs brokerage firm of C.W. Irwin in downtown Toronto. Recently passed over for a promotion, he was about to depart for home when he overheard a senior executive chastising a young lad for attempting to sell raffle tickets at the counter for a charitable cause. Feeling sorry for the boy, he bought a ticket outside the building. That ticket, of course, won the prize, a Gray Dort automobile.

The car was presented to him on the steps of what is now the Old City Hall by the mayor of Toronto and Theresa Small, the wife of Ambrose J. Small, the theatre magnate and mysteriously disappeared millionaire, in one of her rare public appearances. W.G. McKay, unable to drive, had his brother James drive the car to the family home. He immediately sold the car which provided the needed capital for him to open his own customs brokerage business in 1914.

The new firm was first located at 37 Yonge Street, where it remained until 1924 when it moved to the new, but now demolished, Commerce and Transportation Building at Bay and Front Streets. Expansion forced a move to University Avenue in 1977, and again in 1981 to 40 University Avenue, the company's current address.

W.G. McKay led the company until his death in 1953, but it has continued to flourish under the guidance of his son, Winfield Cleland McKay, the current President. Although W.C. McKay did not become President until 1965, he was very involved with the company before his father passed away. His wife Noreen, a former Canadian junior golf champion, works in the accounting department. The third generation, Winfield Laing McKay, is already an account executive at the head office.

W.C. McKay has also been active in a civic role. In 1968 he was a federal P.C. candidate for Toronto's High Park Riding, finishing a strong second to a Liberal in the Trudeau landslide. From 1972 - 1982 he was a Metropolitan Toronto Police Commissioner, and then, from 1985 - 1988, an Ontario Police Commission member. He has served as Chairman of the Ontario Chapter of the Young President's Organization, and is a past President of the Downtown Kiwanis Club. W.C. McKay still serves on a number of boards and committees, and, in addition, takes particular pride in furthering the service and goals of the Canadian Automobile Association - Toronto Division, of which he is a member of its board and Executive Committee.

Today, W.G. McKay Limited, which employs approximately fifty-five people in its offices across Ontario, deals with customs brokerage, customs and traffic consulting, international freight forwarding, airfreight, pool cars and containers. Their accounts range from the large companies such as Petro-Canada and Pitney-Bowes to little shops around the corner.

Win McKay, as he is best known, point outs that it is because of good management that the company has continued to grow. The company "did not outgrow itself, was financed carefully, and only took business that it could handle." For over seventy-five years, W.G. McKay Limited has prospered by providing consistent, dependable services to the Canadian importing public.

1. *The founder of W.G. McKay Limited, Winfield George McKay, 1888-1953.*
2. *Current President and son of the Founder, Winfield Cleland McKay.*

2

Photo Credits

Chapter 1

8   David J. Koene

10 1. NAC/POS-000472; 2. NAC/POS-000959; 3.This aerial photograph ©1980 Her Majesty the Queen in Right of Canada, reproduced from the collection of the National Air Photo Library with permission of Energy, Mines, and Resources Canada

12 1. MNR

14 GOAC, Toronto/Tom Moore Photography, Toronto/colour transparency/George Agnew Reid, O.S.A., R.C.A. *Evening, Lake Temegami*, 1984

15 1.Bainbrigge/NAC/C-011809; 2. Phillips/NAC/C-111276; 3.Bainbrigge/NAC/C-0119114.

16 1. Mercer/NAC/C-035939; 2. Back/NAC/C-93002; 3. Bon Echo Provincial Park; 4. Bon Echo Provincial Park; 5. Bon Echo Provincial Park; 6. Bon Echo Provincial Park

19 1. Bon Echo Provincial Park; 2. MNR; 3. Bon Echo Provincial Park; 4. Bon Echo Provincial Park

21 1. David J. Koene; 2. Bon Echo Provincial Park; 3. NAC/POS-431

23 1. MNR; 2. Bon Echo Provincial Park; 3. MNR; 4. MNR

24 1. This aerial photograph ©26/5/72 Her Majesty the Queen of Canada, reproduced from the collection of the National Air Photo Library with permission of Energy, Mines, and Resources Canada; 2. AO/Acc.2432/S5627; 3. Moodie/NAC/C-174; 4.AO/Acc.13881-3

25 1. NAC/PA-26505; 2. AO/Acc.2432/S5652; 3. NAC/POS-417

26 1. NAC/PA-18575; 2. NAC/PA-16427; 3. NAC/PA-70006; 4. Bon Echo Provincial Park

29 1. This aerial photograph

©1980 Her Majesty the Queen in Right of Canada, reproduced from the collection of the National Air Photo Library with permission of Energy, Mines, and Resources Canada; 2. Phillips/NAC/C-110910; 3. R. Maynard/NAC/PA-120188; 4. NAC/POS-943; 5. Bon Echo Provincial Park

31 1.Bon Echo Provincial Park; 2. MNR; 3. Bon Echo Provincial Park; 4. MNR; 5. Phillips/NAC/C-110849

32 1. Callington/NAC/C-5846; 3. Erskine/NAC/C-11209

33 1. MTRL, J. Ross Robertson Collection T16866; 2. NAC/PA-84780; 3. NAC/PA-28610

35 1. NAC/PA-60827; 2. Simcoe/NAC/C-13917a; 3. Photo by J.D. Soper/NAC/PA-101439

37 NAC/NMC2910

38 1. NAC/C-44633; 2. MNR; 3. NAC/PA-12494; 4. NAC/PA-139334

40 1. NAC/PA-57653; 2. Nicholas Morant/NAC/PA-37548; 3. AO/Acc.9258/S14323; 4. AO/Acc.14313-23

42 1. NAC/PA-86262; 2. NAC/PA-11535

43 1. Holdstock/NAC/C-045487; 2. Bon Echo Provincial Park; 3. NAC/C-11210

45 1. Cackly/NAC/C-46497; 2. MNR; 3. NAC/POS-1229; OLL. NAC/C-24379; OLR. NAC/C-30195

49 1. NAC/C-30234; 2. Hamer, W.M. Collection/NAC/C-19890; 3. NAC/POS-620;

51 1. Bainbrigge/NAC/C-11803; 2. Bon Echo Provincial Park

52 1. NAC/POS-721; 2. Armstrong/NAC/C-114492

54 1. NAC/POS-722; 2. Smyth/NAC/C-1041

57 1. Chavane/NAC/C-1011995; 2. Jefferys/NAC/C-103059; 3.

NAC/POS-952

58 1. NAC/POS-431; 2. Ernest Voorhis Collection/NAC/PA-122303; 3. NAC/PA-42333; 4. AO/S17663

60 1. AO/Acc.6785/S12390; 2. AO/Acc.9164/S14484; 3. AO/S14226

61 NAC/POS-930

Chapter 2

64 1. NAC/POS-360; 2. NAC/POS-285

65 1. AO/AO378; 2. MTRL/T30788; 3. NAC/PA-9390; 4. NAC/C-4913

66 1. NAC/PA-44342; 2. Jefferys/NAC/C-28332; 3. AO/AO374; 4. AO/AO388 5. MTRL/T-31616

68 1. NAC/C-5749; 2. Armstrong/NAC/C-114494

71 GOAC, Toronto/Tom Moore Photography, Toronto/black and white glossy print F.S. Challenger, O.S.A., R.C.A./*Etienne Brule at the Mouth of the Humber*, 1956, after a drawing by C.W. Jefferys

73 1. NAC/C-1471; 2. NAC/PA-54905; 3. NAC/PA-54772; 4. MTRL/T-15468; 5. Huret/NAC/C-1664

75 2. AO/AO-373; 6. NAC/C-013158

78 1. NAC/C-1470; 2. Bigsby/NAC/C-1107; 3. MTRL/T-14868

80 1. Heming/NAC/C-5746; 2. Belier/NAC/C-015497; 3. Bud Glunz/NFB/NAC/PA-145602; 4. OA/AO369

82 1. Marchland/NAC/C-17560; 2. Kelly/NAC/C-7962; 3. MTRL/J. Ross Robertson Collection/T-15220; 4. NAC/C-1225

84 Bigsby/NAC/C-11666

85 NAC/POS-2520

87 1. Heming/NAC/C-5746; 1. AO/Acc.2210/S1994; 2. AO/S-18118; 3. NAC/C-17727

88 1. OA/Acc.2475/S7578; 2.

AO/Acc.2210/S1952; 3. Ellis/NAC/PA-121287; 4. NAC/C-4299; 5. AO/S2525; 6. AO/Acc.15830-97;

90 1. NAC/C-083143; 2. NAC/C-6007

91 NAC/C-79641

92 1. F.W. Michlethwaite/NAC/PA-68377; 2. AO/Acc.10748/S16351; 3. PAC/C-14253; 4. Brown/NAC/C-1229

94 2. NAC/C-34786; 3. MTRL/J. Ross Robertson Collection/T-15216; 4. MTRL/J. Ross Robertson Collection/T-15213

96 1. AO/Acc.6326/S8518; 2. 4. NAC/C-2645; 3. AO/S790; 4. NAC/C-7223;

91 1. NAC/C-14523; 2. Smyth/NAC/C-788; 3. NAC/C-11043

Chapter 3

100 GOAC/Tom Moore Photography, Toronto/black and white glossy print George Agnew Reid/The Homeseekers; MTRL/Baldwin Room/MS Maps 912.71354067

104 NAC/NMC 21404

107 1. MTRL/T14670; 2. Alfred Bobbett/NAC/C-11250; 3. AO/S893

108 1. NAC/C-15127; 2. AO/AO381; 3. AO/AO484

111 1. Frances Anne Hopkins/NAC/C-2774; 2. W.H. Bartlett/NAC/C-2336; 3. MNR; 4. AO/AO382

112 1. NAC/C-29925; 2. AO/S18096; 3. Col. J. Bouchette/NAC/C-977

113 1. AO/Acc.2210/S1951; 2. NAC/C-4219; 3. MTRL/J. Ross Robertson Collection/T16985

114 MTRL/J. Ross Robertson Collection/T-16567

115 J. Walder/NAC/C-6046

117 1. AO/S2076; 2. NAC/POS-2521; 3. MTRL/J. Ross Robertson Collection/T15499; 4. NAC/C-5197

118 1. NAC/C-2847; 2.

AO/S4277; 3.
AO/Acc.18010/S3054

119 1. MTRL/T13485; 2.
NAC/NMC-3000

120 1. NAC/POS-267, with permission of the CPC; 2.
AO/Acc.13098-95

121 J. Lambert/NAC/C-1459

122 John David Kelly/NAC/C-1829

124 Robert Petley/NAC/C-115424

126 NAC/NMC-9896

128 1. AO/S2109; 2. MTRL/J.
Ross Robertson Collection/T15717; 3. C.W. Jefferys/NAC/C-96362

130 1. NAC/C-3903; 2. C.W.
Jefferys/NAC/C-73449; 3.
NAC/PA-121296; 4.
NAC/C-1725; 5.
NAC/NMC-15712

132 1. William Henry Bartlett/NAC/C-2339; 2.
NAC/NMC-7369

135 1. William Henry Bartlett/NAC/C-2334; 2.
NAC/C-61557

136 1. AO/S3845; 2. NAC/C-110101; 3.
AO/Acc.4952/S7400; 4.
NAC/C-121590

138 L. Laborde/NAC/C-84448

139 1. AO/AO375; 2.
AO/AO377

140 Elizabeth Posthuma
Simcoe/NAC/C-20006

141 NAC/NMC-5006

142 AO/AO330

Chapter 4

144 MTRL/J. Ross Robertson
Collection/T10271

146 NAC/NMC 48588

147 1.,3. AO/S3892a and
AO/S3892b; 2. Charles
Walter Simpson/NAC/C-13941

148 1. MTRL/T30854; 2.
AO/AO384

150 1. W.L. Thomson/NAC/C-12559; 2. AO/S628; 3.
MTRL/T30674; 4.
AO/AO380; 5. AO/S1072

153 1. NAC/NMC-11237; 2.
Burland Lith., Co./NAC/C-44625; 3. NAC/NMC-288

154 1. AO/Acc.2624#8; 2.
AO/S633; 3.
MTRL/T32296; 4.
OA/S18300

157 1. Ontario Legislative
Library; 2. MTRL/J. Ross
Robertson Collection/T16767

159 4. Ontario Legislative

Library; 5. Ontario Legislative Library; 6. MTRL; 7.
Troy D. Rhodes

160 1. NAC/POS-2522; 2.
NAC/C-10738; 3. This
aerial photograph ©25/4/87
Her Majesty the Queen in
the Right of Canada, reproduced from the collection of
the National Air Photo
Library with permission of
Energy, Mines, and
Resources Canada; 4. This
aerial photograph ©26/7/65
Her Majesty the Queen in
the Right of Canada, reproduced from the collection of
the National Air Photo
Library with permission of
Energy, Mines, and
Resources Canada; 5. This
aerial photograph ©20/8/86
Her Majesty the Queen in
the Right of Canada, reproduced from the Collection
of the National Air Photo
Library with permission of
Energy, Mines, and
Resources Canada; 6. This
aerial photograph ©20/8/96
Her Majesty the Queen in
the Right of Canada, reproduced from the collection of
the National Air Photo
Library with permission of
Energy, Mines, and
Resources Canada

162 1. MTRL/J. Ross Robertson
Collection/ T15089; 2.
AO/S2248/Acc.1544

163 NAC/C-2710

165 1. Ontario Legislative
Library; 2. AO/S2148; 3.
AO/S2169; 4.
AO/Acc.2624-17

166 Edward W. Battye/NAC/C-29792

167 AO/Acc.2579/S17696

168 AO/AO386

169 AO/Acc.9978/S15868

170 1. AO/AO385; 2. Philip
John Bainbrigge/NAC/C-11848; 3. Henry
DuVernet/NAC/C-608; 4.
J.P. Newell/NAC/C41680

172 AO/Acc.1456/S1130

173 1. OA/Acc.6807/S11828;
2. AO/S1711

175 John T. Lee/NAC/C-7470

176 1. Ontario Legislative
Library; 2. NAC/C-95294;
3. AO/S1427; 4. GOAC,
Toronto/Tom Moore photograph, Toronto/black and
white glossy print Hamilton
P. MacCarthy, O.S.A.,

R.C.A./*Portrait Bust of
Tecumseh*, 1986; 5.
NAC/POS-565

178 1. NAC/C-025014; 2.
NAC/C-024171

179 MTRL/J. Ross Robertson
Collection/T15212

180 1. NAC/C-7045; 2. NAC/C-7018; 3. MTRL/T14987;
4. AO/S17866b

182 1. MTRL/J. Ross Robertson
Collection/T15248; 2.
NAC/C-111307; 3.
AO/AO383; 4. MTRL; 5.
GOAC/Tom Moore Photography/black and white
glossy print/C.W. Jefferys,
O.S.A., R.C.A., LL.D., The
Death of Brock at
Queenston Heights, c.1908

185 1. MTRL/J. Ross Robertson
Collection/T15268; 2.
AO/S1439; 4. AO/AO379;
5. AO/S1431; 6. NAC/C-95295

186 1. MTRL/J. Ross Robertson
Collection/T15241; 2.
AO/Acc.9258/S14334; 3.
MTRL/J. Ross Robertson
Collection/15242; 4.
MTRL/J. Ross Robertson
Collection/T15245; 5.
MTRL/J. Ross Robertson
Collection/T15211

188 1. MTRL/J. Ross Robertson
Collection/T15228; 2.
MTRL/J. Ross Robertson
Collection/T15243; 3.
AO/Acc.6355/S9088a; 4.
AO/S8492

190 1. NAC/POS-2523; 2.
Bainbridgge/NAC/C-011869; 3. MTRL/J. Ross
Robertson Collection/T15457

Chapter 5

192 AO/S13288

194 1. AO/AO387; 2.
MTRL/T15365; 3. NAC/C-6556

196 1. AO/Acc.2469/S7458; 2.
NAC/C-3904

198 1. MTRL/T14369; 2.
MTRL/T33825

199 OL. MTRL/J. Ross Robertson Collection T15382;
1. AO/AO391; 2.
AO/Acc.13281-70

202 1.MTRL/J.V. Salmon Collection SI-4056B; 2.
MTRL/T10485

203 AO/Acc.9082/S13031

204 MTRL/J. Ross Robertson
Collection/T15097

205 MTRL/TEC253B

206 AO/S2126

207 W.J. Thomson/NAC/C-7466

209 1. AO/MUI847#951; 2.
AO/S235

210 1. MTRL/Broadside Collection; 2. AO/S8365; 3.
MTRL/T30645

212 1. AO/S12755; 2.
AO/OA367; 3. AO/AO9;
4. AO/S17472; 5.
AO/S12753

214 1. George Russell
Dartnell/NAC/C-13302; 2.
AO/Acc.3619/S12652; 3.
MTRL/T31223

217 1. AO/Acc.10015/S16217;
2. AO/Acc.4822/S4747; 3.
AO/AO389; 4. AO/AO390

219 1. AO/AO370; 2.
AO/AO392; 3.
AO/Acc.1372/S1137; 4.
AO/S16259; 5.
NAC/NMC2851

221 2. AO/Acc.2331/S4192; 3.
NAC/POS-685; 4.
AO/S657

222 1. David J. Koene; 2.
AO/Acc.4137-43; 3. David
J. Koene; 4. C.W. Jefferys/NAC/C-27570, with
permission of NCC/CCN

224 1. AO/Acc.3964/ST551; 3.
AO/Burrowes #14; 4.
David J. Koene

226 1. AO/AO396; 3.
NAC/POS-933; 4.
E.K.W./NAC/C-20878

229 1. MTRL; 2. AO/AO68

230 1. AO/S2123; 2. AO/S159;
3. MTRL/T11121

232 AO/AO406

233 NAC/C-4500

234 AO/AO407

235 AO/S78

236 1. AO/S18023; 2.
GOAC/Tom Moore Photography, Toronto/black and
white glossy print/C.W.
Jefferys, O.S.A., R.C.A.,
LL.D. *The March of the
Rebels upon Toronto in
December, 1837*. c.1912;
3. AO/Acc.11115-4

238 1. AO/S13291; 2. G. Tattersall/NAC/C-4788

239 William Bengough/NAC/C-4785

240 NAC/C-1242

241 1. OA/S13289; 2.
AO/AO405

243 1. AO/MUI844#831; 2.
AO; 3. NAC/C-15231

244 AO/S155

Chapter 6

246 AO/S2639

248 AO/AO368
249 AO/Acc.9789/S16348
250 1. AO/AO364; 2. AO/S2079; 3. AO/AO365
252 NAC/POS-548
253 NAC/C-8640
254 1. AO/Acc.6899/S13897; 2. AO/S1388
256 AO/S2150
257 AO/S894
258 1. Charles Walter Simpson/NAC/C-13945; 2. AO/S261; 3. MTRL/J. Ross Robertson Collection/T16028
260 1. AO/S167; 2. AO/S2128; 3. MTRL/T31612
262 1. AO/AO371; 2. AO/S158; 3. Andrew Morris/NAC/C-315
263 1. NAC/C-2726 2. MTRL with permission of the *Globe and Mail*; 3. Martin Somerville/NAC/C-6729
264 MTRL/J. Ross Robertson Collection/T30898
265 Troy D. Rhodes
266 1. AO/S201; 2. NAC/PA-66584
267 AO/AO376
268 A.J. Russell/NAC/C-3525
269 AO/AO362
271 1. AO/Acc.11778-4/S16944; 2. AO/Acc.3026/S4841; 3. AO/Acc.1623
272 1. William England/NAC/PA-165997; 2. NAC/C-79134; 3. AO/Acc.6643/S12235; 4. AO/Acc.10103/S16147; 5. AO/AO35; 6. AO/Acc.13281-200
274 AO/S1159
275 NAC/C-20603
276 1. AO/S1186; 2. AO/S1188; 3. AO/S1189; 4. AO/Acc.16630-4; 5. AO/S15341; 6. AO/ACC.15081-26
278 AO/Acc6326/S8512
279 1. AO/Acc.9436/S15072; 2. AO/Acc.16518-18
281 1. AO/AO366; 2. NAC/C-10746; 3. AO/S165
283 1. AO/S175; 2. AO/Acc.1750/S264; 3. AO/S227; 4. AO/S2124
285 1. MTRL/T12103; 2. AO/Acc.6355/S9456
286 AO/Acc.13888-4
287 AO/Acc.1750/S325
288 1. AO/AO363; 2. J.D. Kelly/NAC/C-6799
291 1. AO/Acc2455/S5714; 2. David J. Koene

293 1. NAC/C-21873; 2. MTRL with permission of the *Globe and Mail*; 3. AO/S3491 and S3492
296 OL. MTRL with permission of the *Globe and Mail*; 1. NAC/POS-500; 2. NAC/POS-217; 3. AO/P1956

Chapter 7

298 City of Toronto Archives
300 1. AO/Acc.6355/S9101; 2. Troy Rhodes; 3. MTRL; 4. Consumer's Gas Company Ltd.
302 1. NAC/C-79629; 2. Troy Rhodes; 3. Troy Rhodes; 4. Troy Rhodes; 5. Troy Rhodes
305 1. AO/S2998; 2. AO/S16187; 3. AO/S16180; 4. AO/S16160
306 1. MTRL/T12776; 2. Troy Rhodes; 3. MTRL/T10282
307 1. AO/Acc.4113 Docket Box IV; 2. AO/AO462
309 AO/P2230
310 1. MTRL/T13816; 2. AO/S76; 3. W.L.L. Lawrence Collection/Cochrane Museum/AO/S13795
312 1. AO/S1620; 2. MTRL/T12276; 3. MTRL/T10064
314 1. © Bell Canada, courtesy Bell Canada Telephone Historical Collection; 2. AO/S4589
315 1. AO/S15452; 2. AO/S2835
316 1. Thomas Moore Photography Inc., Toronto/GOAC/Astin Shaw/*Portrait of The Hon. Sir William Howard Hearst, K.C.M.G., K.C.*; 2. NAC/PA22806
317 MTRL
318 1. AO/S16040; 2. MTRL; 3. AO/S1430; 4. Acton Free Press/A.T. Brown Collection/AO/Acc.9339/S15042
320 1. Thomas Moore Photography Inc., Toronto/GOAC/J.W.L. Forster/*Portrait of The Hon. Ernest Charles Drury, 1923*; 2. Thomas Moore Photography Inc., Toronto/GOAC/Kenneth Forbes/*Portrait of Howard Ferguson, K.C., LL.B., 1931*; 3. AO/S332
322 1. AO/Acc.16856-17603B;

2. AO/Acc.16856-19100
324 1. Thomas Moore Photography Inc., Toronto/GOAC/John Russell/*Portrait of The Hon. George Stewart Henry, LL.D.*; 2. Thomas Moore Photography Inc., Toronto/GOAC/Cleve Horne/*Portrait of The Hon. Mitchell Frederick Hepburn*; 3.Thomas Moore Photography Inc., Toronto/GOAC/Evan Macdonald/*Portrait of The Hon. George Alexander Drew, P.C., O.C.*
325 1. AO/S2837; 2. AO/S2841;
326 1. Rhebergen Family; 2. Isaac J. Koene; 3. De Roos Family
327 Troy D. Rhodes
329 1. AO/AO472; 2. AO/AO479; 3. Thomas Moore Photography Inc., Toronto/GOAC/Istvan Nyikos/*Portrait of The Hon. William Grenville Davis, P.C., C.C. O.C., 1989*
330 Troy D. Rhodes
331 Troy D. Rhodes
333 1. Troy D. Rhodes; 2. Troy D. Rhodes

Chapter 8

341 2. Gary Beachy, BDS Studios
345 2. *Toronto Star* U333-12
372 1., 2. The Hospital for Sick Children Archives
396 Lenscape Incorporated
397 Lenscape Incorporated
399 1. *Toronto Star* 90-09-26-24-3A

***

CPC   Canada Post Corporation
GOAC   Government of Ontario Art Collection
HCHS   Hastings County Historial Society
MNR   Ministry of Natural Resoures (Ontario)
MTRL   Metropolitan Toronto Reference Library
NAC   National Archives of Canada
AO   Archives of Ontario

All reproductions from archival sources are based on originals supplied, with no alterations made on actual images other than cropping as required.

Index